Ramesses II, Egypt's Ultimate Pharaoh

Frontispiece: Ramesses II. Turin, Museo Egizio 1380. Courtesy Museo Egizio, Turin.

Ramesses II, Egypt's Ultimate Pharaoh

Peter J. Brand

LOCKWOOD PRESS

Columbus, GA

2023

RAMESSES II, EGYPT'S ULTIMATE PHARAOH

© 2023 Lockwood Press
ISBN 978-1-948488-49-5

Cover design by Susanne Wilhelm.
Cover image: Black granodiorite colossus of Ramesses II from the Luxor Temple forecourt named "Ramesses, the Re of Rulers." Photograph by Peter Brand.

Library of Congress Cataloging-in-Publication Data

Names: Brand, Peter J. (Peter James), 1967- author.
Title: Ramesses II, Egypt's ultimate pharaoh / Peter J. Brand.
Description: Columbus, GA : Lockwood Press, 2023. | Includes bibliographical references and index.
Identifiers: LCCN 2022046379 (print) | LCCN 2022046380 (ebook) | ISBN 9781948488488 (hardcover) | ISBN 9781948488471 (paperback) | ISBN 9781957454962 (epub) | ISBN 9781948488495 (adobe pdf)
Subjects: LCSH: Ramses II, King of Egypt. | Pharaohs--Biography. | Egypt--History--Nineteenth dynasty, ca. 1320-1200 B.C. | Egypt--Foreign relations.
Classification: LCC DT88 .B73 2023 (print) | LCC DT88 (ebook) | DDC 932/.014--dc23/eng/20220927
LC record available at https://lccn.loc.gov/2022046379
LC ebook record available at https://lccn.loc.gov/2022046380

Printed in the United States of America on acid-free paper.

Contents

Preface

Ramesses II was Egypt's most magnificent, iconic pharaoh. His reign, monumental in every way, served as a model for future Egyptian rulers. Indeed, the very name "Ramesses" would become synonymous with "Pharaoh," just as "Caesar" meant "Emperor" in Rome. Forty years after Kenneth Kitchen's seminal *Pharaoh Triumphant*, we have a great deal of new information about the reign of Ramesses II. His revealing, sometimes shocking correspondence with the formidable Hittite queen Puduhepa is just one example. New books appear frequently about Tutankhamun, Akhenaten, Nefertiti, and other Egyptian royalty. The time is ripe for a fresh look at Egypt's ultimate pharaoh.

This book provides both general readers and scholars with a readable, up-to-date survey of Ramesses II. It offers a reassessment of the Nineteenth Dynasty and Egypt's relations with the Hittite Empire, drawing on the latest scholarship and archaeological data. While the focus is on Ramesses himself, we will also meet his royal wives and children, his high officials, and contemporaries. Several foreign rulers, especially the Hittite kings Urhi-Teshub and Hattusili III, and the latter's consort Puduhepa, also share the stage. For readers unfamiliar with all the names of ancient kings, gods, places, and things, there is a handy glossary at the back of this book.

Here we will also "dig deeper" into Egyptian archeology, looking at history's actual sources, often eroded and fragmentary, and doing some detective work to see what they have to tell us. We will examine key royal monuments—temples, tombs, statuary, and stelae. The most iconic and unique are the temples of Abu Simbel, salvaged in the world's greatest archeological rescue operation. The larger temple, with its bold architectural vision, towering colossi, and elaborate relief decoration, is the perfect symbol of Ramesses II. It neatly encapsulates the key events and themes of his remarkable reign.

A Word on Egyptian Dates

The Egyptian calendar consisted of twelve months, each thirty days long, to which they added five "extra days," said to be the birthdays of the gods, to make 365. The twelve months were grouped into three seasons: "Inundation Season," called *Akhet* in Egyptian; the "Season of Emergence," or *Proyet*; and "Harvest Season," called *Shomu*. ("Inundation" referred to the annual flooding of the Nile. "Emergence" referred to the sprouting of new crops.)

Years were numbered by a pharaoh's "regnal year." The first year of Ramesses's reign was "regnal year 1," his last "regnal year 67." A new pharaoh's reign began the day after the death of the previous pharaoh. Historical events are cited by the year of the pharaoh at that time. Due to gaps in the historical record, matching Egyptian regnal years with our Western dating system must be approximate at best. For more on ancient dates and chronology, see p. xxxiii.

Akhet (ꜣḫt)				Proyet (prt)				Shomu (šmw)				5 extra days
I	II	III	IV	I	II	III	IV	I	II	III	IV	
30	30	30	30	30	30	30	30	30	30	30	30	

Civil New Year's Day
I *Akhet* 1

Accession of Ramesses II
III *Shomu* 27

Diagram of the ancient Egyptian calendar showing the civil New Year's day and Ramesses II's accession day. Each month has 30 days, with five "extra days" added at the end of the civil calendar representing the birthdays of the gods.

In this book I have attempted to walk the line between offering a lively, accessible account of Ramesses II and providing scholars with an up-to-date assessment. Egyptologists and ancient historians will find in my notes the scholarly citations and commentary they require. Since the special characters Egyptologists use to transcribe the ancient language would baffle many readers, I have anglicized key Egyptian words and phrases in the main text, but my notes have the Egyptian and Akkadian transliterations familiar to experts.

Ancient texts are usually damaged in some way; seldom are they perfectly intact. Reconstructing them can be as much an art as a science. Where a text is damaged, it is customary to insert brackets [ ]. Words or parts of words within these brackets are damaged or destroyed in the original, but may be restored with various levels of confidence. For passages that cannot be restored the reader will see an ellipsis [...]. In my translations, words in parentheses ( ) are not found in the ancient text, but are added to assist the reader in comprehending the meaning or context of the passage. Most of the translations of ancient Egyptian texts in this book are my own, especially those from the Ramesside period. For cuneiform texts in the Akkadian and Hittite languages, including the diplomatic letters Ramesses II exchanged with the Hittite court, I have relied on published translations by cuneiform specialists.

As a mentor once told me, good history writing should be fine literature. While striving to present a balanced and thoughtful analysis of Ramesses II, I do take the liberty of recreating three scenes from a participant's point of view, in the introduction and chapters five and nine. Hopefully this will enliven the book for most readers without trying the patience of my colleagues in Egyptology.

Ancient history is a messy, uncertain enterprise. We cannot claim to be revealing the definitive, objective truth about the past. Rather, as my graduate mentor Bill Murnane told me, we are having an ongoing conversation, offering up a "best guess" about what may have been and how it might have occurred. We must accept that most of the distant past is lost to us, and be thankful for what we have.

I would like to express my heartfelt thanks to friends and colleagues who have aided me in this project over the past several years. If I omit anyone due to lapse of memory, I am sorry. I am grateful to my colleagues at the University of Memphis, Joshua Roberson, Chrystal Goudsouzian, and Bradford Pendley, as well as current and former graduate students including Erika Feleg, Dennys O'Connor, Cristina Rose, Mark Janzen, Katie Fincher, Rebekah Vogel, Amr Shahat, Roy Hopper, Kevin Johnson, and David Larson.

A warm thank you goes to Ray Johnson and Brett McClain at Chicago House. I would also like to express my sincere gratitude to Jean Revez, codirector of the Karnak Hypostyle Hall Project, for his invaluable collaboration, unparalleled collegiality, and an abiding friendship for many years. My research and fieldwork at Karnak have been greatly facilitated by the former and current directors of the Franco-Egyptian Center at Karnak, François Larché, Emmanuel Laroze, Christophe Thiers, and Luc Gabolde, to all of whom I express my thanks. Thanks go to colleagues in North America, the UK, and Europe including Ron Leprohon, Benoît Lurson, James Hoffmeier, Benedict Davies, Heather McCarthy, Jana Mynářová, Dana Bělohoubková, Katja Goebs, Ogden Goelet, Sameh Iskander, Hourig Sourouzian, Aidan Dodson, and in the southern hemisphere to Boyo Ockinga in Sydney and Jennifer Hellum in Auckland. I wish to express my sincere thanks to my Egyptian colleagues including the Minister of State for Antiquities Dr. Khaled El-Anany and the Chairman of the Supreme Council of Antiquities Dr. Mostafa Waziri. Thanks go also to Mohammed Rafat Abbas, Adel Kelany, Hazem Shared, and Mariam Ayad. For their insights into matters Hittite, I am grateful to Gary Beckman and Trevor Bryce.

A special callout goes to Anthony Spalinger in Auckland. I have benefited immensely from his friendship and consultation. His research has had a profound influence on my own thinking since I first encountered his writings in my undergraduate days in the mid-1980s. As my notes will attest, his seminal work on all aspects of Ramesside history is indispensable. To him I owe countless references and crucial observations through an ongoing correspondence and face to face visits in Auckland, Memphis, and elsewhere for the past two decades.

Writing and editing this book has profited immeasurably from friends and colleagues who are not Egyptologists, but who are well versed in the craft of good historical writing and who have generously offered their editorial advice and assistance. Thanks go to Jan Sherman, Aram Goudsouzian, Roger Long, Dan Veach, and most especially to Carol Conaway, for her tireless efforts in helping me refine multiple chapter drafts. For his love and emotional support, I thank my spouse Glenn Forsythe. Finally, I am most grateful to my editor Billie Jean Collins for her editorial expertise and patience for supporting me in this project for several years. As Tolkien observed, the tale grew in the telling, and I am profoundly grateful that she has helped me reach the end of this quest.

A final expression of profound gratitude goes to two men whose prodigious and meticulous scholarship and personal kindness and generosity have inspired me deeply and served as paragons of the historian's craft to which I aspire. The late Bill Murnane (1945-2000) was my mentor and dear friend. He tutored me in the craft of field epigraphy at Karnak Temple in the 1990s. As a mentor, he trained me in the methods of rigorous historical analysis, which his own work exemplified. Professor Kenneth A. Kitchen through his lifetime of prolific and exacting scholarship made it possible for all Egyptologists to delve into the history and culture of the Nineteenth and Twentieth Dynasties through his Ramesside Inscriptions series, a monumental sequence of volumes of hand copies, translations, and analysis of all the hieroglyphic inscriptions of this era. His interpretive work overflows in countless books and articles he penned over the course of more than sixty years. Kitchen's engaging prose shines through in his captivating biography of Ramesses II, *Pharaoh Triumphant.* I stand on the shoulders of these two colossi. To them I dedicated this book.

Peter J. Brand
Memphis, Tennessee
August 2022

List of Figures

Abbreviations

CG	Catalogue générale des antiquités du musée du Caire
Champollion, *Monuments*	Champollion, Jean-François. *Monuments de l'Egypte et de la Nubie: D'après les dessins exécutés sur les lieux sous la dir. de Champollion le-Jeune, et les descriptions autographes qu'il en a rédigées.* 4 vols. Paris: Didot, 1835–1845.
CHANE	Culture and History of the Ancient Near East
COS	Hallo, William W., and K. Lawson Younger, eds. *The Context of Scripture.* 3 vols. Leiden: Brill, 1997, 2001, 2002.
CRIPEL	*Cahiers de recherches de l'institut de papyrologie et d'égyptologie de Lille*
Description de l'Égypte	*Description de l'Égypte: Ou, Recueil des observations et des recherches qui ont été faites en Égypte pendant l'expédition de l'armée française.* Paris: Imprimerie Impériale.
EES	Egypt Exploration Society
GM	*Göttinger Miszellen: Beiträge zur ägyptologische Diskussion*
HÄB	Hildesheimer ägyptologische Beiträge
IEJ	*Israel Exploration Journal*
JAEI	*Journal of Ancient Egyptian Interconnections*
JAOS	*Journal of the American Oriental Society*
JARCE	*Journal of the American Research Center in Egypt*
JCS	*Journal of Cuneiform Studies*
JdE	Journal d'Éntrée (register of the Egyptian Museum, Cairo)
JEA	*Journal of Egyptian Archaeology*
JEH	*Journal of Egyptian History*
JNES	*Journal of Near Eastern Studies*
JSSEA	*Journal of the Society for the Study of Egypitan Antiquities*
KBo	Keilschrifttexte aus Boghazköi
KRI I–IX	Kitchen, Kenneth A., and Joshua Roberson. *Ramesside Inscriptions, Historical and Biographical.* 9 vols. Oxford: WileyBlackwell; Wallasey: Abercromby, 1969–2018.
KUB	Keilschrifturkunden aus Boghazköi
KV	King's Valley (tomb number)
LD	Lepsius, Carl Richard. *Denkmäler aus Ägypten und Äthiopien.* 12 vols. Berlin: Nicolaische Buchhandlung, 1849–1859.
Le Ramesseum I	Goyon, Jean-Claude, and H. el-Achirie. *Le Ramesseum I: Hypostyle N (travée centrale).* Collection scientifique 30. Cairo: Centre de documentation et d'études sur l'ancienne Égypte, 1973.
Le Ramesseum IV	Youssef, A. A.-H., Ch. Leblanc, and M. Maher. *Le Ramesseum IV: Les Batailles de Tunip et de Dapour.* Cairo: Centre d'études et de documentation sur l'ancienne Égypte, 1977.
Le Ramesseum VI	Goyon, Jean-Claude, and H. el-Achirie. *Le Ramesseum VI: La salle des litanies.* Collection scientifique 32. Cairo: Centre de documentation et d'études sur l'ancienne Égypte, 1974.
Le Ramesseum IX-2	Leblanc, Ch., and S. el-Sayed Ismaïl. *Le Ramesseum IX-2: Les piliers "osiriaques."* Collection scientifique 34. Cairo: Centre d'étude et de documentation sur l'ancienne Égypte, 1988.
Le Ramesseum IX-1	Leblanc, Ch. *Le Ramesseum IX-1: Les piliers "osiriaques."* Collection scientifique 33. Cairo: Centre d'étude et de documentation sur l'ancienne Égypte, 1980.

Le Ramesseum X	Desroches Noblecourt, Ch., G. Moukhtar, Ch. Adam, Ch. Leblanc, M. Nelson, H. el-Achirie, B. Fonquernie, G. Thorel, J.-Cl. Goyon, F. Hassanein, A. Sayed Youssef, and R. Schumann-Antelme. *Le Ramesseum X: Les annexes nord-ouest I; Architecture - archéologie - essai d'interprétation*. Collection scientifique 35. Cairo: Centre d'études et de documentation sur l'ancienne Égypte, 1976.
Le Ramesseum XI	Maher-Taha, M., and A.-M. Loyrette. *Le Ramesseum XI: Les fêtes du dieu Min*. Collection scientifique 36. Cairo: Centre d'étude et de documentation sur l'ancienne Egypte, 1979.
MÄS	Münchner ägyptologische Studien
Medinet Habu II	Epigraphic Survey, *Medinet Habu*, vol. II, *Later Historical Records of Ramses III*. OIP 9. Chicago: University of Chicago Press, 1932.
Medinet Habu VIII	Epigraphic Survey, *Medinet Habu*, vol. VIII, *The Eastern High Gate, with Translations of Texts*. OIP 94. Chicago: Oriental Institute of the University of Chicago, 1970.
MIFAO	Mémoires publiés par les membres de l'institut français d'archéologie orientale
MDAIK	Mitteilungen des Deutschen Archäologische Studien
MMA	Metropolitan Museum of Art (New York)
NEA	*Near Eastern Archaeology*
NeHeT	*NeHeT: Revue numérique d'Égyptologie*
OBO	Orbis Biblicus et Orientalis
OIP	Oriental Institute Publications
OLA	Orientalia Lovaniensia Analecta
OLZ	*Orientalistische Literaturzeitung*
Or	*Orientalia* N.S.
PdÄ	Probleme der Ägyptologie
PIHANS	Publication de l'institut historique et archéologique néerlandais de Stamboul
PM I–VIII	Porter, Bertha, Rosalind L. B. Moss, and Jarimir Malek. *Topographical Bibliography of Ancient Egyptian Hieroglyphic Texts, Reliefs, and Paintings*. 8 vols. Oxford: Oxford University Press, 1927–2012.
RdÉ	*Revue d'égyptologie*
RITA	Kitchen, Kenneth A., and Benedict G. Davies. *Ramesside Inscriptions, Translated and Annotated: Translations*. 7 vols. Oxford: WileyBlackwell; Wallasey: Abercromby, 1993–2020.
RITANC	Kitchen, Kenneth A., and Davies, Benedict G. *Ramesside Inscriptions, Translated and Annotated: Notes and Comments*. 4 vols. Oxford: Wiley-Blackwell, 1993–2014.
SAOC	Studies in Ancient Oriental Civilization
SAK	*Studien zur Altägyptische Kultur*
UF	*Ugarit-Forschungen*
Urk. IV	Sethe, Kurt, and Wolfgang Helck. *Urkunden der 18. Dynastie*, vol. IV of *Urkunden des ägyptischen Altertums*. Leipzig: Hinrichs, 1955–1958.
YES	Yale Egyptological Studies
ZÄS	*Zeitschrift für ägyptische Sprache und Altertumskunde*
ZDPV	*Zeitschrift des Deutschen Palästina-Vereins*

Chronology

Note: All dates before 690 BCE are approximate. Dates prior to the Roman period are BCE. Some dates are concurrent due to multiple kings or even dynasties ruling at the same time. Dates adapted from Hornung et al. 2006. Foreign contemporaries of New Kingdom pharaohs are from Assyria, Babylonia, Hatti, and Mitanni.

EARLY DYNASTIC PERIOD

First Dynasty (2900–2730)
Second Dynasty (2730–2590)

OLD KINGDOM

Third Dynasty (2590–2544)
Fourth Dynasty (2543–2436)
Fifth Dynasty (2435–2306)
Sixth Dynasty (2305–2118)

FIRST INTERMEDIATE PERIOD

Seventh and Eighth Dynasties (2150–2118)
Ninth and Tenth Dynasties (2118–1980)
Eleventh Dynasty (earlier) (1989–2009)

MIDDLE KINGDOM

Eleventh Dynasty (Nebhepetre Monthuhotep II onward) (2009–1940)
Twelfth Dynasty (1939–1760)
Thirteenth Dynasty (1759–1659)

SECOND INTERMEDIATE PERIOD

Fourteenth and Fifteenth Dynasties (? – 1540)
Sixteenth and Seventeenth Dynasties (? –1540)

NEW KINGDOM   Foreign Contemporaries

Eighteenth Dynasty (1539–1290)
    Ahmose
    Amenhotep I
    Thutmose I
    Thutmose II
    Hatshepsut
    Thutmose III

Amenhotep II
Thutmose IV   Artatama I (Mitanni)
Amenhotep III   Kadashman-Enlil I (Babylon);
                                     Tushratta (Mitanni)

Amenhotep IV/Akhenaten   Suppiluliuma I (Hatti);
                                     Tushratta (Mitanni)

Smenkhkare
Neferneferuaten
Tutankhamun   Suppiluliuma I (Hatti)
Ay
Horemheb   Mursili II (Hatti); Muwatalli II
                                     (Hatti)

Nineteenth Dynasty (1292–1191)

Ramesses I (1292–1290)
Sety I (1290–1279)   Muwatalli II (Hatti)
Ramesses II (1279–1213)   Adad-Nirari I (Assyria);
                                     Kadashman-Turgu (Babylon);
                                     Kadashman-Enlil II (Babylon);
                                     Muwatalli II (Hatti);
                                     Urhi-Teshub (Hatti);
                                     Hattusili III (Hatti);
                                     Tudhaliya IV (Hatti)

Merenptah
Sety II
Amenmesse
Siptah
Twoseret

Twentieth Dynasty (1190–1077)

Sethnakhte
Ramesses III
Ramesses IV
Ramesses V
Ramesses VI
Ramesses VII
Ramesses VIII
Ramesses IX
Ramesses X
Ramesses IX

THIRD INTERMEDIATE PERIOD

Twenty-First Dynasty (1076–944)
Twenty-Second Dynasty (943–746)
Twenty-Third Dynasty (845–812)
Twenty-Fourth Dynasty (736–723)
Twenty-Fifth Dynasty (722–655)

SAITE and LATE PERIOD

Twenty-Sixth Dynasty (664–525)
Twenty-Seventh Dynasty (Persian) (525–404)
Twenty-Eighth Dynasty (404–399)
Twenty-Ninth Dynasty (399–380)
Thirtieth Dynasty (380–343)
Thirty-First Dynasty (342–332)

HELLENISTIC PERIOD (332–30)

ROMAN PERIOD (30 BCE–395 CE)

Ancient Dates and Chronology

Students of ancient Egypt are faced with the uncertainties and complexities of two different but related dating systems, each with their chronological problems. The first is the system of date keeping the Egyptians themselves used. The Egyptian civil calendar consisted of twelve months, each thirty days long, to which they added five "extra days," said to be the birthdays of the gods. The twelve months were grouped into three seasons, "Inundation Season," called *Akhet* in Egyptian, the "Season of Emergence," or *Proyet*, and "Harvest Season," called *Shomu*.

Since the Egyptians did not account for the fact that a solar year lasts 365.24 days, which the Julian and Gregorian calendars allow for, the Egyptian New Year, called "Opening of the Year," which fell on the first day of the first month of the Inundation Season (*Akhet*), gradually drifted backward through the year relative to the true solar year. At the beginning of Ramesses II's reign (ca. 1279 BCE), the New Year began on June 28. By his death in 1213 BCE, it had receded to June 22.

There was no system for counting the years from a key event like the birth of Christ. Instead, the Egyptians chronicled the sum total of all the years every king reigned for as far back as they had records. Each new ruler who came to the throne began a new count of his years of rule, which we call "regnal years." The first year of Ramesses II's reign was therefore "regnal year one" and his last came in "regnal year sixty-seven." His successor Merenptah started his own "regnal year one" and so on until his death. In the New Kingdom, the first day of a new king's reign, called his "accession date," came the day after his predecessor had died. Ramesses II's accession date was on the 27th day of the third month of the Harvest Season (*Shomu*), hence III *Shomu* 27.

To compile a full chronology of ancient Egyptian history, it is necessary to know the number of years each king reigned as well as the date each ruler ascended the throne according to the Egyptian civil calendar. But many dates are lost to us and we are unsure of the accession dates of some kings (like Ramesses I), while for others we are not certain of the total number of years they reigned (including Horemheb and Sety I).

A final chronological challenge is determining precisely when these ancient kings ruled by our own system of dating based on the Gregorian calendar. This is called "absolute chronology" and is an ongoing and fiercely debated field of study among scholars of antiquity. Prior to the eighth century BCE, pinning down absolute dates for key events is problematic. What year, for example, did Ramesses II come to the throne? In what year did the Battle of Kadesh occur? Inscriptions tell us the battle took place in his fifth regnal year. An ancient document records an astronomical observation of the moon that allow us to narrow down the the absolute date for Ramesses II's accession to three possibilities: 1305, 1290, and 1279 BCE. For decades Egyptologists have argued vigorously among themselves over which is the correct year. There is still no consensus, although the most widely accepted date is

1279, which I have used here mainly for convenience. But this should not be taken as definitive.

As one of my professors, Ron Leprohon, told his students: "In Egyptology dates are like prices, they are subject to change." Nor should the reader place too much faith in absolute dates for earlier pharaohs since the lengths of some of their reigns is unclear. The farther back we recede from Ramesses II's accession, the more unreliable they become, so that fixing the date of, say, Amenhotep III's reign a few generations earlier is hazardous. Even more tricky is establishing precise chronological sychronisms between Egyptian kings and their Assyrian, Babylonian, and Hittite contemporaries.

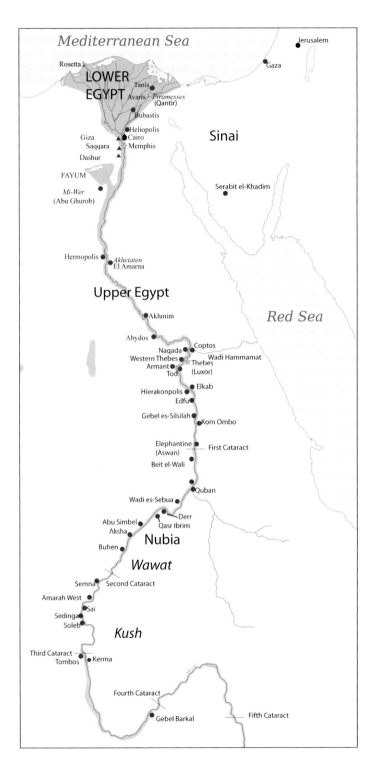

Map of Egypt and Nubia

Introduction

On the last day of her long winter journey to Egypt in 1245 BCE, the Hittite princess gazed apprehensively about her. For several weeks she had traveled through snowbound highlands in her native land, endured blustery storms as her wedding cortege trekked slowly through the cold, rainy expanses of Syria and Canaan, and across the sand-blown desert of northern Sinai before entering the strange, flat countryside of Egypt's Nile Delta. Now, as her retinue with its large military escort entered the Egyptian capital city of Piramesses, the young princess again wondered about her soon-to-be husband, Egypt's mighty Pharaoh.

Who was this man to whom her parents, the Hittite king and queen, had bartered her away? For what kind of husband had they exiled her from her homeland, never to see her family again or view the lofty mountains and high meadows of Hatti? They said Pharaoh was a great warrior once, many years ago. Her people and his had fought before the fortified towns of Syria before they forged the Eternal Treaty of Peace and Brotherhood. They said Pharaoh was old and that his many wives had borne him countless children. They even called him a living god!

As her entourage approached the wide processional avenues of Pharaoh's capital, she began to understand just why his people called him not merely the king of kings, but even the Sun God of kings. All around her stretched an urban vista utterly different from the craggy citadel of Hattusa, her father's capital in the highlands of Anatolia. At every turn Piramesses overwhelmed visitors with its gargantuan stone monuments. On the vast pylon gateways of its temples, she saw vivid war scenes carved in relief, depicting the pharaoh defeating his enemies single-handedly or ruthlessly slaying hapless foreign captives. Leaning against these towers stood tall flag masts sheathed in bronze, with gilded pinnacles flying brightly colored pennants. Dozens of huge obelisks—a veritable forest of tall granite needles carved with hieroglyphic texts and capped with gold—vied with colossal statues representing the god-king himself.

Scarcely had she arrived at Pharaoh's palace than her escort turned her over to attentive court officials and servants of his royal residence. Stripping away her native garb, they clothed the princess in a pleated linen robe. Around her neck they set a broad collar of gold and precious stones. Her arms they adorned with golden bracelets. On her head they placed an outlandishly large wig and a tall golden crown. The princess's feet were now shod with gilt leather sandals.

At last she saw the familiar face of Hatti's ambassador. Her father's envoy explained the ceremonial protocol in her native Hittite tongue, for Egyptian speech still baffled her after months of tutoring. Attendants led her through a labyrinth of corridors and rooms into Pharaoh's main audience chamber.

Throughout the majestic pillared hall an exotic crowd of people milled: foreign ambassadors, Egyptian courtiers, priests, and military officers. Closer to Pharaoh, at the far end of the hall, stood a line of royal bodyguards. Suddenly every eye gazed upon her. As she processed slowly forward they parted, revealing a ceremonial pathway on the audience hall's ornate plaster floor. There she saw painted images of prostrate foreign rulers. As she trod upon them, she realized with horror that some were her own people!

She approached the far end of the hall, where, amid dazzling pomp, she caught a first glimpse of her matrimonial destiny. Atop a dais stood a golden canopy of state. Standing to either side of this pavilion was a small crowd of men, women, and children, a fraction of Pharaoh's hundred sons and daughters. Standing closest to the throne, five women garbed as royal wives stared haughtily at their new colleague. She could hardly believe what she had been told: They were not only wives, but also his daughters!

Soon, the princess stood all alone before the podium as her escort discretely withdrew. Beneath his golden canopy sat Ramesses II, Pharaoh of Egypt. He was a tall man with a long neck, aquiline profile, and a sharp chin. Fine lines creased at the corners of his eyes. He looked remarkably hale and vigorous for a man in his mid-fifties, but she could not help noticing that he had grown stout. There was grandeur here, and unquestioned authority. Bedecked in stately robes and regalia, with a golden circlet bearing the cobra emblem resting on his brow, Pharaoh peered at his new Hittite bride with the sublime assurance and regal dignity of a living statue. A hushed silence pervaded the chamber, broken only when a herald loudly proclaimed his royal names and titles (fig. 1.1): "Insi-biya Wasmu'aria-Satepnaria, Si-Ria Riamessesa-Maiamana!"

***

It is 1245 BCE in Egypt's capital city of Piramesses, a new royal metropolis of palaces and temple complexes, all adorned with dozens of great obelisks and colossal statues that scraped the Nile Valley's blue skies. As Ramesses II first sets eyes upon his Hittite princess bride, he reigns at the height of his powers. In the thirty-fourth year since he ascended Egypt's throne, Ramesses is exactly halfway through his reign of almost seven decades. Already the pharaoh has surpassed nearly all his forebears in kingly accomplishments. Ramesses has constructed dozens of temples and palaces in cities across his realm, stretching from the

Nile Delta in Egypt's north to the far reaches of Nubia in the south, endowing them with rich offerings and precious gifts for Egypt's gods. To his glory and for his worship as a deity, Ramesses has dedicated temples and myriads of statues graven in his image, many colossal in size. In every corner of his realm thousands of monumental inscriptions exalt his royal names, extolling his warlike deeds in foreign lands and his pious acts of devotion to Egypt's gods.

During the first two decades of his reign, the king fought bravely and gloriously as Ramesses-Great of Victories, most famously at the Battle of Kadesh where—so he claimed—he faced countless Hittite foes and defeated them single-handedly. Glorifying his military exploits, his artisans sculpted panoramic battle scenes to adorn the monuments. In 1258 BCE, the twenty-first year of his reign, he forged the Eternal Treaty of Peace and Brotherhood with his Hittite counterpart Hattusili III, ending more than six decades of warfare between their empires. Peace now came to a broad swath of the ancient Near East, stretching from Anatolia across Syria, Lebanon, Canaan, Egypt, and Nubia.

FIGURE 1.1. Cartouches of Ramesses II containing his royal names and titles. From Luxor Temple. Photograph by Peter Brand.

Now, as he celebrates the second of fourteen royal Jubilees, Ramesses II rules as the living incarnation of the sun god Re-Horakhty. Here at the zenith of his reign, his people enjoy prosperity at home and peace with foreign lands. After three decades on the throne of Horus, Ramesses has transformed Egypt. Ahead lie three more decades as a living god.

Half a century earlier, his grandfather Ramesses I had founded a new royal line, the Nineteenth Dynasty. This brought an end to decades of turmoil, as the once glorious Eighteenth Dynasty convulsed in its death throes amid religious upheaval, military defeats, and epidemics besetting Egypt at every turn. These calamities rocked pharaonic kingship to its foundations.

The Rise of Imperial Egypt

In the sixteenth century BCE, two and a half centuries before Ramesses II was born, the Theban kings of the Seventeenth Dynasty expelled the foreign Hyksos rulers and reunited Egypt after a time of humiliation and political division. Their successors, the Thutmoside rulers of the early Eighteenth Dynasty forged an empire stretching from the Third

⬆ **FIGURE 1.2.** Statue of Thutmose III. Luxor Museum. Photograph by Peter Brand.

➡ **FIGURE 1.3.** Statue of Amenhotep III. Luxor Museum. Photograph by Peter Brand.

Cataract of the Nile in Nubia to the Syrian coast.[1] Their aggressive wars in the Levant culminated in Thutmose III's epic series of campaigns.[2] At the Battle of Megiddo, Thutmose (fig. 1.2) defeated a coalition of Syrian and Canaanite kingdoms led by the ruler of Kadesh, a Syrian city-state on the Orontes River. After his Megiddo victory, he led his army back into Canaan and Syria more than a dozen times, bringing most of the Levant under Egypt's dominion, including the Syrian kingdoms of Amurru and Kadesh. A strategic crossroads of the ancient Near East, the Syrian borderlands had long served as a battleground where imperial powers vied for supremacy.[3]

As the Thutmosides extended Egyptian sway northward into Syria, they inevitably collided with the Hurrian rulers of the powerful empire of Mitanni.[4] From its homeland east of the Euphrates River in northern Mesopotamia, Mitanni sought to control the Syrian lands lying to its west. Many of the petty kingdoms and city states in the Syrian heartlands fell within Mitanni's orbit during the fifteenth century BCE. A century of hostilities between the two empires ensued, until Pharaoh Thutmose IV concluded a lasting peace with Artatama I of Mitanni. Cordial relations reached an apogee when Pharaoh Amenhotep III married both a sister and a daughter of Artatama I's successor Tushratta, cementing an alliance between the two great powers (fig. 1.3).[5]

With Egypt's empire at peace after decades of conflict, Amenhotep III now enjoyed the military and diplomatic windfall his ancestors bequeathed to him.[6] He presided over a golden age of Egyptian civilization, which attained unparalleled heights of prosperity and sophistication.[7] Amenhotep built temples across Egypt and Nubia and erected hundreds of royal statues to glorify himself, including dozens of colossi consecrated to his cult of divine kingship. In his last decade Amenhotep III reigned as a living incarnation of the sun god, celebrating his apotheosis in three magnificent Jubilee festivals and a vast campaign of monumental construction.[8]

The Amarna Period: Egypt in Crisis

When Amenhotep III died in the thirty-eighth year of his reign, Egypt's throne passed to his young heir Amenhotep IV, better known as Akhenaten (fig. 1.4).[9] Historians call the tumultuous two decades when Akhenaten and his ephemeral successors ruled Egypt the Amarna period. Forsaking Egypt's ancient pantheon, the new king undertook a religious revolution, establishing the worship of a new

FIGURE 1.4. Colossal bust of Akhenaten. Luxor Museum. Photograph by Peter Brand.

sun god called the Aten in the form of the solar disk. Changing his name from Amenhotep, meaning "Amun is Content" to Akhenaten, "Beneficial for the Sun Disk," he built a new capital called Akhetaten, "the Horizon of the Sun-Disk," in Middle Egypt at the modern site of El-Amarna.

Closing all temples across Egypt except those of the Sun God, Akhenaten shunned the cults of the old gods, depriving their temples of patronage. Next, he unleashed a program of iconoclasm against them. His agents smashed statues of the gods and chiseled their names and images from temples and monuments. None suffered more than the imperial deity Amun-Re, whom the king singled out as the special target of his ire, along with Amun's consort, the goddess Mut, and their son, the moon god Khonsu. At Thebes the iconoclasts defaced Amun's holy places, especially the great temples of Karnak and Luxor.

Akhenaten's religious revolution faltered once he died, but it wrought incalculable damage, disrupting Egypt's administrative, economic, and social systems. He had brutally severed the ties binding Pharaoh and his people to their gods. The deities Akhenaten spurned now seemed to take revenge in a series of misfortunes that struck Egypt in the waning days of the Eighteenth Dynasty, even as it faced a new rival in Syria—the resurgent Hittite Empire (fig. 1.5).

Egypt and the Hittite Empire

Hatti was the most powerful kingdom in Anatolia (modern Turkey) during the late Bronze Age. Surrounded by hostile neighbors, the Hittites were, by necessity, fierce warriors. In the fifteenth century BCE success on the battlefield fueled imperial ambitions and brought Hatti the status of a great power, the peer of empires like Babylonia, Egypt, and Mitanni. During the first half of the Eighteenth Dynasty, Egypt and Hatti did not share a mutual border in Syria that would have led to friction. Instead, the Thutmoside pharaohs vied with Mitanni. A Hittite ruler sent an embassy to Thutmose III, congratulating him after he crossed the Euphrates and raided the Mitanni homeland.[10] It was likely in the reign of Thutmose, or his successor Amenhotep II, that Egypt and Hatti concluded a treaty of peace and friendship called the Kurustama Treaty.[11] This pact remained in effect for over a century, even after Egypt came to terms with its former enemy Mitanni. But the early fourteenth century BCE saw Hatti's fortunes decline, as hostile neighbors attacked it on all sides and burnt its capital city of Hattusa to the ground.

With the accession of Suppiluliuma I, sometime during Amenhotep III's reign, a resurgent Hatti seized the initiative in Syria.[12] Shortly after Akhenaten ascended Egypt's throne, the Hittite king Suppiluma I shattered decades of relative peace that had becalmed the ancient Near East since Thutmose IV's entente with Mitanni. Suppiluliuma invaded Mitanni, compelling King Tushratta to flee his capital of Washshukani in disgrace. Hittite forces then swept down into Syria, overcoming vassal kingdoms once subject to Mitanni.[13]

Pharaoh also possessed subject kingdoms in Syria (fig. 1.6), and these now came under Hittite control.[14] Under pressure, Egypt's northernmost satellite, the costal trading center of Ugarit, switched its allegiance to Suppiluliuma without a fight.[15] Farther south, despite Hatti's long-standing peace treaty with Egypt, the city-state of Kadesh also entered the Hittite fold.

Since Thutmose III first conquered Kadesh in the fifteenth century BCE, the Eighteenth Dynasty pharaohs regarded this strategic town

Black Sea

KASKA
Nerik

ARAWANNA
Hattusa
Troy   Samuha

HATTI

SEHA RIVER
LAND   HAPALLA   PITASSA

MIRA
                                              Kummanni   Tigris R.
ARZAWA   KIZZUWATNA   HANIGALBAT
                        TARHUNTASSA   Carchemish
LUKKA   MUKISH
                                     Alalah Aleppo   MITANNI   Nineveh
                                          Emar   Assur
                        UGARIT   ASHTATA
                        Ugarit   NUHASSE   ASSYRIA
                    AMURRU   Tunip
Cyprus   Dapur Qatna
                Ullaza   Kadesh
                Byblos   Ribla
                Beirut AMKI
                Sidon   UPE
Mediterrnean Sea   Tyre   Damascus
                Acre
                Megiddo
            Jezreel Valley Beth Shean   Babylon KASSITE
            Ashkelon   Gezer   BABYLONIA
            Jerusalem   Nippur
                EGYPT
                Piramesses

Memphis

                                              N   0   200 km
Amarna

as their rightful possession.[16] Later Hittite accounts claimed Suppiluliuma sought to avoid encroaching on Egypt's sphere of influence, but
that Shutatarra, the king of Kadesh, attacked Hittite forces operating
near his border. Suppiluliuma crushed the upstart, making Kadesh a
Hittite tributary. The troublesome city-state now became the chief bone
of contention between Egypt and Hatti, a dispute that would drag on
another six decades.

Bordering on Kadesh, another erstwhile Egyptian vassal, the Syrian
kingdom of Amurru, also slipped from Pharaoh's grasp. Aziru, Amurru's canny king, played a dangerous double game with Egypt and Hatti. For years he manipulated both sides diplomatically, seeking to gain
autonomy. Exploiting the political chaos Suppiluliuma's Syrian wars
had unleashed, he even expanded his realm by attacking nearby city-
states like Sumur and Byblos. During Akhenaten's reign, Aziru at last
succumbed to Hittite pressure and swore allegiance to Suppiluliuma.
When the dust had settled, Akhenaten confronted the loss of his three
northernmost satellites.[17]

FIGURE 1.5. The ancient Near East in the Late Bronze Age. Map by Tina Ross.

FIGURE 1.6. Syria in the Ramesside period (ca. 1300–1100 BCE). Map by Tina Ross.

The Struggle for Syria

In the face of these setbacks, Akhenaten at first seemed to dither. In the Amarna Letters—a cluster of diplomatic messages found in the ruins of his capital Akhetaten—his Syrian and Canaanite vassals sound the alarm about Suppiluliuma's aggression and the perfidy of his new henchman, the treacherous Aziru of Amurru. They also grumble about the pharaoh's studied indifference to their plight, and his refusal to even respond to their messages.[18]

In light of these missives, for most of the twentieth century, scholars of antiquity took a dim view of Akhenaten's record as a statesman and warrior. They concluded that he was a pacifist and a religious fanatic, so absorbed by his new solar cult that he ignored Egypt's empire. More recently, historians have questioned this alarmist reading of the Amarna Letters.[19] Regardless, Akhenaten left the petty rulers of the Levant to their own devices. But this policy of imperial nonchalance proved hazardous to Egypt's interests there.[20] Akhenaten miscalculated and lost his border provinces.[21] Ugarit was a permanent loss, but he refused to concede Amurru and Kadesh. Late in his reign, Akhenaten sent his army to reconquer Kadesh, but the mission failed.[22]

Tutankhamun's Life and Death

Soon after his failed bid to recapture Kadesh, Akhenaten died. His immediate successors, Smenkhkare and the female Pharaoh Neferneferuaten, reigned only briefly. They revived worship of the old pantheon, returning Amun-Re to his seat as King of the Gods. Egypt's throne shortly fell to Akhenaten's nine-year-old son Tutankhamun.[23] Under the tutelage of high officials like the chamberlain Ay and General Horemheb, Tutankhamun decreed a program of religious restoration (fig. 1.7).[24]

But, after decades of royal inbreeding, with pharaohs often marrying close female relatives, genetic maladies crippled the last scion of the royal house. The sickly young king failed to beget an heir by his sister-wife, Queen Ankhesenamun. The Eighteenth Dynasty, whose monarchs forged Egypt's empire two centuries before him, now fell into terminal decline.[25]

The Niphururiya Affair

Toward the end of the Eighteenth Dynasty, one of the most remarkable events in the late Bronze Age transpired between Egypt and Hatti, when Suppiluiluma I and a pharaoh's widow sought to make peace between their kingdoms through a marriage pact. We only know of this from cuneiform texts unearthed in the Hittite archives, which tell how an Egyptian king the Hittite sources call "Niphururiya" died shortly after he sent his troops in a failed bid to reconquer Kadesh. Niphururiya's widow wrote to Suppiluliuma with an extraordinary proposal. Declaring that her husband lacked a son, the Egyptian queen pleaded with him to send one of his own sons to marry her and become the next Egyptian king.[26]

This would have ended the conflict in one bold stroke by placing a Hittite prince on Egypt's throne.

FIGURE 1.7. Relief of Tutankhamun from the Colonnade Hall of Luxor Temple. Photograph by Peter Brand.

After tense negotiations, Suppululiuma agreed and sent a prince named Zannanza to Egypt. After Zannanza died mysteriously on his journey, an enraged Suppululiuma accused the Egyptians of assassinating him. Another pharaoh succeeded Niphururiya. He denied complicity in these charges and attempted to smooth the incident over.[27] Suppiliuma now took revenge for attacks on Kadesh and Zannanza's death, invading Egyptian-held Amki despite Hatti's treaty with Egypt.

Adding to the chaos, a deadly pandemic now gripped the entire Near East. Soon after Suppiluliuma took Amki, it struck down the great warrior king and his short-lived heir.[28] Seeking to understand the plague that killed his father and brother, the next Hittite ruler, Mursili II, divined that Hatti's gods had punished them for breaking the ancient Kurustama Treaty with Egypt.[29]

Scholars are fiercely divided about the identity of "Niphururiya." The two most plausible candidates are Akhenaten and Tutankhamun.[30] Amid the ruins of the temples of Karnak and Luxor, archaeologists have found fragments of a battle scene depicting Tutankhamun and his army assaulting a fortified Syrian town.[31] Was this Kadesh? No inscription identifying the enemy town has been unearthed. This evidence for his Syrian campaign, and the fact that he lacked a natural heir, bolster the case that Tutankhamun was Niphururiya.

After Tutankhamun died, his aged royal Chancellor Ay mounted Egypt's throne, only to die four years later without a son to replace him.[32] For the second time in a few short years, kingship passed not from father to son, but from one high official to another, undermining the principle of inherited succession.

Horemheb and the End of the Eighteenth Dynasty

Ay's successor was Horemheb, Egypt's top military commander (fig. 1.8). Under Tutankhamun and Ay, Horemheb had ascended to the highest echelons of Egypt's military and administrative power structure. In addition to his title of "supreme general of the army," Horemheb held several high offices including that of vizier, and honorific titles marking him as the presumptive heir to the throne.[33] After three decades of turmoil since the death of Amenhotep III, Egyptians hoped that Horemheb would usher in an era of renewal and stability.[34] For years, greedy officials exploited the disruption arising from Akhenaten's policies and the weakness of his successors by plundering state resources. At Karnak Temple, Horemheb issued an edict to stamp out this corruption.[35]

Seeking to distance himself from the Amarna pharaohs, Horemheb suppressed their memory by demolishing Akhenaten's constructions and erasing the names of Tutankhamun and Ay from temples and monuments, replacing them with his own cartouches. Egyptologists often assume domestic affairs so preoccupied Horemheb that he did not engage in foreign wars during his reign.[36] Yet the historical annals of his Hittite contemporary Mursili II record that Horemheb contested Hatti's claims in Syria by force of arms.[37]

Recently fragments of another battle scene, from a temple Horemheb built at Thebes, have come to light. They depict him assaulting a Syria citadel. This time, a part of the hieroglyphic caption text identifies the enemy fortress as "the town His Person captured in the land of Ked—." The end of the name is missing, but it is likely Kadesh, indicating that Horemheb reconquered the city.[38] Another text dated to Horemheb's sixteenth regnal year reports that his armies penetrated deep into Hittite-controlled territory as far north as Carchemish.[39]

For Horemheb, military success in Syria was fleeting. Kadesh quickly reverted to Hittite control. This was only the midpoint in a bitter struggle between Egypt and Hatti that continued under his Nineteenth Dynasty successors Sety I and Ramesses II. Although Akhenaten, Tutankhamun, and Horemheb all waged aggressive wars in Syria, Egypt's former provinces of Kadesh and Amurru remained in Hatti's grasp.

Egypt now faced an uncertain future. Despite his able and vigorous rule, Horemheb, like Tutankhamun and Ay before him, failed to produce a natural heir. Amid this crisis, an infant we now know as Ramesses II came into this world, the offspring of a line of military officers from the Nile Delta. While he later claimed to have been born as a prince whom the gods ordained to "rule while in the egg," little Ramesses began life as a private subject under a dying royal house.

FIGURE 1.8. Statue of Horemheb as Vizier and Great General of the Army under Tutankhamun and Ay. New York, Metropolitan Museum of Art.

Introducing Ramesses II

Superlatives naturally attach themselves to Ramesses II, Egypt's greatest pharaoh, its most colossal builder, a prolific father of at least one hundred children, and husband to more than a dozen royal wives. A fierce warrior on the battlefield, he also distinguished himself as a statesman and peacemaker, concluding one of history's first-known peace treaties with Egypt's long-time enemy, the Hittite Empire. Ramesses II was one of history's first "sun kings"—for much of his reign he governed as the living incarnation of the sun god Re-Horakhty. Ruling longer than most monarchs in human history, he presided over ancient Egypt during its imperial age for almost sixty-seven years and died in his late eighties or early nineties. Few ancients lived longer.

Ramesses II's exploits do not impress his modern detractors, who regard him as the worst sort of ancient despot, a vainglorious and tiresome poohbah who accomplished little of substance beyond excessive self-promotion. Yes, they concede, he built many monuments, but they view these as of poor quality and in bad taste. More often, they protest, he stole credit for works his predecessors created by erasing their names from monuments and carving his own in their place. Further, they complain, he was a military bungler who fell gullibly into a trap that his enemies set for him at the Battle of Kadesh, and blatantly lied about its outcome. His arrogance supposedly exceeded that of any other Egyptian monarch, as if feelings of royal superiority were unique to Ramesses II. Modesty has never been accounted among the virtues of kings.

Too often historians fall into the trap of judging Ramesses II by modern standards. Today, many despise the tireless self-promotion and the cults of personality authoritarian rulers cultivate, even if avid fans admire these qualities in celebrities. But what kind of man, we wonder, lurked behind this pharaoh's grandiose façade? He appears to us only in the guise he wanted us to see—an awesome god-king and mighty warrior.

Egyptian rulers conceal their true selves behind the mask of royalty, presenting themselves through idealized literature and art. This mask rarely slips, and even when it does, another lies behind it. When a pharaoh like Ramesses II chooses to display his emotions—praising his dead father Sety I, or calling out to his celestial protector Amun-Re when Hittite troops ambush him at Kadesh—we must always remember he has an ideological agenda, and his words are thoroughly scripted.

Too often modern observers ascribe motives, emotions, and personalities to ancient Egyptian kings. Most of this "analysis" is pure fantasy or rubbish pop psychology. This book aims to take a fresh, more dispassionate look at a truly remarkable historical figure, resisting the temptation to pass judgement or to accept his image at face value.

A more balanced and nuanced perspective on the king and his accomplishments reveals that Ramesses II's artists and scribes had mastered the art of ancient "spin control" and "image management." They created one of history's first political cults of personality, by which Ramesses restored the prestige of his kingly office, damaged by recent turmoil, to unquestioned authority. Not a stale imitator of older traditions, he was an innovator who adapted traditional images and themes and introduced bold new ones.

History and Ideology

So, how do we approach such a larger-than-life, yet historically remote, figure as Ramesses II? Historians should avoid the extremes of hero worship or hatchet job. This book seeks neither to idolize the pharaoh nor to debunk him. It has twin aims: first, to reconstruct his reign within the broader historical context of Egypt and the ancient Near East during the thirteenth century BCE. Second, it attempts to illuminate the ideological foundations of the ancient texts and monumental art that constitute our main sources for the history of his reign.

Ancient Egypt's worldview, and its sophisticated ideology of kingship, permeate all the texts and monuments of Ramesses II's age. The king's formal inscriptions are profoundly dogmatic. In using them to reconstruct events of the past, we must first penetrate a dense ideological filter. We may define ideology as the mental construct by which ancient Egyptian civilization viewed and justified itself. Ancient Egypt possessed no abstract concept of "the State," or "the Government." Instead, Pharaoh embodied all political authority and ruled his kingdom as if it were one great household, with him as its father. If France's Louis XIV allegedly quipped "I am the State," Ramesses would retort "I am the Civilization." In the ancient Egyptian worldview, the monarch stood at the epicenter of the universe; its survival depended on him exercising his powers to maintain Maat, or Universal Order.

The concept of Maat is fundamental to ancient Egyptian thought. It connotes a range of meanings encompassing notions of Truth, Justice, Order, and Cosmic Balance. Maat constituted the universal order that the creator god established at the dawn of time, which the Egyptians called the "first event" (sep-tepy). The opposite of Maat was Isfet, meaning Chaos, but also Falsehood and Wrongdoing.

Pharaoh upheld Maat through all his words and actions. In the human realm, he governed his people as the sole lawgiver. Religiously, he served as chief intermediary between humanity and the gods, and he himself was quasi-divine. To placate the gods, he constructed temples and monuments for worshiping them and presented rich offerings in their sanctuaries. Pharaoh's symbiosis with Egypt's deities was the essence of Maat. On the battlefield, he fought as a champion of Maat against the chaotic forces Egypt's foreign enemies embodied.[40] He was a leader who, according to traditional royal dogma, single-handedly defeated his foes in war. Modern viewers often criticize Ramesses II's claim to have fought alone at the Battle of Kadesh, but in fact the ideological trope of Pharaoh as a lone warrior overcoming countless enemies was fundamental to all Egyptian kings. [41]

In attempting to reconstruct the history of Ramesses II, we should regard the ideology pervading his hieroglyphic inscriptions and monumental art not as an obstacle, but as a proper subject for study itself. Monumental texts and images are the normative product of ancient Egyptian culture. We must accept that the ideological filter prevents us from learning much we would dearly like to know. Disregarding the dogmatic bent of pharaonic texts and artworks and taking them at face value can lead to naïve and credulous reconstructions. At the opposite extreme, dismissing them all as propaganda devoid of historical import is an oversimplification. Far better to steer a middle, but uncertain, course between these extremes than to cling to false certainties at either end of the spectrum.[42] By examining the hieroglyphic texts and monumental imagery on their own terms, we can gain a deeper understanding of the Egyptian worldview and, hopefully, of historical events.

Notes

1. Redford 1992, 125–213.
2. Redford 2003; Spalinger 2005, 83–100, 110–39.
3. Redford 1992; Bryce 2003, 34–40.
4. Redford 1992, 129–40.
5. On Tushratta and his diplomatic interactions with Amenhotep III and Akhenaten, see Liverani 2000; Zaccagnini 2000b. See also Bryce 2003, 61–153.
6. O'Connor and Cline 1998. For a recent general overview, see Dodson 2014a.
7. Kozloff, Bryan, and Berman 1992; O'Connor and Cline 1998.
8. See Johnson 1998.
9. The literature on Akhenaten and his reign is virtually endless and grows constantly. For comprehensive and authoritative recent studies see Laboury 2010; Hoffmeier 2015. For a recent historiographical overview see Ridley 2019.
10. Redford 2003, 250–54.
11. In tandem with this earliest accord, the two kingdoms also agreed to transfer a large group of captive people from the Hittite-controlled territory of Kurustama into Egyptian lands. The relationship between these protocols was so close that Hittite bureaucrats inscribed this Kurustama memorandum on the reverse sides of tablets containing the peace treaty itself. Only fragmentary copies of either text still exist, but enough remains to show this pact included a mutual nonaggression and defense clause. Sürenhagen 1985, 2006; Singer 2004; Simon 2007; Groddek 2008; Breyer 2010a, 2010c; Devecchi 2015. See p. 313 below.
12. On the chronology of his reign see Bryce 2005, 154–89; Wilhelm 2012; Stavi 2015.
13. Bryce 2005, 154–89. See most recently Stavi 2015, 79–182; Wilhelm 2015.
14. Darnell and Manassa 2007, 142–70.
15. See most recently Eßbach, 2020.
16. Redford 2003; Klengel 1992; Warburton 1997; Brand 2007a.
17. Murnane 1990, 1–38; Stavi 2015, 79–182.
18. Since they first came to light in the late nineteenth century at the site of Akhenaten's capital at El-Amarna, the corpus of cuneiform tablets called the Amarna Letters has been our main historical source for Egypt's relations with the ancient Near East during the late Eighteenth Dynasty. For translations of the Amarna Letters, see Moran 1992; Rainey 2015. The literature on these precious documents is prodigious. For key historical analysis of the letters, see Liverani 1982; Cohen and Westbrook 2000; Bryce 2005, 154–89; Darnell and Manassa, 2007, 147–56; Morris, 2018, 141–86.
19. Earlier scholars took the harangues of these "faithful vassals" at face value: e.g., Breasted 1905, 382–89. Beginning with the pioneering work of Liverani historians took a more skeptical view of the blatantly self-serving agendas Egypt's vassal kings pursued and the alarmist and obsequious language they employ in their letters to the pharaoh. Akhenaten's Canaanite liegemen deliberately exaggerated the gravity of the threats their neighbors posed in lurid reports they sent him—both to curry favor as his loyal henchmen, and to elicit his military intervention on their behalf; Liverani 1982, 3–13; Morris 2018, 165–86.

20. Bryce 2003, 145–69. Liverani (1982) calls the infighting between the pharaoh's Canaanite and Syrian vassals a state of "permanent abnormality."

21. Some have argued that Akhenaten cut his losses after deciding that holding Syria was not worth the effort: Darnell and Manassa, 2007, 170–72; Morris, 2018, 188. This is doubtful. Such clear-eyed *Realpolitik* is rare enough in modern times when ideology still trumps pragmatism and states often doggedly pursue military action even after major setbacks or when facing unending conflict. Witness the failure of two decades of US involvement in Afghanistan, or the previous British and Soviet experiences in that "graveyard of empires."

22. For Akhenaten's Kadesh campaign, see Darnell and Manassa 2007, 172–76.

23. Gabolde (2015) and Eaton-Krauss (2016) both provide authoritative historical analyses of Tutakhamun's reign. For a general overview, see Dodson 2018, 61–88. On his tomb and its treasures see most recently the essays collected in Connor and Laboury 2020.

24. Gabolde 2015; Eaton-Krauss 2016, 33–54; Dodson 2018, 63–64.

25. When the English archaeologists Howard Carter discovered Tutankhamun's tomb in 1922, he found the mummified remains of two stillborn girls suffering from severe birth defects, offering sad but poignant testimony of the young king's failure to sire a natural heir.

26. Recorded in The Deeds of Suppiluliuma; see Hoffner 1997, 185–92.

27. In a fragmentary letter to Suppiluliuma, Niphururiya's unnamed successor denied complicity in Zannanza's death; van den Hout 1994.

28. Bryce 2005, 188–91.

29. From Mursili II's Second Plague Prayer. For translations see Singer 2002, 57–61; Beckman 1997a.

30. This notorious incident has provoked fierce debate among Egyptologists and Hittitologists as to Niphururiya's identity. In one view, accepted here, he was Tutankhamun; see Bryce 2003, 187–98; 2005, 179; Darnell and Manassa 2007, 184–86; Brand 2008; Breyer 2010a, 171–96; Dodson 2018, 89–95. Others make the case for Niphururiya as Akhenaten or even Smenkhkare; see Gabolde 2015; Wilhelm 2009, 2012; Laboury 2010, 329–34. More recently Miller and Devecchi have offered new cuneiform evidence for a synchronism of Egyptian and Hittite chronology that requires Nipkhururiya to have been Akhenaten; see Miller 2007; Devecchi and Miller 2011. Embraced by some (e.g., Stavi 2015), their interpretation has not gone unchallenged (by, e.g., Simon 2009). It is unlikely that a consensus will ever be reached and the problem may be insoluble.

31. Johnson 1992, 2009; Darnell and Manassa 2007, 178–84.

32. Eaton-Krauss 2016, 119–21; Dodson 2018, 95–108. Ay was likely the king who denied involvement in Zannanza's death.

33. Redford 1995; Dodson 2018, 65–66; Kawai 2010; Martin et al. 2016, 143–46.

34. For an overview of Horemheb's reign see Dodson 2018, 109–34.

35. For a convenient translation, see Redford 1995, 235–40, no. 108.

36. Some go so far as to claim that Horemheb was too exhausted from his military service at the behest of Tutankhamun to lead campaigns of his own once he became Pharaoh: Darnell and Manassa 2007, 176.

37. The evidence for Horemheb's military campaigns in Syria as king in the Egyptian and Hittite sources is scattered and fragmentary but reveals that he fought aggressively there during the reign of the Hittite king Mursili II: Redford

1973; Spalinger 1979a; Johnson 1992, 128–29; Bryce 2005, 201–2; Miller 2008; Wilhelm 2009; Devecchi and Miller 2011; Grimal 2018.

38. Johnson 1992, 186, fig. 71. Alternatively, it could be Qode, another Syrian kingdom.

39. A granite bowl records Horemheb's "first campaign of victory" against Carchemish in northern Syria in his sixteenth regnal year. Redford first described the piece in the early 1970s, but it soon vanished and most scholars long rejected it as a forgery. But Grimal has now located and published the bowl, proving beyond all doubt that it is genuine: Redford 1973; Grimal 2018.

40. For a more nuanced view of Maat in the context of warfare, see Allon 2021.

41. Liverani, 2001, 80–85; Brand forthcoming. See pp. 116–17 below.

42. Kitchen (1982) often takes the sources at their word, especially in his popular biography of Ramesses II. At the other extreme, Liverani (2001) tends to reject the historical veracity of ancient texts altogether, especially the Battle of Kadesh narrative. In a related vein, Van der Mieroop (2007) sees the traditional pursuit of "event history" as futile, even for a well-documented period like the early Nineteenth Dynasty, taking inspiration from Braudel and the *Annales* school.

Chapter Two

Rise of the Ramessides: The Reigns of Ramesses I and Sety I

The Queen's Bones

In the burial shaft of a tomb at Saqqara, the necropolis of ancient Memphis, excavators discovered the remains of a woman who died while pregnant around 3,300 years ago. Mingled with her remains were the tiny bones of her unborn child. This sad domestic tragedy has even greater historical significance because archaeologists believe she was none other than Queen Mutnodjemet, Horemheb's (fig. 2.1) chief consort. When anthropologists examined her pelvis, they observed deep scarring arising from multiple difficult and unsuccessful pregnancies. Mutnodjemet's bones reveal both a personal tragedy and a political crisis, as Horemheb desperately attempted to father an heir by his chief queen.[1]

New Kingdom pharaohs were polygamous and Horemheb surely had other wives by whom he could sire male offspring. For reasons we do not fully understand, if any sons born to lesser wives existed, they were ineligible to succeed him. Lacking male offspring born to the Great Royal Wife Mutnodjemet, Horemheb faced a vexing decision. As his Queen lay dying, the last Eighteenth Dynasty pharaoh knew he must ensure a stable transmission of royal power, even though his successor would not be of his bloodline. If he chose wisely, Horemheb would ensure Egypt's future political stability. Failing this, his kingdom would plunge into a succession crisis—perhaps even civil war. We cannot overstate what shaky foundations the principle of inherited succession rested on as the Eighteenth Dynasty drew to an end.[2] According to the archetypical myth of pharaonic rule, each new monarch embodied Horus, god of kingship, who inherited his office from his divine father Osiris. But now, Horemheb's chosen heir would ascend Egypt's throne as the third consecutive appointee to the throne with no royal blood flowing in his veins.

General Pramessu, the Heir Presumptive

Horemheb could only appoint another high official to succeed him. He knew just the man: General Pramessu, a trusted confidant with military

FIGURE 2.1. Horemheb offering wine to Amun-Re in a scene from the gate of the Tenth Pylon at Karnak. Photograph by Peter Brand.

credentials like those Horemheb once held during his own preroyal career. Pramessu descended from a military family hailing from Avaris, a city in the northeastern Nile Delta. His father, the elder Sety, served as a middle-ranking army officer.[3] Pramessu rose through the ranks and joined Egypt's military high command as a "great general of the army" (*imy-ra mesha wer*). Horemheb also bestowed signal honors on Pramessu's eldest son Sety, a man in his twenties named after his grandsire. In fact, Pramessu could boast of two generations of potential heirs, for the younger Sety gave the general a grandson born during Horemheb's reign.[4] Sety named the child Pramessu in honor of his grandfather, but we know him as Ramesses II.

Upon designating General Pramessu as his successor, Horemheb groomed him for kingship just as Tutankhamun and Ay had once prepared his own path to power (fig. 2.2). Transitions from one ruling dynasty to another were often fraught with ideological conundrums and political difficulties. Yet no one must question or challenge the right of Horemheb's designated heir. Smoothing his way to power, Horemheb granted Pramessu Egypt's highest military and civilian offices, including that of vizier, the ancient equivalent of a prime minister. In New Kingdom times, two viziers stood at the apex of the royal administration, second only to Pharaoh himself. One, based in Memphis, supervised Lower Egypt, while his colleague oversaw affairs in Upper Egypt from his headquarters at Thebes. Horemheb also chose Sety as his father's colleague in the vizierate.

We can reconstruct Pramessu's extraordinary rise to power from a series of impressive offices and epithets his regal mentor bestowed upon him. Lists of his titles appears on a pair of statues depicting Pramessu as vizier, which archaeologists discovered in the ruins of Karnak Temple:[5]

> *What was given through royal favor to the chief of archers, overseer of horses, overseer of the border fortress, and overseer of the Nile mouths, charioteer of His Person, royal messenger to every foreign country, royal scribe, commander of archers, general of the army of the Lord of the Two Lands, overseer of the priests of all the gods, king's deputy in Upper and Lower Egypt, chief justice and warden of Nekhen, priest of Maat, heir*

apparent, city mayor, vizier, and overseer of the great courts, Pramessu.[6]

Like their royal masters, Egyptian officials loved to acquire impressive titles and rehearse them in monumental lists. An additional text on the statue's base describe Pramessu as: "The hereditary noble (*iry-pat*) and courtier, [mouth that pacifies the] entire [land] ... fan bearer on the king's right side, hereditary noble, city mayor, and vizier, Pramessu." Pramessu's statue credits his father, the elder Sety, with a more modest rank: "judge and chief of archers."[7]

Originating in Egypt's earliest dynasties, the honorific "hereditary noble" (*iry-pat*) traditionally distinguished high officials as members of the court elite. In the late Eighteenth Dynasty, kings who lacked natural heirs conferred the title *iry-pat* on their hand-picked successors. It takes pride of

place in the myriad civilian and military titles bestowed on Generalissimo Horemehb as heir presumptive. As king, Horemheb conferred it on Pramessu for the same reason.[8] Later, Nineteenth and Twentieth Dynasty pharaohs, including Sety I and Ramesses II, often granted this title to their eldest sons, distinguishing them as Crown Prince. Another unique epithet Pramessu received from Horemheb was "deputy of His Person in Upper and Lower Egypt," recalling the honorific "king's deputy in the entire land," which Horemheb held before he was king.[9]

Through these honorifics, we can trace General Pramessu's meteoric ascent in Horemheb's regime. Originally a "chief of archers" like his father, Pramessu soon attained the more prestigious rank of overseer of horses, Egypt's chariot forces being the elite branch of its military. Pharaoh charged Pramessu with guarding Egypt's northern frontier, making him responsible for protecting several mouths of the Nile Delta branches along Egypt's Mediterranean coast. He also took command of the massive garrison fortress of Tcharu at the Delta's northeastern frontier. Strategic gateway to the Levant, Tcharu stood at the entrance to the Ways of Horus, a military highway stretching across northern Sinai into Canaan.[10]

Further evidence for the preroyal careers of Pramessu, who later became Ramesses I, and his son Sety, comes from a unique edict his grandson Ramesses II issued decades later, the so-called Four Hundred Year Stela, originally from Piramesses but unearthed at Tanis.[11] Carved on a large granite tablet, this hieroglyphic text marked the four hun-

FIGURE 2.3. Ramesses II's "Four Hundred Year Stela." In the scene, Ramesses II and the Vizier Sety (right) worship Seth of Avaris. Cairo, Egyptian Museum JdE 6039. Photograph courtesy of Erika Feleg.

dredth anniversary of some momentous occasion, which the surviving text never mentions.[12] Ramesses II's decree dates to the middle years of his long reign but recalls events that took place several decades earlier in Horemheb's later years, when Pramessu and his son Sety were the viziers of Upper and Lower Egypt.[13] Following Ramesses II's own names and titles, it reports (fig. 2.3):

> *His Person commanded a great stela of granite be made in the great name of the fathers of his father, to establish the name of the father of his fathers: King Menmaatre, the Son of Re Sety-Merenptah, established and enduring for eternity like Re, every day.[14] Year four hundred, fourth month of Harvest Season (Shomu), day four (of) the Dual King Seth-Great of Strength, the Son of Re, He of Ombos, beloved of Re-Horakhty, may he exist eternally and forever.*
>
> *Arrival of the Hereditary Noble, City Mayor and Vizier, Fan-bearer on the King's Right Side, Chief of Archers, Overseer of Foreign Lands, Overseer of the Border Fortress of Tcharu, Chief of the Madjay-police, Royal Scribe, Overseer of Horses, Festival Leader of the Ram-Lord of Mendes, High Priest of Seth, Lector-priest of Wadjet, Judge of the Two Lands, Overseer of the Priests of all gods, Sety, true of voice, son of the Hereditary Noble, City Mayor and Vizier, Troop-commander, Overseer of Foreign Lands, Overseer of the Border Fortress of Tcharu, Royal Scribe, Overseer of Horses, Pramessu, true of voice, born to the Mistress of the House and Chantress of Re, Tiu, true of voice.[15]*

Sadly, the rest of the text has decayed beyond legibility, but Ramesses II's Four Hundred Year Stela constitutes our chief source for Sety I's preroyal career. Sety acquired many offices that his father Pramessu had held, but garnered further distinctions, including the priesthoods of several deities. Although his grandfather Pramessu was Ramesses II's senior ancestor, the Four Hundred Year Stela emphasizes Sety's career. A male figure follows behind Ramesses II in a scene above the text. Unfortunately, the stela has eroded, obliterating this man's head and any hieroglyphic captions identifying him. Yet he wears a pharaoh's ceremonial bull's tail, so we can identify him as Sety I.[16]

Although Sety may have become vizier only after Horemheb's death, this is unlikely. On ascending the throne, Pramessu, now Ramesses I, bestowed the title of "king's eldest son" (*sa nesu semsu*) on Sety as his designated heir. After Ramesses died, Sety took his place, the first pharaoh since Tutankhamun to succeed his father.

Ramesses I's Brief Reign

Ramesses I's ascent marked the beginning of a new royal house, the Nineteenth Dynasty. Ramesses understood this. Upon ascending the throne he chose his titulary, the sequence of five unique ceremonial names and titles distinguishing each pharaoh. The most important and prestigious element of the titulary was his first cartouche name, which Egyptologists call the prenomen or coronation name. Ramesses I modeled his prenomen on that of Ahmose, who had founded the Eighteenth Dynasty two and a half centuries earlier. Ahmose's prenomen *Neb*-Pehty-Re means "Lord of Strength Is Re." Ramesses now chose *Men*-Pehty-Re, "Established Is the Strength of Re."[17] His preroyal name Pramessu now became "Ramesses," which could be spelled *Ramessu* or *Ramesses* (fig. 2.4)[18]

Reigning for less than two years, Ramesses I erected few monuments, and no hieroglyphic inscriptions of any historical importance have come down to us.[19] His most impressive legacy was completing the relief decoration on Karnak Temple's Second Pylon gateway, which Horemheb had constructed and partially inscribed in his last years. Sculptors carved new reliefs depicting Ramesses I conducting rituals before the gods inside the vestibule and passageway of the gateway standing between the Pylon's two massive towers (fig. 2.5). Ramesses also plastered over Horemheb's cartouches

FIGURE 2.4. Ramesses I offering to Seth, divine patron of the Ramesside line. Recently discovered stela from ancient Tcharu (Hebua). Cairo JdE 100012. Photograph by Peter Brand.

FIGURE 2.5 Ramesses I. Relief from the Second Pylon at Karnak. Photograph by Peter Brand.

on its façade, and carved his own in their place, thereby taking credit for the whole structure as his own work.[20]

Ramesses I may have obtained his royal status after he had passed middle age, if the mummy belonging to an elderly individual and recently attributed to him is in fact his.[21] If so, he knew he would not reign for many years, and as the founder of a new dynasty it was imperative to ensure his succession. Fortunately, his eldest son and heir, Crown Prince Sety, was a man in his prime.

Crown Prince Sety: A Star at His Side

Acutely aware he was the first pharaoh since Tutankhamun to inherit his father's throne, Sety I dedicated several monuments to Ramesses I's memory throughout his own reign.[22] Given his nascent dynasty's non-royal heritage, such conspicuous acts of filial piety carried an overt political message. In Abydos, the holy city of Osiris in Middle Egypt, Sety I erected a small cult chapel in his deceased father's honor next to his own royal cult temple. Sety's dedicatory stela announcing this act of filial devotion constitutes our primary historical source for Ramesses I's reign, and highlights Sety's own role as heir apparent.[23] Sety also built a suite of rooms for his father's cult in his royal cult temple at Gurnah in Western Thebes (fig. 2.6).[24]

Time, the elements, and human carelessness have battered the stela, obliterating much of its hieroglyphic text, which alluded to turbulent events of the late Eighteenth Dynasty. Ideologically, Sety I's memorial for his father's cult chapel belongs to a traditional genre of official decrees having the theme of the restoration of Maat, "Universal Order," after a time of troubles.[25]

Two similar royal edicts dating from the late Eighteenth Dynasty, the Restoration Stela of Tutankhamun and Horemheb's Coronation Inscription, obliquely recall the disruptions of the Amarna period.[26] Yet these decrees do not "name names," since neither document refers to Akhenaten or to the Aten solar deity. While these proclamations may serve as useful sources of historical data, we must remember their primary function was ideological. Tutankhamun's Restoration Stela states: "If an army was sent to Djahy (the Levant) to expand the boundaries of Egypt, it met with no success."[27] The Restoration Stela never provides further, crucial details necessary to place this statement in a firm historical context. We can only be certain Egypt experienced a military setback during the Amarna period.[28] Moreover, the author employs this snippet of historical data to characterize the time before Tutankhamun's accession as one of unrelieved chaos. It exaggerates this turmoil for rhetorical effect before heralding the arrival of a savior-king—the

FIGURE 2.6. Sety I anointing Ramesses I in the guise of Osiris. Chapel of Ramesses I in Sety I's Gurnah Temple in Western Thebes. Photograph by Peter Brand.

edict's royal author—who duly suppresses Chaos and returns Maat to its place. These pharaonic decrees are deliberately vague as to the duration of the "time of troubles" they invoke.

Similar themes crop up in Sety I's Dedicatory Stela for his father's Abydos chapel. A fragmentary passage recalls some danger facing Egypt, lamenting: "There were none who overcame it, because [strife and trouble] were [abroad in the whole land ...]."[29]

Without referring to Horemheb by name, Sety's Dedicatory Stela heralds Horemheb's appointment of Pramessu as his heir, who succeeded him as Ramesses I:

> So, my father began (to exercise) the kingship of Re, being seated upon
> the throne-dais like him. His purification was performed in the Upper-
> Egyptian Shrine. He assumed [the crowns ... ruled ... with the stren]gth
> of a falcon.[30]

The main intent of Sety I's Dedicatory Stela was to prove his filial piety and to highlight his own status as Ramesses I's duly anointed heir. It dwells at length on Sety's role as Crown Prince:

> It was he (Ramesses I), indeed, who created my perfection, and
> magnified my family in (people's) minds. He gave me his counsels as
> my protection, and his teaching was like a fortress around my heart.
> See, I am a son who is beneficent for the one who created me [...] I was
> [...] adept at doing what(ever) he said.

> *I declare (all) I did for him until I became Ruler of the Two Lands. I came forth from the womb as a Champion-Bull of Maat, imbued with (his) counsels and teachings. While he was the radiant Sun God, I was with him like a star at his side.*[31]

The text portrays Ramesses as a font of wisdom for his son. Although Crown Prince Sety remains subordinate to his father—a mere star beside Ramesses I's solar brilliance—it is Sety who emerges as the main actor during Ramesses's reign in his recollections. This language might indicate Sety acted as his father's "staff of old age." But Sety I had a vested interest in playing up his role in his father's government as a way of promoting his own legitimacy as pharaoh once he succeeded him. In keeping with this theme, Sety expounds on his military leadership on his father's behalf:

> *I [subdued] for him the Fenkhu Lands (i.e., Lebanon). I drove back the rebels in foreign lands, and I protected Egypt for him as he wished. I united to him his dominion there, just like Horus (did) on the throne of Wennofer (i.e., Osiris). I selected Maat for him every day and I carried it [...]*
>
> *I marshaled his army and caused it to be of one mind. I sought out for him the condition of the Two Lands, so I might act on his behalf with my strong arm as his bodyguard in nameless foreign lands. I acted energetically in his presence, so that he opened his eyes to my perfection.*[32]

Although Ramesses I carefully prepared his son to assume power after him, he never crowned Sety as a second king ruling beside him in a political arrangement called a coregency. Coregencies were rare in Egypt, and most pharaohs—even those in need of shoring up an uncertain succession or easing the burden of ruling for an aged incumbent—were loath to share even a portion of their regal dignity with their heirs. In the Great Hypostyle Hall of Karnak there are a handful of scenes depicting Ramesses I worshiping the gods that alternate with others featuring Sety I. While some take this as evidence the two kings ruled jointly, we now know Sety I carved these inscriptions several years after his father's death as pious memorials.[33] In fact, Ramesses I did not build the Great Hypostyle Hall, a project that Sety I conceived and undertook.[34]

On coming to the throne, Ramesses I lost no time beginning work on his tomb in the Valley of the Kings.[35] When he died less than two years later, the royal tomb makers had cut only a descending passageway and the first antechamber of his sepulture into the limestone bedrock of the Valley. With their master's sudden, but not unexpected, demise, they hastily converted the antechamber into a makeshift burial vault. Unlike

FIGURE 2.7. Ramesses I before Anubis. From his tomb in the Valley of the Kings (KV 16). Alamy.

the much larger tombs of Horemheb and Sety I—both with elaborate carved and painted wall scenes—tomb makers barely had time to paint murals on his burial chamber's walls (fig. 2.7).

Renaissance: Sety I Takes the Throne

The man who now assumed the throne of Horus as Sety I possessed youthful vigor and keen ambition.[36] Determined to set Egypt upon a new path, he signaled his goals and aspirations when he chose his elaborate protocol of royal names and titles. Sety proclaimed his reign to be a renaissance, literally a "repeating of births" (*wehem-mesut*). As his father did before him, Sety modeled his titulary on glorious kings of old.[37]

The pharaohs were highly conscious of Egypt's past, evoking their ancestors to bestow an air of legitimacy on their own deeds. Sety I looked to illustrious Eighteenth Dynasty kings as inspiration, modeling his ceremonial names and epithets on its two greatest monarchs: the warlike Thutmose III, and Amenhotep III, the grand builder and self-proclaimed god-king. Fusing Thutmose III's prenomen *Men*-Kheper-Re with Amenhotep III's Neb-*Maat*-Re, Sety I's prenomen became Men-Maat-Re, meaning "The Truth of Re is Established."

Having chosen his royal stylings, Sety I now undertook the somber duty of conveying Ramesses I on his journey into the netherworld. Once embalmers completed the elaborate process of mummification during the traditional period of seventy days after death, Sety escorted his father's mortal remains to Thebes. There he presided over Ramesses's funeral rites and interred him in his hastily finished tomb in the royal valley. After performing his filial duties, Sety I embarked on an ambitious program of grand building projects at home and aggressive military campaigns abroad.

Sety I's Restoration of Monuments

Four decades before Sety I came to power, Akhenaten had suppressed the cults of Egypt's traditional gods, unleashing a widespread program of iconoclasm against them. A special target of Akhenaten's antipathy was Amun-Re, and that god's temples were in a sorry state at the end of his tumultuous reign.[38] Beginning with Tutankhamun, the last Eighteenth Dynasty pharaohs were not remiss in their pious efforts to repair the damage.[39] In his Restoration Stela, Tutankhamun evokes the derelict state of Egypt's shrines:

> *When His Person appeared as king, the temples and cities of the gods and goddesses, starting from Elephantine to the Delta marshes, had fallen into decay and their shrines had fallen into ruin, having become mounds overgrown with grass. Their sanctuaries were like something that never existed, and their buildings were a footpath, for the land was in rack and ruin.*[40]

Tutankhamun boasts of taking elaborate measures to redress the desecration Amun-Re had suffered. The young king dedicated new golden cult images and donated rich offering gifts to Amun-Re's cult establishment. Meanwhile, artisans methodically repaired vandalized icons and

reengraved their names anew on temple walls wher-
ever Akhenaten had defaced them (fig. 2.8).

Sety I also endeavored to prove his worthiness
to rule through acts of homage and pious generosity to Egypt's gods. While he laid plans for an ambitious program of new temple construction, Sety realized these projects would only bear fruit after several
years. Meanwhile, he quickly stamped his name on
existing monuments after repairing icons that Akhen-
faten's agents had defaced. Even where damage had
already been repaired, Sety made minor changes to
justify adding his name.

To herald these efforts, Sety's craftsmen inscribed
"restoration inscriptions," brief formulaic label texts
adjacent to the mended icons. Beginning with Tutankhamun, Sety I's predecessors sometimes marked
their monumental repairs with these renewal texts.[41]
Sety now employed them on a large scale.[42] A typical
example reads:

FIGURE 2.8. Restored image of Amun-Re on one of Hatshepsut's obelisks at Karnak. Sety's restoration text is at the top left corner. Photograph by Peter Brand.

Restoration of monuments that the Dual King Menmaatre made for his father Amun-Re.

Sety I's restoration texts appear frequently on Theban monuments,
especially in Amun-Re's chief shrines at Karnak and Luxor (fig. 2.9).[43]
Pharaoh's scribes chose the most prestigious and visible locations
within temple complexes when placing these labels.[44] They appear in
clusters along processional routes, on grand gateways and pylon towers, on stelae of earlier kings, and in columned halls and outer court
yards. Sety rarely inscribed these texts in the temples' inner recesses,
such as storage chambers, side chapels, or even the holy of holies
where Amun's cult statue rested in its gilded shrine. Off limits to all
but the higher echelons of the priesthood, these restricted locations
would deprive Sety's renewal texts of the wider audience he desired
for them.

Historical Background to Sety I's Foreign Wars

Meanwhile, in his first regnal year, Sety I also embarked upon his "first
campaign of victory," a large-scale military expedition into the Levant

(fig. 2.10).[45] Historians have long regarded Sety I as one of Egypt's bold-
est warrior pharaohs, crediting him with restoring Egypt's empire after
Akhenaten and his successors allegedly lost their grip on its subject
territories.[46] More recently, however, scholars have rejected claims of
a collapse during the Amarna period. Akhenaten's contemporary, the
Hittite king Suppiluliuma I, expanded into northern Syria after destroying Egypt's old ally, Mitanni.[47] So sudden was this development that
there was little Akhenaten could have done about it. With the help of
the treacherous Aziru, king of Amurru, the Hittites took over Amurru,
Kadesh, and Ugarit.[48] South of this line, however, the Canaanite kingdoms still paid tribute to Egypt. The loss of Kadesh and Amurru rankled
the pharaohs of the late Eighteenth Dynasty. Akhenaten, Tutankhamun, and Horemheb each fought to reconquer these territories, but all
their efforts proved futile.[49]

In the aftermath of these military setbacks, and given the relative stability of Egypt's hold over Canaan, Lebanon, and southern Syria, what
did Sety hope to achieve on the battlefield? Like his predecessors, Sety's
ultimate strategic objective was recapturing Amurru and Kadesh.

But Sety also strove to fulfill his role as a warrior pharaoh and guarantor of Maat against the forces of Chaos, embodied by Egypt's foreign
enemies. Leading his armies to the Levant during his first year in a
robust *tour de force*, the new king asserted his dominance over Canaan
and Lebanon. Later in his reign, he invaded Amurru and Kadesh, defeating Hittite forces on Syrian soil. He also fought Libyan tribesmen
on Egypt's western frontier, and overwhelmed Irem, a small Nubian
polity, in his eighth year. Near the end of his reign, Sety I celebrated his
military career with a war monument at Karnak Temple.

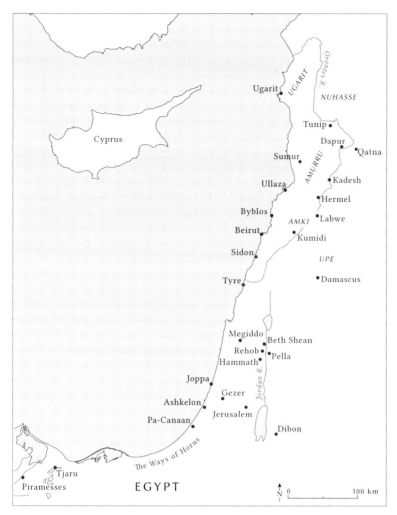

FIGURE 2.10. Egypt and the Levant in the early Nineteenth Dynasty (1305–1212 BCE). Map by Tina Ross.

Sety I's Karnak War Monument

Our chief source for Sety I's military campaigns derives from the spectacular war scenes he left on the north exterior wall of Karnak Temple's Great Hypostyle Hall (fig. 2.11).[50] A panoramic sequence of narrative battle scenes glossed with hieroglyphic captions, Sety's war monument is pharaonic Egypt's most brilliant example of military art.[51] Indeed, the triumphal message these scenes convey is so persuasive it has led historians to overestimate the king's military accomplishments.[52] Unlike the more complex account of Ramesses II's Battle of Kadesh, the thrust of Sety I's war monument is straightforward and unequivocal: Pharaoh single-handedly defeated every foe.

Egyptian battle scenes like Sety I's Karnak war monument are ideological documents, not sober historical records.[53] They evoke Pharaoh's

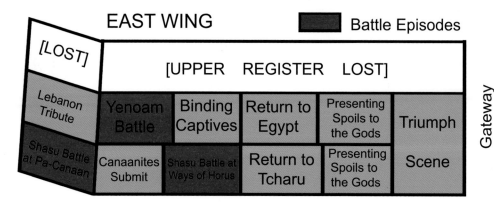

triumph as champion of Maat. Keeping this dogmatic purpose in mind, we must tread carefully when employing these records to reconstruct actual history, steering a middle course between accepting them as accurate historical chronicles or rejecting them as bombastic subterfuge devoid of truth.

Sety I's Campaigns in Canaan, Libya, and Syria

Before his first regnal year ended, Sety I led Egyptian troops and charioteers to Canaan and Lebanon on his "first campaign of victory," which he later immortalized on the eastern wing of his Karnak war panorama.[54] This was not the glorious reconquest of a lost empire as earlier generations of scholars once envisioned. Instead, Sety's first campaign was a brazen show of force to intimidate his vassals and burnish his military credentials—in essence, chariot diplomacy.[55] On Egypt's western frontier, Sety's Libyan war foreshadowed later conflicts during the reigns of his grandson Merenptah and later under Ramesses III (fig. 2.12).[56]

Having reasserted his authority in Canaan and suppressed unruly Libyan tribesmen, Sety unleashed his armies on Syria, invading Amurru, laying siege to Kadesh, and defeating a Hittite army to boot (fig. 2.13). With these crucial Syrian victories, he reached the culmination of his military career.

In his Syrian campaigns, Sety pursued the same dogged strategy as his late Eighteenth Dynasty predecessors, for Egypt refused to concede Kadesh and Amurru to the Hittites. Yet, given the poor results earlier pharaohs obtained, one might fairly ask if Sety I also came up short. His Karnak battle art portrays these clashes as victories. Should we dismiss this as mere hyperbole?

Remarkably, amid the ruins of ancient Kadesh archaeologists unearthed a battered victory stela Sety I left behind to celebrate his con-

	WEST WING		
▢ Non-Battle Episodes			
[SCENES LOST]		Kadesh Assault	Battle Episode
Triumph — Presenting Spoils to the Gods	Return to Egypt	King Slays Libyan Chief — Libyan Battle	[HIDDEN]
Scene — Presenting Spoils to the Gods	Return to Egypt	Hittite Battle	[HIDDEN]

Gateway

quest (fig. 2.14).[57] It was one thing to capture the city, but another to keep it. Kadesh reverted to Hittite control soon after his armies withdrew. Instead of destroying this reminder of Egypt's victory, Kadesh's canny rulers must have stashed it away in some secret spot. With such a token they might protest their "loyalty" to some future Egyptian conqueror.[58]

According to his Karnak monument, Sety I battled local Syrian forces, not Hittites, when he assaulted Kadesh.[59] His Syrian incursions prompted Hittite reprisals. Some time after he captured Kadesh the pharaoh clashed with a Hittite army and claimed another triumph over "the despicable land of Hatti, amongst whom His Person, L.P.H., has wrought great slaughter."[60] All told, Sety's military record, especially against the Hittites, was one that past and future pharaohs might well envy.

← ↑ FIGURE 2.11. Schematic diagram of Sety I's Karnak war monument. North exterior wall of the Great Hypostyle Hall of Karnak. Battle scenes are shown in red and nonbattle scenes in blue. Drawing by Peter Brand.

FIGURE 2.12. Sety I fighting Libyans. Karnak war monument. Photograph by Peter Brand.

FIGURE 2.13. Sety I assaulting Kadesh. Karnak war monument. Photograph by Peter Brand.

Sety I's Building Projects

Sety I undertook an ambitious building program, constructing temples at major Egyptian religious centers including Abydos, Heliopolis, Memphis, and Thebes.[61] Today, little remains of these structures in northern sites like Heliopolis and Memphis, where residents of Cairo plundered stupendous quantities of ancient masonry over the centuries.

Sety I's monuments in Upper Egypt and Nubia have fared much better. At the holy city of Abydos, sacred to Osiris and burial ground of

FIGURE 2.14. Battered victory stela of Sety I found in the ruins of Kadesh (Tell Nebi Mend). Drawing by Peter Brand.

Egypt's earliest kings, Sety constructed an elegant and architecturally innovative temple (fig. 2.15).[62] A virtual pantheon, he dedicated it to the Abydos Triad of Osiris, Isis, and Horus; and to three grand imperial deities, Amun-Re, Re-Horakhty, and Ptah. Six chapels sanctified to these gods stand in a row, next to a seventh consecrated to worship of the deified Sety himself.

FIGURE 2.15. Sety I offering incense to the Bark of Amun-Re. Temple of Sety I at Abydos. Photograph courtesy of Paul Smit.

Sety took a keen interest in his Abydos project, sending his most talented craftsmen to embellish its walls with some of the most exquisite bas-relief decoration found in all Egyptian art. In several chambers, artisans completed their work by painting the bas-reliefs in brilliant colors. Sadly, the king died before he finished the project, and it fell to his successor Ramesses II to oversee its completion. Behind his Abydos temple, Sety also constructed a unique subterranean edifice—a royal cenotaph known as the Osireion.[63] It functioned as a symbolic tomb linked to the cult of Osiris, whose own burial place Egyptians believed lay amid the cemetery of Egypt's earliest kings on the desert edge at Abydos.[64]

The Great Hypostyle Hall of Karnak

In honor of Egypt's chief god Amun-Re Sety I built his most spectacular monument, the Great Hypostyle Hall at Karnak in Thebes (fig. 2.16).[65] Standing at the heart of Amun's huge temple complex, the Great Hypostyle Hall's massive walls enclose a forest of gigantic sandstone col-

⬆ **FIGURE 2.16.** Aerial view of the Great Hypostyle Hall of Karnak Temple. Courtesy of the Franco-Egyptian Center, Karnak.

⬇ **FIGURE 2.17.** Central colonnade and clerestory windows in the Great Hypostyle Hall of Karnak. The great papyrus columns of the central aisle reach heights of 70 feet (21 meters). Alamy.

umns shaped like papyrus stalks (fig. 2.17). These support a high clerestory roof in its central aisle and a network of outsized architraves and ceiling slabs in its northern and southern wings. The largest structure of its kind the Egyptians ever built, it is an eighth wonder of the ancient world. Remarkably, the Great Hypostyle Hall remains largely intact. Covering an acre of land, the hall is vast. On every surface—its walls, columns, and even its roof—sculptors carved hundreds of hieroglyphic texts and elaborate scenes in elegant bas-relief (fig. 2.18).[66]

Hypostyle is a Greek word describing a building with columns supporting its roof. Along the hall's central east–west processional axis stand twelve great columns, with broad open papyrus-blossom capitals. Attaining heights of seventy feet (twenty-one meters), these central columns tower above 122 shorter closed-bud papyrus columns occupying the hall's northern and southern lateral wings, which still attain an impressive height of forty-five feet (fourteen meters).[67] This difference in height permitted Sety's architects to fashion the Hypostyle Hall's lofty clerestory roof with its enormous windows. Giant stone grilles filtered sunlight entering through these windows, providing an ambience of diffused illumination within the hall.

Religious themes prevail inside the Great Hypostyle Hall. Sety I embellished its interior walls and columns with elaborate pictorial scenes (all carved in elaborately painted bas-relief) and hieroglyphic captions depicting the daily cultic rituals performed within Karnak Temple.[68] Here too, his sculptors carved panoramic scenes representing the grand yearly festivals honoring Amun-Re, like the Beautiful Festival of the Valley. Sety's reliefs also portray rites of kingship and Pharaoh's close relationship with Egypt's gods.[69]

On the Great Hall's north exterior wall, Sety left his magnificent war monument. By representing the king upholding Maat through force of arms, these battle scenes imposed a magical barrier protecting the temple and its divine inhabitants from chaotic supernatural forces lurking outside its walls. After completing work in its northern wing, sculptors had just begun to decorate parts of its south aisle when Sety died. It fell to his successor Ramesses II to inscribe the rest during his own reign.[70]

The Egyptians called their temples "mansions of the gods" and built them on a three-part plan consisting of an outer court, a columned hall, and an inner complex of chapels, treasuries, and storerooms. Standing in front of the outer courts and hypostyle halls were huge double-towered gateways called pylons. Larger temples like Karnak had multiple sets of pylons, courtyards, and columned halls. This design mimicked the basic plan of human dwellings but on a far grander scale. The Egyptians built their own houses, including royal palaces, of

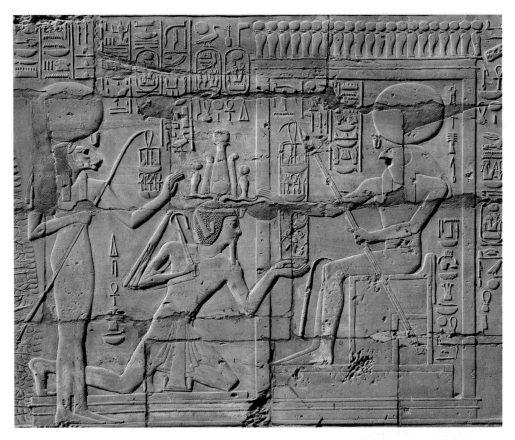

FIGURE 2.18. Sety I kneeling to receive symbols of jubilees and many years from the sun god Re-Horakhty (right) and the goddess Weret-Hekau (left). North wall of the Great Hypostyle Hall at Karnak. In temple art Sety often kneels before the gods. Photograph by Peter Brand.

humble mud brick. For their gods they erected temples in stone, which they called "the good work of eternity." Within Amun-Re's sprawling temple complex at Karnak, the Great Hypostyle Hall corresponded to the public rooms of a house. It was, in essence, Amun's living room. In dedicatory texts inscribed on its massive architraves, we learn that the Great Hypostyle Hall provided a spectacular venue for elaborate ceremonies. Here, during festivals, priests carried images of Amun-Re, Mut, and Khonsu, enshrined in sacred barks, in solemn processions along the main axis of the structure.[71]

An Egyptian temple also functioned as a model of the cosmos at the moment of creation.[72] The Egyptians envisaged each temple as sitting atop the primeval hill that arose from the primordial ocean at the beginning of time, when the creator god willed the universe into existence. The Great Hypostyle Hall evoked a thicket of papyrus reeds growing at the marshy edges of this primordial mound. It also belonged to a special class of temples called "mansions of millions of years," which served both as a temple for the gods and for the cult of the pharaoh's own divine aspect.[73] The Great Hall was a testament to Sety's devotion toward the gods and his status as one of their number.

FIGURE 2.19. Sety I offering a symbol of Maat to Amun-Re and Isis. In temple art, Sety often bows before the gods. Unrolled image from column 97 of the Great Hypostyle Hall at Karnak. Courtesy of Owen Murray/Karnak Hypostyle Hall Project.

Royal Piety and Divinity under Sety I

In Sety I's conception of pharaonic kingship two starkly divergent trends emerge. Before Egypt's gods, he projected an image of pious humility (fig. 2.19). He is often portrayed in temple wall art as bowing or kneeling when performing cult rituals (fig. 2.18).[74] While earlier pharaohs occasionally adopted these deferential postures, Sety I's art is remarkable for their prevalence.[75]

But why would Pharaoh abase himself in this fashion? A possible answer lies in Egypt's social atmosphere following the religious upheaval in the Amarna period. The years after Akhenaten's failed religious revolution were a time of intense personal piety among the Egyptian people. We see this heightened reverence in tomb scenes and votive stelae showing average Egyptians, and even high officials, bowing or kneeling before their gods. Sety I's own nonroyal origins inspired him to portray himself with pious deference once he became king.

Sety I's conspicuous humility did not diminish his standing as a diety in his own right (fig. 2.20).[76] Sety emulated his predecessor Amenhotep III by reviving his style of royal godhood. In his royal cult temple at Abydos a special avatar of the deified king called Menmaatre-the Great God resided.[77] Sety also planned to erect colossal statues of himself. In his ninth regnal year the king tasked his quarrymen with hewing a multitude of colossi and grand obelisks—those potent symbols of

FIGURE 2.20. The *Iuwnmutef*-Priest (center) and Isis (left) offering to the deified Sety I in the guise of Osiris (right). Abydos temple of Sety I. Photograph courtesy of Paul Smit.

FIGURE 2.20. The *Iuwnmutef*-Priest (center) and Isis (left) offering to the deified Sety I in the guise of Osiris (right). Abydos temple of Sety I. Photograph courtesy of Paul Smit.

pharaonic glory and divinity—from the granite beds at Aswan. It was at this point, almost a decade after Sety ascended his throne, that his eldest son, Crown Prince Ramesses, made his first recorded appearance as Pharaoh's heir apparent.

Notes

1. Strouhal et al. 2008; Strouhal and Horáčková 2011; Dodson 2018, 116–17.

2. Murnane 1995b.

3. His major monument is a battered stela fragment now in the collection of the Oriental Institute of the University of Chicago, OI 11456, which gives his title as "chief of archers," *ḥry-pḏwt*. The stela honors two of his male relatives, "his beloved brother, the Fanbearer of the Retinue, Khaemwaset" and "his son, the Stablemaster Ramose." Ramose, may be an alias for Pramessu, the future Ramesses I. See PM VIII.4, 247; Gaballa and Kitchen 1968; Murnane 1995a, 192–96; van Dijk 1997, 60–62; Brand 2000, 336–43; Obsomer 2012b, 22–24; Dodson 2019, 9–10 with fig. 8.

4. Ramesses II was likely in his early twenties when he ascended the throne, about twelve years after his grandfather's accession, so he was probably eight or ten years old at the time. The length of Horemheb's reign is uncertain, but he reigned into his sixteenth regnal year at least. Less convincing is the claim that he ruled for twenty-seven years or more. See most recently van Dijk 2008; Bryson 2015; Wiener 2015; Grimal 2018; Dodson 2018, 131–32.

5. Cairo JdE 44863 and 44864: *Urk.* IV, 2175–2176.

6. *Urk.* IV, 2175:7–16

7. *Urk.* IV, 2176:9–10.

8. Murnane 1995a, 193. Obsomer (2012b, 22 with notes 18–19) observes that Middle Kingdom viziers held the title "hereditary noble on the throne of Geb" (*iry-pʿt ḥr nst Gb*) and that Ramesside viziers revived it.

9. The practice by a king who lacked natural heirs of designating his vizier as "heir presumptive" by showering him with grandiose titles and epithets occurred when the last ruler of the Eleventh Dynasty distinguished the Vizier Amenemhet as his eventual successor, who then became Amenemhet I, founder of the Twelfth Dynasty. At the end of the Eighteenth Dynasty, Horemheb and Pramessu both held the vizierate along with other high offices and elaborate honorifics. See Murnane 1995a, 193–96. Horemheb's preroyal titles appear in reliefs from his tomb and on two statues depicting him as a scribe: New York MMA 23.10.1 (*Urk.* IV, 2089–2094) and British Museum 551 (*Urk.* IV, 2094–2099). For the Memphite tomb reliefs see Martin et al. 2016, with app. I, 143–46 for Horemheb's preroyal career, including his extensive roster of titles and epithets.

10. On the huge Ramesside fortress at Heboua, ancient Tcharu, see Abd el-Maksoud 1998a, 1998b; Abd el-Maksoud and Valbelle 2011.

11. Cairo JdE 60539: K*RI* II, 287–88; *RITA* II, 116–17; *RITANC* II, 168–72. Most scholars now agree that the two viziers this text names are the future Ramesses I and Sety I: Polz 1986, 160–66; Murnane 1995b, 193–95; Brand 2000, 336; Obsomer 2012b, 22–24; Dodson 2019, 9–11 with fig. 9.

12. Egyptologists traditionally regard this as the four-hundredth anniversary since one of the Hyksos kings founded Seth's temple in Pramessu's hometown of Avaris in the northeastern Delta. While this might be true, decay of the lower part of the stela has obliterated the second half of its inscription deprives us of knowledge of the precise significance of this four-hundred-year anniversary.

13. Although the stela lacks a year date, the form of Ramesses II's titulary in the main text was current no earlier than regnal year 34: *RITANC* II, 169. See pp. 76–78 below.

14. In keeping with the Four Hundred Year Stela's ideological bent, Ramesses II refers to Sety I as "the father of his father," an idealized term that can be read literally as "grandfather" or more broadly as "ancestor." Although Sety is just one generation removed, Ramesses describes him as a more distant relation, perhaps equating him with the god Seth.

15. *KRI* II, 288.

16. Murnane 1995b, 194.

17. Kitchen 1987, 132; For a different translation of Ramesses I's prenomen, see Leprohon 2013, 109. For the variations in the hieroglyphic writing of his prenomen, see Brand 2000, 29–31.

18. In the later New Kingdom, the name of the sun god Re was written with the definite article as *Pre* (*p3 R*ꜥ), literally "The Re," hence, Pramessu. Once he became king, Ramesses dropped the definite article reflecting an archaic version of his name more appropriate for a king. The variant forms *Rꜥ-ms-sw* and *Rꜥ-ms-s* reflect differences between the spoken dialects of Upper and Lower Egypt. See Kitchen 1979 and 2001. Both forms of the nomen occur on Ramesses I's own monuments and on posthumous ones Sety I and Ramesses II later dedicated in his memory. Ramesses II also used both forms for his nomen; see pp. 85–88 below.

19. For these meager sources, see *KRI* I, 1–5; *RITA* I, 1–5; *RITANC* I, 1–8; *KRI* VII, 1–6; Roberson, *KRI* IX, 1. Ramesses I's accession date is unknown, while his latest preserved inscription, a donation stela from Buhen (Louvre C 57), dates to regnal year 2, II *prt* 20. Obsomer (2012b, 26) concludes he reigned for seventeen and a half months. By contrast, Hornung, Krauss, and Warburton (2006) maintain that Ramesses ruled two full years and died early in his third.

20. Seele 1940, 7–22. Later still, his grandson Ramesses II once again re-inscribed these cartouches with his name. Egyptologists were able to read all three names and untangle the Second Pylon's complex history.

21. The mummy came to North America in the late nineteenth century and remained with others of unknown provenance in a museum in Niagara Falls, Canada. The Michael C. Carlos Museum in Atlanta, Georgia purchased the mummy and then repatriated to Egypt once it was identified as Ramesses I's mortal remains. See Trope and Lacovara 2003; Hawass and Saleem 2016, 1–3. This identification, while plausible, is by no means certain. Likewise, pinpointing the age at death of ancient mummies is an inexact science. While Ramesses I may have been past his middle years, we should not assume he lived into his sixties, seventies, or beyond like his famously long-lived grandson.

22. Among the monuments attesting to Sety I's filial piety are a tall siliceous sandstone pedestal for an image of Horus from Qantara and the base of a royal statue of Ramesses I from Medamud, each inscribed with the cartouches of both kings. See *RITANC* I, 90–91, 131–32; Brand 2000, 128–29, 190; Obsomer 2012b, 29–31; Sourouzian 2019.

23. At Abydos, Sety I constructed a small chapel whose limestone walls were embellished with the fine bas relief for which his artisans are famous. Several limestone slabs with elegant reliefs are now in the collections of the Metropolitan Museum of Art in New York: Winlock 1921 and 1937. For the dedicatory stela see Schott, 1964; *KRI* I, 110–114; *RITA* I, 93–96; *RITANC* I, 93–94.

24. *RITANC* I, 94–95; Brand 2000, 230–32; Stadelmann, 2013, 2015, forth-coming.

25. For the theme of the dissolution and restoration of Maat in royal texts, see Redford 1986, 259–75.

26. For Tutankhamun's Restoration Stela, *Urk.* IV, 2025–2032, see Murnane 1995a, 212–14; Eaton-Krauss 2016, 32–38. For Horemheb's Coronation Inscription, see Gardiner 1953; Murnane 1995b, 190–91; 1995a, 230–33; Dodson 2018, 109–11.

27. *Urk.* IV, 2027:13–14; Murnane 1995a, 212–14.

28. Murnane 1995a, 213; Redford 1986, 265.

29. *KRI* I, 110:15; *RITA* I, 93.

30. *KRI* I, 111:3–5; *RITA* I, 93.

31. *KRI* I, 111:5–9; *RITA* I, 93.

32. *KRI* I, 111: 10–14. On this much-discussed passage, see Spalinger 1978, 227–31; Murnane 1990, 48.

33. Brand 2000: 206–8; Brand et al. 2018, 29, 178. See the following note. There is no reliable evidence for a period of joint kingship between Ramesses I and Sety I, and monuments naming or depicting both men as kings are posthumous creations of Sety I and Ramesses II by which they established the legitimacy of their young dynastic lineage: *RITANC* I, 131–132; Brand 2000, 310–12.

34. Brand 2000, 192–219; Brand, Feleg, and Murnane 2018, 1–9. On the Great Hypostyle Hall, see below.

35. Reeves and Wilkinson 1996, 134–35; Masquelier-Loorius 2013, 282–86.

36. Since the nineteenth century, historians have characterized Sety I as a vigorous and able king and his reign as marking a new era and a return of Egypt's imperial might after the Amarna interlude: Breasted 1905; Wilson 1956; Steindorff and Seele 1957; Gardiner 1961. Murnane (1995b), however, cautions that the self-confident expressions of royal power we see on the monuments of Sety I and Ramesses II might disguise their political insecurity at the advent of the Nineteenth Dynasty.

37. On Sety's titulary see Kitchen 1987, 132–33; Leprohon 2013, 109–14. Previously, Amenemhet I in the Twelfth Dynasty and Horemheb at the end of the Eighteenth Dynasty incorporated the term *wḥm-mswt* in their titularies, which Sety now employed in both his Horus and Nebty names.

38. Brand 1999a; 2000, 45–118.

39. Brand 1999b; McClain 2007; Eaton-Krauss 2016, 38–52.

40. *Urk.* IV, 2027. Translation adapted from Murnane 1995a, 213.

41. On restoration inscriptions of the post-Amarna kings, see McClain 2007, 74–123.

42. Brand 2000, 45–46; McClain 2007, 124–60; Eaton-Krauss 2016, 38.

43. Brand 2000, 56–102.

44. Historians often credit Sety I with a pious reputation for his program of mending these sacred icons on temple walls. More recently, we have learned that Sety often inserted his restoration labels next to images of the gods that Tutankhamun had repaired before him. Forensic scrutiny reveals that Sety's artists had retouched these icons by augmenting the proportions of their limbs, modifying their facial profiles, and, with Amun-Re's images, by extending the lofty plumes on his headdress. Following Horemheb's rejection of the legitimacy of his immediate predecessors, Sety I now regarded even the sacred

icons that Tutankhamun had repaired as being tainted, thereby justifying these secondary restorations. See Brand 1999b; 2000, 45–118.

45. On Sety I's first regnal year and its chronology, see Murnane 1990, app. 2, 75–94; Degrève 2006, 61; Obsomer 2012b, 33–34.

46. Breasted 1905, 379–98; Gardiner 1961; Steindorff and Seele 1957, 220–21; Wilson 1956, 230–31.

47. See pp. 8–9 above.

48. Murnane 1990, 1–30; Bryce 2003, 145–69.

49. See pp. 6–11 above.

50. The definitive publication is Epigraphic Survey 1986.

51. For historical and iconographic analysis of Sety's war monument, see Broadhurst 1989; Murnane 1990, 39–66; Heinz 2001; Degrève 2006, 49–52; Masquelier-Loorius 2013, 44–55; Spalinger 1979b; 2005, 187–208; 2011, 27–46, 125–34.

52. Breasted 1905, 408–13; Wilson 1956, 240–41; Kitchen 1982, 20–25.

53. Heinz 2001; Spalinger 2011; Brand forthcoming.

54. *RITANC* I, 12–21; Murnane 1990, 39–50; Spalinger 1979b; 2005, 188–93; 2018b. Degrève's (2006) reductionist notion, followed by Obsomer (2012b, 35–44), that Sety I waged one grand campaign in the Levant, from Sinai to Kadesh, all in his first regnal year, is wrongheaded. A handful of triumphal stelae that he left in the Levant further augment the historical record of this expedition, but these fragmentary inscriptions from Tell esh-Shihab in south Syria and Tyre in Lebanon reveal little historical information: *KRI* I, 17, 117; *RITA* I, 14, 98–99; *RITANC* I, 21–22, 96; Brand 2000, 122–24.

More valuable are two stelae dating to his first regnal year from the Canaanite town of Beth Shean in the Jezreel Valley: *KRI* I, 11–12, 15–16; *RITA* I, 9–10, 12–13; *RITANC* I, 17–19, 20–21. In the early Nineteenth Dynasty, Beth Shean functioned as an administrative outpost of Egypt's empire in Canaan; Morris 2005, 350–51; 2018, 195–98; Spalinger 2016.

55. See Brand forthcoming.

56. *RITANC* I, 23–25; Murnane 1990, app. 4; Spalinger 2005, 197 and 202–5; Masquelier-Loorius, 2013, 63–68. We should discount Degrève's (2006, 53) idea that a scene depicting Sety brandishing his khepesh-scimitar against his Libyan foe as an indication that Sety did not personally lead his troops against the Libyans.

57. *KRI* I, 25; *RITA* I, 20; *RITANC* I, 26; Brand 2000, 120–22.

58. Murnane 1990, 53.

59. Epigraphic Survey 1986, pl. 22. Only the king's face and his arm drawing the bow string is visible. This is consistent with a chariot scene.

60. *KRI* I, 17; Epigraphic Survey 1986, pl. 34. Egyptologists, and even Hittitologists have taken Sety's victory claim at face value: Murnane 1990, 58–62; Bryce 2005, 228–30.

61. Brand 2000, 350–65; Masquelier-Loorius, 2013, 111–84.

62. Calverley and Broome 1933, 1935, 1938, 1958. On the construction of the temple and chronology of its relief decoration under Sety I and Ramesses II, see Brand 2000, 155–70.

The newest edition of Rosalie David's invaluable study of the temple (2018) provides readers with a detailed description of the architecture and decorative program, as well as translations and analysis of the ritual texts. See also Eaton's (2013) discussion of temple ritual. More general descriptions of Sety's temple include O'Connor 2009, 42–61; Masquelier-Loorius 2013, 132–41; Dodson 2019, 31–43.

63. On the date and construction of the Osireion, see Brand 2000, 174–78. A group of ostraca tells us something of the logistics of its construction: K*RI* I, 127–28; *RITA* I, 107–8; *RITANC* I, 103–5. For general descriptions of the building and its meaning, see O'Connor 2009, 50–51; Masquelier-Loorius 2013, 141–43; David 2018, 31–32; Dodson 2019, 43–45.

64. O'Connor 2009.

65. Brand 2000, 192–219; Blyth 2006, 146–51; Brand, Feleg, and Murnane 2018; www.mcmphis.edu/hypostyle.

66. Brand, Feleg, and Murnane 2018, 11–17.

67. On Sety I's innovative design and decorative template for papyrus columns, see Brand 2018.

68. On temple ritual in the Ramesside period, see Eaton 2013; David 2018. Lurson (2016) has explored the role of cultic scenes, including representations of his idealized coronation, as expressions of Sety I's royal ideology through a meticulous examination of reliefs on the north interior wall of the Great Hypostyle Hall.

69. For photographs of the interior wall scenes with translations of the hieroglyphic texts, see Brand, Feleg, and Murnane 2018.

70. Murnane 1975, 170–83; Revez and Brand 2015; Brand, Feleg, and Murnane 2018, 17–24.

71. Bell 1997.

72. McCarthy 2007.

73. Haeny 1997; Ullmann 2002, 2016. See pp. 399–400 below.

74. Brand 2000, 8–15.

75. Eaton 2013, 154–60.

76. Brand 2000, 384–93.

77. Calverley and Broome 1958, 4:pl. 42; Brand 2000, 390. On the main cult chapel of Sety I at Abydos Calverley and Broome 1935, 2:pls. 29–38, see David 2018, 190–209.

CHAPTER THREE
CROWN PRINCE RAMESSES AND HIS CAREER UNDER SETY I

In the third year of his reign, Ramesses II held council with his advisors. Hearing of the hardships of his gold miners in Nubia's parched desert, he proposed to dig a well to bring them water. Knowing their part in this royal drama, his grandees responded by singing their pharaoh's praises, lauding him as a prodigy since childhood:

> *Every matter passed through your ears since you were deputy of this land. You made plans while you were (still) in the egg in your office of (royal) child and heir apparent. The affairs of the Two Banks were told to you while you were still a boy wearing the side-lock. No monument came forth that was not under your authority and no judgement came about without you. You acted as a supreme chief of the army when you were still a youth of ten years. (As for) every construction project that came about through your hands, its foundation was (well) made.*[1]

A stela discovered at remote Quban in Nubia records this panegyric. Nor is this our only account of Ramesses II's precocity as a princeling. Shortly after Sety I died, Ramesses visited his father's unfinished cult temple at Abydos. There he left his Abydos Dedicatory Inscription on the porch of the temple's second court.[2] Vowing to complete Sety's edifice as an act of filial piety, the new king—then in his early twenties—summoned his officials and reminded them how Sety had prepared him to be king (fig. 3.1):

> *I came forth from Re, while (as) you say, it was Menmaatre who nurtured me. The All Lord magnified me while I was a child until I could rule. He gave the land to me while I was in the egg. Officials kissed the ground before me when I was inducted as eldest king's son and heir apparent upon the throne of Geb and when I reported the [affairs] of the Two Lands as chief of the infantry and chariotry.*
>
> *When my father appeared before the people, I being but a child in his embrace, he said about me "crown him as [king so] I might [see] his perfection while I am alive." [He summoned] chamberlains to set crowns upon my brow (saying) "place the Great Diadem upon his head," so he said concerning me while he was on earth, "so he might administer this land, so he might care for [Egypt], so he might command the people." [And when he spoke of me, his eyes filled with] tears, so great was his love for me!*[3]

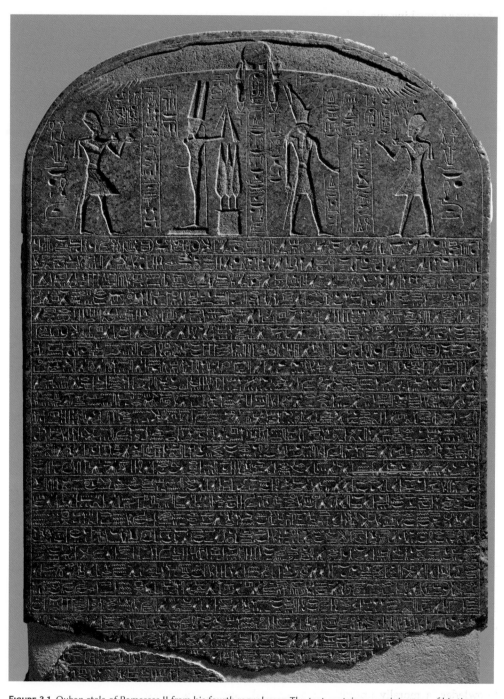

FIGURE 3.1. Quban stela of Ramesses II from his fourth regnal year. The text contains a reminiscence of his time as crown prince under Sety I. Grenoble Archaeological Museum MG 1937-1969-3565. Courtesy Grenoble Archaeological Museum.

Here was a touching spectacle, a great pharaoh of Egypt shedding tears of joy as he placed the crown on his young son's head. Some Egyptologists take this passage to mean that Sety I installed Ramesses II as king to rule beside him, in what is called a coregency.[4] Did it happen this way? We have good reason for skepticism. According to the mythological foundation of Egyptian kingship, every living ruler embodied Horus. At death, he became Osiris, lord of the Underworld, and his son assumed his place as a new Horus incarnate. For two avatars of Horus to rule jointly, or for Osiris to reign on earth beside Horus, was unthinkable.[5]

Only rarely in Egypt's long history did two pharaohs rule together.[6] What role did Ramesses play during his father's reign? Ramesses II's own later accounts like the Abydos and Quban inscriptions claim his father had bestowed administrative authority and high military honors on his young son. How did Sety educate his eldest son and prepare him for the Throne of Horus?

Ramesses the Child Heir

Ramesses II was born into a family of military officers during the middle years of Horemheb's reign and lacked royal blood. He was in late childhood or early adolescence when his grandfather, the general and vizier Pramessu, succeeded Horemheb as Ramesses I.[7] Given the high status his grandfather and father enjoyed in Horemheb's court, Ramesses grew up in an institution called the *Kap*, or royal nursery. The *Kap* served a vital political function, educating and socializing Pharaoh's sons alongside those of the court elite and the children of foreign vassal kings sent to Egypt as hostages. In the *Kap* Prince Ramesses received his education alongside youths who would one day serve as high functionaries and trusted confidants in his own administration. The institution of the *Kap* forged bonds of trust and loyalty between the children of the elite and their future royal masters.[8]

A key function of the *Kap* was to teach literacy. Prince Ramesses and his schoolmates learned the cursive hieratic script used to write everyday documents on papyrus. They also studied the formal hieroglyphic script found on monuments and art works. Within the *Kap* scribal mentors gave Prince Ramesses the traditional education of an elite bureaucrat. Tutors instilled in their young charges the ethics of Egypt's caste of high officials, encouraging virtues like wisdom and knowledge, a morally upright character, and constant awareness of where they stood in Egypt's rigid social hierarchy.

Students learned to read and write by copying classical works of Egyptian literature.[9] Wisdom texts, like the Old Kingdom classic The

Instructions of Ptahhotep, gave pointers on how to behave in society as one's social position dictated. A Middle Kingdom work, The Instructions of a Man for His Son, instilled loyalty to Pharaoh's regime.[10] The Satire of the Trades used humor to belittle every sort of military and civilian manual labor, describing the physical torments and misery soldiers and common laborers suffered daily, in contrast to a scribe's privileged and pampered lifestyle.[11] For a future king, a "must read" was The Instructions of King Amenemhet I for Senwosret I. After his father's own bodyguards had assassinated him, Senwosret I commissioned this warning against the treachery of servants. Perhaps, too, Prince Ramesses read the decrees of great pharaohs before him like Ahmose, Thutmose III, and Amenhotep III.

As the scion of the fledgling Nineteenth Dynasty, Prince Ramesses was crucial to its survival.[12] Upon ascending the throne Sety I named Ramesses as his heir. As he approached adolescence, Prince Ramesses received the titles of "heir apparent" (*iry-pat*), and "king's eldest son" (*sa nesu semsu*).[13] Henceforth Sety carefully groomed his son for his future role as monarch, offering him an excellent model of Egyptian kingship to emulate. He schooled Ramesses in the arts of war, the administration of Egypt, supervision of large building projects, and pious observance of sacred rites in the temples of Egypt's gods.

Crown Prince and Builder-Pharaoh-in-Training

Grand monuments were a defining hallmark of ancient Egyptian civilization. Pharaohs like Sety I built passionately, and their massive construction projects were central to their royal ideology. New Kingdom kings erected numerous temples and decorated them with elaborate wall carvings and hieroglyphic inscriptions, colossal statues, and soaring obelisks, dedicating all these monuments to Egypt's gods and their own glory. Following this tradition, Sety I took pains to train his eldest son in planning and supervising these grand construction projects (fig. 3.2).

During his ninth year, shortly before he died, Sety I commissioned a multitude of granite obelisks and colossal statues to embellish his building projects in Heliopolis and Thebes. To commemorate this momentous event, Pharaoh's entourage traveled to the granite quarries near Elephantine, modern-day Aswan, on Egypt's southern frontier. In one of the stelae Sety erected there, the future Ramesses II makes his first appearance in the historical record, albeit anonymously:

> His Person, L.P.H., has ordered the commissioning of a multitude of works for making very great obelisks and great and wondrous statues in the name of His Person, L.P.H. He made great barges for transporting them, and ships' crews to match them (for) ferrying them from the

FIGURE 3.2. Enhanced photograph of the larger Year Nine Stela of Sety I from Aswan. It records the opening of granite quarries to produce colossal statues and obelisks. The future Ramesses II is described as "eldest king's son" at the end of the text. Image by Peter Brand.

quarry while officials and transport-men hastened, and his eldest son was before them doing what is beneficial for His Person.[14]

Sety allowed Prince Ramesses to leave his own memorial to this quarrying expedition (fig. 3.3). On a tiny island near Aswan called Hassawanarti, archeologists unearthed a graffito scratched on a rocky outcropping.[15] Here Sety I makes an offering to Khnum, the ram-headed god of Elephantine. In a scene below, Crown Prince Ramesses kneels as he adores both his father and Khnum. Ramesses wears the garb of a high official and grasps a flabellum with a single ostrich plume as a symbol of his courtly rank. A hieroglyphic text lists his names and titles:

Fanbearer on the king's right side, great general of the army for all monuments, true king's scribe, his beloved, the heir apparent and king's son Ramesses.[16]

FIGURE 3.3. Enhanced image of a rock inscription from the small island of Hassawanarti depicting Sety I offering to Khnum. Below, Crown Prince Ramesses kneels in adoration. His name and titles are in the lower left corner. Image by Peter Brand, after Seidlmayer 1999, 141.

Prince Ramesses must have left this memorial during his father's expedition to Aswan's granite quarries. The graffito entitles the prince a "great general of the army for all monuments," indicating he commanded his father's corps of engineers. But Sety did not limit his son's education to monuments. He also initiated Prince Ramesses in the arts of war.

A Prince's First Taste of War

An essential element of a future king's education was preparing him to lead Egypt's armies in battle. Vigorous physical and martial training tutored the prince to conform to the ideological mold of the sportsman and warrior king—a deadly hunter of wild game in the desert and of human prey in war.[17] The Eighteenth Dynasty monarch Amenhotep II represented a paragon of this muscular style of kingship. In a decree he set up beside the Great Sphinx at Giza, Amenhotep II recalls his training for military leadership while he was still a prince under his father Thutmose III.[18] In this idealized "autobiographical" text, Amenhotep stresses his athleticism and skill with weapons and military hardware, particularly his excellence as an archer and charioteer. He boasts of his unrivaled strength, his consummate skill with the bow, and his special bond with horses:

Now His Person appeared as king as a perfect youth who had developed his body, having completed eighteen years upon his haunches in valor. He knew all the works of Monthu. There was no equal to him on the battlefield. He knew about chariot teams and he had no equal in this innumerable army. None could draw his bow and he could not be overtaken in running…

Now when he was still a royal child, he loved his horses and rejoiced over them. Strong willed was he when working with them, learning their nature, being skilled at controlling them, and entering their counsels. When this was heard in the palace by his father … (Thutmose III), His Person's heart was pleased when he heard it. Rejoicing at what was said about his eldest son, he thought to himself: "It is he who will act as ruler of the whole land without being attacked. His desire ranges far after valor and rejoices in strength, while still a beautiful youth without wisdom. He is not (yet) at the right age for doing the work of Monthu, yet he ignores the thirst of the body and he loves victory. It is the god inspiring him to act to protect Egypt, so (they) shall bow down on earth before him."

His Person said to those at his side: "Have the most perfect horses given to him from My Person's stable in White Walls (Memphis), telling him:

'look after them, train them, exercise them, and care for them even if they struggle against you.'" ... *He raised horses without equal. They did not grow weary while he held the reins. They did not sweat at high speed.*[19]

Amenhotep II's early training as a warrior emphasized horsemanship and proficiency with the composite bow, as did Prince Ramesses's own military education during his youth. These skills served Ramesses well in campaigns he waged during his first two decades as pharaoh, especially at the Battle of Kadesh. Given his military ancestry, Sety I adhered to family tradition by instituting a regimen of vigorous martial drills for his son, preparing him for his eventual role as supreme commander of Egypt's armed forces. In the Nile kingdom's political and military structure, Pharaoh was a warlord who personally led his troops into battle.[20]

According to Ramesses II's Quban stela, Sety I appointed his eldest son as an army commander while he was a mere lad of ten years. Once he rose to be Pharaoh, Ramesses II bestowed high military offices on some of his own sons while they were still children or adolescents, including the rank of "great general of the army."[21] And just as some of Ramesses II's sons later witnessed the Battle of Kadesh and his later wars during their childhoods, Prince Ramesses followed the warlike Sety I on his campaigns abroad. Scenes from Sety I's Karnak war monument and military art from a small temple Ramesses II built during the first year of his reign at Beit el-Wali in Nubia offer glimpses of his earliest military adventures.

In several of his father's Karnak war scenes, Prince Ramesses follows after Sety I.[22] Examining these scenes closely, we see that sculptors inserted the prince's name and image into the composition as an afterthought, carving them over the figure of someone else. It was once thought that this was an older brother whom Ramesses allegedly pushed aside to take the throne.[23] We now know that no such prince existed. Instead, it was a commander of archers named Mehy, who was "rubbed out" of history to make room for Ramesses (fig. 3.4).[24]

Yet, it is likely the prince did campaign with Sety, if only as a spectator. In Sety I's eighth regnal year his army fought in Irem, a Nubian territory.[25] In his Nubian temple at Beit el-Wali, built in the first year of his reign, Ramesses II depicts himself at war in Nubia.[26] The Viceroy of Kush, Amenemopet, brings the booty and prisoners to Ramesses.

FIGURE 3.4. Prince Ramesses superimposed over the commander of archers, named Mehy, from Sety I's Karnak war monument. Photograph by Peter Brand.

But another man named Yuny had replaced Amenemopet as Viceroy of Kush just before Sety's death.[27] Additional war scenes at Beit el-Wali—with Ramesses II battling Libyans, Asiatics, and Shasu Bedouin—may also recall his part in Sety I's wars. They take events that happened while Ramesses was sill a prince and recast him in the role of Pharaoh. Apparently, like monuments, even military operations could be appropriated.

Prince Ramesses Starts a Family

After the death of his father Ramesses I, less than two years after he founded the Nineteenth Dynasty, Sety I took a keen interest in propagating the newly founded Ramesside line. Sety knew—as all ancient people did—how death often struck quickly and unexpectedly. Ramesses was now "heir apparent" (*iry-pat*) and "king's eldest son" (*sa nesu semsu*). It was imperative for the prince to beget sons of his own, and soon. Once Ramesses reached puberty, Sety promptly took steps to ensure this. In his Abydos Dedicatory Inscription Ramesses II recalled how his father established a household for him, complete with multiple wives, while he was still crown prince:

> *He (Sety I) furnished me with a female household and royal apartments comparable to the beautiful maidens of the palace. He selected for me wives throughout [the land(?) ...] taking khener-women for [me ...] his ... [... children ...] ... being suckled ... the kheneret-household of female companions.*[28]

Despite some lamentable gaps natural decay has inflicted after three millennia, the text offers us a crucial glimpse of Ramesses's earliest family life. Preparing his son for his future office, Sety I created a domestic establishment for the prince, literally a "female household" (*peryet*). Within this homestead, he received his own "private royal apartments," (*ipet nesu*), staffed with "beautiful maidens," (*neferut*) and "*khener*-women" (*kheneru*) within the "*kheneret*-household (*per kheneret*).[29]

Sety chose his son's brides from the eligible daughters of Egypt's high officials. By arranging marriages with women from elite families across the kingdom Sety secured cordial relations, both for himself and for his heir, with Egypt's ruling class.

When his father presented him with several attractive young women and told him to "get busy," it's unlikely Ramesses had to be told twice. The atmosphere in the prince's new household quarters took on the character of a "baby race." Each of his new wives ardently wished to present Ramesses with his first-born son, enhancing her own status by giving him an heir.[30] That honor fell to a woman named Nefertari, who gave her husband a baby boy they named Amunhirkhopeshef.

It is impossible to overstate the importance of Amunhirkhopeshef's birth for his father Prince Ramesses and his grandfather Sety I.[31] The future of this new dynasty hung by a genetic thread, so it was vital for Ramesses to become a father. His first wives bore him at least four sons before he became pharaoh once Sety I died. The first-born Amunhirkhopeshef and the fourth eldest, Khaemwaset, appear in the battle scenes at Beit el-Wali, indicating they were alive in Ramesses II's first regnal year.[32] Two more sons, the second-born Ramesses Junior and the third-ranked Prehirwenemef, also arrived before their father ascended the throne. These four lads soon gained many more brothers and sisters, but as Prince Ramesses's eldest sons the four enjoyed a privileged status their younger siblings could only envy.

Their mothers also gained lasting prestige. As mother of the first-born son Amunhirkhopeshef, Nefertari enjoyed special eminence, while her colleague Isetnofret delivered the second-born son, named Ramesses after his father. By presenting their new husband with his first male offspring, these young women secured preeminence for themselves as his most favored wives. Upon taking the throne Ramesses II conferred the supreme queenly title of "great royal wife" (*khemet nesu weret*) upon Nefertari.[33]

Aside from Nefertari and Isetnofret, no record of his other earliest wives has come down to us. Even their names are lost to history.[34] Nefertari's preeminent rank and prestige as mother of the first-born son overshadowed all his wives, including Isetnofret, mother of Ramesses "Junior."

Fortune smiled on Nefertari. Both she and her infant son Amunhirkhopeshef survived pregnancy and childbirth. Not all of Ramesses's wives were as fortunate. Ancient women endured horrific rates of miscarriage and infant mortality. Tragically, for those infants surviving birth, as many as fifty percent died before their fifth year. Many mothers also perished from complications of pregnancy and delivery. [35] To counter such dismal realities, gynecological prescriptions loom large in Egyptian medical texts. Magic tinged all these remedies.[36]

Ancient Egyptians believed evil spirits caused all sickness and misfortune that befell the innocent. Egyptian women relied on aid from a small pantheon of household gods, goddesses, and benevolent spirits to protect them and their children. The hippopotamus goddess Taweret, "She Who is Great," personified pregnancy. Like hippos, Taweret was powerful, dangerous, and temperamental, but she used her formidable strength to safeguard women and children by slaying any demon who dared approach them.

Evil spirits lurked in every house, striking their victims as they slept at night. Fortunately, a hideous little god called Bes was on guard duty. This bandy-legged dwarf had a lion's face. Growling ferociously, banging on a tambourine or waving sharp knives in the air, Bes danced wildly about the bedroom, terrorizing harmful demons and driving them back to the spirit world even as mother and child slept peacefully. Despite medicinal treatments and magical protections, some of Prince Ramesses's new brides doubtless suffered tragic miscarriages or infant deaths. Some may not have survived their pregnancies.

Sety I lived long enough to become the happy grandfather of several children of both sexes. Despite the dangers of childbearing and high rates of mortality, Prince Ramesses's burgeoning brood grew rapidly, swelling to *at least* one hundred offspring in later years. His family's vast size and prominence on his monuments became hallmarks of Ramesses II's singular reign.[37]

Ramesses as Crown Prince in Sety I's Abydos Temple

Sety I initiated Prince Ramesses into temple rituals in service to Egypt's gods, as we can see in wall reliefs from Sety's temple at Abydos. In the so-called Gallery of Kings, a few scenes portray an adolescent Ramesses joining Sety in temple worship.[38] In the most significant episode, father and son render homage to a grand list of Egypt's past kings, from King Menes, legendary founder of dynastic Egypt, down to Sety himself.[39] Pharaoh holds an incense censer in one hand and raises the other in a salute to his regal forbearers. Standing alongside him, Prince Ramesses unrolls a papyrus scroll and recites a liturgical incantation on behalf of the kings of old. The king list is grid-like, with two rows of boxes containing the prenomen cartouches of past monarchs (fig. 3.5).

The Abydos King List does not record the names of all previous Egyptian rulers. For both practical and ideological reasons, the roster offers an edited selection of pharaonic names.[40] Wall space was at a premium, leaving insufficient room for enrolling every royal ancestor. Sety's king list omits whole groups of earlier pharaohs for this reason, particularly the lesser ones from the so-called Intermediate Periods following glorious epochs like the Old and Middle Kingdoms. But in compiling his honor roll of Eighteenth Dynasty kings, Sety deliberately excluded several he considered "politically incorrect" and unworthy of his act of pious remembrance. Tainted, in Sety's view, for failing to uphold the tenets of Maat, several rulers are conspicuous by their absence from this list: the female Pharaoh Hatshepsut and pharaohs of the Amarna period from Akhenaten down to Ay.[41] A caption beside

Prince Ramesses declares: "Reciting the (royal) offerings by the Heir Apparent and King's Eldest Son of his body, Ramesses, true of voice."[42]

Additional ritual scenes on the opposite wall of the Gallery of Kings depict Sety and Prince Ramesses jointly worshiping the gods. With slight variations from one episode to another, these bas-reliefs offer visual and textual markers of Ramesses's status as heir apparent. Artists portrayed him as an adolescent. Standing shorter than his father, Ramesses wears the side lock of youth, a hairstyle symbolically marking him as a king's son (fig. 3.6). By custom, Egyptian princes displayed this token of childhood even as adults.[43]

But Prince Ramesses still lacks any regalia indicating kingly status. He wears no crown, nor does the Uraeus serpent—the sacred cobra emblem of pharaonic rule—perch on his forehead. Hieroglyphic captions identifying Prince Ramesses in the Gallery of Kings never enclose his name in cartouches, because he had not yet attained pharaonic status.

But even as the craftsmen were decorating the Gallery of Kings, Sety I died suddenly. In one unfinished scene depicting Ramesses as prince alongside his father, the newly crowned Ramesses II now instructed his artisans to insert an ornamental brooch on the sash of his princely kilt displaying his new cartouche names. With this small decorative flourish, Ramesses signaled his transition from heir apparent to pharaoh in his own right (fig. 3.7).[44]

Otherwise, Ramesses always bears the princely titles of "eldest king's son" (*sa nesu semsu*), and "heir apparent" (*iry-pat*) where he appears with Sety I, proving he was not yet Pharaoh when artisans began decorating the Gallery of Kings.[45] This fact is crucial to understanding any claims Ramesses made after his father's death.

Sety I left his Abydos temple and its exquisite wall carvings incomplete when he died.[46] Ramesses finished them as an act of homage. A year or more after ascending the throne, Ramesses II ordered his

FIGURE 3.5. Sety I and Prince Ramesses before the King List in Sety's Abydos temple. Courtesy Manna Nader Gabana Studios Cairo.

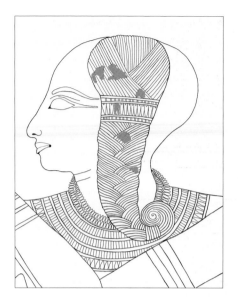

FIGURE 3.6. Prince Ramesses wearing the side-lock of youth. From the Gallery of the Kings in Sety I's Abydos Temple. Drawing by Peter Brand.

FIGURE 3.7. ➡ Ramesses as Crown Prince in the Gallery of the Kings in Sety I's Abydos temple. Nineteenth Century drawing by A. Mariette. Inset: cartouches on the prince's sash. The scene was completed after Sety I's death when Ramesses II inserted his royal cartouches. Inset photograph by Peter Brand.

craftsmen to decorate another passageway adjoining the Gallery of the Kings, known today as the "Corridor of the Bull." Unlike the Gallery, sculptors carved the Corridor's walls in sunk relief by following painted designs that the draftsmen had laid out during Sety I's lifetime.[47] Several episodes in this passageway were updated to depict Ramesses II conducting sacred rites alongside his eldest son Prince Amunhirkhopeshef for the gods and for the deified Sety I himself (fig. 3.8).[48]

Here we witness a dramatic scene that gives the Corridor of the Bull its modern name. Ramesses and Amunhirkhopeshef chase a stampeding wild bull, seeking to lasso it for sacrifice.[49] Not wishing to end up as a god's dinner, the unruly long-horned beast gallops away with its tongue lolling out. Pharaoh has just secured one lariat around its horns even as he readies to cast another loop of rope. Meanwhile Prince Amunhirkhopeshef gamely grasps the bull with both hands—not by

FIGURE 3.8. Ramesses II and Prince Amunhir-khopeshef offering ducks. From the Corridor of the Bull in Sety I's Abydos temple. Carved in sunk relief with the long form of Ramesses II's prenomen, the scene was carved after his first regnal year. Traces of Sety I's erased names, which were in raised relief, remain in the cartouches, indicating that Sety I's men began carving it just before his death. Courtesy of the Griffith Institute.

the horns, but by the tail. And with both hands! This arresting scene is among the most dynamic images in pharaonic art (fig. 3.9). By adapting Sety's preliminary sketches for his own carvings in the Corridor of the Bull, Ramesses II emphasized the continuity of three generations of his royal line.[50]

Ramesses II's Later Accounts of His Role as Prince and Other New Kingdom Royal "Autobiographies"

Much of our evidence for Ramesses II's career as crown prince is artistic, including Sety I's Karnak war scenes and bas-reliefs from the Gallery of Kings at Abydos. During Sety I's lifetime, some of his courtiers acknowledged Prince Ramesses's status as heir apparent on their own funerary monuments.[51] The earliest stage of Ramesses II's biography would be much slimmer without later statements he made in his

FIGURE 3.9. Ramesses II and Prince Amun-hirkhopeshef lassoing a bull from the Corridor of the Bull in Sety I's Abydos temple. Alamy.

Abydos Dedicatory Inscription and the Quban Stela. But we must be careful, as these accounts blend historical fact with political mythology (fig. 3.10).

Ramesses II is one of several New Kingdom pharaohs who commissioned "autobiographical" texts describing their preroyal careers. Each king relates how the gods themselves preordained his kingship from childhood and even before his birth.[52] Such royal origin stories were a genre of ancient mythic-political fiction. Among the most famous of these concerns Thutmose IV and the Great Sphinx.

In a stela he erected before the Great Sphinx at Giza, Thutmose IV recalls how he learned of his regal destiny while still a prince.[53] After hunting wild game in the high desert near the Great Pyramids, Prince Thutmose took an afternoon nap in the shadow of the Great Sphinx—at that time buried up to its neck by sand dunes. Thutmose dreamed the Sphinx spoke to him as an avatar of the sun god Horemakhet, commanding the prince to free his mighty statue from its sandy prison. Horemakhet then foretold how Thutmose would duly succeed his father Amenhotep II as his reward.

At the end of the Eighteenth Dynasty, Horemheb used the traditional doctrine of the pharaoh's divine parentage to justify his own peculiar nonroyal heritage. In his Coronation Inscription Horemheb explained how the gods predestined him to rule, although he grew up as a commoner.[54] It identifies Horus of Henes, his hometown god, as his divine father. After a distinguished career serving other kings—whom the text never names—Horemheb journeys to Thebes with Horus during the annual Festival of Opet. There, Amun-Re reveals Horemheb to be the true king and adopts him as his own son.

FIGURE 3.10. Stela of Amenwahsu and Tia adoring Sety I and Crown Prince Ramesses. Chicago, Oriental Institute Museum 10507. Courtesy of the Oriental Institute of the University of Chicago.

In the broader context of such pharaonic "autobiographies," we can recognize the ideological purpose of Ramesses II's Abydos Dedicatory Inscription and his Quban Stela.[55] Ramesses wished to emphasize his status as Sety I's duly appointed and legitimate heir, and show how the gods predestined him to rule "in the egg." Given his youth and the newness of his dynastic line, this was even more vital. Both texts intermix idealized rhetoric with genuine details. The Abydos text even relates the poignant spectacle of Sety I shedding tears of joy as Prince Ramesses is crowned before him, but we should not take this political mythology as historical fact.[56] Even though Ramesses later exaggerated his role during Sety's rule, he did hold important offices under his father's tutelage.

Artwork with Both Kings Together and the Issue of Coregency

Proponents of the coregency theory look to temple reliefs Ramesses II created in his first regnal year as proof.[57] On Karnak's Great Hypostyle Hall and Sety I's temples at Gurnah and Abydos, both kings sometimes appear together in the same scene. But is this evidence they were both alive and ruling jointly as coregents when the sculptors carved them? All these scenes portray Ramesses II as the sole actor in temple rituals, while Sety passively receives his son's cultic worship, or stands by as witness to Ramesses's interactions with Amun-Re and other deities. Here Sety plays the role of a deceased ancestor, not a living king (fig. 3.11).[58]

In the earliest temple reliefs showing Ramesses II as king in the Karnak Hypostyle Hall and in Sety I's temples at Abydos and Gurnah, we never see him acting in consort with his father, who always appears as a deified ancestor.[59] This contrasts with art of Hatshepsut and Thutmose III as coregents, where they act in unision while performing temple rituals, or reliefs from the Abydos Temple of Sety I in the Gallery of Kings where Ramesses is still a prince. Ramesses II also has temple art showing him paying homage to his deified grandfather Ramesses I at Gurnah, who died more than a decade before they were carved (see fig. 4.7 on p. 83 below). Clearly, these cannot be evidence of coregency.

Scenes of Ramesses II worshiping Sety I and Ramesses I are best understood as the new pharaoh's homage toward his recently deceased father. Such overt acts of filial piety legitimated Ramesses, whose royal line had governed Egypt for just over a decade when he assumed power.[60]

Further doubt about the coregency theory arises when we consider that imagery of Ramesses II as king alongside his father are largely found in Sety I's temples at Abydos, Gurnah, and in the Great Hypostyle Hall at Karnak. Yet, we rarely see Sety himself in Ramesses II's own temple at Abydos and never at Beit el-Wali, which coregency proponents claim were built and decorated in Sety's lifetime. If the two monarchs did rule jointly, with Sety being the senior partner, why would he tolerate this anonymity on his newly crowned son's monuments while sharing the limelight so generously with Ramesses in his own temples?[61] Coregency advocates view this alleged power shar-

Figure 3.11. Ramesses II offering incense and libation to the deified Sety I on the south wall of the Great Hypostyle Hall of Karnak. Photograph by Peter Brand.

ing from Ramesses II's perspective, but from Sety I's vantage point, it makes no sense. Sety I died in the prime of life. Not being old and feeble, he had no reason to yield greater authority and prestige to his son, then only a youth in his late teens or early twenties.

The End of Sety I's Reign

By his ninth regnal year Sety I's gargantuan building program neared fruition in cities across Egypt. At Karnak architects had finished constructing his Great Hypostyle Hall and sculptors were busy embellishing its walls and columns with elegant bas-reliefs.[62] Across the Nile in western Thebes artists were also decorating his royal cult temple at Gurnah. At Abydos Sety's architects had largely completed his splendid cult temple and the mysterious Osireion cenotaph tomb. Other projects were well under way at Memphis, Heliopolis, and the king's new Delta residence near Avaris.[63] Not content with these achievements, Sety I envisioned even more ambitious projects, including a grand entrance at Luxor Temple complete with a pylon gateway, obelisks, and colossi, and he undertook further constructions in Heliopolis and Memphis.[64] Sadly, he never lived to see them finished.

The last known dated inscription of Sety I comes from his ninth year, but precisely when his reign ended is uncertain.[65] The anniversary of Sety's accession to the throne fell on the twenty-fourth day of the third month of the Harvest Season (*Shomu*).[66] Ramesses II arose as king on the twenty-seventh day of this same month.[67] Therefore,

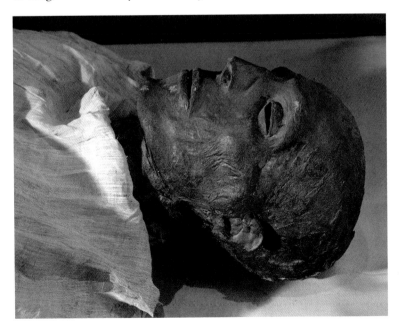

FIGURE 3.12. Mummy of Sety I. Egyptian Museum, Cairo. © akg-images / De Agostini Picture Lib. / W. Buss.

Sety I must have died either at the beginning of either his tenth or his eleventh year.[68]

After a decade as Lord of the Two Lands, Sety I died well before his time. His mummy belongs to a man in vigorous middle age, likely in his forties (fig. 3.12). Although determining the age of Egyptian mummies is not an exact science, he had not reached his fiftieth year when he succumbed to some fatal illness.[69] Once Sety breathed his last, amid keening wails of palace women, a solemn report went out from the palace and spread like wildfire throughout Egypt: "The Falcon has flown to heaven!" With this traditional euphemism, Sety's subjects learned that he was dead. Now, after a decade of careful training and preparation, his eldest son and heir, a young man in his early twenties, assumed the awesome mantle of Pharaoh of Egypt. The reign of Ramesses II had begun.

Notes

1. *KRI* II, 356; *RITA* II, 188–93; *RITANC* II, 214–16.

2. *KRI* II, 323–36; *RITA* II 162–74; *RITANC* II, 191–97; McClain 2007, 178–86; Spalinger 2009.

3. *KRI* II, 327–28. Translation adapted from Brand 2000, 315.

4. Seele 1940; Murnane 1975. Others use terminology like "regency" (Spalinger 1978) or "prince regency" (Kitchen 1982, 27–30; *RITANC* II, 194–95), but still view Ramesses II as being pharaoh with cartouches and regalia while Sety was still alive. Kitchen and Spalinger reject Murnane's contention that Ramesses began his own system of regnal year dates prior to his father's death, a theory Murnane himself later renounced.

5. A notable exception is the indisputable Eighteenth Dynasty coregency between the female Pharaoh Hatshepsut and her junior partner Thutmose III. Few women ever held the inherently masculine office of kingship and Hatshepsut's coregency was a highly unorthodox affair born of political and ideological necessity. It was not a model that later rulers would seek to emulate. On the ideological and evidentiary objections to most coregencies, see Laboury 2010, 87–92; Dodson 2014b; Brand 2020b.

6. Although hypothetical coregencies have been fashionable among some Egyptologists for over a century, today most are skeptical. The evidence is sparce or highly ambiguous. Most of the hypothetical coregencies Murnane (1977) proposed are dubious. The most controversial case remains the alleged joint rule of Amenhotep III and Akhenaten, which several scholars have convincingly refuted: Murnane 1977, 123–68; Dorman 2009. Still, a vocal minority clings to the hypothesis. Laboury (2010) aptly dismisses the notion of an Amenhotep III–Akhenaten coregency as "un fiction égyptologique."

7. Ramesses II likely lived to be in his later eighties or early nineties. See p. 459 n. 2 below. Since he ruled for just over sixty-six years, he would have been in late childhood or his early teens when his grandfather came to power. When his father Sety I died a little more than a decade later, Ramesses II ascended the throne in his late teens or early twenties. For different estimates for his age at accession, see Murnane 1995a, 192; Leblanc 1999, 22 n. 5; Obsomer 2012b, 63–64.

8. Feucht 1985; Mathieu 2000; Meltzer 2001.

9. For translations of these classic works of Egyptian literature, see Simpson 2003.

10. On the role of Middle Kingdom literature in the training and acculturation of members of the New Kingdom elite, see Ragazzoli 2016; Navrátilová 2019, 146.

11. This literature was "updated" in the Ramesside period with new compositions designed to give scribes a sense of superiority over soldiers, including elite officers of the chariotry; Spalinger 2006, 5–50.

12. There was a political taboo against calling attention to a pharaoh's brothers. Since Sety never named any other sons besides Ramesses on his monuments, any potential younger brothers of Ramesses would have languished in relative obscurity once he became king. The word "brother" had the connotation of "equal" but also of "rival/opponent"; see Revez 2003. A Ramesside literary work, The Tale of the Two Brothers, casts the sibling protagonists as

bitter enemies. Likewise, in The Contendings of Horus and Seth, the two gods, who were nephew and uncle, were also called "brothers," meaning "rivals."

13. For discussion of these titles, see Murnane 1995a, 193; Fisher, 2001, 62–64, 85, and 125–26. As Fisher notes, *iry-pꜥt* does not always designate the king's official heir, but in most cases it does. In practice, with Prince Ramesses during Sety I's reign and for Ramesses II's sequence of designated successors over the course of his long reign: Amunhirkhopeshef, Ramesses "Junior," Khaemwaset, and Merenptah, the title effectively meant "heir apparent." Likewise, at the end of the Eighteenth Dynasty, the high officials Horemheb and Pramessu both used *iry-pꜥt* at the beginning of their roster of titles and epithet as a key marker of their status as "heirs presumptive" despite their lack of royal blood; see p. 21 above. For the title as a marker of the current heir to the throne among Ramesses II's sons, see pp. 263 and 279 n. 93 below.

14. *KRI* I, 74:12–14; translation after Brand 2000, 274.

15. Seidlmayer 1999, 2003; Brand 2000, 269–70; *KRI* IX, 2.

16. Translation after Brand 2000, 269.

17. On the theme of the sportsman king, see Redford 1995, 167–68.

18. For Amenhotep II's athleticism, see Der Manuelian 2006, 423–26.

19. *Urk.* IV, 1279–82.

20. Spalinger 2005, 101–6; 2020.

21. Murnane 1995b, 205; Fisher 2001, 63–64.

22. Epigraphic Survey 1986, 91–92 and pls. 6, 10, 12, 23, 29.

23. Breasted 1899; 1905, 418–20.

24. Murnane's comments on Mehy's origins and his supposed political influence during Sety I's reign are intriguing but impossible to verify: Murnane 1990, 107–14; 1995b, 199–202. We need not conclude Mehy fell into political disgrace. Instead, Ramesses's desire to highlight his role as his father's eldest son and designated heir easily took precedence over Sety's initial urge to glorify a mid-level officer, no matter how bravely he fought. What, then, can we conclude from Ramesses's presence in his father's war monument? Sculptors inserted his image after they had finished the original composition of Sety's battle scenes. Moreover, Ramesses only appears where Mehy's figure had stood previously, in only some of Sety's war scenes. It is unlikely that Mehy was Horemheb's son. He may not even have been a real person, but an idealized figure of a dutiful Egyptian soldier following his king as a stand-in for the army as a whole.

25. A pair of triumphal stelae in Sety's name commemorate this event, although Sety himself may not have led his troops against Irem in person. When this minor war occurred, the highest crown official in colonial Nubia was the Viceroy of Kush Amenemopet. Amenemopet dedicated his own stela recording a hymn in praise of his king as a warrior at Qasr Ibrim in Lower Nubia, likely during Sety's Irem campaign in year eight. Prince Ramesses's name never crops up in any of these stelae, where all glory goes to Sety I. For the two stelae from Amara West and Sai in Nubia, see *KRI* VII, 8–10; *RITA* I, 85–87; *RITANC* I, 81–90; Murnane 1990, 100–102; Darnell 2011; el-Saady 2011; Masquelier-Loorius 2013, 96–98; Nielsen 2018.

26. Ramesses in his chariot storms into a mass of Nubian foemen who flee in terror toward their home village. Damage to hieroglyphic captions prevents us from identifying the precise Nubian location or population group involved, but it is likely in Irem. In an adjoining image, the Viceroy of Kush Amenemopet presides

as tribute bearers present Nubian war booty and lead enemy prisoners before Ramesses, who sits enthroned in state. Although some take the Beit el-Wali war reliefs as faithful chronicles of Ramesses II's earliest combat experiences, their historical value is not so clear cut; see Ricke, Hughes, and Wente 1967, pls. 8–15; Spalinger 1980. For iconographic analysis of these reliefs and their relationship to Sety I's Karnak war scenes, see Spalinger 2011, 28–38. On the temple as an expression of Egyptian cosmological thought, see McCarthy 2011.

27. The presence of Amenemopet in the Beit el-Wali scenes is not evidence for a coregency between Sety I and Ramesses II as was long believed (Seele, 1940); see Brand 2000, 327–28. Kitchen's (2001) objections are unfounded.

28. *KRI* II, 328:4–5; Spalinger 2009, 35–36; Brand 2016, 8–9.

29. On the *kheneret*-household (*pr-ḥnrt*), the so-called royal harem, and the women of the king's household, see pp. 204–10 below.

30. Brand 2016, 8–12.

31. On this prince, see Fisher 2001, 43–70. See pp. 263–65 below.

32. These boys were far too young to participate actively in the fighting, especially since the Beit el-Wali scenes portray events during Sety's reign. We cannot be certain these princelings even came along on campaign. Their brothers Ramesses Junior and Prehirwenemef must also have also come into the world by their father's first regnal year. See pp. 258–59 below.

33. See pp. 215–16 below.

34. How many additional wives Crown Prince Ramesses had is unknown, but the Abydos Dedicatory Inscription implies several women married him simultaneously, in keeping with Egypt's tradition of royal polygamy. Since he urgently needed to beget sons to continue his father's dynastic line, it is unlikely Nefertari and Isetnofret wed him before his other early wives. Instead, he took multiple spouses at once and soon impregnated several them, siring an ever-growing brood of children. Certainly, he had every dynastic incentive to do so; see Brand 2016, 9–10.

35. Robins 1994; Brand 2016, 10 with nn. 13–15.

36. Pinch 2006; Robins 1994.

37. See pp. 249–53 below.

38. Mariette 1869, pls. 42–46; *RITANC* I, 117–23; Brand 2000, 162–63, 318; Obsomer 2012b, 53–55; Shaikh Al Arab, 2019.

39. Mariette 1869, pl. 43; *KRI* I, 177–79; Redford 1986, 18–20.

40. Redford 1986, 19.

41. Redford 1986, 19–20; *RITANC* I, 118–19.

42. Mariette 1869, pl. 43; *KRI* I, 177:10. On the ambiguity of the term "true of voice," *mꜣꜥ-ḥrw*, for determining if a king was alive or dead when the inscription was made, see Murnane 1977, 270–72. The Abydos relief was carved several decades before Ramesses died. Not yet a king, Ramesses here recites the liturgy for the royal ancestors, so it was vital that he speaks truly, hence the epithet. In the adjoining Corridor of the Bull, Prince Amunhirkhopeshef's titles also include *mꜣꜥ-ḥrw* in two scenes carved long before he died.

43. Fisher 2001, 47–49, 69, 127–28; Xekalaki 2011, 60–62.

44. The written form of his prenomen cartouche indicates it dates to Ramesses II's first regnal year. Yet, a hieroglyphic caption above his head titles him "king's eldest son," *sꜣ nsw smsw* and "heir apparent," *iry-pꜥt*, not king.

45. Discussing the cartouche ornament in my study of Sety I's monuments, I concluded that the sculptors completed this scene during Sety's lifetime and

that Ramesses II's prenomen must have been chosen for him before he became king (Brand 2000, 162). I now believe the artists carved the prince's image in this relief after Sety's death once Ramesses II ascended the throne and chose his prenomen. Obsomer (2012b, 85) has reached the same conclusion.

46. Brand 2000, 155–70, esp. 169–70.

47. In his Abydos Temple, Sety I realized it would take some time for his craftsmen to execute the intricate bas-relief he demanded. Instead of the traditional red and black sketches, his draftsmen painted their designs with a wider color palette of red, yellow, and white as a temporary substitute for the exquisite bas-relief sculptors would later carve. In the inner chambers of the Abydos Temple's annex, some painted sketches still exist because sculptors never began their work before Sety died. Once he became king, Ramesses II set about to convert designs Sety's draftsmen laid out into reliefs naming himself; see Brand 2000, 161, 164–67.

48. Brand 2000, 165–67 and figs. 83–87.

49. Mariette 1869, pl. 53; Baqué 2002.

50. The composition of wall scenes in the Corridor of the Bull provides several clues indicating Ramesses II did not conceive them but employed painted designs Sety I's artist had prepared earlier but adapting them for his own purpose. Two images of the deified Sety I were likely modified images originally sketched as other male deities in Sety's own prepatory sketches: Brand 2000, 165–66, and figs. 84–85.

Artists completed another episode in sunk relief showing Ramesses II and Prince Amuhirkhopeshef offering captured waterfowl to the gods. The long form of his prenomen Usermaatre-Setepenre indicates the carving dates to after the first regnal year. Close examination of the cartouches reveals palimpsest traces of the suppressed nomen and prenomen of Sety I carved incompletely in raised relief. It is unclear whether these traces were Sety's own work or an aborted instance of Ramesses II's posthumous honoring of his father. On Amenhirkhopeshef's role in these scenes, see Fisher 2001, 43–46.

51. Two examples of such loyalist expressions are a relief tablet belonging to a pair of royal scribes named Amenwahsu and Tiya from Abydos, and the stela of Miya, a "scribe of offering tables," from Abydos. On both tablets, Prince Ramesses appears as a shorter adolescent figure standing behind his father Sety I. In each case, Ramesses wears the side lock of youth and grasps an ostrich feather flabellum as an emblem of his honorary rank of "fan bearer on the king's right side." Captions identify him as "the king's bodily son, Ramesses." For the Mia stela, see *RITANC* I, 238–39; Brand 2000, 187 and fig. 138; Petersen and Kehrer 2016, 90. For the Amenwahsu relief, see *RITANC* I, 212–13; Brand 2000, 151 and fig. 137; Obsomer 2012b, 53–55. It was long thought to be from Saqqara, but Scalf (2022) convincingly argues it comes from Abydos based on the writing of Sety I's nomen.

52. A prime example of these ideologically tinged royal "autobiographies" is Hatshepsut's Coronation Inscription: *Urk.* IV, 242–65; Müller 2005. Key to her program of self-legitimation as a female pharaoh, it relates in exquisite detail her alleged coronation during her father Thutmoe I's lifetime—an event that never happened. Yet, we need not resort to calling Hatshepsut a "liar" for these ideologically tinged distortions of historical reality. Nor would anyone today take her Coronation Inscription literally as a "historical" document. Its ideological purpose shines through. Another text of this genre is Thutmose III's

Texte de Jeunesse from Karnak: *Urk.* IV, 155–75. On its historical and ideological context, see Laboury 1998, 569–71.

53. *Urk.* IV, 1539–44; Cumming and Davies 1984, fasc. 3, 247–51.

54. Gardiner 1953; Murnane 1995a, 188–91; 1995b, nos. 106 and 107.

55. A common thread connecting all these texts is how the gods foretell the future sovereign's destiny, which is then presented after the fact as having been preordained. Huyeng (2014) discusses the common ideological themes and ahistorical quality of the so-called coronation inscriptions of Hatshepsut, Thutmose III, and Horemheb.

56. Brand 2000, 315–16, 330–32; Huyeng 2014. Too often scholars have taken this tale of Sety having Ramesses crowned in his own lifetime at face value as a genuine historical event: Seele, 1940, 26–30; Murnane 1977, 58; *RITANC* II, 194–95, 215; Spalinger 2009, 33–34. Murnane (1995a, 207–8) later admitted that Ramesses II's claims were self-serving and of questionable veracity. Rejecting a coregency, Obsomer (2012a) describes the incident as something like a case of play-acting where a doting Sety I stages a mock investiture ceremony for the child Ramesses. But pharaonic kingship, with its sacred overtones, potent regalia, and ceremony were not mere "royal trappings." For this same reason, we must reject the concept of a "prince regency" or "regency" whereby Ramesses was somehow not a king but entitled to wear the regalia and enclose his names in cartouches as Kitchen and Spalinger advocate. No Egyptian monarch would lightly confer the royal titulary and crowns on his intended successor during his own lifetime, contra Kitchen 1980, 171; see Brand 2000, 316–30, 333–35.

57. Seele 1940; Murnane 1975 and 1977; Spalinger 1979c; Costa 2017.

58. Brand 2000, 319–26, 329–30.

59. Brand 2000, 309–10.

60. Masquelier-Loorius 2013, 331–40.

61. Brand 2000, 309–10.

62. Brand 2000, 212–13, 216–19; Brand, Feleg, and Murnane 2018, 11–17; Blyth 2006, 147–49; Masquelier-Loorius 2013, 122–26.

63. Brand 2000, 350–55.

64. Ramesses II completed the Luxor Project, a peristyle forecourt complete with a towering pylon gateway, in his own name along with a pair of obelisks and several colossal statues; see Brand 1997; 2000, 271–75, and pp. 90–95 below. By the end of his reign, Sety I's men had inscribed one side of a single large obelisk, the Falminian Obelisk now in Rome. Ramesses II later completed this monolith's hieroglyphic texts in his own name and erected it in Heliopolis; see *RITANC* I, 97–98; Brand 1997, 102; 2000, 133–34 and fig. 63. Later still, the Roman Emperor Augustus transported this monolith to Rome. It now stands in the *Piazza del Popolo.*

65. The length of Sety I's reign has been controversial, with estimates ranging from fourteen or fifteen years, to as few as nine; see Brand 2000, 305–9; Hornung Krauss, and Warburton 2006, 210–11; van Dijk 2011; Wiener 2015; 210–11; Revez and Brand 2015, 258 n. 8; Aston 2016.

66. This is known from later administrative documents. For III *šmw* 24 as the anniversary of Sety's accession and discussion of the alternatives, see Helck 1959, 117–18; Brand 2000, 301–2; Hornung Krauss, and Warburton 2006, 210–11; Obsomer 2012b, 32–33.

67. Helck 1959, 118–20 first proposed the date of III *šmw* 27 for Ramesses II's accession. For an overview of the question, see Brand 2000, 302–5. Helck's

date is now widely accepted; Hornung Krauss, and Warburton 2006, 211; Obsomer 2012b, 62–63; *RITANC* II, 191–92. Therefore, Sety must have died a day before, on the twenty-sixth, a mere two days into a new regnal year: Brand 2000, 301–5; Wiener 2015, 659. But which year? Some believe Sety reigned for fifteen or sixteen years, but this is doubtful since we have no contemporary evidence for such a long reign; see Brand 2000, 305–9. If Sety had lived for five or six additional years, he surely would have completed more of the colossal statues and obelisks he commissioned in his ninth year. Ramesses II's grand pylon gateway and forecourt at Luxor Temple would now be known as Sety I's monument instead.

68. The date on Sety I's Gebel Barkal stela was long thought to be an alleged regnal year eleven: *KRI* I, 75:8; *RITANC* I, 65–66; Brand 2000, 296–97 and 305. Van Dijk (2011) has now demonstrated that this reading is in error, and it likely dates to Sety's third year instead. This leaves year nine as the highest attested regnal year, but was likely not his last. Sety was active during his ninth regnal year and he surely did not die in its earliest months. Also dating to year nine is the threefold dedicatory inscription recording an arduous journey through the desolate wastes of the Eastern Desert to the gold mining at Kanais, where he consecrated a small temple cut into the mountainside. Contra van Dijk 2011, 330–31.

Wine jar dockets from Sety's tomb date to his eight regnal year (Aston 2016), but this need not preclude his death at the beginning of a regnal year ten or even year eleven. Wine jar dockets from royal tombs in the Valley of the Kings are not by themselves infallible proof that a king died in the year they record. On the ambiguity of this type of evidence, see Bryson 2015; Dodson 2018, 130–32; 2019, 69. On the other hand, I am not convinced by their reasoning that wine jars of the regnal year 14 vintage of Horemheb's reign were prestocked in his tomb many years in advance, which he supposedly then occupied himself after a hypothetical year 27. Horemheb reigned for little more than half the three decades that Dodson and Bryson would credit him with, even if he died two or more years after his fourteenth regnal year as van Dijk (2011) argues. A granite bowl presented to an army general records Horemheb's first campaign in regnal year 16: Redford 1973; Grimal 2018. But an eleven-year gap in dated sources between year 16 and a putative year 27 is hard to accept.

69. The condition of Sety I's mummy suggests that he died sometime between the ages of forty and fifty; Wente 1980; Hawass and Saleem 2016, 151, 152–60. Although determining the age of Egyptian mummies is tricky, Hawass and Saleem note that moderate degeneration of the spine and knees, along with tooth ware suggest Sety was still in middle age. Although the mummy was broken into several pieces post mortem, there is no sign of violence and the cause of death was likely some disease or illness.

CHAPTER FOUR
| THE EARLY REIGN OF RAMESSES II

Ramesses II's First Royal Journey to Upper Egypt

Sety I died on the twenty-sixth day of the third month of Harvest Season (*Shomu*) in early June of 1279 BCE. Following hallowed tradition, Ramesses II arose as king the next day on the twenty-seventh.[1] Ramesses II may have taken power at Memphis or in his father's new royal residence in the Delta, but we know surprisingly little about where and when—or even if—he underwent a formal coronation.[2] Western scholars often view coronation rites in Christian Europe as analogues for the investiture ceremonies attending Egyptian kings upon their accession. This subtle bias is misleading.[3] It is conceivable a New Kingdom pharaoh did not undergo one "coronation" ceremony but performed similar observances in major temples throughout his realm.[4] Temple wall scenes often depict the monarch receiving crowns and regalia from the gods. While he enacted these rituals in the temples, the scenes are idealistic and ideological, and none should be taken as marking a specific historical occasion.[5] Rather, they proclaim an endless cycle of idealized crowning rituals by which the gods reconfirm the pharaoh's right to rule (fig. 4.1).[6]

After the traditional seventy-day period of mummification, Ramesses II dutifully escorted his father's embalmed body to Thebes for interment in the splendid tomb Sety I prepared for himself in the Valley of the Kings.[7] In sweltering August heat, Egypt's nobility anxiously awaited the somber flotilla bearing Sety's mummy and their new sovereign to arrive. After a two-week journey from Memphis, Pharaoh's barge and its escorts docked at the Southern City (fig. 4.2).

Even for a young man in his early twenties, Sety's funeral taxed Ramesses physically and emotionally. The last miles of the dead pharaoh's final earthly journey traversed desolate wastes in the Valley of the Kings as the canyon twisted and turned, burrowing its way into the Eastern Desert's rugged limestone hills on the outskirts of western Thebes (fig. 4.3). Outfitted in their finery and roasting under the oppressive summer sun—unbearable even in early morning—Pharaoh and his courtiers plodded along rocky tracks shimmering with heat. With them came oxen dragging a catafalque bearing Sety's encoffined corpse to its house of eternity in the royal necropolis Egyptians called the Great

FIGURE 4.1. Idealized scene of Ramesses II's "coronation" by the gods. He sits enthroned between the goddesses Nekhbet and Wadjet while Horus and Thoth place the crowns of Upper and Lower Egypt on his head. Photograph by Peter Brand.

Place (*set weret*).[8] Behind the dignitaries came a long file of servants and necropolis personnel bearing the late monarch's tomb equipment and earthly possessions, all for his use in the afterlife. As Sety I's eldest son, Ramesses II presided over his father's burial, with the high priest of Amun-Re and a host of lesser clergy supporting him. By laying Sety in his tomb, Ramesses legally affirmed that he was the dead king's rightful heir.

Sety I's funeral cast a somber pall over a normally festive time in ancient Thebes, for it came just as the magnificent annual celebration in honor of Amun-Re began in late summer: The Beautiful Festival of Opet.[9] Yet, this confluence of sacred observances—a pharaoh's burial and the most important celebration in the Theban religious calendar—marked an auspicious beginning to Ramesses II's relationship with his celestial father Amun-Re.

Opet was a solemn observance of the cyclical renewal of Amun-Re and the king. Each year Amun-Kamutef, the god's fertility aspect, journeyed from his main shrine at Karnak to Luxor Temple, which the Egyptians called the Southern Sanctuary, one and a half miles (two kilometers) to the south.[10] Amun-Kamutef's name means "Amun-Bull of His Mother"—the god who created himself by impregnating his own

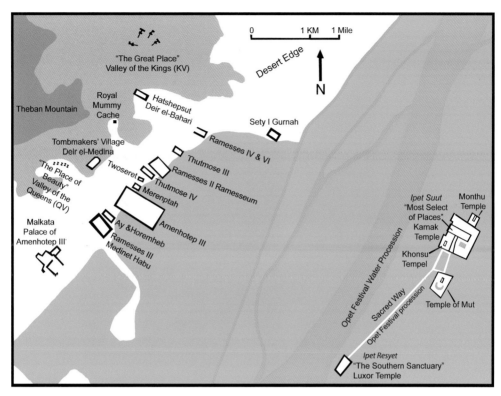

Map labels:
"The Great Place" Valley of the Kings (KV)
Theban Mountain
Royal Mummy Cache
Hatshepsut Deir el-Bahari
Sety I Gurnah
Desert Edge
N
0   1 KM   1 Mile
Tombmakers' Village Deir el-Medina
Ramesses IV & VI
Thutmose III
"The Place of Beauty" Valley of the Queens (QV)
Twoseret
Thutmose IV
Ramesses II Ramesseum
Merenptah
Malkata Palace of Amenhotep III
Ay & Horemheb
Amenhotep III
Ramesses III Medinet Habu
Ipet Suut "Most Select of Places" Karnak Temple
Monthu Temple
Khonsu Tempel
Opet Festival Water Procession
Sacred Way
Temple of Mut
Opet Festival procession
Ipet Resyet "The Southern Sanctuary" Luxor Temple

FIGURE 4.2. Map of Thebes (modern Luxor) showing the locations of the major New Kingdom monuments. The overland religious processions of the Opet Festival traveled from Karnak to Luxor along the sacred way while the divine barges voyaged by river. On the west bank, the Ramesseum stands at the center of the "kings' row" of New Kingdom royal cult temples at the desert edge, which the cult images of the Theban Triad visited during the Beautiful Festival of the Valley. Further west are the royal tombs in the Valley of the Kings and Valley of the Queens.

mother.[11] Within Amun's Southern Sanctuary, king and god renewed their mutual energies, guaranteeing Egypt's fertility for another year. Over weeks of celebrations, Pharaoh and Amun's clergy proffered huge quantities of food and drink to the Theban Triad on hundreds of temple altars: roasted oxen, geese and waterfowl, a dozen varieties of bread and cakes, fruits and vegetables of all kinds, and scores of tempting delicacies.[12] Once the gods and spirits of the royal ancestors took their fill from the essence of these offerings, priests and populace feasted too, washing it down with free-flowing draughts of wine and beer.

Opet was a divine pageant inspiring awe and wonder in all who beheld its spectacle. Festivities opened with a grand cavalcade from Karnak to Luxor. Under Pharaoh's lead, companies of priests carried the sacred barks of the Theban Triad: Amun-Re, his consort Mut, and their son Khonsu (fig. 4.4). Sacred barks were portable model boats resting on platforms with carrying poles, borne on the shoulders of priests.[13] As befitted a god's mode of transport, they were sheathed in gold foil and encrusted with semiprecious stones like lapis lazuli, turquoise, and carnelian, along with faience and colored glass inlays. Figureheads at prow and stern represented the god's image, or that of its sacred animal, and embodied its spiritual presence.[14] The bark itself was as much

FIGURE 4.3. View of the Valley of the Kings (KV). On the slope in the foreground are the entrances to the tombs of Sety I (KV 17) and Ramesses I (KV 16). Alamy.

a divine avatar as the cult statue housed within its cabin-shrine. Sacred barks could act as oracles through which deities expressed their will. Ram figureheads representing Amun's sacred animal festooned Amun's bark both fore and aft. Ramesses II's own sacred bark, with effigies of his crowned head at prow and stern, and a portable cult-statue of his predecessor Sety I, escorted the barks of the Theban Triad on their festal journey.[15]

Following behind these processional icons marched members of the royal family, cadres of officials, hosts of soldiers, troops of musicians and dancers, droves of sacrificial animals, and companies of priests and temple staff bearing cultic paraphernalia and food offerings for Amun's altars.[16] These multitudes paraded southward to Luxor along stone-paved sacred roadways connecting the Temples of Karnak and Luxor. Jubilant mobs thronged these sacred ways to observe the spectacle.[17] More crowds gathered at the riverside to witness an even more breathtaking waterborne procession.

In Ramesses II's day, an awesome flotilla of divine and royal barges transported the sacred barks from the quay at Karnak to a dock by Luxor Temple. Amun-Re's river barge was a virtual floating temple called *Amun-Userhet*, "Amun-is-Mighty-of-Prow (fig. 4.5)."[18] Like the sacred bark it carried, imposing figureheads at the *Userhet*'s prow and stern took the form of gilded ram's heads wearing elaborate crowns.[19] Ceremonial objects and cultic equipment filled its deck: statuary, offering

FIGURE 4.4. Ramesses II offering incense to Amun-Re's sacred bark carried by priests wearing falcon and jackal masks. Located on the south wall of the Great Hypostyle Hall of Karnak, the relief dates to the first regnal year. Courtesy of the Franco-Egyptian Center of Karnak.

tables laden with incense, flowers, food and drink; and tall standards with divine and royal emblems. At its center a massive cabin-shrine lodged the portable barks and sacred icons, shielding them from profane eyes during their waterborne progress.

From the riverbank onlookers would have squinted in amazement, for *Amun-Userhet* was plated to her waterline with a heavy sheathing of pure gold.[20] Gold cladding overlaid its ram figureheads, cabin-shine, and other fixtures. Engraved sheets of this precious metal, adorned with scenes of Pharaoh worshiping Amun, lined the sides of her hull.[21] *Amun-Userhet* possessed no sails or means of propulsion. Instead Pharaoh's own barge would tow it, while groups of the faithful, hauling at ropes on the Nile embankment, assisted in heaving the mighty ship southward against the river's current. In their wake came a flotilla of attending vessels—most prominently Mut's barge, which the Queen's barge of state would tow, and Khonsu's vessel. Temple reliefs depict smaller boats escorting *Amun-Userhet*. Shaped like geese, also sacred to Amun, these were floating altar tables heaped with offerings of food, libations, floral bouquets, and incense—truly a movable feast.[22]

The processions on land of notables, clergy, and sacrificial animals converged with the sacred flotilla at Luxor Temple. Ramesses II now escorted the portable barks of the Theban Triad into Luxor Temple to enact mysterious rites unseen by all but the highest clergy. Deep within its inner sanctum, his *Ka*-spirit merged with Amun's *Ka*.[23] This mystical union of Amun and Pharaoh recharged their mutual energies. Doctrinally, Opet epitomized and reinforced the king's relationship with Amun-Re as his heavenly progenitor. Once these arcane sacre-

FIGURE 4.5. The great river barge of Amun-Re called *Amun-Userhet*, meaning "Amun is Mighty of Prow." Relief from the west wall of the Great Hypostyle Hall of Karnak Temple. The huge vessel was a floating temple overlaid with gold plating. Drawing by Peter Brand.

ments concluded, the divine cortège returned to Karnak with additional pomp, a mirror of the opening festivities.

Ramesses II's Royal Titulary

Upon ascending the Throne of Horus, every pharaoh chose his official set of ceremonial names and titles, which Egyptologists call his titulary.[24] In the two millennia of Egyptian civilization that elapsed before Ramesses II's time, Egyptian kings accumulated an elaborate sequence of five sets of regal names and titles.[25] The first and oldest was the Horus name.[26] Its origins stretched back before 3000 BCE, into remote prehistory when the proto-pharaohs of Upper Egypt ruled as living incarnations of the falcon-god Horus.

Scribes enclosed the Horus name in a rectangular box, called a *serekh*, meaning "to make known." This device represents an archaic palace façade. It enclosed one or more descriptive epithets the king chose to identify himself. A falcon perched atop the *serekh* represented the king as Horus. New Kingdom ideology linked Pharaoh's Horus name with his "living royal *Ka*," (*ka nesu ankh*), an aspect of his divine nature.[27] Starting with Thutmose I, most New Kingdom rulers began their Horus name with the title "mighty bull," to which they added one or two further epithets. For his Horus name, Ramesses II chose Mighty bull: beloved of Maat (fig. 4.6). In his thirty-fourth regnal year he added the epithet "lord of Jubilees like his father Ptah-Tatchenen."[28] On his monuments, especially temples and obelisks, Ramesses II displayed a bewildering variety of novel epithets in his Horus name.[29]

The most recognizable elements of the Egyptian royal titulary were Pharaoh's two cartouche names. The cartouches represented loops of rope enclosing and protecting his sacred names and symbolizing his

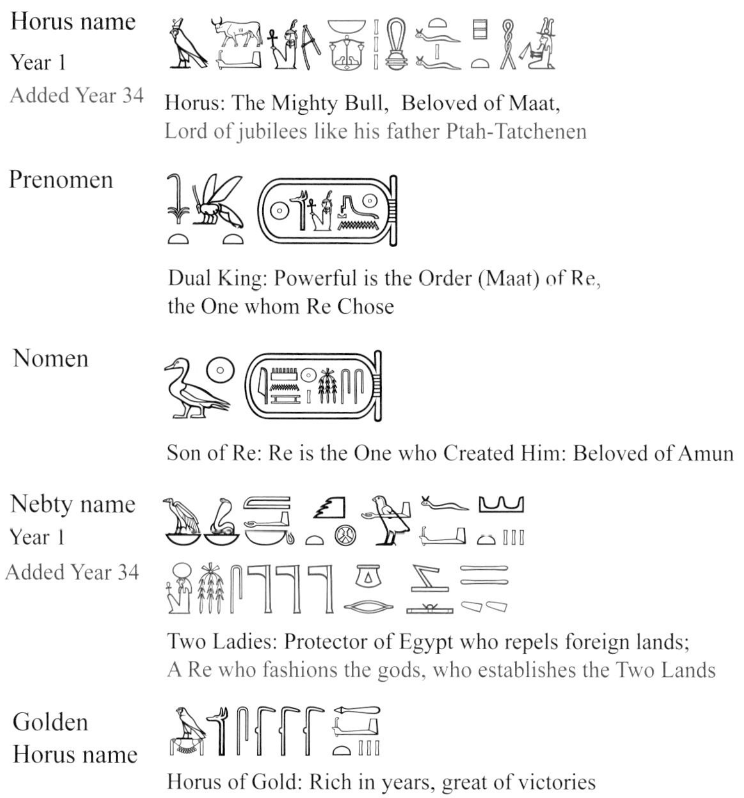

Horus name

Year 1

Added Year 34

Horus: The Mighty Bull, Beloved of Maat,
Lord of jubilees like his father Ptah-Tatchenen

Prenomen

Dual King: Powerful is the Order (Maat) of Re,
the One whom Re Chose

Nomen

Son of Re: Re is the One who Created Him: Beloved of Amun

Nebty name

Year 1

Added Year 34

Two Ladies: Protector of Egypt who repels foreign lands;
A Re who fashions the gods, who establishes the Two Lands

Golden
Horus name

Horus of Gold: Rich in years, great of victories

FIGURE 4.6. The five-fold titulary of Ramesses II. He added the elements in red beginning in regnal year 34. Diagram by Erika Feleg.

dominion over all creation.[30] Standing before his first cartouches was the title  (*nesu-bity*). Egyptologists often translate it as "King of Upper and Lower Egypt," but it may not have had a geographic meaning.[31] Instead, it conveyed two modes of kingship with separate origins lost in the mists of Egyptian prehistory. It is translated here as "Dual King." It preceded Pharaoh's most important name, enclosed within his first cartouche, which Egyptologists have labeled variously as his prenomen, coronation name, or throne name.[32] King lists, like Sety I's honor roll of royal ancestors at Abydos, designate each ruler by his prenomen. Likewise, when New Kingdom monarchs corresponded with foreign rulers, they identified themselves by their prenomens in diplomatic letters.

Egyptian kings first adopted the prenomen in the early Old Kingdom. They usually compounded it with the name of Re, thereby expressing a theological statement about the monarch's nature and his relationship to the sun god. Kings frequently modeled their prenomen cartouches on those of their forebears, either from their own dynastic line or kings of old they wished to emulate.[33] Sety I chose Men-Maat-Re, or "Enduring is the Truth (*Maat*) of Re" for his prenomen. Now, Ramesses II selected  User-Maat-Re, "Powerful is the Truth

(*Maat*) of Re." Ramesses also experimented with various hieroglyphic spellings of his prenomen and he sometimes fixed terminal epithets to it. As we shall see, this culminated in his adoption of the longer pre-nomen Usermaatre-Setepenre beginning in his second year.

The title 𓅭𓇳 (*sa Ra*), meaning "Son of Re," introduced the pharaoh's second cartouche name, which Egyptologists call his nomen because it was usually the name he received at birth.[34] A New Kingdom ruler typically attached further epithets to his nomen, expressing some aspect of kingship or his relationship to particular deities. The individual we call Ramesses II, born Pramessu, now became 𓉘𓂋𓄿𓐝𓐠𓉙 (*Ramesses-Mera-mun*), meaning "Re is the One who Created Him: Beloved of Amun."[35]

Egyptian pharaohs chose two more names, but they were merely strings of titles and epithets. The Nebty or "Two Ladies" name honored two goddesses who protected the king: Nekhbet appeared as a vulture and personified Upper Egypt, and Wadjet of Lower Egypt was a sacred cobra.[36] For his Nebty name, Ramesses chose "Protector of Egypt who Subdues Foreign Lands." Last came his Golden Horus name, "Rich in Years and Great of Victories."[37]

During his sixty-seven-year reign Ramesses inscribed numerous variants of his royal names on hundreds of monuments, often with different epithets attached to his Horus names. As we will see, scribes wrote his cartouche names in several forms with a wide range of hieroglyphic spellings, especially during his first year. Beginning in his thirty-fourth year, he expanded his Horus and Nebty names to celebrate his Jubilee festivals and divine kingship.

Ramesses II's First Visit to Abydos as King

After celebrating his first Opet Festival as king, Ramesses II stayed in Thebes for another month, conferring with local dignitaries, including the Upper Egyptian Vizier Paser, and inspecting temples in Amun's city. After a busy late summer of solemnities and administrative tasks in Thebes, the "Southern City," Ramesses II departed for his new capital in the Delta. We do not even know its original name, because Ramesses II lost no time in rebranding the city as Piramesses-Aanakhtu, meaning the Domain of Ramesses who is Great of Victories.[38] But Pharaoh had an important stop to make at Abydos, the holy city of Osiris. There, Sety I had left his own cult temple incomplete when he died. Ramesses described his visit in his Abydos Dedicatory Inscription, a lengthy edict he inscribed on the columned porch of Sety's temple:[39]

> *One of these days it happened in regnal year one, month three of Inundation Season (Akhet), day twenty-three, wh[en His Person] came after causing Amun to sail south to Opet (Luxor Temple). With praise in*

> *valor and victory before Amun-Atum-in-Thebes he went forth ... when*
> *His Person came from the Southern City ... setting forth on the way,*
> *setting sail, the king's barks illuminating the waters, setting a course*
> *northward toward the seat of valor, Piramesses-Great of Victories.*
> *His Person arrived to see his father (Osiris) cruising on the waters of*
> *the canal of the Thinite Province (Abydos) and to present offerings to*
> *Wennofer (Osiris).*[40]

Upon his arrival Pharaoh surveyed conditions in the holy city with
dismay. The shrines of Egypt's ancestors lay in ruins while Sety I's cult
temple languished, after the builders and artisans charged with its completion seemingly abandoned their work:

> *It was falling into ruin that he found the temple enclosures of the Sacred*
> *Land belonging to the kings of old, and their cenotaphs in Abydos; half*
> *of them were still under [construction], and [the other half of them*
> *covered] with earth, while their walls [lay] on the ground. Not a brick*
> *touched the next one. What had been a divine abode had turned into*
> *dust [...] their owners having flown up to heaven. But there was no son*
> *who restored the monument of his father in the necropolis.*[41]

Although he certainly indulges in some dramatic license, Ramesses II
presents a sad picture of the hoary ancestral cemetery of Abydos as it
sat moldering into dust and ruin. It was every Egyptian son's solemn
duty to complete and maintain his father's funerary monument, but
the ancient tomb chapels in the City of Osiris had no one left to repair them.[42] This pathetic scene served as a timely backdrop to efforts
by this young Pharaoh, who boasts how he took care of his father's
Abydos shrine after finding that—to his profound shock—workmen had
neglected it since Sety I's death:

> *Now (as for) the temple of Menmaatre, its front and its back end were*
> *(still) under construction after he entered heaven. There was no one who*
> *completed its monument. There was no one who erected the pillars on*
> *its terrace. Its cult statue lay on the ground; it had not been fashioned*
> *according to the (proper) specifications for it in the Mansion of Gold. Its*
> *divine offerings had come to a halt and the priests of the temple likewise*
> *were taking away and bringing back (things) from its fields without*
> *(properly) establishing their boundaries on the land.*[43]

We may easily imagine workmen hesitating at their task upon learning of Sety's demise and before their new royal master arrived to inspect their handiwork. Yet, Ramesses surely exaggerates the condition
of his father's temple, thereby enhancing his filial piety. Upon seeing
Sety's unfinished edifice the new king summoned his courtiers and
proclaimed he would complete it. Here Ramesses recalled his princely

career under his father's tutelage, including the fictive account of Sety crowning him as a child.[44] Politically, the Abydos Dedicatory Inscription stresses two key ideological themes: that Sety I designated his eldest son as king, and that Ramesses II acted piously to fulfill his father's monumental legacy:

> I fashioned (the cult statue of) my father from gold anew in the first year of my appearing (as king). I decreed that his temple might be supplied; I established its fields [...] I [endowed] offerings on his behalf for his Ka (consisting of) [provisions of bread, beer, oxen and fowl], wine, incense, every sort of fruit, [every kind of] fresh vegetables, and orchards that flourished for him.
>
> See, his temple was under my authority and all its works were under my supervision since [I became king(?)]. Now, I was (only) a child [when I was given charge over the temple(?)] of my father. I will make it great by restoring its monuments. I will not neglect his (cult) place like those children who forget [their] fathers [...] it will be said [about me he was(?) ...] a son who performed beneficent acts.
>
> As for my mighty deeds (that I did) for my father as a child, I will (now) complete them as Lord of the Two Lands. I will complete them in proper fashion. [...]; I will [build up] the walls in the temple of the one who begat me; I will put in charge a man of my choosing to direct this work in it; I will rebuild what was mis[sing] on its walls; [I will construct] its pylon gateway in [sandstone(?) ...]; I will roof his house; I will erect its pillars; and I will place stones in the foundation trenches. It is good to make monument after monument, two beneficent deeds at one time, they being in my name and in the name of my [father]. So with a son [...], so with the one who begat him.[45]

Despite stating his dismay for the alleged neglect of the priests and craftsmen responsible for Sety's Abydos temple, Ramesses decided to promote the local High Priest of Abydos, a man named Nebwenenef.[46] Pharaoh now appointed Nebwenenef to Egypt's preeminent sacerdotal office: The High Priesthood of Amun-Re in Thebes. Yet, this man bore ultimate responsibility for any lack of progress on Sety's temple. Clearly his new lord was pleased with Nebwenenef. The priest himself later recalled as much in his "autobiography" inscribed on the walls of his Theban tomb that records his promotion:[47]

> Then His Person said to him: "You are (now) High Priest of Amun. His treasury and his granary are under your signet ring. You are the master of his temple and every endowment of his is under your authority."[48]

Pharaoh informs the new High Priest how Amun himself had elected him via an oracle:

> *As Re lives for me and loves me, and as my father Amun praises me,*
> *I displayed for him the whole entourage, and the chief of troops. The*
> *(names of) the priests of the gods, while the officials of his Estate [who*
> *were in front of him] were announced to him. But he was not content*
> *with a single one of them, except when I told your name to him. [Do*
> *what is beneficial for him], since he has preferred you. I know you are*
> *efficient. Exceed expectations [and] his [Ka will praise you] and my Ka*
> *will also.*[49]

Ramesses II's Earliest Monuments: Honoring His Father and Grandfather

At his death, Sety I left several major building ventures incomplete.[50] For Ramesses II, filial duty required him to bring these works to fruition. Even as he ordered work to resume at Sety's Abydos temple, Ramesses took his father's other projects in hand.

At Karnak architects had finished constructing Sety's Great Hypostyle Hall. Sculptors had carved fine bas-reliefs throughout its northern wing and had just started embellishing its southern half when Ramesses came to power.[51] Determined to leave his own mark on this vast edifice, the young king directed his men to carve reliefs in the Hypostyle Hall's central processional axis with its double row of giant papyrus columns. Here Sety's draftsmen had laid out painted versions of the scenes and texts on these mighty columns, but sculptors had not yet engraved them in bas-relief. Now they carved this decoration following Sety's painted designs, but in the name of Ramesses.[52] Other teams labored on the Hall's south and southwestern walls, drafting new scenes in paint and sculpting them in the bas-relief style Sety had favored.[53] But Ramesses quickly abandoned his father's humble ritual pose. No longer would Pharaoh be pictured constantly bowing or kneeling before the gods.[54]

By completing the Great Hypostyle Hall, his father's most magnificent edifice, Ramesses II also paid homage to Sety's memory. Several scenes depict him offering cult service to images of his deified father. In one scene Sety takes the form of a portable statue following the sacred barks of Amun-Re, Mut, and Khonsu during the Festival of Opet.[55] In later years, to emphasize his own divinity, Ramesses altered images of the deified Sety I on the Hypostyle Hall's southern gateway.[56] Here he erased Sety's cartouches and inserted his own, so that now he worships Amun-Re and his own divine alter ego.

His grandfather, Ramesses I, never built a royal cult temple during his short reign. Sety I provided a suite of rooms for this purpose in his Gurnah Temple, just south of its hypostyle hall.[57] Sety designed this space as a temple within a temple. Its chapel lodged Ramesses I's cult statue, which received daily offerings from priests to nourish his *Ka*. It also accommodate Amun-Re's sacred bark during the Beautiful Festival of the Valley, an ancestor feast when Amun visited cult temples of current and previous kings in western Thebes.[58]

By the end of Sety's reign craftsmen had decorated his father's chapel with reliefs depicting Sety adoring Amun-Re's sacred bark and anointing a statue of Ramesses I in the guise of Osiris. But the walls of a small vestibule in front of the inner chapel remained unadorned. Once Ramesses II became Pharaoh, he conceived a new decorative program for this vestibule, featuring his pious ritual worship of cult images of his father and his grandfather alongside those of the gods (fig. 4.7).[59]

Here we detect a subtle shift in the themes Ramesses II stresses in his wall reliefs. Sety I no longer takes any active role in the rituals. Instead he stands behind Amun-Re, receiving cultic worship from his son.[60] Ramesses I, long dead when his grandson ascended the throne, is also present in some scenes, receiving the new pharaoh's offering gifts. Both Ramesses I and Sety I bear emblems signifying their divinity. Each grasps the crook and flail scepters folded across his chest with one hand while the other dangles by his side clutching the *ankh*-sign of life, an emblem normally held by the gods themselves.

One scene on the vestibule's northern wall fires the imaginations of some Egyptologists who view it as representing Ramesses II's coronation during Sety I's lifetime. We see Ramesses II kneeling before Amun-Re, while Mut extends her arms protectively as she confers symbols of a long reign and many Jubilees on him.[61] Behind Amun-Re, the divine Sety I witnesses the ceremony. But this is not a "historical" document proving a coregency or even a record of Ramesses's coronation.[62] Instead, it represents the mythic world where the gods confer their blessings on Pharaoh (fig. 4.8).

Within a year or two Ramesses II's zeal for paying homage to Sety waned, even as he continued to decorate his father's temples at Gurnah and Abydos.[63] In the outer hypostyle hall of Sety I's Abydos Temple, Ramesses added new scenes and inscriptions in his own name, and even carved over earlier decoration of his father. They were carved in his own preferred style of sunken relief, rather than bas-relief.

In one peculiar case, an architrave inscription displays Ramesses II's regal titles superimposed over those of Sety I (fig. 4.9). Amid the weird jumble of overlapping hieroglyphs, some naïve viewers and conspiracy theorists see images of modern war machines, including an attack helicopter, as though the ancient Egyptians possessed such advanced technology. Much like seeing images of people and animals in the forms of clouds, these suggestive shapes are no more real than a cloud-dragon

FIGURE 4.7. Ramesses II offers to Amun-Re, Mut, Khonsu, and his deified grandfather Ramesses I. Displaying the short form of Ramesses II's prenomen, Usermaatre, this scene dates to his first regnal year. Vestibule of the Ramesses I chapel in the Gurnah Temple of Sety I. Nineteenth century drawing by Champollion. NYPL digital collections. Public domain.

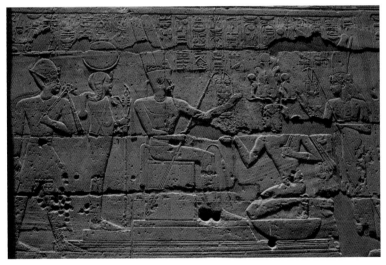

FIGURE 4.8. Idealized scene of Ramesses II receiving crowns and regalia from Amun-Re, Khonsu, and Mut in the presence of the deified Sety I. Carved in raised relief with Ramesses II's short prenomen Usermaatre, the scene dates to the earliest months of Ramesses's reign. Gurnah Temple of Sety I, vestibule to the Ramesses I chapel, north wall. Photograph by Peter Brand.

floating across the sky.[64] These wrongheaded conspiracy theories often thrive on the internet but are easy to debunk.[65]

Evolution of Ramesses II's Relief Decoration and His Early Cartouche Variants

Today, we can trace the chronology of Ramesses II's earliest monumental inscriptions by observing the style of his temple art as it rapidly evolves. In his earliest months as king, Ramesses followed tradition by using both raised and sunk relief in his temple decoration. In raised, or bas-relief, sculpted images project out from the wall surface, after the artist carves away the background plane surrounding them. In sunk relief, the sculptor carves the image into the wall, but does not remove

FIGURE 4.9. The so-called Abydos helicopter inscription. In reality, this is a palimpsest relief with Ramesses II's titulary superimposed over Sety I's on an architrave (ceiling beam) of Sety's Abydos temple, as is common elsewhere in the Abydos Temple and in the Karnak Hyposytle Hall. Hieroglyphs in black are Sety I's version. The red hieroglyphs are Ramesses II's names and titles that were later carved over Sety's. In the upper right, the first element of the Horus name, "Living Horus, Mighty Bull," were not recarved because they are identical for both kings. Courtesy Manna Nader Gabana Studios Cairo. Hieroglyphic diagram by Peter Brand.

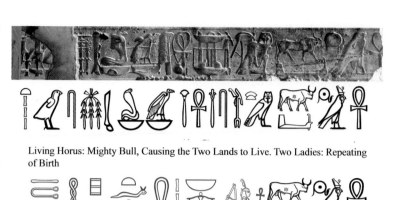

Living Horus: Mighty Bull, Causing the Two Lands to Live. Two Ladies: Repeating of Birth

Living Horus: Mighty Bull, Beloved of Maat, Lord of Jubilees like his father Ptah-Tachenen

Menmaatre

Powerful of Scimitar, Who Suppresses the Nine Bows

Usermaatre-Setepenre

Two Ladies: Protector of Egypt Who repels foreign lands

the background matrix. Instead a narrow, sharp-edged trough outlines each figure.

Before Ramesses II's time, Egyptian kings employed raised relief for interior decoration. But under the intense rays of Egypt's sun, sunk relief accentuates the play of light and shadow along the edges of sculpted figures dramatically. For this reason Egyptian kings long preferred sunk relief for exterior walls and other monuments exposed to sunlight.[66]

At the beginning of his reign, sculptors executed Ramesses II's interior artwork in the traditional raised-relief style, just as they had under Sety I. Within a few months of taking power, however, Ramesses decided to employ sunken carvings exclusively on both the interior and exterior surfaces of his temple buildings. His modern critics often disparage this decision, accusing him of preferring quick and allegedly shoddy workmanship in sunk relief as opposed to Sety I's exquisite raised reliefs.[67] But Ramesses II's early sunk reliefs also achieved a high standard of artistic quality.[68]

In fact, Ramesses II's motive for abandoning raised relief had more to do with visibility than hastiness. Although centuries of decay have left most Egyptian temples unroofed today, exposing them to a flood of sunlight, in ancient times their interiors were dark. Even the colossal window grilles of the Great Hypostyle Hall admitted only a diffuse light into its deep recesses. In the dim interiors of the temples sunk relief stood out more vividly due to the play of light and shadow along the edges of the carvings.[69]

The second criteria Egyptologists use to date the earliest phases of Ramesses II's monumental reliefs and inscriptions is the form of his cartouche names.[70] Here we must distinguish between the form of the name—what it means and how the Egyptians pronounced it—and its hieroglyphic spelling. The hieroglyphic writing system possessed so many different signs that scribes could combine and arrange a variety of different glyphs to spell out the same name. At the beginning of his reign Ramesses exploited this flexibility to display his cartouche names in a myriad of spellings (see figs. 4.10 and 4.11).

Upon his accession to the throne he adopted a prenomen with the simple form Usermaatre ⌻, without a terminal epithet, and usually spelled out.[71] Throughout his first regnal year this simple form was the most common one, although Ramesses sometimes appended epithets like "image of Re" and "heir of Re," among others, yielding more complex forms.[72] In most cases these epithets occurred on cartouches arranged horizontally, while most vertical cartouches were simple Usermaatre (figs. 4.10 and 4.12).[73]

This practice continued until sometime in his second year. Henceforth, Ramesses II decided, his prenomen would be Usermaatre-Setepenre, which scribes often spelled ⌻. The terminal epithet *setep-en-Ra* means "the One whom Re Chose." This long form of the prenomen remained definitive for the remaining six and a half decades of his rule. The anglicization Usermaatre-Setepenre is artificial, but well established. Cuneiform diplomatic texts indicate that the contem-

FIGURE 4.10. Variant forms and writings of Ramesses II's prenomen cartouche. Diagram by Erika Feleg.

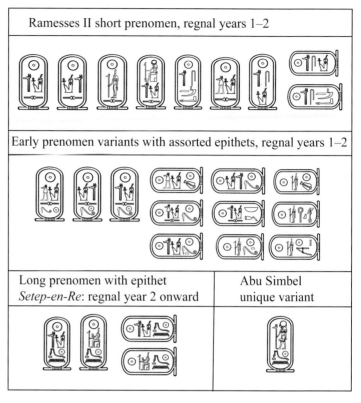

Ramesses II short prenomen, regnal years 1–2

Early prenomen variants with assorted epithets, regnal years 1–2

Long prenomen with epithet *Setep-en-Re*: regnal year 2 onward	Abu Simbel unique variant

porary pronunciation of the long prenomen sounded something like *Wasmu'aria-Satepnaria*.[74]

Although scribes enjoyed some leeway in selecting and arranging hieroglyphic elements of the long prenomen, they did not change the meaning of his name. After his first regnal year, he abandoned all other

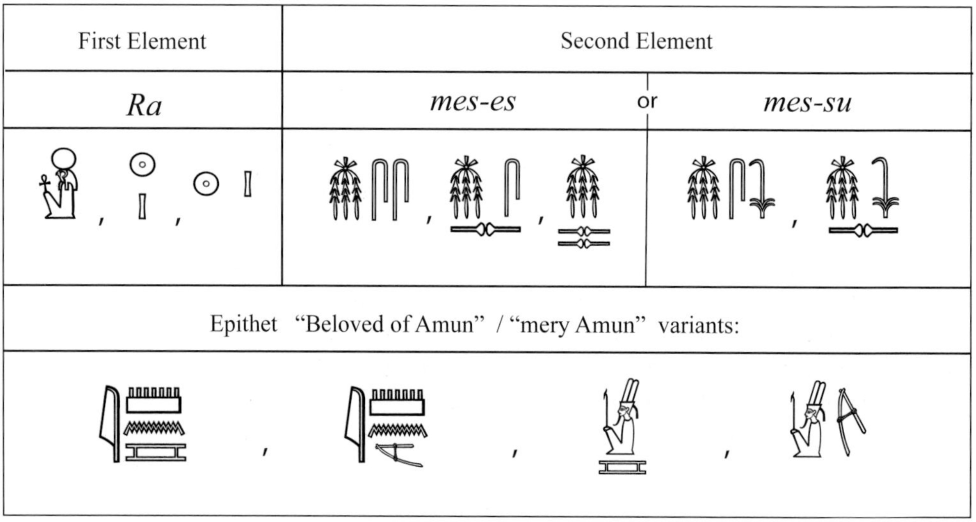

FIGURE 4.11. Variant writings of the three elements of Ramesses II's nomen cartouche. Diagram by Erika Feleg.

First Element	Second Element		
Ra	*mes-es*	or	*mes-su*
Epithet "Beloved of Amun" / "mery Amun" variants:			

FIGURE 4.12. Variant writings of Ramesses II's cartouches. Left: The Ramessu and Ramesses forms of the nomen. Right: The long and short forms of the prenomen. Photographs by Peter Brand.

epithets along with simple Usermaatre. The two most common spellings of the definitive long prenomen were ⊙𝕄△ and ⊙𝕄△, although different spellings sometimes occur.[75]

As was traditional, the king's nomen cartouche reflected the name he received at birth, in this case "Ramesses," meaning "Re-Created-Him."[76] To this the young pharaoh appended a regal epithet "Mer-Amun," meaning "He-whom-Amun-Loves." Scribes wrote the name Ramesses with two different endings: one represented an obsolete archaic pronunciation; the other was a "modern" variant reflecting how the name was voiced in the spoken dialect of the later New Kingdom.

After the name of the Sun-god Re, both forms have the *mes*-sign 𝕄, meaning "to create." After this comes a phonetic compliment *s*, written either with the vertical folded cloth glyph ∏, or the flat door-bolt sign ⊷ .

The final glyphs of the name Ramesses represent the dependent pronoun *sw* meaning "him." In the classic Egyptian dialect this was spelled with the sedge plant glyph ⥾ or as ⥾𖾚 with the quail chick being a phonetic compliment.

By Ramesses II's day, the long *su* sound had shortened to a clipped *se*, with the vowel unsounded. To render this modern pronunciation in hieroglyphs scribes replaced the glyph with simple *s*, using ∏ or the flat door bolt sign ⊷, in addition to the phonetic compliment *s* following *mes* (see fig. 4.11). The obsolete vocalization sounded something like *Riamesesu* but was now pronounced *Riamesesa*.[77]

Although the terminal epithet naming the god Amun was pronounced last, scribes wrote it at the beginning of the cartouche in keeping with a convention called "honorific transposition," whereby the name of a major god was written first. Amun's name could be inscribed phonetically or with a glyph representing the seated god. Re's name could also be indicated with a seated falcon-headed god crowned with a solar disk, or with the simple sun-disk. In some writings, the gods sit face-to-face at the beginning of the cartouche (figs. 4.11 and 4.13).

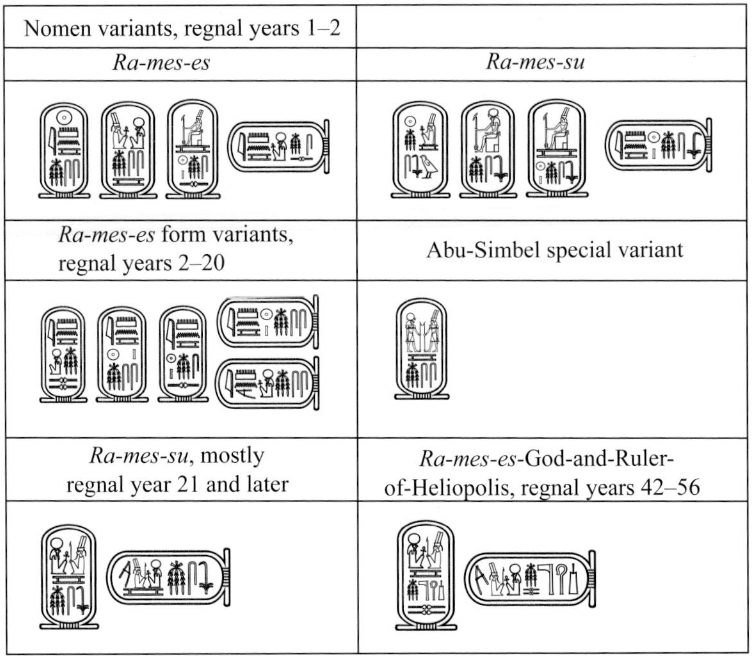

FIGURE 4.13. Variant forms and writings of Ramesses II's nomen cartouche. Diagram by Erika Feleg.

Nomen variants, regnal years 1–2	
Ra-mes-es	*Ra-mes-su*
Ra-mes-es form variants, regnal years 2–20	Abu-Simbel special variant
Ra-mes-su, mostly regnal year 21 and later	*Ra-mes-es*-God-and-Ruler-of-Heliopolis, regnal years 42–56

In his first year Ramesses II employed both the *Ramesses* and *Ramessu* forms of his nomen, both in Upper and Lower Egypt (fig. 4.13). During this early period the forms and hieroglyphic spellings of his two cartouche names varied profusely.[78] Indeed, the king and his scribes delighted in writing out his cartouches in an array of novel and unusual spellings.[79] This rich diversity does not betray any wavering or indecision on his part. Rather it indicates a youthful royal eclecticism. Craving variety, this energetic and adventurous young pharaoh simply refused to accept one staid form or spelling of his cartouche names, but experimented restlessly with numerous variations during the earliest months of his reign.[80]

By observing the style of his temple reliefs and the forms and spellings of his cartouches, we can detect three successive stages in temple inscriptions of the first two years of Ramesses II's reign:[81]

Phase 1: In the first months of his reign he used raised relief and the short form of his prenomen Usermaatre, sometimes with epithets like "image of Re" and "heir of Re," these being mostly horizontal cartouches.[82] Both forms of the nomen occur: *Ramesses* and *Ramessu*. During this period work progressed in the Great Hypostyle Hall of Karnak, Sety's Gurnah Temple, the two Abydos temples,[83] and at Beit el-Wali.[84]

Phase 2: As sculptors labored at all these temples, Ramesses became dissatisfied with bas relief in the latter months of his first year. Now he adopted sunken reliefs exclusively but kept the short prenomen. Both forms of the nomen appear, often on the same monument, and both cartouches now feature many exotic spellings.[85]

Phase 3: From some point during his second regnal year onward, Ramesses continued using sunk relief exclusively, and now adopted the long prenomen Usermaatre-Setepenre. The nomen *Ramesses* predominates, especially in Upper Egypt, until his twenty-first year, when he began to prefer *Ramessu*, with few exceptions, until his death.[86]

New Building Projects in Upper Egypt

Ramesses II was not content simply to complete the works of his father, he wished to glorify himself with new building projects of his own. Among the first to emerge were the small temple of Beit el-Wali in northern Nubia and his own royal cult temple at Abydos, situated just to the north of Sety I's larger shrine in this city. Ramesses's masons and craftsmen built and decorated both temples largely during his first two regnal years, and they bear reliefs from all three of his early decorative phases.

Meanwhile, Pharaoh's architects laid the foundations for two new constructions, one on each side of the river at Thebes. On the west bank, New Kingdom pharaohs raised temples dedicated to their own godhood as local avatars of Amun-Re.[87] From Sety I's temple at Gurnah, just east of the entrance to the Valley of the Kings, these cultic foundations are strewn along the desert edge, southward to Ramesses III's shrine at Medinet Habu near the entrance to the Valley of the Queens.

In the middle of this "king's row" Ramesses II began constructing his royal cult temple known today as the Ramesseum.[88] There archaeologists discovered foundation deposits of small ritual objects inscribed with the early form of his prenomen, indicating that work on the Ramesseum began during his first year.[89] Blocks from this sanctuary are carved in the same delicate bas-relief found in the work of Sety I and Ramesses's earliest carvings in Sety's Gurnah Temple; craftsmen from the same workshop executed them.[90]

Ostraca from the Ramesseum bear the jottings of scribes overseeing the construction of Ramesses II's new temple. They record deliveries of shiploads of blocks from the sandstone quarries at Gebel es-Silsilah.[91] From these we know the cargo manifests of several ships, and even the names of their captains. Operating in flotillas of several vessels, each ship carried five to seven blocks of varying sizes.[92]

On the western side of Gebel es-Silsilah, a recently discovered stela dating to the king's first regnal year commemorates the quarry work in the sandstone beds that provided stone for the Ramesseum (fig. 4.14).[93]

Much of the text is a eulogy of the monarch and of his piety to the gods. Beside it, a marginal inscription records the name of an official named Hapi as he adores his monarch's cartouches. A miniature scene depicts gangs of men hauling sandstone blocks, including a stela, down to the riverbank to load them on ships bound for Thebes.[94]

It's not surprising that Ramesses made rapid progress on his new cult temple. The sandstone quarries were operating at peak performance in the wake of his father's grand constructions at Karnak and Gurnah. Now sandstone blocks poured forth from the quarries on both sides of the Nile at Silsilah, destined for the grand forecourt of Luxor Temple and for the Ramesseum.[95]

Below the peak of the tallest mountain in Western Thebes lies the Valley of the Kings. Nearby is Deir el-Medina, the village of the royal tomb builders. No sooner had they left off their labors on Sety I's grand sepulture than they started on a tomb for Ramesses II (KV 7).[96] The entrance corridor of the tomb features a scene depicting Pharaoh adoring the sun god Re-Horakhty. Here the artisans inscribed his prenomen Usermaatre oddly, inverting the second and third signs, perhaps unsure of the proper way of writing their new king's cartouche.[97] They decorated this passageway with elegant bas-relief even before they cut the deeper chambers of this vast underground mausoleum (fig. 4.15).[98]

The Luxor Temple Pylon and Forecourt

As the venue for the annual Opet Festival, Luxor Temple (figs. 4.16 and 4.17) had been sacred to Amun-Re since at least the early Eighteenth Dynasty. Ramesses II now built a spectacular entrance, erecting a massive pylon gateway fronting a peristyle forecourt.[99] The interior wall reliefs celebrated the Opet and Min Festivals.[100] But there were numerous innovations in the scenes and texts, like the processions of Ramesses's royal children.[101] Ramesses II further embellished the complex with a pair of tall monolithic granite obelisks (one of which now stands in the Place de la Concorde in Paris) and several colossal statues of himself.[102] A dedicatory inscription on the pylon presents the king both as a scholar who delves into the temple archives and a master architect overseeing the work on this grand pylon gateway and forecourt:[103]

> [As for] this good god (the king), he is a scribe who excels in gaining wisdom through knowledge like Thoth … Then His Person researched in the archives, and he unrolled the scrolls of the House of Life.[104] He learned about the enigmas of Heaven and of every mystery on earth. He discovered that Thebes is the Eye of Re, the primeval hill which came into being since this land [... when] Amun-Re was king and illuminated the

FIGURE 4.14. Rock inscription dating to regnal year one from Gebel Silsila East showing the transportation of sandstone from the quarries by ships. Masons cut blocks for the walls and columns from the quarry face (upper) while a gang of laborers drags one large block to a waiting ship. The stone was destined for the Ramesseum and the Luxor Temple pylon and forecourt, then under construction. Drawing by Peter Brand after Martinez 2009, 163.

FIGURE 4.15. Left: Scene from the entrance of Ramesses II's tomb in the Valley of the Kings (KV 7). Dating to the king's first regnal year, the scene includes an unusual variant of his short prenomen Usermaatre. Right: facsimile drawings of unusual writings of Ramesses's cartouches. In the prenomen (upper right), the positions of the Maat and the jackal-staff glyphs are reversed. The nomen (lower right) has a human-headed Re-glyph instead of the usual falcon-headed god. These strange early variants are unique to the tomb but are common in its outer corridor. Drawing by Peter Brand after Leblanc 2009b, 202

FIGURE 4.16. View of Ramesses II's pylon gateway with colossal statues and obelisks at Luxor Temple. A second obelisk was moved to Paris in the nineteenth century. Both obelisks were partly decorated during the king's first regnal year. The seated colossus to the right of the obelisk in the photograph is bicolored. Its body is black granodiorite, but a layer of red granite runs through its crown. Photograph by Peter Brand.

sky and shone in the solar circuit, looking for a place on which the rays of his Eye might alight. His Right Eye is Thebes in the City of Southern Heliopolis. His Left Eye is in Adj-Heka the Northern Heliopolis. (He is) the Dual King Amun-Re. His name is everlasting, his image is eternal, and his Ka-spirit is all that exists.

Then King Usermaatre-Setepenre said to the nobles who were with him: "I am one who proclaims effective [deeds ...] See, my mind is set upon making works [... for my father Amun-Re ...] erecting constructions in his temple which is in [Southern] Opet (Luxor Temple) [...]. [It was] the king himself who spoke, giving instructions for directing the work [...].[105]

The middle part of the inscription is badly damaged, but it referred to craftsmen who sculpted the statues, soldiers who likely hauled stone from the quarries, ships and crews that transported the blocks, and to the abundant quantities of grain the king provided to feed all who toiled on the project until it was completed:

The work was finished in regnal year three, month four of Inundation Season (Akhet), day [...] making [...] in all its work in the craftsmanship of South-of-His-Wall (=Ptah), consisting of granite [...], hard white [sand]stone, and every genuine precious gemstone.[106]

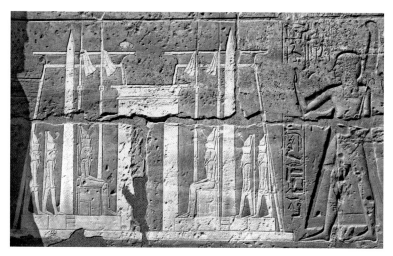

FIGURE 4.17. Enhanced image of a relief from Luxor Temple depicting Ramesses II's pylon gateway with colossal statues and obelisks. At right, his eldest son Prince Amunhirkhopeshef approaches. Photograph by Peter Brand.

While Ramesses II could rightfully take credit for constructing and decorating the great pylon and forecourt of Luxor Temple, it was likely Sety I who envisioned the project and began work on it shortly before he died.[107] Although Sety's name appears nowhere on the edifice, telltale clues suggest these obelisks and four large seated colossi were fruits of his year nine quarrying expedition to Aswan a year or two before his death.[108] Ramesses II's short prenomen Usermaatre appears on both obelisks, indicating that sculptors began inscribing them during his first year.

The ancient Egyptians could quarry these gigantic monuments more quickly than we might imagine. Queen Hatshepsut boasted how quarrymen extracted her two Karnak obelisks from the granite bedrock of Aswan in only seven months (figs. 4.18 and 4.19).[109]

At Luxor Temple, the four seated colossi are monoliths of black granodiorite, but one of them has a thick vein of pinkish-red granite running through its crown. This is no accident. In his quarry text, Sety I vowed to make black granite colossi with red colored crowns. At least two other black granodiorite statues of Ramesses II from his earliest reign have similar veins of pink or red granite in their crowns.[110] These bicolored colossi came from the quarry Sety I opened in his ninth regnal year. One is the famous Younger Memnon colossus from the Ramesseum.[111] Now broken in two, its handsome bust became one of the treasures of the British Museum.[112] While its torso and lower body consist of black granodiorite, Younger Memnon's head and crown were cut from a stratum of red granite. Egyptian quarrymen went to considerable trouble to isolate contiguous beds of back and red granite and to hew massive blocks of stone from them so the resulting statues would be bicolored.

FIGURE 4.18. Black granodiorite colossus of Ramesses II from the Luxor Temple forecourt named "Ramesses, the Re of Rulers." Photograph by Peter Brand.

FIGURE 4.19. ↗ Bicolor black granodiorite statue of Ramesses II dating to his first regnal year. It has a thick patch of dark pink granite in its crown, similar to a colossus from Luxor Temple and the Young Memnon colossus from the Ramesseum now in the British Museum. Luxor museum. Head: formerly Cairo, Egyptian Museum, CG 824. Photograph by Peter Brand.

The two enthroned colossi inside Ramesses II's Luxor Temple Forecourt were so large his architects were obliged to install them before building up the walls and columns around them.[113] Transporting and erecting such huge statues and obelisks—monoliths weighing hundreds of tons—was a prodigious feat of engineering and logistics.[114] As Sety I's Aswan stela reports, the Egyptians built massive transport vessels to ferry them from the quarries.[115]

Erecting the Obelisks

Equally impressive was the method they used for erecting the two obelisks in front of the Luxor pylon. The pink granite spires reached heights of seventy-five and eighty-two feet (twenty-three and twenty-five meters). Although they weighed several hundred tons, they were relatively fragile.[116] To erect them on their pedestals the Egyptians built long rampways of mud bricks.[117] At the end of the elevated rampway, high above the obelisks' pedestals, engineers built hollow mud-brick silos and filled them with desert sand. From openings at their base, workmen could drain the sand like an hourglass.[118] Next, workmen positioned each obelisk's butt end at the top of this sand funnel. As the sand drained away, the enormous shaft floated gradually downward until it came to rest on its pedestal (fig. 4.20).

During this tricky operation a few skilled and courageous workmen labored inside the funnel to ensure the giant stone needle descended smoothly and evenly, and did not crash into the mud-brick walls of the silo chamber.[119] The obelisk had to be exactly aligned on its pedestal. To ensure this, masons first carved a shallow trough called a turning groove on one side of the pedestal's upper surface.[120] With luck, one edge of the obelisk's base would catch on this groove so that its sides were parallel with the pedestal's.

The obelisk was not yet fully vertical, so gangs of men hauling at ropes tilted it the last few degrees until it stood upright.[121] Everyone no doubt held their breath during this final, nerve-wracking maneuver. If the engineers applied too much pressure the obelisk might crack or even snap in two. The huge shaft might wobble slightly when it landed, leaving it standing askew on its pedestal.[122] Once they had set both obelisks in place, workmen dismantled the mud-brick causeways and sand funnels. Remains of one such large mud-brick construction ramp can still be seen at Karnak Temple beside the unfinished First Pylon.[123]

Quarrying Royal Colossi

Among the most prestigious and personal monuments Ramesses II created in his zeal for grand building projects were colossal royal statues in his image.[124] Today they still invoke wonder in all who behold them, as they surely did in antiquity. The most famous of all his colossal statues is the romantic wreckage now sprawling amid the ruins of the Ramesseum in Western Thebes, which inspired the English poet Percy Bysshe Shelley to compose his celebrated sonnet "Ozymandias." (The name comes from the Greek pronunciation of Ramesses II's prenomen Usermaatre.) This colossus stood intact in the first century BCE, when the Roman travel author Diodorus Siculus penned his own account of it.[125] By the early nineteenth century it had shattered into giant fragments. Christian or Muslim iconoclasts also attacked the king's face, obliterating his features. Yet, in its heyday the Ozymandias was a super-colossus bearing the official name "Ramesses-Meramun-The Re of Rulers," embodying his concept of divine kingship.[126]

The Ozymandias was indeed titanic in scale. Estimates of its original height range between sixty to sixty-five feet tall (eighteen to twenty meters)—and this was a *seated* colossus! A monolith, it easily surpassed nine hundred tons, and rested on a separate pedestal weighing over a hundred tons. The Ozymandias was one of two super-colossi Ramesses II dedicated to his own cult and glory. The other, perhaps even larger

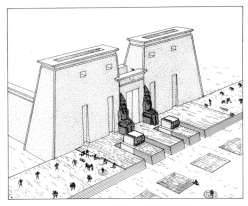
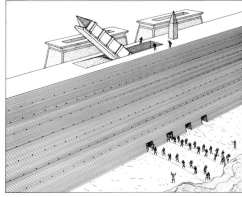
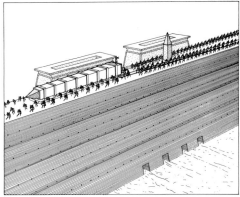
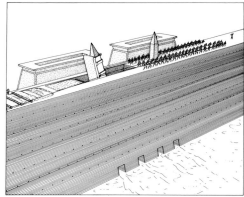

FIGURE 4.20. Ancient method for erecting an obelisk using a mud-brick ramp and sand funnel. After Golvin and Goyon 1987, 132–33.

than the Ozymandias, he erected in Piramesses, but only a handful of large fragments now attest to its grandeur.[127] Later pharaohs cut it up into blocks and used them to construct a monumental gateway at Tanis.

Besides these gigantic colossi, and the four mighty statues carved into the cliff face of Abu Simbel, the "garden variety" colossi, which Ramesses II commissioned by the dozen, reached heights of twenty to thirty-five feet (seven to eleven meters). They seem mere dwarves beside their giant cousins.

Producing immense colossi and obelisks was backbreaking work that occupied thousands of sweating workmen in the vast granite quarries at Aswan, one of the hottest places in Pharaoh's domains. Lacking iron tools, which did not come into regular use until long after Ramesses II ruled, the king's quarrymen relied on large nodules of dolerite, a stone harder than granite. Wielding dolerite pounders the size of bowling balls, dozens of men toiled in narrow trenches along the sides of the future obelisk or colossus to free it from its stony prison. They did this not by driving wedges into the granite to crack it open as was done in Roman times. Incredibly, they bashed away at the bedrock with their dolerite pounders, laboriously pulverizing it into dust and minute chippings. For every granite obelisk or colossus the Egyptians made this way, they smashed the equivalent volume of two more into small particles.

Choking on the dust, the men ached to their very bones and their arms and hands quickly went numb from slamming the heavy dolorite pounders against the implacable bedrock. The staccato sound of the pounders was earsplitting. Men inhaled rock dust into their lungs. Their eyesight was endangered by flying chips of granite. Accidents and injuries must have maimed some, while scores of others died of heat and exhaustion. They labored day after weary day, inch by agonizing inch under the merciless heat of the Aswan sun.

The monoliths, once freed from the quarry bed and set to moving through the labor of hundreds of men, could easily crush any unfortunates caught in its path. The dangerous conditions at these projects must have cost many workmen their lives as they toiled for Pharaoh's eternal glory.[128]

Ramesses II took an active interest in his colossi before the quarrymen and sculptors ever set their hands to the work. Like Sety I, Ramesses portrayed himself as an avid prospector after quality stone in the granite quarries of Aswan. In his eighth regnal year, Ramesses led his entourage to another quarry, the siliceous sandstone beds of the "Red Mountain" near Heliopolis on the eastern outskirts of modern Cairo.[129] There Pharaoh "discovered" a suitable outcropping of reddish siliceous sandstone. From this rock his sculptors hewed a colossal statue destined for one of his temples in Heliopolis. An impressive stela recording Ramesses II's official proclamation of the project offers us a vivid glimpse of Pharaoh as builder (fig. 4.21):[130]

> *Regnal year eight, second month of the Season of Emergence (Proyet), day eight of the Dual King, Usermaatre-Setepenre, the Son of Re, Ramesses-Meramun: Now, His Person was in Heliopolis doing what his father Re-Horakhty-Atum, Lord of the Two Lands, the Heliopolitan, praises. Now His Person was striding in the desert hills south of the (temple) Domain of Re and north of the (temple) Domain of the Divine Ennead, opposite to the (temple Domain of) Hathor, Lady of the Red Mountain. Then His Person discovered a great quartzite rock, whose like had not been discovered since the time of Re. It was taller than a granite obelisk. It was His Person himself who achieved this, as it sparkled like his (=Re's) horizon.*
>
> *Then His Person himself commissioned it (as a statue) from among chosen workmen who know the skill of their hands in regnal year eight, third month of Harvest Season (Shomu), day twenty-one. It emerged complete in regnal year nine, third month of Harvest Season (Shomu),*

FIGURE 4.21. Stela of Ramesses from Manshiyet es-Sadr describing quarry work in the siliceous sandstone quarries at "the Red Mountain" (Gebel Ahmar) near Cairo. The text includes the king's speech to the quarrymen. Cairo, Egyptian Museum CG 34503. © akg-images / De Agostini Picture Lib. / W. Buss.

day eighteen, making one year: The great statue (named): Ramesses-Meramun-the-God."

Then His Person rewarded the overseer of construction works with silver and gold in abundant quantities; and the strong-armed men who worked on it with praise from the King. His Person looked after them every day while they worked for His Person with loving hearts toward the Dual King, Lord of the Two Lands, Usermaatre-Setepenre, the Son of Re, Ramesses-Meramun.[131]

So-called Egyptian quartzite, more accurately siliceous sandstone, occurs in shades ranging from tawny pink to deep red and golden brown. Red was a solar color to the Egyptians, and siliceous sandstone symbolized light emanating from Re himself. They named this type of rock *iner en biat*, meaning something like "wonder stone."[132] Its most precious characteristic was the marvelous way it glittered, especially when newly cut, due to tiny crystals of quartz embedded in its stony matrix. These flecks of quartz caught and reflected the dazzling rays of sunlight Re himself emitted. Like his Eighteenth Dynasty paragon Amenhotep III, Ramesses II sought to present himself as an avatar of Re by creating giant statues from this exotic stone.[133]

The quarrying expedition of year eight also served as a forum in which Ramesses harangued the workmen with a grand speech while his scribes obediently scribbled down every word to include in this monumental decree. Noteworthy is Pharaoh's chatty rapport with and generous concern for workmen laboring on the project in difficult conditions in the parched and sultry desert. Ramesses boasts how he provided them with generous rations for their sustenance:

The Dual King Usermaatre-Setepenre, the Son of Re Ramesses-Meramun, he himself said: "O you chosen workmen; O you strong-armed men who know (the skill of) their hands, who hew monuments for me in any quantity! O those who adore working in costly exotic stone, who are experienced with granite, and accustomed to quartzite, who are valiant and vigorous in working on monuments, so that I may fill every temple, and achieve their lifetime. O good men, who do not grow weary, who are vigilant in performing their duties energetically and effectively, of whom it is said 'they will do (it)!' according to the plans that have gone out to their worksite in the divine mountain. Listen to what we say to you. See, benefits will be yours (just as your) deeds have matched (your) words!"

"I am Ramesses-Meramun, who fosters the youths by providing for them. Food overflows before you and there is no (saying): 'Oh, for (more) of it!'—food abounds all around you. I shall meet your needs in every way, so you might work for me with loving hearts. I am reliable as patron for your needs. The rations given to you exceed the (required) labor, through (my) desire (to) sustain (you) and make you thrive. I know your work is vigorous and excellent, since one rejoices in work when the belly is full."

"The granaries are overflowing with grain for you to prevent (you) from spending (even) a day lacking sustenance, each one among you is satiated monthly. I have filled storerooms for you with everything: with bread, meat, and cakes to sustain you, and sandals, clothing, and ointments aplenty to anoint your heads every ten days, your clothing every year, and sandals (on) your feet every day.[134] *None of you will lie down grieving about poverty. I have assigned many people to provide for you against misery: fishermen to bring you catches of fish, others in gardens to grow vegetables, a potter to make pots, and to make jars to cool the water for you in summertime.*[135] *For you Upper Egypt ferries (supplies) northward and for you Lower Egypt ferries (supplies) southward, consisting of barley, emmer, wheat, salt, and beans without limit. (I) have done all this so you might prosper and be of one mind while working for me."*

"I traveled to Elephantine (Aswan) to search and (my) gaze (fell) upon a perfect mountain. I have assigned its work site to you. Thus, I have decreed for you work in the quarry named: 'The Quarry of Ramesses-Meramun-Beloved-Like-Re,' so shall it be called. I found another quarry for you for black granodiorite beside it, for colossal statues whose crowns are of quartzite (named): 'The Quarry of Ramesses-Meramun-Ruler-of-the-Two-Lands,' so shall it be called. I (have) found for you (yet) another quarry in the [mountain] its color being like washed silver (named): 'The Quarry of Ramesses-Meramun-Beloved-of-Ptah,' so it shall be called."[136]

Like all kings, Ramesses II takes credit for every achievement. So he claims to have personally "discovered" not one but three major quarries.[137] In fact, one was the black granodiorite beds Sety I opened in his ninth year, where Ramesses, as crown prince, once oversaw production of colossal statues on his father's behalf. Ramesses II's year eight quarry stela presents him as a generous patron of his workers' every need.[138] He also showed concern for the welfare of gold workers toiling in the remote desert valleys of Nubia.

Gold Mining Ventures in Nubia

Ramesses II issued a large variety of official decrees in his earliest years as king. Indeed, Pharaoh's word was law in Egypt, so anything he uttered was a *wedj-nesu*, "royal command."[139] Typically, he summoned his courtiers and proclaimed some bold plan of action scribes jotted down on papyrus scrolls. Seldom have these fragile documents survived the intervening ages intact. But in some instances craftsmen immortalized his fiat in the more durable medium of a carved stone stela. Three millennia since Ramesses II's time, some of these stelae still exist today.

One decree that escaped destruction is the Quban stela (fig. 3.1). Far from being his most momentous edict, its chief importance lies in the fact that it has not vanished like so many others. Enthroned in his palace, Ramesses ponders a problem in far-off Nubia:

> *Now His Person was in Hut-ka-Ptah (Memphis), doing what his fathers, all the gods of the South and North, praise, according to how they give him valor and victory, and a great lifespan of millions of years. One day His Person sat on an electrum throne, crowned with the Seshed-fillet and tall-plumed headdress, thinking about the desert mountains from which gold is brought, and deliberating on plans for digging wells along roads made difficult because of (a lack of) water, after it was reported:*
>
> *"Gold is plentiful in the foreign country of Akayta, but the road is made very difficult because of (a lack of) water. If some crews of gold-washers travel to it, only half of them reach it because they die of thirst on the way, along with donkeys that were (driven) before them. They cannot not find (enough of) what they need to drink when going up or coming back down from (their) water skins. No gold was brought from this foreign land due to lack of water."*[140]

When Ramesses summons his courtiers to discuss the problem, they commence with the flattering eulogy about his time as crown prince that we've already seen. Returning to the subject at hand, they report:

> *As for the foreign country of Akayta, this is what has been said about it: The Viceroy of despicable Kush has said in Your Person's presence: "It has been in this horrible condition because of (a lack of) water since god's time. They die of thirst (there) because of it. Every king in past times desired to open a well in it, but they did not succeed. King Menmaatre (Sety I) did too. He caused a well 120 cubits deep to be dug in his time, (but) it was abandoned when no water came out of it."*[141]

Responding to his courtiers, Pharaoh vows: "I am the one who will open a well there, bringing forth water every day just as in [... Egypt]."[142] At this point the text becomes fragmentary, but we know Ramesses II ordered the Viceroy of Kush to organize a survey expedition to prospect for water along routes to the gold mining region, which amazed the local Nubian populace. In due course, a jubilant report arrived in Memphis from the Viceroy: "O Sovereign, [my] lord, every[thing has happened just as] Your Person has said with his own mouth! Water has appeared in it at a depth of twelve cubits, there being (water) four cubits deep in it."[143]

Ramesses II's First Campaign of Victory

Unlike Sety I, Ramesses II undertook no formal military campaign abroad in the opening year of his reign. He first led his armies into the Levant in his fourth regnal year, ca. 1274 BCE, on his "first campaign of victory."[144] But his earliest years were not entirely peaceful. We find hints of conflict with foreign peoples before year four, but our sources lack definite chronological or historical contexts. Much of this is the timeless rhetoric of pharaonic military ideology. Historians cannot avoid wrestling with such rhetorical texts, but extracting historical data from them is decidedly tricky. Typical in this regard is a rhetorical stela from Aswan dated to Ramesses II's second regnal year. The scribe provides no specific occasion or setting for this text, which presents a hymn in praise of Ramesses as a warrior:[145]

> *Live O good god, O Monthu of millions,*
> *Strong like (Seth), son of Nut,*
> *Who fights on the battlefield (like) a fierce lion,*
> *He has attacked myriads in an instant.*
> *A great rampart for his army on the day of fighting,*
> *Terror of him has broken all lands.*
> *While Egypt rejoices (over) the Ruler within her,*
> *He has extended her borders forever.*
> *The Asiatics are destroyed, and their towns are plundered,*
> *He has trampled the Northern foreign countries.*
> *The Libyans are fallen through terror of him,*
> *The Asiatics (say) "if only we had a mouthful of his air (to breathe)!"*
> *I caused Egypt to go on campaign,*
> *Their hearts filled with his plans.*
> *As they sit in the shade of his strong arm,*
> *They did not fear any foreign country.*
> *He has destroyed the warriors of the Great Green (Sea),*
> *So Lower Egypt might rest and sleep.*
> *O vigilant King, exact of counsels,*
> *Nothing he said has (ever) been overturned.*
> *Foreign peoples come to him bringing their children (as hostages),[146]*
> *To request the breath of life.*
> *His war-cry is powerful in Nubia,*

His awesome majesty subdues the Nine Bows.
Babylon and Hatti come bowing down to his power.

What, if any, historical event does this florid poetry record? Certainly, much of it is standard fare for such eulogies. It reflects an ideology envisaging Pharaoh as ruler of the whole world and considered all foreign peoples to be vanquished supplicants "begging for the breath of life." In reality, Egypt's relations with Babylon were peaceful. While envoys from the Great Kings of Assyria and Babylon might bring diplomatic gifts to Pharaoh, they did not come groveling in submission, and Ramesses would have returned the favor to his regal counterparts.

Against Hittites forces, Ramesses had not yet been tested in battle, although the two kingdoms had remained hostile since Akhenaten's reign. There is no evidence of active warfare with the Hittites after Sety I encountered them in Syria, until Ramesses II's Kadesh campaign in his fifth year. Egypt's western and southern neighbors, the Libyans and Nubians, were traditional opponents. References to them here are either wholly rhetorical or may allude to conflicts late in Sety I's reign, much like the contemporary war scenes in Ramesses II's Beit el-Wali temple.

We can extract at least one snippet of new historical data from the Aswan stela's hyperbole, a passing reference to "warriors of the Great Green Sea." The Sea in question is the Mediterranean, as a reference to the Nile Delta indicates. These maritime warriors also turn up in Ramesses's account of the Battle of Kadesh. Along with his own Egyptian infantrymen and chariot officers, Pharaoh bolstered the ranks of his armies at Kadesh with "Sherden warriors His Person captured, when he brought them by the triumph of his strong arm."[147] A later stela equates these Sherden with the sea-warriors and offers a fleeting glimpse of Ramesses II's military actions in his earliest days on the throne:

> *The Dual King Usermaatre-Setepenre, the Son of Re, Ramesses-Meramun, whose power has crossed over the Great Green Sea (so that) the Islands-in-the-Middle (=Aegean Sea) are in fear of him. They come to him, bearing gifts from their chiefs, [his awesome majesty having overpowered] their minds. The rebellious minded Sherden—against whom none knew how to fight since eternity—now came with ferocious [hearts as they voyaged in] war[ships] from the middle of the Sea, and no one could stand against them! [(But) He plundered them by the victories of his valiant strong arm and carried (them) off to Egypt]: (namely) the Dual King Usermaatre-Setepenre, the Son of Re Ramesses-Meramun, given life like Re.[148]*

Egyptian artists depict Sherden warriors in Ramesses II's artistic narrative of the Battle of Kadesh. Unlike bare-headed Egyptian soldiers, these foreign auxiliaries wear distinctive helmets decorated with a pair of horns and a disc-like symbol.[149] Instead of sickle-shaped Egyptian *khepesh*-swords, they brandish straight-bladed longswords. The Sherden's reputation for ferocity preceeded them. Even after he defeated these pirate raiders, their mettle impressed Ramesses so much he placed them among his foreign auxiliaries.[150] In fact they appear beside Pharaoh in the Kadesh battle scenes, suggesting he recruited them into his personal bodyguard.

Ramesses II's forces fought the Sherden in Egyptian territory along the Mediterranean seaboard. It is not clear the king himself took part in these hostilities directly.[151] Aside from a passing reference in his year two Aswan Stela and a later stela from Tanis, we know of no triumphal decree or monumental battle scenes recording this incident. Ramesses did not view this conflict as a full-scale campaign. Shortly after his accession Egyptian forces must have intercepted one of the periodic raids the Sherden and other Sea Peoples staged across the eastern Mediterranean. But Ramesses II's first official military campaign did not unfold until his fourth regnal year.

Traditionally New Kingdom rulers accorded great symbolic importance to their "first campaign of victory" to display Pharaoh's power and to fulfill his ideological role as champion of Maat. For Ramesses II, his second campaign against Kadesh, a year later in 1275 BCE, overshadowed his first formal military expedition. Indeed, we have no battle scenes or inscriptions from Egypt referring to a "first campaign of victory." But we know it must have taken place, because the Battle of Kadesh narrative identifies this event specifically as his second campaign. Two stelae that Ramesses left in the Levant during his fourth year constitute our only sources for this early military foray.

From the harbor town of Byblos in Lebanon comes a fragmentary stela with a date in regnal year four corresponding to late May of 1276 BCE.[152] Six months later, in late September, Pharaoh's army stopped at a headland near the mouth of Nahr el-Kelb, the "Dog River," eight miles north of Beirut, where he dedicated the first of three stelae marking his military expeditions in the first decade of his reign.[153] Carved into porous limestone cliffs, the hieroglyphic text of his year four stela has

FIGURE 4.22. Lepsius's drawing of the year four stela of Ramesses II at the "Dog River" (Nahr el-Kelb) north of Beirut in Lebanon. Little more than the date and the king's names and titles are preserved. It is one of three stelae Ramesses II left at Nahr el-Kelb during his military campaigns in the Levant in the first decade of his reign. NYPL digital collections. Public domain.

weathered badly, and little more than its date and Pharaoh's names and titles remain legible today (fig. 4.22). This expedition occupied seven months as Ramesses II and his armies trekked northward from Egypt's north-east border fortress at Tcharu, across the Ways of Horus in North Sinai, and on into Canaan and up the Phoenician coast.[154] They took the traditional military route into the Levant, following in the footsteps of the Eighteenth Dynasty warrior kings Thutmose III and Amenhotep II. Like Sety I's first campaign, Ramesses II's year-four expedition was largely a show of force meant to overawe Egypt's vassals in Canaan and along the Lebanese and south Syrian coast.[155]

Did Ramesses venture farther north, deep into Hittite-controlled Syria? Perhaps his forces laid the groundwork for his Kadesh campaign the following year by attacking the Hittite vassal kingdom of Amurru.[156] If so, no direct evidence for such an incursion survives. Later Hittite sources hint that Benteshina, king of Amurru, gave aid—or at least insufficient resistance—to an Egyptian king who invaded his territory. For this dereliction of duty his Hittite overlord Muwatalli II removed him from power. But the Hittite source never identifies the pharaoh in question, and this incident could also refer to Sety I's campaign against Amurru or any of Ramesses II's later Syrian campaigns.[157]

Whatever transpired during his first campaign, it encouraged Ramesses to plan a new expedition for the spring of his fifth regnal year (ca. 1275 BCE). He intended to penetrate even deeper into Syria, beginning with an assault on Kadesh, which had reverted to Hittite control after Sety conquered it. This Kadesh campaign would mark a political, military, and ideological watershed in Ramesses II's reign.

Notes

1. See pp. 69–70 n. 67 above.

2. Barta (1980) stresses the distinction between the king's accession immediately following his predecessor's death and the new pharaoh's coronation. See also Leclant, Bonhême, and Forgeau 1988, ch. 6; Obsomer 2012b, 61–63.

3. Irsay-Nagy (2018) takes exception to this Eurocentric view while exploring the possibility that pharaonic enthronement rites were more akin to the accession rituals of Japanese emperors.

4. If so, Ramesses would soon receive his diadem from Amun-Re himself during his first official visit to Thebes as king, just as he did at Memphis and Heliopolis. For Obsomer (2012b, 89–91) Ramesses II's "coronation" at Karnak Temple in Thebes occurred sometime between Sety I's funeral around II *ꜣḥt* 1 and his departure from Thebes on III *ꜣḥt* 25. The theme of the king's "coronation" by the gods still appears in monumental reliefs created throughout his reign, not just at its beginning. Even in Theban and Upper Egyptian temples, the ideal venue for the king's coronation by the gods is Heliopolis, often beside the *Ished*-tree with Re-Horakhty and other solar deities confirming the king's power; see Lurson 2016, 40–44, 102–8, 161–74. It is evident from Lurson's analysis that the royal coronation as depicted in temple reliefs depicts an idealized event that is not limited temporally or geographically to a single location at the beginning of his reign, but can recur endlessly, ideally in Heliopolis, but by implication in any temple. It is not a historical event but a mythological one.

5. A number of so-called coronation inscriptions may or may not commemorate specific events. Hatshepsut's alleged coronation by her father Thutmose I is certainly fictitious (see p. 68 n. 52). Horemheb's coronation accounts, preserved on a statue now in Turin and two fragmentary inscriptions from Karnak, are more plausible as records—albeit idealized—of actual events: *Urk.* IV, 2113–26; Gardiner 1953; Murnane 1995a, 230–32. Even so, we must be on guard against taking these texts at face value.

6. For discussion of scenes from Karnak depicting Ramesses receiving regalia from the gods, see Obsomer 2012b, 92–96. On the iconography and meaning of such "coronation scenes" depicting Sety I on the north wall of the Great Hypostyle Hall, see Lurson 2016, esp. 136–50. A relief now in Bath, England portrays Ramesses receiving crowns and regalia from Atum of Heliopolis; see Shorter 1938. The relief dates more than two decades after his accession, an elegant demonstration of the ahistorical, idealized nature of such temple art and of the "coronation event" itself.

7. Sety I's tomb is superlative in every respect. Not only was it one of the largest and most completely decorated tombs in the Valley of the Kings, it boasts well-preserved wall reliefs of the highest quality, painted in a rich palette of colors. Its decorative program is almost perfectly intact and contains a priceless set of the "books of the Underworld" representing the nocturnal journey of the sun god through the underworld and his mystical union with Osiris. No definitive publication of the tomb yet exists. For its decoration, history, and religious meaning, and the remnants of Sety I's burial goods, see Hornung 1991; Weeks and De Luca 2002, 194–221; Dodson 2019, 79–113. Dodson provides an overview of the later history of Sety I's tomb, from the time it was robbed during the Twentieth Dynasty (twelfth century BCE), and its modern history, from its rediscovery in the early nineteenth century CE down to recent

efforts to conserve and record it; Dodson 2019, 115–18, 123–38. For Sety's calcite sarcophagus and his canopic equipment, see Taylor 2017.

8. Taylor 2019a, 49–50.

9. Bell, 1985; Epigraphic Survey 1994 and 1998; Bell 1997; Darnell 2010; Fukaya 2019, 15–43.

10. On Luxor Temple and its role in the Opet Festival, see Bell 1985, 1997; Darnell 2010.

11. Gabolde 2018, 513–39.

12. See plates in Epigraphic Survey 1994.

13. Bell 1985, 1997; Karlshausen 2009. The outward and return journey of the barks of the Theban Triad and the king are depicted in great detail in Tutankhamun's reliefs from the Colonnade Hall of Luxor Temple; Epigraphic Survey 1994.

14. Karlshausen 2009; Eaton 2007.

15. Brand, Feleg, and Murnane 2018, pl. 53.

16. Epigraphic Survey 1994; Darnell 2010.

17. The Egyptian populace had access to and played a significant role in the Opet festival; Bell 1997; Fukaya 2019, 15–43.

18. Foucart 1921; Epigraphic Survey 1936, pl. 84 and 90; 1994, pls. 76–81.

19. The barges of the Theban triad were deified and became the objects of royal and private devotion. A stela from Deir el-Medina (Cambridge, Fitzwilliam Museum E.SS.52· PM I.2, 715) depicts Amenemheb and his wife kneeling in worship of the barges of the Theban Triad. In the Great Hypostyle Hall at Karnak, a relief of Ramesses IV on column 28 depicts the deity *Amun-Userhet* in the form of a ram-headed man who personifies Amun-Re's barge.

20. Amenhotep III offers a vivid description of the golden barge in a stela from his royal cult temple in western Thebes: *Urk.* IV, 1652–53.

21. These scenes on the barge's hull are depicted in the Colonnade Hall of Luxor Temple Epigraphic Survey 1994, pls. 77–80 and on the Third Pylon at Karnak (PM II, 61 [183]; El-Sharkawy 1997, 287–91. The scenes on barge's hull on the Third Pylon date to the post-Amarna era, although the original scene was created by Amenhotep III; see Brand 1999b.

22. Epigraphic Survey 1936, pl. 86.

23. Bell 1985 and 1997; Darnell 2010. Bell's 1985 article remains the seminal work on this. For a reassessment of the nature of the "living royal *Ka*," *k3 nsw* ʿnḫ, see Winnerman 2018. Winnerman concludes that each king had a royal *Ka*, but they did not collectively share the royal *Ka*, a common spirit of divine kingship that settled on each pharaoh generation after generation as Bell had argued.

24. Von Beckerath 1999, 1–6; Leprohon 2013, 5–12.

25. Leprohon 2013, 7–19.

26. Von Beckerath 1999, 6–10; Leprohon 2013, 12–13.

27. Bell 1985; Winnerman 2018, 13–17 offers new analysis and a critique of Bell's theory and its reception by Egyptologists (27–40). See pp. 382–84 below.

28. Kitchen 1987, 133.

29. For a comprehensive, yet not exhaustive, catalog of these, see Leprohon 2013, 115–18. Amenhotep III and Sety I also inscribed variants of their Horus names on monuments, but on a smaller scale; Leprohon 2013, 102–4 and 109–14.

30. Von Beckerath 1999, 27–29.

31. Von Beckerath 1999, 21–25; Leprohon 2013, 17.

32. Von Beckerath 1999, 10–16; Leprohon 2013, 17–18.

33. Kitchen 1987; Leprohon 2010.

34. Von Beckerath 1999, 25–26; Leprohon 2013, 18–19.

35. The Egyptians did not assign ordinal numbers to like-named kings, so Ramesses II is a modern designation. Each pharaoh was distinguished by his unique sequence of names, especially his prenomen. While Egyptian kings often selected certain names and epithet borne by royal ancestors, no two pharaohs had identical titularies.

36. Von Beckerath 1999, 10–15; Leprohon 2013, 13–15. For additional variants of Ramesses II's Nebty name, see Leprohon 2013, 118.

37. Von Beckerath 1999, 17–21; Leprohon 2013, 15–17.

38. On the city, see ch. 14.

39. *KRI* II, 323–36; *RITA* II, 162–74; *RITANC* II, 191–97; McClain 2007, 178–86; Spalinger 2009.

40. *KRI* II, 325; translation adapted from Spalinger 2009, 22–24; *RITA* II, 165.

41. *KRI* II, 325–26; translation adapted from Spalinger 2009, 25; *RITA* II, 165; McClain 2007, 180.

42. McClain 2007, 184.

43. *KRI* II, 326; translation adapted from Spalinger 2009, 26–27; *RITA* II, 165–66; McClain 2007, 180.

44. See pp. 47–49 above.

45. *KRI* II, 328; translation adapted from Spalinger 2009, 131; *RITA* II, 168; McClain 2007, 180–82.

46. On his career and family background, see Raedler 2017.

47. *KRI* III, 282–85; *RITA* III, 201–3; *RITANC* III, 233–34; Frood 2007, 35–39.

48. *KRI* III, 283.

49. *KRI* III, 283.

50. Brand 2000, 346–65.

51. Brand, Feleg, and Murnane 2018, 15–17.

52. Brand 2000, 214–16; Brand, Feleg, and Murnane 2018, 15–17.

53. Murnane 1975, 171–73; Revez and Brand 2012, 25–28; Brand, Feleg, and Murnane 2013, 196; Brand, Feleg, and Murnane 2018, 17–20.

54. Brand 2000, 15–16. For other changes Ramesses II introduced in his conception of wall decoration in the Great Hall, see Lurson 2005.

55. Brand, Feleg, and Murnane 2018, pl. 53. Images of the deified Sety I appear in several other cult scenes on the south wall of the Hall Nelson and Murnane 1981, pls. 42, 48, 57, 61, 65, 72 and on column thirteen. For photos, translations, and commentary see the relevant plates in Brand, Feleg, and Murnane 2018. In each case Ramesses II offers cult worship to his father. Murnane's discussion of these reliefs (1975, 173–79) wrongly concludes Sety was alive and ruling jointly with Ramesses when these scenes were inscribed. Iconographically, Sety appears as the cult statue of a deified king; Brand 2000, 43–44.

56. Brand, Feleg, and Murnane 2018, pls. 57 and 61. For commentary and photos, see Brand, Feleg, and Murnane 2018, 115–16, 120, and figs. 74, 76, 78.

57. Brand 2000, 230–32.

58. Haeny 1997; Ullmann 2002; Fukaya 2019, 41–78.

59. Brand 2000, 238–44; Stadelmann forthcoming.

60. Brand 2000, 239 and figs. 122–23, 127–28.

61. Seele 1940, 28, fig. 9. Photos in Brand 2000, figs. 122–23.

62. Costa 2017 is misguided in viewing the scene as a "historical" record of the alleged coronation of Ramesses II during Sety I's lifetime.

63. Brand 2000, 164–67.

64. Pareidolia is the human tendency to misperceive meaningful patterns of familiar persons, animals, or objects in inanimate objects they find in the world around them. The two most familiar examples of pareidolia are when we see suggestive shapes in cloud formations or human faces in inanimate objects These familiar shapes are also conditioned by our culture, meaning that we only see things with which we are already familiar. Nineteenth century visitors would not have seen a "helicopter" in the Abydos inscription because helicopters did not exist at that time.

65. Roberson 2016.

66. Vandersleyen 1979; Woods 2015.

67. See most recently Brand, Feleg, and Murnane 2018, 17–21.

68. Seele (1940, 89) speculated that Ramesses "may have fallen under the influence of a rising school of sculpture which maintained that the old style of bas-relief was a relic of another age—an outmoded archaism which ought to go. After all, the young Ramses was not far removed in time from the Amarna age, in which incised relief had for the first time really come into its own." This is fanciful. By contrast, Winlock (1921, 44–49) imagined Sety I's art represented the triumph of a sophisticated and complex modern style of relief that had not yet "resulted in the stagnation and shoddiness of Rameses II and his successors." Winlock attributes this to Sety I's personality and his noble mien, with the physical traits allegedly preserved on his mummy reflecting an intellectual refinement mirrored in his art: "Seti's features show a fineness which his descendants lacked in greater and greater degree as time went on, and that their degradation of features is exactly paralleled by the degradation of art in their reigns" (Winlock 1921, 47 n. 1). Such views are hopelessly biased, outdated, and without merit.

69. Sunk relief may also be linked with the solar cult; Manouvrier 1996, 447–49.

70. Sethe 1927; Seele 1940, ch. 4; Murnane 1975, 158–61; Brand 2000, 34–36; Spalinger 2008.

71. In the contemporary dialect, the final *r* of *wsr* was not pronounced. Scribes reflected this silent *r* by writing the final voiced consonant *s*.

72. Seele 1940, 27–31; Spalinger 2008. As with Sety I, Ramesses II's early use of prenomen epithets is most common with horizontal texts, although vertical examples do sometimes occur, especially on the columns Ramesses decorated in the hypostyle hall of his father's Gurnah Temple where the form *Wsr-M3ʿt-Rʿ-tit-Rʿ* is common.

73. Brand 2000, 31–36. Sety I and Ramesses II both used several different prenomen epithets on the abbaci of the 134 columns in the Great Hypostyle Hall at Karnak: Brand et al. 2013, 196–98 and figs. 11–12; Revez and Brand 2012, 17–21; 2015, 254–57. The use of such epithets with the prenomen was a characteristic feature of the format of abacus decoration and has parallels in other contemporary Ramesside monuments, both with Sety I and Ramesses II.

74. See *ÄHK* I, passim. On the orthography and phonetics of transcriptions of Ramesses II's prenomen into Akkadian by Egyptian scribes, see Cochavi-Rainey 2011, 192 and Müller 2010, 424. Both authors discuss the morphology and phonology of Egyptian names and terms transcribed into Akkadian.

75. There are not as many variant orthographies of the long prenomen, and they have not received as much scholarly attention as the short form in use during the first year or so of the king's reign. The two most common variants are distinguished by the squatting and enthroned Maat figures. A third writing, unique to Abu Simbel, has a standing Re figure holding the *wsr*-staff and a Maat-feather (see fig. 4.10). A number of rare, exotic orthographies turn up in the forecourt of Luxor Temple on the walls, columns, and colossal statues.

76. Like Ramesses I, Ramesses II was probably named Pramessu at birth. In the later New Kingdom, Egyptian scribes introduced Re's name with the definite article *p3*, hence Pre. When Ramesses I became king, he adopted a more archaic mode for writing his nomen by dropping the definite article.

77. Kitchen (1979, 383–89; 2001, 382) first called attention to the two forms and explained how the *Rᶜ-ms-sw* form reflected an archaic pronunciation and the *Rᶜ-ms-s* was a "modernist" form in keeping with contemporary dialect. However, he was wrong in claiming the archaic form was distinctive of the allegedly more urbane Memphite scribes of Lower Egypt. The *Rᶜ-ms-s* form does occur in the north as well. For the cuneiform transcription of the nomen as Riamesesa-Maiamana, see *ÄHK* I, passim. The cuneiform scribes confused Akkadian *š* with Egyptian *s*, resulting in the erroneous transcription Riamašeša. See Cordani 2017, 35; Cochavi-Rainey 2011, 191; Müller 2010, 424.

78. Spalinger 2008; Brand, Feleg, and Murnane 2018, part 3, figs. 66, 69–71, 337–56. For a table of variant forms and writings of Ramesses II's cartouche names in the Great Hypostyle Hall at Karnak, see Brand, Feleg, and Murnane 2018, appendix B. Goelet and Iskander (2012) reject any chronological pattern in Ramesses II's cartouche variants, preferring to emphasize stylistic criteria, but their analysis is based solely on this temple and does not take into consideration early dated inscriptions and the king's other early relief decoration. What they term as "calligraphic" issues certainly did influence the orthography of cartouches, yet these chronological criteria cannot be dismissed so easily.

Nevertheless, the chronological and geographical boundaries for the *Rᶜ-ms-s* and *Rᶜ-ms-sw* forms are not as stringent as Kitchen believed. Both forms occur frequently during the first regnal year or so. Once Ramesses adopted the long prenomen sometime in his second regnal year, he commonly used the *Rᶜ-m-s* nomen form, but not only in Upper Egypt. Examples also occur in Lower Egypt and in the Levant. Even while *Rᶜ-ms-s* predominates in Upper Egypt during this two decade interval, the king did not banish the *Rᶜ-ms-sw* form there, since it crops up sometimes, especially in horizontal texts, as on the east interior wall of his forecourt at Luxor Temple (*KRI* II, 607; Feleg 2020, 456, fig. 102). One suspects that many of his Memphite and Lower Egyptian monuments displaying the *Rᶜ-ms-sw* form date to the Jubilee period after he largely ceased using the *Rᶜ-ms-s* form. See pp. 411–12 below.

79. This is especially true of reliefs from the second phase, which combine sunk relief and the short prenomen as we see in the eastern half of the south wall of the Great Hypostyle Hall at Karnak (Brand, Feleg, and Murnane 2018, pls. 62–86); portions of the Abydos Temple (Iskander and Goelet 2015); and the vestibule of the Ramesses I suite at the Gurnah Temple. Most telling is a frieze of cartouches on the cornice above the doorway leading into the main chapel of Ramesses I's cultic suite, which displays several variant orthographies side by side; see Brand, Feleg, and Murnane 2018, figs. 69–70.

80. Kitchen (2001, 382) asserts that "it is in the highest degree likely that Ramesses II deliberately adopted his full prenomen of Usimare Setepenre on the first anniversary of his accession, which was the beginning of Year 2. And not at the end of Year 2, as Brand suggests without any scrap of explicitly-dated evidence." But what evidence does Kitchen have to offer? The fact remains that there is a dearth of texts dated to the second regnal year. A stela of Amenemopet and Ashahebused at Serabit el-Khadim in Sinai has a year two date, but no season, month, or day. Interestingly, it displays both the R^c-*ms-s* and R^c-*ms-sw* nomen forms alongside the long prenomen. Otherwise, Ramesses II's Aswan stela, dated to regnal year two, III Šmw 26—the day before the beginning of his third year—remains the earliest dateable occurrence of the long prenomen *Wsr-M3^c t-R^c-stp-n-R^c*: KRI II, 344–45. It remains possible Ramesses adopted the long prenomen earlier in the second year, but there is no evidence for it, much less for 364 days before the date on the Aswan stela on the very first day of that regnal year as Kitchen maintains.

81. Murnane 1975, 158–61; Brand 2000, 34–36; Brand, Feleg, and Murnane 2018, 19–21.

82. As we see on a doorway in the Ramesses I vestibule at Gurnah Temple where the horizontal prenomens of Sety I and Ramesses II on the lintel have epithets while the vertical ones on the door jambs do not; Seele 1940. This pattern is not without exceptions and there are a few examples of the prenomen *Wsr-M3^c t-R^c-tit-R^c* in the vertical format in the vestibule and on the columns of the adjoining hypostyle hall.

83. Murnane 1975; Iskander and Goelet 2015.

84. Ricke, Hughes, and Wente 1967; Murnane 1975, 161–62; Spalinger 1979c; RITANC II, 112–13. The observations of Kitchen, Murnane, and Spalinger are all premised on the assumption that Sety I was still alive when Ramesses II built and decorated the Beit el-Wali temple, a view I have challenged; see Brand 2000, 327–28. Kitchen's rebuttal 2001, 383 does not convince.

85. So, in wall reliefs from the Great Hypostyle Hall at Karnak: Brand, Feleg, and Murnane 2018, passim.

86. See p. 411 below.

87. Haeny 1997; Ullmann 2002, 2016; See ch. 13 below.

88. PM II², 431–43; RITANC II, 431–49. See 399–400 below. To date, seven volumes of the Centre d'étude et de documentation sur l'ancienne Égypte series on the reliefs and inscriptions from the Ramesseum have been published: *Le Ramesseum* vols. I, IV, VI, IX¹⁻², X, and XI. For the results of ongoing excavations, conservation work, and analysis of the temple complex, see also the annual reports published in the journal *Memnonia*. For a synthesis of the temple and its historical and archaeological evolution, see Leblanc 2019.

89. Leblanc 2019, 65–67, 82 n. 31, and fig. 98, opposite p. 171.

90. For the Ramesseum blocks bearing the short prenomen, see Leblanc 2019, figs. 44–47. Leblanc identifies them as coming from the main sanctuary of the temple. In favor of this interpretation is the Egyptians's tendency to build and decorate the innermost portions of their temples first. The style of the raised relief and paleography of the hieroglyphs on these blocks is strikingly similar to the reliefs of Sety I and from Ramesses II's first period of decoration at Gurnah Temple. This temple atelier working in Western Thebes is stylistically distinct from the work of the craftsmen laboring in the Great Hypostyle Hall across the Nile at Karnak.

91. *KRI* II, 667–71; *RITA* II, 448–52; *RITANC* II, 443–44.

92. Kitchen 1991; Goyon et al. 2004, 188–89; Leblanc 2019, 65–68.

93. Martinez, 2009; Leblanc 2019, 67–71 and figs. 12–13.

94. The largest block shown in this scene depicts a round-topped stela, presumably the one set up in the inner sanctum of the Ramesseum, of which only the foundations remain. It was presumably of the false door type: Leblanc 2019, 158–58. While false doors were often made of granite, royal cult temples also had sandstone (Gurnah Temple of Sety I, chapel of Ramesses I) and limestone (six chapels of Sety I's Abydos Temple).

95. On the sandstone quarries and methods of extraction, see Goyon et al. 2004, 144–56; Klemm and Klemm 2008, 167–214; Harrell and Storemyr 2013; Harrell 2016.

96. *LD* III, 172g; Leblanc 2009a, 202, fig. 3.

97. This reversal appears in some of the litany text carved on the east wall of the outermost corridor of KV 7 before giving way to the more conventional orthography of the short prenomen. A unique variant of the nomen cartouche appears in these texts where the ideogram for Re is a squatting human-headed figure crowned with the solar disk instead of the conventional falcon-headed glyph. To my knowledge, this occurs nowhere else.

98. *LD* III, pl. 172g; Leblanc 2009a, fig. 3.

99. PM II², 305–6; Bell 1997.

100. Bell,1997; Feleg 2020.

101. Fisher 2001, 38–40; Boraik 2008; Klotz 2020. Feleg (2020) offers an analysis of the decorative program of cultic scenes on the interior walls of the forecourt, including improved translations and commentary on the grand offering lists and other ritual texts in the southeast quadrant.

102. PM II², 302–4, 312–13; *KRI* II, 598–605, 629–33; *RITA* II, 392–400, 417–21; *RITANC* II, 405–6, 422–25; Brand 1997; Sourouzian 2019, cat. nos. 50–56, 158–60, 179–82.

103. Abd el-Razik 1974, 1975; *KRI* II, 346–47; *RITA* II, 183–84; *RITANC* II, 208–10.

104. The temple library was called "the House of Life"; see Redford 1971, 1986.

105. *KRI* II, 346–47.

106. *KRI* II, 347.

107. Brand 1997, 107–14; *RITANC* II, 209, 405–6; Brand 2000, 271–75.

108. Brand 2000, 308; Revez and Brand 2015, 258, n. 18. See p. 63 above.

109. *Urk.* IV, 367:3–5.

110. Brand 1997, 112–13; Sourouzian 2019, cat. nos. 180 (Luxor colossus), 200 (seated statue, former Cairo CG 824 + torso, now in the Luxor Museum).

111. Leblanc and Essmoignt 1999; Garnett 2015; Sourouzian 2019, cat. no. 184.

112. See pp. 472–74 below.

113. Brand 1997, 110–11.

114. For the erection of colossal statuary, see Goyon et al. 2004, 334–38.

115. On the problem of loading large monoliths onto ships, transporting them by Nile, and unloading them, see Goyon et al. 2004, 190–96.

116. The smaller obelisk, now in the Place de la Concorde in Paris is seventy-four feet (twenty-two and a half meters) tall. For the texts: *KRI* II, 598–605; *RITA* II, 392–400; *RITANC* II, 405–6. On the peculiar geometry of these obelisks,

see Isler 1987. Spalinger (2010) presents an exhaustive analysis of their inscriptions.

117. Golvin and Goyon 1987, 131–37; Goyon et al. 2004, 329–34. A curious sequence of mathematical problems recorded on a Papyrus Anastasi I details the construction of such a ramp, the transport of an obelisk, and the erection of a large monolith—likely a colossal statue—by means of a sand-filled funnel: Gardiner 1911, *16–*19; Fischer-Elfert 1992; Wente 1990, 104–5. For interpretation of these passages, see Gardiner 1911, *31–*34; Schwela 2012; Nishimoto 2014; Monnier 2020.

118. Golvin and Goyon 1987, 131–37; Goyon et al. 2004, 331, fig. 431.

119. Chevrier (1954) discusses the problem of guiding the obelisk onto its pedestal.

120. Goyon et al. 2004, 332, fig. 432.

121. Chevrier 1954. Idealized images the king erecting pairs of obelisks with ropes in the presence of the gods occur in Ramesses II's decoration on the enclosure wall of Karnak Temple (Helck 1968, fig. 52; Goyon et al. 2004, 335, fig. 434) and a Ptolemaic relief from the temple of Horus at Edfu (PM VI, 124). The obelisks are miniature examples and there is no depiction of the mud-brick ramp and sand funnel in these scenes, making them of limited value in reconstructing the method the Egyptians used on large obelisks weighing hundreds of tons. On the cultic significance of these scenes, see Goyon et al. 2004, 335.

122. This happened to Hatshepsut's northern obelisk in the hall behind the Fourth Pylon and Thutmose III's eastern obelisk in front of the Seventh Pylon. Hatshepsut's obelisk failed to catch on the turning groove and wobbled a bit, but with no ill effects. Thutmose III's obelisk came to rest skewed 20 degrees off its proper axis and off center toward the northeast corner. To disguise the error, masons added an angular stone slab to the northern face of its pedestal. Luc Gabolde, pers. comm.

123. Arnold 1991, 95–97; Goyon et al. 2004, 204–10, 213–17.

124. For an exhaustive catalog of Ramesses II's statuary, including his colossi, see Sourouzian 2019.

125. Leblanc 1985.

126. PM II², 433; RITANC II, 431–32; Leblanc 1993b; 2011; 2019, 114–15 and figs. 21, 65, 67–68; Sourouzian 2019, cat. no. 183.

127. PM IV, 14; KRI II, 439, nos. 5–6; RITANC II, 294–95; Sourouzian 2019, cat. no. 187. Kitchen and Sourouzian concur that this must have been the largest of all Ramesses II's colossal statues. On popular devotion to the cult of this and other royal colossi at Piramesses see pp. 394–99 below.

128. We lack any statistics for the casualty rate on any of Ramesses II's building projects, or for most other periods in pharaonic history. A partial exception to this are a few cases where we hear of the numbers of men on certain quarrying expeditions who survived against the total numbers sent. In his third regnal year, Ramesses IV dispatched a large crew to quarry stone in Wadi Hammamat under the leadership of the High Priest of Amun, Ramessesnakht: KRI VI, 12–14; RITA VI, 12–15. The rock inscription commemorating the expedition lists its personnel in detail, breaking them down by category for a grand total of 8,368 men, but this total did not include "the dead who are omitted from this list: 900 (men)": KRI VI, 14:9. Nine hundred is a suspiciously round figure, but given pharaonic Egypt's heightened bureaucratic mindset and the practice of keeping detailed logbooks for every official institution of the state, it is likely

scribes kept detailed records of casualties from quarrying and building operations, but these are lost to us. Throughout history, the royal passion for building cost many workers their lives. One thinks of the human cost of another Sun King's grand project, the hundreds of workers killed building Versailles at Louis XIV's command or the thousands who perished building the Great Wall of China.

129. The name of the site is identical in ancient Egyptian, *Dw-dsrt*, and modern Arabic, Gebel Ahmar.

130. Hamada 1938; *KRI* II, 360–62; *RITA* II, 193–95; *RITANC* II, 216–18; Putter 1997.

131. *KRI* II, 361; Hamada 1938, 217–30.

132. On siliceous or silicified sandstone, see Klemm and Klemm 2008, 215–32; Harrell 2013. The ancient term was *inr n bi3t*: Harris 1961, 76–76. On the solar qualities of this stone, see Aufrère 1991, 698–700.

133. Kozloff, Bryan, and Berman 1992, 138–42.

134. If the king is promising his workmen new sandals every day, it implies they were made of rushwork and not leather. Even if such sandals were flimsy and amid the harsh working conditions in the desert quarries, Ramesses may be exaggerating the frequency with which he supplied new footwear to his workmen.

135. Traditional ancient and modern Egyptian water jars use the principle of evaporative cooling to chill drinking water. Although fired in a kiln, the porous unglazed clay of these jars slowly secretes water at the bottom, removing heat by evaporation and cooling the remaining water inside the jar. The method is still used in rural Egypt today.

136. *KRI* II, 361–62; Hamada 1938, 223.

137. Putter 1997, 136–41.

138. The theme of Pharaoh's paternalistic concern for his men turns up in other Ramesside quarrying and expedition texts including Ramesses II's Quban stela.

139. Vernus 2013.

140. *KRI* II, 354–55.

141. *KRI* II, 356–57.

142. *KRI* II, 357.

143. *KRI* II, 359.

144. Attesting to this campaign, Ramesses left two stelae dating to regnal year four at Byblos (*KRI* II, 224; *RITA* II, 78; *RITANC* II, 135–36) and Nahr el-Kelb (*KRI* II, 1; *RITA* II, 1; *RITANC* II, 1–2).

145. *KRI* II, 344–45; *RITA* II, 181–83; *RITANC* II, 207–8.

146. Since at least the reign of Thutmose III, Egyptian kings had compelled their vassal kings to send their children to the Egyptian court both as hostages to their fathers' good behavior and to indoctrinate them as future vassals who would be loyal to Pharaoh; see Morris 2018, 154–56.

147. *KRI* II, 11.

148. *KRI* II, 290.

149. On the Sherden and their role as mercenaries in Ramesside Egypt, see Cavillier 2015; Emanuel 2013; Abbas 2016.

150. Abbas 2016.

151. Obsomer (2012b, 121), following Morschauser (1988), takes the reference to the king's "strong arm," *ḥpš*, in the Aswan stela as an indication that

Ramesses dispatched his armies without participating himself. Given the rhetorical nature of the text this is unclear.

152. PM VII, 383; *KRI* II, 223; *RITA* II, 78; *RITANC* II, 135–36.

153. PM VII, 385; *LD* III, 197b; *KRI* II, 1; *RITA* II, 1; *RITANC* II, 1–2; Wimmer 2002; Loffet 2009; Thum 2016.

154. *RITANC* II, 135–36. Three more damaged stelae from Adhlun, Tyre, and Byblos date to the early part of the reign and may attest to the king's sojourn in Lebanon during the year four campaign. The scenes on these stelae depict the king smiting enemies in the presence of a deity. The text of the Adhlun stela has eroded beyond legibility: PM VII, 383; *KRI* II, 223; *RITA* II, 78; *RITANC* II, 135. A small stela fragment from Byblos contains the nomen cartouche in the *Rᶜ-ms-s* form: *KRI* II, 401; *RITA* II, 228; *RITANC* II, 261. Isolated snippets of text refer to someone (perhaps the king?) "sailing northward," *ḥd*, and to "the victories of His Person," *nḫtw n ḥm=f*. Much better preserved is the top of a triumphal stela discovered at Tyre in 1975 with a scene of the king slaying captives before Re-Horakhty: Beirut 2030. It now appears that these fragments belong to the same stela: Loffet 1999, 2000. It is a pity the main text is largely destroyed, for it would have recorded details of one of Ramesses II's campaigns in the Levant that are now lost to us.

155. Brand forthcoming.

156. Kitchen 1982, 50–53; *RITANC* II, 1–2, 136; Spalinger 2020, 142–43. In Obsomer's view (2016, 138–40), the *Na'arin* force or "vanguard troops" (*skw tpy*) who intervened at the crucial moment during the Battle of Kadesh did not split off from the main Egyptian army on the march to Kadesh in regnal year five but had been prepositioned in Amurru during Ramesses II's "first campaign of victory" during the previous year. See p. 127 below.

157. See p. 158 below.

CHAPTER FIVE
THE BATTLE OF KADESH

For a moment Ramesses forgot himself. His face flushed and his head spun. He stared in horror at the news his advisors brought him, then flew into a clamorous rage at the hapless underlings cowering before him. As the vizier and generals traded nervous glances, someone noticed a smudge of dust forming low on the southeast horizon. It billowed and rolled to the north and west. Soon they sensed a faint tremor. Pharaoh now realized his ministers feared more than his furious recriminations. As the dust cloud towered upward, the faint hum grew into a deafening roar as the hooves of countless horses thundered on the plain. A horde of war chariots carrying a host of Hittite warriors and their allies sped toward them. Ambush! Now even Ramesses II—however briefly—knew fear. With a prayer to Amun, he leapt into action. Grabbing his composite bow and mounting his waiting chariot, Ramesses charged out of his camp toward the enemy. A small entourage of royal attendants and bodyguards raced desperately after him, even as pandemonium seized the military encampment around them.

***

A Thorn in Egypt's Side

One of the largest conflicts of the Late Bronze Age, Ramesses II's famous Battle of Kadesh in ca. 1274 BCE was the last of a protracted series of Egyptian-Hittite conflicts for dominion over this Syrian citadel. Situated at the modern site of Tell Nebi Mend on the Orontes River, some fifteen miles (twenty-three kilometers) southwest of modern Homs, the ancient city of Kadesh occupied the frontier between the Beqaa Valley, the region of Damascus to the south, and central Syria to the north (figs. 5.1 and 5.2).[1] Its strategic location on the main inland corridor of the northern Levant had long made it both the crossroads and the plaything of rival empires—Egypt, Hatti, and Mitanni—throughout the Late Bronze Age.[2]

Kadesh had been a thorn in Egypt's side since the fifteenth century BCE, when its ruler led a coalition of Syrian and Canaanite kingdoms that Thutmose III defeated at the Battle of Megiddo. Thutmose III and his successor Amenhotep II both conquered Kadesh. It remained within Egypt's orbit until the Amarna period when the Hittite king Suppiluliuma seized and held the city against all efforts by Akhenaten, Tutankhamun, and Horemheb to recapture it.[3] Ramesses II's father

FIGURE 5.1. The ancient mound at Tell Nebi Mend (ancient Kadesh) in the Homs region of Syria. Courtesy Sally Pei.

Sety I gained a fleeting victory when he stormed the town, but it promptly returned to the Hittite fold after his forces departed.[4] Recent history should have persuaded Ramesses II that contesting Hatti's dominion over this strategic citadel was hopeless. But this did not deter the belligerent young pharaoh.

Following his first campaign to the Levant in the previous year, Ramesses II embarked on his famous Kadesh campaign in a final bid to wrest control of this troublesome city from the Hittites. The incident has come down to us as the best known and possibly the largest military engagement of the Late Bronze Age.[5] The Battle of Kadesh owes its ancient and modern fame to the pharaoh's unprecedented efforts to commemorate it, through literary accounts and monumental war scenes carved on the walls of temples throughout Egypt and Nubia.

FIGURE 5.2. Kadesh citadel in a relief from the first court of the Ramesseum. Photograph by Peter Brand.

Ramesses II's scribes and artists composed and propagated a sophisticated set of textual and pictorial accounts documenting incidents of the battle—and putting a positive spin on them. This elaborate record offers us a wealth of evidence unrivaled by any single event in pharaonic history, presenting us with a unique opportunity to reconstruct a remote historical incident in minute detail. Yet, we must also be cautious. Dense layers of royal ideology and symbolic rhetoric permeate these sources, the ultimate purpose of which was to glorify Ramesses.

The Ideological Filter

Formal royal inscriptions from pharaonic Egypt and other ancient Near Eastern civilizations are not "historical" in the modern sense but serve propagandistic ends, name-ly, to convince the audience of the author's point of view.[6] When using Egyptian texts to reconstruct pharaonic history we must first penetrate a dense ideological filter. Ramesses II's Kadesh accounts exemplify this ten-dency. His scribes and image makers tailored their narrative to conform with traditional doctrines of Egyptian kingship, seeking to persuade us that the battle ended with Ramesses triumphing over countless enemies single-handedly. The main conceits of this elaborate narrative are that: (1) the Hittites acted treacherously, breaking "the rules" by ambushing Pharaoh's army;[7] (2) his own soldiers withered before this onslaught and deserted him;[8] (3) Ramesses nevertheless fought bravely and ferociously all alone, defeating innumerable foes;[9] and (4) despite their craven disloy-alty, his own troops witnessed his solo victory (fig. 5.3).

Even the most credulous modern observers find all this hard to ac-cept. Historians often castigate Ramesses II for peddling an unbeliev-able tale, a grandiose outpouring of propaganda devoid of historical accuracy.[10] Some would condemn him as a fabulist who sought to hood-wink his people—and us—with a massive program of disinformation to cover up his military failures.

We can profit by comparing Ramesses II's Kadesh chronicle with the war accounts of earlier pharaohs, and the kings of various an-

FIGURE 5.3. Ramesses defeats the Hittites single-handedly in his chariot. Prisse d'Avennes's facsimile of a scene from the first court of the Ramesseum showing the color still preserved in the early nineteenth century. NYPL digital collections. Public domain.

cient Near Eastern civilizations. The theme of the monarch as a lone champion vanquishing countless foes also pervades their war accounts. Egyptian texts and military art depict the pharaoh single-handedly defeating myriads of enemies.[11] Indeed, a chief difference between Ramesses II's Kadesh narrative and the records of other pharaohs is the remarkable amount of information Ramesses gives us. When describing their wars, kings like Thutmose III and Sety I essentially proclaim: "I won." End of story.[12]

Another element of the Kadesh narrative—common to most official Egyptian texts about foreign peoples—is the colorful and derogatory language with which Egyptian scribes demeaned Egypt's enemies. Ancient Egyptians believed Pharaoh alone was a true "king," (*nesu*); every foreign ruler was merely a "chief," (*wer*), or at best a "great chief," (*wer a'a*), like the Hittite king. Ramesses II's scribes disparage the Hittite monarch Muwatalli II as "the despicable Chief of Hatti," (*wer khesy en Kheta*), without mentioning his name.[13] Another epithet they hurl at the Hittite king literally means "fallen one," (*kheru*), but in Egyptian slang it meant "loser."

When examining the Kadesh narrative, we must strike a balance between credulity and cynicism. Some modern observers take most of Ramesses's claims at face value; others dismiss the whole effort as an Egyptian historical fantasy, or even a boldfaced lie.[14] Today we can verify few of Pharaoh's claims about the fighting, and much remains unclear. The only surviving Hittite records that may touch on these events are fragmentary and never mention Kadesh by name. The Hittites also claim they won. We are left at the mercy of these ideological, fragmentary, and sometimes contradictory sources.

Sources for the Battle

Ramesses II's complex Kadesh narrative has come down to us through epic battle scenes and three textual compositions: The Poem, the Bulletin, and hieroglyphic captions glossing the artwork.[15] The elaborate artistic narrative of Kadesh unfolds in two main pictorial scenes. The king ordered his scribes and artisans to immortalize these events with a series of monumental relief sculptures carved on the walls of temples across his realm.[16] Today, the textual and pictorial accounts survive largely intact on the walls of Luxor Temple, the Ramesseum, and the king's temple at Abu Simbel. Fortunately we still possess a version of the Poem on fragile papyrus that has miraculously survived for thirty-three centuries.[17] The Poem, the Bulletin, and the captions to the battle scenes complement one another in style and content.[18] Crucial details of these events may turn up in one source but not in

Figure 5.4. Text of the Bulletin above part of the camp scene from Champollion's facsimile of the Kadesh reliefs in the great temple of Abu Simbel, showing the original colors as they appeared in the early nineteenth century. Below the text, Ramesses II's chariot driver Menna holds the reigns of the royal team. On the lower left, four Egyptians beat two Hittite scouts. NYPL digital collections. Public domain.

the other two. We can reconstruct a comprehensive picture only by drawing on all three.[19]

The longest and most sophisticated textual chronicle is the so-called Poem.[20] As its name implies, court scribes composed much of this text in epic verse.[21] Cast as a eulogy of Ramesses II's heroism, the Poem opens with a hymn in praise of his valor. Changing to a style midway between poetry and prose, the Poem recounts the departure of the Egyptian forces, the secret gathering of the Hittites and their allies at Kadesh, and their subsequent ambush of Pharaoh's encampment. Reverting to high poetic style, a large section of the Poem imagines a dialogue between Ramesses II and his divine father and protector Amun-Re, as fierce combat rages around the king.[22] Reciting the many services he had performed for Amun, Ramesses petitions the god for aid. Amun now intervenes, ensuring Pharaoh's triumph.[23] The Poem highlights the king's single-handed counterattack against the Hittite foe.[24] When the fighting dies down, he upbraids the army for deserting him in the crisis. Despite containing much crucial data, the Poem is patently ideological and rendered in a flamboyant style (fig. 5.4).

Our second textual source, which Egyptologists often label "the Bulletin," has a more prosaic format, but sometimes lapses into verse.[25] The Bulletin offers crucial details omitted in the Poem, but dwells only on incidents of the first day of the battle. After stating blandly that "His Person was in Syria on his second campaign of victory," it picks up the story a month after Pharaoh's armies departed Egypt, at dawn on the day of battle, as Ramesses and his soldiers arise in their overnight campsite twelve miles (twenty kilometers) south of Kadesh.[26] Later the same day, as Pharaoh and the first division of his army set up camp on the plain west of Kadesh, the Egyptians capture and interrogate two enemy scouts. After a severe beating, they reveal that the Hittite king, with a huge army including numerous allies, lurks in wait on the far side of the citadel.

While Pharaoh rebukes his councilors and officers, a vast wave of Hittite chariots ambushes the second Egyptian division as it marches toward him. The Hittites then descend on the king's encampment. Ramesses springs into action, and the Bulletin now lapses into epic verse as it glorifies his ferocious counterstrike.[27] After claiming he won the fight unaided, Pharaoh swears an oath: "As Re lives for me and loves me, and as my father Amun praises me, regarding everything My Person said, I truly did these things in the presence of my soldiers and my chariotry."[28] Although the Bulletin lacks the lyrical quality of the Poem, the ideological filter colors both texts.

Hieroglyphic captions accompanying the pictorial scenes form a third textual component. These range from mere name labels and brief quotations by actors in the scenes to extended descriptions of key events.[29] The most important caption reveals the timely arrival of the *Na'arin*, a force of elite Egyptian troops who intervene at a crucial moment, turning the tide of battle against the Hittite attackers.[30] Parallel examples of all three textual compositions survive on temple walls, along with a manuscript of the Poem on fragile papyrus.[31]

Amplifying these textual chronicles, Ramesses II's artisans sculpted panoramic battle scenes on the temple walls (figs. 5.5 and 5.6).[32] This pictorial narrative consists of two unique episodes that are among the most sophisticated scenes in Egyptian art. Both are complex and "busy" with innumerable details. Each condenses a sequence of incidents into one pictorial whole. This is most obvious in the first scene, at the Egyptian camp. As his soldiers set up their bivouac, Pharaoh receives word from his advisors of the impending Hittite ambush. Below Ramesses, a miniature vignette portrays Egyptian troops savagely beating two Hittite scouts to interrogate them. This occurred *before* the king's meeting with his advisors. We also see what happened shortly after: the Hittite

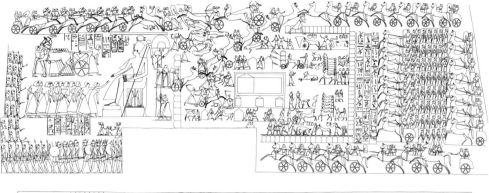

ambush begins, as enemy chariots burst into Pharaoh's encampment while startled Egyptian troops mount sporadic resistance.

When attempting to reconstruct the Battle of Kadesh as a historical event, we must keep two things in mind. One, we are at the mercy of Pharaoh's ideological narrative, having little evidence from the Hittite side, or anywhere else, with which to confirm or deny Ramesses II's claims. On the other hand, Ramesses's elaborate narrative offers us the most detailed chronicle of any single event of the entire Bronze Age. To reject it outright as unmitigated propaganda—or even worse as a tissue of lies—is counterproductive. What follows is just one *possible* reconstruction of the Battle of Kadesh. It attempts to place the conflict in its broader historical and ideological contexts.[33]

FIGURE 5.5 (TOP). The Battle of Kadesh camp scene on the pylon of Luxor Temple, west tower. Drawing after Rosellini. NYPL digital collections. Public domain.

FIGURE 5.6 (BOTTOM). Ramesses II fighting the Hittites at the Battle of Kadesh on the pylon of Luxor Temple, east tower. Drawing after Champollion. NYPL digital collections. Public domain.

Weaponry and Tactics of the Opposing Forces

The grand host Ramesses II mustered for his campaign against Kadesh marched under the standards of four *mesha*, an Egyptian word that can have three meanings: (1) "the army" as the sum total of the Egyptian military forces; (2) individual "divisions" named after Egypt's great gods, such as the "army of Amun," or; (3) the infantry in contrast to the chariot forces. The divine namesakes for the four *mesha*-divisions at

Kadesh were Amun, Ptah, Re, and Seth.[34] How many men did Ramesses command? Modern commentators often number them in thousands of chariots and tens of thousands of infantrymen, citing a figure of 5,000 men as typical for an Egyptian division. By this logic, Ramesses II fielded at least 20,000 soldiers.[35]

In fact, we have no idea how many men the Egyptians brought.[36] Yet, this was not a thoughtless oversight. Figures for the size of the army are conspicuously absent from the Kadesh narrative.[37] In keeping with royal dogma, Ramesses II presented himself as a solitary warrior fighting against innumerable enemies. He had no incentive to boast of the size of his army. In contrast, the Kadesh inscriptions offer up suspiciously large integers for the Hittites: 3,500 chariots and 37,000 infantrymen. We should regard these figures for the enemy host with caution, as too round and bloated.[38] As with Pharaoh's own troops, it is impossible to verify the actual size of the Hittite forces.

The four divisions of the Egyptian army consisted largely of infantrymen, conscripts levied from Egypt's towns and villages.[39] They wielded spears, composite and simple bows, sickle-shaped *khepesh*-swords, and axes. They defended themselves with tall, round-topped shields of animal hide stretched over wooden frames (fig. 5.7).[40] Logistical support for the Egyptian forces consisted of two- and four-wheeled ox-drawn carts and wagons, gangs of human porters, and long trains of donkeys laden with panniers full of supplies, all trudging along with the footsore troops.[41]

The Chariot Forces

Charioteers formed the most renowned and storied branch of every Late Bronze Age army.[42] Ancient elites prized horse-drawn chariots as war machines and status symbols, and the Kadesh accounts dwell on their role in the battle, especially Ramesses II's team.[43] By contrast, the sources underplay the lowly infantrymen, who vastly outnumbered the charioteers.[44] Given this bias, modern historians often misinterpret the tactical role and capabilities of these early war wagons.[45] The iconic impact of Pharaoh in his chariot team, charging the ill-fated enemy, is deceptive. Some imagine that these vehicles functioned as the ancient equivalent of armored tanks.[46] But Egyptian artists grossly exaggerate the chariot's power. In some battle scenes we see Pharaoh's chariot run down an enemy whose limbs are entangled and crushed by the spokes of its wheels. In reality such a collision would wreck the wooden vehicle in a crash that might also kill its royal passenger (fig. 5.8).[47]

Experts fiercely debate the capabilities and tactics that Late Bronze Age chariot forces employed. Some dismiss them altogether as imprac-

FIGURE 5.7. Egyptian infantrymen with their shields slung over their shoulders. Part of a scene from the pylon of the Ramesseum. Photograph by Peter Brand.

FIGURE 5.8. Idealized image of Syrian enemies entangled in the royal chariot wheel. Detail of a scene depicting the Battle of Dapur from the first hypostyle hall of the Ramesseum. Photograph by Peter Brand.

tical war machines, claiming they served as nothing more than "battle-field taxis" transporting warriors to the front, where they fought on foot as they do in Homer's *Illiad*.[48] Others view them as armored ve-hicles, ploughing through ranks of hapless foot soldiers.[49] In fact, Late Bronze Age chariots were not robust enough to use this way (fig. 5.9).

Much of our evidence for ancient chariotry comes from idealized Egyptian artistic and textual sources, hindering our understanding of how effective they were in battle.[50] Built of organic materials like wood and leather, few ancient chariots have survived, except for a handful from Egypt, including six from Tutankhamun's tomb.[51] No Hittite char-iots still exist (fig. 5.10).

FIGURE 5.9. Egyptian chariots with two-man crews. Relief from the temple of Ramesses II at Abydos. Courtesy Manna Nader Gabana Studios Cairo.

FIGURE 5.9. Egyptian chariots with two-man crews. Relief from the temple of Ramesses II at Abydos. Courtesy Manna Nader Gabana Studios Cairo.

FIGURE 5.10. Hittite and allied chariots with three-man crews. On the right, the Hittite shield bearer carries an hourglass-shaped shield. On the left, Syrian allies have rectangular shields. From Ramesses II's Abydos temple. Photograph courtesy of Ogden Goelet.

Egyptian chariots were small, lightweight contraptions. Ancient craftsmen manufactured these Late Bronze Age "high-tech" war machines from composite materials: bent wood, leather, and sinew, with few metal parts beyond bronze horses' bits and minor pieces of tack and hardware (fig. 5.11).[52] Royal examples like Tutankhamun's pair of state chariots were often sheathed in gold foil, but this contributed nothing to their durability. While surprisingly resilient and effective as high-speed transport, Egyptian chariots could not withstand the punishing conditions ancient artists and fanciful modern imaginations place on them. Their tactical role—and their practical limitations—compare with modern fighter jets: They combined advanced composite materials technology, great expense, and elite status as battlefield superiority weapons. They also tended to require as much time in maintenance as in the field.[53]

Chariot Logistics and Performance

Although royal couriers traversed long distances in their chariots, such journeys inflicted severe wear and tear on their vehicles.[54] Pharaoh,

Figure 5.11. Modern replica of a New Kingdom Egyptian war chariot, based on examples from Tutankhamun's tomb. The wide axle set at the back of the cab gave these vehicles exceptional stability and turning capacity. Courtesy Romer- und Pelizaeus Museum, Hildesheim.

and perhaps a fraction of his chariot forces, would have ridden them daily during the month-long journey across Sinai, Canaan, Lebanon, and on to Kadesh in Syria.[55] But logistical teams transported the bulk of the disassembled Egyptian chariots on sturdier supply carts, beasts of burden, and the shoulders of human porters. A chariot was so light that one or two men could carry one.[56] By transporting dismantled vehicles this way, Pharaoh's army spared most of these finicky contraptions from excessive wear and tear and the need for frequent repairs. Unharnessed from their chariots and led by grooms, horses also arrived less fatigued. Only the army's small, wiry scouts habitually rode their horses.[57] With the army traveling at the slow walking pace of infantrymen, donkeys, and ox-drawn carts (averaging a daily rate of about fourteen miles/twenty-two and a half kilometers), long distance riding would only have squandered the horse-drawn chariot's potential, inflicting needless attrition on horses and equipment.

Ramesses II's Kadesh scenes illustrate the apparent differences between Egyptian and Hittite chariots. Textual and visual sources consistently represent Hittite chariots with three-man crews—a driver, a shield bearer, and a warrior—suggesting their war wagons were larger and heavier than their Egyptian counterparts.[58] In the two-man Egyptian units, drivers doubled as shield bearers, as with Pharaoh's driver and shield bearer Menna, whom the Poem singles out by name.[59] Like Ramesses himself, the second Egyptian crewman brandished weaponry: composite bow, javelin, and sword.[60]

With their array of weaponry and crewmen, chariots were not as speedy as today's motorized vehicles, but were lightning fast by ancient standards.[61] A pair of horses drawing an Egyptian chariot with two men in its cab was of course much slower than an unharnessed horse by itself.[62] The heavier Hittite war wagons, carrying three passengers, were even slower.[63] This assumes these wheeled units could operate on flat, even ground with few if any troublesome obstacles.[64] There were few areas suitable for battles with massed chariots in the ancient Near East, but the plain surrounding Kadesh was one of them.

Chariot Weaponry and Tactics

We know both sides at the Battle of Kadesh fielded chariots carrying similar armament.[65] Although Ramesses II's artists have provided us with an unprecedented quantity of pictorial detail, they made deliberate choices that can mislead us. In the scenes, only one member of the three-man Hittite crews bears offensive arms—typically a single javelin. Some Hittite vehicles lack weapons altogether. Unlike Egyptian chariots, they have no bow case or quivers mounted on the cab, nor does a single Hittite charioteer wield a bow. Sety I's war reliefs are surely more accurate in showing Hittite chariots carrying archers.[66] The Poem states that Hittite chariots did have archers, but claims they were useless against Pharaoh's power as their arrows scattered harmlessly like chaff.[67] In fact, we never see a single Hittite *using* his weapon against *any* Egyptian, much less against Ramesses himself. Instead, Hittite warriors grasp their lances as mere props. We must be on guard against such ideological distortions in the texts and imagery.

While the chariots of both sides at Kadesh would have relied on archery as their primary offensive capability, this was not their only armament.[68] In the Kadesh scenes, the third Hittite charioteer grasps a lance except when unarmed. This was surely a casting weapon, since a thrusting spear was ineffective in chariot warfare.[69] Ramesses II's chariot has multiple quivers attached to the side of its cab, each containing a pair of javelins and a bundle of arrows. He may have carried several of these larger missile weapons. Archery provided a long range "standoff" capability, allowing bowmen to target opposing chariots and infantry from a safer distance. When they drew too near to the enemy, they danced away and circled around for another attack run.[70] If the tide of battle placed charioteers at a closer range, the javelin became their weapon of choice.

Chariots were armed with limited supplies of javelins, which were essentially single-use pieces of ordnance. A warrior could only cast a javelin accurately at close range, with just one opportunity to hit his opponent, obliging him to choose his mark with care. While humans were possible targets, a more effective tactic was to impale an enemy horse. Even if the horse wasn't killed, a hit could disable an enemy's chariot and turn its passengers into foot soldiers.[71] When opposing chariots came within range, the shrieks of dying and injured animals would have been horrific once these javelins found their targets.[72]

Ramesses Sets Out for Kadesh

> Now His Person equipped his army, his chariotry, and the Sherden-warriors His Person captured by the victory of his strong arm; they were supplied with all their weaponry and instructions for fighting were given to them. His Person proceeded northward, his army and chariotry being with him. He began a good journey for marching in regnal year five, month two of the Harvest Season (Shomu), day nine, to the despicable land of Kharu on his Second Campaign of Victory.
>
> His Person passed the border fortress of Tcharu, and he was powerful like Monthu when he ventures forth. Every foreign land trembled before him, their chiefs bringing their tribute offerings. Every rebel came bowed down through fear of the power of His Person. His army proceeded upon the narrow roads, which were just like traveling on the roads of Egypt.[73]

So, in the beginning of April in 1275 BCE, Ramesses II and the four divisions of his army departed from Egypt's frontier at the great fortress of Tcharu in the northeast corner of the Nile Delta.[74] Across the coastal plain of north Sinai, into Canaan and onward to Lebanon and Syria, these armies plodded along at an average daily rate of fourteen to fifteen miles (twenty-two to twenty-four kilometers) per day.[75] A week later they reached Gaza after traversing the "Ways of Horus," Egypt's ancient military highway interspersed at regular intervals with fortified watering cisterns, along the north coast of Sinai.[76]

Although we can only guess at the number of troops Ramesses II fielded, it was a vast host by the standards of its time: men, horses, donkeys lugging their panniers and bundles, and oxen hauling two- and four-wheeled supply carts.[77] Like every army that ever marched overland, from the early Bronze Age down to Napoleon's Grande Armée, its momentum seemed painfully slow but inexorable. During his march through Canaan—we are not sure exactly when—Pharaoh organized a separate detachment of elite troops "drawn from the first battle-line (*seku tepy*) of all the leaders of his army," also called the *Na'arin* in the scene captions.[78] Ramesses ordered this crack unit to proceeded northward by a separate route along the Lebanese coast into the Syrian kingdom of Amurru.[79] There it would turn eastward, under orders to rendezvous with the main corps at Kadesh. Meanwhile Ramesses led his four main divisions further inland into Lebanon, entering the Beqaa Valley between the Lebanon and Anti-Lebanon mountain ranges (fig. 5.12).[80]

FIGURE 5.12. Map showing the route Ramesses II and his four divisions took to reach Kadesh from northern Canaan and through the Beqaa Valley. Once it split off from the main army, the *Na'arin*-force would have followed the coastal route through Lebanon to reach Amurru and then cut inland to Kadesh via the Nahr el-Kebir River Valley. Map by Tina Ross after Obsomer 2016, 159, fig. 15.

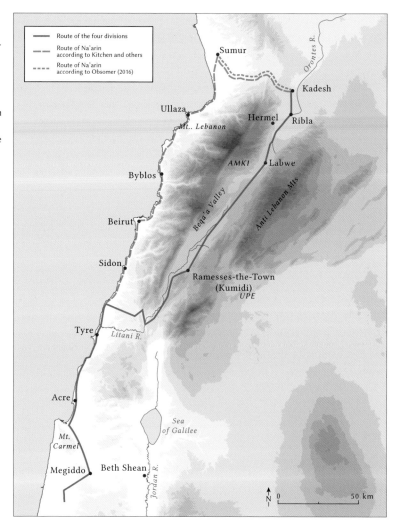

Military Intelligence Fails

What did Ramesses expect to find at the ramparts of Kadesh? Certainly not what he did find: namely, the combined hosts of the Hittite Empire.[81] It is easy to judge Ramesses as a reckless young hothead for pressing forward, allegedly with nothing more than a personal bodyguard, while the lead division of Amun—a mere quarter of his army—barely kept pace behind him.[82]

Some accuse the pharaoh of trying to deceive us by claiming he did not expect to meet the Hittites at Kadesh, while others view the battle as a prearranged encounter; a test of honor and mettle—even a "show down"—to decide once and for all the ownership of the citadel.[83] Ramesses likely knew that Muwatalli II and his Hittites were on the march: spring, as the Bible tells us, was the season when kings went to war.[84] But keeping track of enemy forces deep within hostile territory was far from easy.[85] Sources of news were haphazard. From the Amarna letters we know Egyptian royal envoys preceded deployments of Pharaoh's soldiers.[86] They issued detailed instructions to garrison commanders and vassal kings to supply his hungry and thirsty troops.[87] There was no guarantee the contents of these communiques remained secret. Reports and rumors flew northward from Ramesses's capital at Piramesses and the towns of his Levantine subjects. Messengers, merchants, travelers, spies—all reported their observations and repeated rumors of Pharaoh's expeditionary preparations. No doubt the flow of information went both ways.[88]

We have one such "front line report" from around this period of history, the letter a military officer dispatched to the king of the Syrian coastal city of Ugarit, a Hittite satellite.[89] Even in the cold and rainy days of winter, rumor had it that Egypt's king was on the march. No one knew the size of this force or when it might appear, but the officer grumbles that his own troops, horses, and chariots were in poor condition and stood little chance against an Egyptian army. If this hearsay could elicit such anxious speculation and distress among the petty kings of the Levant, imagine their horror at news of the vast host Ramesses II now mobilized.

This raises an issue historians tend to neglect: what were Ramesses's own expectations for his Second Campaign of Victory? Was Kadesh his only objective, or did he plan on ranging farther afield?[90] Did he think he would find the Hittites at Kadesh (Sety had not, after all), or elsewhere in northern Syria? Did he imagine he could avoid them altogether? Or, having been raised on a steady diet of Egyptian triumphalism, did he perhaps assume that Muwatalli II would be afraid to engage him?[91]

As they threaded their way northward through Canaan and into the Beqaa Valley, any citadel, town, or village lying in the path of Pharaoh's armies—even if not the target of his ire—must have looked upon their arrival with the same dread one feels toward a descending swarm of locusts. Surely Egypt's king and his men would strip them of every provision, practically eating them alive.[92] Months before, Ramesses and his armies descended on their towns, his officials and messengers brought arrogant and impossible demands for supplies and rations to feed his insatiable troops, all to be prepositioned in ready stockpiles.[93] Now, to each rural hamlet and hilltop citadel, the dreaded day came and the locals were no better off for these warnings.

Canaanite rulers could not easily fulfill Ramesses's demands for food, water, and supplies. Nor were his soldiers very picky about whether the storerooms they plundered, the fields they trampled, the orchards and vineyards they stripped belonged to "friend" or "foe." But settlements in the path of any army never received gentler treatment from Sargon I of Akkad, Thutmose III of Egypt, Suppiluliuma I of Hatti, Ashurbanipal of Assyria, or Darius the Great of Persia. Indeed, those unfortunates in Anatolia and northern Syria along the route of Muwatalli II's assembled hosts surely fared little better.

The Day of Battle

One day early in May of 1275 BCE, exactly one month after they departed from the Egyptian border fortress of Tcharu, the division of Amun under Ramesses II's command awoke near Hermel just as the sun crested the eastern horizon:

> Regnal year five, month three of the Harvest Season (Shomu), day nine under the incarnation of Horus: The Mighty Bull, beloved of Maat, the Dual King Usermaatre-Setepenre, the Son of Re Ramesses-Meramun, given life eternally. Now His Person was in Djahy during his Second Campaign of Victory. A perfect awakening in life, prosperity, and health in the tent of His Person on the ridge top south of Kadesh. Then, at dawn, His Person appeared as when Re shines, taking for himself the battle gear of his father Monthu.[94]

From the high ridge of Hermel at the northern end of the Beqaa Valley the Amun division bestirred itself some fifteen miles (twenty-four kilometers) south of Kadesh on the Orontes River (fig. 5.13).[95] Their final leg would take most of a day's march. Later that morning the troops of Amun began crossing the Orontes ford about eight miles (thirteen kilometers) to the south of the town. By late spring the river was flowing at a lower ebb, and many men and horses simply waded and splashed their way across the fords. For supply carts, donkeys, and the lightweight but finicky chariots, the Egyptians may have fashioned rafts or a bridge of pontoons.[96]

While the Orontes is not a large river, neither is it a mere brook, and it was vital to prevent kit and supplies from becoming waterlogged (fig. 5.14). Nor would the donkeys laden with packs—beasts who are wont to bray with earsplitting cries of protest under even the best conditions— have enjoyed a quick dip in the river. By Ramesses II's day, the Egyptian army drew on over 250 years of experience fording rivers in the Levant. Two centuries earlier Pharaoh Thutmose III boasted of how he crafted river boats and carted them overland to cross the Euphrates when his armies raided the empire of Mitanni in northeastern Syria.[97]

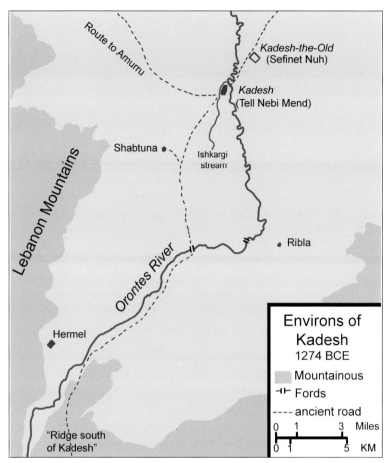

FIGURE 5.13. Map of the environs of Kadesh. On the morning of the day of battle, Ramesses II and the Amun division departed from the "ridge south of Kadesh" near Hermel and proceeded northward along the east bank of the Orontes River before crossing the fords south of the town of Shabtuna. Note the Ishkargi stream (also called the Mukaddiya) a small tributary of the Orontes River running south and west of Kadesh.

FIGURE 5.14. View of the Orontes River from the mound at Tell Nebi Mend (Kadesh) taken in March. Courtesy www. holylandphotos.org.

Ramesses II's Kadesh account passes over the fording of the Orontes in silence, suggesting his forces completed it without difficulty. Around midday the division of Amun reached the outskirts of the town of Shabtuna, just north of the Orontes fords. They were still a couple of hours south of the plain of Kadesh, where they would pitch camp that afternoon.[98] The second Egyptian army, named for the sun god Re, trudged along one *iter* (six and a half miles/ten and a half kilometers) behind Amun, still south of the Orontes fords.[99] Crucially for the day's events, the army of Ptah lagged behind Re, away to the south near Hermel, where Ramesses had awakened that morning. Under the standards of Seth, the fourth corps straggled still farther behind. As Egyptian scouts from Amun, mounted on horseback, fanned out to reconnoiter the territory ahead,[100] Pharaoh's vanguard met two apparent deserters from the enemy alliance:

> *The Lord proceeded northward and reached the environs south of the town of Shabtuna. Arrival by two Bedouin of the tribes of the Shasu to speak to His Person (saying): "Our brothers who are chiefs of the tribes belonging to the loser of Hatti caused us to come to His Person to say: 'It is to perform service for Pharaoh, L.P.H., and to leave the dominion of the loser of Hatti that we have come.'"*
>
> *Then His Person said to them: "Where are they, these brothers of yours who sent you to speak of this matter to His Person?" Then they said to His Person: "They are where the despicable Chief of Hatti is. In fact, the loser of Hatti (still) sits in the land of Aleppo to the north of Tunip. He is too afraid of Pharaoh, L.P.H., to come southward since he heard it said that Pharaoh, L.P.H., was coming north."*
>
> *Now when the Shasu said these things, they spoke lies to His Person, for (in fact) the despicable loser of Hatti made them come to see where His Person was through a desire to prevent the army of His Person from preparing itself for fighting with the loser of Hatti.[101]*

Reporting this startling turn of events, the narrator of the Bulletin speaks from an omniscient perspective Ramesses and his troops lack. As the Egyptians soon learned, the Hittites lay in wait on the far side of Kadesh:[102]

> *Now the loser of Hatti caused the Shasu Bedouin to come to tell these things to His Person as he (the Hittite king) came with his army, his chariotry, and with the chiefs of every land in the districts of the land of Hatti, along with their armies and their chariotry, (all of) which he had brought with him as champions to fight with the army of His Person. They stood, ordered and prepared, behind Kadesh-the-Old. But His Person did not know they were there. Then the two Shasu Bedouin were beaten in the (royal) presence.[103]*

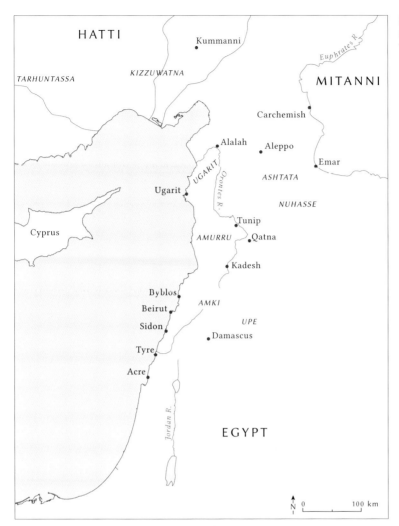

FIGURE 5.15. Hatti's Syrian allies. Map by Tina Ross.

The Poem elaborates on this theme, stressing the vast size and mercenary quality of Hatti's allies (fig. 5.15):

> *Now the despicable loser of Hatti came; he had gathered to himself every foreign country as far as the ends of the sea: the whole of the land of Hatti came, Nahrin likewise, and Arzawa, Dardany, the Gashgash (i.e., Kaska), those of Masa, those of Pitassa, the Arawanna, the Karkisa, and Lukka, Kizzuwatna, Carchemish, Ugarit, Qode, the entire land of Nuhasse, Musnatu, and Kadesh. He did not leave (a single) foreign land which was not brought among every distant foreign country.*
>
> *Their chiefs were there with him, every man with his own army. Their chariotry was exceedingly numerous without equal, and they covered the mountains and valleys. They were like a locust swarm in their multitudes. He (Muwatalli) did not leave (any) silver in his land, having*

stripped himself of all his property which he gave to every foreign land to bring them with him to fight. Now the despicable loser of Hatti, together with numerous foreign countries who were with him, stood concealed and ready to the northeast of Kadesh.[104]

Hittite monarchs normally required their vassal kings to fight alongside them.[105] But this elaborate roster of enemy forces also served an ideological purpose: it stressed their overwhelming numbers and would maximize Pharaoh's triumph in defeating them single-handedly.[106] From this perspective his own army was merely a witness and a narrative foil. Moreover, if any Canaanite vassals or foreign auxiliaries fought alongside their Egyptian overlord—aside from the contingent of Sherden warriors in the royal bodyguard— Pharaoh never reports it.[107] Conforming to the trope of the lone king arrayed against innumerable foes, Ramesses had no incentive to report the numbers and diversity of his own soldiery.

The Poem emphasizes Pharaoh's relative isolation as he approached the town, accompanied only by his bodyguard:

Now His Person was completely alone with his followers while the army of Amun was marching behind him. The army of Re was crossing the ford in the area south of the town of Shabtuna at a distance one iter from the (place) in which His Person was.[108] *The army of Ptah was south of the town of Arnama and the army of Seth was marching on the road.*[109]

Should we take this evident display of royal audacity at face value and conclude that Ramesses really outpaced even the division of Amun? Military leadership, too, has a performative aspect, so the king must be seen marching at the head of his army. With a little artistic license, his scribes portray him charging forward to glory all alone, but we need not take such effusions seriously.[110]

Although the Egyptians interrogated the two Shasu agents with a severe beating, the Bulletin never informs us whether they revealed the Hittites's true location (fig. 5.4). As modern intelligence services have discovered, torture does not always lead to actionable intelligence. Meanwhile, Ramesses and the Amun division arrived at their destination:

His Person traveled northward and arrived at the northwest of Kadesh, setting camp by the army of His Person there. His Person sat upon his stool of electrum to the north of Kadesh, upon the West side of the Orontes River.[111]

By accepting the false report the Shasu decoys offered him, Ramesses II took the fateful decision to press onward toward Kadesh and encamp there, expecting he would lay siege to it the next day (fig. 5.16). Mod-

FIGURE 5.16. Ramesses II enthroned in the Camp of Amun takes counsel with the vizier and other officials. Below Ramesses are his Sherden warrior bodyguard (left) and a group of Egyptian soldiers (right). Rosellini's facsimile of the Kadesh reliefs from Abu Simbel with the original colors that were still preserved in the early nineteenth century. NYPL digital collections. Public domain.

ern observers have roundly condemned the pharaoh for this, berating him as a hotheaded fool.[112] But hindsight is perfect, and military intelligence often proves faulty. In fact, the Shasu's disinformation matched the reports of Ramesses's own scouts and vassal kings were giving him for days.[113] Egyptian reconnaissance also believed the Hittites were far from Kadesh.

Perhaps Ramesses hoped to steal a march on his adversaries, and besiege Kadesh before Muwatalli could stop him. He was taking a calculated risk. Based on his scouts' reports, the king's decision was militarily sound: to set up his base camp, apparently uncontested, at the very site of his strategic objective.[114] Nor can we blame the scouts too much: it would have been hard, moving days ahead of the army and deep into hostile territory, to discover the actual whereabouts of the Hittites.

And what became of the Shasu agents? Perhaps Ramesses turned them loose with a vow to bring their kinfolk over to his service, but it is just as likely he detained them. Historians often assume he released them immediately—only to tell Muwatalli his clever ploy had succeeded.[115] But nothing in our sources confirms this. Even if the Shasu's lies convinced Ramesses, he could have held one or both for further questioning, or as hostages for the fulfillment of their promise. We cannot confirm or disprove this Shasu Bedouin narrative—which some scholars view as a fiction. The Bulletin presents it with dramatic flair, as proof of the enemy's cunning perfidy.[116] But the Poem never mentions the incident.

This close to Kadesh, the two Bedouin were surely not the Hittites's only intelligence assets keeping tabs on Egypt's approaching armies for Muwatalli. By Ramesses II's own account, Hittite scouts were active nearby.[117] Watchmen on the ramparts of the citadel and messengers from surrounding villages could spread the news as well.

Did Ramesses have much choice in the disposition of his forces? The Egyptians could not get around the fact that four large divisions—each with thousands of men, hundreds of horses and beasts of burden, and creaking baggage trains laden with supplies and equipment—had to string out as they plodded along the roads, narrow chokepoints, and high ridges lying in their path.[118] Though a god in Egyptian royal dogma, Ramesses was only a man leading other men.[119]

The Encampment of Amun

Around midafternoon, Amun's division reached the plain northwest of Kadesh and set to bivouac in the fields, to the dismay of local farmers. The elaborate records emblazoned on the walls of temples at Luxor, the Ramesseum, and Abu Simbel vividly illustrate the teeming buzz of camp life, offering us the most detailed pictorial evidence for military logistics from the Bronze Age (fig. 5.17).[120]

At the heart of Amun's encampment stood a "royal district" housing the king's own large pavilion and a group of smaller tents surrounding it. A perimeter fence enclosed this zone, segregating the royals and their entourage from the military rank and file. Pharaoh's tent had a leather and cloth roof and sidings gaily painted with multicolored geometric and pictorial designs—all mounted on a wooden framework complete with elaborately carved and gilded fixtures befitting the mobile palace of an Egyptian monarch. Subsidiary tents housed members of the royal family and their retainers. Among the noncombatants and camp followers in the king's train were some of his young sons. A caption text from the Ramesseum tells how Ramesses dispatched heralds to warn members of the royal family to avoid danger once enemy chariots broke into the camp's western perimeter:

> *Arrival of the fan-bearer of Pharaoh, L.P.H., to tell the royal children (mesu-nesu) and the [servants(?)] of the God's [Moth]er: "[Do not] leave by the west side of the camp, keep yourselves clear of the fighting."*[121]

Figure 5.17. Lepsius's facsimile of the camp scene on the Ramesseum pylon. NYPL digital collections. Public domain.

In Ramesses II's fifth regnal year, most if not all his sons were likely still too young to participate in combat, even if he had appointed a few to the ceremonial rank of generals and chariot officers. His first-born son and heir, Prince Amunhirkhopeshef, could scarcely have been more than fifteen. He may have been younger.[122] In the camp scene at the Ramesseum we see the king's third son Prehirwenemef— entitled a "Generalissimo and First Charioteer to His Person" despite his youth— fleeing in a chariot once combat ensued.[123] Royal women also sheltered in the camp.

Ramesses II brought his mother Queen Tuya, Sety I's widow, on his Kadesh campaign. Were the Great Royal Wife Nefertari and some of his other wives also present? Royal women and young princes (and princesses?) might appear to be strange companions for a king on the march to war. In fact, there are ancient and modern parallels for just such a royal "family outing." When Alexander the Great defeated the Persian Emperor Darius III at the Battle of Issus in 333 BCE, Darius fled, leaving his wife, daughters, and mother, who had joined him on campaign, to fall into Alexander's hands. In the eighth century BCE the Kushite pharaoh Piankhy besieged the Egyptian king Namlot in Hermopolis. Namlot's wife went to Piankhy's siege camp to plead with the Kushite royal women who were with their lord.[124] Likewise, when Louis XIV went on campaign, members of his family and court, including the queen and the Sun King's official mistress, attended him

FIGURE 5.18. Detail the Camp of Amun with oxen and supply carts (right), unharnessed war chariots (center), and patrolling soldiers and a donkey (left). From the pylon of the Ramesseum. Photograph by Peter Brand.

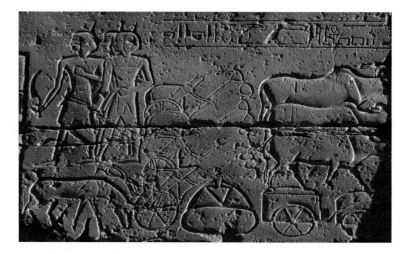

in his encampment.[125] Another Egyptian parallel occurs in the Middle Kingdom Tale of Sinuhe.[126] A New Kingdom pharaoh's "campaign of victory" was more than a military action. It was a grand ceremony he enacted while much of his entourage, including his royal women and offspring, attended as witnesses to his martial prowess and glory.

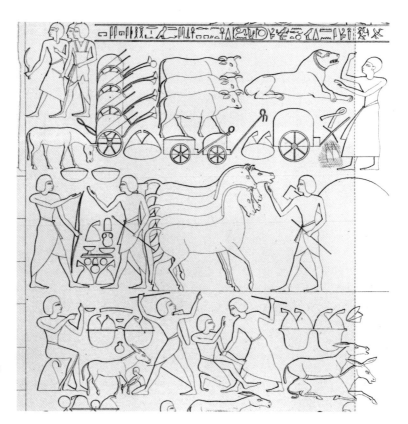

FIGURE 5.19. Detail of Lepsius's facsimile of the camp scene from the Ramesseum pylon, including Ramesses II's pet lion. NYPL digital collections. Public domain.

Elsewhere in the Ramesseum's pictured camp, soldiers attend to the mundane routines of army life. While a few look smart and patrol the grounds, others feed themselves and drink from animal skins. Grateful to have arrived at their destination, some lounge after yet another wearying day of marching. They squat with their heads on their laps or sit sprawled on bags of supplies. One man examines an injury to his comrade's foot. Some troops mend weapons and restring their bows. Two show enough pep to engage in a wrestling match.

Figure 5.20. Ramesses II's pet lion from the pylon of the Ramesseum. Photograph by Peter Brand.

Logistical concerns also occupy the soldiers (figs. 5.18 and 5.19). Quartermasters marshal ranks of ox-drawn supply carts and oversee the unpacking of supplies. One man brandishes his staff at an obstinate donkey, which bellows resentfully even after being relieved of its pack. Even the horses look tired as they stand picketed in a row, unharnessed from their chariots. Meanwhile, a keeper attends to Ramesses II's pet lion, wielding a staff so as not to become its next meal (fig. 5.20). A caption identifies the magnificent male specimen as "a living lion, follower of His Person, (named) Slayer-of-his-Foes."[127] The ferocious beast was a tangible symbol of Pharaoh's might and glory.

The Ambush

Muwatalli II had lured the vanguard of Ramesses II's armies to the plain northwest of Kadesh, on the west bank of the Orontes (fig. 5.21). The main Hittite force lay hidden behind Kadesh-the-Old, the crumbling ruins of a Middle Bronze Age fortress standing two miles (three kilometers) to the northeast of Kadesh. The main citadel sat atop a mound at the modern site of Tell Nebi Mend, where the Orontes River merges with its tributary the Nahr El-Iskargi (figs. 5.2 and 5.13 above).[128] Upon hearing from his scouts that three quarters of Pharaoh's army were too far away to give timely aid to their lord, Muwatalli took the momentous decision to spring his trap on Ramesses.[129] The Hittite ruler was taking a gamble, but he had to exploit this tactical advantage and, to be sure, he could scarcely believe his luck.

Thousands of the *Teher*-infantry warriors comprised the bulk of Hatti's army according to Egyptian accounts (fig. 5.22). Hieroglyphic captions identify two separate groups of 18,000 and 19,000 foot soldiers, but these numbers appear suspiciously large and even. Whatever their actual number, the *Teher*-warriors could never reach Pharaoh's camp on foot before the army of Re reinforced the Amun division. Only a task force of

FIGURE 5.21. Phase 1 of the Battle of Kadesh. After crossing the Orontes River, Ramesses II and the Army of Amun proceed northwest. Along the way, the Egyptians intercept two Shasu Bedouin who have been sent as decoys. Meanwhile, the Hittite chariot force moves from its base camp at Kadesh-the-Old to lie in ambush just south of Kadesh.

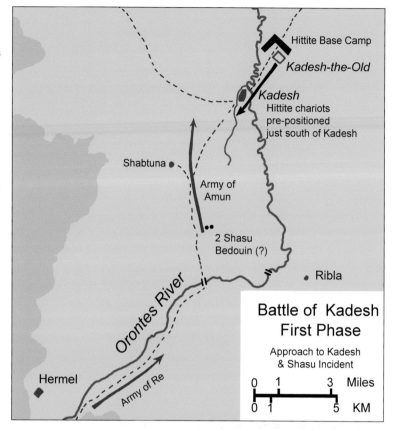

Hittite Base Camp

Kadesh-the-Old

Kadesh
Hittite chariots
pre-positioned
just south of Kadesh

Shabtuna

Army of
Amun

2 Shasu
Bedouin (?)

Ribla

**Battle of Kadesh
First Phase**

Approach to Kadesh
& Shasu Incident

0   1   3   Miles

0 1   5   KM

Orontes River

Hermel

Army of Re

FIGURE 5.22. A group of 18,000 Hittite *Teher*-warriors, from the Ramesseum. Photograph by Peter Brand.

140

charioteers could ambush the Egyptians, striking a quick knockout blow by killing or capturing Ramesses.

We cannot be certain how many chariots Muwatalli II deployed. The Poem claims the first wave of Hittite chariots numbered no fewer than 2,500 vehicles bearing three-man crews, totaling about 7,500 warriors. Again, these figures are suspect. Modern estimates range from two hundred to over a thousand.[130] Whatever their quantity, the Hittite wheeled force was extraordinary by ancient standards.

Where did the Hittites launch their attack and how soon did the Egyptians sense their presence?[131] Departing from Kadesh-the-Old, they would have traveled for about two and a half miles (four kilometers) before entering the fray. Was this a frenzied sprint to ford the Orontes and break out onto the plain to the west of Kadesh? We have no idea what challenges the Hittite chariots faced in crossing the Orontes, and historians debate how much time and effort it involved.[132]

Perhaps Muwatalli had carefully rigged the ambush by shifting his chariot squadrons beforehand, across the Orontes to its western side? If so, they would now be stationed just south of the looming walls of the citadel, with only the much smaller Nahr El-Iskargi—more a stream than a river—between them and their target.[133] In antiquity, as today, lines of trees and scrub on the banks of this smaller watercourse would have screened the mass of Hittite chariots.[134]

Once Muwatalli gave the final signal, wave after wave of Hittite squadrons began rolling out. As the staccato beat of horses' hooves resounded, first in their dozens, then hundreds, then thousands, a deafening percussion rolled like thunder across the plain west of Kadesh, as great clouds of dust billowed skyward. After crossing the Nahr El-Iskargi, the attackers followed an arcing trajectory westward and north as they swept through the plain toward Ramesses II's hapless encampment. They were keeping a pace of twelve to fifteen miles per hour (nineteen to twenty-four kilometers per hour). At full throttle, they would reach the camp of Amun within minutes.[135] Flying westward from Kadesh, they were poised to draw first blood (fig. 5.23).

The division of Re had just completed its own crossing of the Orontes, at a ford to the south and west by the town of Ribla.[136] Now its troops trekked northward across the plain of Kadesh, toward the camp of Amun. As the long files of Re's men and animals marched along, oblivious to danger, they blundered directly into the path of the oncoming enemy strike force. According to the Poem, the Hittites "sliced through the army of Re in its middle while they were marching, unaware and not prepared to fight."[137] Although some of Re's chariots were operative, many would have been disassembled and unharnessed from their horses, and so in no state to respond. Trudging along with

FIGURE 5.23. Phase 2 of the Battle of Kadesh. The Army of Amun sets camp and soon learns of the imminent Hittite attack. The first wave of Hittite chariots (black) ambush the Division of Re and then turn north and west to attack the encampment of Amun.

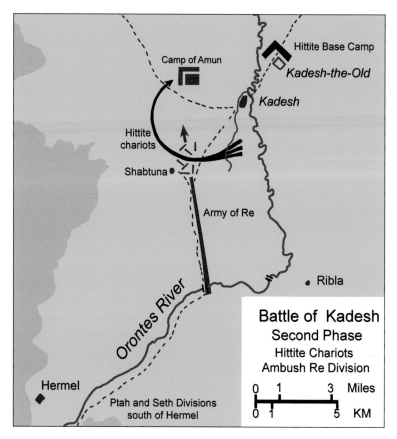

Camp of Amun

Hittite Base Camp

Kadesh-the-Old

Kadesh

Hittite chariots

Shabtuna

Army of Re

Ribla

Battle of Kadesh
Second Phase
Hittite Chariots
Ambush Re Division

0   1   3   Miles

0   1   5   KM

Orontes River

Hermel

Ptah and Seth Divisions
south of Hermel

no expectation of combat, Re's infantrymen were hardly better prepared to resist the Hittite ambush.

About this time, amid the bustle of Amun's camp, Egyptian military intelligence had learned of the danger to which Pharaoh was now exposed. As Ramesses II sat on his gilded camp stool holding council with his officers and ministers, the Bulletin reports:

> *Arrival of a scout in the following of His Person bringing two scouts of the loser of Hatti. They were dragged into the (royal) presence.*
>
> *Then His Person said: "Who are you?"*
>
> *They said: "We belong to the Chief of Hatti. It was he who sent us to see where His Person was."*
>
> *Then His Person said to them: "Where is he, himself, the loser of Hatti? See, I have heard it said he is in the land of Aleppo to the north of Tunip."*
>
> *They said to His Person: "See, the despicable Chief of Hatti has come along with all the lands which are with him, which he brought with him as champions from every foreign land in the districts of the land of Hatti. ...*
>
> *They are equipped with their infantrymen and their chariotry and with their weapons of warfare. They are more numerous than the sands*

of the shore. See, they are standing equipped and prepared for fighting behind Kadesh-the-Old!"[138]

Thunderstruck by this horrific news, Ramesses became apoplectic with rage. Shouting for his officers, he roared at them with cutting sarcasm:

Then His Person had the officials summoned into the (royal) presence, making them hear all the words the two scouts of the loser of Hatti had said in the (royal) presence. Then His Person said to them: "See the (bad) situation which the governors of foreign countries and the chiefs of the lands of Pharaoh, L.P.H., are in! They stood saying to Pharaoh, L.P.H., every day: 'the despicable Chief of Hatti is in the land of Aleppo to the north of Tunip, and he fled before His Person since he had heard it said: "See, Pharaoh, L.P.H., has come!" So they say to His Person daily!"'

"But look, I have heard this (very) hour from these two scouts of the loser of Hatti who said: 'the despicable loser of Hatti has arrived with the numerous foreign countries that are with him, with men, and all the horses which are as numerous as the sands! Look, they are waiting concealed behind Kadesh-the-Old.' But my governors of foreign countries and my chiefs of the lands of Pharaoh, L.P.H., did not know about them (or) tell us they were coming!"[139]

Terrified and ashamed, Pharaoh's grandees confessed to being guilty of a "great crime" for not keeping better tabs on enemy maneuvers.[140] No doubt grateful for the opportunity to flee from his master's displeasure, the vizier decamped post haste by chariot with orders to alert the division of Ptah to hurry forward to aid their lord.

While Ramesses still huddled with his ministers and officers, the first wave of Hittite chariots crashed into the long file of Re's troops.[141] From scenes of the battle, we know the standard marching formation of an Egyptian division had several files of infantry with chariots flanking both outer wings to escort them (fig. 5.24).[142] But it is likely that only a fraction of the unit's chariots were operational on a routine daily march.

Re's soldiers were strung out in a file extending nearly a mile, plodding along at a walking pace of about two and a half miles per hour toward the Amun encampment. The Poem states they were now one *iter* from their comrades in Amun. Charging at full speed, Hittite charioteers took Re's men by surprise (fig. 5.23).[143] As the Hittites drew within range they shot volleys of arrows, wreaking havoc on the troops and any escorting chariots. The hapless infantrymen of Re were left to scatter, as their wheel-borne compatriots dashed to safety or tried to mount a disorganized response.

The Poem and the Bulletin both describe the results in blunt terms: "Then His Person's infantry and chariotry withered before them."[144] The

FIGURE 5.24. Formation of Egyptian chariotry and infantry from Ramesses II's Abydos temple. Marching between the chariots and the regular infantry carrying their large shields are a group of soldiers called "runners." They lack shields. Courtesy Manna Nader Gabana Studios Cairo.

Hittites, had they wished, could have cut a large swath of the army of Re to pieces, then turned again to destroy it in detail. But this was not their main objective. Unless a large Hittite force could roll north and ambush the pharaoh's camp, Muwatalli's trap would not be sprung.

Moreover, the afternoon was wearing on.[145] Their hard-pressed teams of two horses, hauling chariots with three-man crews, must eventually tire. Not holding back to decimate Re's troops, the Hittites cut through and arced around them, racing toward Amun's encampment. As they flew past the scattering Egyptian soldiers, a grand ancient "drive-by shooting" ensued. But even here, amid all these easy pickings, Hittite bowmen could not afford to expend too much ammunition.[146] They did not destroy the army of Re, only mauled and disrupted it.[147]

As this mayhem occurred, an Egyptian vizier and his small entourage of retainers were flying south. Ramesses had dispatched them from his camp to warn Ptah's division of the danger. According to the Poem, Ptah's men were well south of Re's troops. The vizier and his posse peeled away to the south and west to avoid any oncoming Hittite chariots. Reaching the Ptah division, they began shouting "Hurry up! Pharaoh stands amid the enemy all alone!"[148]

Meanwhile, with the disrupted columns of the Re division lagging far behind, the Hittite attack's leading edge now collided with Amun's encampment, smashing through its palisade of round-topped shields. Within the camp pandemonium ensued as the panicked Egyptians tried to defend themselves.[149] Dividing into four large squadrons, most Hit-

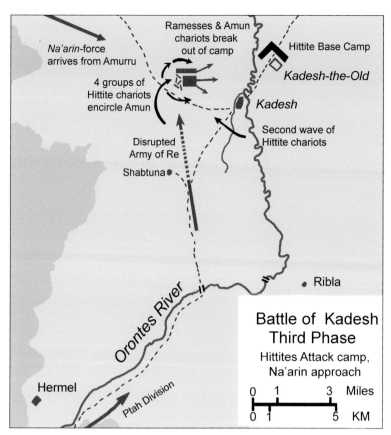

FIGURE 5.25. Phase 3 of the Battle of Kadesh. The first wave of Hittite chariots divides into four groups. Some assault the camp while others move to encircle it. Ramesses II and his followers break out of the camp. The *Na'arin*-force arrives from Amurru to the northwest of Kadesh. The second wave of Hittite chariots now engages.

tite chariots moved to encircle the camp, harrying its defenders with bowshot but keeping clear of Egyptian infantrymen (fig. 5.25).

The full impact of the Hittite charioteers' attack on Pharaoh's camp remains open to question, although historians often assume they routed the Egyptians. In the elaborate Kadesh scenes at Abu Simbel and the Ramesseum, much of the bivouac appears blissfully unaware of the impending assault. By now, the two captured Hittite spies had revealed to Pharaoh what the thunderous roar of hooves was also telling his soldiers. The blithe atmosphere of the camp looks too calm to believe. In fact, the scene depicts two different moments in time: the state of the camp prior to any warning of the imminent attack, and—for dramatic effect—the moment when Hittite chariots burst into its west side.

From this point, in both the textual and pictorial narrative, events happen chiefly from Ramesses II's own perspective, and we can only guess how the action unfolded beyond his immediate vicinity. Modern observers often fill this gap in our knowledge by assuming the worst of the Egyptian troops, just as Ramesses berated them once the fighting died down. Aside from Pharaoh's claim that his soldiers "abandoned" him, neither the Bulletin nor the Poem indicates how Amun's division performed under assault or what losses they suffered. In keeping with traditional royal dogma, Ramesses confronted and defeated his enemies alone. His soldiers and chariotry were redundant to the ideological purpose of the Kadesh narrative, which—like all Egyptian war accounts—seeks only to laud the pharaoh.

We need not conclude the Hittite chariots routed the Amun division. Comparing Ramesses II's narrative with Thutmose III's account of the Battle of Megiddo is instructive. Both single the army out for failing in its duty. Blaming the army was a well-established trope. Egyptian troops serve as an incompetent foil, making Pharaoh's own martial valor more praiseworthy.[150] In fact, Egyptian rhetoric overflows with stock phrases lauding the king as defender of his soldiers. A eulogy of Ramesses II in the opening verses of the Poem calls him: "Rescuer of his army on the day of fighting; great protector of his chariotry; who brings his followers (safely) back; who rescues his troops; his heart being like a mountain of copper."[151] Far from being an effective force, Egyptian ideology casts the army as a damsel in distress at best, or a band of deserters and incompetents at worst.

Ramesses Strikes Back

Ramesses himself, after issuing a flurry of commands to his retainers, mounted his chariot and sped off into the fray (fig. 5.26). Although the textual and pictorial narratives portray Pharaoh's counterattack in vivid detail, dogmatic motifs suffuse these accounts, obscuring the true sequence of events and presenting us with contradictory details. Various components of the narrative disagree over specifics of the king's supposedly solitary counteroffensive (figs. 5.3 and 5.6 above).

In the battle scenes Ramesses II charges alone into the mêlée, the reins of his chargers tied gamely around his waist. Such bravado was a traditional conceit of New Kingdom battle art.[152] The Bulletin also casts him as a lone champion battling a multitude of Hittites. Yet, in the Poem, Pharaoh's chariot driver and shield-bearer Menna plays a role.[153] The Poem also mentions an entourage of royal "cup-bearers of the audience chamber," his most intimate personal servants, who stick by him during the fight.[154] These attendants serve as first-hand witnesses to Ramesses II's valor. As a narrative foil, the Poem contrasts Menna's panicky state of mind with Ramesses's resolute bravery amid the onslaught:

> Now when Menna my shield-bearer saw a multitude of chariotry surrounding me, he became weak, his heart was craven, and stark fear entered his body. Then he said to His Person: "O my good Lord, O mighty Ruler, O great Protector of Egypt on the day of fighting, we stand alone

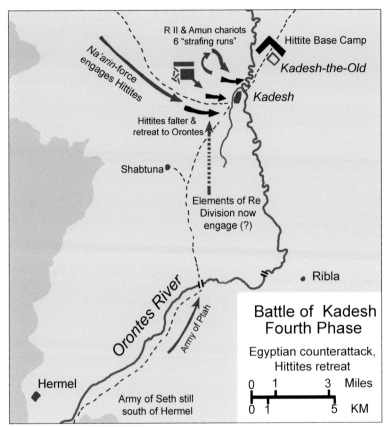

FIGURE 5.26. Phase 4 of the Battle of Kadesh. The Hittite attack looses momentum as the *Na'arin*-force, Ramesses II, and troops from the Army of Amun seize the initiative. The flagging Hittite chariots retreat eastward to the Orontes.

amid the enemy. See, the infantry and the chariotry have abandoned us. Why do you stand to rescue them? Let us get clear (away)! Save us O Usermaatre-Setepenre!"

Then His Person said to his shield-bearer: "Be strong, be strong in your heart O my shield-bearer. I will enter among them like the strike of a falcon as I slay, slaughter, and fell (them) to the ground! What are these (effeminate) back-turners to your mind?[155] Millions of them do not concern me.

Then His Person galloped off quickly. He swiftly entered into the midst of the enemy for the sixth time of entering among them. "I was like Baal in pursuit of them in the moment of his power. I wreaked havoc among them and I could not let up!"[156]

What should we make of Ramesses II's claim to have stormed into the thick of the Hittite chariots six times? We might dismiss it as pure hyperbole, although six is not a particularly symbolic number here.[157] Tactically, what sense did it make for Pharaoh and his small group of loyal attendants and bodyguards to expose themselves to overwhelming numbers of enemy chariots? According to the text, four groups of Hittite chariots hemmed Ramesses in on all sides. But charging into the throng of enemy vehicles would have been a suicide mission. We should discount this passage as hyperbole. Instead, Ramesses leveraged the speed and agility of his light Egyptian chariot to make a series of strafing runs.[158]

By charging within bow range of the Hittites and firing salvos of arrows at them—then speeding away to a safer distance—Ramesses, and any operational Egyptian chariots with the presence of mind to resist the ambush, tried to stay out of range of the horse-killing, hand-tossed Hittite javelins. Both Egyptian and Hittite chariots were also supported by a class of soldiers the Poem calls "runners" (fig. 5.23 above) who fought on foot alongside their wheel-borne comrades, lending aid to disabled vehicles while targeting enemy chariots and personnel. Perhaps they were a form of ancient "mechanized infantry" who could hitch rides on chariots and hop on and off as combat required.[159]

While both sides wielded composite bows, the Egyptians may have enjoyed an edge with their lighter two-man vehicles. If Pharaoh was isolated on the battlefield—not entirely alone, but with only a small escort of bodyguards and loyal attendants—it made better sense to keep his distance by making a series of hit and run attacks to harass the larger Hittite squadrons. Perhaps some of Amun's chariot forces rallied to their king, even if Ramesses chose not to credit them. Or perhaps it was every man for himself. Either way, it would have been suicidal for Pharaoh and his small band of chariots to plunge into the horde of Hittite attackers. Whether Ramesses made six strafing runs or some other number, he took full advantage of his chariot as a speedy, mobile missile platform, following standard military doctrine of the Late Bronze Age.[160]

Aside from Ramesses II, how did the rest of Amun's division acquit themselves in the fray? Here again we face a set of unknowns.[161] How chaotic were the conditions in the camp? What percentage of Amun's horses and chariots were yoked and operational? Did Pharaoh and other Egyptian chariots get clean away before the Hittites broke into the camp? How many Hittites breached its perimeter? What resistance did the infantry, many armed with their bows, offer? Did any elements of the Re division arrive in time to render aid to their comrades?

One factor soon impacted the Hittite attack. Their horses began to tire.[162] After their furious charge through the division of Re and their encirclement of the camp of Amun, the Hittite chargers were surely becoming winded. Colliding with the Egyptian bivouac had reduced the momentum of their attack.[163] How soon did the Hittites run out of steam? Like any good commander, Muwatalli II foresaw this eventuality. He kept a significant portion of his chariots in reserve, for use as a relief force.[164]

Now, the Poem reports, the Hittite king deployed his most high-status warriors: his key vassal kings and even his own brothers.

> *Now the despicable Chief of Hatti was standing in the middle of his army and his chariotry watching the fighting by His Person—who was entirely alone, for his army was not with him, nor was his chariotry— while he (Muwatalli) stood there, turning back, cringing and fearful. Then he caused many chiefs to come forth, each one with his chariots. They were equipped with their weapons for fighting:*
> > *This Chief of Arzawa, the One from Masa,*
> > *The Chief of Arawanna, this One of the Lukka,*
> > *This One from Dardany, the Chief of Carchemish,*
> > *The Chief of Karkisa, and this One from Aleppo,*
> > *Along with the brothers of this One of Hatti:*
> *All together as one unit, they totaled one thousand chariots, who came straight forward into the fire!*[165]

Again, the figure of a thousand is inflated and too round; how could the Egyptians possibly make an accurate count as battle raged? Yet, once this second wave sped off, Muwatalli had expended all the arrows in his quiver. His infantrymen could never hope to catch up with their wheel-borne compatriots and play a meaningful role in the fighting that late afternoon.

About this time, an Egyptian relief force arrived from the northwest and entered combat—the *Na'arin* troops Ramesses had sent to Amurru, an elite detachment picked from "the first battle line from all the leaders of the army" (fig. 5.27).[166] A long caption announces:

> *The arrival of the Na'arin of Pharaoh, L.P.H., from the land of Amurru. They found the enemy losers of Hatti had surrounded the camp of Pharaoh, L.P.H., upon its western side, while His Person sat alone, without his army being with him. The enemies and the horses [of Hatti] came and surrounded the [camp of Pharaoh, L.P.H., and] his army, while the army of Amun—which Pharaoh, L.P.H., was in—had not finished setting up camp. Now the army of Re and the army of Ptah were still marching, but their troops had not yet come from the woods of Labwe.*[167]
> *The Na'arin attacked the enemies belonging to the despicable loser of Hatti as they entered the camp of Pharaoh, L.P.H., and the servants of Pharaoh, L.P.H. slaughtered them. They did not permit (even) one of them to escape, their hearts were confident in the great strength of Pharaoh, L.P.H., their good lord, while he surrounded them like a copper mountain, like an iron rampart, forever and ever, eternally.*[168]

Neither the Poem nor the Bulletin ever mentions the *Na'arin*. Their focus rests squarely on the pharaoh's valor as a one-man army, in contrast to his inept troops.

FIGURE 5.27. Orderly ranks of the *Na'arin*-force (left) engage a chaotic mass of Hittite chariots. Rosellini's facsimile of a relief from Abu Simbel. NYPL digital collections. Public domain.

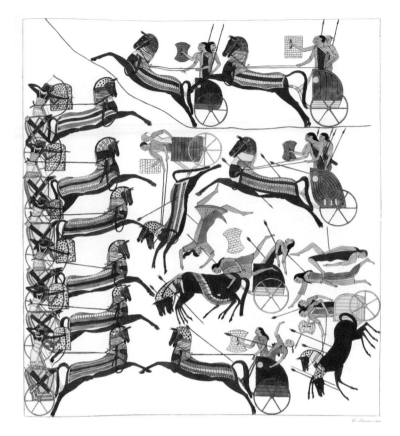

Once the *Na'arin* engaged, the flow of battle apparently turned against the Hittites, as a cascading series of factors broke their momentum, causing their *esprit de corps* to falter. Horses and men grew weary. The Hittite formations broke down in the milling chaos of the camp as they desperately searched for Ramesses, their ultimate prize. Gradually, men from the Amun division would have recovered, mounting a more effective and organized resistance. This likely included the infantry, whom the Kadesh narrative largely ignores. Perhaps they were the unsung heroes of the battle. The functional Egyptian chariots, including the bodyguard of Ramesses II, exploited their superior speed and agility against the fatigued Hittite attackers.

Did the *Na'arin* turn the tide or merely deliver the coup de grace? Here again the narrative leaves us with more questions than answers. Did only the *Na'arin* chariots engage, as the scenes imply? Did they arrive at the critical moment, like the cavalry in a Hollywood movie?[169] It is not surprising that the Poem and Bulletin do not mention them, their purpose was to glorify Pharaoh as the lone hero of the battle. But this elite detatchment gave new momentum and cohesion to the Egyptian

FIGURE 5.28. Hittite dead in Orontes with hieroglyphic labels naming high-ranking enemy casualties. First court of the Ramesseum. Photograph by Peter Brand.

side just as the Hittite attack waned. The *Na'arin* may have executed the decisive maneuver in countless battles down through history: a classic flank attack. Charging in by surprise from the side or rear, they would throw the enemy into a panic and create a rout.

At any rate, Egyptians forces now seized the initiative and pushed back the flagging Hittite attackers (fig. 5.28). With characteristic bombast the Bulletin describes the ensuing mayhem as a rout. In keeping with Egyptian royal dogma, it credits Pharaoh alone for this sudden reversal of fortune:

> *Then His Person saw them, and so he rose quickly and raged against them like his father Monthu Lord of Thebes, taking up his fighting gear and his coat of armor. He was like Seth in his moment of power. Then he took the reigns of "Victory in Thebes," his great (chariot) steed and he led them off in a hurry, alone, by himself.[170] His Person was powerful, his heart was stout, no one could withstand him. All around him were the flames of a fire, for he had incinerated every foreign country with his fiery blast. His eyes were fierce after he saw them, and his power flared like an inferno against them.*
>
> *He gave no heed to millions of foreigners. He viewed them as (mere) chaff. His Person entered among the enemies belonging to the loser of Hatti along with numerous foreign countries that were with them. His Person was like Seth great of strength, like Sakhmet in her moment of rage!*
>
> *His Person killed all enemies belonging to the Loser of Hatti along with their chiefs, their great ones, and his brothers—all of them—and*

FIGURE 5.29. Lepsius's facsimile of Hittite casualties in the Orontes. *Teher*-infantry men stand on the east bank and rescue some of the survivors. First court of the Ramesseum. NYPL digital collections. Public domain.

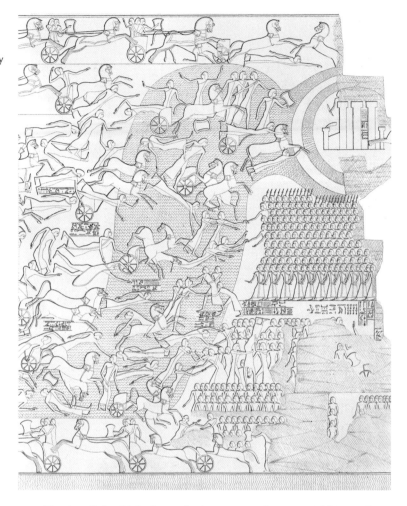

likewise, all the chiefs of every foreign country who came with him, and their infantry and chariotry. They were (all) fallen on their faces, one atop the other. His person massacred and slew them where they were, and they piled up in front of his horses. Yet, His Person was alone, no other being with him.

Next, His Person caused the enemy forces of the Hittite losers to fall on their faces, piling up one on top of the other and plunging like crocodiles into the waters of the Orontes: "I pursued them like a griffon. I vanquished every foreign country by myself; though my infantry and my chariotry abandoned me. Not one among them stood by, looking back."[171]

To appreciate the ensuing spectacle, no doubt exaggerated in the poet's flamboyant retelling, we must turn to the pictorial record (fig. 5.29). In depicting Ramesses II's counterattack, the artist places all emphasis on Pharaoh's larger-than-life figure charging his doomed adversaries,

FIGURE 5.30. Hittite troops holding the king of Aleppo upside down to empty him of water. First court of the Ramesseum. Photograph by Peter Brand.

who fall in a chaotic mass like scythed wheat, shot down by his arrows. Hittite survivors bolt eastward toward the Orontes River, crashing into it as men and horses drown, their listless bodies floating in the waters. Some swim to its opposite shore where ranks of Hittite foot soldiers, otherwise powerless to intervene in combat, attempt to rescue the survivors. It is all high drama and patent Egyptian triumphalism, and deeply humiliating to the Hittites.

Egyptian scribes and artists could not resist having a laugh at the enemy's expense. Their mockery targeted Aleppo's unfortunate king— the very town that the deceitful Bedouin had falsely claimed as the whereabouts of Muwatalli's army. After nearly drowning in the Orontes as he escaped, this leading Hittite vassal now suffered great indignity when two soldiers held him upside down to drain the water he had gulped. A caption text gleefully reports his mortifying predicament (fig. 5.30): "The despicable Chief of Aleppo being emptied (of water) by his infantrymen after His Person threw him into the water."[172]

If we believe the artistic record, a large group of Hittite foot soldiers, and Muwatalli himself, witnessed the carnage from the east bank of the Orontes and the battlements of Kadesh. They soon realized, to their horror, that Muwatalli's plan had gone horribly wrong. Now their own attack force stood in mortal jeopardy.

Once again, we are left with a set of unanswerable questions. How many casualties did each side suffer? Among the two waves of Hittite chariots, how many returned safely to the east bank of the river? Aside from rescuing survivors of the chariot force who swam across, what role, if any, did Hittite infantrymen huddled on the east bank of the river play? Did elements of Re's division arrive in time to offer effective support? Did they block the escape route for surviving Hittite chariots retreating to the south? We can only guess.

The Egyptian accounts omit much vital data. The day's events were surely more complex than Ramesses II's scribes and artists portrayed. However, if the outcome was not a lopsided Egyptian victory, we should not assume that Ramesses tried to conceal a catastrophic defeat. Pharaoh and most of his forces did survive the fighting, as did Muwatalli's.

The Evening After

As dusk fell and the dust began to settle, both sides took stock of the day's events.[173] Whatever debates and recriminations disturbed the equanimity of Muwatalli's headquarters that evening are now lost to us. On the Egyptian side a more familiar story transpired, as Ramesses II congratulated himself for his own bravery and castigated his feckless men for deserting him in his hour of need. The Poem reports how Egyptian troops sheepishly filtered back into their Lord's presence:

> Then they presented themselves one by one, approaching the camp at evening time, and found every foreign country among whom I engaged now lying overthrown in their blood—all the fine warriors of Hatti including the children and brothers of their Chief. For I had made the fields of Kadesh white (with corpses) and no one knew where to walk because of their multitude.
>
> Then my infantry came to praise me, their faces [amazed] at seeing what (I) had done. My officials came to exalt my mighty arm, and my chariotry likewise, (all) boasting of my renown:
>
> "O what a fine warrior who makes hearts strong—so you might rescue your infantry and your chariotry.
>
> You are the Son of Amun who acts with his arms as you destroy the land of Hatti with your valiant strong arm.
>
> You are the finest warrior, without equal—a King who fights for your army on the day of battle.
>
> You are great-hearted, first in combat, paying no heed to every country gathered together in one place.
>
> You are great of victories in the presence of your army and before the entire land without speaking boastfully—Egypt's protector who curbs foreign countries.
>
> You have broken the back of Hatti forever!"[174]

The Poem vividly recounts this scene, but we must remember that blaming the army was a well-worn cliché. Nevertheless, his diatribe against his underlings surely reflected the pharaoh's mood, whether or not he spoke these actual words. Incandescent with rage, Ramesses derides and shames his officers and soldiers in a tirade dripping with sarcasm, while he singles out his horses for sticking by him in the crisis:

> *What is the matter with you O my officials, my infantry, and my chariotry who are ignorant of fighting? Does not a man make himself great in his hometown when he returns after acting bravely in the presence of his Lord? It is good, indeed, to win fame by fighting again and again. From ages past a man is respected because of his strong arm. Indeed, have I done nothing good for (even) one among you, so that you should abandon me alone amid the enemy? How truly fortunate is he among you who is still alive to draw breath while I was all alone! Do you not know in your hearts that I am your iron rampart? What will they say when they hear you abandoned me, alone without a comrade? Neither an official nor a chariot officer nor a soldier came to give me a hand while I fought. I repulsed a million foreign lands all alone, upon "Victory in Thebes" and "Mut Is Content," my great chariot steeds. It was they whom I found to give me support while I fought alone against a multitude of foreign lands. I will personally stoop to having them fed in my presence every day I am in the palace. For it was they whom I found amid my enemies—along with the charioteer Menna, my shield bearer, and my palace attendants who were at my side. They can bear witness for me about the fighting. See, (at least) I found them!*[175]

Whatever losses of men and materiel the Egyptians suffered in battle remains a mystery. The texts state only that the men and horses of the Re division "withered" under the Hittite onslaught.[176] In the pictorial record, we do see some Egyptian infantry and charioteers involved in the fighting. Yet, we never read of Egyptian casualties in either text or see them in the scenes. Once again, ideology trumps reality. Just as Pharaoh's artists never portray the Hittites fighting with their weapons, we do not see a single Egyptian suffering death or injury. Nor do the inscriptions tally the Egyptian dead.

By contrast, the scene captions list seventeen high-ranking Hittite casualties by name and rank. Although these represent a mere fraction of the Hittites killed, they were a huge propaganda coup for Ramesses due to their close ties to Hatti's monarch. Among those slain were two of Muwatalli's own brothers, Sippazili and Himmu-zalama, his royal secretary, and over a dozen high-ranking officers.[177] Frustratingly, and unlike other New Kingdom war accounts, totals of enemy dead and captured are absent from the Kadesh texts. But scenes from Abu Simbel and Karnak depict Egyptian soldiers rounding up groups of Hittite and allied prisoners, and depositing as gruesome trophies the severed hands of the enemy dead, which scribes tally up in the presence of Pharaoh.[178]

Another casualty in Ramesses II's subsequent propaganda war was Muwatalli II's dignity (fig. 5.31). Allegedly witnessing the debacle from

FIGURE 5.31. An ideological representation of Hittite king (center) surrounded by his *Teher*-infantry, as he supposedly avoided combat. In the upper left, Hittite soldiers hold the king of Aleppo upside down to drain water from him. Lepsius's facsimile of a scene from the Ramesseum pylon, south tower. NYPL digital collections. Public domain.

the safety of the east bank of the Orontes, where a multitude of his *Teher*-infantry stood protectively around him, Muwatalli prepares to flee in his chariot as a caption beside his figure snidely insinuates:

> *The despicable loser, the Chief of Hatti, standing amid his troops and chariotry, his face averted, shrinking back, his heart fainting. He could not come out to fight for fear of His Person, since he saw His Person overpowering the Hittites, along with the chiefs of every foreign land who came with him.*[179]

Here is yet another time-worn Egyptian trope—a cowardly foreign king fleeing in terror from Pharaoh's might.[180] It is all too neat.[181]

The Aftermath of the Battle

The next morning further combat ensued, but we know almost nothing about it. The Poem describes this second day of skirmishing in brief and rhetorical terms, giving us no real details. The Bulletin and artistic record both ignore this event, although this has not prevented historians from pondering it.[182] At last, when the melée played itself out, Muwatalli II sent an offer of truce to Pharaoh—or so the Poem claims:

> *It was then that the despicable loser, the Chief of Hatti, sent a message honoring my name like Re saying: "You are Seth, Baal in the flesh! Dread of you is like a fiery brand in the land of Hatti." Then he sent his messenger with the document in hand (addressed to) the great name of My Person:*
> *"This humble servant speaks, to let it be known that you are the Son of Re who came forth from his flesh. He has given to you all lands gathered*

together in one place. As for the land of Egypt and the land of Hatti,
they are yours, your servants, under your feet. Re your august father
has given them to you.

Do not set your power against us. See, your might is great, and your
strength lies heavily upon the land of Hatti. Is it good to kill your servants
with ferocity and without mercy? See, you spent yesterday killing
myriads. Today you came and left no heirs (alive). Do not speak harshly O
victorious king. Peace is more beneficial than fighting. Let us breathe!"[183]

We need not doubt that Muwatalli II parleyed with his Egyptian adversary after the battle. But this "quotation" from his message is pure fiction, tailored to suit Ramesses II's vanity and allowing him to save face.[184] Upon receiving this message, Pharaoh assembles his courtiers and officers in council, seeking their advice. After hearing the Hittite missive—which the Poem so obviously distorts—Egyptian grandees respond in unison: "Most excellent is peace, O Sovereign our Lord! There is no blame in peace when you make it. Who can resist you on your day of wrath?"[185]

The Poem's account of this peace overture conforms to a literary genre called the "king's novel."[186] According to the traditional plot of the king's novel, Pharaoh presents some bold plan of action, which his advisors gainsay. Disregarding their advice, the king always carries out his plan with resounding success. The Poem makes an odd twist on this theme. Here his advisors approve of the Hittite peace offer, but Ramesses himself remains silent.

Muwatalli may have offered a truce for both sides to withdraw. But otherwise, it was *status quo ante*, with Kadesh remaining under his dominion. Accepting these terms, after failing to take the city, would have humiliated Ramesses. To save face, the mercurial Pharaoh ignored any talk of peace, leaving the onus for discussing it on his counselors. Without further comment, the Poem announces:

His Person commanded that his word be obeyed. He turned southward
in peace. His Person set off in peace toward Egypt together with his
infantry and his chariotry, all life, stability, and dominion being with
him.[187]

Before departing the field of battle, Ramesses presided over a triumphal ceremony while sitting enthroned in his chariot (fig. 5.32). Soldiers, high officials, and even his young sons led bound Hittite and allied captives in review before him. Nor were enemy dead exempt from the spectacle. Egyptian soldiers brought the severed right hands of foemen they had killed, dumping these grisly trophies in piles under the king's gaze as scribes assiduously tallied the dead.

FIGURE 5.32. After the battle, several princes lead Hittite and Syrian captives before their father Ramesses II who reviews the spectacle from his chariot. As officials rejoice, officers pile the severed hands of enemy dead before Pharaoh while scribes tally these grizzly tokens. From Abu Simbel. Drawing after Desroches-Noblecourt et al. 1971.

The Poem then reports Ramesses II's safe return to his capital, Pi-ramesses-Great of Victories, where Egypt's gods welcome him home as a conquering hero.[188] This sudden and oddly anticlimactic ending to the Poem masks a more problematic upshot to the two days of fighting at Kadesh. What would Ramesses do now? He had no option but to make an orderly withdrawal from Hittite territory.

Although the Poem describes the homecoming as happy and un-eventful, cuneiform sources indicate Muwatalli provided Ramesses with a hostile escort out of Syria.[189] In what might be one of the only surviving Hittite references to the battle, Muwatalli II's brother and successor, King Hattusili III, later recalls:

> Because my brother Muwatalli campaigned against the king of Egypt and the king of Amurru, when he defeated the kings of Egypt and Amurru, then he (the Egyptian king) went back to the land of Upe. When Muwatalli, my brother, defeated Upe, he [... and wen]t back to Hatti, but [he left] me in Upe.[190]

Scholars often assume Hattusili's statement recounts the aftermath of Kadesh, but it never mentions the city. Instead, it singles out the ren-egade vassal kingdom of Amurru. Sety I had fought there and now Ramesses II sent his *Na'arin* through Amurru. This may imply that Amurru was under Egyptian control.[191] Hattusili's memoir also refers to a Hittite assault on the Egyptian province of Upe near modern Da-mascus.[192] This conformed to a pattern of Hittite incursions into Egypt's client states after Egyptian attacks on Kadesh and Amurru.[193]

We can gain further insight into the immediate aftermath of the Bat-tle of Kadesh from a diplomatic letter Ramesses II sent to Hattusili III well over a decade later, once they brokered a peace treaty. The two former opponents were engaged in an ongoing epistolary dispute about what really happened at Kadesh years earlier. In relating his version of events, Pharaoh takes issue with a statement Hattusili made in an earlier message, where he reminded Ramesses how the Egyptian army took refuge in the Lebanese coastal town of Sidon.[194]

If Muwatalli did compel Ramesses and his army to withdraw southward with a stopover in Sidon, Pharaoh did not stay cooped up there long. Nor did the Hittites lay siege to the place. The Egyptians and Hittites had shed enough blood for this season. Muwatalli dispersed his vassal allies and brought most of his forces home. His brother Hattusili's incursion into Upe came only after the main Egyptian force had left the field. The Hittites would not retain control of Upe; it soon came back into Egypt's orbit.

Who Won?

In the final analysis, we can make only educated guesses as to who the real victor was. Both sides claimed victory, of course. Hittitologists and Assyriologists often credit Hattusili III's statement about defeating the Egyptian king as "proof" the Hittites won.[195] We should keep in mind that all these sources, Egyptian *and* Hittite, are ideological in nature. Ancient kings rarely admitted defeat.

As for Ramesses II's narrative, his superheated rhetoric tends to leave modern readers jaded and suspicious.[196] But let's remember, the only evidence we possess for *doubting* Pharaoh's version of events are what he gives us himself, by reporting what went wrong for the Egyptians. Ramesses washed his dirty laundry in public, so to speak. Such bitter truths were rarely seen in Egyptian royal narratives. Nor should we assume the Hittite counter narrative—brief though it is—represents the unvarnished truth.

The result of Kadesh was neither a crushing defeat nor a resounding victory for either Ramesses II or Muwatalli II. Ramesses and his troops escaped destruction, repelling the Hittite surprise attack and perhaps even routing them.[197] Tactically, the result was a draw. Both armies survived, bloodied but largely intact. Having survived a deadly ambush and rallied his panicked troops, Ramesses might well consider this a personal victory.

At the strategic level, however, there is no question Ramesses II failed to achieve his objective: the capture of Kadesh. Compelling the Egyptian king to abort his quest, and perhaps taking Upe as well, Muwatalli II could also claim victory. Still, this was only a temporary setback for Ramesses. He and his armies would penetrate even deeper

FIGURE 5.33. Palimpsest relief of an unfinished image of Ramesses II in his chariot. Later the camp scene was carved over the king and his chargers. Luxor Temple pylon, west tower. Photograph by Peter Brand.

into Syria in the coming years. As is often the case in military history, indecisive results allowed both sides to cry victory.[198]

What about the Kadesh Narrative? Was Ramesses II's elaborate memorial of these events a colossal effort at disinformation? Beyond its inflated rhetoric and traditional exaggerations, it is crucial to understand the specific nature of his claims. It is plausible, if not certain, that the Hittite ambush of the Amun encampment failed, after which Egyptian troops drove the enemy chariots into the Orontes River. Ramesses asserts his own valor and fortitude in combat—something even his harshest critics often concede.[199] The claims we find hardest to swallow, the failure of his troops and his single-handed victory, are all traditional elements of royal dogma. Ramesses is no more "dishonest" in this regard than other pharaohs—Thutmose III, Amenhotep II, Sety I—or indeed any ancient king.[200]

Nowhere in the Kadesh record—and this distinction is crucial—does Ramesses II ever claim he *captured* the city. We can see this by comparing the hieroglyphic name labels affixed to conquered towns with similar captions in his later war scenes. In most Ramesside military art, an enemy town the king assaults bears a label describing it as "the town His Person plundered" or similar, and gives its name.[201] By contrast, in Ramesses II's Kadesh scenes, of which we have multiple versions, the caption reads simply: "The despicable town of Kadesh."[202]

Modern critics who accuse him of "lying" about the battle would do well to keep this in mind.

A Propaganda War

Soon after Ramesses II returned to Egypt, his scribes and artist began composing the grand narrative of the battle. Soon, copies of the Poem inscribed on papyrus were circulating among his courtiers.[203] About the same time, draftsmen and sculptors undertook the bold effort to immortalize the battle with panoramic war scenes on temples across the realm.[204]

A closer look at the Kadesh reliefs on various temples at Thebes and Abu Simbel reveals that sculptors reworked them by carving later versions on top of deleted or unfinished originals—resulting in palimpsests in stone (fig. 5.33).[205] Rejecting the artistic compromises in these "first drafts" of his Kadesh narrative, Ramesses ordered a do-over. The final product was both grander and more refined.

The Kadesh Narrative exposes some "bitter truths." In relating how the Hittites outwitted him and surprised his forces with their deadly ambush, Ramesses II revealed his human vulnerability—something earlier pharaohs never admitted to. But why? By overcoming these perils when all seemed lost, Ramesses became a hero.

Notes

1. On the archaeology of Tell Nebi Mend, see Pézard 1931; Parr 1991.

2. Murnane 1990; Klengel 1992, 157–60; Warburton 1997; Singer 2002.

3. See pp. 6–11 above.

4. See pp. 32–33 above. For Syria in the early Nineteenth Dynasty, see Klengel 1992.

5. The literature on the battle is immense. For key reviews of the literature, see *RITANC* II, 21–42; Obsomer 2016. See also the essays in Guidotti and Pecchioli Daddi 2002 and Pecchioli Daddi and Guidotti 2005.

6. Liverani's work (2001, 2013) on ideological themes in Egyptian and ancient Near Eastern textual sources is fundamental and has profoundly influenced my own research. On ideological aspects of Egyptian art, see Leprohon 2015; Brand forthcoming.

7. Liverani (2001, 81, 109, 119–21) contends that a key theme of Ramesses II's Kadesh narrative is how the Hittites broke the rules of proper warfare by ambushing him. For Liverani, this even extends to the "unfair" number of three men to a chariot instead of the "proper" number of two.

8. What Liverani (2001, 119) calls a "polemical theme" about the disloyalty of the army recurs through the Kadesh texts alongside that of the enemy's perfidy. But the notion that Egyptian troops are at best helpless and at worst disloyal crops up in Thutmose III's Megiddo account and Tutankhamun's Restoration Inscription. See also Shirun-Grumach 1998, 1069–71.

9. Liverani 2001, 17.

10. On the counterfactual and propagandistic aspects of the Kadesh narrative, see Liverani 1990, 211–13; 2001, 102. Still, Liverani emphasizes the ideological nature of this "celebrative apparatus." If the Kadesh narrative deceived anyone, Ramesses II himself must be counted the first casualty. Like so many other ancient and modern rulers, he seems to have believed his own hype. Certainly, he maintained his version of events in his correspondence with his Hittite counterpart Hattusili III. See pp. 329–31 below.

11. The theme of the king as a lone champion fighting myriads of enemies is widespread in other ancient Near Eastern royal inscriptions: Liveranni 2001, 79–85.

12. The textual records of these battles are often sophisticated and complex, incorporating a variety of rhetorical devices, colorful language, and well-crafted narratives. They employ hallowed literary conventions like the *Königsnovelle*. Form-critical analyses of New Kingdom military texts have yielded much historical insight: Redford 2003; von der Way 1984; Spalinger 1982; Manassa 2003. Yet, even in the most complex of these narratives, the pharaoh encounters few genuine impediments, which at most only briefly delay his swift and inevitable triumph; see Brand forthcoming.

13. Mynářová 2011.

14. Kitchen regards the account—divorced of supernatural elements, of course—as largely reliable, while Liverani emphasizes the ideological themes and considers them to be so pervasive as to render the historical veracity of the events at Kadesh unknowable.

15. Kuentz (1928) issued the first comprehensive edition of the texts. Kitchen republished all the relevant inscriptions in a convenient synoptic hand copy, along with translations in *KRI* II, 2–147 and *RITA* II, 2–26. His invaluable

commentary provides a summary and discourse on previous scholarship down to the late 1990s: *RITANC* II, 3–54. Other key translations and textual analysis include Gardiner 1960; Lichtheim 1976; Fecht, 1984; von der Way 1984; Davies 1997, 55–96; *COS* 2.5:32–40.

16. Wreszinski 1925, pls. 16–25, 63–64, 68–70, 76, 81–90, 92–106, 169–78; Desroches Noblecourt, et al. 1971; Heinz 2001, 281–93; James 2002, 99–102; Petersen and Kehrer 2016, 358–59; Iskander and Goelet 2015, pls. 2.1.1–2.2.43. For further references see *RITANC* II, 3.

17. The so-called Poem of Pentaweret recorded on two Papyrus manuscripts: P. Raifé/Sallier III and P. Chester Beatty III; see Gardiner 1935. For recent analysis of P. Sallier III, see Spalinger 2002. For meticulous analysis of the linguistic and grammatical structure of the Poem see Spalinger 2021.

18. Gardiner 1960; Fecht 1984; von der Way 1984; *RITANC* II, 5–10. More than anyone, Anthony Spalinger has contributed to our understanding of the Kadesh texts through his meticulous and penetrating analyses: Spalinger 1982, 1985b, 2002, 2003a, 2003b, 2005, 2006, 2007a, 2012, 2018a, 2020, 2021, and forthcoming. On the thematic and structural distinctions between the three textual sources, see Gardiner 1960, 2–4; Spalinger 2012, 376–77.

19. *RITANC* II, 10–13, 42–49.

20. But it is not composed entirely in verse, hence Gardiner's preference for labeling it the "Literary Record." On this distinction, see Gardiner 1960, 2–4; *RITANC* II, 5; Spalinger 2012, 373–77. I have chosen to use the more traditional label of "Poem," abbreviated P, for convenience given how well established it is.

21. This multifaceted literary composition draws from various genres of Egyptian writing and serves multiple aims: von der Way 1984, 95–278; Spalinger 2002, 317–65. In terms of genre, a more appropriate designation of the Poem would be a "victory text," *nḥtw*, as the opening rubric states clearly: "Beginning of the victories of the Dual King Usermaatre-Setepenre, the Son of Re Ramesses-Meramun, given life everlastingly, which he made against the land of Hatti...": P 1–2: *KRI* II, 3. On *nḥtw* as a genre of royal inscriptions lauding the king's prowess in battle, see Spalinger 1982, 224–32. The Poem presents a comprehensive account of Ramesses II's year-five campaign, opening with a royal encomium. It is clear that the narrative sections describing the journey from Tcharu to Kadesh draw heavily on the daily logbooks of the army.

22. P 92–122: *KRI* II, 34–42.

23. See pp. 184–85 below.

24. On the literary devices and thematic tropes in the Poem, which serve to valorize Ramesses II by contrasting his heroism to the dereliction of his soldiers, see von der Way 1984, 152–58; Spalinger 2012, 376–77.

25. It has also been called the "Report," "Record," or "Official Record": Gardiner 1960, 3–4; von der Way 1984, 33–34; *RITANC* II, 7–8; Spalinger 2012, 373. See also Spalinger 1985b.

26. The Bulletin, abbreviated B, thus offers a periscope of the Kadesh campaign by dwelling on one day.

27. B 84–110: *KRI* II, 119–24.

28. B 109–110: *KRI* II, 123:14–124:3. Breasted (1904, 5–7) considered the Bulletin to be merely the largest of these epigraphs, resulting in a bipartite structure for the Kadesh texts. Scholars have almost universally rejected Breasted's view in favor of the conventional tripartite division: Gardiner 1960; *RITANC* II, 5–10; Spalinger 2012. Still, it is true that the Bulletin text is typically

placed adjacent to the camp scene, often beside the king, whereas the text of the Poem is often divorced from the two main scenes on the monuments. On the juxtaposition of the textual and pictorial elements of the Kadesh narrative on temple walls, see Spalinger 2012, 383–89.

29. Reliefs (R) 1–97: *KRI* II, 125–47; *RITANC* II, 8; Spalinger 2003a.

30. R 11: *KRI* II, 131–33; Spalinger 2003a; Servajean 2012; Obsomer 2016. For a detailed critique of the literature on this question, see Obsomer 2016, 109–38.

31. P. Raifé-Sallier III and P. Chester Beatty III. For analysis, see Spalinger 2002.

32. Gaballa 1976, 113–19; Spalinger 1985a; 2003b; 2006, 137–56; Broadhurst 1989; Heinz 2001, 126–48.

33. My interpretation owes much to Spalinger's masterful research on the battle over the past four decades, culminating in his most recent works. If I part ways with his analysis at times it is due to my giving more weight to ideological aspects of the Kadesh accounts and their tendency to conceal and distort the events of the battle.

34. When *mšꜥ* refers to a specific detachment like the "division of Amun," *mšꜥ n 'Imn*, it comprises both infantry and chariotry. The term can distinguish foot soldiers from charioteers in the phrase "infantry and chariotry," *mšꜥ nt-ḥtri*. Derived from the verb "to march," *mšꜥ* literally means "marchers." In this chapter, I have used the terms "army" and "division" interchangeably.

Ramesses II's four armed divisions named for the gods Amun, Re, Ptah, and Seth have a parallel in the larger Beth Shean stela of his father Sety I who named three divisions Amun-Powerful of Bows *'Imn-wsr-pḏwt*, Re-Prodigious of Valor *Rꜥ-ꜥꜣ-ḳnt*, and Seth-Mighty of Bows *Swtḫ-nḫt-pḏwt*: *KRI* I, 12:10–12.

35. On the oft-quoted figure of 5,000 men per division, see *RITANC* II, 39–41; Spalinger 2005, 229; Heagren 2010, 450. This derives from an expedition of soldiers Ramesses IV sent to quarry stone in the Wadi Hammamat that consisted of 5,000 "men of the army/infantry" (*rmṯ mšꜥ*) but only 50 charioteers (*ḳtn*): *KRI* VI, 14:5–6. The ratio of only 50 charioteers to 5,000 infantrymen seems too small, but a quarry expedition in the Egyptian desert is different than a campaign to Syria. The satirical letter in P. Anastasi I also gives a figure of 5,000 soldiers in the context of the rations required to sustain them: Gardiner 1911, 19–20; Fischer-Elfert 1992, 148–57; Heagren 2010, 176–77. Kitchen guesses that the four divisions at Kadesh fielded 500 vehicles with 1,000 crewmen. For calculations on the amount of space an Egyptian division composed of infantrymen and chariots occupied on the march, see *RITANC* II, 40–41; Heagren 2010, 450; Spalinger 2018a, 100–104.

36. Spalinger 2018a, 106–7 considers factors that undermine the putative accuracy of the figure of 20,000 fighting men in Ramesses II's army including the presence of camp followers whose purpose was solely logistical; scribal personnel who documented the events and managed the administration of the army in the field; and inevitable attrition in the ranks that would deplete fighting strength due to men who died or were incapacitated by injury or illness even before the fighting began. These might variously shrink or swell the number of total men in the Egyptian force. To these we might add courtiers, members of the royal family, their attendants, Ramesses II's cup bearers (*wbꜣw*), his bodyguards (*šmsw*) including the Sherden warriors, and non-Egyptian auxiliaries including any Canaanite vassals.

37. This contrasts with the seemingly bureaucratic mindset of some quarry inscriptions like the Wadi Hammamat text dating to the third regnal year of Ramesses IV, which enumerates the numbers and occupation of 8,368 men who survived the trip plus a frank—albeit even—tally of 900 of the dead: K*RI* VI, 14; *RITA* VI, 14–15. More modest was the list of 388 men on another Hammamat quarry trek in Ramesses IV's first regnal year: K*RI* VI, 1; *RITA* VI, 1–2. Here, the author omits a grand total and does not reports any casualties.

38. The texts refer to 2,500 Hittites chariots in the first attack wave and 1,000 for the second. Captions from the scenes identify one corps of 19,000 *Teher*-warriors and "another" (*ki*) consisting of 18,000, but all these figures are suspect: Beal 1992, 290–93; Spalinger 2005, 214–15; 2018a, 92–93 with n. 12, 105; 2020, 140.

39. Spalinger (2005, 152–55 203–4) estimates that the maximum number of troops the economy of New Kingdom Egypt could sustain was at most 40,000 men.

40. On Egyptian infantry combat and weaponry, see Healy 1993, 30–39; Darnell and Manassa 2007, 20; Heagren 2010, 57–73.

41. On the logistics of baggage trains in the New Kingdom army, see Heagren 2007; 2010, 189–209. On supply carts, see Köpp-Junk 2016. For the underappreciated importance of the lowly donkey as a universal beast of burden vital to ancient societies, see Mitchell 2018. Heagren 2010, 196–202 also discusses the logistical importance of donkeys and oxen for supply trains in New Kingdom Egypt's army. The Hittites also relied on donkeys and four-wheeled oxcarts, as illustrated in reliefs from Ramesses II's Abydos temple: Wreszinski 1925, pl. 22; Iskander and Goelet 2015, pls. 2.2.14–2.2.15.

42. Spalinger 2007b and 2011; Veldmeijer and Ikram 2018.

43. On the ideological and iconographic significance of chariots in elite culture of Egypt and the ancient Near East, see Feldman and Sauvage 2010; Sabbahy 2018.

44. Indeed, Drews (1996, 127–34) discounts the role of infantry in combat involving chariot forces in the Late Bronze Age, taking the Battle of Kadesh as paradigmatic. Other scholars have largely rejected Drew's claims: Littauer and Crouwel 1996; Nefedkin 2005; Trimm 2017, 209–10.

45. Littauer and Crouwel (1996) stress that chariots were neither the primary element of Late Bronze Age armies, nor could densely packed masses of chariots charge against each other, which, in their words, "would immediately result in a melée of broken legs and wheels." Moreover, charioteers would have to maintain precise timing and spacing in such formations to avoid colliding with friendly vehicles due to the fact that their axles projected almost ten inches (twenty-five centimeters) from the wheel on both sides like the six chariots from Tutankhamun's tomb.

46. For detailed analyses of the versatile role of chariots in combat, see Nefedkin 2005; De Backer 2009. Both scholars reject the notion of chariots as ancient "armor" that plowed through ranks of enemy foot soldiers.

47. For further objections to the notion that horse-drawn chariots trampled the enemy, see Trimm 2017, 205–6; Spalinger 2020, 166. Here again ideological iconography is at play. Scenes of royal chariots running over the foe are no more real than images of enemy captives stuffed into the cab of Sety I's chariot as it paraded in victory or of Ramesses III standing on prostrate foes as he fires

arrows from the shoreline at their compatriots in ships in a scene from Medinet Habu: Epigraphic Survey 1986, pls. 6, 31; *Medinet Habu I*, pl. 36.

48. For this now-defunct view of chariots, see Schulman 1980.

49. Drews 1996, 127–29. See critiques in Littauer and Crouwel 1996; Heagren 2010, 82 n. 245.

50. On the iconic potency of images of the king in his war chariot, see Spalinger 2011; Sabbahy 2018. Even when he was not in battle, appearing in his chariot displayed and enhanced the pharaoh's glory and divinity. Long after it became obsolete in warfare after the end of the Late Bronze Age, the image of the triumphant warrior parading in his chariot remained a staple of military iconography of the Greeks and Romans, and even in European art until the seventeenth century, as with paintings of Louis XIV riding in triumph in a gilded chariot in murals from Versailles.

51. Littauer and Crouwel 1985; Crouwel 2013.

52. On chariot workshops and manufacturing, see Pusch and Herold 1999; Herold 2006; Morkot 2007; Heagren 2010, 247–49; Crouwel 2013, 82–85; Veldmeijer and Ikram 2018, 97–119.

53. On the problem of chariots breaking down in field conditions, see Nefedkin 2005, 9. The bent pole that attached the cab to the horse yokes was subject to fracture as modern tests confirmed. Chariot wheels and axles were also vulnerable even in ideal conditions. The ancient Chinese annals warn that wheels could break even when marching and inopportunely in battle. The axle of Julius Caesar's ceremonial chariot broke as he rode through Rome for his Gallic Triumph, which nearly threw him from the vehicle: Suetonius, *The Twelve Caesars*, book 37.

54. Royal messengers and other elites often traveled by chariot in the Levant; Abbas 2013. Their vehicles might easily suffer mechanical failure at various points along the way. In one vivid anecdote from the Satirical Letter of P. Anastasi I, the scribe Hori recounts the misfortunes of a nameless chariot officer who loses his way while traveling in the Levant; Gardiner 1911; Wente 1990, 106–9. In a treacherous pass surrounded by hostile Shasu Bedouin, his chariot is damaged under rough conditions, and he attempts to make ineffective repairs. Later, his horses bolt and the chariot crashes. The charioteer longs to enter an armory where craftsmen skilled in leather and woodworking might repair it. The piece exploits the theme of the misfortunes of the soldier's life common in New Kingdom literary works; see Spalinger 2006, "The Paradise of Scribes and the Tartarus of Soldiers." Even as a worst-case scenario, the tale in P. Anastasi I rings true in revealing the many potential types of mechanical failures chariots might suffer and the constant need to maintain them. Chariots, especially in large numbers on expeditions, required daily maintenance once the day's march had ended. One expects that camp followers in Ramesses II's four divisions included wheelwrights and other craftsmen who maintained them. Likewise, there were men who saw to the needs of horses, which—even when not harnessed to their vehicles—walked the entire distance and required care.

55. Ramesses likely traveled most or all of the distance from Tcharu to Kadesh by chariot, but he likely had multiple vehicles at his disposal. If he spent most of the month-long journey riding the same chariot, it would have suffered considerable wear and tear, not least to the precious gilding and inlays of the sort that Tutankhamun's state chariots display. Even with spare parts

and daily maintenance, it would be a challenge to keep one vehicle in good order and—equally importantly—to maintain its appearance for the sake of the king's glory. Nor were all royal chariots gilded, as the four wood-framed chariots in Tutankhamun's tomb demonstrate. Their leather coverings were badly decayed when Carter cleared the tomb, but the leatherwork of the Tano chariot reveals the sophistication and artistry of these vehicles; Veldmeijer and Ikram 2018. The king surely had other horses as a backup in addition to the two steeds named in the Kadesh record.

56. Heagren 2010, 75–76; Spalinger 2018a, 96.

57. The classic study on horseback riding in New Kingdom Egypt is Schulman's 1957, but see now Turner 2021, 253–55. On scouts, see Heagren 2010, 88–89; Trimm 2017, 229.

58. Spalinger 2018a, 96.

59. Menna is designated as a ḳrꜥw, "shield bearer"; see Schulman 1963, 88–89; Spalinger 2013, 238–39.

60. Egyptian *khepesh*-swords would have been of relatively little use to a mounted chariot warrior, except in the most pressing close-range combat. An image of Sety I brandishing his *khepesh*-sword over his head preparing to strike down a Libyan chieftain on foot must be taken as highly artistic license: Epigraphic Survey 1986, pl. 28. In this scene, Sety has one leg hiked over the forward rail of his chariot cab with his foot resting on the yoke pole. With his other hand, he grasps his bow, using it to snare his enemy like a noose around the Libyan chieftain's neck. His chargers' reigns, of course, are tied around his waist. The iconography is magnificent, but none of it is believable. Cf. Ramesses II at Beit el-Wali; Ricke, Hughes, and Wente 1967, pl. 13; see Brand forthcoming.

61. Practical experiments with a modern replica of an Egyptian chariot with one man yielded a top speed of 23.6 mph (38 km/hour); see Spalinger 2018a, 95–96 and nn. 17 and 21.

62. On the potential velocity of Egyptian and Hittite chariots with two and three crew members respectively, see Spalinger 2018a, 95–98.

63. Spalinger 2018a, 96–97. He calculates the theoretical mass of chariots with two horses at 400 kg, the vehicle at 20 kg, and either one (70 kg), two (140 kg), or three (210 kg) crew members. Presumably, the three-man Hittite chariots were larger and more robust than Egyptian vehicles, but slower. For the Hittite chariots, Spalinger posits an average velocity of perhaps 6.8–15.5 mph (11–25 km/hour), with a top speed of 23.6 mph (38 km/hour). Kitchen estimates a velocity of roughly 10–15 mph (10–24 km/hour) for Hittite chariots, with a top speed of potentially 20 mph (32 km/hour); *RITANC* II, 42 and 44. How these estimates would compare to real-world experience is uncertain. Most importantly, how long and across what distance could the Hittite chariots sustain top speed with a full crew?

64. While the smooth sandy dunes in some regions of Egypt's desert wilderness might furnish ideal arenas for encounters pitting massed squadrons of Egyptian chariots against myriads of enemy vehicles in dramatic running battles in ideal conditions, such encounters more often take place in Hollywood movies and historical fiction. One thinks of the departure of Pharaoh's chariots to pursue the Israelites at the climax of Cecil B. DeMille's 1956 epic film *The Ten Commandments*. The Hollywood prop makers manufactured them from steel, not wood, leather, and sinew.

65. On Egyptian chariots and their weaponry, see Darnell and Manassa 2007, 77–80; Heagren 2010, 74–87; Trimm 2017, 210–17. For Hittite chariotry and charioteers, see Beal 1992, 142–91; Trimm 2017, 217–18. For the Hittite side, the data is mostly textual, describing the classes of chariot officers and the role of their vehicles in combat. From the Egyptian side we enjoy a wealth of archaeological evidence of the vehicles and numerous artistic representations of chariots in combat. Textual data is often rhetorical and, like the iconography, highly ideological in nature.

66. The Egyptian artists may have omitted archers from the Hittite chariots in the Battle of Kadesh scenes for aesthetic reasons. With three men crammed into a chariot, their upper bodies take up more space according to the conventions of Egyptian art, which usually depicts the shoulders in a frontal view. The shield held by one of these warriors occupies so much space, it allows just enough space for his comrade to hold a slender lance. There was no room for a bow without making a serious artistic compromise.

67. P 204–205: *KRI* II, 65–66: "As for all who were shooting directly at me, their arrows would scatter when they reached me."

68. Archery went hand-in-glove with the chariot since the latter's introduction into the armory of the Hittites and other ancient Near Eastern cultures: Nefedkin 2005; Genz 2013.

69. Wernick 2013 demonstrates that thrusting a spear at a target from a fast-moving chariot, with a team of horses directly in front of the cab, was not practical. The horses blocked most of a would-be chariot spearman's field of attack, and the warrior could only brandish his spear at an angle from the vehicle's side, increasing the likelihood of snapping his weapon in two on even a glancing blow. Otherwise, the kinetic force of impact would disarm the spearman, or even knock him flying from the back of his vehicle, injuring or killing him outright. At the very least, he would lose the advantage of mobility his chariot offered. Wielding a spear from a speeding chariot was more dangerous to the aggressor and his own horses than to his intended target.

70. Nefedkin 2005; De Backer 2009; Heagren 2010, 82–876.

71. Littauer and Crouwel (1996) emphasize the relative fragility of the chariot as a system due to the vulnerability of its horses to death or injury from enemy weaponry and even from obstacles on the battlefield that could render them lame.

72. Nefedkin (2005, 9) paints a vivid picture of the chaos of the battlefield with the wreckage of disabled vehicles and the agony of wounded and dying men and horses amid the carnage.

73. P 25–33: *KRI* II, 11–13.

74. For the departure of the army from Tcharu, see Spalinger 2013.

75. *RITANC* II, 41–42; Spalinger 2005, 211–12; 2020, 84–87; Heagren 2010, 198–202, 206. Spalinger calculates a rate of 1.8–2.5 mph (3–4 km/hour) owing to the slower speed of the donkeys burdened with supplies and oxen hauling carts and assumes five or six hours of marching per day. I suspect the actual progress varied from day-to-day and includes the possibility that there were layovers at specific points. Did Ramesses stop anywhere in Canaan or at the administrative center at Kumidi Kamid el-Loz in the Beqaa Valley to receive ceremonial homage from his vassals? One of Sety I's war scenes depicts just such an occasion with a crowd of petty kings kowtowing before him: Epigraphic Survey 1986, pl. 4. See Brand forthcoming. On Kamid el-Loz–Kumidi, which he had renamed

"Ramesses-Meramun-the Town,", see *RITANC* II, 15–16. On the archaeological history of Kamid el-Loz, see Charaf 2017. The town is described as being in "the Valley of Conifers"—namely, the Beqaa Valley, which had stands of cedars on the eastern slopes of the Lebanon Mountains.

76. On the army's march across north Sinai and the fortified waypoints with their logistical support facilities, see Heagren 2010, 211–19; Spalinger 2018b, 109–28.

77. Wreszinski 1925, pls. 52 and 92; Desroches-Noblecourt, et al. 1971.

78. P 63: *KRI* II, 23.

79. This is the traditional interpretation: Kuschke 1979; *RITANC* II, 42–43 and map 3. For a different view, see Obsomer 2016.

80. For analysis of the route through Canaan and into the Beqaa, see Kuschke 1979; Heagren 2010, 219–22; Obsomer 2016. Kitchen discusses several key topographical terms from the Kadesh texts: *RITANC* II, 15–21.

81. On this point Spalinger (2005, 211–13) concludes that Pharaoh's strategy was simply to take Kadesh but that he did not expect to fight the Hittites there. Instead, Ramesses planned to take the field at Kadesh, encamp there, and either fight a pitched battle with the citadel's much smaller army or lay siege to the place on the following day, but the Egyptians were clearly unaware of Muwatalli's presence. See also Spalinger 2020, 150–55.

82. The king's "followers," *šmsw*, consisted of his bodyguard and personal attendants including the Sherden: Spalinger 2013, 239–40, 244; Abbas 2016. Its members may have included high-ranking courtiers. On the question of whether Ramesses and his personal entourage were truly isolated from the army, see below.

83. Goedicke 1985, 84–87; Healy 1993, 25–27. Kitchen effectively rebuts the notion of a prearranged battle: *RITANC* II, 28–29, 34. Nevertheless, there may have been a tacit protocol to hostilities, what Spalinger (2007a; 2020, 45) calls "ludic war" or "chivalry." In his view, when an invading army laid siege to a Near Eastern citadel, the local forces often fought a pitched battle in a plain outside the town. Even this did not preclude further resistance necessitating a prolonged siege. Thutmose III's Megiddo campaign illustrates both phenomena.

84. 1 Chr 20:1; 2 Sam 11:1.

85. Spalinger (2005, 214; 2020, 144) cites modern examples of armies that failed to detect large enemy forces even at close range. History provides numerous examples of this phenomena. While Egyptian reconnaissance came up short, it was operating in hostile territory. Who knows how many isolated Egyptian scouts, even in small groups, were intercepted and either killed or taken captive?

86. A select dossier from the Amarna Letters consists of messages to Akhenaten in which vassal kings acknowledge instructions to prepare for arrival of Egyptian troops for a campaign against Kadesh: EA 141, 143–44, 155; see Murnane 1990, 18–19; Darnell and Manassa 2007, 173.

87. On the coercive administrative policies that the Egyptians used to provide revenue for the empire and supplies for their armies during the Eighteenth Dynasty, see Morris 2018, 144–49. Even with a significantly larger army than the one Thutmose III fielded, Ramesses II was able to feed them; Spalinger 2020, 43–44. On the operational logistics of provisioning and watering the army in the field, see Heagren 2010, 161–94. A sufficient supply of potable water was also crucial. During the spring runoff, river courses in the Levant offered ample

supplies, but the Ways of Horus along the north coast of Sinai may have been more challenging. How brackish were the wells and cisterns there?

88. *RITANC* II, 34; Cohen 2000; Spalinger 2020, 44–45.

89. For the importance and date of this much-debated letter, see most recently Spalinger 2005, 162–63; Obsomer 2016, 133–35; Eßbach 2020. For a review of earlier scholarship on the "general's letter," see Rainey 1973; Izre'el and Singer 1990; *RITANC* II, 30–31. Various dates for the letter and for the identity of the Egyptian king have been proposed, including the Amarna period (Izre'el and Singer; Kitchen); Sety I (Eßbach); Ramesses II's year-four campaign (Obsomer); around the time of his Kadesh campaign or shortly afterward (Spalinger).

90. A few scholars have gone so far as to deny that Kadesh was even a target of the year-five campaign, or that the location of the battle was only incidental to the king's strategic purpose. Recently, Obsomer (2016, 123–28) has rebutted one such claim. Spalinger (2020, 138–44) reviews Ramesses II's tactical objectives, order of march, and expectations of enemy resistance as he approached Kadesh. Despite a prudent approach to maneuvering his forces into the combat theater and establishing his command center with the Army of Amun to the north and east of Kadesh, Pharaoh was at the mercy of his intelligence service's failure to detect the presence of Muwatalli's forces, which had reached Kadesh before the Egyptians; Spalinger 2020, 144–55. Nor did the Hittite side escape the fog of war. It is likely Muwatalli was unaware of the *Na'arin* as they approached Kadesh from Amurru and linked up with the Amun division at the crucial hour: Spalinger 2005, 214; 2020, 150.

91. The trope of a fearful enemy king fleeing ahead of Pharaoh turns up in the Kadesh narrative and in Thutmose III's account of crossing the Euphrates River when the king of Mitanni supposedly abandoned the field: *Urk.* IV, 1232: 9–10.

92. For detailed analysis of the provisioning required to support men and animals and the logistics of supplying a New Kingdom army in the field, see Heagren 2010, 159–242.

93. During Thutmose III's reign we learn that the Egyptians organized supply depots at harbor towns along the coast of the Levant from Canaan to as far north as Ullaza to supply his armies during his annual campaigns: Redford 2003, 255–57. See now: Morris 2018, 141–64.

94. B 1–6: *KRI* II, 102–3.

95. *RITANC* II, 16.

96. On fording the Orontes, see Kuschke 1979, 34; Healy 1993, 45–47; *RITANC* II, 39 and 44. Healy points out that historians often dismiss the fording of the Orontes as being of no consequence, but he views it as a more difficult obstacle for the Egyptians and the Hittites, claiming it would have taken the Amun division "a very long time." Kitchen refutes this, reasoning that the Egyptians were long familiar with the problem. Kuschke's comments are based on firsthand knowledge of the area.

97. *Urk.* IV, 587:13–15, 1232:1–6. Thutmose I had also crossed the Euphrates *Urk.* IV, 697:3–5, while Amenhotep II records his crossing of the Orontes during his year seven campaign *Urk.* IV, 1302:7–8. On river crossings in Western Asia, see Heagren 2010, 385.

98. *RITANC* II, 43–44; Spalinger 2005, 212–15; 2020, 138–40.

99. There were two values for this unit of distance. The long *iter* was 6.5 mi. (10.5 km) and the shorter one 1.65 mi. (2.65 km). Spalinger (2005, 212 with n. 9) prefers the long *iter* in this case.

100. For the ensuing intelligence debacle, modern observers often criticize Ramesses for his supposed reckless gullibility, blaming him for the Egyptians' blindness toward the Hittite ruse. Some commentators fault the Egyptian forces for not having adequate scouts. This all seems unlikely. Shortly before the battle, an Egyptian scout captured two of his Hittite counterparts. At Kadesh, the Egypt's intelligence system failed, but this was not due to the lack of such operations. Likewise, it is all too easy to pin the blame on Ramesses himself, but just as he did not fight the battle alone, the king was not the only Egyptian responsible for reconnaissance that day. For scouts in the New Kingdom Egyptian army, which comprises operational or tactical intelligence by contrast with strategic-level intelligence, see Heagren 2010, 88–89, 443–44; Darnell and Manassa 2007, 69. For Ramesses II's scouts at Kadesh, see Spalinger 2020, 141, 145–46.

101. B 7–20: *KRI* II, 103–6.

102. Spalinger (2020, 144) argues that Muwatalli deliberately left the Amun division unmolested on the final leg of its march, preferring to attack only after the Egyptians set to pitching camp.

103. B 21–28: *KRI* II, 107–8.

104. P 41–55: *KRI* II, 16–21. Liverani (2001, 81–82) emphasizes this grand list of names as conforming to the ideological theme of the king fighting alone against myriads of enemies, which is common in royal inscriptions from Egypt and other ancient Near Eastern civilizations. This pattern emerges in other New Kingdom accounts, including the Battle of Megiddo narrative of Thutmose III and Ramesses III's record of his wars against the Sea Peoples and Libyans. The fact that these pharaohs employ this trope need not force us to dismiss their war accounts as ahistorical. At Kadesh, the Egyptian armies likely included Canaanite, Nubian, and Libyan soldiers who could have been subdivided based on differing ethnic groups and homelands. Did Ramesses II also require his Canaanite vassals to send some of their chariots to accompany him to Kadesh? If so, one could imagine Muwatalli commissioning his own account of the battle claiming he had defeated the king of Egypt and his countless allies and mercenaries all alone. Certainly, the theme of Hatti surrounded by enemies and fighting on all fronts is common in Hittite historical texts and Hittite rulers like Suppiluliuma I, Muwatalli II, and Hattusili III frequently take sole credit for victory in war. On the names of foreign peoples and places, see *RITANC* II, 50–52.

105. Bryce 2010, 76.

106. On the Hittite allies at Kadesh, see Bryce 2010, 76 and Trimm 2017, 118–20. They also discuss the role of nonallied contingents in other Hittite wars. See also Hasel 1994.

107. In the Satirical Letter from P. Anastasi I, the scribe Hori tasks his rival with the problem of the food rations needed to support a force of 5,000 soldiers consisting of 1,900 Egyptian men, 500 Sherden, 1,600 Kehk, [100] Meshwesh Libyans, and 880 Nubians: Gardiner 1911, 29:3–6; Wente 1990, 106. A better designation for these foreign contingents in New Kingdom armies is auxiliaries. They were not mercenaries in the sense of hired soldiers; see Spalinger 2005, 6–8; Heagren 2010, 68 and n. 178.

In his Kadesh narrative, Ramesses had no incentive to reveal the size and diversity of his own forces. The Sherden are a special case, being an "exotic" royal bodyguard, and the accounts imply they were few in number. On non-Egyptian troops in pharaonic armies, see Spalinger 2005, 7–8; Trimm 2017, 114–17. While they turn up in various textual and iconographic sources before and during the New Kingdom, including Ramesses II's singling out of the Sherden and the various foreign elements in Ramesses III's war records, the Kadesh Narrative—like most New Kingdom military texts—generally ignores the role of non-Egyptians in Pharaoh's war machine, doubtless for ideological reasons.

108. On the distance and timing of the last stretch of the march from Shabtuna to the Amun camp site, see Spalinger 2005, 212.

109. P 56–62: *KRI* II, 21–23.

110. The image of heroic generalship is a staple of military history. One thinks of Plutarch's accounts of Alexander the Great or Julius Caesar, or the latter's self-aggrandizing *Gallic Wars*.

111. B 29–32: *KRI* II, 108–9.

112. Darnell and Manassa (2007, 177) are more charitable than some, crediting Ramesses with snatching a tactical victory from the jaws of defeat, yet, they also fault him for "racing ahead with but a portion of his force and leaving his other army groups strung out behind ..." The image of Ramesses II outpacing his army with only a small entourage of bodyguards and palace attendants is likely part of the trope of the king as a lone warrior. In any case, the Hittite ambush did not unfold until the whole division of Amun had arrived.

113. Like other ancient polities, New Kingdom Egypt had a system for collecting and digesting intelligence about foreign lands both within and beyond its imperial possessions. Scribes of the "diplomatic corps" situated within the chancery, called the "office of the correspondence of Pharaoh," solicited, received, and translated messages from vassal kings in the Levant as we see in the Amarna Letters. Meanwhile, army scribes and Madjay-police posted with even small garrisons of soldiers in military outposts in places like Nubia recorded data on troop patrols and the movement of local Nubians as we know from surviving daily logs of these institutions from the Middle and New Kingdoms. On intelligence in the Amarna Letters, see Cohen 2000. For Egyptian military intelligence operations, see Heagren 2010, 441–45; Darnell and Manassa 2007, 69–70; Trimm 2017, 76–77. Spalinger's recent study on the generalship of Egyptian kings emphasizes the critical importance of intelligence for effective military leadership and operational success as well as its failures at Kadesh: Spalinger 2020, 12, 39, 44 and n. 85, 113, 141, 144–46, 150–51, 181. The Kadesh narrative indicates that Ramesses II relied on two sets of responsible officials to keep him informed on enemy movements whom he excoriates upon learning of the imminent Hittite ambush: "The chiefs of the lands of Pharaoh" *wrw n pꜣ tꜣw n pr-ꜥꜣ*, namely the vassal kings of the Levant, and "the overseers of foreign lands" *imyw-r ḫꜣswt*, who were Egyptian officials stationed in Canaan and Syria to manage their master's interests there; see Morris 2005, 461.

We should not imagine that Egypt's vassals were reliable informants meekly surrendering crucial and unfiltered intelligence to their Egyptian overlords. It was well within their interests and *modus operandi* to ply Pharaoh with outright disinformation including slanderous accusations of disloyalty to Pharaoh that they frequently lodged against neighboring kings and even Egyptian officials: Murnane 1990, ch. 1; Morris 2018, 177–82.

114. In his recent study on royal generalship Spalinger 2020, 138–40, 142–46 convincingly demonstrates that Ramesses II's advance to Kadesh and his chosen campsite was a prudent tactical maneuver executing a well laid plan, while the spatial disposition of his four large divisions was an operational necessity, not an error in judgment.

115. *RITANC* II, 44. Spalinger 2020, 154 is less certain the Shasu were turned loose.

116. For the ideological theme of the cunning and ruthless enemy in Egyptian texts, see Liverani 2001, 108–21.

117. Spalinger 2020, 148. The evidence for reconnaissance troops in Hittite texts, including mounted scouts and "spies," is ambiguous: Beal 1992, 192, 238, 260–61, 266–68. On Hittite intelligence gathering, see Trimm 2017, 78–81.

118. Spalinger 2020, 140–41 emphasizes these operational constraints, arguing Ramesses did not err by dividing his forces into four large units with an interval of one iter between them. On the marching formation of pharaonic divisions based on interpretation of the Kadesh reliefs, see Heagren 2010, 26–34; Spalinger 2018a, 101–3; 2020, 41–43.

119. On the competence of his generalship, see Spalinger 2020, passim.

120. For analysis of the camp of Amun in the context of logistics, see Heagren 2010, 194–207.

121. R 9: KRI II, 130:11–12; *RITA* II, 19. This broken passage was more complete when Lepsius copied it: LD III, pl. 154. Obsomer 2012b, 231–32 disputes the reading of "god's mother," insisting that the bird's legs, the only part of the crucial sign still visible today, do not belong to a *mwt*-vulture, but to a *w*-quail chick. He also points to the fact that another avian glyph in an adjacent column that Lepsius took to be a *mwt*-vulture is in fact an *ꜣ*-bird. He considers the reading of "god's [mother]" to be impossible, preferring a reading of "[…] goddess." Still, what goddess could this refer to if not a senior royal woman and why is she mentioned in the context of a caption recording the warning to other members of the royal family? Did the goddess need to escape? It is plausible, then, that one or more royal women—the dowager Tuya and/or Nefertari—were present. Tuya held the title "god's mother." As mother of the heir apparent Prince Amunhirkhopeshef, Nefertari also held this title.

122. See p. 263 below.

123. On the military careers of Prehirwenemef and some of his brothers see pp. 258–61 below.

124. Spalinger 2020, 218–20.

125. On his 1667 campaign in Flanders during the War of Devolution, Louis XIV's queen, Marie-Thérèse, the king's current mistress Françoise-Athénaïs the Marquise de Montespan, and Henriette-Anne the Duchesse d'Orléans all attended him, along with other court ladies. On another campaign, the queen tolerated the presence of two royal mistresses, Louise de La Vallière and Madame de Montespan. Louis demanded all the luxuries and spectacles of his royal court be present while he warred in keeping with his regal glory, prompting one observer to note: "All that you have seen of the magnificence of Solomon and the grandeur of the king of Persia does not equal the pomp displayed on this trip": see Fraser 2007, 111; Lynn 2002, 106.

126. The protagonist of the eponymous Tale of Sinuhe is a courtier in service to the princess and royal wife of Senwoseret I named Neferu. Sinuhe states: "I was an attendant who attended his lord, a servant of the royal apartments

(*ipt nsw*), waiting on the king's daughter, the highly praised Royal Wife of King Senwosret in Khenemsut, the daughter of King Amenemhet I in Kanefru, Nefru, the revered." Translation adapted from Lichtheim 1973, 1:223. The tale opens while Senwosret is on a campaign in Lybia where Sinuhe is present. If Sinuhe was performing his regular duties, this implies Senwosret I's wife accompanied him along with her servant Sinuhe.

127. R 2: *KRI* II, 129:6.

128. The tributary is also called Nahr El-Mukadiyah. On the ruins of this Middle Bronze Age fortress the locals call Sefinet Nuh, "Noah's Ark," as Kadesh-the-Old and site of Muwatalli's base camp, see Kuschke 1979; *RITANC* II, 17. At three points B 25, 50, 63 the Bulletin refers to the Hittites as lurking behind Kadesh-the-Old. In the Poem, P 55 they "stood concealed and ready to the northeast of Kadesh."

129. Spalinger 2020, 146–53.

130. *RITANC* II, 44. We are left with no basis for making a more refined assessment other than pure guesswork.

131. Spalinger 2005, 213–14 is incredulous that the massed Hittite chariots would have failed to give rise to so much dust and noise as to alert the Egyptian forces to the impending ambush, but suspects the city and its mound obscured their movements from the Egyptians on the plain. He also wonders that Pharaoh's scouts had not detected them and reported back. But scouts could be intercepted and picked off, and in any case at least one scout returned with enemy agents in tow and alerted his king at the last moment.

132. Healy 1993, 45–47 views the Orontes fords as a major bottleneck, concluding it took the Hittites hours to cross the river. Kitchen takes a more sanguine view of the Orontes as a challenge to either the Egyptian or Hittite forces: *RITANC* II, 39, 44. See p. 170 nn. 96–97 above.

133. The Egyptians would have learned that the Hittite base camp was at Kadesh-the-Old after the battle. On the timing of the Hittite movements, see Spalinger 2018a, 96–99.

134. Healy's contention (1993, 50–51, 54–55) that, "in the absence of scouts," Muwatalli was blind to the approach of the Egyptian forces is unfounded. Clearly they did have scouts and other sources of reconnaissance, not least sentries posted on the ramparts of Kadesh as shown in all the reliefs.

135. *RITANC* II, 44–45; Spalinger 2018a, 96–99.

136. Kuschke 1979, 32–33 and fig. 1.

137. P 72–73: *KRI* II, 26–27. The key Egyptian term is the verb *šfꜥ*, meaning "to cut/slice"; see Spalinger 2018a, 97 and n. 24. He notes that this terminology is more literary than military.

138. B 33–51: *KRI* II, 109–12.

139. B 52–67: *KRI* II, 112–15.

140. B 69: *KRI* II, 116. So, *bṯ ꜥꜣ*. Pharaoh uses the same term in the Poem when he berates his troops for deserting him. P 193: *KRI* II, 62; see Spalinger 2002, 148–51.

141. We can only guess where or how they intersected the Re division.

142. On these formations, see *RITANC* II, 41; Spalinger 2003b; 2005, 217–21; 2018a; Heagren 2010, 26–35; Iskander and Goelet 2015, pls. 2.1.1–2.1.7.

143. Perhaps 20–23.6 mph (32 to 38 km/hour). See p. 167 n. 63 above.

144. B 81: *KRI* II, 118. Even this admission of the army's inadequacy served the ideological narrative.

145. How far the Hittite chariots traveled on their sprint to the Amun encampment depends on whether their starting point was at the Hittite base camp at Kadesh-the-Old (Sefinet Nuh) or, as Obsomer (2016) argues, if Muwatalli had shifted his chariots to a closer starting point just south the citadel. Spalinger provides detailed estimates for the timing of this operation and distance the Hittite chariots covered on their attack run, including their curving velocity as they cut through the division of Re and arced around to the west and north to strike the encampment of Amun on its western side: Spalinger 2018a, 97–99.

146. The sufficiency of the stores of ammunition that Late Bronze Age armies carried—in particular chariots operating in the field—is uncertain. On the one hand, the Egyptians and other ancient civilizations had employed archery since prehistoric times and would have been well aware of the need for adequate stores of arrows. For large armies of the Late Bronze Age operating in the field far from their home base, the logistical challenge of keeping adequate stores of ammunition was likely a challenge. Composite bows and bronze tipped arrows were costly. Likewise, the attrition rate for arrows that might break or be lost in heat of battle was significant; see Heagren 2010, 69 n. 184, 160, 259. He also hypothesizes that a detachment of 50 chariots each carrying a quiver of 80 arrows, the capacity of a quiver according to Pap. Koller, would have 4000 arrows at their disposal: Heagren 2010, 81–82. While chariots often carried more than one quiver, it is also possible these held fewer than 80 arrows each. In battle, one wonders if the Egyptian and Hittite charioteers faced a situation similar to the Spanish Armada and English navy in 1588, when both sides quickly expended most of their stock of gunpowder and cannon shot during their initial encounter. Being isolated from their base camp in the thick of the fray, Hittite charioteers at Kadesh faced a similar dilemma.

147. This distinction is crucial: Spalinger 2020, 149–50.

148. R 12: *KRI* II, 133.

149. R 19: *KRI* II, 135.

150. Like Ramesses at Kadesh, Thutmose III faced a coalition of many enemy kingdoms at Megiddo, where he rallies his troops for a siege with the call "the capture of Megiddo is the capture of a thousand towns." Here again, Thutmose places emphasis on the overwhelming numbers of his opponents. It is surely no coincidence both narratives blame the Egyptian army for failing to do its duty, which Liverani 2001, 119–20 calls the "polemic against the army." See also Shirun-Grumach 1998. I would take issue with her label of "the betraying army" for this theme. The alleged incompetence of Pharaoh's army serves as a foil to his own martial brilliance. Likewise, Tutankhamun's Restoration stela recalls the army's failure prior to his accession, stating bluntly that Egyptian armies had failed in Djahy: *Urk.* IV, 2027:13–14. Here, the army's incompetence is part of the larger "time of troubles" motif. In all these cases, the feckless conduct of the king's officers and troops contrast with his own courage and success on the battlefield. It is one stock theme in the larger genre of the *Königsnovelle*, which often contrasts the boldness and success of Pharaoh's plans and endeavors with the naysaying and timidity of his courtiers, who advise against his initiatives. Inevitably, his action succeeds. On the *Königsnovelle* theme in the Bulletin, see Spalinger 2012. It recurs in the conclusion of the Poem when Ramesses rejects the Hittite king's peace offer after the fighting ends despite his officials speaking favorably of it. See below.

151. P 22–23: *KRI* II, 10. On rhetoric comparing the king to a metallic fortress shielding his troops, see Liverani 2001, 84–85.

152. This imagery dates back to the early Eighteenth Dynasty. In many New Kingdom war scenes, including Sety I at Karnak, no Egyptian other than the king appears on the battlefield, who defeats his enemy single-handedly. When Egyptian soldiers do appear, they conduct "mopping up" operations in the wake of the pharaoh's rampage, capturing prisoners, severing hands of the fallen as war trophies, or finishing off enemies cut down by the king's arrows. In Ramesses II's Kadesh narrative, a few Egyptian soldiers fight in the camp scene or engage in secondary action against surviving remnants of the Hittite foe in the wake of the pharaoh's solo offensive.

153. For analysis of the Menna episode, see Spalinger 2002, 134–56. In Egyptian art, ideology demanded that the king was usually alone in his chariot. In the Amarna Period, Nefertiti sometimes—but not always—rides with her husband Akhenaten in parade scenes. A deity might also accompany the king, as with a scene on Thutmose IV's chariot cab depicting Monthu guiding the king's aim as he shoots arrows at his enemies. This is likely a visual representation of a common trope in New Kingdom military texts that describe Pharaoh "appearing in his chariot as Monthu"; see P 76 and 279; B 84. While it is possible that a king could drive into battle with the reigns of his steeds strapped around his waist while he shot arrows, this does not mean that he would attempt such a reckless stunt: Brand forthcoming.

154. P 274: *KRI* II, 84:1. On these cup-bearers or "royal butlers," see Schulman 1976.

155. The term *ḥm* is often translated as "effeminate," especially in the context of a passive recipient in same-sex activity. It literally means "one who turns backward." It is one component of a larger theme of the gendered stereotype of the effeminate male foreign enemy in Egyptian rhetoric and iconography. See most recently Matić 2021, 114–15.

156. P 205–223: *KRI* II, 66–71.

157. P 221: *KRI* II, 70:13–15 Spalinger 2002, 136–37.

158. The standard tactic for Late Bronze Age chariots was to make a circular hit and run maneuver with chariot drivers rushing toward the enemy and turning away at closer range while the archers fired volleys of arrows: Nefedkin 2005; De Backer 2009; Heagren 2010, 81–84.

159. Schulman 1963, 89–90 considers these "runners" *pḥrrw* to be the third man in Hittite chariots, a view Beal 1995, 202–3 rejects. "Runners" were a class of infantrymen who supported chariot forces in Late Bronze Age chariot warfare; Drews 1996, 141–47. Manassa (2003, 78–80) notes this role was often fulfilled by Sherden warriors and other Sea Peoples in service to Pharaoh. Yet Egyptian troops also served as runners. They appear in the Kadesh reliefs from Ramesses II's Abydos temple as foot soldiers, but do not carry shields like the regular infantry and their weaponry varies as well: Iskander and Goelet 2015, pls. 2.1.2–2.1.7; Spalinger 2003b, 171–73; 2013, 251.

As for the Hittite "runners," or as Spalinger 2013, 245 and 2020, 165 and n. 89 calls them, "fast troops," even if they were not always the third man in the Hittite vehicle, it seems likely they would have relied on chariots to carry them long distances. De Backer (2009, 6–7) emphasizes the use of chariots as "mechanized infantry" and as "personalized carriers for dragoons." As the Egyptians clearly showed, it was possible for a driver to do double duty as a shield bearer.

Another challenge for the runners was keeping up with their speedier chariot-borne comrades.

160. Nefedkin 2005; De Backer 2009; Heagren 2010, 74–87. Heagren (2010, 85–86) emphasizes the point that chariots would close the distance with opposing infantry only after the latter broke formation. Like cavalry, chariots were best suited to harassing foot soldiers or pursuing them in a rout.

161. Spalinger 2005, 215 raises additional imponderables.

162. On the problem of horse fatigue during charges, see Nefedkin 2005, 5–6, 10. He makes the reasonable suggestion that the intensity of combat waxed and waned, with periodic lulls where winded charioteers and their animals took respite and reformed their ranks. While chariot archers could fire on the run, they could also pick their targets with care and fire at a measured pace so as to preserve ammunition. Briefly stopping the vehicle facilitated this.

163. Of course, this depends on how they approached the mass of foot soldiers lodged in the camp. While the artistic record shows some Hittite chariots breaking into the western side of the camp, others seem to envelop it. A significant percentage of Hittite vehicles encircled the camp taking shots at the concentrated troops within and seeking to pick off any Egyptian chariots or foot soldiers who ventured forth. How effective this tactic might have been is impossible for us to know. Groups of Egyptian chariots, including Pharaoh and his posse, would have broke free of the confines of the camp before the Hittite surrounded it.

164. Bruyn (1989) claims the Hittites launched a two-pronged attack, one force crossing the Orontes north of Kadesh and the other to its south. Kitchen refutes this, noting that the Hittite chariots struck the west side of Pharaoh's camp, but not the east as one would expect if a second force crossed the river north of the citadel: *RITANC* II, 33.

165. P 143–153: *KRI* II, 48–51.

166. P 63–64: *KRI* II, 23–24. The identity of this "first battle line" or "front-line troops" *skw tpy* has prompted much debate, although it is likely identical to the *Na'arin* troops named in the long caption text R 11; see *RITANC* II, 42; Servajean 2012, 1–14. For the most recent and detailed overview of the debate concerning these terms and their significance for reconstructing the battle, see Obsomer 2016, esp. 99 104 (*n'rn*), 104–7 (*skw tpy*), with a review of the literature and conclusions (110–40).

167. The location of this wooded area is likely at modern El-Labwe 12 mi. (18 km) south of Qamuat Hermel: *RITANC* II, 18. See also Obsomer 2016, 96 and fig. 22 there.

168. R 11: *KRI* II, 131–33. For a detailed reconstruction and analysis of this crucial text, see Obsomer 2016, 93–98,

169. Few scholars question this notion.

170. Ramesses mounted his chariot, not the horse himself. As Spalinger (forthcoming) has now shown, "Victory in Thebes" refers not to the paired team of horses, but the leading stallion himself. Elsewhere, the Poem also names his teammate "Mut Is Content." See p. 155 above.

171. B 84–108: *KRI* II, 121–24.

172. R 40: *KRI* II, 138. Illustrated at Abydos (Iskander and Goelet 2015, pls. 2.2.10–11) and the Ramesseum (Wreszinski 1925, pl. 106; Kitchen 1982, 62, fig. 21.).

173. *RITANC* II, 46–47.

174. P 229–250: *KRI* II, 73–77.

175. P 253–275: *KRI* II, 78–84.

176. P 74: *KRI* II, 27; B 81: *KRI* II, 118. The term used is *bdš*, "to grow weak."

177. Relief captions from the Ramesseum's second court: R 23–39: *KRI* II, 137–38; see *RITANC* II, 53–55; Spalinger 2005, 226.

178. Abydos Temple of Ramesses II: Wreszinski 1925, pls. 16–17; Iskander and Goelet 2015, pls. 2.2.18–2.2.23. Abu Simbel: Wreszinski 1925, pls. 170–71; Desroches Noblecourt et al. 1971. Karnak Great Hypostyle Hall: Wreszinski 1925, pl. 76; Kuentz 1928, pl. 8f, 25. Karnak, south axis: Wreszinski 1925, pl. 70. For the practice of taking hands as trophies, see most recently Matić 2019, 2021.

179. R 42: *KRI* II, 139.

180. Prakash 2011; Mynářová 2011.

181. Had Muwatalli and his *Teher*-warriors marched from the ruins of Kadesh-the-Old to gather in and around the city?

182. For a meticulous analysis of the second day of fighting, see Spalinger 2007a. He emphasizes the "ludic" quality of the event as a prearranged battle in the morning when both sides tacitly consented to engage.

183. P 295–320: *KRI* II, 90–95.

184. Brand 2007a, 26–28.

185. P 328–330: *KRI* II, 97.

186. The Bulletin account has three separate incidents of the *Königsnovelle* type: (1) Ramesses II's interview with the Shasu Bedouin, (2) the revelations of the captured Hittite scouts when Pharaoh upbraids his officials, and (3) when he receives the Hittite king's message after the second day of fighting. On the *Königsnovelle* theme in the Kadesh account see most recently Spalinger 2012, 381–83, 389–93; see also Shirun-Grumach 1998.

187. P 332–334: *KRI* II, 98–99.

188. In the mundane world, delegations of high officials and priests bearing bouquets from temple altars greeted the king on his return as we see in a scene from Sety I's Karnak war monument: Epigraphic Survey 1986, pls. 40, 43.

189. *RITANC* II, 14; Bryce 2005, 239.

190. KUB 21.17 i 14–21 with duplicate KUB 31.27:2–7 (CTH 86): Translation by Beal 1992, 307; see also Edel 1950, 212; Mauer 1985; Bryce 2005, 240.

191. Alternatively, Hattusili might be referring to events following one of Sety I's campaigns.

192. Called Aba in CTH 86 (i 17, 18, 20; see n. 190).

193. Brand 2007a.

194. *RITANC* II, 14; Bryce 2005, 239–41. The tentative reference to Sidon is partially preserved in KBo 1.15 + KBo 1.19 obv. 38′ (CTH 156): *ÄHK* I, 60–61, no. 24. Cordani (2017, 85–87), in her much more judicious translation of the missive no. 13, omits the key passage, considering it too fragmentary for translation. On the epistolary dispute over Kadesh between Ramesses II and Hattusili III see pp. 329–31 below.

195. Bryce 2005, 238–41.

196. Nor did it fail to irk the Hittites, particularly Muwatalli's successor Hattusili III: Liverani 1990. See pp. 329–31 below.

197. See *RITANC* II, 45–46; Spalinger 2005, 226.

198. A modern example of this phenomenon is the 1973 Arab-Israeli War. The Israelis and Western observers regard the final outcome as a victory for the Jewish State. Yet the Egyptian leader Anwar Sadat claimed the Egyptian

crossing of the Suez Canal at the outset of the October War, as the Egyptians call it, constituted a triumph for Egypt. October sixth remains a public holiday in Egypt. There is a museum and war monument complete with Egyptian tanks and jet aircraft, along with the wreckage of a downed Israeli fighter jet, in the Heliopolis district of eastern Cairo. On the concept of decisive battles in history, see Harari 2007.

199. Murnane 1995b, 210–11 argues that the point of the Kadesh narrative is straightforward: to laud Ramesses II's personal bravery. Such an obvious purpose often escapes modern observers who seek a more subtle meaning, subtext, or polemic. An example is Assmann's misguided historical reconstruction of the lead-up to Kadesh, in which he claims Ramesses sought to discredit a "war party" among the military high command by pinning the blame on his generals for the Kadesh debacle. He imagines that bellicose generals plunged Egypt into a long war with Hatti after the death of Tutankhamun/Niphururiya: Assmann 1984; 2002, 247–71; von der Way 1984, 379–83. This is fanciful and misreads the evidence. Ramesses was no dove, as his aggressive campaigns after the Battle of Kadesh attest and his own resistance to peace overtures from the Hittites amply shows. See chs. 6 and 9.

Coming at the issue from a historical viewpoint, Murnane 1995b, 209–11 refutes Assmann's scenario, arguing that the king's opprobrium was not directed at the army as a whole but against both his military and civilian advisors. Goedicke 1985 offers a bizarre interpretation of the Kadesh narrative, arguing the king decimated his own troops as "rebels" on the second day of the incident, repeated by Healy 1993. For Kitchen's devastating critique, see *RITANC* II, 27–29.

200. See Spalinger's pertinent remarks 2012, 381. He notes that Ramesses stood in mortal peril at Kadesh, while Thutmose III had the tactical advantage at Megiddo. Nor was Ramesses any less "truthful" than his predecessors. On the quality of these two kings as field commanders, see also Spalinger 2020.

201. Examples abound in Ramesses II's later war scenes from Karnak and Luxor: *KRI* II, 153:5, 155:11, 156:5, 158:5, 159:15, 181: 2–3 and 11, 182:5–6 and 12–13. Ramesses II's Kadesh labels are comparable to two examples from Sety I's Karnak war scenes constructed on the formula *pꜣ dmi NN*, "the town N": *KRI* I, 8:16 Pa-Canaan; 13:4 Ycnoam; 14:7 Qader in the land of Hinuma. But while Sety attacked and captured Yenoam and Qader, he only fought a battle against the Shasu in open country beside the town of Pa-Canaan. In Sety's Kadesh battle scene, the label refers to the king's "ascent," *ts*, against Kadesh and Amurru. See ch. 2.

The most commonly used phrase in fort labels from Ramesses II's later war scenes are *dmi fḫ.n ḥm=f*, "the town that His Person destroyed." On the term *fḫ*, literally "to loosen" but meaning "to destroy," see Hasel 1998, 33–34. Other variants include *dmi in.n ḥm=f*, "the town that His Person captured," literally "brought": *KRI* II, 170:15, 173:1; Hasel 1998, 65–67 and *dmi ḥꜣq pꜣ ḫpš tnr pr-ꜥꜣ*, "the town that the mighty arm of Pharaoh plundered": *KRI* II, 172:5, 180:3, 181:4; Hasel 1998, 71–73.

202. R 49: *KRI* II, 140.

203. The copy of the Poem on P. Sallier includes a colophon crediting the manuscript as being made in regnal year nine of Ramesses II by the hand of a scribe named Pentaweret. As Spalinger (2002, 106–15) has clarified, the specific copy that Pentaweret, a prominent scribe during the reign of Merenptah,

made does not date to Ramesses II's ninth year, but the composition itself had appeared shortly after the battle.

204. See Spalinger 2006, 137–56.

205. Spalinger 1985a; Brand 2011.

Chapter Six

Great of Victories: Ramesses II's Later Wars

Ramesses II's epic encounter with Muwatalli II at Kadesh did not end the long Egyptian-Hittite conflict. In the coming year the war continued on two fronts. Abroad, Ramesses fought aggressive wars in Canaan and Syria on at least two more occasions, in the eighth and tenth years of his reign. At home, Pharaoh ordered his scribes and artisans to immortalize his Kadesh campaign through monumental inscriptions and bas-reliefs conceived on a scale far surpassing accounts of any single event in pharaonic history. In telling this story, his court poets dared to transform the traditional image of the warrior king.

Without a doubt, Ramesses II suffered a military setback at Kadesh. But how did this impact Egypt's hegemony in the Levant? Just after Kadesh, Muwatalli's forces occupied Egypt's northern province of Upe. Their grasp proved to be ephemeral, just as Suppiluliuma's incursions had been during the Amarna period.[1] Kadesh and Upe stood as the effective border between these rival empires, with neither able to dislodge the other across the frontier.[2]

But what of Pharaoh's Canaanite subjects? Did they now perceive Egyptian weakness and rise up in rebellion?[3] Ramesses marched his armies through Canaan and Galilee in his eighth and tenth regnal years, assaulting any citadels that dared to oppose him. He also penetrated deep into Syria on both occasions, capturing towns well north of Kadesh: Dapur, Tunip, and Ullaza.[4] In the long run his aggressive strategy failed to wrest control of these lands from the Hittite Empire, but Egypt maintained its traditional hegemony over Canaan and Lebanon.

The Literary War: Transforming the Image of Pharaoh in Battle

Ramesses II's Kadesh account was revolutionary, not only in its epic scale but in the way it portrayed him. Along with the usual elements of royal dogma, it presents Pharaoh, for the first time, facing genuine peril. His vulnerability heightens the dramatic impact of the story, but conflicts with the age-old image of the pharaoh as invincible warrior. To appreciate this fundamental change we must first consider traditional metaphors describing the king in battle.

In the rhetoric of their battle accounts, Egyptian kings portrayed themselves as akin to fierce predatory animals. Scribes evoked vivid imagery comparing their sovereigns to dangerous beasts: lions and leopards, cobras and crocodiles, wild bulls and baboons.[5] A caption from Sety I's battle scenes at Karnak epitomizes this imagery:

> Divine falcon, dappled of plumage, sailing across the heavens like the incarnation of Re. Upper Egyptian jackal, swift running, who traverses this land in a moment. Savage lion treading secret paths in every foreign land. Mighty bull, sharp horned and strong willed, who tramples the Asiatics, who crushes the Hittites, who slays their chiefs, casting them down in their own blood, who goes among them like a blast of fire, making them nonexistent.[6]

While scribes colored their descriptions with graphic imagery and striking metaphors, subtle shades of meaning in their jargon may still elude us. Fortunately, scribes provided clues called semantic determinatives. Determinatives are additional hieroglyphic signs placed at the ends of words. Rather than giving the sound of a word, they use imagery to convey a more precise meaning. Terms denoting movement have a pair of walking legs ⏁ indicating a verb of motion. Vigorous and violent actions receive the determinative of a man brandishing a staff 𓀜 to bludgeon some opponent. When indicating an abstract concept, scribes inserted a papyrus scroll glyph ⊠ as the symbol for an abstract idea.

Determinatives representing animals may offer clues when we consider that creature's natural behavior. A hymn in praise of Thutmose III's warlike deeds describes him as lightning-quick when he attacks his enemies:

> He is a king who fights alone without a multitude backing him up. He is more effective than a million numerous soldiers, and his equal has never been found, (he is) a warrior with a strong arm on the battlefield. There is no one left standing around him, who immediately overpowers every foreign land at the head of his army when he flashes among the two (groups) of (enemy) bowmen like a star when it crosses the sky.[7]

The key phrase here is "flashing (*seshed*) … like a shooting star" The Egyptian verb *seshed* conveys instantaneous movement by a meteor or a streak of lightning in the night sky, winking in and out of existence in a split second.[8] But what exact shade of meaning does the term convey? Offering us a clue, the scribe employs a crocodile hieroglyph 𓆊 as its determinative.[9] The action is instantaneous. As for the term *seshed*, the crocodile determinative indicates movement as quick as a crocodile's ambush.

Another word describing Pharaoh on the attack is *khar*, which means something like "to rage."[10] According to the Kadesh Bulletin, Ramesses II "raged" against his enemies in the heat of battle.[11] Here, the scribe inserts a baboon hieroglyph as its determinative. We can grasp the nuance of this word by considering the aggressive behavior of baboons, especially the vicious threat displays by the alpha male troop leader. With his long incisors he savagely dominates his troop and keeps all rivals at bay. As the ultimate alpha male, Pharaoh in battle transforms into a berserker who metaphorically "goes ape."

Similes casting Pharaoh as an ambush predator first appear at the dawn of Egyptian civilization and remain pervasive in art and literature for over two millennia.[12] The script remains identical, whether in Thutmose III's account of the Battle of Megiddo or the war records of Thutmose I, Amenhotep II, or Sety I. Girded in armor and equipped with his panoply of war, Pharaoh mounts his glittering chariot as the living incarnation of the war god Monthu. He hurtles at his doomed foes, who collapse immediately under his ferocious onslaught.

Court poets delight in likening their sovereign to a blast of fire, a raging panther, a ravenous lion, a swooping falcon, a rampant griffon, or the deadly cobra goddess affixed to his brow, spitting fiery venom at his enemies. Egypt's ruler has no equal in battle, only helpless prey. It is not a fight; it is a slaughter. Egyptian texts recount this carnage in gruesome detail. Shot down by his arrows and trampled under the hooves of his chariot team, the king's victims pile up into mounds of corpses.

Pharaoh as Hero in the Kadesh Narrative

By placing Ramesses II in mortal peril, the Kadesh chronicle introduces a novel element to this traditional narrative. After the enemy ambushes him and his own troops desert him, the outcome, for the first time, hangs in doubt. By exposing Pharaoh's vulnerability in combat, the authors of the Kadesh narrative deviate from traditional dogma stretching back two millennia. Before Ramesses II, the narrative arc of Egyptian battle accounts was simple—Pharaoh massacres his enemies in an instant.[13] The narrative of Kadesh puts the lie to this age-old doctrine of royal omnipotence and omniscience. The enemy dupes Ramesses with false intelligence. His own troops abandon him in the fray. While Egyptian battle accounts always present the king as an army of one—a solo warrior who triumphs over millions—no Pharaoh ever appeared as isolated and vulnerable in battle as Ramesses II does at Kadesh.[14] The hunter stands at bay as his enemies stalk him like roving packs of hyenas encircling a lone lion:

Then His Person sped off at a gallop, entering into the midst of the enemy forces of the losers of Hatti, being entirely alone without another beside him. His Person went to look around and found himself surrounded by 2,500 chariots cutting off his escape—all the runners of the losers of Hatti together with numerous foreign countries who were with them: from Arzawa, Masa, Pitassa, from Gashgash (Kaska), from Arawanna, Kizzuwatna, from Aleppo, from Ugarit, Kadesh, and Lukka. They were three men to a chariot team acting as a unit. But there was no official with me, no charioteer, no soldier of the army, no shield-bearer, for my infantry and my chariotry retreated before them. Not one of these stood firm to fight with them![15]

In the Poem, Ramesses beseeches his divine father Amun-Re in his moment of crisis, reminding the god of all the pious works and generous acts he has performed on Amun's behalf. Nor does Pharaoh shy away from reproaching the deity for his current plight:[16]

What is this O my father Amun?
Does a father ignore his son?
Would I do something without you?
Indeed, do I not go forward and stand still at your word?
I have not disobeyed a plan you have decreed
How much greater is he, the Great Lord of Egypt,
than to permit foreigners to draw near his path?
What are they to you, O Amun, these Asiatics, despicable and ignorant
*   of god?*
Indeed, have I not made for you great myriads of monuments?
I have filled your temple with my plunder
I have built for you my Mansion-Temple of Millions of Years
I gave to you all my property as a testament
I have presented to you every land gathered together to supply your
*   divine offerings*
...
What will they think if something bad happens to one who relies on your
*   counsel?*
I have called out to you O my father Amun, amid a multitude whom I
*   know not*
Every foreign country is united against me, and I am alone in (their)
*   midst without another beside me*
My numerous infantrymen have abandoned me; no one has looked for
*   me among my chariotry*
When I was shouting to them, not one of them heard me as I called out.[17]

In response to this pious harangue Amun intervenes, turning the tide of battle against his Hittite foes:

I found Amun to be more effective than millions of infantrymen, or hundreds of thousands of chariots, or tens of thousands of men, whether

brothers or sons, though united with one will. There is no deed of many
men but Amun is more effective than they. I have achieved (all) this by
the counsels of your mouth O Amun. I have not exceeded your counsel.

Now I have made a petition from the ends of the earth, my voice
echoing in Southern Heliopolis (Thebes). As soon as I called out to him,
I found Amun came. He gave his hand to me and I rejoiced. He called
out (all) around me as though we were face-to-face: "Go forward, I am
with you, I am your father, my hand is in your hand. I am more effective
than hundreds of thousands of men. I am the lord of victory who loves
bravery!"[18]

Ramesses II now rallies and triumphs single-handedly over the Hittites. Here his Kadesh account differs from those of his regal forebears only in its epic scale. But the route to victory has exposed his vulnerable human side. Pharaoh lacks omniscience and cannot choose the time and place of battle. His foes are treacherous and waylay him in ambush. His own troops are cowards who desert him in the fray. Facing these calamities, Ramesses is indignant, perhaps even fearful, doubting for a moment even the justice of Egypt's greatest god.

All these plot points expose Ramesses II to harsh criticism from his modern detractors, who declare him rash, naïve, reckless, and incompetent.[19] Furthermore, his critics accuse him of deceit. For considering all the misadventures and blunders leading up to that fateful day, how can we regard the king's claim of victory over the Hittite ambush as anything less than a boldfaced lie? Surely, they contend, he suffered a crushing defeat. But every adverse detail we know about the battle is one that Pharaoh and his scribes *chose* to tell us.

Ramesses II took an ideological risk by introducing this complex and ambivalent storyline to his retelling of the battle. But why? By highlighting the adversity that he faced at Kadesh, this narrative transforms Ramesses into a genuine hero. He confronts a moment of crisis and mortal peril. Only then does he win the support of his god and triumph in the end. This real doubt and danger magnifies his final victory.

By tradition, Pharaoh was a supernatural warrior who instantly and effortlessly prevailed over his foes as the champion of Maat against Chaos. Yet, in his Kadesh narrative, Ramesses II tells how he faced real danger, but overcame it to become the first truly *heroic* Pharaoh.[20]

Ramesses II's Military Campaigns after Kadesh

Although it was a pivotal event in his reign, the Battle of Kadesh did not end Ramesses II's active military career. He returned to Canaan and Syria at least two more times.[21] As with his first campaign in year four, our sources for his later expeditions are sparser and much less detailed than the Kadesh chronicle. We are not even sure how many campaigns Ramesses led, and none of the records assign a number to these forays, such as a "third" or a "fourth campaign of victory."[22]

The offensive in year eight is the best attested of these. A large triumphal inscription from the Ramesseum is our primary source for this expedition.[23] Battle scenes from various temples are undated and less informative than the Kadesh narrative.[24]

Ramesses II also left three triumphal stelae at Nahr el-Kelb, the "Dog River," in Lebanon north of Beirut.[25] Carved in chalky limestone cliffs, over the centuries all three inscriptions have weathered badly, and we can recover little of their hieroglyphic texts. One stela dates to year four, marking the king's first campaign. Next to it a second is dated as regnal year ten, but its text has eroded beyond legibility. In the 1860s the soldiers of the Emperor Napoleon III engraved the third stela with a French text before anyone recorded its ancient inscriptions scientifically. It likely celebrated either the year five Kadesh campaign or his year eight expedition.

The Year Eight Campaign

A relief on the Ramesseum's Pylon gateway displays a list of fortified towns that Ramesses II conquered in his eighth year (fig. 6.1).[26] His artisans conceived of this triumphal panorama on a vast scale. It depicts a large group of defeated citadels, each bearing a label text identifying it as "the town His Person captured in regnal year eight," followed by its name. Departing from each of these towns, one of Ramesses II's sons leads a small group of bound captives (fig. 6.2).[27]

The north wall of the Ramesseum that once adjoined the year-eight list has vanished (fig. 6.3), but we can gain a sense of the lost war scenes that once graced it by analogy with intact examples from Ramesses III's nearby royal cult temple at Medinet Habu,[28] which features a curious mixture of contemporary and anachronistic battle episodes.[29] One sequence depicts Ramesses III fighting against Syrians and Hittites in citadels in Amuru, Tunip, Ullaza.[30] His artisans took inspiration from out-of-date battle art from the Ramesseum[31] since, by Ramesses III's day, no Egyptian army had set foot this far north in ninety years.[32]

The list of captured towns on the Ramesseum's pylon, although fragmentary, reveals that this campaign was no less ambitious than his earlier Kadesh offensive, ranging across the Levant from Canaan to Syria.[33] At least two towns in Galilee appear in the Ramesseum's year eight list, and others turn up in undated war scenes at Karnak and Luxor.[34] Had mutiny erupted among Pharaoh's Canaanite subjects far to the south of the Egyptian-Hittite front line?[35] If so, the pharaoh swiftly

FIGURE 6.1. Lepsus's drawing of a scene from the pylon of the Ramesseum with a pictorial list of Canaanite and Syrian towns Ramesses II captured in his eighth regnal year. From each town one of his sons leads away groups of prisoners. NYPL digital collections. Public domain.

FIGURE 6.2. A prince drives Syrian and Canaanite prisoners from one of the towns captured in year eight. Photograph hy Peter Brand.

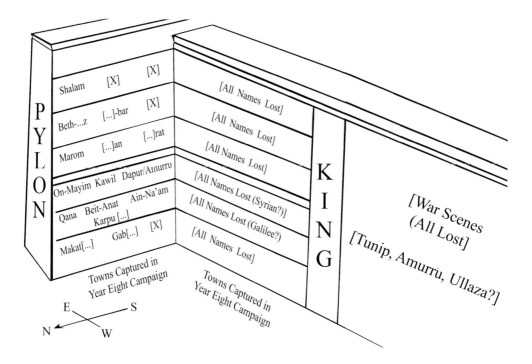

FIGURE 6.3. Hypothetical reconstruction of the north exterior wall of the Ramesseum. Only the west face of the pylon still stands. Drawing by Peter Brand.

crushed them. Defeating his most wayward vassals quickly overawed the rest. Perhaps Ramesses followed the strategy of Sety I's first campaign, picking fights with his vassals at the slightest provocation, to dispel any lingering sense of Egyptian weakness after the events at Kadesh.

After quelling any mutiny in Canaan, Ramesses II invaded Syria once again, striking deep into the heart of Amurru, where he attacked several enemy towns subject to Hatti. In this daring riposte to his setback at Kadesh, a number of Syrian citadels, including Dapur and Kawil and perhaps Tunip and Ullaza as well, fell before Pharaoh's onslaught.[36] How many Syrian towns Ramesses besieged in year eight is unclear, because at least a dozen names on the Ramesseum list of conquered strongholds are damaged or missing. Despite venturing even deeper into Hittite territory, the pharaoh avoided tangling with Kadesh. Had his previous encounter spooked him? Or did he plan to cut it off from Hittite support, so that it would fall into his grasp?[37]

The Battle of Dapur

One of the proudest moments in Ramesses II's military career came when he conquered Dapur, a key Hittite stronghold near Tunip in Syria (fig. 6.4).[38] Dapur turns up in the year-eight list from the Ramesseum and in two battle scenes, one from the Ramesseum's hypostyle hall

(fig. 6.5) and the other on the west exterior wall of the Luxor Temple forecourt. In the Luxor version, Pharaoh storms Dapur on foot; at the Ramesseum he attacks in his chariot.[39] Adjoining these pictorial records is a hymn extolling Ramesses as a valiant warrior:

FIGURE 6.4. Ramesses II assaults Dapur on foot. Scene from the west exterior wall of the Ramesside forecourt at Luxor Temple. Behind the king, a text records a speech in which Ramesses boasts of fighting without wearing his body armor. Courtesy Erika Feleg.

> *The Good God, mighty of valor in foreign countries, stout-hearted in battle, firm with the horse team, brilliant in the chariot; who, when he takes up a bow, shoots and captures because he cannot miss. One who grips the reins knowing the skill of his own hand, who leads in battle and returns only after he has triumphed over the loser of Hatti, scattering him like chaff in the wind. He (the Hittite king) has abandoned his town through fear of him (Ramesses). He has set his power on him daily, his might being in his limbs like fire.*
>
> *The bull who fights on his borders and seizes his rebels. He has not permitted (even one) to escape from his hand. He is a thunderstorm over foreign countries, great of war cry, who sets a hurricane against the chiefs to plunder their cities, who turns all their places into red mounds. His arrows pursue them like Sakhmet, stifling breath in the noses of the defiant ones from the land. Hatti is strangled for opposing him, the Dual King Usermaatre-Setepenre, the Son of Re Ramesses-Meramun, given life.[40]*

This panegyric exalts Pharaoh as an all-conquering warrior. In this sense it is traditional. The second element of the Battle of Dapur texts revisits the new theme of Ramesses as a risk-taking, and potentially vulnerable, "action hero," which his scribes first developed in the

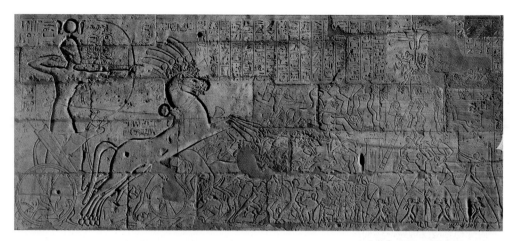

FIGURE 6.5. Ramesses II assaults Dapur in his chariot. Scene from the first hypostyle hall of the Ramesseum. Photograph by Peter Brand.

Kadesh narrative.[41] Here, Ramesses boasts of his reckless bravado in a long-winded speech. In extoling his own courage, Pharaoh belabors the point by repeating himself. Still this address offers a fascinating insight into an Egyptian king's personal speech patterns and self-image:

> *The King himself said: "As I live, as Re loves me, as my father Atum praises me, and makes my nostrils youthful with life and dominion when My Person is on the throne of the Two Lands: As for this matter of (my) standing and fighting against this Hittite town in which there is a statue of Pharaoh, L.P.H., His Person, L.P.H., has very truly done it in the presence of his infantry and his chariotry! His Person, L.P.H., was in front of his infantry and his chariotry fighting against the town of those losers of Hatti who were in the region of the town of Tunip in the land of Naharin.*
>
> *His Person took up his body armor to place it on himself (only) after His Person, L.P.H., had spent two hours standing and fighting against the town belonging to the Hittite enemies in the presence of his infantry and his chariotry [without his] body armor being on him. His Person returned to take up his body armor to place it on himself (only) after he had already spent two hours attacking the town of the Hittite enemies in the district of the town of Tunip in the land of Naharin (when) he did not have body armor on him."*[42]

The chief point of this chatty statement is that the valiant king gamely exposed himself to danger. History would have unrolled differently had some enemy bowman landed a lucky shot! In the Battle of Dapur scene at Luxor Temple, Ramesses does wear his coat of armor, consisting of an ankle length shirt of leather studded with overlapping bronze scales. Although it offered less protection against a cutting or bludgeoning weapon, this armor was most effective against an arrow shot.[43]

Ramesses does not stand behind an arrow shield as some of his sons do, fighting beside him in the Ramesseum version of his assault on Dapur.[44] The Egyptian army and Pharaoh's own sons bear witness to his heroism, even as they too engage the foe. As with Kadesh, the narrative introduces this novel element of royal vulnerability. This time, however, he takes the risk voluntarily. His sons and his army also get at least some credit for taking part in the battle (fig. 6.6).

Some view Ramesses II's comment about his statue standing in Dapur as proof he captured the place on two separate occasions. In this scenario, Ramesses first conquered Dapur in his eighth year and erected a statue of himself there, then returned in year ten to recapture the city after it fell back into Hittite control. However, this stretches the evidence too far, and we may safely conclude he took Dapur only once, during his year-eight campaign.[45]

FIGURE 6.6. Detail of the Battle of Dapur from the Ramesseum. The king's sons lead the assault on the town. Photograph by Peter Brand.

The Moabite Campaign

From war scenes carved on the eastern wall of his forecourt at Luxor Temple, we know Ramesses II's forces ventured across the Jordan River into the biblical land of Moab, east of the Dead Sea.[46] These battle scenes lack dates, but Ramesses invaded Moab sometime after his Kadesh campaign, likely during the first decade of his reign, perhaps in year seven.[47] Among the damaged and obscure place names attached to enemy towns in these reliefs, one stands out as being familiar: the town of Dibon named in the biblical book of Exodus.[48] Another is labeled "the town which the valiant arm of Pharaoh, L.P.H., conquered in the land of Moab: Butaru."[49] Two texts on a stela and an obelisk from Northern Egypt refer to the king's triumph over Shasu Bedouin at "the Mountain of Se'ir," in biblical Edom, hinting that his armies ventured north of Moab.[50]

But why did Ramesses campaign in Transjordan? Captions from the Luxor Temple war scenes hint that the Hittites were stirring up Moabite opposition to Egypt. In one episode the pharaoh addresses his eldest son Prince Amunhirkhopeshef, deputizing him as an envoy to the defeated Moabites: "The King speaks to the Hereditary Prince and Senior King's Son, Amunhirkhopeshef: 'Speak with the chief of the foreigners—make him understand his evil deed.'"[51] The young prince berates these vanquished enemies, denouncing them for associating with his father's greatest foe (fig. 6.7):

> You are evil. One does not know your good deeds, so One (= the king) says in the palace, L.P.H., for you have allied yourself with the Hittite (king), another evil one just like every other (one) of your kind.[52]

Given Ramesses II's ongoing aggression against their own Syrian provinces, the Hittites would be eager to stir up resistance to Egypt in Canaan.[53] But surely no Hittite army ever ventured so far south. As for the petty kings of the ancient Near East, receiving envoys from any Great King besides their imperial overlord was treason. Whether Moab and Edom were rebellious vassals of Egypt's Levantine empire or independent realms beyond its border, Pharaoh brooked no Hittite interference in the region. They now became targets of his wide-ranging campaigns in the aftermath of the Battle of Kadesh, allowing him to burnish his image as a victorious warlord.

Syrian Stalemate

Ramesses II's last-known military offensive in the Levant came in his tenth regnal year. Our slim evidence for this expedition includes one of the three stelae he left in Lebanon at Nar el-Kelb, and perhaps some of his undated war scenes from the temples of Karnak and Luxor. The stela has eroded badly after thirty-three centuries, and we can read little more than the king's name and the date. Clearly, his forces ranged at least as far as Egypt's northern frontier in the Levant. But we do not know what Ramesses accomplished on this foray. A few war scenes at Karnak and Luxor depict fighting in Hittite-controlled Amurru, but

FIGURE 6.7. Prince Amunhirhopeshef leads Moabite prisoners before Ramesses II in a scene from the east exterior wall of the Ramesside forecourt of Luxor Temple. Photograph by Peter Brand.

these could refer to events either in year eight or ten. Given Egypt's long-standing feud with Hatti, Ramesses may have invaded Amurru once again in year ten, in a last-ditch effort to wrest control of the region from his enemy. Although we don't know the short-term outcome of these military operations, the final result is clear: stalemate.

Like the late Eighteenth Dynasty pharaohs, and his own father Sety I, Ramesses II learned a hard lesson on the limits of Egyptian military power. They could not hold Kadesh or Amurru in the face of implacable Hittite opposition. Any successes on Syria's battlefields were fleeting. They would not—or could not—leave sufficient garrisons to defend their conquests once their armies withdrew. Soon thereafter, Hittite officials, perhaps with soldiers backing them up, revisited any towns Pharaoh had captured. Willingly or not, all these Syrian citadels returned to Hatti's orbit.

The penalty for any Hittite vassal who failed to resist the Egyptians could be the loss of his throne. This fate befell Benteshina, the hapless king of Amurru, when his overlord Muwatalli II deposed him. Although Hattusili III later pardoned Benteshina, their new treaty of vassalage reminded him of his punishment:

> To my brother Muwatalli, Benteshina was (politically) dead in [the land] of Amurru. Benteshina had acceded to the throne of kingship in Amurru, but my brother Muwatalli removed Benteshina from the throne of kingship in the land of Ammuru.[54]

Benteshina suffered the misfortunes of governing a key Hittite satellite along the disputed frontier with Egypt during the reigns of the aggressive pharaohs Sety I and Ramesses II.

Shortly after the Battle of Kadesh Muwatalli II died. His son assumed power with the throne name Mursili III, although he is better known by his personal name Urhi-Teshub.[55] Urhi-Teshub now contended with Ramesses II, who remained undaunted in his Syrian ambitions. But after his year-ten campaign, the long Egyptian-Hittite war devolved into a standoff. The strategic status quo favored the Hittites, but political turmoil soon erupted in their homeland, which Ramesses would exploit.[56]

Great of Victories

After his tenth regnal year, evidence for Ramesses II's military career evaporates. Ramesses left a handful of stelae in the Levant after the first decade of his reign (fig. 6.8).[57] A well-preserved rhetorical stela from Beth Shean dates to his eighteenth year, but offers no hard evidence for any additional campaigns.[58]

With no permanent territorial acquisitions to his credit, today some might conclude Ramesses II's military career ended in failure. Yet, he

FIGURE 6.8. Upper part of a victory stela of Ramesses II from Tyre, Lebanon. The king slays captives in the presence of Re-Horakhty who offers him a *khepesh*-sword. Wikimedia Commons.

fought the enemy to a standstill in Syria, far from the Nile but on Hatti's front doorstep. Active hostilities only ceased because Pharaoh chose to refrain from further belligerence. In the Egyptian worldview, Ramesses had achieved victory (*nakhtu*) and valor (*keniyet*) in combat.[59] As champion of Maat, Pharaoh's rule encompassed the whole world, and all foreign kings were mere rebels. Yet, Pharaoh could never eliminate the Chaos (*isfet*) his foreign enemies personified; he could only hold it at bay. Of the foreign enemy, the author of the *Instructions for King Merikare* laments: "he neither conquers nor can he be conquered."[60] Against such chaotic foes, there could be no permanent victory.

From this ideological perspective, Ramesses II could spin his campaigns at Kadesh and Amurru not as ignominious failures but a series of famous victories. At Kadesh, in the face of Hittite treachery and the disloyalty of his own troops, Pharaoh had proved his courage and audacity. All the Canaanite and Syrian towns he captured during his later campaigns, especially his conquest of Dapur, redounded to his personal glory. When he lay aside his composite bow, the reins of his chariot team, and his *khepesh*-sword for the last time, Ramesses II could boast he had lived up to his personal epithet "great of victories." And finally, a decade after the campaign of year ten, he was ready to make peace with the Hittite Empire.

Notes

1. For the Hittite perspective, see Bryce 2005, 238–41.

2. Warburton 1997 makes the case for seeing the result at Kadesh as a stalemate. See also: *RITANC* II, 49; Brand 2007a.

3. As Kitchen has suggested: 1964, 69; 1982, 67; *RITANC* II, 59. War scenes depicting a string of Ramesses II's victories against Canaanite or Syrian towns during his later campaigns may inflate both the outcomes of these encounters and their strategic importance. As Spalinger (2020, 53) notes: "We must be careful when evaluating the overwhelming pictorial data of Ramesses II, for example. He reaps success against one Asiatic city after another, but were the engagements that successful? What is made to appear as a major series of revolts, may, in fact, be something less. Thus we must treat the numerous images of triumph with some degree of caution." The traditional ideological framework that casts all military resistance to the king as "rebellion" is a fixture of Egyptian and ancient Near Eastern ideology: Liverani 2001, 86–90. Much like Sety I during his regnal year-one campaign, Ramesses could have conjured up the specter of "rebellion" to justify a conspicuous display of military power in the wake of the Kadesh campaign. Still, he considered it politic to go on the offensive even if his grip on his tributaries had not weakened after Kadesh.

4. Kitchen 1964; *RITANC* II, 55–60, 63–72; Obsomer 2012b, 173–93.

5. Hsu 2013, 2014a.

6. *KRI* I, 17:15–18:2; Epigraphic Survey 1986, pl. 34.

7. *Urk.* IV, 1229–30.

8. Winkler (2013) discusses other cases where the king is compared to a star, including his lightning-quick movement.

9. McDonald 2002, 442–45, esp. 444 with references. Although the term *sšd* may convey the idea of the brightness of a star or meteor as McDonald suggest, it is also linked to the concept of fast movement. The context is the king's prowess in battle fighting alone among the enemy. I am dubious of McDonald's translation "he shines between the two wings of the army like a star as it sails across the sky" (p. 444). The two groups of "bowmen" are liable to be enemies, not Egyptian soldiers.

10. *Wb.* III, 244.

11. B 85; *KRI* II, 119. On royal rage, see Köhler 2021.

12. Hsu 2013, 2014a.

13. Inscriptions commemorating the king's warlike deeds are replete with declarations that he overcomes his foes in an instant (*m wnwt*) and employs similes emphasizing the violent speed and ferociousness of his attacks, including predatory animals who ambush prey and blasts of fire: Winkler 2013.

14. On the theme of Ramesses II's isolation at Kadesh, see Liverani 2001, 119–21.

15. P 80–91; *KRI* II, 28–33.

16. Assmann (1984, 216–21; 2002, 247–71) discusses the religious connotations of the Poem, viewing the king's plea to Amun in the heat of battle as a manifestation of the phenomenon of personal piety in the post-Amarna and Ramesside periods. Ockinga (1987) challenges his view of the episode and its bearing on the larger Kadesh narrative. While the king may have made a plea to the god in the heat of battle (Spalinger 2020, 167 nn. 96–97), the version recorded in the Poem is an artful literary composition with parallels in other

New Kingdom royal inscriptions: von der Way 1984, 174–97, 202–18; see also Liesegang 2014.

17. P 92–116; *KRI* II, 34–41.

18. P 117–127: *KRI* II, 41–44.

19. Examples include: Breasted 1905, 435–37; Wilson 1956, 244–47.

20. Despite Bolshakov and Soushchevski's claim (1998a, 21) that "a significant degree of heroization had been achieved by Kamose"—neither Kamose nor his pugnacious successors during the Eighteenth Dynasty ever present themselves as enduring hardship or overcoming it "heroically." Rather, they perform their mighty deeds effortlessly by means of their innate divine powers. So too, Thutmose III's experience at Megiddo fails to reach this standard, even as he risks the narrow pass at Arunna. His regal bluster and the nervous naysaying of his advisors are part of a set piece of the *Königsnovelle* genre; a moment of heightened tension perhaps, but not a trial by fire. As Spalinger (2012) notes, Ramesses II was in mortal danger at Kadesh; at the Arunna pass, Thutmose III was not.

On Ramesses II as a hero, see Brand forthcoming. Bolshakov and Soushchevski (1998a, 22–23) briefly touch on Ramesses II at Kadesh, stating that his "heroic presumption" and "outstanding contempt for death" both ensnares and frees him from the Hittite ambush. By late antiquity, Greek authors like Herodotus adapted received Egyptian folklore about earlier pharaohs and conflated it into a new tradition centered on the figure of King Sesostris. An amalgam of various Middle and New Kingdom kings, Herodotus and other Greco-Roman authors reinvented Sesostris, casting him in the mold of the classical warrior hero; see Pouwels 2014; Widmer 2014.

21. Kitchen 1964; 1982, 67–70; Obsomer 2012b, 187–92.

22. Our main sources for these later campaigns are undated war scenes from Karnak and Luxor. Other records, mostly administrative papyri like the daily logs of the army, and perhaps the now illegible inscriptions on the Nahr el-Kelb stelae in Lebanon, would have numbered these campaigns, but are now lost.

23. Bolshakov and Soushchevski are right in asserting that New Kingdom warrior pharaohs did not quite meet the classic archetype of "genuine heroism," this despite being "heroized" (1998a, 23). Here again, Egyptologists have bandied the terms "hero" and "heroic" about too glibly. Ramesses came closer to adversity than other kings—at least according to royal texts. It is a pity we lack all but the introduction to the Ramesside tale *The Quarrel of Seqenenre and Apophis*, for we would dearly like to know how the story ended. As his mummy so gruesomely attests, the historical Seqenenre Tao II's heroic journey—like that of Achilles—ended with his violent death in battle.

24. Gaballa 1976, 106–13; Heinz 2001, 252–58, 262–78; Spalinger 2011, 47–53, 58–140; Brand 2011.

25. *LD* III 197a–c; *KRI* II, 1 and 149; PM VII, 385 *RITA* II, 1–2, 27; *RITANC* II, 1–3, 60; Maïla-Afeiche 2009; Loffet 2009; Thum 2016.

26. *LD* III, pl. 156: *KRI* II, 148–49; *RITA* II, 26–27; Wreszinski 1925, pls. 90–91; Heinz 2001, 278.

27. *KRI* II, 148–49; *RITA* II, 26–27; *RITANC* II, 55–60; Obsomer 2012b, 174–75. The massive scene once spread across the outer wing of the Ramesseum's pylon and continued on its northern exterior wall. On the pylon, there were once eighteen forts, but only sixteen survive partly or completely intact, while

their identifying labels have decayed so badly that we can only decipher four-teen names in part or in full. Kitchen estimates that the entire triumphal scene may once have shown thirty-six or even fifty-four captured enemy towns.

28. Nims 1976. A century after Ramesses II built the Ramesseum, his Twen-tieth Dynasty descendant Ramesses III modeled his own temple closely on that of his admired paragon, modeling large swathes of its wall decoration on reliefs from the Ramesseum.

29. The corresponding portion of Medinet Habu is not a slavish copy of the Ramesseum: it lacks a pictorial list of defeated towns comparable to the year eight list on the rear face of the Ramesseum pylon, having Syrian war scenes instead. If these were replicas of battle art from the Ramesseum, the originals were displayed on that temple's adjoining south wall, which has vanished en-tirely since antiquity.

30. *Medinet Habu* II, 87–96; *KRI* V, 78–86; *RITA* V, 60–66. But a century after Ramesses II's wars in the thirteenth century BCE, the political face of the an-cient Near East had changed drastically. After 1200 BCE, as the Late Bronze Age drew to its chaotic close, several civilizations fell into decline, including the Hittite Empire. Ramesses III's war scenes display his military actions against present day enemies among the Libyans and migratory Sea Peoples.

31. Nims 1976. It is hard to know which of the Medinet Habu reliefs are facsimiles of lost parallels on the north exterior wall of the Ramesseum. By analogy with scenes at Medinet Habu, Kitchen *RITANC* II, 56–57 and fig. 13 avers that the north wall of the Ramesseum once had three scenes depicting Ramesses II's fighting against Tunip and Ullaza. For Ramesses III's war reliefs naming these towns, see *Medinet Habu* V, pls. 87–89; *KRI* V, 78:15 and 79:12. Kitchen also restores a third episode to the north wall of the Ramesseum de-picting an assault on Dapur, although there is no Medinet Habu parallel for this. He bases his conjecture on the dubious notion that Ramesses II conquered Dapur twice. Scholars often consider the Medinet war scenes of Ramesses III fighting Hittites in Syria as anachronisms inspired by Ramesses II's war scenes; Nims 1976. Redford (2018, 140–42) rejects them as being facsimiles of Ramess-es II's lost war scenes and claims they are historically accurate accounts of Ramesses III's Syrian wars.

32. In Ramesses III's day, Egypt and Hatti were long at peace, while the Hit-tites and many of the minor kingdoms of the Levant were now in steep decline amid environmental, economic, and military upheaval at the end of the Late Bronze Age. It remains possible that reliefs portraying Ramesses III's phantom "Syrian campaign" are neither historical accounts nor facsimiles of lost scenes from the Ramesseum, but are idealized: Obsomer 2012b, 175.

33. Only a handful of the towns named in the year eight Ramesseum list can be identified, but these are clustered in Galilee and Syria. *RITANC* II, 57–59; Obsomer 2012b, 174.

34. These scenes may also commemorate battles Ramesses fought in year eight. Name labels affixed to many enemy towns on the south exterior wall of the Great Hypostyle Hall at Karnak represent several Levantine toponyms, but most are damaged or name unknown locations. Kitchen locates some in Canaan including Accho, Acre, and Afka in Lebanon: *KRI* II, 152–59; *RITA* II, 29–35; *RITANC* II, 63–65. When these battles happened is less certain, as none are dated, but they likely occurred in regnal year eight or ten. War scenes on the west exterior wall of the great forecourt of Luxor Temple depict events in

Qode and at Dapur, both in Syria, and the town of Mutir south of Tripoli in Lebanon. More puzzling is a scene depicting an assault on the town of Satuna. It famously includes a vignette of a man climbing a cedar tree to escape a bear. Satuna was likely somewhere in Lebanon, but the defenders of the town are unaccountably depicted as Libyans.

35. Kitchen 1982, 67–68; *RITANC* II, 59.

36. *RITANC* II, 59–60. Severe damage to the year-eight list has deprived us of most of the Syrian toponyms aside from Dapur "in the land of Amurru" and a place called Kawil. For other Syrian towns Ramesses attacked in his eighth year we must turn to more ambiguous sources including hypothetical parallels in Ramesses III's Medinet Habu scenes depicting his assaults on Tunip and Ullaza. On Tunip and its location, see Helck 1973. Topographical lists from Ramesses II's triumphal scenes at Karnak, Luxor, and elsewhere preserve the name of Ullaza (*Inrt*) but other northern names are clearly aspirational—e.g., Hatti, Arzawa, Babylon, Ashur—and do not reflect genuine conquests. On the identification of some potential Syrian toponyms in the triumphal lists at Karnak and Luxor, see *RITANC* II, 65–72 and 86–88. More frequent are identifiable polities in Canaan and Lebanon. Undated war scenes from Karnak and Luxor include possible Syrian names, but the pharaoh may have targeted some of these during his year-ten campaign. While intriguing, we cannot simply take the names appearing on such triumphal lists as proof the king fought there. Surely Ramesses II never invaded Assyria and Babylonia!

37. Kenneth A. Kitchen, pers. comm. He also reasoned (*RITANC* II, 59–60) that the pharaoh sought to deter any interference from Kadesh as he moved against the north Syrian coast against Ullaza(?) and in central Syria, Dapur, and perhaps Tunip. More speculative is Kitchen's assertion that Ramesses divided his forces into two prongs sending one into the Beqaa Valley and onward to Upe Damascus while another proceeded up the coast against Ullaza and the Syrian interior north of Kadesh, thereby surrounding the trouble spot; *RITANC* II, 59 and map 12. While possible, he conjures this elaborate scenario up from disparate sources including topographical lists of Ramesses II, battle scenes of Ramesses III at Medinet Habu allegedly copied from lost originals from the Ramesseum, and by comparison with the Kadesh campaign of regnal year five. In fact, we can only guess at the exact itinerary and deployment of forces during the year-eight campaign.

38. On the location of Dapur, in the vicinity of Tunip, see *RITANC* II, 58; Obsomer 2012b, 189.

39. Luxor: Wreszinski 1925, pls. 77–80; *KRI* II, 172–73; Heinz 2001, 274. Ramesseum: *LD* III, pl. 166; Wreszinski 1925, pls. 107–9; *KRI* II, 173–74; Youssef, Leblanc, and Maher 1977; Heinz 2001, 278. As Obsomer (2012b, 175) notes, it was unusual to decorate the hypostyle halls of temples with battle scenes. The outer hall of Ramesses II's grand temple of Abu Simbel, which bears war scenes on both the north and south walls, might seem to be an exception, but it functions more as an outer court—albeit carved inside the mountain—than a conventional hypostyle.

40. *KRI* II, 173; *RITA* II, 46; *RITANC* II, 82–83.

41. Bolshakov and Soushchevski (1998a, 23 with n. 56) miss the mark by contending that Ramesses II "did not behave recklessly anymore" after Kadesh and that his later campaign records "became more impassive."

42. *KRI* II, 174–175; *RITA* II, 47; Obsomer 2012b, 177.

43. Indeed, Ramesses wears this coat of mail in the Luxor Temple version of the Battle of Dapur in which he fights on foot. Kitchen mistakenly interprets this "as linen? 'T-shirt', without body-armor": *RITANC* II, 83. But Ramesside artists were not as literal minded as he, nor did they feel the need to make the Luxor relief match the rhetoric of their royal master's speech. Likewise, the pharaoh fights in his chariot in the Ramesseum. We need not—indeed we must not—take such images literally.

44. On the military role of the king's sons, see pp. 258–61 below.

45. As Kitchen asserts: 1982, 69–70; *RITANC* II, 59. This contention hinges on a phrase in Ramesses II's speech about his assault on Dapur, describing it as "this Hittite town in which there is a statue of Pharaoh"; *KRI* II, 174. This refers not to a second battle in regnal year ten but to the fact that he left the statue there after he defeated it during his campaign of year eight but before he later recalled this event in his speech; Obsomer 2012b, 188. The settlement has not been identified in the archaeological record, and its precise location is unknown. No trace of Ramesses II's statue has ever emerged.

46. Three scenes from the lower register of the eastern exterior wall of the forecourt of Luxor Temple commemorate the Moabite campaign: PM II², 334–35; Kitchen 1964, 48–56 and pls. 3–4; Heinz 2001, 272; *KRI* II, 179–81; *RITA* II, 45–51. The Moabite place names are palimpsests that were later filled in with plaster and replaced with more northerly toponyms including Shabtuna, a town near Kadesh known from the Kadesh narrative; see Darnell and Jasnow 1993; *RITANC* II, 96. Kitchen (1964, 64–65) first identified the palimpsest toponyms in these reliefs as being Moabite, and his views are widely accepted; Hasel 1998, 159–65; Obsomer 2012b, 189–90. See also *RITANC* II, 89–97 for the state of the question in 1999. Na'aman (2006) rejected this assessment, but see Kitchen's later (2007) riposte. The objections to identifying these toponyms as Moabite are unconvincing and reflect an adherence to the minimalist school of biblical studies, which too often denies the identification of toponyms and peoples known from the Bible with New Kingdom Egyptian texts. One need not view every *event* recorded in the Bible as being historical fact while still accepting that numerous places and peoples named in scripture already existed in the Late Bronze Age and can turn up in extrabiblical sources like New Kingdom Egyptian inscriptions.

47. On the date of this campaign, see *RITANC* II, 96–97. Kitchen places the Moabite campaign either a year before or a year after the Battle of Dapur of year 8—thus, either in year 7 or year 9. As Obsomer (2012b, 189–90) notes, Kitchen's proposed dating and detailed itinerary for the Moabite campaign is speculative. The occurrence of the nomen form R^c-*ms-s* indicates the reliefs themselves predate regnal year 21. Obsomer dates the Moabite campaign to Ramesses II's fifteenth regnal year or later due to the presence of Prince Amunhirkhopeshef, assuming that the princeling had to have reached a sufficient age to have carried out his diplomatic task as an envoy. Like the Beit el-Wali war scenes from the first regnal year depicting this prince and his younger brother Khaemwaset riding in chariots, the Luxor Temple scenes are idealized.

48. Kitchen convincingly demonstrates that the toponym Tabunu (*Tbnw*) is in fact Dibon; *RITANC* II, 92–93.

49. *KRI* II, 180:2. On the possible location of Batora, see *RITANC* II, 90–92; Hasel 1998, 165.

50. Obelisk from Tanis: *KRI* II, 408; *RITA* II, 235; *RITANC* II, 275. Rhetorical stela from Gebel Shaluf: *KRI* II, 303:6; *RITA* II, 137; *RITANC* II, 182. See also *RITANC* II, 93–95.

51. Darnell and Jasnow 1993; *KRI* IX, 37.

52. *KRI* IX, 37.

53. A similar incident occurred during the reign of the Eighteenth Dynasty ruler Amenhotep II when the Egyptians apprehended a messenger from another hostile superpower, the Kingdom of Mitanni: *Urk.* IV, 1304:16–19. That courier carried a letter from the Mitannian king aimed at igniting rebellion among Pharaoh's Canaanite vassals. While each incident is plausible, the possibility remains that they constitute yet another ideological trope about Egypt's cunning and deceitful foreign adversaries.

54. Beckman 2008, 101.

55. For Urhi-Teshub's reign, see Bryce 2005, 246–65. For his interactions with Egypt, see chs. 9–11 below.

56. See p. 287 below.

57. Wimmer 2002; Thum 2016; Levy 2017. Most are fragmentary.

58. Kitchen takes the Beth Shean stela as proof of a campaign, perhaps a final military crisis in the lead-up to his peace treaty with the Hittite King Hattusili III in regnal year 21: *RITANC* II, 60–63. This is highly speculative, and the Beth Shean stela contains nothing but traditional rhetorical praise of the king's martial prowess without referring to any specific event: Obsomer 2012b, 190–92. A fragment of another stela dating to some point between regnal years two and twenty was discovered reused inside a mosque in the Jordanian town of At-Turra near Tell es-Shihab, where it was known locally as the "Job Stone": Wimmer 2002. A third stela dating to regnal year 56 recently came to light at the site of Al-Kiswah in the region of Damascus, near the ancient Egyptian administrative center of Upe; Taraqji 1999. Kitchen (1999) attempts to place this inscription within the context of Egyptian-Hittite relations, but nothing in the text indicates that it is anything other than ceremonial.

59. Galán 1993.

60. Simpson 2003, 161.

Chapter Seven

All the King's Wives: Ramesses II's Royal Women

Few aspects of pharaonic Egypt seem more enviable than the lives of its queens.[1] Egyptian art evokes visions of slim, gorgeous women who, we imagine, led lives of languid elegance among all the splendor of Pharaoh's domains.[2] Surely they resided in spacious palaces overflowing with luxuries and pleasures. Were they not bedecked with exquisite diadems, gossamer linen gowns, and every sort of finery imaginable—broad collars, pectoral necklaces, bracelets, anklets, earrings, and hair ornaments—all made of gold, silver, lapis lazuli, carnelian, and turquoise? They possessed sumptuous arrays of luxury goods crafted in royal workshops and exotic imports from faraway lands: exquisite furniture of ebony, ivory, and cedar wood, all embellished with costly inlays of gemstones, gilding, and colored glass. They enjoyed fine toiletries too: glass perfume bottles, faience *khol*-flasks, silver mirrors, bronze tweezers, ivory hairpins, and delicate ointment vessels, to name but a few of the lovely personal effects and trinkets Pharaoh showered upon them.[3] And surely they held real power and influence as Ladies of the Two Lands, did they not?

The Egyptian word for "queen," *khemet-nesu*, means "royal wife," literally "Wife of the King."[4] A hierarchy of wives and children existed within the king's family. At its summit sat the "great royal wife," *khemet nesu weret*, his favored consort and often the mother of his eldest son and heir. The wives and mothers of the pharaohs were central to the ideology of Egyptian kingship. They embodied goddesses like Hathor and Mut, and were feminine counterparts to the king's masculine divinity.[5] Pharaoh's wives ensured the renewal of kingship. Just as the "king's mother," ideally his father's principal wife, gave birth to the pharaoh, so his wife brought forth his successor.[6] By bearing his children, royal wives enabled the pharaoh to express his own procreative energy, thereby guaranteeing the fertility of Egypt itself.

Pharaoh's wives participated in court ceremonies and religious festivals and wore elaborate regalia, insignia, and costumes attesting to their exalted status.[7] In New Kingdom times the royal wives and mothers wore a rich and complex array of crowns and ornaments that set them apart from other women as virtual goddesses.[8]

FIGURE 7.1. Nefertari from her tomb in the Valley of the Queens (QV 66). Courtesy Manna Nader Gabana Studios Cairo.

For all their elegant splendor, we should avoid idealizing and romanticizing Egyptian queens. The pharaohs were polygamous. For every preeminent consort like Nefertari (fig. 7.1), there were several, even dozens, of lesser wives living in her shadow. In his lifetime Ramesses II married well over a dozen women and fathered more than one hundred children by them.[9] In the early decades of his reign, residential palaces at Memphis, Mi-Wer, and his capital of Piramesses overflowed with an ever-burgeoning population of wives, foreign princesses, and scores of little boys and girls.

All the pharaoh's wives fulfilled their marital duties by spending their childbearing years in multiple pregnancies, giving birth to as many children as possible, sometimes at ruinous cost to their own health.[10] Ramesses II's chief consort Nefertari gave him at least eight sons and daughters, while her colleague Isetnofret delivered six or more babies, not counting any failed pregnancies or infant deaths they may have suffered. For ancient women childbearing was dangerous and frustrating. Too often they miscarried, or their infants died at alarming rates. Amid the painful rigors of labor and birth, women also died with tragic frequency.[11]

Pharaoh's So-Called Harem and the Flawed Ottoman Paradigm

The precise nature of what Egyptologists often call the royal "harem" remains imperfectly understood and controversial.[12] Since the nineteenth century, when men dominated Egyptology, scholars took the existence of the pharaonic harem for granted in all periods of Egyptian history, likening it to the Ottoman sultan's household.[13] In Ottoman civilization, harem referred collectively to a sultan's wives, mother, other female relations, and his younger children—all of them secluded in private quarters within his rambling Topkapi Palace in Istanbul.[14] Derived from an Arabic term, the harem consisted of women who were "inviolable." However, this concept of the restricted "harem" is inappropriate for pharaonic Egypt.[15]

While the Ottoman paradigm is most familiar today, polygamous kings in many ancient and modern cultures maintained domestic quarters housing their numerous women and offspring. These include the

FIGURE 7.2. *Ramses in His Harem* (1886) by Jean Jules Antoine Lecompte Du Noüy. Courtesy Stéphane Mahot.

ancient Near Eastern civilizations of Assyria, Babylonia, and Hatti, Islamic civilizations of the modern Middle East, and kingdoms and empires ranging from Benin in West Africa to Mogul India, imperial China, and feudal Japan.[16]

In Western culture, where Christian monogamy remains the rule, "harem" is a loaded term, freighted with prejudicial notions about "decadent" oriental potentates. It conjures up stereotyped imagery of sexual excess and fantasy, and forms a cornerstone of a larger system of cultural bias called Orientalism.[17] Beginning in the eighteenth century, Orientalism pervaded European intellectual and artistic responses to eastern cultures, particularly the Islamic and Middle Eastern world. Since Mozart wrote his famous opera *Abduction from the Seraglio*, western artists and intellectuals have obsessed over the sultan's harem as a prison-palace of sexual bondage, where, they imagine, the potentate indulged his limitless erotic appetites in a never-ending orgy of debauchery.[18] In lurid European fantasies, sexless eunuchs guard scantily clad concubines who populate the potentate's harem as his sex slaves (fig. 7.2).

For over two centuries Europeans imposed this cultural bias on various so-called oriental civilizations, including Egypt.[19] As a paradigm for understanding Pharaoh's household, the Ottoman harem is deeply flawed.[20] Egyptian royal wives were not confined to their residential quarters within the palace, although outsiders had no direct access to their private living spaces.[21] Instead, Pharaoh's women resided in several palace complexes across Egypt, where they played active, public roles in court ceremonies and religious rituals both within and outside their domiciles. Nor were any of his women "concubines."[22]

Over the past fifty years, western scholarship began casting off outdated orientalist prejudices.[23] Meanwhile, feminist theory has taken root in historical studies and anthropology. New generations of Egyptologists, especially women scholars, reject any notion of an Egyptian harem as a sexist and racist delusion.[24] Still, Egyptian kings were undeniably polygamous, and they kept households with numerous women and children. The royal domain comprised a complex administrative and economic infrastructure, with a large staff of male officials and servants of both genders who supported the royal family. Pharaoh's mother and his senior consort sat atop a hierarchy of women and children in his extensive household, supervising all their attendants and servants.

The Structure of Pharaoh's Household

Egyptian Pharaohs presided over an extensive domain called the *per nesu*, or "king's household," consisting of his family, all the people who served them, and all property belonging to his estate.[25] This included a network of residential and ceremonial palaces, rest houses called the "mooring places of Pharaoh" all along the Nile, provincial estates, farmlands, and other administrative and economic facilities throughout Egypt and Nubia.[26] A host of officials and servants staffed these palaces and far-flung estates.[27] Within several palatial complexes, including residential facilities at Memphis and Mi-Wer (Medinet Ghurob) in the Fayum region, resided the king's many women and children.[28] Living alongside Pharaoh's family were additional women and girls, children of Egyptian courtiers, and sons and daughters of foreign vassal kings. A network of agricultural lands, workshops, storerooms, and related infrastructure supported the royal household's dependents.

Egyptologists have often identified two related institutions within Pharaoh's larger estate as his would-be harem. One, called the *ipet nesu*, existed from early dynastic times, more than two millennia before Ramesses II ruled Egypt.[29] Within the *ipet nesu*, the king's women attended him, prompting some to label it his harem. But an *ipet* was a private chamber or sanctuary, so *ipet nesu* is best understood as the "private apartments of the king."[30] The pharaoh slept and relaxed within these privy chambers, in the company of female companions, when he was not carrying out public duties. From Middle and New Kingdom texts, we know senior queens resided in the "*ipet nesu* of the king's wife." Surely this was her private apartments and not her harem. [31] One late Eighteenth Dynasty tomb scene depicts the consort of King Ay holding court with women of the palace elite. This was within her own palace suite, separate from her husband's chambers.[32]

Another term Egyptologists sometimes translate as harem refers to an institution called the *per kheneret*, or "*kheneret*-household."[33] This seems to be synonymous with another term, *pa khenty*.[34] The much-debated term *kheneret* designated groups of musicians, mostly women, who sang, danced, and played musical instruments during temple rituals, religious festivals, and court ceremonies.[35] Music and dance were key elements of Egyptian temple liturgy and palace life. Egyptian gods and goddesses could have *kheneret*-groups of female musicians who performed in their cultic rites. These women often came from well-connected families in the upper echelons of Egyptian society.[36]

Pharaoh's mother, wives, and daughters also provided musical liturgy in temple worship and grand festivals of the gods. Temple art depicts Ramesses II's mother Tuya and his principal spouse Nefertari chanting and playing sacred rattles called sistra as he conducts offering rituals before Amun-Re. In wall scenes at Luxor temple, Nefertari leads a procession of royal children, including twenty-two princesses.[37] Each holds a sistrum aloft and sings. Label texts identify each daughter as the *shemayet*, or "chantress," of a particular male or female deity, including local avatars of Hathor, goddess of love, sex, and regeneration.[38]

Queens, princesses, and other elite women offered musical performances and rhythmic dancing both in temple cults and palace ceremony. Tomb scenes dating to the Amarna period and late Eighteenth Dynasty depict court women dancing and making music as a central element of palace life.[39] Even in Pharaoh's abode, music and dance were not simply entertainment; they also fulfilled a religious function. Female companions magically soothed and rejuvenated the king, just as Hathor herself placated her father Re in mythology.[40]

As hallmarks of religious practice and the rhythm of courtly life, *kheneret*-groups became synonymous with royal women in New Kingdom times. *Per-kheneret*, "the household of the *kheneret*," refers collectively to women in Pharaoh's household, who are also called *kheneret*-women. Both terms appear in Ramesses II's Abydos Dedicatory Inscription, where he describes the "female household," *pereyet*, that Sety I established for him while he was still crown prince.[41] The *kheneret*-household included Pharaoh's wives, his mother, his daughters, and other court women, who were not royal wives, but who came from elite families and were married to court officials. Not a cloistered "harem" in the Ottoman sense, the *per-kheneret* functioned both as a domestic space and a ceremonial institution within the royal estate.

Both the "royal apartments," (*ipet nesu*), and "*kheneret*-household," were branches of the larger "king's estate," (*per nesu*). But how did they relate to each other? Administrative texts indicate the pharaoh's apartments were enclosed within the larger *kheneret*-household.[42] When the king traveled through his realm, a perambulating entourage of favored women and children came with him, even abroad on military campaigns.[43]

We should not imagine Egyptian royal women were confined or segregated from Pharaoh's court or the outside world. Nor was there an impermeable barrier between the larger *kheneret*-household and the royal apartments. Women could be found in both.[44] Ramesses II's numerous palaces all offered him a domestic sanctuary, an *ipet nesu*. Even the smallest facilities had some room for the women and children traveling with him.

Royal Polygamy in New Kingdom Egypt

As in all dynastic monarchies, an Egyptian king sought to beget a viable male heir to ensure his family line. This imperative was never more pressing than for Sety I and his son Crown Prince Ramesses, scions of a brand-new dynasty. Historians often assume that Ramesses II fathered more than one hundred offspring to ensure his succession. But most of these children had little chance of inheriting the throne. Even with high rates of child mortality and the short life expectancy of even the high born, his extensive progeny of almost fifty sons far exceeded what was required to guarantee an heir.

How can we explain his prolific procreation?[45] Like polygamous kings in other cultures, Egypt's ruler begat many offspring to flaunt his sexual potency and assert his masculine authority. Ideologically, Pharaoh entrenched his status as a regal alpha male as much through his sexual virility as through his fighting prowess.[46] The vast brood he sired by numerous women was living proof of his stamina, much like his record of "valor and victory" on foreign battlefields. In Egyptian ideology, he was the "Mighty Bull," bosting all the sexual vigor such imagery evokes.[47] Pharaoh's own procreative fecundity ensured that the yearly flooding of the Nile would bring bountiful harvests and prosperity for Egypt's people.

While Ramesses was still a prince, Sety I chose young brides for him from Egypt's leading families. Cross-cultural studies from a broad range of civilizations show a similar pattern: kings who practiced polygamy enhanced relations with social elites by marrying daughters of courtiers and officials.[48] Likewise, interstate relations benefited when the monarch wed princesses from other countries, both vassals and peer kingdoms. This holds true for the ancient Near East and an array of historical cultures, ranging from Africa to China and Japan.[49] Social and political dynamics—not merely the need to beget an heir—motivated polygamy throughout history.

The same pattern of matrimonial politics holds true across the ancient Near East, where daughters and sisters of court elites and vassal kings became wives in polygamous households of Great Kings in

Assyria, Babylonia, and Hatti. Princesses were also a diplomatic commodity, whom Great Kings exchanged with their peer monarchs or married off to their imperial vassals to strengthen bonds of loyalty and trust.[50] Children born from these alliances were living barometers of peaceful relations between kingdoms.[51]

Polygamy and exuberant procreation also came with political risks for ancient kings. Far from safeguarding the dynastic line by ensuring an heir, having numerous sons could inflame political tensions and prompt a succession crisis. Younger sons vying to supplant the designated heir—or even their father—might plot assassination or foment civil war.

Having a collection of women available to the king did not always permit him to indulge his unbridled lust. Due to a lack of sources and the decorous restraint of the few texts describing the erotic life of the pharaohs, we know nothing about sexual dynamics within the palace beyond what our imaginations conjure up.[52] In other civilizations, political and cultural factors limited a polygamous king's libido, determining when and how frequently he could have sex with any of his wives. Royal sex was a political act, not just an amorous pleasure.[53]

Pharaoh's Women

Egyptian texts identify the monarch's relatives with titles stressing their relationship to him, including "king's mother" (*mout nesu*), "royal wife" (*khemet nesu*), "king's sister" (*senet nesu*), "king's son" (*sa nesu*), and "king's daughter" (*sat nesu*). Among royal siblings, only sisters (*senet nesu*) are mentioned in text, while the king's brothers are not.[54] Egyptologists translate these titles with western terms: "queen," "prince," and "princess." Sometimes this is harmless, but other words, especially "concubine," are inappropriate and misleading, and it is best to follow Egyptian terminology.

The Egyptian term for "queen" (*khemet nesu*), means "wife of the king," or "royal wife," but never "female ruler."[55] Still, a hierarchy existed among the pharaoh's women. The most privileged, like Nefertari, attained the rank of *khemet nesu weret*, "great royal wife." However, monumental inscriptions do not display these titles consistently. Nefertari and other wives of Ramesses II who held the distinction of "great royal wife" can also be entitled simply "royal wife."[56] We need not conclude they were promoted—or demoted—over time.[57] Instead, artists sometimes lacked enough room to inscribe the longer title of "great royal wife." Ramesses bestowed further epithets including "Lady of the Two Lands" and "Mistress of South and North" on his most favored wives, marking their elevated status in the hierarchy of palace women. As his supreme consort and mother of his first-born son, Nefertari boasted the largest array of honorary distinctions.

Aside from Nefertari and Isetnofret, the women who gave Ramesses II most of his children are now anonymous. We know neither their names nor their ranks. They were also designated "royal wives," but none is ever named on his monuments.[58]

Other women, lacking the title "royal wife," populated the Egyptian court and the *kheneret*-household. One group in palace society was the *khekherut nesu*, the "ornamented ones of the king," or "royal ornament-women."[59] Earlier scholars mistook them for "concubines," but this is a faulty orientalist notion. Artists depict these court women bedecked in long, pleated linen gowns, luxuriant wigs, fine jewelry, and elaborate golden diadems. They were not married to the king and had no sexual relations with him. Instead, these "royal ornament-women" attended the pharaoh's wives and daughters and were married to high officials of the court.[60]

Another female group within the king's household was the *neferut en akh*, the "beautiful maidens of the palace." The *neferut*, literally "beautiful ones," were young women and girls who had not yet given birth.[61] Although not his wives, they played a key role in entertaining the king as he relaxed in his apartments (*ipet nesu*). Scenes from Ramesses III's temple at Medinet Habu show him lounging within his private quarters with small groups of *neferut*-maidens.[62] They acted as incarnations of Hathor, who soothed her father Re in Egyptian mythology.[63]

The King's Mother Tuya

Ramesses II's mother Tuya, like her husband Sety I, was not of royal blood, but descended from a line of military officers. Before he arose as Ramesses I, Pramessu arranged for his son to marry Tuya, daughter of a chariot officer named Raia and his wife Ruia.[64] Though she was Sety I's great royal wife, Tuya seems invisible to us during her husband's lifetime. Every known monument with her name dates to Ramesses II's reign (fig. 7.3).[65]

Scribes wrote her name both as Tuya and Tuy. As consort of one king and mother of another, her name was always enclosed by a cartouche. Ramesses II also established a cult for his mother as a living embodiment of Mut, Amun-Re's consort, who personified motherhood. Some inscriptions call her Mut-Tuy, literally "Mother Tuy." Another alias was Muty, meaning "She of Mut," just as her late husband Sety was "He of Seth." This eclectic variety of names signaled Tuya's prestige and ideological role as Pharaoh's mother.[66]

FIGURE 7.3. Relief depicting Ramesses II and his mother Tuya. The form of the king's name indicates that this relief dates two or three decades after her death. Vienna, Kunsthistorisches Museum Inv. 5091. © akg-images / De Agostini Picture Lib. / W. Buss.

As his principal consort, Sety I distinguished Tuya with honorifics including "lady of the Two Lands" and "mistress of all lands." When Ramesses II came to power, the dowager Tuya retained these distinctions and gained those of king's mother and god's mother.

Texts on a broken statue from the Ramesseum list many of Tuya's titles and epithets:

> *Hereditary noblewoman, great one of the* khetes-*scepter, royal mother of the Dual King Usermaatre-Setepenre, the Son of Re, Ramessu-Meramun, mistress of all lands ... lady of charm, [sweet] of love [... wife(?)] of Horus, who gave birth to his son for Re [...] the god's wife and king's mother Tuy, may she be healthy.*[67]

Her titles include: "mistress of [all] the [royal] wives," "chief of the *kheneret*-musicians of Amun," "sistrum player of Mut," and "*Menat*-bearer of Hathor."[68] A fragmentary text recently unearthed at the Ramesseum heralds Tuya as "king's mother, [mistress of the *neferut*-maid]ens,

FIGURE 7.4. Statue of Tuya originally made for Amenhotep III's wife Tiy. The statue's nose and chin were restored in modern times. Vatican Museum. Alamy.

[mistress of] the ornamented ones of the king, Muty, alive and youthful eternally."[69] From these texts, we know Tuy had a senior role in providing musical liturgy for the cults of goddesses like Mut and Hathor and in overseeing the king's wives and the *nefrut*-maidens within the royal household.

Great royal wives and king's mothers exerted influence with the pharaoh via their ideological role as feminine counterparts to masculine kingship.[70] Their power was informal and much of it depended on individual personalities and emotional attachments. As in other historical monarchies, pharaohs shared strong emotional, ideological, and political bonds with their mothers. A royal wife lost most of her status at court after her husband died, unless her son succeeded him. The dowager relied on him for her continued influence and eminence, deriving much prestige as "king's mother," *mout nesu*, and "god's mother," *mout netcher.*[71]

Pharaoh knew his mother was wholly loyal to him, and bonds of trust enabled her to advise and influence his decisions, granting her a degree of "soft power" through him.[72] We catch a rare glimpse of a dowager queen's influence in a diplomatic letter Tushratta, king of Mitanni, sent to Amenhotep III's widow Tiy, imploring her to intercede in a dispute with her son Akhenaten.[73]

After Sety I died, Tuya consoled herself by acquiring increased honor and influence as Ramesses II enhanced the public role and monumental visibility of his family. He continued paying homage to Tuya long after her death, commissioning statuary, temple reliefs, and a special temple at the Ramesseum consecrated to her cult.[74] The two best preserved images for Tuya are statues representing earlier queens that Ramesses reinscribed for his mother, including a magnificent sculpture in black granodiorite of Amenhotep III's Great Royal Wife Tiy, now a treasure of the Vatican Museum's Egyptian collection (fig. 7.4).[75] Ramesses II also commissioned original sculptures of his mother, including two effigies on the façade of his grand temple at Abu Simbel.

Tuya's most glorious memorial was a colossal statue Ramesses erected next to his celebrated Ozymandias colossus in the first court of the Ramesseum.[76] Sculpted in black granodiorite, Tuya sat enthroned and wore a tall-plumed headdress surmounting her voluminous wig.

Her statue remained intact when the ancient Greek author Diodorus Siculus visited the Ramesseum in the first century BCE.[77] Diodorus describes it as being thirty feet (nine meters) tall. Today, only a few large fragments attest to its lost splendor.

During Ramesses II's first two decades as king, Tuya played a prominent role in court ceremonies and temple rituals, alongside his chief consort Nefertari. On a gateway in the first hypostyle hall at the Ramesseum, a damaged scene shows two queens participating in temple rituals.[78] Of the first, undoubtedly Nefertari, only her wig and headdress are left. Beside her stands the intact image of a second woman entitled "King's Mother and Great Royal Wife Mut-Tuy." She wears a long wig and a vulture-shaped crown, common to queens and goddesses, as she plays the sistrum, offering musical worship to the gods (fig. 7.5).

FIGURE 7.5. Left: relief depicting Tuya from the Ramesseum. Right: her names and titles from Abu Simbel: "King's Mother and God's Wife Mut-Tuya, given life." Photograph by Peter Brand.

A key element of New Kingdom ideology was its doctrine of the king's divine birth through theogamy, or "divine marriage," a sexual union between Amun-Re and the queen.[79] Eighteenth Dynasty rulers expounded this mythology in a cycle of temple wall reliefs and texts. The best-preserved examples are Hatshepsut's from Deir el-Bahari in Western Thebes and Amenhotep III's in Luxor temple, but the cycle may date back to the Twelfth Dynasty.[80] A thousand years after Ramesses II, Ptolemaic kings asserted their divine origins by building shrines called *mammisi*, or "birth houses" next to temples of deities like Hathor at Dendera and Horus at Edfu.

One of the earliest known *mammisi* was a small double temple Ramesses II constructed at the Ramesseum, attached to the main temple's north wall. He consecrated this shrine to the cults of his mother Tuya and his senior wife Nefertari.[81] Sadly, little more than its foundations exist, but later kings reused inscribed blocks from Tuya's shrine when they enlarged the Eighteenth Dynasty temple of Amun-Re at Medinet Habu. These preserve fragments of Tuya's theogamy and Ramesses II's miraculous birth.[82]

According to doctrine, Amun-Re begat the future king by impersonating his earthly father and seducing his mother in her bedchamber. A well-preserved text about Amenhotep III's miraculous birth recounts his mother Mutemwia's amorous encounter with the god:

Words spoken by Amun-Re, Lord of the Thrones of the Two Lands, Preeminent in his Inner Sanctuary, after he transformed himself into *the bodily form of this <her> husband: The Dual King Menkheperure (Thutmose IV), given life. It was while she was resting in the innermost chamber of the palace that he found her. At the god's scent she awoke, and she laughed (with delight) in front of his incarnate form. He went to her at once, for he lusted after her. He caused her to see him in his godly form after he approached her, and she rejoiced at seeing his perfection. Love of him coursed through her limbs, and the palace was flooded <with> the god's scent ... After this, the incarnate form of this god did all he desired with her.*

Words spoken by Amun-Re, Lord of the Thrones of the Two Lands in front of her: "Amenhotep-Ruler-of-Thebes is the name of this child I have [placed] in your womb."[83]

Amun-Re commands the potter god, Khnum, who fashions each person from clay, to create his son's body. Khnum models the royal babe and its royal *Ka* on his potter's wheel.[84] Resembling an identical twin, his *Ka* embodies his animating life force and unique identity. As the king's mother completed her gestation, a company of protective gods and goddesses escort her to the birthing chamber, where they assist her in delivering the infant king and his *Ka*.[85] Both resemble small children more than infants. Hathor presents them to their celestial father Amun-Re. Taking the infant and his *Ka* into his arms, Amun proclaims how he will one day rule Egypt.

As the vessel through which this miracle occurred, the king's mother achieved supreme honor once her husband died, and her son took his place on the Throne of Horus. Now she was also called "mother of the god," an epithet she shared with Isis, divine mother of Horus.

More than Ramesses himself, Tuya was the main protagonist in this mythic event. She is unique among mortals, having experienced physical intimacy with a god and giving birth to his divine son.[86] The shrine Ramesses II built for her at the Ramesseum highlights her exceptional prestige and her theological role.

In these scenes of Ramesses II's miraculous birth, the divine and human worlds intersect at the crucial moment. While Amun-Re transforms himself into Sety I, Tuya embodies Mut. History and myth merge, transposing the terrestrial event of the king's birth into the supernatural realm. Ramesses never denies his earthly origins, nor did his divine birth supersede the mundane fact that Sety and Tuya were not yet royalty when he was born. Instead, these alternate realities— mythic and historical—coexisted without contradiction in the ideology Ramesses II formulated.[87]

Tuya lived into the third decade of her son's reign, and her honor and prestige exceeded that of any of Ramesses II's women except for her daughter-in-law Nefertari. After Ramesses sealed his peace treaty with the Hittite ruler Hattusili III, he granted Tuya the privilege of addressing a pair of cordial letters of friendship to Hattusili and his consort Queen Puduhepa.[88] But Pharaoh's venerable mother, by then in her late fifties or early sixties, was approaching the end of her days.

Ramesses II prepared a sumptuous tomb for Tuya in the Valley of the Queens (QV 80) alongside others he built for his most favored women.[89] Tuya's sepulture equaled the fabulous tomb of her daughter-in-law Nefertari (QV 66), both in size and the splendor of its decoration. Sadly, QV 80 suffered a tragic fate; natural disaster and human vandalism ravaged the tomb, leaving it a wreck. Its beautiful painted wall reliefs are largely destroyed. Nor did Tuya's mortal remains rest in peace for long. Ancient thieves plundered her rich burial goods and destroyed her mummy amid a wave of tomb robberies at the end of the New Kingdom. One object they left behind is a lovely sculpture of Tuya wearing an elaborate wig, in the form of a calcite stopper from one of her canopic jars (fig. 7.6).[90] Few fragments of her burial goods remained intact when archaeologists unearthed QV 80. But an ink note scribbled on a wine jar shard gives a vintage of Ramesses II's twenty-second regnal year, suggesting he laid Tuya to rest soon after this date.[91]

FIGURE 7.6. Calcite canopic jar stopper of Tuya from her tomb in the Valley of the Queens, now in the Luxor Museum. Photograpy by Peter Brand.

The Great Royal Wife Nefertari

Ramesses II's preeminent consort, the Great Royal Wife Nefertari, surpassed all his women aside from his mother Tuya. Nefertari's exquisite tomb in the Valley of the Queens (QV 66) and her majestic temple at Abu Simbel testify to her unrivaled esteem. Nefertari's parents are unknown, but inscriptions bearing her name never include the titles "king's daughter" or "king's sister," so no regal blood flowed in her veins when Sety I chose her as one of his eldest son's brides.

Yet some claim her heritage was regal, based on a minor artifact unearthed in her plundered tomb, a decorative knob bearing King Ay's gilded cartouche (fig. 7.7). This charming blue-glass object was affixed to an ornamental casket, like examples from Tutankhamen's tomb. But is this proof Nefertari was Ay's kinswoman? This is far-fetched. Ay

FIGURE 7.7. Glazed knob from a chest inscribed with the name of Ay found in the tomb of Nefertari in the Valley of the Queens. Turin, Museo Egizio S 5162. Courtesy Turin, Museo Egizio.

himself was an old man when he succeeded Tutankhamun as pharaoh, two decades before Sety I arranged for Prince Ramesses to marry Nefertari. Surely Ay was not her father. Was she instead his young niece or granddaughter, as some suppose?[92] Should we accept this small object as reliable testimony to her family origins? Too often Egyptologists' imaginations run wild when even tiny bits of evidence emerge, leading them to expound grand theories from meagre sources. The Ramessides regarded Ay as one of Akhenaten's illegitimate successors. Why would Sety I choose Ay's female descendant as one of his son's earliest wives? And why would Ramesses II have elevated her as his chief consort?

We are left to ponder how this little curio naming Ay came to rest in Nefertari's house of eternity. There is a prosaic but likelier scenario. As they stocked the queen's tomb with goods for her journey to the netherworld, palace functionaries rummaged through a royal residence looking for surplus furnishing. Their gaze fell upon a decorative box, a forgotten heirloom of the previous dynasty, which they selected to fill the quota of goods Nefertari took to her afterlife.

Nefertari was probably a well-connected courtier's daughter, as were most of Ramesses II's wives. Who knows? Perhaps she was a beautiful—and exceptionally fortunate—village maiden Sety I plucked from poverty and obscurity. But such a romantic vision belongs in fairytales.[93] Neither a princess nor a peasant girl, Nefertari's people were likely members of Egypt's official class. As far as we know, Nefertari never looked back on her preroyal origins after she wed Ramesses, nor did her relatives boast of their pharaonic son-in-law.[94]

From the Abydos Dedicatory Inscription we know Sety arranged for Prince Ramesses to marry several brides. A "baby race" ensued among the heir's new wives.[95] Nefertari won the day by delivering his first viable male offspring, Amunhirkhopeshef. In all she gave birth to at least four boys and four girls.[96] We know this because images of each of them stand beside statues of their parents on the façades of the twin Abu Simbel temples. If Nefertari gave Ramesses any more children, they would appear in temple lists of his sons and daughters. Unfortunately, these lists never identify the mothers of his children.[97] Ideologically, only their father mattered in monumental inscriptions.

Nefertari stood at the apex of the royal family's hierarchy, eclipsing all Pharaoh's other wives. Whatever beauty she possessed, whatever affection Ramesses had for her, Prince Amunhirkhopeshef was her greatest achievement and the lynchpin of her husband's esteem. Nefertari and her eldest son appear beside Ramesses in statuary and wall reliefs created during the first two decades of his reign, including colossi from Luxor temple and his celebrated Turin statue. His other wives are nowhere to be seen (fig. 7.8).[98]

The name Nefertari's received at birth means "She-has-become-beautiful." When Ramesses became pharaoh, her name was inscribed within a cartouche and she acquired the epithet "Beloved-of-Mut," in parallel to her husband's "Beloved-of-Amun."[99] Ramesses showered an array of ceremonial titles and laudatory epithets on Nefertari, attesting to her ascendancy over all his wives:

> *Hereditary Noblewoman*
> *Great Royal Wife, his Beloved*
> *God's Wife*
> *Great One of the Kheneret-Women of Horus, Lord of the Palace*
> *Mistress of the Neferut-Maidens of the Palace*
> *Mother of the God*
> *The Good Mother*[100]
> *The Greatly Praised One*
> *Lady of the Two Lands*
> *Wife of the Victorious Bull*

FIGURE 7.8. Amun-hirkhopeshef (left) and Nefertari (right) on the Turin statue of Ramesses II. Turin, Museo Egizio 1380. Courtesy Museo Egizio, Turin.

Mistress of the North and South
Mistress of All Lands
Mistress of Charm
Great of Love in the Circlet-Diadem
Sweet of Love
She Who Unites with the Sovereign
She Whom Horus Remembers
The Greatly Beloved One
She who Makes Hearts Joyous
Mistress of Beauty
Radiant of Limbs
Beautiful of Face
Beautiful with the Tall Plumed-Diadem
Lofty of Plumes
She who Propitiates the Gods
She who Appeases Horus (the King) with Her Voice
[Sweet?] of Voice when She Chants
Lovely of Hands while Holding the Sistra
Who Plays the Sistra in Karnak[101]

Praising Nefertari's virtues, an inscription from Luxor temple exclaims: "One is pleased with (any word) she utters—whatever she says is done for her—since every good thing (happens) according to her wish."[102] Being at her every command, courtiers and servants were fortunate, for "her every word pleases the [ear] and one lives by hearing her voice!"[103]

Nefertari's Cultic Role and Queenly Iconography

Along with these laudatory epithets, Nefertari held titles denoting religious and ceremonial duties she fulfilled as great royal wife.[104] Her most important sacerdotal office was "God's Wife" of Amun. Ramesses I, Sety I, and Ramesses II also conferred the office of "god's wife" on their chief consorts Satre, Tuya, and Nefertari.[105] The god's wives played a key liturgical and political role in Amun-Re's extensive cultic establishments in Thebes.[106]

Reliefs in Ramesses II's forecourt at Luxor temple show Nefertari performing festival rites alongside him. Like other elite women, including Pharaoh's daughters, Nefertari served as a "chantress" (*shemayet*) in temple ceremonies, where she sang and played a pair of sistra to placate the gods. Or she clasped a sistrum in one hand and a *menat*-necklace, token of Hathor's cult, in the other.[107] Shaking two sistra during the Opet Festival, Nefertari leads a procession of the king's daughters, each playing a sistrum (fig. 7.9).

On the south face of the Luxor pylon, Nefertari accompanies Ramesses II in two rituals honoring the ithyphallic god Min, an alter ego

FIGURE 7.9. Nefertari playing the sistra in two scenes from the eastern pylon of Luxor Temple. Photographs courtesy of Erika Feleg.

of Kamutef, the fertility aspect of Amun.[108] In one episode the couple escorts Min's processional statue. Nefertari agitates two elaborately decorated sistra, while a *menat*-necklace hangs from the crook of her left arm. A caption records her chant to the god:

> *Words spoken by the Great Royal Wife Nefertari-Beloved of Mut to her father Min-Amun-Kamutef: "May you be at perfect peace O Lord of the Gods in your Mansion of Millions of Years. I play the sistra to your beautiful face so I might propitiate your beautiful face. May you protect your son, whom you love. May you be content on account of him: (namely) the Lord of the Two Lands, Usermaatre-Setepenre, given life like Re eternally."*[109]

Nefertari is resplendent in sumptuous panoply in the painted wall reliefs of her well-preserved tomb in the Valley of the Queens (QV 66).

FIGURE 7.10. Statue of Nefertari attached to a colossus of Ramesses II in the forecourt of Luxor temple. Photograph by Peter Brand.

She wears a long, pleated linen gown with a wide hem and flaring sleeves. Women of the king's household made this "royal linen" in palace residences. The elite prized these luxurious fabrics. Egyptian art idealizes these costumes as brilliant white with a gossamer texture, leaving the woman's body contours visible beneath. In sculpture, pleated gowns cling to every voluptuous curve of her figure (figs. 7.10 and 7.11).

Nefertari also wore an assortment of ostentatious wigs and exquisite jewelry common to high-born women: broad collars composed of tubular beads, large earrings, intricate bracelets, and anklets. These and other precious adornments were worked in gold and silver with inlays of amethyst, carnelian, lapis lazuli, turquoise, and beads of colored glass and faience.

As the personification of Hathor, a queen's ornate regalia distinguished her from other court women, even from princesses. The golden headdress perched atop her elaborate wig announced the queen's supremacy among Egyptian women. Over a long tripartite wig, Nefertari

FIGURE 7.11. ← Nefertari's statue attached to a colossus of Ramesses II from the forecourt of Luxor temple. She wears an enveloping Hathoric wig and the double uraeus serpents of queenship. Photograph by Peter Brand.

FIGURE 7.12. Nefertari wearing a vulture head-dress and enveloping wig offering wine to Hathor from her tomb in the Valley of the Queens (QV 66). Courtesy Manna Nader Gabana Studios Cairo.

often wore a golden cap crown in the form of a vulture goddess. Atop this, a circular platform called a modius supported a solar disk and two lofty feathers. Nefertari's honorary epithet "beautiful in the tall-plumed diadem" evokes this elegant crown, her usual regalia in wall paintings on her tomb (fig. 7.1 above).

Nefertari also wore the "enveloping" wig that evokes Hathor. This immense hairdo covered her head and shoulders, hiding her ears beneath a dense mass of wavy tresses, while her earrings peek out through this voluminous coiffure (fig. 7.12).

Along with assorted shorter and longer wigs, Nefertari might don a golden circlet with twin uraeus cobras, symbolizing the protective goddesses Nekhbet and Wadjet and her own queenship. Her modius crown could have a circle of rearing uraeus serpents facing out in every direction. These cobra symbols evoked the fierce power of the goddesses who protected both king and sun god. Even Hathor, goddess of love and sex, had her dangerous side. As the "Eye of Re," she took the form of a divine cobra spitting fiery venom at his enemies.[110]

Inside her own Abu Simbel shrine, Nefertari appears with a rich array of wigs and crowns, including one golden circlet usually reserved for Pharaoh himself, signaling her exclusive role as his feminine counterpart.[111] Nefertari's exotic regalia testifies to her preeminence among all Ramesses II's women and hints at her political influence.

Nefertari's Prestige and Influence

Along with Ramesses's mother Tuya, Nefertari's jurisdiction extended to all the king's women, children, and palace attendants dwelling within the *kheneret*-household. Residing in her own suite of palace apartments, she presided over a society of highborn women at court.[112]

But how much clout did she have with Ramesses II in political affairs? We can only guess how often she advised him in official matters, or how successfully. But hers was an informal, "soft power," now hidden from our eyes. Nefertari's rank and prestige as Ramesses II's first great royal wife and mother of the heir ensured her regular access to her husband, granting her opportunities to sway him. As with royal women throughout history—and the wives of modern presidents and prime ministers—the influence of a pharaoh's senior consort varied according to the situation and the personalities of both spouses.

Some, bedazzled perhaps by their queenly regalia, may overstate the power of wives like the famous Nefertiti, Akhenaten's chief consort and alleged power behind his throne. Some also believe his mother Tiy dominated both her son Akhenaten and her husband Amenhotep III. This is not to say these women had no influence, only that we have no way of measuring it.[113] Late in her career, Nefertari did participate in at least one affair of state. Shortly after Ramesses II concluded a peace treaty with the Hittite monarch Hattusili III, Nefertari addressed a pair of diplomatic letters to her Hittite counterpart, Queen Puduhepa. Both messages are entirely formal and congratulatory. Yet, they were not without significance, for they reflected Nefertari's privileged rank in the royal family's hierarchy.[114]

Although Nefertari lived to witness the Egyptian-Hittite peace treaty in Pharaoh's third decade of rule, she died soon after, just as work on the temples at Abu Simbel came to fruition. Some historians depict her final days as a tragic romance, with Ramesses II dedicating his shrine to her at Abu Simbel as she lay dying on the royal barge.[115] In fact, we know nothing of her cause of death, but no later than regnal year thirty, and probably several years earlier, Ramesses interred her in the splendid tomb (QV 66) he prepared for her in the Valley of the Queens.[116]

In the Twentieth Dynasty her tomb fell victim to robbers, who ransacked almost every tomb in the Valleys of the Queens. Aside from parts of her legs, they destroyed Nefertari's mortal remains in their greed to pluck every piece of jewelry and the

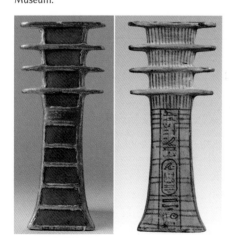

FIGURE 7.13. Gilt wood *djed*-pillar amulet inlaid with blue glass from the tomb of Nefertari. The inscription painted on the back (right) reads: "The Osiris-Great Royal Wife, his beloved, Nefertari, true of voice like Re." Turin Egyptian Museum 5163. Courtesy Turin Egyptian Museum.

amulets that once adorned her mummy. Archaeologists discovered a few minor objects the robbers overlooked.(fig. 7.13).[117]

Isetnofret

Among several brides Sety I chose for the adolescent Prince Ramesses was Isetnofret (fig. 7.14), a young woman whose name means "The Beautiful Isis."[118] She gave her youthful husband his second viable son, also named Ramesses, securing an honored place for herself and her children within Ramesses II's extensive household. Isetnofret's origins are a mystery.[119] Like Nefertari, she lacked the titles of "king's daughter" and "king's sister," so she was not a princess.

Figure 7.14. Bust of a small statue of Isetnofret. Her cartouche is inscribed on her right shoulder. Brussels Inv. E 5924. Courtesy Musées Royaux d'Art et d'Histoire.

Nominally, Isetnofret's rank of great royal wife equaled Nefertari's. In practice, Nefertari far outstripped her in prestige and influence. Few, if any royal monuments portray Isetnofret. She was not alone: Ramesses honored no other woman on his monuments but Nefertari—and his mother Tuya—until after his favorite consort died.

Some imagine these women competed as beautiful but bitter rivals for their husband's affections, Nefertari jealously guarding her prerogatives and Isetnofret envying her preeminence.[120] Although they coexisted as his leading spouses for two decades or more, ancient sources tell us nothing of how they interacted. Speculating about a glamorous feud between Nefertari and Isetnofret revives outdated gender stereotypes and is best left to tawdry fiction.

Most of our knowledge about Isetnofret comes from monuments her son, Prince Khaemwaset, created to honor his mother and her children three decades after his father ascended the throne.[121] Beginning around regnal year thirty, as Ramesses II celebrated his first Jubilee festival, Khaemwaset traveled across Egypt to herald the event. As he passed through the far south of the realm, the prince left two stelae at Aswan and Gebel es-Silsilah depicting him alongside both his parents, his elder brother Ramesses Junior, his younger brother Merenptah, and his eldest sister Bintanath (fig. 7.15).[122]

By his first Jubilee, power dynamics within the pharaoh's family had shifted decisively in favor of Isetnofret's children.[123] Nefertari and Amunhirkhopeshef were dead. Now Isetnofret's eldest son Ramesses "Junior" was heir to the throne, while Ramesses II designated Bintanath as a great royal wife. Prince Khaemwaset himself prospered in his sac-

FIGURE 7.15. Reinforced photo of Prince Khaemwaset's "family stela" from the shrine of Horemheb at Gebel es-Silsila. From right to left, Prince Khaemwaset, Ramesses II, Queen Isetnofret, and Bintanath worship Ptah (far right). The relief dates to around the time of the first jubilee in regnal year thirty, after Isetnofret had died. Photograph and drawing by Peter Brand.

erdotal career as the high priest of Memphis and master of ceremonies for his father's Jubilee festivals. But what about Isetnofret herself?

In monumental inscriptions Khaemwaset dedicated in her honor, Isetnofret is called both "royal wife" and "great royal wife." By this time, her eldest son Ramesses Junior was heir. On the Aswan stela she is royal wife, but the Gebel es-Silsilah inscription heralds her as great royal wife.[124] Since they both date to the first Jubilee, it is unlikely Pharaoh increased Isetnofret's rank at that time. Instead, this discrepancy may arise because the Aswan stela's format left no room for the longer title. Even Nefertari is called by both titles on the monuments, although she was certainly great royal wife from the outset of her husband's reign.

While a great royal wife outranked a royal wife, multiple women could hold this exalted title at the same time.[125] Given Nefertari's singular eminence, it is possible Ramesses II conferred the title of great royal wife on Isetnofret only after Nefertari and Amunkhopeshef were dead and Prince Ramesses Junior became heir.[126] Isetnofret likely received the honor posthumously.[127] Years later, Isetnofret's youngest son Merenptah honored her memory with the title "king's mother" once he had succeeded Ramesses II, long after her own death.[128]

By their longevity, her sons Ramesses Junior, Khaemwaset, and Merenptah each served in turn as crown prince, until the youngest of the three eventually succeeded his father as Pharaoh.[129] Two of her daughters, Bintanath and Nebettawy, took her place as great royal wives during the Jubilee period. In this way, Isetnofret and her children won a kind of genetic revenge after living in the shadow of Nefertari and Crown Prince Amunhirkhopeshef for over twenty years.[130]

Isetnofret would have been proud of her children's advancement, but she did not live to see it. Had she survived Nefertari and ascended to the rank of great royal wife in her own lifetime, it is strange Ramesses II never permitted Isetnofret's name and image to appear beside his own on the colossal statues he erected and the temple reliefs he produced during his Jubilee years. Instead, her eldest daughter Bintanath stands beside him as great royal wife.

Given her absence, and her daughter's presence, on her husband's monuments, we may conclude that Isetnofret died before Ramesses II marked his first Jubilee in regnal year thirty, perhaps even before Nefertari's death.[131] But she is conspicuously absent from the Valley of the Queens, where Pharaoh prepared tombs for his mother Tuya, his preeminent wife Nefertari, and his senior daughters.[132]

FIGURE 7.16. Relief from Saqqara depicting the Great Royal Wife Isetnofret. Drawing by Peter Brand.

Aside from Khaemwaset's "family stelae," every known text naming Isetnofret comes from the Memphis region, leading some to believe she was born or resided there.[133] Perhaps Ramesses laid Isetnofret to rest in the vast Memphis necropolis of Saqqara, where her children, including the future Pharaoh Merenptah, attended her funeral (fig. 7.16). As in life, so in death, Isetnofret left a host of unanswered questions behind. Archaeologists have yet to discover her tomb.

Ramesses II's Other Wives

It is unclear how many women Ramesses II married over the course of his long reign, but we can divide them into three general categories: his Egyptian spouses from elite families, including Nefertari and Isetnofret; his two Hittite brides and other foreign princesses; and at least five of his own daughters whom he took as consorts in the middle and later years of his reign. Of all these women, we can identify only Isetnofret, Nefertari, the five daughter-wives, and the first Hittite bride by name. His second Hittite spouse is anonymous, but an official decree confirms the match.[134] Aside from these nine women, enumerating Pharaoh's additional wives becomes precarious. Diplomatic sources hint at further marriages to foreign brides, including a Babylonian princess and possibly others from three Mesopotamian kingdoms.[135] They might increase the number of wives to thirteen. Yet, the final tally is surely larger, since we know Ramesses sired at least one hundred children.

We know Nefertari and Isetnofret had at least fourteen children between them. Several other women gave birth to the majority of Ramesses's more than one hundred children.[136] All trace of these early wives has vanished, even their tombs, coffins, or personal monuments. We don't even know their names. Only the Abydos Dedicatory Inscription and the grand temple rosters of Ramesses II's offspring testify to their existence. This anonymity is the counterpoint to Nefertari's supremacy as his preeminent consort.

Pharaoh's Daughter-Wives

The most controversial—and to modern views, unsettling—aspect of pharaonic marriage practices were incestuous unions between kings and their close female relatives: sisters, half-sisters, and daughters.[137] Unlike several Eighteenth Dynasty kings, Ramesses II never, as far as we know, wed his sisters.[138] Instead, he took no fewer than five of his daughters as spouses: the Princess-wives Bintanath, Merytamun, Henuttawy, Nebettawy, and Henutmire. What this meant in practice has long exercised the imagination and moral indignation of historians.

Ramesses accorded each of his daughter-wives the dignity of great royal wife. Two were daughters of Nefertari and two were Isetnofret's, while Henutmire's mother is unknown. The pharaoh could have married their daughters after his senior queens died, or while they still lived.[139] Ramesses II's five daughter-wives fulfilled the same courtly roles as their mothers. He provided each with a splendid tomb in the Valley of the Queens next to those of Nefertari and the King's Mother Tuya, in a row along the north slope of the Valley.[140]

When sculptors carved the façade of Ramesses II's grand temple at Abu Simbel, no later than the mid-twenties of his reign, they honored six daughters of Nefertari and Isetnofret, along with the king's mother and his two eldest sons, beside the massive legs of Pharaoh's four towering colossi (fig. 7.17).[141] All six princesses are entitled "king's daughter," but their names are not enclosed by cartouches as with the statues of Nefertari and Tuya.

Statues of the daughters at Abu Simbel vary in scale and attire, and some bear queenly regalia. Bintanath, Merytamun, and Nebettawy all wear the enveloping Hathor wig and a vulture cap with a modius and two tall plumes, instead of the flowing sidelock of a princess. Does this

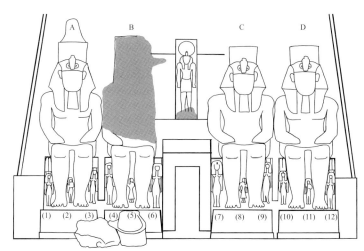

FIGURE 7.17. Diagram of the façade of the great temple of Abu Simbel showing the members of the royal family and the names of the four colossal statues of Ramesses II. Drawing by Peter Brand.

Named Colossi	Royal Family Members	
A: Beloved of Ruler-of-the-Two Lands	(1) Nebettawy	(7) Nefertari (Queen)
B: [Beloved of Re-of-Rulers]	(2) [Isetnofret (Princess)]	(8) Ramesses Junior
C: Beloved of Amun	(3) Bintanath	(9) Baketmut
D: Beloved of Atum	(4) Mut-Tuya	(10) Merytamun
	(5) Amunhirkhopeshef	(11) Nefertari (Princess)
	(6) Nefertari (Queen)	(12) Mut-Tuya

hint at their eventual rise to queenship? Princess Baketmut also dons a queenly Hathor wig and modius but hers lacks the tall plumes. Ironically, this means Baketmut's statue is taller than the other three, yet she is never attested as a daughter-wife. Two more princesses—standing between the legs of their father's colossi, Nefertari II and an unnamed woman who might be Isetnofret II—are shorter than the others and sport the side-lock of princesses.[142]

The daughter-wives can appear both as queens and as princesses on contemporary monuments. On the smaller Abu Simbel temple, small figures of Merytamun and her sister Henuttawy standing beside Nefertari's colossi depict them as princesses with long side locks and simple modius platforms atop their wigs. In the list of princesses inside their father's Abu Simbel temple, Bintanath, Merytamun, Henuttawy, and Nebettawy lack queenly attributes, but they wear such regalia on the façade, blurring the iconographic and textual distinction between princess and queen.

These daughter marriages enhanced Ramesses II's prestige and reconfirmed the ascendency of the children of Nefertari and Isetnofret at the pinnacle of the royal family's hierarchy. Another question remains unresolved. Why did Ramesses II marry these particular four daughters of Nefertari and Isetnofret instead of their sisters Baketmut, Nefertari II, and Isetnofret II? Perhaps these four outranked their sisters for some reason that now eludes us. Or the other three may have died before their father decided to wed them.

FIGURE 7.18. Bintanath and an anonymous "king's daughter" from her tomb in the Valley of the Queens (QV 71). The princess is not her daughter or sister but represents Bintanath herself in her aspect of "royal daughter." Drawing by Peter Brand.

The five daughter-wives are attested on a range of monuments: as subsidiary figures on their father's colossal statues, in temple lists showing processions of Ramesses II's many daughters, and in their tombs in the Valley of the Queens. Discerning the career trajectory of these women is difficult. None of the monuments is precisely dated, and we have only a rough idea of when an inscription was carved. The titles of the daughter-wives also fluctuated. They can be called "king's daughter," "royal wife," and "great royal wife," on the same monument, even in the same inscription. Therefore, we cannot say any of them were "promoted" from a lower to a higher status.[143] Even after they achieved queenship, lists of royal daughters in the temple of Wadi es-Sebua in Nubia, which Ramesses built in the forties or fifties of his reign, name them as royal daughters, without queenly cartouches or regalia.

An uncomfortable question looms over these father-daughter marriages: did Ramesses II consummate them? The idea that any man would have sexual relations with one—to say nothing of five—of his own daughters morally repels us. The squeamish, or those seeking to defend the king's reputation, insist these unions were only ceremonial. To those who regard Ramesses as a depraved despot, the mere existence of five daughter-wives signals his perverted tendencies. We simply cannot tell, because we cannot identify any offspring of these daughter-wives, and no reliable evidence for a child born to them exists today.[144] But the mothers of most of his hundred-odd children remain a mystery, so we cannot exclude the possibility.

Bintanath

Princess Bintanath was the eldest daughter of Isetnofret, born in the reign of her grandfather Sety I.[145] Her name means "Daughter of Anath" in the Canaanite tongue of the ancient Levant and honors the Canaanite war goddess Anath, whom New Kingdom pharaohs revered. Historians usually conclude she was the eldest of all his daughters (fig. 7.18).[146]

In Ramesses's first two decades as ruler she was entitled "king's bodily daughter" like her sisters. A processional scene from the west wall of the Luxor Forecourt labels each princess as a "chantress" of a particular goddess but designates Bintanath with the more exalted title "great one of the *khenerut*-women of Amun," a distinction she shared with Tuya and Nefertari.[147] She was in late childhood or adolescence when artists created this scene, around the third year of Ramesses II's reign, but already her prestige was greater than any of her sisters. Bintanath's star continued to rise over the coming decades.

Determining when Ramesses made Bintanath one of his consorts is difficult.[148] It was likely after both Nefertari and Isetnofret had passed into the underworld.[149] Several colossal statues erected on or after his thirty-fourth regnal year include smaller images of Bintanath as consort, with the titles "king's daughter" and either "great royal wife" or "royal wife."[150] At times she bears additional honors. On her father's limestone colossus from Hermopolis, she is "Hereditary Noblewoman (*iryet-pat*), Great of Praises, Mistress of the South and North, King's Daughter, Great Royal Wife, Bintanath."[151]

In the Queens' Valley, Ramesses II built an impressive tomb for Bintanath (QV 71) near those for Tuya and Nefertari.[152] The wall decoration is typical of Ramesside queen's tombs, showing Bitnanath adoring the gods of the underworld. Two scenes in the burial chamber are unique because an unnamed princess accompanies the queen. On the east wall, Bintanath worships a symbol of Osiris. The caption identifies her as "the Osiris Great Royal Wife, Lady of the Two Lands, Mistress of South and North, Bintanath, True of Voice." Standing just behind the queen is a princess identified only as "king's bodily daughter (fig. 7.18)."[153] On the opposite wall, Queen Bintanath worships the god Res-Wedja, an aspect of Osiris, while this anonymous princess, wearing the side lock of a royal daughter but lacking a queenly diadem, adores the goddess Nepthys. Could she be a child of Bintanath by Ramesses II, and therefore her sister-daughter?[154]

Elsewhere in the Queens' Valley, only the tomb owner appears before the gods. No relative, not even Pharaoh, is present or named.[155] As the tomb owner, Bintanath's name is prefixed by that of Osiris, allowing her to merge her identity with the Ruler the netherworld as The Osiris-Bintanath. This, it turns out, is our clue to the phantom princess's identity.

The caption identifies this princess as "the Osiris king's daughter."[156] This princess *is* the tomb's owner: Bintanath herself.[157] These images

FIGURE 7.19. Relief depicting Merytamun as a daughter-wife. Inset upper left: titles and cartouche of Binanath from another Luxor colossus. Both women are entitled "king's daughter and king's wife." In the later decades of his reign, Ramesses ordered identical images of Merytamun and Bintanath carved on some of his standing colossi at Luxor temple. Reinforced photograph by Peter Brand.

depict both a younger Bintanath as a princess and an older one as royal wife, just as the *Book of the Dead* may show the deceased, in the same scene, as youthful and elderly. In life, Bintanath kept her title "king's daughter" even after she attained the rank of great royal wife.[158] Likewise, in the afterlife, she was reborn for all eternity both as a princess and a queen.

Bintanath survived her father, living on into the reign of her brother Merenptah, Isetnofret's youngest son. On a statue originally made for Amenhotep III, Merenptah inscribed his own names and inserted an image of his older sister beside his striding leg. It depicts Bintanath as a queen with the titles: "king's daughter, king's sister, and great royal wife."[159] Having outlived her father, did she now become her brother's ceremonial spouse as well? Or, like her grandmother, the dowager Tuya, did an elderly Bintanath retain her queenly title after Ramesses II died?[160]

Merytamun: "She Whom Amun Loves"

Ramesses II selected Merytamun to be his consort sometime in the twenties of his reign.[161] She appears beside her father on a stela the Viceroy of Kush, Hekanakht, dedicated at Abu Simbel, showing Pharaoh and his daughter offering to Amun, Re-Horakhty, and the divine Ramesses himself.[162] In a scene below them, Hekanakht kneels before Nefertari, who sits on her throne as he intones a hymn in praise of the three gods shown above. The form of the king's nomen cartouche indicates Hekanakht dedicated his stela no earlier than year twenty-one. As with her statue carved on the façade of the grand temple nearby, Merytamun's regalia is queenly. On the stela she bears the title "king's daughter," but her name appears in a cartouche.

When Merytamun became a great royal wife along with Bintanath, whether before or after Nefertari died, is uncertain. In the thirties of his reign, as Ramesses celebrated his Jubilees, he honored both of these daughter-wives with images standing beside him on his colossi and with statues of their own.[163] Merytamun is often paired with her half-sister Bintanath (fig. 7.19) or with the pharaoh's first Hittite consort, Maahorneferure.[164]

A colossus of Ramesses II originally from Piramesses, now at Tanis, depicts a princes-queen named Merytre, which means "She Whom Re Loves."[165] We never see her on other monuments, nor does she possess a tomb in the Queens Valley. Not a "new" daughter-wife of Ramesses, Merytre is simply an alias for Merytamun. Like her older brother Amunhirkhopeshef, Merytamun sometimes went by a different name in northern Egypt.[166]

Ramesses also honored Merytamun with a splendid colossal statue of her own. Archaeologists uncovered it in 1991 amid the ruins of a temple to the fertility god Min at Akhmim (fig. 7.20).[167] This exquisite limestone colossus, with its tall plummed diadem, towers above large statues of her mother Nefertari at Abu Simbel.[168] The Akhmim statue was originally crafted for a late Eighteenth Dynasty queen. In the second half of his reign, Ramesses II repurposed it for his favored daughter-wife, just as he reinscribed statuary of earlier pharaohs for himself.[169]

We have no idea when Merytamun died, but Ramesses interred her in a splendid tomb in the Queens' Valley (QV 68), which matches Bintanath's tomb in size and layout.[170] Little of QV 68's carved plaster wall decoration survives, and most of its colors have faded, but Merytamun's tomb once equaled her mother Nefertari's in beauty and sophistication.

Nebettawy and Henuttawy

These two daughter-wives rarely appear outside the lists of princesses. Nebettawy's name means "Lady of the Two Lands" (fig. 7.21).[171] Although the evidence is ambiguous, it is more likely that Iset-nofret was her mother.[172] We know little else about Nebettawy's life.[173] Princess Henuttawy, "Mistress of the Two Lands," was a younger daughter of Ne-

FIGURE 7.20. Limestone Colossus of Merytamun as a queen from the temple of Min in Akhmim. Originally made for a late Eighteenth Dynasty queen, Ramesses II reinscribed it for Merytamun as his daughter-wife. Alamy.

fertari.[174] Small statues of her as a princess flank Nefertari's colossi on the façade of the smaller temple of Abu Simbel. Ramesses II gave both these daughter-wives tombs in the Queens' Valley, but they are not identical. Nebettawy's tomb (QV 60) is unique, with a vaulted ceiling in its antechamber and a large number of side chambers.[175] Henuttawy's house of eternity (QV 73) is a small "prefabricated" tomb.[176] Craftsmen left the cartouches empty, to be filled in once its eventual occupant died.[177] Perhaps she died prematurely, before Pharaoh could build her a more elaborate tomb.

Henutmire: "A Mistress Like Re"

Henutmire, the fifth of Ramesses II's daughter-wives, held the titles king's bodily daughter, royal wife, great royal wife, hereditary noble-

Figure 7.21. ➡ An early nineteenth-century color facsimile of an image of Nebettawy from her tomb in the Valley of the Queens (QV 60) by Prisse d'Avennes. Today, little of the paint in the tombs of Ramesses II's royal women still survives, aside from Nefertari's tomb. NYPL digital collections. Public domain.

Figure 7.22. ➡ ➡ Relief of Henutmire as daughter-wife, from a granite colossus of Ramesses II, now in the Sohag Museum. Courtesy of Manna Nader Gabana Studios Cairo.

woman (*iryet-pat*), great of praises, lady of the Two Lands, and mistress of North and South (fig. 7.22).[178] Her precise relationship to Ramesses is debated, and theories can verge on the bizarre. Some consider her the daughter of Sety I and Tuya, and therefore Ramesses II's sister-wife, because Henutmire's image appears on the side of Tuya's magnificent Vatican statue.[179] Others claim Henutmire was born to an unknown sister-wife of Ramesses, with Tuya being both her maternal *and* paternal grandmother, a close relationship indeed.[180] Or was she the child of a royal daughter-wife?[181] If so, Ramesses would have been, astonishingly, Henutmire's father, grandfather, and husband! But no solid evidence for any of these notions exists.[182] It is more likely she was Ramesses II's daughter whom he later took as a consort.[183] The identity of her mother remains a mystery to us.[184]

Henutmire outlived her father, dying amid a schism between his grandson, Sety II, and the usurper pharaoh Amenmesse, a dozen years or so after Ramesses II died.[185] Amid political turmoil, a crooked foreman named Paneb from the village of the royal tomb builders, dared to raid her tomb. Listed among his crimes was the following: *Accusation about his going to the burial of Henutmire, L.P.H., and stealing a goose.*[186] Was the goose a valuable statue or a fresh food offering Paneb hoped to eat for supper? Sadly, it was not the last postmortem indignity she suffered, for thieves looted her burial several decades later, taking everything of value. In the ninth century BCE, a High

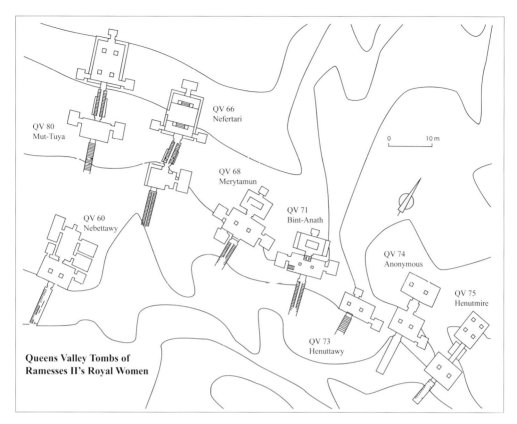

FIGURE 7.23. Map of the eight grand tombs Ramesses II constructed for his most favored female relatives in the Valley of the Queens. Drawing by Daniel Warne.

Priest of Amun named Harsiese even took Henutmire's sarcophagus for himself.[187]

Tombs of the Queens in the Place of Beauty

Across the Nile from Thebes lies a small desert valley the ancients called *Ta Set Neferu*, "The Place of Beauty."[188] Known today as the Valley of the Queens, this desolate landscape was consecrated by pharaohs of the Nineteenth and Twentieth Dynasties who built tombs for their favored royal women and sons. Unlike previous dynasty, the Ramessides, and Ramesses II most of all, created large tombs with elaborate painted reliefs to honor their royal women—and provide them with unique, independent afterlives.[189]

When pharaohs of the Eighteenth Dynasty had begun tunneling into the Valley of the Kings to fashion grand tombs for themselves, the provisions they made for their wives were far more modest.[190] A king might allot space for his great royal wife within his own tomb. Lesser wives were deposited in small undecorated burial chambers at the bottom of a deep shaft, often sharing a communal tomb, as with the burial of three Syrian wives of Thutmose III.[191]

In the Nineteenth Dynasty, the first Ramesside pharaohs transformed both the eternal destiny of their wives and daughters and the landscape of the Valley, renaming it The Place of Beauty. Ramesses I and Sety I built at least five tombs for their women, which grew progressively more complex in their design and decoration.[192] Among the earliest of these (QV 38) belonged to Ramesses I's principal wife Satre. Her burial vault seems abbreviated and hurriedly finished, but its decorative program served as the basis for all later Ramesside queens' tombs.[193] Sety also constructed four more tombs on the south slope of the valley for great royal wives and king's daughters, but these were "prefabricated."[194] Builders left the cartouches blank until the eventual occupant was laid to rest.[195]

Tombs in the Place of Beauty attained the height of intricacy and grandeur under Ramesses II, who commissioned no fewer than eight of them, for three generations of his highest-ranking women. These formed a "queen's row" along the north flank of the valley (fig. 7.23).[196] Most have fared badly over the millennia, suffering from collapsed ceilings, destroyed walls, ruined portals, and damage from torrential rains, tomb robbers, fires, and vandals. These misfortunes have wrecked their fragile stucco surfaces and scoured or blackened their once vibrant painted reliefs.[197]

The miraculous exception to this devestation is QV 66, the spectacular tomb of Nefertari, who was favored as much by fate itself as by Ramesses II. When Italian archaeologists uncovered it in 1904, they were dumbstruck to find its exquisite murals virtually intact (fig. 7.24). Over the next several decades the tomb began to deteriorate rapidly, forcing Egyptian authorities to close it to visitors. In the 1980s, an international team of conservators expertly cleaned, consolidated, and restored this astonishing tomb.[198] Their work revealed colors so vibrant that viewers might think the artists had just painted them. But Nefertari's exquisite murals were not unique. In their heyday, all these queens' tombs rivaled QV 66 in the quality of their polychrome and the iconographic richness and variety of their wall scenes.

The earliest and grandest of these tombs belonged to Nefertari (QV 66) and Ramesses II's mother Tuya (QV 80). Just as elaborate, but smaller, were the burial vaults for the two eldest daughter-wives, Bintanath (QV 71) and Merytamun (QV 68). Ramesses II appears to have prefabricated three more tombs, assigning the smallest (QV 73) to Henuttawy and a slightly larger one (QV 75) to Henutmire. He also commissioned QV 74, but it remained empty until Ramesses IV pressed it into service for his consort Duatentipet.[199] Just to the south of the tombs of Tuya and Nefertari is the tomb of Nebettawy.

In their design and decoration, the tombs of Ramesses II's women were innovative. Graceful figures of their queenly owners interacting

with gods of the netherworld filled every wall beneath a deep-blue ceiling filled with yellow stars. These charming images were not merely decorative, but functioned magically, enabling the deceased to be reborn in the afterlife by merging her identity with Osiris and Re.[200]

The most surpising feature of the tombs Ramesses II commissioned for his royal women is his complete absence from their decoration. Nowhere in any of these tombs do we see the image or read the name of the pharaoh himself. This taboo enabled royal women to make their own way in the Afterlife, where their identities merged with Osiris and they were reborn each day like the sun god Re. The presence of a male spouse, it seems, would interfere with this process (fig. 7.25).[201]

These magnificent sepultures were reserved for Ramesses II's most favored women. There were no additional tombs in The Place of Beauty for his numerous wives and daughters: Isetnofret, his Egyptian and foreign brides, or even his first Hittite wife Maahorneferure.[202] They were buried elsewhere in more modest graves.

The tombs of Nefertari and his senior royal women are perhaps the only monuments Ramesses II ever built devoid of his own name and image. Yet, he still gained prestige from these splendid tombs. In life and in death, his wives, playing Hathor to his Re, fulfilled their roles in the larger mythological drama of his god-kingship. And the hundred children they gave him, marching in grand processions in temple wall scenes, were living evidence of his godlike powers and potency.

FIGURE 7.24. ↖ Nefertari offering wine to Isis from her tomb in the Valley of the Queens (QV 66). Courtesy Manna Nader Gabana Studios Cairo.

FIGURE 7.25. ↑ Horus leading Nefertari from her tomb in the Valley of the Queens (QV 66). Courtesy of Manna Nader Gabana Studios Cairo.

Notes

1. Ziegler 2008; Roth 2009.
2. Robins 2008.
3. Ziegler 2008, 134–51.
4. Dodson and Hilton 2004, 26–31; Roth 2009.
5. Troy 1986; 2008; Roth 2009.
6. On the title "king's mother" (*mwt-nsw*), see Roth 2001; Dodson and Hilton 2004, 31–32. Since the king was considered divine, his mother was entitled "god's mother" (*mwt-nṯr*); Roth 2001.
7. Troy 1986; Roth 2006, 2009.
8. Troy 1986, 2008; Robins 2008.
9. Leblanc 1999; Brand 2016. See pp. 256–57 below.
10. Brand 2016, 10–12
11. Robins 1994; Brand 2016, 10 and n. 13–14. See p. 56 above.
12. Reiser's seminal study 1972 is now outdated. For a critical review see Kemp 1976. For overviews of the Egyptian royal "harem," see Callender 1994; Roth 2012; Yoyotte 2008.
13. Roth 2012.
14. Peirce 1993.
15. Roth 2012.
16. See the essays collected in Walthall 2008.
17. Said 1979.
18. On the harem in western perceptions, see Elie 2004.
19. On Orientalism in Egyptology, see Vasiljević 2016; Hellum 2020; forthcoming.
20. See comments of Roth 2012.
21. The *pr-ḫnrt* had door keepers who acted as security guards. They were compromised in the assassination conspiracy against Ramesses III; see Redford 2002; Vernus 2003; Hawass 2014.
22. The concubine theory has been thoroughly refuted: Nord 1970; Ward 1983; Hellum 2020.
23. In Ottoman studies, scholars like Pierce have moved on from the myth of the harem and related orientalist fallacies to address the institution of royal polygamy in its true historical and cultural context: Peirce 1993 and 2008; Elie 2004; Lewis 2004. The same is true for historical and cultural studies of other polygamous royal systems. See the essays collected in Walthall 2008. For the ancient Near East, see Solvang 2006 and the studies in Budin and Turfa 2016. Regarding ancient Near Eastern palace women, Solvang (2006, 398) concludes: "Even freed from its Orientalist baggage, the Ottoman harem analogy does not fit well with the Mari and Neo-Assyrian data. Applying this analogy to these contexts necessitates qualifying the term and the institution it represents and can result in missing or misreading the ancient sources."
24. Picton 2016, 231–32: "It would have been better for our attempt to understand the subtleties and realities of how the New Kingdom administration dealt with the plethora of women thrust over Egypt's border, if the first translator had picked a random word, real or invented, which might have elicited a more intelligent assessment of their place in society than the culturally loaded term 'harem.'"
25. On the royal administration and court of the Ramesside period, see Grandet 2013.

26. On the "mooring places of Pharaoh," see Grandet 2013, 856 with n. 69.

27. Grandet 2013, 862–87.

28. Remains of a residential palace complex at Medinet Ghurob in the Fayum dating to the Eighteenth and Nineteenth Dynasties constitute the clearest archaeological evidence for the living quarters of royal women and children in the New Kingdom. Textual records and artifacts found in the settlement and its nearby cemeteries indicate that it housed members of the royal family and their attendants: Kemp 1978; Lacovara 1997; Shaw 2011; Yoyotte 2008; Picton 2016. More difficult to identify in the archaeological record are the family quarters within late Eighteenth Dynasty palaces of Amenhotep III at Malkata and of Akhenaten at El-Amarna and the compact palaces of Ramesside royal cult temples at Thebes like Medinet Habu: Reiser 1972, 32–47; O'Connor 2010. For Memphis, we have only textual sources—administrative documents and the funerary monuments of officials who served in the *ipt-nsw* and *pr-ḥnrt*: Reiser 1972, 48–87; Gohary 2011; Roth 2012.

29. The translation of *ipt nsw* and the precise function of this institution is hotly debated. It has often been regarded as the term for the king's women, namely, the so-called royal harem: Reiser 1972, 1–11; Kemp 1976; Callender 1994, 9–10; Roth 2012. This meaning has also been challenged by Gardiner (1948, 91), Nord (1975, 145), and most recently Picton (2016, 231–32). Before the New Kingdom, the *ipt-nsw* clearly designated the residential quarters of the royal palace, wherein the king and his women and children lived: Nord 1975; Callender 1994, 10–17. In the New Kingdom, it can be distinguished from a related section of the royal residence, the *pr-ḥnr/pꜣ ḫnty*, where his family resided. See below.

30. Nord 1975, 145. Ward (1983, 69–70) considers "royal apartment" as one possible translation of *ipt nsw*, along with "royal accounting-house" and "royal granary." While possible in some instances, it is clear that the term usually designates palace living quarters.

31. Callender 1994, 17; Roth 2012, 4.

32. Pereyra De Fidanza 2000.

33. Reiser 1972, 11–16; Roth 2012; Brand 2016, 8–9 with n. 10.

34. The term *pꜣ-ḫnty* seems to be a New Kingdom variant of *pr-ḥnrt*: reflecting linguistic changes in the New Kingdom dialect: Reiser 1972, 13–14; Picton 2016, 232. It can refer both to a palace structure and to the women who dwelled therein.

35. Nord 1981; Bryan 1982; Callender 1994, 7–9; Roth 2012, 2–3; Guégan 2020.

36. Onstine 2005, 2016.

37. PM II², 308, 20; Feleg 2020, 190–96 with figs. 39–40.

38. *KRI* II, 919–20; *RITA* II, 600; *RITANC* II, 620–21.

39. Fantechi and Zingarelli 2002.

40. O'Connor 2010.

41. *KRI* II, 328:4–6; Brand 2016, 8–10. See ch. 3.

42. The Turin Juridical Papyrus suggests the *ipt-nsw* was located within the larger *pr-ḥnrt*. Likewise, inscriptions from the tomb of a Ramesside high official named Tjuroy name him as a "great overseer of the royal apartments (*ipt nsw*) of the *kheneret*-household (*pr-ḥnrt*) of the Lord of the Two Lands"; Gohary 2011.

43. In the Turin Juridical Papyrus, this is called "the royal apartments of the kheneret-household in-the-following" (*ipt nsw n pr ḥnr ḥr šmsw*).

44. Female inhabitants of the *pr-ḥnrt* were collectively called *ḥnrw(t)*-women in the Abydos Dedicatory Inscription; K*RI* II, 328:5. See Reiser 1972, 14–16. Adult women and younger *nfrwt*-maidens also attended the king within the *ipt-nsw*; see O'Connor 2010.

45. Polygamous kings fathered numerous children to demonstrate their fecundity and enhance their prestige, not merely to beget heirs; see Walthall 2008, 13–14.

46. Even as we reject Orientalist fantasies about harems and study Egyptian women in their own right, we cannot forget that Egypt was a male-dominated society.

47. On the bull as a symbol of royal power, see Hsu 2015.

48. Barbara Watson Andaya shows how kings in various premodern and modern civilizations in Asia and Africa used royal polygyny as a powerful tool for securing the loyalty of elite subordinates and vassals, and diplomatic alliances with foreign rulers. Throughout history, dynastic marriage alliances enabled kings to secure good relations between royal and elite power centers, both in polygynous cultures and in Christian Europe where monogamy was the rule: Watson Andaya 2008, 24–27. In the Sixth Dynasty, Pepy I married two daughters of a regional official in Upper Egypt named Khui. Both sisters were renamed Ankhesenpepy and gave birth to the next two kings, Merenre and Pepy II. Amenhotep III's senior consort Tiy was the daughter of a well-connected official named Yuya and his wife Thuya. Although pharaohs often married their sisters or half-sisters, cases like Tiy were more frequent than we might imagine—even if we can identify relatively few such women bearing the title great royal wife.

49. See the essays in Walthall 2008.

50. See pp. 354–56 below.

51. The Great Kings of Assyria, Babylonia, and Hatti married the daughters of their vassal kings as well as those of their peer monarchs; Meier 2000.

52. On the Orientalist stereotype of the lascivious pharaoh, see pp. 475–77 below.

53. Walthall 2008, 13–14.

54. Notably absent from the range of titles for Pharaoh's kin is a term meaning "royal brother." A king's living male siblings were an implicit threat to his sovereignty, and the term *sn*, "brother," could also mean "rival/opponent"; see Revez 2003. The god Horus and his uncle Seth were also labeled "brothers" in mythic accounts of their violent competition for the right to be Osiris's successor. Two contemporary Ramesside folktales, The Tale of the Two Brothers and The Blinding of Truth by Falsehood, depict pairs of brothers as bitter rivals. In The Tale of the Two Brothers, some scholars find allusions to dynastic strife in the late Nineteenth Dynasty.

55. Kingship was a masculine office and women, like the female Pharaoh Hatshepsut, rarely ruled. Hatshepsut was a great royal wife while her husband Thutmose II lived and, in the earliest years of Thutmose III, she acted as regent. Once she assumed the mantle of kingship, she became "King" Hatshepsut, taking on masculine titles including *nsw-bity*, Dual King. Hatshepsut sometimes feminized titles like *s3t Rˤ*, "Daughter of Re," but she projected a masculine image in statuary and relief decoration, which usually depicts her as a man.

56. Although Nefertari is well attested as "great royal wife," *ḥmt-nsw wrt*, from the beginning of Ramesses II's reign, inscriptions sometimes give her the lesser title of "royal wife," *ḥmt-nsw*, with both variants sometimes appearing on the same monument, as with the lid of her sarcophagus: *KRI* II, 851: 5–7. Likewise, in her temple at Abu Simbel, Nefertari often bears the shorter title where insufficient wall space precluded the fuller one. This is especially true when she is given more epithets like "female heiress," *iryt-pʿt*, "great of praise," *wrt ḥswt*, and the like: Desroches-Noblecourt and Kuentz 1968, pls. 23–27, 35–36, 43–44, 47–48, 53–54, 57–58, 66–67, 93–96, 98–99, 119–22.

57. As has sometimes been suggested in the case of daughter-wives like Bintanath and Merytamun. See below.

58. In the Eighteenth Dynasty, three of Thutmose III's foreign wives buried in a single tomb each held the title *ḥmt-nsw*; Lilyquist 2003.

59. Nord 1970; Ward 1983; Stefanović 2015.

60. As a courtly rank indicator, *ḥkrt-nsw* might be the equivalent of "matron" or "lady in waiting"; Troy 1986, 77–79.

61. Troy 1986, 78–79. They are explicitly described as "having not yet opened up to give birth" in a tale about King Snefru from P. Westcar: Simpson 2003, 16–18.

62. Epigraphic Survey, *Medinet Habu VIII*, pls. 630–646, 648–655. The *nfr-wt*-maidens are associated with the royal apartments (*ipt-nsw*), where senior royal wives and palace officials supervised them; Gohary 2009 and 2011.

63. O'Connor 2010; Troy 1986, 78–79.

64. *KRI* II, 664; *RITA* II, 446; *RITANC* II, 440; Gaballa and Kitchen 1968, 261–63; Habachi 1969b; Leblanc 1999, 26–27; 2019, fig. 2; Obsomer 2012b, 218. The beginning of the wife's name is damaged and could be read either as [Ru]ia or [Tu]ia.

65. Habachi 1969b; Desroches-Noblecourt 1982; Manouvrier 1996, 37–42; Leblanc 2009b, 174–83 ; Obsomer 2012b, 219–25.

66. Desroches-Noblecourt 1982, 233–34, 236.

67. *KRI* II, 846; *RITA* II, 551–52; *RITANC* II, 552–54.

68. For Tuya's titles, see Manouvrier 1996, 38–39.

69. So, *mwt-nsw [ḥnwt nfrwt ḥnwt] ḥkrt-nsw Mwt ʿnḫ.ti rnp.ti ḏt*; see Obsomer 2017, 45–53. Most interesting is Tuya's title "[Mistress] of the Ornamented Ones of the King." Earlier scholars wrongly took this as "concubine," but we now know it was a rank indicator for elite women associated with the royal court. Common in the Middle Kingdom, the title seems to have fallen into abeyance by the end of the Middle Kingdom. The new inscription from Tuya's temple at the Ramesseum suggests Ramesses II revived the title as a mark of his mother's prestige among court women. On the title *ḥkrt-nsw*, see most recently Stefanović 2015.

70. Troy 1986, 2008; Robins 2008.

71. Roth 2001.

72. The strong political bonds of trust and support between the king and his dowager mother are a recurrent pattern in monarchical systems throughout history. The dowager's status often surpassed that of the preeminent royal wife. See Walthall, 2008, 11–13; Lal 2008, 104–8.

73. EA 26–28 Rainey 2015; Xekalaki 2011, 166–67.

74. A relief, Vienna 5091, depicting Ramesses II and Tuya in adoration of Osiris can be dated to the forties or fifties of his reign because of the form of his

nomen cartouche containing the epithet "god and ruler of Heliopolis": *KRI* II, 847; *RITANC* II, 555–56. See pp. 425 and 428, fig. 14.21 below.

75. Vatican Museum 22678: Kozloff 1996; *KRI* II, 844; *RITA* II, 550; *RITANC* II, 549–50. From Tanis comes another granite statue originally made for a wife of Senwosret II, which Ramesses II repurposed to honor his mother; Cairo JdE 37484.

76. *KRI* II, 845; *RITA* II, 551; *RITANC* II, 551; Leblanc and Esmoingt 2014; Leblanc 2019, 114–16 and figs. 66–68.

77. Diodorus Siculus, *Bibliotheca Historica* I.47; Leblanc 1993b.

78. PM II², 437 14b; *KRI* II, 648; *RITA* II, 433; *RITANC* II, 433; Schmidt and Willeitner 1994, 57, fig. 72; Leblanc 2019, fig. 3.

79. Brunner 1986; Lurson 2015.

80. Lurson 2015, 113.

81. Habachi 1969b; Desroches-Noblecourt 1990; Obsomer 2012b, 220–20; Lurson 2015, 2017a, 2017b.

82. Desroches-Noblecourt 1990; Lurson 2015.

83. *Urk.* IV, 1714–15. Translation adapted from Murnane 1995a, 22–23.

84. This episode is not preserved among the fragments of Tuya's temple, but a parallel occurs on the south wall of the Great Hypostyle Hall at Karnak: Brand, Feleg, and Murnane 2018, pl. 66.

85. Brunner 1986, pls. 8–9, 12.

86. Lurson 2015, 114–23.

87. Lurson 2015, 123–37.

88. See p. 320 below.

89. Desroches-Noblecourt 1982, 232–35; Leblanc 1989, pls. 222–24; 2009b, figs. 210–13; McCarthy 2011, 197–222; Demas and Agnew 2012–2016, 1:60, 2:478–90; Elleithy and Leblanc 2016, 245–56, 346, pl. 70A–B.

90. Romano 1979, 142–43, cat. no. 215; Freed 1987, 140–41, cat. no. 8. For other fragments of her burial equipment, see Desroches-Noblecourt 1982, 232–35.

91. *KRI* II, 847:3–4; *RITA* II, 552; *RITANC* II, 554–55.

92. Hari 1979. Leblanc (1993a, 331–33; 1999, 24–25) and Obsomer (2012b, 232–33) flirt with the notion that Nefertari could have been, if not a daughter, then perhaps a granddaughter of Ay.

93. Amenhotep III's senior wife Tiy was not a princess but came from a prominent family among the elite. In popular culture, the 1954 film *The Egyptian*, based on Mika Waltari's 1945 novel of the same name, presents Queen Tiy as the aging, alcoholic daughter of a common bird catcher. As a worldly dowager in the reign of her effete son Akhenaten, this cinematic version of Tiy still weaves fishing nets while drinking cup after cup of beer that a servant ladles from a large jar as she sits in palatial splendor decked out in full queenly regalia in front of her loom. Campy and entertaining, this Hollywood fantasy bears no relationship to historical reality. Rather, it derives from naïve modern readings of Queen Tiy's portraiture, which often depicts her with a slight moue and narrow almond-shaped eyes, leading to fanciful conjectures about her supposedly strong-willed character.

94. The same is true of the relatives of Queen Tiy, Amenhotep III's great royal wife. Her parents Yuya and Thuya received a tomb in the King's Valley but it lacked a decorated tomb chapel. Her brother Anen, despite holding high administrative and priestly offices, never boasts of his sister's position as queen

in his own tomb chapel. Another possible brother, the courtier and eventual Pharaoh Ay, also avoids doing so. Given the political advantage and prestige these men enjoyed through their royal connections, we can safely conclude that they were either not permitted or felt it best to remain silent about their sister's marriage to the pharaoh in inscriptions on their tombs and funerary monuments.

95. Brand 2016, 16–17. See pp. 54–56 above.

96. Nefertari's known sons are Amunhirkhopeshef (no.1), Prehirwenemef (no. 3), Meryre I (no. 11), and Meryatum (no. 16). Her daughters are Baketmut, Nefertari II, Merytamun, and Henuttawy. Prince Sety (no. 9) might be one of her sons too, if he is the individual identified as "the King's Son Sety, born of Nefertari" on Ostracon Louvre 2261 along with "the King's Son and heir apparent (*iry-pᶜt*) Sethhirkhopeshef" (*KRI* II, 914:12–915:2; *RITANC* II, 617). The second prince is surely Ramesses II's eldest son. Gomaà (1973, 8) objects to Prince Sety being the son of the Great Royal Wife Nefertari, suggesting he was the son of Sethhirkhopeshef and his sister, Princess Nefertari II, and therefore the grandson of Ramesses II and his senior consort, since this Nefertari lacks a title. Given the nature of this document, a "work note" drafted in haste by a clique of officials making the rounds in the bowels of KV 5, the absence of a title for Nefertari is conceivable. Moreover, the wording of the text does not show that Sety was the son of Sethhirkhopeshef. Gomaá's view was accepted by Fisher (2001, 1:109) and previously by myself (2016, 11 n. 16). As with Isetnofret (see below), it remains possible that other individuals known from the lists of princes and princesses were also born to Nefertari, but these cannot be identified with certainty. See pp. 256–57 below.

97. By contrast, inscriptions naming the six daughters born to Akhenaten's preeminent wife Nefertiti name her as their mother.

98. Turin 1380: PM II², 214; *KRI* II, 590–91; *RITANC* II, 400–401; Connor 2017. The four seated colossi from the forecourt of Luxor temple depicted Nefertari, and one of them depicted the prince as well. PM II², 304 (7–8), 313 (70–71); *KRI* II, 629–30; *RITA* II, 417–18; *RITANC* II, 422–23; Obsomer 2012b, figs. 8a–b. A battered schist statue from Karnak dating to the king's first regnal year has a relief of the queen on the side of her husband's throne and her eldest son on the other: Cairo CGC 42140 (JdE 36652): PM II², 141(a); *KRI* II, 586; *RITA* II, 384; *RITANC* II, 399–400; Fisher 2001, 1:pls. 128–129.

99. Two other conventional translations of the name Nefertari are "Beautiful Companion" and "She to Whom Beauty Pertains." Both are grammatically problematic considering how Egyptian scribes wrote her name. Instead we can best understand the construction as a stative and an adverb, *Nfr.t(i) iry*.

100. *KRI* II, 848:6.

101. For an inventory of Nefertari's titles and epithets, see Manouvrier 1996, 44.

102. *KRI* II, 849.

103. *KRI* II, 849.

104. Xekalaki and Khodary 2011.

105. Kings of the early Eighteenth Dynasty created this important sacerdotal post for their mothers and wives, but it fell into abeyance after Hatshepsut's reign until Ramesses I revived it for his wife Satre: Ayad 2009; *KRI* I, 5:8. The title is also attested for Sety I's wife Tuya: *KRI* II, 844:11 and 16, 845:1–2; 846:5; and for Nefertari: *KRI* II, 850:14, 851:2. Unlike royal women in the early

Eighteenth Dynasty and during Third Intermediate period, the early Ramesside queens are never explicitly designated as "god's wife of Amun." It is possible the god in question could be both Amun and their royal husbands, just as the title "god's mother," *mwt-nṯr* celebrated their status as mother of the next king. While Tuya may have acquired this title once Ramesses II succeeded his father, Nefertari received it in anticipation that her eldest son Prince Amunhirkhopeshef would one day also become king. Schmidt and Willeitner (1994) argue that Nefertari was "god's wife of Amun."

106. Ayad 2009.

107. Troy 1986, 86–88; Onstine 2016, 219–20.

108. Kuentz 1971, pls. 17 and 19 (scenes 13 and 14b); Feleg 2020, 287–93 with fig. 62, 299–303 with fig. 64.

109. PM II², 306 (17); *KRI* II, 349:11–13; *RITA* II, 185–86; *RITANC* II, 212–15.

110. Troy 1986, 30–31; Robins 2008.

111. Desroches-Noblecourt and Kuentz 1968.

112. On the queen's role as the leader of the circle of royal and elite women at court, see Pereyra De Fidanza 2000; Haslauer 2001; Roth 2009.

113. On the idealization of queenly power vis à vis foreign relations, see Roth 2002.

114. For Nefertari's letters to the Hittite queen, see pp. 320–22 below.

115. Nefertari appears on the stela of Viceroy of Kush Hekanakht that appears to date no earlier than regnal year 21 based on the form of Ramesses II's nomen as *Rˤ-ms-sw*. Kitchen dates it to around year twenty-three and views it as contemporary with the dedication of Abu Simbel, when, he believes, Nefertari was either dead or terminally ill; Kitchen 1982, 99–100; *RITANC* II, 562. All this is maudlin speculation, but we have no dated evidence for Nefertari after the early twenties of the reign.

116. Thausing and Goedicke 1971; Leblanc 1989, 24–52 and pls. 152–73; McCarthy 2011, 223–72; Demas and Agnew 2012–2016, 1:49–52, 2:393–408; Elleithy and Leblanc 2016, 157–84. A few objects survived the pillaging, including a handful of rather crude wooden ushabti figurines, and the blue-glazed knob inscribed with Ay's cartouche. The tomb robbers also shattered the queen's massive granite sarcophagus. Fragments of its lid rest in the Egyptian museum in Turin, Italy, along with other remnant of her burial goods: Schmidt and Willeitner 1994, 94–99; Greco 2020, 106–10.

117. Habicht et al. 2016. In their haste, tomb robbers dropped a few scraps of gold regalia when they despoiled her mummy, which conservators found during the restoration of the tomb in the 1980s; Schmidt and Willeitner 1994, 86–87.

118. Leblanc 1993a; 1999, 141–83; Obsomer 2012b, 245–49.

119. Highly speculative is Leblanc's suggestion that Isetnofret is related to the family of Horemheb. Nor is it certain she came from Memphis as Leblanc 1993a, 331; 1999, 142–43 has claimed.

120. So Kitchen (1982, 98) imagines.

121. *KRI* II, 854–55; *RITA* II, 556–58; *RITANC* II, 567; Sourouzian 1989, 2–5; Leblanc 1999, 164–66; Obsomer 2012b, 245–49; Charron and Barbotin 2016, 26–27, 30–30, cat. no. 2.

122. Gebel Silsila stela: PM V, 210 (20); *LD* III, 174c; *KRI* II, 384–85; *RITA* II, 213–14; *RITANC* II, 240–41; Sourouzian 1989, 3–4 and pl. 2. Aswan Stela: PM V, 249; *KRI* II, 854; *RITA* II, 557; *RITANC* II, 565–66; Sourouzian 1989, 2–3 and pl. 1.

123. Isetnofret's known sons are: Ramesses Junior (no. 2), Khaemwaset (no. 4), and Merenptah (no. 13). Her daughters are Bintanath, Isetnofret II, and Nebettawy. Like Nefertari, she could have had more children whom we cannot identify in the lists of royal children.

124. Kitchen notes (*RITANC* II, 565–66) that Isetnofret is only "royal wife" on the Aswan stela while her daughter Bintanath is "great royal wife." This discrepancy is due to lack of space to fit the full title, not because Isetnofret had not yet been "promoted." On Khaemwaset's Gebel es-Silsilah stela Isetnofret has the higher title, leading Kitchen (*RITANC* II, 565) to conclude that she obtained it only after outliving Nefertari. This is dubious.

125. Amenhotep III gave the title to some of his daughters while their mother Queen Tiy was alive. Likewise, two or more of Ramesses II's daughters were great royal wives concurrently, along with his first Hittite bride Maahorneferure.

126. For Prince Ramesses Junior, see pp. 264–65 below.

127. Obsomer (2012b, 247–48) and Brand (2016, 28) suggest she gained the superior title honorifically after her own death.

128. As she appears on a statue of Merenptah now in Copenhagen: AEIN 345: Sourouzian 1989, fig. 21b and pl. 17d.

129. See pp. 439–40 below.

130. This did not extend to any official persecution of Nefertari's memory as Janssen (1963) contends. See Leblanc 1993a, 320–21 with n. 32.

131. Christophe 1965, 118; Sourouzian 1983, 366. Kitchen (1982, 100) places her death around year 34. Leblanc (1993a, 327–28), too, argues that Isetnofret died between regnal years 30 and 34, a decade after Nefertari, because she appears on Khaemwaset's stela from the shrine of Horemheb at Gebel es-Silsila, but lacks the epithet "true of voice" (*mȝꜥ-ḫrw*), but this is tenuous. The living can hold the title, as Ramesses II does as prince in the Gallery of the Kings in Sety I's Abydos Temple, while others who were certainly dead when posthumous images of them were created can lack it.

132. Scholars long thought that a reference to the burial of a certain Isetnofret in the King's Valley, O. Cairo JdE 72460, belonged to none other than Ramesses II's wife: *KRI* II, 855–56; *RITA* II, 558; *RITANC* II, 567–68; Leblanc 1999, 168–73. Dorn and Polis (2016) have now rebutted this claim, noting that the woman in question lacks the titles one would expect for a queen. Aside from Nefertari and his five daughter-wives, the burials of Ramesses II's other wives are unknown.

133. Leblanc 1993a, 331.

134. See pp. 424–27 below.

135. See p. 356 below.

136. Brand 2016, 21–23. Few of these scores of children can be assigned to the Hittite brides or the five daughter-wives, all of whom married Ramesses decades after most of his offspring were born, that is, during Sety I's lifetime and in the first two decades of his own reign.

137. For a definition of consanguineous marriage and its occurrence among nonroyal Egyptians, see Robinson 2020.

138. Prior to the Ptolemaic era, the clearest evidence for consanguineous marriage between kings and their sisters and daughters stems from the Eighteenth and early Nineteenth Dynasties. Its prevalence in earlier periods is largely veiled from our view. While individual cases have received much atten-

tion, especially among the Thutmoside and Amarna pharaohs, few systematic studies of the phenomenon of royal consanguineous marriages have appeared; see Middleton 1962.

139. Amenhotep III made at least two of his daughters, Sitamun and Isis, great royal wives while their mother Tiy was still alive. Tiy lived on into the reign of Akhenaten.

140. Leblanc 1989; 1999, 97–98 with fig. 30; McCarthy 2005; 2011, 186–96.

141. Christophe 1956; Leblanc 1999, 61–69.

142. Christophe 1956, 110. While the identification of this anonymous princess as Isetnofret II is possible—even likely—it is not certain. Only the daughters of Nefertari and Isetnofret appear on the façade of the great temple. On their privileged status in the royal family hierarchy, see Brand 2016, 19–21.

143. The same is true of their mothers Nefertari and Isetnofret.

144. Hellinckx 1999; Brand 2016, 16 with n. 42. See n. 173 below.

145. On Bintanath's life and monuments, see Leblanc 1999, 185–206; 2009b, 216–25; Obsomer 2012b, 251–55.

146. In monumental lists depicting Ramesses II's daughters marching in procession, Bintanath always comes first: Brand 2016, 15. It is reasonable to conclude she was the eldest, but perhaps she was merely the first girl born to either Nefertari or Isetnofret and she could have had an older sister or two born to mothers of lesser standing. If so, Bintanath attained her unrivaled status among Pharaoh's daughters because her brother Ramesses Junior was the second born son; Brand 2016, 14–15. See p. 275 n. 43 below.

147. KRI II, 919:9: wr(t) ḫnrt n im[n].

148. Desroches-Noblecourt (1997, 277) argues Bintanath became great royal wife when her grandmother Tuya died in Ramesses II's twenty-second or twenty-third regnal year. Leblanc (1999, 192–94) disputes this, positing that Merytamun only became great royal wife upon the death of Nefertari, which he places in regnal year twenty-six.

149. This was likely during the mid-twenties of the reign, when Pharaoh consecrated his newly finished temples at Abu Simbel. On the date and chronology of the grand temple's decoration, see Christophe 1956, 125–28; Spalinger 1980; Obsomer 2012b, 241–43. Kitchen (RITANC II, 481) states that the four great colossi on the façade were completed by the fifth regnal year, but without giving evidence for this assessment. Certainly, the inscriptions on the temple exterior, including those associated with the colossi and of the royal family, were finished by regnal year twenty-one as the form of the king's nomen as Rꜥ-ms-s indicates. But when were the subsidiary figures of Bintanath and her sisters on the larger temple's façade completed? And why do the captions designate Bintanath, Merytamun, and Nebettawy as princesses, while their costumes are queenly? We have no clear answers to these questions.

150. See cross-references listed at: KRI II, 924:9–10; RITA II, 604; RITANC II, 624–26. See now Sourouzian 2019, cat nos. 42, 44, 45, 63, 89, 103, 175, 177, 190, R-2, R-9, R-15, R-18, R-56, R-61, R-63.

151. KRI II, 504; Sourouzian 2019, cat no. R-61.

152. For QV 71 see KRI II, 923–24; RITA II, 603–4; RITANC II, 623–25; Leblanc 1989, pls. 187–92; 1999, 237–43; McCarthy 2011, 301–46; Demas and Agnew 2012–2016, 1:54, 2:423–37; Elleithy and Leblanc 2016, 195–205. Bintanath's tomb, and that of her half-sister Merytamun (QV 68), are comparable in scale, although Bintanath's is slightly larger and its architecture is more complex.

Pharaoh's workmen excavated both just north of the earlier and larger tombs of his mother Tuya and his Great Royal Wife Nefertari. Although its carved plaster decoration is better preserved than in the tombs of her sisters, flooding, fire, and decay have blackened the walls of Bintanath's tomb and obscured its once brilliant paint; see Demas and Agnew 2012–2016, 2:428–37.

153. Leblanc 1989, pl. 174; 1999, 197, fig. 55; Elleithy and Leblanc 2016, pl. 55.

154. Egyptologists have often assumed she was Bintanath's daughter by Ramesses: Kitchen 1982, 110; Leblanc 1999, 195–97. Dodson and Hilton (2004, 169) admit that she might not be.

155. McCarthy 2011, 344–46.

156. *LD* III, pl. 172.

157. McCarthy 2011, 346.

158. So she has the title and costume of a king's daughter, *s3t-nsw*, in procession scenes of princesses carved in the second half of the reign at Abydos and Gebel es-Silsila by which time she had been named great royal wife. As in her tomb, Bintanath served both as royal wife and royal daughter simultaneously, with the two roles being distinguished in monumental inscriptions.

159. Luxor JdE 131: *KRI* II, 63–64; Romano 1979, cat. no. 129; Sourouzian 1989, 159–61 and pl. 30; 2019, cat. R-20; Leblanc 1999, 197–98.

160. She would have been in her early seventies when her younger brother Merenptah succeeded their father on the throne; Leblanc 1999, 198.

161. On Merytamun's life and monuments, see Leblanc 1999, 207–22; 2009b, 226–35; Obsomer 2012b, 255–57.

162. PM VII, 118 (17); *LD* III, pl. 195d; Champollion, 1835–1845, pl. IV-3; *KRI* III, 71; *RITA* III, 49–50; *RITANC* III, 61; Leblanc 1999, 43, fig. 14.

163. For colossi of her father with subsidiary figures of Merytamun in relief or sculpture in the round, see Sourouzian 2019, cat. nos. 46, 48(?), 178, 190, R-10, R-14, R-16, R-56, R-58. In addition, a sandstone bust of a daughter-wife that likely belongs to a fallen sandstone colossus of Ramesses II from Wadi es-Sebua Sourouzian 2019, cat. no. 90 may represent Merytamun, while the mate to this statue (cat. no. 89) depicts her sister Bintanath. The lower part of the fallen colossus is missing, depriving us of the inscription that would identify the daughter-wife with certainty. Her bust is now kept in the Nubian Museum at Aswan.

164. *RITANC* II, 628–29. For colossi with subsidiary figures of Mertyamun, see Sourouzian 2019, cat. nos. 46, 48, 57, 58, 178, 190, R-10, R-14, R-16, R-56, R-58.

165. Sourouzian 2019, cat. no. 44. Kitchen restored the damaged cartouche as Merytamun: *KRI* II, 440:6. It is now certain that Merytre is the correct reading; Payraudeau 2020.

166. Payraudeau (2020, 257–58) explicitly denies this solution and the analogy of Prince Amunhirkhopeshef's alias but he offers no convincing evidence for this assessment. The name Merytamun does occur on another siliceous sandstone colossus from Tanis, likely the mate to the one with her alternate moniker Merytre: Sourouzian 2019, 46. On Amunhirkhopeshef's alias Sethhirkhopeshef, see pp. 263–64 below.

167. Alas, the queen's name is damaged, so attributing it to Merytamun, while likely, is not certain: *KRI* VII, 106:14–107:1; Leblanc 1999, 210–11; Obsomer 2012b, 255–56.

168. The Akhmim colossus closely resembles the "white queen," a smaller painted limestone statue bust Petrie discovered in the ruins of a chapel near the

Ramesseum. It is now in Cairo CG 600 (JdE31413): PM II2, 431; *KRI* II, 845; *RITA* II, 551; *RITANC* II, 552; Freed 1987, 142–43 cat. no. 9; Leblanc 2009b, 227–28; 2019, with figs. 31–32. The Ramesseum statue was originally attributed to Ramesses II's mother Tuya, but its striking resemblance to the Akhmim colossus prompted scholars to reattribute it to Merytamun. Unlike the colossus, the gown of the "white queen" is unpleated but has rosettes on the breasts. The long echelon wigs are identical, and both images have the double uraeus of queenship, but the colossus has a vulture cap whereas the smaller piece has a circlet diadem.

169. Dodson (2018, 103–4) dates the Akhmim colossus to Ay's reign, stating that it represented his wife Tey. Johnson (1994, 148) ascribes it to Ankhesenamun, Tutankhamun's great royal wife. The colossus's eyes have been recut. Ramesses II also left three large limestone statues of himself at Akhmim, one of which dates to the later decades of his reign and has a subsidiary figure of Merytamun herself: Sorouzian 2019, cat. nos. 48, 190, 191.

170. *KRI* II, 924–25; *RITA* II, 604; *RITANC* II, 626–27; *KRI* VII, 107; Leblanc 1989, pls. 174–77; 1999, 207–22; McCarthy 2011, 273–300; Demas and Agnew 2012–2016, 1:53, 2:409–22; Elleithy and Leblanc 2016, 185–93.

171. Leblanc 1999, 223–36; Obsomer 2012b, 257–58.

172. Leblanc 1999, 223–27; McCarthy 2011, 441–44.

173. She never appears on her father's colossal statues, and there is no reliable evidence she or any other daughter-wives of Ramesses II had children by him. On the basis of a tiny carnelian amulet called a "name bead" and inscribed with Nebettawy's name, Leblanc (1999, 227–29) claimed she bore Ramesses II a daughter allegedly called "Isetemakh." This proved to be erroneous. The supposed "name" of this illusory daughter of a daughter on this little talisman is a phrase referring to the goddess Isis; Hellinckx 1999. For the carnelian amulet (Cairo JdE 27739), see *KRI* II, 926:11; *RITA* II, 606; *RITANC* II, 629–30.

174. Subsidiary figures of Henuttawy appear with those of her sister Merytamun next to Nefertari's colossi on the façade of the smaller temple at Abu Simbel; Christophe 1956, 114–15.

175. *KRI* II, 926; *RITA* II, 605; *RITANC* II, 629; Leblanc 1983, 1984; McCarthy 2011, 441–79; Demas and Agnew 2012–2016, 1:43–48, 2:376–92; Elleithy and Leblanc 2016, 145–56.

176. Although the draftsmanship in QV 60 is fine and the paintings iconographically complex, the artists employed a simpler, less vibrant color palette when compared to Nefertari's tomb (QV 66). Leblanc 1986; 1989, 24–55 and pls. 187–92; McCarthy 2011, 415–40; Demas and Agnew 2012–2016, 1:55–56, 2:438–50; Elleithy and Leblanc 2016, 207–15.

177. Henuttawy's name was painted in one of these blank cartouches but all the rest that survive are empty; see Leblanc 1986, 211–12, 215 and pl. 21A; Demas and Agnew 2012–2016, 1:55.

178. Sorouzian 1983; Leblanc 1999, 244–53. With Bintanath, she stands beside Ramesses on a colossus from Hermopolis in Middle Egypt dating to the forties or fifties of his reign. The king's nomen cartouche includes the epithet "God-and-Ruler-of-Heliopolis" in use between his forty-second and fifty-sixth regnal years. See p. 425 below. *KRI* II, 503–4; *RITANC* II, 355; Obsomer 2012b, 253; Sorouzian 2019, cat. no. R-61. A large granite statue of Ramesses II from Canopus (Abukir) also depicts Henutmire in relief on the left side of the statue's support pillar. Formerly in the Greco-Roman Museum

in Alexandria, it has now been transferred to the new museum in Sohag: Sourouzian 2019, cat. no. 102.

179. Vatican Museum no. 28: *KRI* II, 844; *RITA* II, 550; *RITANC* II, 549–50. Proponents of Henutmire as Ramesses's sister include Kitchen 1982, 98; *RITANC* II, 569–70; Dodson and Hilton 2004, 164. For the image of Henutmire, see Leblanc 1999, figure facing p. 246; 2009b, 176; Obsomer 2012b, pl. 12b. An early-modern restoration of the lower legs of Tuya's statue included a maladroit attempt by the artist to depict Henutmire's image in relief with a short kilt and legs, perhaps after the classic fashion of a male figure in ancient Egyptian art.

180. Sourouzian 1983, 370–71. A woman named Tia is Ramesses II's only known sister; Sourouzian 1983, 365–71; Schmidt and Willeitner 1994, 34–35; Leblanc 1999, 245–46; Brand 2000, 346; Obsomer 2012b, 229. Tia bears the title king's sister (*snt-nsw*) in her tomb, but she lost the title king's daughter (*s3t-nsw*) after their father Sety I died. Nor is it clear whether Tuya was her mother. For Tia and the Memphite tomb she shared with her husband, also named Tia, see Martin, van Dijk, and Aston 1997; Obsomer 2012b, 225–29; Bács 2019.

181. Leblanc 1999, 246.

182. Hellinckx 1999, 113–21. The consanguous mariages between pharaohs and their sisters and daughters make these possible.

183. Her name seems absent from temple lists of the princesses, but these inscriptions are damaged and some names are incomplete or destroyed. A certain Princess Henut-[...] appears in the twenty-third position on the second list of royal daughters from Sety I's Abydos temple; *KRI* II, 919:4. She might be Henutmire, but this is not certain. Henut means "mistress" and it appears in the names of several of the king's daughters. See my numbered list on p. 257 below: Henuttawy (no. 7), Henutakh (no. 14), Henutiunu (no. 16), Henutmerut (no 20), Henutpahar (no. 24), Henutsekhemu (no. 25), Henuttaneb (no. 42), Henutshedesh(er)et (no. 44), and Henutttatemu (no. 47). This numbering system differs somewhat than Kitchen's in *KRI* II, 916–22.

184. Like Bintanath, Merytamun, Henuttawy, and probably Nebettawy, Henutmire may have been selected as a daughter-wife because her mother was either Nefertari or Isetnofret. Admitedly, this is speculative, but given the royal family's hicrarchy it is plausible; Brand 2016, 19–21.

185. Henutmire's tomb (QV 75) is one of the last queenly sepulchers Ramesses constructed in the Queens' Valley: Leblanc 1988; 1999, 244–56 and figs. 66–70; McCarthy 2011, 387–414; Demas and Agnew 2012–2016, 1:58–59, 2:464–77; Elleithy and Leblanc 2016, 231–44. Like Henuttawy's tomb (QV 73) it was smaller and prefabricated with the cartouches left empty. Later, her name was inserted quickly in red paint: Leblanc 1988, 137–38 and pl. 10A–B.

186. P. Salt 124, verso 1:10. Černý 1929; *KRI* IV, 413:14; Leblanc 1988, 131–32. This burial, literally a "uniting-with-the-earth," could refer to Henutmire's tomb, or to her interment rites.

187. Cairo JdE 60137: Leblanc 1988, 132–33 and pl. 8; *KRI* II, 857; *RITA* II, 558; *RITANC* II, 569; Sourouzian 1983, 369; Leblanc 1988, 132–33 and pl. 8; 1999, unnumbered photo between 246 and 247.

188. Alternatively, its name can be translated "Place of the Beautiful Ones." On the history of the Queen Valley (QV) and its tombs, see Leblanc 1989, 3–23; 1999, 90–96; McCarthy 2005 and 2011, 1–54; Demas and Agnew 2012 2016, 1:11–26; Elleithy and Leblanc 2016.

189. Roth 1999; McCarthy 2002, 2005, and 2011, 29–45.

190. Bickel 2016; Demas and Agnew 2012–2016, 1:25–29.

191. Lilyquist 2003.

192. McCarthy 2011, 69–74 and 179–85; Demas and Agnew 2012–2016, 2:143–47.

193. Leblanc 1989, pls. 67–72; McCarthy 2011, 72–109; Demas and Agnew 2012–2016, 1:36–38, 2:217–29; Elleithy and Leblanc 2016, 37–42.

194. Tombs QV 31, 33, 34, 36: McCarthy 2011, 110–38; Demas and Agnew 2012–2016, 1:30–32, 2:168–216; Elleithy and Leblanc 2016, 13–42. QV 40 is more elaborate and might date to the reign Sety I or of Ramesses II: McCarthy 2011, 139–78; Elleithy and Leblanc 2016, 43–52.

195. The eventual owner of QV 33 was Tanedjemy, who is entitled king's wife and king's daughter. Her name was inscribed in black ink in a single pre-served cartouche: Desroches-Noblecourt 1982; Leblanc 1989, pls. 60–62; 1999, 143–44 and fig. 37; McCarthy 2011, 110–14; Demas and Agnew 2012–2016, 1:34; 2:188–93; Elleithy and Leblanc 2016, 19–22.

196. Leblanc 1989, 1999; McCarthy 2005, 2011; Demas and Agnew 2012–2016, 1:30–32.

197. Bianchi and McDonald 1992.

198. Bianchi and McDonald 1992; Schmidt and Willeitner 1994, 101–3; Mc-Donald 1996.

199. McCarthy 2011; Demas and Agnew 2012–2016, 1:57, 2:451–63; Elleithy and Leblanc 2016, 217–30.

200. McCarthy 2002; 2011, 29–37, 698–700, 715–20.

201. Roth 2002; McCarthy 2005; 2011, 682–91.

202. No trace of the burial or tomb equipment of Ramesses II's first Hittite wife Maahorneferure has ever come to light. Politi (2001) argues that the "burnt groups" of destroyed personal effects that Petrie discovered at Ghurob reflect a Hittite burial custom, perhaps bearing witness to the burial of Hittite wom-en, perhaps even one of Ramesses II's Hittite wives. More recently, Gasperini (2018) challenged this interpretation, arguing that these destroyed objects at-test to tomb robbery in the late Twentieth Dynasty.

Chapter Eight
The Royal Children and Their Ideological Role

The Unusual Prominence of Ramesses II's Family

Egyptian kings embodied the Nile Kingdom's fertility, fathering large broods of children by multiple wives. In this respect Ramesses II followed precedent by filling his palaces with bustling hordes of young children during his first decades of rule. Indeed, Ramesses II fathered one hundred or more children—more than are known for any other pharaoh. He marshalled these little ones as vital symbols of his procreative energies through an innovative program of monumental art and inscriptions by which he glorified himself. Ramesses II's myriad sons and daughters march in grand processions in scenes carved on the walls of their father's temples.

We might imagine that royal offspring were prominent in the historical record, but in fact, the opposite is true.[1] Wary of establishing their sons as potential rivals, most Egyptian kings rarely named even their eldest sons on royal monuments.[2] Akhenaten, for example, displays his daughters on countless monuments—but never once mentions his son, who would one day become Tutankhamun. Earlier princes are attested so haphazardly in ancient sources that we know the names of more sons of Ramesses II than of all the rulers of the Eighteenth Dynasty.[3] A pharaoh's daughters posed no threat to his authority, and are often better known than their brothers. Ramesses II broke with tradition, giving both his male and female children unprecedented exposure on his monuments.

Processional Lists of Royal Children

Ramesses II introduced a new genre of temple decoration featuring wall scenes with processions of his sons and daughters marching in long files, with hieroglyphic captions displaying their names and titles.[4] Artists created the first of these processional lists of royal children inside the forecourt that Ramesses built at Luxor Temple during his earliest years as king. These cavalcades of regal offspring embellish several temples he built throughout Egypt and Nubia in the ensuing five decades, becoming a hallmark of his reign.[5] By their sheer numbers,

FIGURE 8.1. Procession of Ramesses II's sons from the Ramesside Forecourt of Luxor Temple. From left to right: Ramesses "Junior," Prehirwenemef, Khaemwaset, Monthu-hirwenemef, and Nebenkharu. Photograph by Peter Brand.

Ramesses II's sons and daughters attested to his status as a paragon of masculine virility, in keeping with the time-honored royal epithet "Mighty Bull."[6] Celebrating these legions of progeny served to enhance his prestige (figs. 8.1 and 8.2).[7]

The temple lists are unevenly preserved. Rosters of princes and princesses at Abu Simbel are intact, but limited wall space curtailed their number to the most senior members of the family. Centuries of ruin and decay have ravaged the once more-extensive lists on the walls of the Ramesseum and several other temples.[8] All together, the names and images of most of Ramesses II's sons and daughters survive on at least one monument, but a few names are incomplete or missing from damaged lists.[9]

Three processions in the forecourt of Luxor Temple are the earliest and served as prototypes for later examples. Here, royal children of both genders participate in the Opet and Min festivals. Princes carry

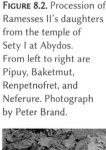

FIGURE 8.2. Procession of Ramesses II's daughters from the temple of Sety I at Abydos. From left to right are Pipuy, Baketmut, Renpetnofret, and Neferure. Photograph by Peter Brand.

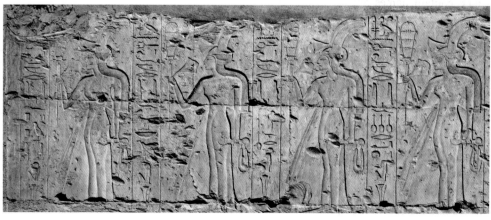

250

FIGURE 8.3. Typical costume of a Ramesside prince and princess. Drawings by Rosellini. Public domain.

tall floral bouquets for Amun-Re's altars, while their sisters play sistra and chant.[10] In subsequent temple lists at Abu Simbel and elsewhere, long files of royal children serve solely to display Ramesses II's fertility. The trains of royal children are always arrayed along the base of the walls, subordinate or unrelated to the scenes above, where their father interacts with the gods.[11] Artists created the latest roster at Wadi es-Sebua during the forties of his reign. Also late are the Abydos lists, which contain names not seen elsewhere.[12]

Pharaoh's offspring march with siblings of the same gender, all wearing costumes and regalia denoting their illustrious heritage.[13] Most of the long lists of princes depict at least twenty-five individuals.[14] Captions identify each with the title "king's bodily son," marking him as Ramesses II's own flesh and blood, unlike certain officials who received the honorary epithet "king's son," but were unrelated to him.[15]

Royal children wore common "uniforms." For princes this consisted of a kilt with a sloping hem and a tight-fitting garment resembling a corslet (fig. 8.3).[16] Long pairs of streamers dangle from their belts. The eldest sons might also don a pleated gown with flaring sleeves and a longer kilt with a wide hem worn over a tunic, like those worn by Ramesses and his courtiers (fig. 8.4).

FIGURE 8.4. Lepsius's drawing of the four eldest sons of Ramesses II with their names and titles. From left to right: Amunhirkhopeshef, Ramesses "Junior," Prehirwenemef, and Khaemwaset. NYPL digital collections. Public domain.

Pharaoh's sons have shaved heads or wear an official's wig if they are older, but all display the sidelock of youth, which emerges from one side of their heads.[17] A traditional badge of childhood, Egyptian boys usually cut their sidelocks at puberty. Adult princes wore the lock as an artificial hairpiece over their wigs, to denote their royal parentage. For most, the sidelock was long and straight.[18] Princes serving in a priestly role display a shorter lock, curled at the end.[19]

Images of Ramesses II's sons in temple lists emphasize their uniformity, not their individuality, portraying all of them as idealized adolescents. Each appears equal in stature and age to his brethren, with identical facial features, as though they were clones. Minor variations in the style of their sidelocks or earrings reflect artistic choices, not specific personalities. The most senior princes, Amunhirkhopeshef, Ramesses Junior, and Prehirwenemef in particular, often wear more elaborate costumes and hold distinctive titles, setting them apart from their younger siblings.[20] But for rank and file princes farther down the roster, only their names distinguish them from their brothers.

Princes bear one or more articles of regalia befitting their royal heritage. Each clutches the *khui*-flabellum, a scepter with a single ostrich plume.[21] Not a practical fan for keeping cool, the *khui*-flabellum denoted its owner's honorary rank of "fanbearer of the king."[22] New Kingdom pharaohs bestowed this distinction on favored courtiers. Kings of the late Eighteenth Dynasty conferred the enhanced title of "fanbearer on the king's right side" on their most favored officials, including the future kings Ay, Horemheb, and Pramessu.[23] Having received this accolade from Sety I while he was a prince, Ramesses II made his own sons fanbearers, giving each a flabellum they proudly wield as their badge of office. The senior sons usually bore the higher rank of "fanbearer on the king's right side."[24]

The sons of Ramesses bear two more emblems of courtly rank, the *heka*-scepter and a strip of red cloth.[25] Resembling a shepherd's crook, but shorter, the *heka*-scepter denoted the word "to rule" in hieroglyphic writing. Along with the pharaoh himself and certain officials like the vizier, princes might carry the *heka*-scepter, indicating the bearer possessed quasi-royal authority.[26] Like the highest administrative officeholders, including the vizier and Viceroy of Kush, princes also bear a strip of red cloth wound about the wrist. With these regalia, Ramesses II signaled to the elite that his sons, with his blood flowing in their veins, outranked even the highest officials of the court.[27]

All of Ramesses II's daughters wore identical costumes (fig. 8.3 above). Their long, pleated gowns are wide at the hem and sleeves, and appear semitransparent. Over a short wig, each princess displays a luxuriant, flowing side-lock falling over her shoulder and reaching to the small of her back (fig. 8.5).[28] These locks are elaborately braided and fixed with bands and hair ornaments appropriate for royal women.[29] A circular modius atop the princess's wig may support a pair of tall feathers. Sometimes they have a lotus blossom worked into their hairdos. In the processional scenes, each daughter shakes a sistrum with one hand and clutches a *menat*-necklace in the other, signifying her cultic role as a chantress in temple ceremonies.[30]

FIGURE 8.5. A daughter of Ramesses II. Relief from the temple of Sety I at Abydos. Photograph courtesy of Paul Smit.

The processional scenes of royal children are an innovative element of temple decoration under Ramesses II, but have antecedents in decorative temple friezes of so-called Nile gods. Beginning in pyramid temples of the Old Kingdom, rows of these fecundity figures carrying trays laden with food, drink, and floral bouquets serve to personify the fertility and agricultural bounty of Egypt's Nile Valley. They appear along the base of walls in hypostyle halls and outer courts in New Kingdom temples, including those of Sety I and Ramesses II at Abydos.[31] The processions of Ramesses II's children in his temples remind the viewer that his procreative energies guaranteed the prosperity of his subjects and of Egypt itself.

Hierarchy among the Royal Children

Processional temple lists reveal a pecking order among Ramesses II's children (see the list of royal sons on p. 256 below).[32] They organize his sons in a strict order, unlike their sisters, whose priority varies from list to list. This reflects the divergent roles that the king's male and female offspring played in his ideological program. Pharaoh's sons strut along in a strict order with rare exceptions.[33] Prince Amunhirkhopeshef always leads his younger brethren. He alone holds the title "King's Eldest son." Next comes Prince Ramesses Junior. This rigidity indicates that birth order governed where each son marched in the queue, not the eminence of his mother.[34] So the younger sons of Nefertari, Meryre I (no. 11) and Meryatum (no. 16), and Isetnofret's youngest son Merenptah (no. 13), come after older siblings born to wives whose names are now lost to history.[35] Yet, these "missing mothers" gave birth to most of his children.[36]

There may be two exceptions to strict birth order among the sons. Prehirwenemef and Khaemwaset occupy the third and fourth slots in temple processionals. Since Ramesses married several brides before his accession, Nefertari and Isetnofret had competitors vying to present him with sons. It seems doubtful they each delivered two boys but before any of his other wives had even one.[37] Perhaps the prestige the two favored wives and their first-born sons enjoyed caused Prehirwenemef and Khaemwaset to be moved forward in the ranks of their bretheren.[38]

Surviving temple rosters of the princesses are more dilapidated. Some names are fragmentary, others destroyed, but we can identify thirty-eight princesses who appear at least once on these monuments.[39] A tally inked on an ostracon, now in the Louvre in Paris, names fifteen more princesses, although one name is missing and two others are incomplete. With one possible exception, these daughters never turn up in the processionals.[40] This brings the sum of Ramesses II's daughters to between fifty-two and fifty-five (see the list of daughters on p. 257 below).[41]

Unlike their male siblings, birth order does not govern the sequence of princesses, which varies between monuments.[42] The sole constant is Princess Bintanath, who always comes first. Historians often assume she was Ramesses's first-born daughter, but perhaps she was simply the first little girl born to either Nefertari or Isetnofret, and not the eldest of all his daughters.[43]

After Bintanath the order of princesses fluctuates in the lists, but there is a pattern. In almost every case, the seven known daughters of Nefertari and Isetnofret occur among the first ten names, suggesting they outranked their sisters.[44] Their birth order is uncertain.[45] Six more daughters appear among the first ten positions in at least one processional scene, sometimes before daughters of the two favored queens.[46]

As with most of their brothers, the mothers of forty-six of Ramesses II's daughters are a mystery. Since princesses were ineligible to succeed their father, birth order was less important than the prestige they derived from their mothers, especially for the daughters of the two favored queens.

The priority given to the children of Nefertari and Isetnofret continued after death. One of Nefertari's sons named Meryre, comes eleventh in the lists, but he died early. Soon after his death, another boy was born and given the same name. Even after his death, the elder prince, whom we call Meryre I, is always in eleventh place, while his namesake Meryre II takes the eighteenth position in the lists.[47] The format of the lists does not distinguish between the living and the dead. But some of Pharaoh's children had passed into the underworld when sculptors carved the lists at Wadi es-Sebua in Nubia.[48] There, more than a decade after he died, Amunhirkhopeshef leads files of his brothers as though he still lived. We are ill informed about the lifespans of most of Ramesses II's sons and daughters, but the monumental tallies at Abydos and Wadi es-Sebua indicate that even in death Pharaoh's children continued to serve his ideological agenda and enhance his prestige.[49]

Endless Ranks of Younger Children

Ramesses II sired at least forty-five sons and more than fifty daughters. Surviving records are incomplete, so he likely fathered more than a hundred. Most were born during his first two decades as king. Older sons like Ramesses Junior, Khaemwaset, Sety, and Merenptah were given names associated with their father's ancestors. After the first twenty-odd princes, Ramesses faced the challenge of finding suitable names for all these little boys. His ingenious solution was to name many of them "Ramesses," plus a unique epithet to distinguish each lad from the rest. The first is Ramesses-Merenre (no. 21). Beginning with Ramesses-Siatum (no. 27), many of the later princes bore such compound names. Well-preserved examples include Ramesses-Sikhepri, Ramesses-Merymaat, and Ramesses-Userkhepesh. Perhaps a dozen others can be reconstructed from imperfectly preserved lists at Abydos and the Ramesseum.[50]

When a prince died, he needed proper funerary equipment for his journey to eternity. One strange and touching case is a hunchbacked prince named Ramesses-Nebweben, who never appears in the temple lists. When he died in his thirties, his father ordered that two granite sarcophagi, once intended for his great grandfather, be recycled for the prince's burial (fig. 8.6).[53] Made for the Vizier Pramessu during Horemheb's reign, they became redundant once Pramessu became Ramesses I. They sat unused for decades in the Memphite necropolis, where Pramessu likely had a tomb. Decades later, inscriptions on both sarcophagi were altered to name the hunchback prince.

One of the repurposed sarcophagi was sent to Thebes, but if Pharaoh intended to lay his son to rest in the Valley of the Kings, this never

Why did Ramesses compound the names of these sons with his own? In one sense they were "political," stressing each lad's fealty to his father's regime, not unlike the loyalist names of officials at all periods of pharaonic history that were compounded with the sovereign's.[51] For princes of the blood, these compound names marked each boy as a living subset of Pharaoh's identity just as they were physically "king's sons of his body."[52]

FIGURE 8.6. One of two sarcophagi of Prince Ramesses-Nebweben that was originally made for his great grandfather Pramessu before he became Ramesses I. Cairo, Egyptian Museum JdE 77203. Upper right: the central text gives the name and titles of the Vizier Pramessu. To either side is the name of Prince Ramesses-Nebweben written with his father's nomen cartouche. Bottom: Inscription on the side of the sarcophagus's trough with the titles of the Vizier Pramessu. At the right end, the inscription was altered to Nebweben's name. Photograph and enhanced image of texts by Peter Brand.

The Sons of Ramesses II[143]

(N) = son of Nefertari   (I) = son of Isetnofret   R.- = Ramesses-

1. Amunhirkhopeshef (N)[144]
2. Ramesses "Junior" (I)
3. Prehirwenemef (N)
4. Khaemwaset (I)
5. Monthuhirkhopeshef
6. Nebenkharu
7. Meryamum
8. Amunemwia[145]
9. Sety[146] (N)?
10. Setepenre
11. Meryre I (N)
12. Horhirwenemef
13. Merentpah (I)
14. Amenhotep
15. Itamun
16. Meryatum (N)
17. Nebentaneb
18. Meryre II
19. Amenemopet
20. Senakhtenamun
21. R.-Merenre
22. Thutmose
23. Simonthu
24. Monthuemwaset
25. Siamun
26. Siptah[147]
27. R.-Siatum[148]
28. Monthuenhekau
29. [Mery]monthu[149]
30. [R.(?)-me]rpare[150]
31. [R.-M]eritimire
32. R.-Userkhepesh
33. R.-Merysutekh[151]
34. R.-Sikhepri
35. R.-Merymaat
36. [R.]-Meryastarte
37. [R.(?)]-Mahyranath
38. R.-Sethemnakht[152]
39. [R.(?)]-Geregtawy
40. [R.(?)]-Shepsesemiunu
41. [R.(?)]-Astartekhirwenemef
42. R.-Paitnetcher
43. R.-Maatptah
44. R.-Nebweben
45. R.-Userpekhty[153]

The Daughters of Ramesses II[154]

(N) = daughter of Nefertari   (I) = daughter of Isetnofret

1. Bintanath (I)	2. Baketmut (N)
3. Nefertari II (N)	4. Merytamun (N)
5. Nebettawy (I?)	6. Isetnofret II (I)
7. Henuttawy (N?)	8. Werel
9. Nedjemmut	10. Qedmerut
11. Nebetiunu	12. Nebetnuhet
13. Tuy[155]	14. Hcnutakh
15. Merytsakhmet	16. Henutiunu
17. [...][156]	18. Nebukherkhesbed
19. Shepsykherites	20. Henutmerut
21. Meretmihapi	22. Merytites
23. Nebuemiunu	24. Henutpakher
25. Henutsekhemu	26. He[nut...]isep (?)
27. Pipuy	28. Renpetnofret
29. Neferure	30. Merytnotcher
31. Merytptah	32. [...]etnofret
33. [...]hab	34. [...]maat
35. [...]uiunes	36. [...][157]
37. [...]emmeret	38. [...]em[...]mut
39. [...][158]	40. [...]nofret[159]
41. [...]taweret	42. Henuttaneb
43. Tuya	44. Henutshedesh(er)et
45. Hotepuemamun	46. Nebetiamnedjem
47. Henuttatemu	48. Nebetananash
49. Sitamun	50. Tia-Satre[160]
51. Tuya-Nebettawy	52. Takhat
53. Nebuemweskhet[161]	54. Henut[mire][162]
55. (daughter of Maahorneferure)[163]	56. Isis[164]

came to pass, and it ended up being dumped in a pit. Archaeologists discovered the prince's remains in the second sarcophagus near the royal family's palace at Mi-Wer in the Fayum, where he lived and died. Unusually, on both sarcophagi, the prince's name consists of his father's nomen cartouche followed by the epithet Nebweben.[54] For most princes called "Ramesses" there is no cartouche.[55] Perhaps this is evidence of the tender feeling Ramesses had for his handicapped son.

Royal daughters have more personal and evocative names than do the sons, as with Shepsykherites, "Noble Because of Her Father" and Merytites, "Beloved of Her Father." Most names linked the princess to a deity, especially goddesses, like Baketmut, "Servant of Mut." Or they might signal her royal status, as with several names formed with terms like *Henut* "mistress" or *Nebet* "lady." Some were simply elegant, like Nebukhirkhesbed, "Gold on Lapis Lazuli" and Nebetiamnedjem, "Lady of Charming Sweetness."

Given Ramesses II's longevity and the dynamics of royal polygamy, we should not be surprised he engendered so many children. The same is true of kings in other polygamous royal cultures.[56] Sources recording his youngest offspring are sparse. Later processional scenes from Abydos and Wadi es-Sebua have large gaps. More fragile are records inscribed on papyri and ostraca, and few have come to light.[57] Much evidence has simply vanished, leaving us guessing how many children Ramesses fathered in total.

The Sons of Pharaoh Go to War

Ramesses II instilled the warrior ethos in his sons, granting the senior princes high military rank. Despite their extreme youth, battle art portrays several princes participating in the offensive wars of his first decade as king.[58] Already in year one, idealized battle scenes at Beit el-Wali show Prince Amunhirkhopeshef and his younger brother Khaemwaset riding in chariots. Drivers accompany both princelings, keeping pace with Ramesses II's royal chariot as he charges a group of fleeing Nubians. Each boy carries a bow and flabellum but neither engages in combat. Instead, they witness Pharaoh's valor while enjoying the thrill of a high-speed chase. In fact, both were still young children at the time, Amunhirkhopeshef being ten at most.[59]

The hyperbole on display at Beit el-Wali is most vivid in a scene depicting Ramesses II assaulting a nameless Canaanite town on foot and slaying its oversized chieftain, who emerges from the bastion like some giant balloon.[60] In front of Ramesses, the tiny figure of an unnamed prince batters the walls with an axe. We need not ponder which prince attends him, since he was surely too young for combat. These idealized images, which obscure the true age of Pharaoh's young offspring, must put us on guard when assessing later battle art featuring his sons.

The Beit el-Wali scenes are high theater. Scribes gave young Prince Amunhirkhopeshef (here called Amunhirwenemef) a grown-up's voice as he extolls his father's power:

> Words spoken by the Fan-bearer on the King's Right Side, the Heir Apparent, King's Bodily Son, whom he loves, Amunhirwenemef: "(I) thought there was no end to the sky, (but) the Ruler has made us see its limit to the South. I am jubilant, and (my) heart is joyful as (my) father strikes his enemies. He has set the power of his strong arm against the Nine Bows."[61]

Three years after these scenes were carved Ramesses II undertook his first formal campaign. We know little about this venture and cannot say whether his sons attended him.[62] A year later in 1274 BCE, members of

Figure 8.7. Prehirwenemef (right) and an unknown brother (left) escape from the camp of Amun at the Battle of Kadesh. Lepsius's drawing of a scene from the pylon of the Ramesseum. NYPL digital collections. Public domain.

Figure 8.8. Rosellini's color facsimile of Princes Amun–hirkhopeshef, Ramesses "Junior," and Prehirwenemef in their chariots, from the outer hall of the great temple of Abu Simbel. Public domain.

the royal family were present at the Battle of Kadesh. In the camp scene from the Ramesseum pylon, two princes and a pair of royal fanbearers ride in chariots amid the Hittite ambush on the camp of Amun (fig. 8.7).[63] The lead prince was likely Amunhirkhopeshef or Ramesses Junior, but the top of the wall has vanished, destroying any identifying captions. Riding hard on his wheels comes Prehirwenemef. Neither prince brandishes arms, clutching only their flabellums. Were it not for the chaos milling around them, they might appear to be taking a joyride.

But this was no game. Behind them a fanbearer shouts a warning to the royal children, to avoid the battle now raging on the western side of the encampment.[64] We see them dash off in their chariots to escape the mayhem. This passive stance that the princes take dovetails with battle scenes at Abu Simbel and Beit el-Wali, where they observe their father's heroics from their speeding chariots (fig. 8.8).[65] At once actors and spectators, royal sons play their assigned role peaceably, leaving the fighting to the king.

Later military scenes from Luxor Temple and the Ramesseum, touting wars that Ramesses waged after his famous encounter at Kadesh, depict several princes fighting beside him. Had they now come of age? Or does their belligerence reflect evolving rhetorical themes in his battle

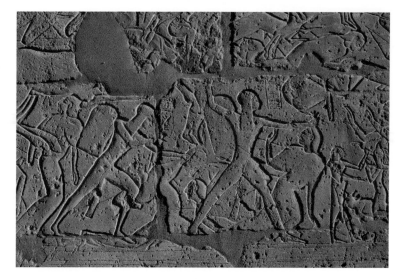

art?[66] Eight princes fight in the splendid Dapur relief at the Ramesseum, with captions naming six individuals.[67] Khaemwaset sets about butchering a prostrate Hittite with grim determination, grasping the enemy by one arm as he plunges a sword into his neck (fig. 8.9). Beside him, Monthuhirkhopeshef seizes a foe by the hair and readies an axe to strike the killing blow. The victim is already fainting, with two royal arrows protruding from his waist and shoulder.

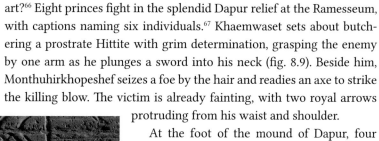

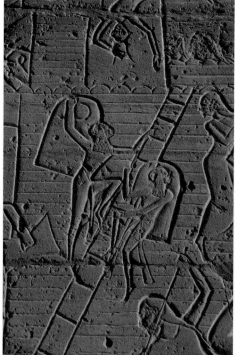

At the foot of the mound of Dapur, four more princes—Amenemwia, Meryamun, Setepenre, and Sety—emerge from the cover of tent-like arrow blinds (see fig. 6.6 above). Defenders on its ramparts fire arrows at them, which they deflect with upraised shields as they ready to storm the walls. Ahead of them, two anonymous princes scaling a ladder are reaching for the parapet (fig. 8.10). In two additional Syrian battle scenes on the west wall of Luxor Temple, princes slay enemies on foot or shoot arrows from their chariots. No captions survive, so we cannot identify them by name.

Conspicuous by their absence from the Dapur scenes are Pharaoh's three eldest sons, Amunhirkhopeshef, Ramesses Junior, and Prehirwenemef.[68] From temple lists, we know all three bore impressive military titles. Was this just for show? Or, did Ramesses II bar them from combat for fear of risking the lives of his "heir and two spares" on the battlefield? We need not read too much into this. The warlike deeds of Khaemwaset and his seven younger brothers must also be viewed with skepticism. Like a cinematic blockbuster "based on true events," Egyptian artists took liberties to heighten the dramatic effect.[69] While still children, a cohort of Ramesses II's sons did follow him on his early campaigns, including Kadesh. In their teens, some participated in the Syrian offensives of years eight and ten, if only as spectators. But artistry serves ideology, distorting their role at the Battle of Dapur.[70]

The military campaigns of New Kingdom pharaohs were equal parts ceremony and strategy. Once the fighting ceased, they staged triumphal rituals to celebrate—rounding up prisoners and spoils of war, marching them back to Egypt, and presenting captives and booty to the gods, just as Caesar did in Rome.[71] In temple war narratives, princes lead small groups of prisoners before Ramesses II on the field of victory. Pharaoh's sons act their parts bravely, dragging subdued foes on tethers or shoving them forward from behind. They even rough up the prisoners, punching, shoving, slapping, and threatening them with batons. The brutality of the Egyptians toward their captives does ring true, whether or not by the hand of Pharaoh's young sons.[72]

Careers of Royal Sons

Ramesses II appointed several of his elder sons as military officers and elevated Khaemwaset and Meryatum to the high priesthood. Yet, we should not overestimate the political influence or power any of them held, even Crown Prince Amunhirkhopeshef.[73] Ramesses lived so long that his first three designated heirs died well before him. By the last decade of his reign, once the king grew wizened and enfeebled, old age forced his hand and his ultimate heir, Prince Merenptah, governed in his name.[74]

Until then, Ramesses guarded his power and prerogatives jealously, just as his predecessors had. Egyptian pharaohs brooked no rivals. Ramesses took a calculated political risk by displaying his innumerable children on royal monuments, bargaining that the prestige they garnered for him outweighed the danger of intrigue against him. If any factions arose in the royal family's ranks, they left no trace in history.[75]

Having fathered numerous sons, we might imagine Ramesses put them to work as ministers of state, thereby keeping the levers of power "in the family." Egyptian kings made different calculations. They largely refrained from granting their sons the authority and resources with which they might become rivals.[76] Thus most princes lacked "career options" aside from ceremonial duties. If Ramesses II gave his sons high

FIGURE 8.11. Procession of royal sons from the Ramesseum. The artist left blank spaces so that various titles could later be inserted once each prince gained military or administrative posts. None of these were ever recorded, except for Merenptah (third prince from the left), who inscribed his prenomen cartouche once he became pharaoh. From right to left: Amunemwia, Sety, Setepenre, Meryre I, Horhirwenemef, Meren–ptah, Amunhotep, and Itamun. Photograph by Peter Brand.

military titles, the army's real general staff consisted of men of nonroyal birth, wholly loyal to him.

At first glance Ramesses II seems to have jettisoned this practice of excluding princes from office, appointing several of his elder sons to posts in the upper echelons of the army and clergy. Amunhirkhopeshef and Ramesses Junior were both made "great general of the army."[77] The third-ranked son Prehirwenemef rose quickly through the ranks, attaining a sequence of lofty military honors. In addition to being a "great general of the army," Ramesses dubbed him "leader of the king's army," "first of the braves," "first deputy of the army," "overseer of horses," and "first charioteer of his person."[78] Prince Merenptah, Ramesses II's eventual successor, also became a "great general of the army" by regnal year thirty. Fifth-ranked Prince Monthuhirkhopeshef was "first charioteer of his person."[79] Khaemwaset served as high priest of Ptah in Memphis.[80] Ramesses appointed Nefertari's youngest son Meryatum as "chief of seers," the high priest of Re in Heliopolis.[81]

Most of Ramesses II's sons lack administrative titles in monumental texts, but some bear the title "royal scribe," indicating they were literate. From year forty-two, an ostracon informs us that Prince Simonthu, the twenty-third son, was in charge of his father's temple estate in Memphis. (Simonthu was also married to a woman named Iryet, the daughter of a Syrian ship's captain![82]) So junior princes might hold sinecures, lucrative to be sure, but conferring no great authority in the sprawling machinery of state.[83]

At first, Ramesses planned for all his sons to receive administrative, military, or priestly offices as they matured. In processional lists from the outer hypostyle hall of the Ramesseum the four eldest sons hold multiple titles in addition to "king's son of his body, his beloved" (fig. 8.4).[84] Their younger brothers lack such offices, but the sculptors left blank spaces to insert them at a later date (fig. 8.11).[85] None of these gaps were ever filled, except for Merenptah, who inserted his royal title and cartouche after he succeeded his father as Pharaoh.

Crown Prince Amunhirkhopeshef

Amunhirkhopeshef was born to Nefertari a few years before his grandfather Sety I died.[86] When Ramesses II ascended the throne, he appointed his eldest son as heir.[87] Amunhirhopeshef's name means "Amun is in Possession of his Strong Arm." Nefertari and Amunhirkhopeshef stand alongside the sovereign in statuary from the earliest years of his reign, including the exquisite Turin statue and the four enthroned colossi in the forecourt of Luxor Temple.[88] At Beit el-Wali, the eldest prince is called Amunhirwenemef, meaning "Amun is on His Right Side."[89] Nor was this Amunhirkhopeshef's sole alias. In the north of Egypt, he went by Sethhirkhopeshef, a variant alias honoring Seth of Avaris, patron god of the Ramesside kings.[90] In his first regnal year Ramesses II experimented further with his heir's name just as he did with his own cartouches.

On one early statue the Crown Prince is called "Usermaatre," the same as his father, but without a cartouche around his name (fig. 8.12).[91] As texts on this statue attests, Ramesses II heaped titles and accolades on his young heir:

> *Heir Apparent (iry-pat), Fanbearer on the King's Right Side, True King's Scribe, whom he loves, Divine Seed which came forth from the Mighty Bull, King's Son, of his body, whom he loves, Great General of the Army, Usermaatre, true of voice.*[92]

The title *iry-pat*, literally "member of the elite class," affirmed Amunhirkhopeshef as heir apparent.[93] As the firstborn of all his father's boys, he was entitled "eldest king's son." Among the ceremonial epithets Amunhirkhopeshef accrued were "effective confidant," "and "first king's son of his body," indicating he was Nefertari's oldest son, while "divine seed that came forth from the victorious bull" lauds his royal

FIGURE 8.12. Image of Prince "Usermaatre," an alias of Amun–hirkhopeshef, on a schist statue of Ramesses II dating to his first regnal year. Cairo Museum CG 42140. Photograph by Peter Brand.

father.[94] Procession scenes emphasize Amunhirkhopeshef's priority as the eldest son over his younger brethren. He wears the pleated gown and long kilt of an adult courtier, complete with an official's wig and the princely side lock.

Despite being a "great general of the army," Amunhirkhopeshef never engages the foe in combat in his father's war scenes. Instead he marshals enemy captives and acts as intermediary between Ramesses II and the defeated Moabites in a relief from Luxor Temple.[95] This burnished the prince's credentials as an extension of Pharaoh's power. At the same time, Ramesses scorns the Moabites as unworthy even of groveling for mercy at his feet.

It is too much to claim that Amunhirkhopeshef had a diplomatic career, but he participated in at least one act of state in year twenty-one, when Ramesses II concluded his peace treaty with the Hittite Empire.[96] Ramesses authorized his eldest son to send two greeting letters to the Hittite king Hattusili III. Scribes wrote his name in cuneiform as Shutahapshap, which corresponds to the Lower Egyptian variant of his name Sethhirkhopeshef.[97]

Exalted above his brothers and flourishing an array of grand titles and high offices on his father's monuments, Prince Amunhirkhopeshef led a life of privilege and distinction. Ramesses, never imagining he would live so long, expected Amunhirkhopeshef to someday inherit his throne. It was not to be. The prince died less than halfway through his father's reign. Precisely when Amehirkhopeshef entered the netherworld is unclear, but as we've seen he was still alive in year twenty-one. A decade on, as Ramesses II marked his first Jubilee in year thirty, his second-born son, Prince Ramesses Junior, had assumed the role of heir apparent. Since the year of Amunhirkhopeshef birth is also a mystery, he might have died young at twenty-three or lived to forty, but he was most likely in his thirties.[98]

Pharaoh laid his eldest son to rest in the massive sepulture he built for his numerous offspring in the Valley of the Kings (KV 5). Amunhirkhopeshef's privileged rank followed him to his grave, where his name and image are prominent in reliefs on the tomb's outer chambers, in which Ramesses II leads his son before the gods of the netherworld.[99] Archaeologists discovered fragments of one of Amunhirkhopeshef's canopic jars in KV 5, proving he was interred there.[100]

Prince Ramesses Junior

Isetnofret gave the future Ramesses II his second son and namesake during Sety I's reign. We have called him Ramesses "Junior" to distinguish him from the pharaoh, but he did not have any such epithet in

FIGURE 8.13. Members of the royal family beside the legs of Ramesses II's colossal statues on the façade of the great temple of Abu Simbel. From left to right: Queen Nefertari, Ramesses "Junior," Baketmut, and Merytamun. Photograph by Peter Brand.

antiquity. Prince Ramesses Junior always comes second in the processionals. He holds the title "first king's bodily son," indicating he was the eldest of Isetnofret's boys (fig. 8.13).[101]

From an early age Pharaoh elevated his second son to the army's highest echelons, conferring the rank of "first great general of the army of His Person" and other titles.[102] He followed Ramesses II on military campaigns during the first decade of the reign, but we never see Prince Ramesses Junior fighting in scenes like those depicting the Battle of Dapur. By his later teens or early twenties, his soldierly career came to an end, though he retained his military titles.

Ramesses Junior played second fiddle to Amunhirkhopeshef for over two decades. By regnal year thirty, if not before, his elder brother was dead. The prince now garnered the titles of "heir apparent," (*iry-pat*), and "eldest king's son," (*sa nesu semsu*), marking him as designated heir. He enjoyed his preeminence for at least two decades, until he died around year fifty-two.[103] Leaving no monuments of his own, he is only named briefly on two stelae left by his younger brother Khaemwaset.[104] Ramesses II interred him in KV 5, the vast tomb of the royal children, where the prince appears with his father and older brother in a relief from an outer chamber.[105]

Khaemwaset the Scholar Prince

We know more about the life and career of Isetnofret's second son, the fourth-ranked Prince Khaemwaset, than the rest of Ramesses's sons combined (figs. 8.14 and 8.15).[106] No fewer than 151 artifacts—statues,

FIGURE 8.14. ⬆ Over life-sized statue of Prince Khaemwaset. British Museum EA 947. Photograph by Peter Brand.

FIGURE 8.15. ⬈ Prince Khaemwaset's "Family Stela" from Aswan. In the upper register, Ramesses II, Isetnofret, and Khaemwaset stand before Khnum. Below from right to left are Ramesses "Junior" as Crown Prince, Bintanath as Great Royal Wife, and Prince Merenptah. Drawing by Peter Brand.

statuettes, stelae, monumental reliefs and inscriptions, shabtis and burial goods—preserve his name and image, attesting to a busy life.[107] Even Amunhirkhopeshef seems a mere phantom by comparison. Through this abundance of inscriptions Khaemwaset achieved lasting fame.[108]

Like his three elder brothers, Khaemwaset was born while Sety I still ruled. The prince makes his first appearance at Beit el-Wali in a battle scene from Ramesses II's first regnal year. He zooms along in hot pursuit of Pharaoh's chariot, while his older brother, here called Amunhirwenemef, keeps pace beside him.[109] A few years later, battle scenes at Luxor Temple and the Ramesseum show Khaemwaset fighting at the Battle of Dapur and herding war captives during later Syrian campaigns, all while he was still a child or adolescent.[110] It is unclear if Khaemwaset's army career was anything more than symbolic, or when it came to an end. Ramesses II never granted him military titles like his three older brothers. Pharaoh had different plans for Isetnofret's second son: a distinguished career in the priesthood.

Prince Khaemwaset rose to the highest echelon of Egypt's religious hierarchy during the middle and later years of his father's long reign. Ramesses made him "great controller of craftsmen," and "*Sem*-priest of Ptah," the High Priest of Ptah in Memphis.[111] Just when Khaemwaset took charge of the Memphite deity's cultic establishment is unclear, although one text claims the god chose him in his youth.[112]

Khaemwaset attained even wider prominence in year thirty when Ramesses II observed his first *Sed*-festival, the so-called Egyptian royal Jubilee.[113] Centuries of tradition linked this most ancient rite of king-

FIGURE 8.16. A restoration inscription that Prince Khaemwaset left in his father's name on the pyramid of the Fifth Dynasty King Unas at Saqqara. Photograph by Peter Brand.

ship with Memphis, Egypt's age-old capital, and with Ptah. Ramesses repeated these festivals at three-year intervals, and tasked Khaemwaset with the duty of heralding these momentous occasions all over Egypt. Khaemwaset acted as master of ceremonies until the fifth Jubilee in regnal year forty-two.[114]

The prince left monumentals recording his deeds and travels during the middle years of his father's reign, ranging from the necropolis of Memphis at Saqqara to Aswan on Egypt's southern border. Among the most noteworthy memorials are a series of restoration inscriptions telling how, on his father's orders, Khaemwaset repaired the ruined pyramid complexes of several Old Kingdom rulers at Saqqara and Abu Sir near modern Cairo.[115] Traces of this work still exist on five pyramids, though there were surely others.[116] His inscription on the pyramid of King Unas at Saqqara is the most legible (fig. 8.16). It juxtaposes the names and titles of Ramesses II with those of his worthy predecessor in large-scale hieroglyphs. Couched as a formal royal decree, a longer text below includes Khaemwaset's personal testimonial:

> *A decree of His Person charging the Great Controller of Craftsmen, the Sem-priest, and King's Son Khaemwaset with perpetuating the name of the Dual King Unas. Now his name was not found upon the face of his pyramid, (yet) very greatly did the Sem-priest and King's Son Khaemwaset wish to embellish the monuments of the Nesut-kings and the Bityu-Kings, because of what they had made, but their durability was (now) falling into ruin ...*[117]

The rest is fragmentary, but snippets of identical texts have survived on other pyramids. We can piece enough together to know that Khaemwaset revived the funerary cults of ancestral kings in their dilapidated pyramid temples centuries after they were built. Ramesses II authorized new endowments of agricultural land and assigned personnel to revive the daily food offerings to nourish the *Ka*-spirits of his remote forebears.[118]

Prince Khaemwaset's keen interest in the blessed dead of times past comes through in a eulogy he inscribed in honor of his ancient predecessor Prince Kawab, whose father Khufu built the Great Pyramid of Giza. While supervising repair work on Old Kingdom shrines on the Giza Plateau, he unearthed a statue of Kawab. Clearly awed and fascinated by the relic, he inscribed an account of its discovery amid the ruins of the Fourth Dynasty royal necropolis. He honored Prince Kawab, who lived thirteen centuries before him, by setting it up in a funerary chapel to receive cult offerings on behalf of Kawab's hallowed *Ka*-spirit:

> *The King's Son Khaemwaset was delighted with this statue of the King's Son Kawab, taking what had been discarded as rubbish in ... canal(?) beloved(?) of his father, the Dual King Khufu. Then the Sem-[priest and King's Son Kha]em[waset] ordered [that it be given(?)] a place in the favor of the gods among the excellent Akh-spirits which are foremost in the Ka-chapel of Ro-Setjau—for he so greatly loved ancient times and the august ancestors along with the excellence of all they made in such proper fashion a million times over!*[119]

Khaemwaset had a human curiosity about people who lived centuries before him. His fascination with ancient artifacts has lead some to call him history's first archaeologist.[120] No doubt Khaemwaset would agree! But antiquarian impulses alone did not fuel his efforts. His prime motive as the *Sem*-priest of Ptah was a religious duty to the blessed dead in the vast cemeteries of Memphis. He worked on the orders of Ramesses II, for whom such conspicuous piety to royal forebears paid ideological dividends, bolstering his legitimacy just as it had for Sety I.

Khaemwaset's religious duties in Memphis included care of the Apis Bull, the living incarnation of Ptah. When the old bull died, a high commission of Memphite clergy roamed the land seeking to discover Ptah's new incarnation—a healthy calf they identified by distinctive symbols on its body. Each Apis had to be black with special white markings on various parts of its hide, and the image of a scarab beetle on its tongue. Plucked from some rural estate or peasant farmer's pen, they transported the new Apis to Memphis with great pomp. There it lived under the meticulous attentions of Ptah's clergy, receiving daily cult worship with rich foods to eat, and taking part in temple ceremonies. If his mother was known, she too was brought to Memphis.

When Ptah's bovine avatar died, priests mummified his corpse and laid him to rest in splendor befitting a god's own flesh. Prince Khaemwaset oversaw the selection and burial of a number of Apis bulls.[121] With the patronage and authority of Ramesses II, he enlarged the Serapeum at Saqqara, the catacombs where generations of Apis bull-mummies were entombed in massive sarcophagi for eternity.[122]

Khaemwaset's wife is unknown, but he had two sons and a daughter. The elder lad, named Ramesses after his grandfather, bears the title "king's son" in an inscription, but should not be confused with his uncle Prince Ramesses Junior. Khaemwaset's other son, named Hori, became high priest of Ptah after his father.[123] Japanese archaeologists recently discovered the tomb of Khaemwaset's daughter, named Isetnofret after her grandmother.[124]

Khaemwaset served as Ramesses II's heir when his older brother Ramesses Junior died, during the early fifties of his father's reign, but he did not enjoy this distinction for long, since he too died no later than his father's fifty-fifth regnal year. His younger brother Merenptah then became the final heir.[125]

This scholar-prince was long thought to have prepared his own final resting place among the Apis bulls in the Serapeum, where the French Egyptologists Auguste Mariette uncovered a richly appointed burial in the 1850s, complete with gold jewelry, amulets, and *ushabti* figures inscribed for Khaemwaset (fig. 8.17).[126] Mariette identified the mummified remains, complete with a rather crude gold foil mask, as that of the prince himself. But the supposed mummy that Mariette found consisted only of resin, crushed bones, and flecks of gold. It has since vanished.[127] Egyptologists now suspect they belonged to an Apis bull, not to Khaemwaset himself. Nor was Khemwaset interred with his many brothers in the Valley of the Kings. Instead he built a tomb for himself at Saqqara, next to his daughter Isetnofret's burial, and perhaps near that of his mother Isetnofret.[128]

FIGURE 8.17. An *ushabti* of Prince Khaemwaset found in the Serapeum in Saqqara. Paris, Louvre Museum N 461A. Photograph by Peter Brand.

Housing the Royal Children for Eternity

In 1825 the English explorer James Burton discovered an unusual tomb in the Valley of the Kings, but was only able to access its three outer chambers.[129] Howard Carter reentered the tomb, known by the acronym KV 5, in 1902.[130] He dismissed it as being of no interest, and moved on to more promising sites, including Tutankhamun's burial. An American team of Egyptologists set about mapping this long-forgotten tomb in the late 1980s. As they retraced the footsteps of Burton and Carter the Americans were not optimistic. Repeated catastrophic floods had washed tons of debris into the tomb over the past three millennia, choking it with a mix of compacted rubble and powdered limestone, often as hard as concrete. Debris filled its chambers nearly to their ceilings, forcing intrepid explorers to crawl on their hands and knees.

After making little headway over several field seasons, they made a sensational discovery.[131] Beyond a pair of tiny entrance rooms, and a large chamber supported by sixteen pillars that Burton and Carter saw, they penetrated the tomb to depths unknown to anyone since antiquity. What they found was a long T-shaped corridor, lined with dozens of doorways opening on tiny, cell-like rooms (fig. 8.18).[132] Were they offering chapels or burial crypts? At the cross axis of the T-shaped corridor, a niche held a statue of Osiris carved into the bedrock.[133] As ruler of the netherworld, the god watched over this tomb's occupants. But who was buried here?

Once they cleared the first two rooms, the Americans knew KV 5 was the resting place for Ramesses II's two eldest sons, Amunhirkhopeshef and Ramesses Junior, who appear in badly damaged wall scenes.[134] The dumbstruck archaeologists realized the pharaoh must have entombed most of his numerous sons in this grand mausoleum. For sheer size, KV 5 surpasses every tomb the ancient Egyptians ever built. Its design is also unique in the annals of funerary architecture. To date, excavators have uncovered more than 130 individual rooms, but they are convinced that others await discovery. With its pillared halls, grand branching corridors, descending staircases, and scores of little chapels lining every passageway, KV 5 sprawls out beneath the floor of the royal valley like the tentacles of a vast subterranean octopus. Not even the burial vaults of the Apis Bulls in the Serapeum rival its size and complexity.

Amid this architectural grandeur, archaeologists sifting through the debris found only a few damaged wall inscriptions, dozens of fragmentary burial goods, and thousands of pot sherds. From surviving inscriptions on shattered canopic jars and ruined stucco reliefs in the outer rooms, we know Ramesses II buried at least several of his sons in KV 5.[135] With so many rooms, there was space for his daughters too. An ancient papyrus recording a series of disturbances in the twenty-ninth regnal year of Ramesses III records that workmen had pilfered stones from atop the entrance to KV 5, which is called "the tomb of the royal children (*mesu nesu*)" of Ramesses II.[136] Aside from the tombs of the five daughter-wives in the Valley of the Queens, the burials of the great majority of Ramesses II's daughters have never come to light. Since the term *mesu nesu* can indicate children of both genders, KV 5 may have housed princesses along with their royal brothers.[137]

While its architectural structure is intact, mere fragments of KV 5's decoration survive on its battered walls, mostly in its two small outer

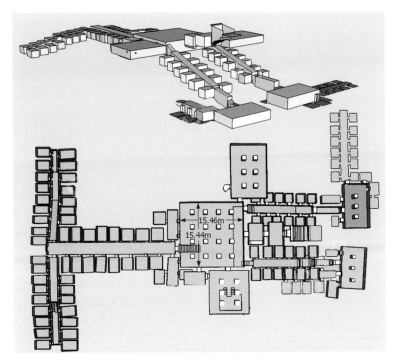

chambers. Repeated flash floods over the centuries stripped the painted plaster decoration from its walls, but enough remain to prove their quality matched the exquisite murals in Queen Nefertari's tomb. Unlike the tombs of his favored women in the Queens' Valley, Ramesses II himself features prominently in KV 5's decorative program.[138] Pharaoh introduces his sons to the deities of the underworld, reminding us that KV 5 was as much a monument to Ramesses as it was to his sons. Its gigantic proportions were worthy of his extensive progeny and his own lofty self-conception as Egypt's ruler. Resting in their massive tomb, the pharaoh's children magnified his glory even in death, as he guided their spirits before the gods of the underworld.

KV 5's potential occupants included all but a handful of Ramesses II's children, whom we know were buried elsewhere. While many rooms have been discovered, only a tiny fraction of them have been excavated. To date, archaeologists have recovered inscriptions naming only seven royal sons.[139] Even rarer are actual human remains. In a shallow pit in the small second chamber, archaeologists unearthed the complete skeletal remains of a man approximately fifty years of age, along with three skulls, also belonging to middle-aged males (fig. 8.19).[140] The skeleton rests in a dignified pose with his arms folded across his chest. All four skulls display a resemblance to the kings of the early Ramesside line. One has a particularly sharp chin, elongated skull, and long aquiline nose. A skull fracture may indicate he suffered a violent

FIGURE 8.19. Skeleton of an anonymous son of Ramesses II found in a pit near the entrance of the tomb of the royal children in the Valley of the Kings (KV 5). At death, this man was probably in his fifties, making it highly unlikely he is Amunhirkhopeshef, who probably died in his thirties. Alamy.

attack, perhaps in battle. But it shows evidence of healing, and likely was not fatal.[141]

Ancient tomb robbers dumped his body here, along with the heads of three other males. Once mummified and bedecked in precious jewelry and amulets, now they are reduced to bones. Thieves took them from deep within the tomb and brought them up to this outer chamber, seeking better light to despoil their mummies. After stripping them of everything of value, they discarded the body and three heads in the pit.

Some would identify the skeleton as none other than Prince Amunhirkhopeshef. This is highly dubious.[142] No inscribed objects were found to identify the skeleton. Since Ramesses had at least forty-seven sons, the chances of the KV 5 skeleton being Amunhirkhopeshef are slim. Nor, to put a more popular rumor to rest, do we have any evidence that Amunhirkhopeshef, as Pharaoh's first-born son, fell victim to the biblical plague recounted in Exodus. Such speculations make for dramatic TV documentaries, but rest only on hype that would make even Ramesses blush.

Notes

1. Royal children cut a low-profile on the monuments of Ramesses I and Sety I, with the future Ramesses II being the main exception. If Sety I had any siblings, no trace of them survives in the historical record. Ramesses II had a sister named Tia who married a man also named Tia. The couple received a tomb at Saqqara during her brother's reign, where she holds the title "king's sister," but not "king's daughter." A royal woman named Tanedjemy has the titles "king's daughter" and "mistress of the Two Lands" in her tomb in the Valley of the Queens: QV 33. See p. 248 n. 195 above. Any other children of Sety I left few traces of their existence, although a handful of additional tombs likely dating to Sety I's reign were prepared for women holding the titles of royal wife and royal daughter, but the cartouches were left blank and they remained unoccupied: McCarthy 2011, 6, 70. See p. 234 above.

2. Indeed, most of our evidence for individual princes of the Eighteenth Dynasty derives from private sources: their own funerary and religious monuments and tomb inscriptions belonging to a cadre of elite men and women the pharaohs appointed to act as their guardians and nurses.

3. Dodson 1990.

4. *KRI* II, 858–68; *RITA* II, 559–63; *RITANC* II, 571–75; Fisher 2001, 1:33–42; Brand 2016, 12–16.

5. On dating the temples containing the various lists, see Fisher 2001, 1:13–30.

6. Hsu 2015.

7. Fisher 2001, 1:135–36; Xekalaki 2011, 50–110; 2015.

8. These include the temple of Wadi es-Sebua in Nubia, and Sety I's Abydos Temple, where wide gaps mar the sequence of names. In Lower Egypt, mere fragments of lists survive from Piramesses, but here too they were an essential feature of his temple decoration in Lower Egypt: *KRI* II, 867; *RITA* II, 23–25; *RITANC* II, 571, 574; Fisher 2001, 1:pls. 17–18. Versions must have existed in Memphis, Heliopolis, and other northern centers, but archaeologists have yet to unearth any trace of them.

9. Examples include sons such as [Mery]monthu (no. 29); [Ramesses-me]r-Pre (no. 30); and [Seth(?)]emnakht (no. 38). The numbers refer to my own list on p. 256. Kitchen's are slightly different: *KRI* II, 859–60, nos. 30, 31, and 39; *RITA* II, 560. Of the thirty-eight known daughters in the monumental lists, the names of two are completely destroyed while six other names are fragmentary: *KRI* II, 916; *RITA* II, 598–99.

10. Kuentz 1971, pls. 22–24 (pylon, south face, east tower); Fisher 2001, 1:38–40 and pls. 42–58; Feleg 2020, 186 with pl. 37; 190–97 with figs. 39-40 (west wall north half); 233 with pl. 21; 247 with fig. 52; 249–51 (south wall, west half); 260–61 with pl. 24; 312–14 with fig. 67 (pylon, south face, east tower).

11. The earliest examples at Luxor show daughters marching behind their brothers: Kuentz 1971, pl. 24; Feleg 2020, 260–61 with pl. 24; 312–14 with pl. 67.

12. *RITANC* II, 469–71; Fisher 2001, 1:19–22, 33–34 and pls. 5–28. On the date of the Abydos and Wadi es-Sebua lists, see Brand 2016, 23–25.

13. Murnane 1995b, 203–6; Fisher 2001, 1:33–41, 132–35.

14. *RITANC* II, 571–75.

15. Nubian viceroys held the honorific title of "King's Son of Kush," although they were not actually royal offspring. The proliferation of the honorific

title "king's son" led New Kingdom pharaohs to distinguish their actual sons with the extended epithet "king's bodily son," *s3 nsw n ẖt=f.*

16. Rosellini 1832, pl. 16; *Medinet Habu* V, pl. 250. Artists rendered this garment in paint, not in relief. It consists of long strips of dyed fabric wound around the midriff and lower torso above the belt line. In the Queens Valley tomb of Prince Amunhirkhopeshef (QV 55), the son of Ramesses III, the prince wears a similar garment that only covers his belly; Leblanc 1989, pls. 135–142.

17. Xekalaki 2011, 60–62.

18. Fisher 2001, 1:42.

19. The earliest examples are reliefs depicting Amunhirkhopeshef alongside Ramesses II in the Corridor of the Bull in Sety I's Abydos Temple: PM VI, 25–26; Mariette, 1869, pl. 53; Brand 2000, 165–66 and fig. 83. See fig. 3.8 above. Fisher (2001, 1:44–49) discusses possible parallels for the prince wearing the curled sidelock with child-gods like Horus, Ihy, and Khonsu, with the *Iuwnmutef*-priest, and the *Sem*-priest of Ptah. Prince Khaemwaset also wears the curled sidelock in his capacity as *Sem*-priest: Fisher 2001, 1:91. On the sidelock with child-gods and New Kingdom princess, see also Xekalaki 2011, 22 and 60–62.

20. Fisher 2001, 1:35; Charron and Barbotin 2016, 29, fig. 3.

21. Fisher 2001, 1:132–33.

22. Murnane 1995a, 200; Fisher 2001, 1:131.

23. Murnane 1995a, 200.

24. Murnane 1995a, 202–3; Fisher 2001, 1:131–32.

25. Murnane 1995a, 203; Fisher 2001, 1:133–34; Xekalaki 2011, 62–63.

26. Fisher 2001, 1:134; Xekalaki 2011, 63.

27. Murnane 1995a, 203.

28. Xekalaki 2011, 88–89.

29. Xekalaki 2011, 90–92.

30. Xekalaki 2011, 93–94. On Ramesses II's daughters as chantresses, see Onstine 2005.

31. Calverley and Broome 1958, passim; Iskander and Goelet 2015, pls. 3.2.1–3.2.22.

32. Brand 2016.

33. *KRI* II, 859–68; *RITANC* II, 573; Brand 2016, 12–15.

34. Brand 2016, 13–14.

35. Among Ramesses II's first twenty sons are fourteen who cannot be identified as children of Nefertari or Isetnofret: Monthuhirkhopeshef (no. 5); Nebenkharu (no. 6); Meryamun (no. 7); Amunemwia (no. 8); Sety (no. 9); Setepenre (no. 10); Horhirwenemef (no. 12); Amenhotep (no. 14); Itamun (no. 15); Nebentaneb (no. 17); Meryre II (no. 18); Amenemopet (no. 19); Senakhtenamun (no. 20). While a few *could* have been born to the senior queens, we have no evidence for this. Most were born to other women who are now completely unknown to us; see Brand 2016, 21–23.

36. Brand 2016, 21–23. See pp. 225–26 above.

37. Did his other wives first have girls, or suffer failed pregnancies? These potentially older half siblings would occupy the fifth through tenth positions; Brand 2016, 13–14.

38. Brand 2016, 13–14.

39. *KRI* II, 916–21; *RITA* II, 598–99; *RITANC* II, 619–21.

40. O. Louvre 666: *KRI* II, 922–23; *RITA* II, 603; *RITANC* II, 623.

41. Kitchen identifies an erroneous daughter "Weretekhau" (his no. *54) by misinterpreting a list from Sety I's temple at Abydos where the daughter in third position is entitled [...] *Wrt-ḥk3w Nbt-t3wy* (*KRI* II, 918.2). This is not a unique occurrence of a daughter by that name (contra *RITANC* II, 620, §1127; *RITA* II, 599, no. *54), but is more probably part of a title [*šmʿyt n*] *Wrt-ḥk3w*, "[chantress of] Weret-Hekau" preceeding the name of Nebettawy, the well-known daughter of Queen Isetnofret who also became a daughter-wife. Many of Ramesses II's daughters are attested as chantresses of various deities in the Luxor Temple list: *KRI* II, 919.11–920.3; *RITA* II, 600–601. This is not true for most of the names in the Abydos princess lists but might be explained by Nebettawy's seniority. The Abydos lists date to the middle years of the reign by which time Nebettawy had become a daughter-wife. See p. 231 above.

42. For discussion of these lists see *RITANC* II, 620–21, §§1126–1129. See the concordance of the temple lists in *RITA* II, 598–99.

43. If so, Bintanath was the *oldest* sister of Prince Ramesses Junior, but not necessarily his *older* sister. Bintanath was likely younger than Ramesses Junior, or else how could their mother Isetnofret give birth to both of them before any male children, aside from Amunhirkhopeshef, were born? Bintanath may have had one or more half-sisters whose mothers were among Ramesses II's anonymous early wives. Admittedly, this is speculative, but how likely is it that Nefertari and Isetnofret between them produced four sons and at least one daughter, Bintanath, before the future king's other wives gave him any children of either gender? See p. 244 n. 146. above.

44. See p. 241 n. 96 and p. 243 n. 123 above.

45. Baketmut is the second daughter at Abu Simbel and third at Derr, but twenty-sixth in the first Abydos list. Henuttawy is in the seventh position at Abu Simbel and Derr and ninth at Abydos but fifteenth at Wadi es-Sebua. Other daughters of the two favored wives—as far as their names are preserved in the various lists—are consistently placed in the first ten positions even if their order varies. So Isetnofret II is sixth at Abu Simbel and Derr and eighth at Luxor Temple, and in the two Abydos lists.

46. They include the Princesses Werel, Nedjemmut, Qedmerut, Nebetiunu, Nebetnuhet, and Pipuy. Princess Werel is always placed within the first ten names in five lists while her sister Qedmerut is the fourth princess in both the Abydos lists and at Luxor Temple. Nedjemmut is the ninth daughter at Abu Simbel and Derr, but fifteenth at Wadi es-Sebua. Nebetiunu is fifth in the two Abydos lists but tenth at Luxor and seventeenth at Wadi es-Sebua. Nebetnuhet is tenth in both Abydos processions and sixteenth at Wadi es-Sebua. Note that Werel, Qedmerut, and Nebetiunu all appear at least once in a higher position in the lists than at least one of the daughters of Nefertari and Isetnofret. Princess Pipuy is fifth in the Luxor Temple list.

47. Ancient sources do not distinguish one as the "first" or "second." We only know there were two sons named Meryre because they both appear in the lists. Meryre I appears beside his father's colossus in the smaller temple at Abu Simbel, indicating Nefertari is his mother. Was Meryre II born after his namesake had died? If so, Meryre I must have succumbed to some illness tragically young. Aside from his name and his eighteenth position on the temple lists, we know nothing about Meryre II, including his mother's identity.

48. Setau, the Viceroy of Kush, oversaw construction of Wadi es-Sebua in the mid-forties of the reign: *RITANC* II, 469; Davies, *RITANC* III, 79–80. See pp. 424–25 below.

49. At Wadi es-Sebua, and perhaps Derr as well, it is clear some of the royal children are represented posthumously, including Amuhirkhopeshef and Meryre I. Given the high rates of infant and child mortality and briefer lifespans for adults in antiquity than today, an unknown number of Ramesses II's children would have predeceased him. For Meryre I, see Fisher 2001, 1:111.

50. At Sety I's Abydos temple, only the lowest courses of the walls in the outer courts bearing these lists of sons remains intact, but examples from the west wall of the first court and east wall of the second court have enough space to accommodate these longer names, and in some instances (e.g, Ramesses-Userkhepesh and Ramesses-Sikhepri) the "Ramesses" element is largely intact: Fisher 2001, 1:pls. 58B–59A, 62A–63B. Several blocks from the Ramesseum re-used in the small temple at Medinet Habu show a lower course of blocks with the waists and legs or an upper course with the heads and tops of the shoulders of several princes. It is clear from the scale of these figures that a middle course of blocks is now missing showing the bulk of the princes' torsos and the "Ramesses" element of their names. Traces of the *ms-s* or *ms-sw* element may remain on at least one block; Fisher 2001, 1:pls. 39A–42A.

51. In Ramesses II's day, these include men named Ramessesnakht, Ramesses-Ashahebused, Usermaatre-Ashanakhtu, and Ramesses-Meryamun.

52. Brand 2016, 26–27. The pattern is similar to the gods "of Ramesses II," conveying the notion that these deities were extensions of his identity; Römer 2004. On these deities, see pp. 388–89 below. Römer sees the ideological agenda such names convey not as a sign of political strength and confidence, but as a marker of potential weakness.

53. Cairo JdE 30707, 46764, and 72203: *KRI* II, 912–23; *RITA* II, 595–96; *RITANC* II, 615–16; Polz 1986.

54. But Ramesses-Nebweben's name lacks a cartouche on an alabaster fragment from Ghurob and a bronze statuette of Amun: *KRI* II, 914; *RITA* II, 596; *RITANC* II, 616.

55. In Kitchen's synopsis, these are sons nos. 21, 27, 34, 35, 36, 44, 45, 47, and 48: *KRI* II, 866–67.

56. See pp. 208–9 above.

57. So, with an ostracon now in Cairo that once named sixteen sons: JdE 72503: *KRI* II, 868; *RITA* II, 563; *RITANC* II, 575. Ramesses-Maatptah is known only from two papyri now in Leiden, nos. 366 and 367: *KRI* II, 910–12; *RITA* II, 594–595; *RITANC* II, 615.

58. Ricke, Hughes, and Wente 1967, pls. 8–15; *KRI* II, 195–99; *RITA* II, 59–62; *RITANC* II, 111–13; Spalinger 1979c, 272, 275–76; Fisher 2001, 1:22–24, 50–52 (Amunhirkhopeshef), 91–92 (Khaemwaset).

59. There is a tendency to read too much into these scenes from a chronological standpoint: Seele 1940, 36; Murnane 1975, 161–62; Spalinger 1979c; Kitchen 1980, 170. They are highly rhetorical, so attempts to calculate when these two princelings were old enough to accompany Ramesses when he fought in Nubia—allegedly during Sety I's reign—are in vain. The issue is also enmeshed in debate about a hypothetical coregency between Ramesses II and Sety. But speculation about their age when Beit el-Wali was built and decorated

is pointless. Certainly, they were alive in the first year of their father's reign; beyond this nothing is certain.

60. Ricke, Hughes, and Wente 1967, pl. 12.

61. Ricke, Hughes, and Wente 1967, pl. 8.

62. See pp. 103–4 above.

63. PM II², 433 (3); *LD* III, pl. 154; Wreszinski 1925, pls. 92–95; Heinz 2001, 291; Spalinger 1985b, 2003a; Schulz 2016.

64. Caption R 10: *KRI* II, 130:15; *RITA* II, 19.

65. Abu Simbel: PM VII, 102–3; Wreszinski, 1925, pl. 183; Heinz 2001, 252. Beit el-Wali: Ricke, Hughes, and Wente 1967, pl. 8.

66. Spalinger 2011, 135 10 and 148–57; Schulz 2016.

67. PM II², 438 (18); Wreszinski, 1925, pls. 107–109; *KRI* II, 174; *RITA* II, 47; *RITANC* II, 82–84; Youssef, Leblanc, and Maher 1977; Heinz 2001, 278; Schulz 2016.

68. One scene from Beit el-Wali shows an anonymous prince swinging an axe at the gate of a nameless Syrian town. Even if this does represent Amunhirkhopeshef, the whole episode is symbolic, and his role is no more "historic" than the speech of the defeated enemy chief in this scene. Ricke, Hughes, and Wente 1967, pls. 10, 12.

69. Schulz (2016) offers a brilliant visual analysis of the Dapur relief in the Ramesseum hypostyle hall. Her notion that the princes are shown assaulting Dapur in the scene to recover some of the honor lost by the supposedly ignominious retreat of their brethren—including Prehirwenemef and another whose name is lost—from the Hittite foe in the Kadesh narrative on the Ramesseum's pylon (fig. 8.7) is unlikely. All these sons were still children in their father's fifth regnal year. If their flight from the Hittite ambush on the camp was so embarrassing, Pharaoh's imagemakers would have avoided depicting it at all. Moreover, why are Prehirwenemef and his older brothers Amunhirkhopeshef and Ramesses Junior absent from the Dapur scene if they were present at Kadesh?

70. See p. 191 and fig. 6.6 above.

71. See Heinz 2001, 155–96; Spalinger 2013.

72. Janzen 2013; Matić 2019, 2021.

73. Murnane 1995a, 204–5. Historically, kings were often wary of empowering their close male relatives as potential rivals. Louis XIV, for example, kept both his brother Phillipe Duc d'Orleans and his eldest son the Dauphin from all affairs of state.

74. Murnane 1995a, 205–6.

75. Less fortunate were his descendants Sety II, who confronted the usurper Amenmesse, and Ramesses III, who fell victim to assassins conspiring to put a junior prince named Pentawaret on the throne. See p. 457 below.

76. In the early Old Kingdom, the highest offices of the royal administration, especially the vizierate, were held by princes. This began to change in the later Fourth Dynasty leading to a dramatic shift in the Fifth Dynasty as men with no royal blood were granted the highest offices; Bárta 2013. Thereafter, the princes had no access to senior administrative posts, a trend that continued in the Nineteenth Dynasty; Murnane 1995a, 204–5.

77. Fisher 2001, 1:62–64 (Amunhirkhopeshef), 76–77 (Ramesses Junior).

78. Fisher 2001, 1:85–87.

79 Fisher 2001, 1.107.

80. Khaemwaset's military service may have been entirely symbolic. Evidence is limited to the Nubian battle scene from Beit el-Wali and the Battle of Dapur episode at the Ramesseum; Fisher 2001, 1:91–92.

81. Fisher 2001, 1:117–18.

82. Ostracon Louvre 2262: *KRI* II, 907; *RITA* II, 592; *RITANC* II, 612–13.

83. So too with men related to Pharaoh by marriage, like his brother-in-law Tia, married to Ramesses II's sister Tia; van Dijk 1997; *RITANC* I, 212; Obsomer 2012b, 225–29.

84. Fisher 2001, 1:131.

85. PM II², 437–39 and 472–73; *LD* III, pl. 168; KRI II, 860–68; *RITANC* II, 571–75; Fisher 2001, 1:34–36 and pls. 28–42.

86. How early or late in Sety I's decade-long reign Amunhirkhopeshef was born is unclear and depends on how old Ramesses was when Sety ascended the throne and when the king established a household for the crown prince with wives of his own. See pp. 54–56 above.

87. This is clear from statuary and reliefs dating to the first years of the reign where Amunhirkhopeshef appears; see Fisher 2001, 1:66–68.

88. Turin 1380: Connor 2017.

89. Likewise, Prince Monthuhirkhopeshef (no. 5) is sometimes called Monthuhirwenemef in temple lists. Here *Imn-ḥr wmn=f*, "Amun is on His Right Side," substitutes for *Imn-ḥr ḫpš=f*, "Amun is in Possession of His Strong Arm"; see Fisher 2001, 1:57–58.

90. Fisher 2001, 1:58–62. Likewise, Prince Amunemwia, "Amun-is-in-the-Divine-Bark" (no. 8) is also called Sethemwia, "Seth is in the Divine Bark": *KRI* II, 863; *RITA* II, 586; *RITANC* II, 603; Fisher 2001, 1:108. Kitchen originally argued that Sethhirkhopeshef was a different individual than Amunhirkhopeshef, but he later revised this view. Leblanc 1999, 77–83 also considers them two individuals. More recently, the consensus among scholars is that Ramesses II's eldest son went by both names. For an overview of the debate, see *RITANC* II, 577; Fisher 2001, 1:58–62; Obsomer 2012b, 266–69. While some viewed Sethhirkhopeshef as a later moniker of the prince, Fisher (2001, 1:61–62) argues persuasively that it was his birth name since his family came from Avaris, an important cult center of Seth, while Amunhirkhopeshef was "his 'public' designation in much of the country." Since many monuments naming the prince stem from Upper Egypt, especially Thebes and the Nubian temples, the alias honoring Theban Amun is much better attested in surviving inscriptions than the Lower Egyptian variant that may once have been common on lost monuments from Heliopolis, Memphis, Piramesses, and other northern centers. Less persuasively, Obsomer (2012b, 269) claims Sethhirkhopeshef was a later alias connected with the Egyptian-Hittite peace treaty of regnal year twenty-one, in the Egyptian transcription of which the Hittite Storm God was identified as Seth. The Sethian alias was also used in two letters the prince sent to the Hittite king Hattusili III after the treaty; Fisher 2001, 1:59. See pp. 320 and 322 below.

91. Obsomer 2012b, 265; Brand 2016, 25 with n. 80. Janssen (1963, 32 n. 5) sees the name Usermaatre as referring to the king, but it lacks a cartouche and appropriate titles like *nsw-bity*. Leblanc (1999, 54 n. 144) claims the name belonged to Amunhirkhopeshef's own son. Both interpretations are unconvincing.

92. Cairo CG 42140: *KRI* II, 586.15–16.

93. Beginning in the late Eighteenth Dynasty, the traditional rank indicator *iry-pꜥt*, "member of the *pꜥt*-class," served to mark the current heir to the throne, beginning with the nonroyal "heirs presumptive" Horemheb and Pramessu. From the start of the Nineteenth Dynasty, it was used alongside the title "king's eldest son," *sꜣ-nsw smsw*, coming first in the sequence of the titles and names of the current heir; Murnane 1995b, 193; Fisher 2001, 1:62–63 (Amunhirkhopeshef), 125. Occasionally, princes other than the designated heir held the title.

94. So *mḥ-ib mnḫ, sꜣ-nsw tpy n ḫt=f*, and *mw nṯry pr m kꜣ-nḫt*; Fisher 2001, 1:64–65.

95. PM II², 334–35; Kitchen 1964; *KRI* II, 180; *RITA* II, 49–59; Heinz 2001, 272; Fisher 2001, 1:51–52 and pl. 108. For the palimpsest texts, see Darnell and Jasnow 1993; Roberson, *KRI* IX, 37. On the Moabite campaign, see pp. 191–92 above.

96. Fisher 2001, 1:52–53. See p. 320 below.

97. *ÄHK* I, nos. 7 and 9; Beckman 2008, 128; Cordani 2017, 69–70.

98. This is the possible interval for his lifespan if we add the twenty-one years of the king's reign when Amunhirkhopeshef was crown prince to an unknown number of years before Ramesses II's accession during Sety I's reign and another uncertain stretch of years after regnal year twenty-one but before year thirty. Scholars have come up with a wider range for his lifespan, with some believing he lived on into the forties or even fifties of the reign, but the evidence indicates he was dead by the early Jubilee period when his younger brother Ramesses Junior had become heir. For an overview of the debate, see Fisher 2001, 1:69–70. Fisher places his death sometime between regnal years 21 and 36, but he probably died before his father's first Jubilee in year thirty.

99. Carved in plaster on the rough-hewn walls of KV 5's two outer chambers, these battered reliefs were once painted in brilliant polychrome in a style like that of Nefertari's tomb (QV 66). Only the names of the two eldest sons, Amunhirkhopeshef and Ramesses Junior, are preserved in two scenes. While some of their younger brothers could theoretically have appeared, it is more likely that, due to their seniority, the two eldest princes each appeared multiple times in these antechambers to the exclusion of their siblings. For the reliefs, see Weeks 2006, 55–94; Fisher 2001, 1:30, 46–47, 71–72. As Obsomer (2012b, 268–69) notes, the form of Ramesses II's nomen in these scenes, *Rꜥ-ms-s*, is consistent with a completion date before regnal year twenty-one. A fragment of one of his calcite canopic jars indicates Amunhirkhopeshef was interred in KV 5.

100. Weeks 2006, 105–6.

101. On the distinction between the epithet *sꜣ-nsw tpy*, "first king's son," meaning the oldest son of a particular royal wife, and *sꜣ-nsw smsw*, "eldest king's son," meaning the oldest (living) of all princes, see Fisher 2001, 1:64–65. Amunhirkhopeshef held both titles as the eldest of all sons and as Nefertari's first born. Ramesses Junior was initially *sꜣ-nsw tpy* as Isetnofret's first son and later *sꜣ-nsw smsw* after Amunhirkhopeshef's death: Fisher 2001, 1:71–73, 77.

102. So *imy-r mšꜥ wr tpy n ḥm=f*.

103. For discussion of the prince's career and various assessments of the date of his death, see Fisher 2001, 1:76–79.

104. Apart from battle scenes dating to the first two decades, a subsidiary statue on the façade of the larger Abu Simbel Temple, and in processional lists

of royal sons, Ramesses II never honored his like-named son on royal monuments; see Fisher 2001, 1:71–79.

105. Weeks 2006, 59–61.

106. *KRI* II, 871–99; *RITA* II, 565–85; *RITANC* II, 581–601; Gomaà 1973; Kitchen 1982, 103–9; Fisher 2001, 1:89–105; Charron and Barbotin 2016.

107. Gomaà 1973; Kitchen 1982, 103–9; Leblanc 1999, 155–60; Fisher 2001, 1:103–5; Snape 2011; Obsomer 2012b, 272–74; Charron and Barbotin 2016.

108. Charron and Barbotin 2016, 290–99; Vinson 2018. See pp. 467–68 below.

109. Ricke, Hughes, and Wente 1967, pl. 8; Heinz 2001, 261; Fisher 2001, 1:pl. 78.

110. Charron and Barbotin 2016, 34–35.

111. Fisher 2001, 1:98–101.

112. A dedicatory inscription from the Serapeum claims the Apis chose him while he was still a child: *KRI* II, 878–79; *RITA* II, 569–70; *RITANC* II, 588; Gomaà 1973, 33. Indeed, the text has autobiographical tones that seem to borrow from the rhetoric of New Kingdom royal inscriptions that claim the gods had destined the king to rule "in the egg." It describes Khaemwaset as predestined "in the womb," to serve Ptah and the Apis Bull.

113. See pp. 351–52 below.

114. *KRI* II, 377, 384–86, 390–94; *RITA* II, 208, 213–14, 219–23; *RITANC* II, 233–34, 239–42, 245–50; Fisher 2001, 1:pls. 84–90, 134.

115. *KRI* II, 873–75; *RITA* II, 566–67; *RITANC* II, 583–85; McClain 2007, 187–89; Snape 2011, 468–70; Navrátilová 2016.

116. Khaemwaset placed his memorial texts on the casing blocks sheathing the coarser stone that formed the bulk of Old Kingdom pyramids, but later generations stripped away this fine Tura limestone, much of it to build medieval Cairo. Did the prince also leave texts on the Great Pyramids of Khufu and Khafre at Giza? Today, the Giza pyramids are missing their casing stones, so we cannot tell. Indeed, some view Khaemwaset more as a recycler than a custodian of Old Kingdom monuments; see Navrátilová 2016.

117. *KRI* II, 874; Gomaà 1973, 77, 105–6. *RITANC* II, 583–84; McClain 2007, 187–88.

118. Snape 2017.

119. *KRI* II, 872; *RITA* II, 566; *RITANC* II, 583; Fisher 2001, 1:pls. 139–140; Snape 2011, 470–73. On Ro-Setjau in the Nineteenth Dynasty and its connection with the royal ancestor cult, see Bács 2019.

120. Kitchen 1982, 107. Charron and Barbotin (2016) characterize Khaemwaset as "le prince archéologue."

121. For the Apis burials in Ramesses II's sixteenth and thirtieth regnal years and later, see *KRI* II, 366–77; *RITA* II, 199–208; *RITANC* II, 220–33. For Khaemwaset's monuments from the Serapeum, see Charron and Barbotin 2016. Inscriptions recording the later Apis burials under Ramesses II are undated but took place under the auspices of Khaemwaset and later his brother Merenptah, who succeeded him as *s3 nsw smsw* and heir during the mid-fifties of the reign; Fisher 2001, 1:112, 114–15.

122. On the Serapeum of Saqqara during the Ramesside period, see most recently Thijs 2018.

123. On a granite statue of Khaemwaset (Vienna 5768), his son Ramesses holds the title of *s3-nsw* (*KRI* II, 883; *RITANC* II, 592) where the younger man

is obviously a grandson of the pharaoh. By contrast, Khaemwaset's son Hori, who later became High Priest of Ptah, lacks the title *s3-nsw* on the only known reference to him, a pillar fragment from Saqqara: Cairo JdE 43271; PM III.2², 703; *KRI* III, 414–15; *RITANC* III, 312. See also Dalino 2017.

124. On a statue, now in Milan, Khaemwaset's daughter Isetnofret is simply titled *s3t=f n ht=f mr=f Ist-nfrt*, "his bodily daughter, his beloved, Isetnofret" (*KRI* II, 887.13–15; *RITANC* II, 593–94). In the burial shaft of a tomb chapel recently discovered by Japanese archaeologists at Saqqara, a sarcophagus of this woman identifies her as *špst Ist-nfrt*, "the noble woman Isetnofret." See Kawai 2010, 2014; Yoshimura and Kawai 2010; http://www.egyptpro.sci.waseda.ac.jp/e-abusir.html. Another woman named Isetnofret was the daughter of Prince Merenptah, Ramesses II's thirteenth son and eventual successor. She is referred to two or three times in P. Leiden I, 350, verso. In the first entry she is entitled *špst Ist-nfrt s3t Mr-n-Pth*, "the noble woman Isetnofret, daughter of Merenptah" (*KRI* II, 807.13). In a second entry the title *špst* is used but the name was left blank and no reference to her father is given (*KRI* II, 809.1). A third entry refers to deliveries to *s3t-nsw Ist-nfrt*, "the king's daughter Isetnofret" (*KRI* II, 812.10). These daughters of Princes Khaemwaset and Merenptah were named after their paternal grandmother Queen Isetnofret and neither should be confused with Princess Isetnofret II, the sister of the two princes, who was their aunt. Dorn and Polis (2016, 149–50) identify the Isetnofret named in the recently discovered Saqqara tomb as the daughter of Merenptah instead of Khaemwaset. They suspect that O. Cairo 72460 refers to the burial of one of these granddaughters of Ramesses II and not his wife or daughter.

125. Fisher (2001, 1:105) places his death no earlier than regnal year 53. In that year, a treasury scribe named Pentawaret wrote a note on an ostracon referring to himself as "scribe and physician of the *Sem*-priest of Ptah, the King's Son Khaemwaset," indicating the prince was still alive: Fisher 2001, 2:106, no. 4.51.

126. See most recently Charron and Barbotin 2016, 272–86 with cat. nos. 120–134.

127. On the state of the Apis "mummies" that Mariette discovered, see Charron 2020.

128. The monumental stone structure of Khaemwaset that the Waseda University team discovered at Saqqara included fragments of a granite false door stela inscribed with his name, suggesting this was his tomb chapel.

129. Weeks 1998, 88–93; 2006, 3–5.

130. Weeks 1998, 105 and 108.

131. Weeks 1998, 81–144.

132. Reeves and Wilkinson 1996, 144–46; Weeks 1998, 209–50; 2006, 6–53.

133. Although the statue lacks any trace of inscriptions, Weeks described it as an image of Ramesses II in the guise of Osiris, basing this on the fact that the god wears a *Shebyu*-necklace, which Johnson's research has linked to the divine king, especially in his solar aspect; Weeks 1998, 225, 242–43; 2006, 36–37. But the *Shebyu*-necklace is, in fact, a common attribute of Osiris in Egyptian art from the late Eighteenth Dynasty and is ubiquitous for the god in the Ramesside era, as can be seen in contemporary private and royal tombs including those of Senedjem at Deir el-Medina (TT 1); Neferrenpet (TT 178); Nefertari in the Queens Valley (QV 66); and Sety I (KV 17). Likewise, in Sety I's Abydos temple, Osiris frequently wears the *Shebyu*-necklace, but the solar god in his

various guises of Re-Horakhty, Khepri, and Atum never does. Nor should we date the Osiris statue in KV 5 to the Jubilee period based on the flawed notion that Ramesses II was not deified before year thirty. Contra Weeks 1998, 242–43. See pp. 413–14 and fig. 14.6 below.

134. Fisher 2001, 1:pls. 102–105; Weeks 2006, 55–93.

135. For the canopics, see Weeks 2006, 104–11. From these we know that at least three princes were laid to rest here: Amunhirkhopeshef (no. 1), Sety (no. 9), and Ramesses-Meryatum. As many as three broken canopic jars attest to Prince Sety, whose name is spelled "Suty," *Swty*, thereby avoiding the Seth hieroglyph in the tomb where the deceased prince was identified with Osiris. Ramesses-Meryatum is more puzzling, if this is not a unique variation of the name of the sixteenth prince, Nefertari's youngest son Meryatum, we would have to increase the number of Ramesses II's known male offspring by one.

136. The Turin Strike Papyrus (P. Turin 1880, recto 4,13–4,14): "The tomb of the royal children of the Osiris-King Usermaatre, L.P.H., the great god," *p3 isy n n3 msw-nsw n nsw Wsir Wsr-m3ʿt-Rʿ-stp-n-Rʿ ʿnḥ wd3 snb p3 ntr ʿ3*: Gardiner 1948, 58:3–4. P. Turin 1880 recto 4,13.

137. Having been robbed in antiquity, KV 5 remains largely unexcavated, and we only have direct evidence for the burials of three sons named on the canopic jars, and a fourth, Ramesses Junior, in the wall decoration. An ostracon (Cairo JdE 72503) listed at least sixteen of Ramesses II's sons, including Sety, prince no. 9, here written "Suty." This ostracon is likely an accounting of burials in KV 5. Another ostracon now in Paris (Louvre 2261) dated to regnal year 53 apparently records the inspection of the burials of Princes Sety and Sethhirkhopeshef, a.k.a. Amunhirkhopeshef, along with "the royal children of His Person, L.P.H. in the following" : *KRI* II, 914:13–915:2; *RITA* II, 596; *RITANC* II, 617. Yet, with so many rooms, it is likely the king buried many of his daughters in KV 5 as well. Another ostracon (Louvre 666) records an inspection carried out by the same officials named in O. Louvre 2261. O. Louvre 666 lists fifteen royal daughters: *KRI* II, 922:9–923:3; *RITA* II, 603; *RITANC* II, 623. Presumably, they too were buried collectively in KV 5, perhaps in a separate wing of the labyrinthine tomb from their brothers.

138. Much better preserved are the five tombs Ramesses III built for his sons in the Queen's Valley: Prehirwenemef (QV 42), Sethhirkhopeshef (QV 43), Khaemwaset (QV 44), Ramesses (QV 53), and Amunhirkhopeshef (QV 55). As with the damaged reliefs in KV 5, the decorative program consists mainly of scenes depicting the king leading his son before the gods of the underworld; Leblanc 1989, pls. 91–100, 134–52; Weeks and De Luca 2002, 312–23; McCarthy 2011, 664–70.

139. Those royal children not entombed in KV 5 include the five daughter-wives—Bintanath, Merytamun, Henuttawy, Nebettawy, and Henutmire—each having a tomb in the Queen's Valley; Khaemwaset, likely interred at Saqqara; and Ramesses-nebweben, buried at Mi-Wer (Ghurob). Ramesses began preparing another tomb for some of his children in the Valley of the Queens. According to one of the tomb-robbery papyri dating to the reign of Ramesses IX, a coppersmith accused of violating the tomb of Isis, the wife of Ramesses III, led officials to "the common tomb of the royal children of King Usermaatre-Setepenre, L.P.H., the great god, in which no burial had been made, and which had been left open": P. BM 10221, Recto, 16: *KRI* VI, 474–75: *RITA* VI, 364.

B. Davies 2018, 356–57, suggests this was a precursor to KV 5. Archaeologists have not yet identified this abandoned tomb.

140. On the human remains, see Weeks 1998, 280–85 and photo opposite 205; 2006, 18–21; C. M. Wilkinson 2008; Wilkinson and Weeks 2019, 393–94.

141. Weeks 1998, 284.

142. The identification of inscriptions in the tomb naming Amunhirkhopeshef set off a frenzy of speculation as the media and armchair archaeologists worldwide latched on to the notion that as Ramesses II eldest son, Amunhirkhopeshef must have been the princely victim of the final plague recounted in Exodus. Weeks and his team (Weeks 1998, 275–79) walked a fine line trying not to add fuel to the fire. When human remains were uncovered in the pit from chamber two, the media and internet lit up with reports that here was the ill-fated Prince Amunhirkhopeshef. Typical in this regard was the documentary "Rameses: Wrath of God or Man," Discovery Channel 2004: https://www.imdb.com/title/tt1024234/. The Discovery Channel presented a computer-generated image of a facial reconstruction of the skull. While this shows an affinity with Ramesses II's mummy that suggests the individual was possibly a male relative, identifying him as the pharaoh's first born is hopeful guesswork since no identifying inscriptions were associated with the skeleton. The whole affair is a perfect example of the uneasy relationship between Egyptology and archaeology as scientific fields and the public's interest in pharaonic civilization and Egypt's ties to the Bible that both feed off of and are fed by the news media and the "infotainment industry," to say nothing of internet and social-media conspiracy theories.

143. This numbering of the princes differs somewhat from the tallies of Kitchen *KRI* II, 859–60; *RITA* II, 560; *RITANC* II, 571–75; Fisher 2001, 2:63–188; and Obsomer 2012b, 261–62.

144. His aliases include Amunhirwenemef, Sethhirkhopeshef, and Usermaatre, the last two of whom Kitchen tentatively listed as his nos. 49 and 50, but later confirmed were alternative monikers of Amunhirkhopeshef.

145. Alias Sethemwia.

146. Also called Suty. The variant writing of Sety's name as *Swty* occurs on O. Cairo JdE 72503 (*KRI* II, 563) and canopic jar fragments from KV 5 (Weeks 2006), indicating that he is the same individual. A separate "Suty" is illusory: Kitchen's no. 43 (*KRI* II, 860); Fisher's no. 46 (Fisher 2001, 2:187); Obsomer's no. 42 (Obsomer 2012b, 261). See p. 282 nn. 135 and 137.

147. So just Siptah in the Abydos list: *KRI* II, 867. This son of Ramesses II is to be distinguished from Ramesses-Siptah, attested on some objects now in the Louvre Museum: *KRI* II, 907–9; *RITANC* II, 613–614; Fisher 2001, 2:181–82. This Prince Ramesses-Siptah was Sety II's younger son who later became Pharaoh Siptah: Fisher 2001, 1:118–19; Johnson 2012, 39–43. For an overview of the debate about these Nineteenth Dynasty princes named Siptah, see Johnson 2012, 40–41. While Ramesses II gave many of his younger sons' names compounded with "Ramesses," Siptah (no. 26) was not one of them. See pp. 452–53 below.

148. Part of the prefix "Ramesses" is preserved in a relief from Sety I's Abydos Temple.

149. Kitchen's "Prince no. 30 [...]monthu" from the first Abydos list is an erroneous dittography of his no. 29; *KRI* II, 867: 2 = "24th Prince." Merymonthu's name is fully preserved in O. Cairo JdE 72503. Due to this dittography, and his

erroneous no. 43 "Suty," Kitchen's numbering tally of princes differs from my own from this point.

150. It appears likely that most of the princes from nos. 27 to 45, along with no. 21, have names formed by compounding "Ramesses" with various epithets. Eleven of these are well preserved, but others can be restored in a damaged temple lists at Abydos and in the gaps between blocks from the Ramesseum re-used in the small temple at Medinet Habu: Fisher 2001, 2:pls. 39–42A, 58A–59B, 61B–63B. Other examples from Abydos clearly lack the room for this prefix: Fisher 2001, 1:pls. 60A–61A.

151. Alias Ramesses-Meryseth: Fisher 2001, 2:183–85.

152. The name is damaged in Ramesseum block reused at Medinet Habu: *KRI* II, 868; Fisher 2001, 1:pl. 42A. The full name was carved over that of Prince Setepenre on a limestone doorway from Piramesses (Qantir): Habachi 1954, 490–94 and pl. 25; *KRI* II, 900–901; *RITANC* II, 604–5.

153. No reliable evidence exists for other princes. Kitchen lists a "*R.-Sth-ḥr-wmn.f*" in his initial tally but he provides no documentation for this phantom (*KRI* II, 860, no. 48). His nos. 49 "Sethhirkhopeshef" and 50 "Usimare" are aliases of Amunhirkhopeshef. See below. Also doubtful are Fisher's nos. 43–45, where, as she carefully notes (2001, 2:186–87), the "names" of three princes in O. Cairo JdE 72503 may be titles. This seems certain, as Kitchen's transcription and analysis makes clear: *KRI* II, 868; *RITA* II, 563; *RITANC* II, 575.

154. The order of names on this list of daughters is based on Kitchen's synopsis with some alterations: *KRI* II, 916–23; *RITA* II, 598–603; *RITANC* II, 619–23.

155. One of two daughters named after their paternal grandmother Tuya. The other is Tuya-Nebettawy (no. 51: *KRI* II, 922:15).

156. The fifteenth name is missing from both Abydos lists, but either, or both, could be preserved on other lists.

157. The missing name of a princess on a Ramesseum block reused at Medinet Habu: *KRI* II, 916:13.

158. Since the name is missing, it is possible she is one of the first thirty-eight princesses.

159. If she is not the same as Renpetnofret (no. 28).

160. Named for her aunt Tia and great grandmother Queen Satre.

161. So not "Nebouemsekhmet," as Obsomer 2012b, 251 reads.

162. The twenty-third name on the second Abydos list, *Ḥnwt*-[...], (*KRI* II, 919:4), if she is not identical to He[nut...]isep (no. 26: *KRI* II, 919:3), might be Ramesses II's fifth daughter-wife Henutmire. See p. 247 n. 183 above.

163. The unnamed daughter born to Ramesses II's first Hittite wife, Maa-horneferure, who is known from the diplomatic correspondence he exchanged with the Hittite court could be added to the list if she is not one of the princesses named in the Abydos lists. See pp. 371–73 below.

164. A mummy said to be from Akhmim and now in Madrid allegedly belongs to a daughter of Ramesses II named Isis who was also a temple singer: Llagostera Cuenca 1998. The mummy belongs to an adolescent female. The coffin associated with it has disappeared, depriving us of the inscriptional data. One wonders if the mummy is genuinely a daughter of Ramesses II and how it came to be in Akhmim.

Chapter Nine

The Path to Peace: International Diplomacy and the End of the Egyptian-Hittite Conflict

Intelligence filtering into the royal courts of Egypt, Babylonia, and Assyria reported political turmoil in the Hittite Empire. A new king, Hattusili III, had overthrown his predecessor. According to rumor, the deposed Hittite monarch escaped his captor's grasp before disappearing. Now Pharaoh received an urgent request from a Hittite delegation newly arrived at his capital Piramesses. Foregoing the usual pomp and ceremony, they pleaded for an immediate—and private—royal audience.

Curious as to their intentions, Ramesses granted the strange request.

Soon palace attendants ushered a small group of Hittite envoys into one of Pharaoh's private audience chambers. They paid formal obeisance to their royal host, as Ramesses demanded even from a Great King's emissaries. But one haughty young Hittite stood aloof from his companions, and refused to bow. As the lead envoy stammered that "their lord" required his aid, Ramesses II inclined his head and smiled—for he realized now who this young Hittite was. Standing before him begging for refuge was Urhi-Teshub, erstwhile Great King of Hatti and mortal rival of the usurper Hattusili III. Pharaoh graciously offered sanctuary to this useful royal guest.

***

Soon after this dramatic scene unfolded, in his twenty-first regnal year (ca. 1258 BCE), Ramesses II concluded one of history's earliest known peace treaties with the Hittite King Hattusili III, ending more than half a century of hostilities. How did this détente come about? During the Late Bronze Age (ca. 1550–1200 BCE), the Great Kingdoms of the ancient Near East seldom forged peace treaties with peer kingdoms, although the Hittites frequently imposed them on vanquished enemies and vassal kingdoms (figs. 1.5 and 5.15).[1] Relations between these empires veered between open hostility and guarded coexistence, supported by intense diplomacy.[2] Diplomatic records unearthed in the ruins

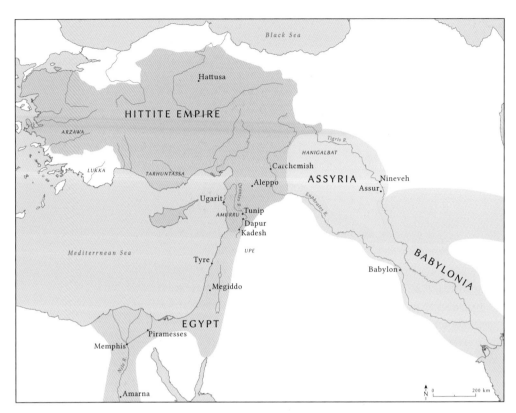

FIGURE 9.1. The Great Kingdoms of the ancient Near East, ca. 1250 BCE. Map by Tina Ross.

of the Hittite capital of Hattusa allow us to follow the dramatic events leading up to the Egyptian-Hittite pact.

Today scholars debate why these powerful rivals forged their alliance after six decades of conflict. Many assume Ramesses II's misadventure at Kadesh led directly to the settlement. But fifteen years of hostilities separated these events, as Ramesses II doggedly pursued his aggressive strategy deep inside Hittite-controlled Syria. Diplomatic intrigues on the eve of the treaty reveal what drove both sides to the negotiating table. To understand this ancient peace process, we must first look at diplomacy among the great powers in the ancient Near East.

The Great Powers Club

A handful of Great Kingdoms dominated the ancient Near East during the Late Bronze Age, wielding hegemony over numerous smaller kingdoms (fig. 9.1). Rulers of these imperial powers called themselves Great Kings, with minor kings being their vassals. Great Kings jealously guarded their superior status and prestige as imperial overlords and formed what historians have dubbed "the Great Powers Club."[3] Within this exclusive group each Great King recognized a small number of royal peers, even as he jealously guarded his own status and prestige.

When they dominated adjacent lands, relations between Great Kings were often hostile. During the first half of the Eighteenth Dynasty, Syria had become a battleground as Egypt and Mitanni fought to control it.[4] Thutmose IV and his Mitanni counterpart King Artatama ended this decades-long conflict and the two empires remained at peace until Akhenaten's reign, when the Hittite king Suppiluliuma I conquered Mitanni and made it his vassal.

Great Kingdoms who were at peace, especially those that did not share a troublesome border, normally pursued diplomatic relations, trading royal envoys, diplomatic letters, and precious gifts. Issues of stature and influence, and not merely economic concerns, motivated these regular exchanges. We know from the Amarna Letters that Amenhotep III and Akhenaten maintained intensive diplomatic contacts with the kings of Assyria, Babylonia, Hatti, and Mitanni.[5]

In the argot of ancient Near Eastern diplomacy, Great Kings referred to each other as "brothers," indicating their status as peers. The messages they exchanged were highly formal. Strict protocols and elaborate formulaic wording expressed bilateral respect and courteous reciprocity.[6]

Despite strict rules of diplomatic courtesy, Great Kings often quarreled with one another, resorting to harsh words and calculated slights to indicate displeasure with their correspondents. Through verbal sparring, each Great King asserted his own sense of superiority, or sought revenge for any perceived affront his royal brother had inflicted on him.[7]

During the Nineteenth Dynasty the Great Powers Club consisted of Egypt, Babylonia, Hatti, and a new member—the resurgent kingdom of Assyria. Among its peers in the international system, Hatti was at war with Egypt for several decades, and its relations with Assyria were often tense. Hatti's relations with other Great Kingdoms played a key role in the political turmoil that rocked the Hittite Empire during the first two decades of Ramesses II's reign.

Political Crisis in Hatti

Shortly after the Battle of Kadesh, Ramesses II's old sparring partner, King Muwatalli II, died, leaving his throne to his son Urhi-Teshub, who took the throne name Mursili III (fig. 9.2).[8] Most of our evidence for his reign comes from the Apology of Hattusili III, a political tract in which Hattusili justifies his seizure of the throne as a divine judgment against his nephew.[9] Even the length of Urhi-Teshub's reign remains unclear, but his tenure spanned the period around Ramesses II's tenth regnal year.[10]

FIGURE 9.2. The royal seal of King Mursili III, better known as Urhi-Teshup. From Hethitologie Portal Mainz, redrawn by Peter Brand.

Urhi-Teshub soon came into conflict with his powerful uncle Hattusili, Muwatalli's brother and close confidant. Muwatalli had entrusted Hattusili with the governorship of Hatti's Upper Lands. Concerned that Hattusili's power threatened his own, Urhi-Teshub distrusted his uncle and begrudged him his fiefdom. Systematically, he stripped Hattusili of his territories and privileges while the older man seethed with resentment.

Urhi-Teshub also suffered from turbulent relations with other Great Kingdoms. Conflict lingered on his southern front as Ramesses II pursued campaigns in Syria following Kadesh. To the east, relations with Assyria were also problematic. Freed from its vassalage to Mitanni after Suppiluliuma I destroyed its former overlord, Assyria was now bent on expanding in northern Mesopotamia, threatening Hatti's interests.

East of the Euphrates River, Hanigalbat, as the rump kingdom of Mitanni was called, now served as a client kingdom and buffer zone, insulating the Hittite Empire's southeast flank. But King Adad-Nirari of Assyria conquered Hanigalbat and absorbed it into his own empire, pushing Assyria's border to the banks of the Euphrates River, dangerously close to Carchemish, Hatti's viceregal seat in Syria and a lynchpin of its empire.[11]

Having secured Hanigalbat as his vassal, Adad-Nirari felt entitled to join the ranks of the Great Kingdoms. Buoyed by his victory, he wrote to Urhi-Teshub, addressing him as a "brother," thereby asserting that he was a Great King of equal status.[12] Still smarting from the humiliating loss of his client kingdom, Urhi-Teshub was in no mood to mince words with his uppity Assyrian counterpart. In his snide reply, the Hittite king ridiculed Adad-Nirari's claim to "brotherhood":

> Have you become a Great King? Why do you keep talking about brotherhood …? What does brotherhood mean? … And for what reason should I write to you about brotherhood? Who writes to whom about brotherhood? Do those who are not on good terms write to one another about brotherhood? Why should I write to you about brotherhood? Were you and I perhaps born of the same mother? As my grandfather and father did not write to the king of Assyria about brotherhood, even so you must not write to me about brotherhood and Great Kingship![13]

Meanwhile, Urhi-Teshub's quarrel with his uncle Hattusili reached its breaking point. According to Hattusili's Apology, his royal nephew envied the prominence and good fortune he enjoyed as governor of the Hittite Upper Lands.[14] He even took credit for installing his nephew on the throne after Muwatalli died. But from Urhi-Teshub's perspective, his uncle had become an overly ambitious subject whose power now

FIGURE 9.3. Relief of Hattusili III (right), pouring a libation at an altar before the Storm God of Heaven (left). Fraktin, Turkey. Courtesy of Tayfun Bilgin, www.hittitemonuments.org.

threatened his own. At first Hattusili held his tongue while his nephew deprived him of more and more of his holdings. Pushed into a corner, Hattusili struck back at last:

> So out of respect for my brother (Muwatalli II) I did not retaliate accordingly, and for seven years I was tolerant. But that one schemed my destruction.... So I was no longer tolerant, and I became his enemy. But when I became his enemy, still I did nothing impure—I did not rebel against him with chariot, nor did I rebel against him within (his) house. I addressed him like a man, saying "You disputed with me, yet you are a Great King, but I, the one fortress which you left me, (I) am king of only that one fortress. So, come! (The goddess) Ishtar of Samuha and the Storm God of Nerik will decide our case." When to Urhi-Teshub I wrote thus—and if someone (should) say the following, "Why at first did you install him (Urhi-Teshub) to kingship, but now you write to him (as an) enemy? (I will answer), "If he had in no way disputed with me, would (the gods) truly have subjugated a Great King to a minor king?" Now, because he disputed with me, the gods have subjugated him to me by (their) verdict.[15]

In the ensuing clash, Hattusili emerged victorious. He captured Urhi-Teshub and brought him to Hattusa as a prisoner, stripping him of his royal status. After this *coup d'état* Hattusili III would labor throughout his reign to justify his usurpation (fig. 9.3). At home and abroad, skeptical audiences impugned his legitimacy. Other Great Kings spurned his offers of friendship, while many of his own subjects harbored loyalty to Urhi-Teshub.[16]

Hattusili III's Diplomacy

However prickly their dealings were with Urhi-Teshub, the rulers of rival Great Kingdoms—Assyria, Babylonia, and Egypt—refused to welcome his replacement with open arms. Instead, suspicion and confusion prevailed as to who was the rightful Hittite king. For Babylonia and Egypt, the incident also presented an irresistible opportunity to meddle in the affairs of a rival kingdom.

The Great Kings had good reason to be perplexed about Hatti's leadership, because Urhi-Teshub and Hattusili III both sent them letters following the coup.[17] While his agents played a cat and mouse game to disrupt Urhi-Teshub's international correspondence, Hattusili launched a diplomatic charm offensive, seeking the Great Kings' recognition of his rule.[18] This would confirm his full membership in the Great Powers Club. In turn, formal ties with these powerful monarchs would reinforce his standing among his own subjects.

Hattusili III's statecraft met with uneven success at first. King Adad-Nirari of Assyria still nursed a grudge against Hatti over Urhi-Teshub's stinging rebuke. Hattusili frankly admitted to him that Assyrian envoys had "experienced aggravation" under Urhi-Teshub.[19] Now he proposed a fresh start. But Adad-Nirari spurned this overture, failing to reciprocate with the customary gifts or even acknowledge his claim to kingship. Hattusili complained:

> Did [my brother (Muwatalli)] not send you appropriate gifts of greeting? But when I assumed kingship, [then] you did not send a messenger to me. It is the custom that when kings assume kingship, the kings, his equals in rank, send him appropriate [greeting-gifts], clothing befitting kingship, and fine [oil] for his anointing. But you did not do this today.[20]

Although Adad-Nirari's reply has not survived, relations between Assyria and Hatti remained cool, if not outright hostile.[21]

Meanwhile, Hattusili still faced the vexing question of Urhi-Teshub's future. According to the norms of Hittite society, it was unthinkable to execute the former ruler.[22] Exile to some remote part of the empire was the usual fate for disgraced members of the Hittite royal family. Hattusili packed his deposed predecessor off to Syria, and made him a regional governor.[23]

Unfortunately for Hattusili, banishment to Syria offered Urhi-Teshub plentiful opportunities to plot his escape, for he was determined to take back the throne. Soon he began intrigues with his former colleagues on the international stage, dispatching letters to the kings of Assyria and Babylonia. The Assyrian monarch offered him no comfort, given his rude rejection of Adad-Nirari's letter. In Babylonia, though,

King Kadashman-Turgu listened with evident interest. Negotiations progressed so far that Urhi-Teshub made plans to depart for Babylon. Hattusili got wind of his scheme just in time, and prevented his nephew's escape.[24]

Unable to contain Urhi-Teshub in Syria, Hattusili transferred his rogue nephew to the Mediterranean coast. But Urhi-Teshub would not sit idly in another provincial backwater. Giving his wardens the slip, he now sought a new foreign haven. Indeed, there was one more Great King with whom Urhi-Teshub had dealings; one only too pleased to host this deposed Hittite potentate to the discomfort of his successor Hattusili III.[25]

Hattusili was outraged and incredulous when his missing nephew resurfaced at the court of Hatti's implacable enemy, Ramesses II. Urhi-Teshub's presence in Egypt also drew unwelcome attention to Hattusili III's shaky legitimacy. With Assyria and Egypt ranged against him, the support of Babylonia was now imperative.

At first, negotiations with the Babylonians bore fruit. Hattusili forged an alliance with old King Kadashman-Turgu, despite that king's previous offer to harbor Urhi-Teshub. All was fair in the rough and tumble world of ancient statecraft. Kadashman-Turgu played a double game, but Hattusili could not afford to be squeamish about his new ally's double-dealing.

When Ramesses II balked at Hattusili's demand to extradite Urhi-Teshub, the Hittite king appealed to Babylonia. Kadashman-Turgu promised to help him recover his nephew, going so far as to sever diplomatic relations with Egypt, as a letter Hattusili later wrote to his successor, Kadashman-Enlil II, informs us:

> [When your father] and I established friendly relations and became brothers, [we] spoke [as follows]: "We are brothers. To the enemy of one another [we will be hostile, and with] the friend of one another we will be friendly." And when the King of Egypt [and I] became angry [with one another], I wrote to your father Kadashman-Turgu: "[The King of Egypt] has become hostile to me." And your father wrote to me as follows: "[If your troops] go against Egypt, then I will go with you. [If] you go [against Egypt, I will send you] such infantry and chariotry as I have available to go." ... My enemy, who [had escaped] to another country, [left] and went to the King of Egypt. When I wrote to him: "[Send me my enemy]," he did not send me my enemy, [then, because of this, I and the King of] Egypt became angry with one another. Then [I wrote] to your father: "[The King of Egypt] is coming to the aid of my enemy." [At that time your father] cut off [the messenger of the King of] Egypt.[26]

A wider war now threatened to engulf the whole Near East. But fate intervened, and Hattusili III's first diplomatic success collapsed when Kadashman-Turgu died shortly after their alliance.[27] The Babylonian king's young successor, Kadashman-Enlil II, had a vizier who opposed the Hittites. Following his advice, Kadashman-Enlil restored diplomatic relations with Egypt, as Hattusili reminded his younger counterpart: "When (you) my brother [became king], you sent [your messenger to the king of] Egypt.... [And the king of] Egypt [accepted] your [gifts, and] you accepted [his gifts]." But Hattusili had no other friends, and could not afford another enemy. He concludes by asking rhetorically, "Now [you are an adult. If] you send [your messenger to the King of Egypt], why would I restrain you in any way?"[28]

Why Hattusili III Wanted Peace with Egypt

Despite Urhi-Teshub's presence in Egypt, and Ramesses II's ongoing aggression in Syria, Hattusili III swallowed his outrage and once again sought to negotiate with Pharaoh. He may have attempted this even before his nephew fled. But once Urhi-Teshub resurfaced in Egypt, Ramesses spurned all requests to extradite him. In the face of Pharaoh's implacability, why did Hattusili persist in seeking peace?

One theory introduces a third party into this ancient geostrategic drama—the rising power of ancient Assyria.[29] Some historians believe the threat from Assyria drove the Hittite king to seek peace with Pharaoh.[30] Hattusili III was caught in a two-front war—while a truculent Assyria encroached on his eastern flank along the Euphrates, Ramesses threatened Kadesh and Amurru on the long-festering southern front.[31] Peace with Ramesses would relieve the pressure on his southern border. This assumes that tangible strategic considerations motivated the Hittite king, prompting him to take the most rational course of action. But did such factors inform his decision?

More recently, scholars have downplayed the Assyrian menace.[32] If Hattusili III tried to mend fences with Assyria, it was not because he feared her. For centuries, hostile kingdoms had encircled Hatti. Yet, Hittite kings aggressively fought all enemies on the battlefield. Why should Hattusili III now fear Assyria, whose apex lay five centuries in the future?[33]

Diplomatic Recognition

The reasons Hattusili sought détente with Egypt—as with his overtures to Babylonia and Assyria—lay closer to home. His chief foreign policy goal—indeed, his overarching political priority—was to bolster his legitimacy as ruler. He hoped to leverage Hatti's membership in the

Great Powers Club, thereby gaining diplomatic recognition of his regime. So far all his efforts had come to naught. However unlikely, Egypt was now his only hope.

It must have galled Hattusili to seek peace with Ramesses II, after more than half a century of Egyptian-Hittite hostilities. He nursed a personal sense of animosity too, for Hattusili had fought alongside his brother Muwatalli II at the Battle of Kadesh. Most troubling of all was Urhi-Teshub's presence at Pharaoh's court, and Ramesses's refusal to extradite him.[34]

But Egypt was a charter member of the Great Powers Club, and Ramesses II the most prestigious ruler of his time. If Hattusili could persuade the Egyptian monarch to come to terms, he would achieve a double victory: peace and security on his southern border, and political legitimacy at home and abroad. A treaty would also neutralize the threat Urhi-Teshub posed to his regime. With luck, an extradition clause would return the fugitive to his uncle's clutches.

Ramesses II Resists Peace

Hattusili III and his predecessors made repeated overtures of peace to Ramesses II. Their desire to end hostilities was not unconditional, for the Hittites held onto Suppiluliuma's conquests of Amurru and Kadesh and balked at ceding them to any pharaoh. From Hatti's perspective, Ramesses could only end the conflict by first agreeing to Hittite claims in Syria. Until Egypt accepted the permanent loss of its former territories, there could be no peace.

This was hard for any pharaoh to accept. Their duty was to defeat the chaos foreign enemies embodied. Why, then, did Akhenaten, Horemheb, Sety I, and Ramesses II continue to wage fruitless wars in Syria? A sober assessment of Egypt's campaigns might give a more thoughtful pharaoh pause. Yet, a stubborn ideology of royal power and aggression long drove Ramesses II and his forebearers to seek war and reject peace as they vainly attempted to wrest control of Kadesh and Amurru from the Hittite Empire.[35]

One inscription suggests the Hittites repeatedly offered Ramesses peace during his first two decades as king. On the occasion of his marriage to the daughter of Hattusili III, in his thirty-fourth regnal year (1245 BCE), Ramesses II's First Hittite Marriage Decree presents a rhetorical—and at times downright fictional—history of his conflict with the Hittites.[36] Submerged within its bombast, one phrase is revealing: "Then the Great Chief of Hatti sent messages to appease His Person year after year, but he never listened to them."[37] Was this proof of Pharaoh's pride and recklessness, which many are quick to see in his

Kadesh accounts? Or did a deeply ingrained ideology prevent Ramesses and his predecessors from coming to terms with their Hittite foes for six long decades?[38] Egyptian monumental texts and war scenes attest to a mindset that could not admit defeat. Pharaoh must impose Maat by force of arms against the "rebellious" foreigner.[39] He must perform feats of valor by "widening the borders of Egypt" and surpassing what his ancestors achieved before him.[40] In the Twelfth Dynasty, Pharaoh Senwosret III left an eloquent statement of this doctrine in a border inscription he set up at Semna in Lower Nubia:

> I am a king who speaks and acts; what my mind thinks happens by my hand. I am ferocious to seize and quickly achieve success. A plan does not sleep in (my) mind. I am merciless to the enemy who attacks me, since silence after an attack empowers the enemy's heart. Bravery is aggression; wretchedness is "turn-and-retreat;" a coward is one forced back from his border. Since the Nubian will fall at a word, answering him makes him retreat. Be aggressive to him and he turns his back. Retreat, and he goes on the attack.[41]

Obliged to conform to this ancient code of valor, no pharaoh could accept defeat. Embedded in his worldview and tradition was the imperative to guard his personal honor, a desire for vindication and revenge, and a need to save face at all costs. Heeding these ideological imperatives, Ramesses II doggedly pursued his aggressive military strategy in Syria, rejecting all peace offers for two decades. An ideology of military adventurism and dreams of glory drove him back into Syria again and again.[42]

Peace with Honor

According to Ramesses II's Hittite Treaty Stela, the peace came in his twenty-first year (1258 BCE). But to use a Cold War analogy, "who blinked first?" In both his Hittite Treaty Stela and later in his First Hittite Marriage Decree, Ramesses implies the Hittite king sued him for peace. It is easy to dismiss this claim, for the trope of foreign chieftains submitting to Pharaoh and "begging for the breath of life" was a staple of Egyptian rhetoric.[43] Moreover, Egypt was arguably in a weaker strategic position in Syria, having failed to wrest any lasting control over the region from Hatti.

While all these factors might cast doubt on Ramesses II's assertion that Hattusili III initiated negotiations, pressing political issues motivated the Hittite king more than strategic ones. Hattusili III *needed* peace to secure his legitimacy.[44] Pharaoh did not.[45] Moreover, Hatti never sought to expand south of Kadesh and Amurru, and only raided there in revenge for Egyptian attacks on their own territory.[46] Ramesses

FIGURE 9.4. "Saving face": workers reconstruct a colossus of Ramesses II from the great temple of Abu Simbel in the 1960s. Getty Images.

could wait his opponents out. Honor and ideology demanded they come to him—as they did time and again—before he relented.

Ramesses II could not set aside his rejectionist policy until conditions allowed him to save face by framing peace as a foreign chieftain submitting to his terrible might (fig. 9.4). Still, however it might be presented to his Egyptian subjects, renouncing his claim to Kadesh and Amurru was hard to swallow. Ramesses was turning his back on decades of Egyptian strategic doctrine, with no territorial gains to show for it.

For Hattusili III a treaty had much to recommend it.[47] Without ceding any land, he lost no face by seeking peace with another Great King, even if he first proposed it. The deal granted Hattusili the political endorsement of the Great Powers Club's most senior member, and recognized his heirs as Hatti's legitimate royal house.

And what was in this deal for Ramesses II? South of Kadesh and Amurru, it secured his Canaanite provinces from Hittite attacks. For two decades he fought for valor and victory in Canaan and Syria. Genuine, albeit temporary, triumphs at Dapur and other citadels, and his personal bravery at Kadesh, garnered Pharaoh an honorable reputation as a warrior king who was "great of victories." Now, by divorcing these glorious memories from any territorial losses, he could spin these accords as a diplomatic triumph and retire from his military career with honor.

To his credit, Ramesses II made a visionary decision: namely, to set aside the militant tenets of pharaonic ideology, whereby his predecessors—from Akhenaten to Sety I—persisted in endless, futile hostilities, instead opting for an honorable peace. Ramesses also adapted traditional doctrine to suit his new role as peacemaker. Having kept the Hittite side waiting and suing for peace for years, Pharaoh portrayed Hattusili III's final appeal as the "Great Chief of Hatti begging for the breath of life." After two decades of belligerence, Ramesses II proved himself to be a strategic realist and a farseeing statesman. Satisfying his need for honor, he presented these accords as what they really were: a genuine personal triumph.

Notes

1. Sürenhagen 1985 and 2006; Beckman 2006; Kitchen and Lawrence 2012; Devecchi 2013, 2015. For translations of many of the Hittite vassal treaties, see Beckman 2008; Devecchi 2015. If the Hittites had accords with other Great Kingdoms including Babylonia, none of them survive. On the earlier Egyptian-Hittite treaty see the sidebar on p. 313 below.

2. See the studies in Cohen and Westbrook 2000. For broad overviews of Late Bronze Age diplomacy, see Bryce 2003; Podany 2012.

3. Liverani 2000.

4. Redford 1992, 2003; Morris 2018, 122–25.

5. See the essays in Cohen and Westbrook 2000. See also: Liverani 2001; Roth 2005, 180–81 and 208–9. A crucial element of this diplomatic system was the maintenance of ongoing and permanent diplomatic contact through visiting envoys, high ranking foreign guests, and marriage alliances between kingdoms; see Gundlach, Raedler and Roth 2005; Roth 2006.

6. Moran 1992, xxii–xxiii. Mynářová (2009, 2011) discusses the different formulas of address and salutations with which the Great Kings opened their letters to each other between the Amarna Letters and the Ramesside correspondence. See p. 325 below.

7. Avruch 2000.

8. On Urhi-Teshub's complex career and scholarly controversies about it, see Wouters 1989; Bryce 2003, 204–13; 2005, 246–65; Singer 2006; Houwink ten Cate 2006; Bányai 2010; Devecchi and Miller 2011. After seizing the throne, Hattusili III consistently referred to his deposed nephew by his birth name Urhi-Teshub, denying his royal status and authority by refusing to call the deposed king by his throne name Mursili (III).

9. For a translation, see van den Hout 1997a. The most recent analysis is in Knapp 2015.

10. According to Hattusili III's self-justifying edict known as the Apology, Urhi-Teshub commanded Hattusili's loyalty as his sovereign for a period of seven years. As a chronological marker, this figure is suspect because the Apology is a political document and this time span may be symbolic; Knapp 2015, 123 with n. 12. Hittite chronology is often uncertain (see, e.g., Beckman 2000, 19–21), but Bryce credits Urhi-Teshub with a reign of only five years; Bryce 2005, xv (chart of Hittite kings).

11. Bryce 2005, 256–59.

12. The beginning of the letter is missing, leaving the names of the sender and recipient open for debate, although it is clear from the content that a Hittite king is addressing his Assyrian counterpart. Some scholars previously assigned to either Hattusili III or Muwatalli, but it now appears that Urhi-Teshub was the likely author of this anonymous letter; Bryce 2005, 258–59; Beckman 2008, 146–47 (no. 24A).

13. KUB 23.102 i 4–18. Translation by Beckman 2006, 281.

14. The Apology justified many of the controversial actions of Hattusili's career, in particular his dealings with Urhi-Teshub, in the form of a legal suit between them brought before the gods; see the discussion in Knapp 2015, 148–59.

15. Apology of Hattusili III, §10c, iii 62–79. Translation adapted from Knapp 2015, 146.

16. Bryce 2005, 263.

17. Bryce 2005, 264; 2003, 205.

18. Bryce 2005, 266–67; Brand 2007a, 19–22.

19. Beckman 2008, 149 (no. 24B, §5).

20. KBo 1.14. Translation after Beckman 2008, 149 (no. 24B, §4).

21. Edel reconstructed a fragmentary passage from a letter Ramesses II sent to Hattusili (KBo 8.14) as the alleged quotation of a stinging rebuke from the Assyrian king stating that Hattusili was "only the substitute for a Great King": ÄHK I, no. 5: 24–25. But Edel wholly invented this reference to the king of Assyria, which many scholars accepted uncritically. More recently, others have rejected it; see, e.g., Cordani 2017, 157–58. Her new analysis of the preserved passage reads "See, you are a Great King" (158). My earlier study (Brand 2007a) took Edel's restoration at face value.

22. Bryce 2003, 205. The Proclamation of Telipinu, a Hittite king from the sixteenth century BCE, sought to end a period of dynastic bloodshed that hobbled the kingdom for a century. It established rules of succession to the throne and forbade the killing of a member of the Hittite royal family; see Bryce 2005, 108–9; van den Hout 1997b, 194–98 (1.76, esp. §§29–31)

23. Bryce 2005, 263–65.

24. Bryce 2003, 205–6.

25. Bryce 2003, 205–7.

26. KBo 1.10+KUB 3.72. Translation adapted from Beckman 2008, 141 (no. 23, §7) .

27. Bryce 2005, 266–67.

28. Translation adapted from Beckman 2008, 141 (no. 23, §7).

29. Rowton 1959, 1–11; Bryce 2006, 3–4.

30. Rowton 1959; Kitchen 1982, 74–75.

31. Rowton 1959, 9–11.

32. Bryce 2005, 275; Brand 2007a, 20–21.

33. Are historians unduly influenced by knowledge of Assyria's eventual rise to military supremacy in the ancient Near East during the eighth and seventh centuries BCE? In Ramesses II's day, powerful neighbors like Hatti and Babylonia hemmed Assyria in on all sides.

34. But when did Urhi-Teshub flee to Egypt—before the treaty or after it? This issue remains unresolved. Although some would place Urhi-Teshub in Egypt only after the treaty, why would Hattusili risk damaging his new alliance with Ramesses? And why on earth would the fugitive king seek refuge in Pharaoh's court knowing only too well that extradition clauses were a standard provision of Hittite treaties? Surely it was to his advantage to seek asylum while Ramesses II remained hostile to his uncle's regime. After the treaty this would be folly. Nevertheless, Urhi-Teshub stayed in Egypt for some time after the treaty, becoming an ongoing irritant in Hattusili III's dealings with the Egyptian court for several years. See pp. 331–36, 361 below. For the view that Urhi-Teshub came to Egypt before the treaty, see Kitchen 1982, 73; Bryce 2003, 206–7; 2006; Roth 2006, 183–86; Brand 2007a, 24–25. Houwink Ten Cate (2006) claims he arrived in Egypt after the treaty. Devecchi and Miller (2011, 163–66) also base their assessment on the date of Urhi-Teshub's flight to Egypt on their determination of synchronisms in Egypt, Hittite, and Babylonian chronology, but these schemes are often based on numerous factors and assumptions such that if only one is false, the whole chronological edifice they erect collapses. For this reason, I remain skeptical of purely chronological arguments for deter-

mining the date of Urhi-Teshub's arrival in Egypt vis à vis the conclusion of the peace treaty in Ramesses II's twenty-first regnal year.

35. Brand 2007a.

36. Brand 2005, 32–33.

37. *KRI* II, 245:13–246:3; *RITA* II, 93; and see pp. 364–68 below. Given the way Egyptian royal texts "telescope" historical events and their avoidance of naming specific foreign kings, this passage might refer to diplomatic overtures any one or all of three Hittite kings—Muwatalli II, Urhi-Teshub, and Hattusili III—made to Ramesses II. On the ideological context of the First Hittite Marriage Decree see pp. 364–70 below.

38. Brand 2007a, 26–29.

39. Liverani 2001, 86–90.

40. Galán 1993, 101–55.

41. Berlin, Egyptian Museum ÄM 1157; Parkinson 1991, 43–46; translation Brand 2007a, 28–29.

42. Brand 2007a, 129–30.

43. Liverani 2001, 97–98. On Egyptian conceptions of *ḥtp*, "peace," which can also mean "pacification," see V. Davies 2018, 1–19, 59–65.

44. See Bryce 2006.

45. One school of thought views Ramesses II's embrace of peace as a matter of economic policy, with the pharaoh seeking access to Syrian trade routes; Kitchen 1982, 75; Allam 2018. This assumes that such factors motivated the Egyptian side and that the Hittites could and would maintain an effective trade embargo against Egyptian merchants and shipping. All of this is questionable. Certainly, peaceful relations allowed for enhanced and free-flowing trade, but this was far from the only, or even the major, calculation; see Roth 2005, 181–82.

46. Brand 2007a, 29–30.

47. Again, see Bryce 2006.

Chapter 10

The Silver Treaty: The Egyptian-Hittite Peace Accords

In the relative cool of a late autumn day in 1259 BCE, six royal envoys of Egypt and Hatti presented themselves in the audience hall of Ramesses II in his capital of Piramesses. Bringing rich greeting gifts from the Hittite king and queen, they also carried a silver tablet, engraved with cuneiform script in the Akkadian language of Babylonia. Here was the rarest gift of all: the peace accord between these two ancient superpowers—an "eternal treaty of peace and brotherhood" bringing six decades of hostilities to an end.[1] Today a replica of the Silver Treaty hangs in the foyer of the United Nations building in New York, as an ancient symbol of harmony between nations.

The Peace Treaty of Year Twenty-One

We have no idea how long the two sides negotiated before they finalized their accords, but the task must have occupied Egyptian and Hittite diplomats for more than a year. Strangely, although we know of several letters Ramesses sent to Hattusili just before they sealed their compact, none mention the nitty-gritty details their envoys must have worked out orally. The kings limited their own discussions to the formal exchange of the silver treaty tablets, and the dawning era of "peace and brotherhood."

Hittite rulers sometimes engraved treaties with their most important vassals upon bronze tablets.[2] Such a modest metal would not suffice for the superlative prestige and strategic importance of this grand alliance. Instead, Hattusili III and Ramesses II agreed to exchange silver tablets incised with reciprocal treaty texts that each side composed for the other. These precious silver tablets were destined to rest in the temple sanctuaries of Re-Horakhty in Heliopolis and the Hittite Storm God in Hattusa, as proof of their solemn oaths before the Egyptian and Hittite gods.

Sadly, these glittering plaques vanished long ago, but by good fortune copies of both versions still exist. Thanks to diligent Hittite chancery scribes, who created multiple "file copies" on clay tablets (fig. 10.1),

FIGURE 10.1. Main fragments of the cuneiform text of the Egyptian Hittite Peace Treaty. This clay tablet was a "file copy" Hittite scribes made of the text engraved on the silver tablet that Ramesses II sent to Hattusa. Wikimedia Commons.

we can reconstruct most of the text that Ramesses II sent to Hattusa. In Egypt, Ramesses made an unprecedented effort to publicize the treaty. He erected monumental stelae, translating the cuniform tablet Hattusili sent him into the Egyptian hieroglyphic script. Only fragments of Pharaoh's stela from the Ramesseum survive, but the copy at Karnak is largely intact. While the Egyptian and Hittite versions are similar, they are not identical.[3]

The Akkadian language of ancient Babylonia served as an international medium of diplomacy in the ancient Near East. Scribes from Egypt and Hatti each composed their king's version of the treaty in Akkadian and engraved it on a silver tablet in the cuneiform script. Amid the ruins of Hatti's capital at Hattusa (modern Boğazköy in Turkey), archaeologists unearthed clay tablet copies of the Akkadian treaty document that Ramesses II's scribes composed and sent to Hattusili on the Egyptian silver tablet. By contrast, the hieroglyphic text Pharaoh recorded on his stelae at Karnak and the Ramesseum is an Egyptian translation of the Akkadian document Hattusili dispatched to Egypt on his silver tablet. So, a bit confusingly, the Egyptian version that Ramesses sent is in Akkadian and turned up in Hattusa, while the Hittite version now exists only as a hieroglyphic transcription on the stela from Karnak Temple.

The Egyptian and Hittite cuneiform documents distinguish Ramesses II and Hattusili III equally with the title "Great King," as ancient Near Eastern diplomatic protocol dictated.[4] Yet, this notion clashed with

Egypt's concept of pharaonic exceptionalism. When Egyptian scribes translated Hattusili III's silver tablet into their own language, they altered it to conform to their worldview. The Egyptian word for "king," (*nesu*), applied uniquely to Egypt's sovereign, and could not be used for any foreign ruler. In the hieroglyphic edition, Ramesses II's scribes distinguished him as the "Great Ruler" (*heka a'a*) of Egypt, while downgrading Hattusili to the "Great Chief," (*wer a'a*), of Hatti, thereby asserting Pharaoh's superiority for a domestic audience.[5]

Linguistic analysis of the Egyptian document found at Hattusa reveals Pharaoh's scribes first drafted the treaty in their native tongue before translating it into the Babylonian language. Finally, they inscribed it in cuneiform on the silver tablet. As they did with diplomatic letters, Hittite bureaucrats drafted Hattusili III's version of the treaty in their own language as well, translating the final product into Akkadian (fig. 10.2).

The only date connected with either version of the treaty appears in Ramesses II's Karnak Treaty Stela, which has a framing narrative recording the delivery of the Hittite king's silver tablet to Piramesses in the autumn of 1259 BCE:

> *Year twenty-one, first month of the Season of Emergence (Proyet), day twenty-one under the incarnation of the Dual King Usermaatre-Setepenre, the Son of Re Ramesses-Meramun, given life forever and ever, who is beloved of Amun, Re-Horakhty, Ptah who is South of his Wall, the Lord of Ankh-Tawy, Mut, Lady of Isheru, and Khonsu-Neferhotep. He has appeared on the throne of Horus of the living like his father Horakhty, forever and ever.*
>
> *On this day His Person was in Piramesses doing what his fathers Amun-Ra-Horakhty-Atum, the Lord of the Two Lands, the Heliopolitan, and what Amun of Ramesses-Meramun and Ptah of Ramesses-Meramun, and Seth Great of Strength, the son of Nut (all) praise as they give him millions of Jubilees and eternally peaceful years, with all flat lands and all hill countries being prostrate under his sandals forever.*
>
> *Arrival of the royal messenger and chariot officer Netcher[wymes]; the [royal messenger...]; and [the royal messenger...], along with the messenger of the land of [Hatti] N[erikkaili]; and of [...] [Tili]-Teshub; and of the second-ranked messenger of Hatti Ramose; and the messenger [of the land of Carche]mish Yapusili; bearing the silver tablet that the Great Chief of Hatti, Hattusili sent to Pharaoh, L.P.H., to beg for peace from the incarnation of the Dual King Usermaatre-Setepenre, the Son of Re Ramesses-Meramun.*[6]

After thirty-three centuries, natural decay and human mischief have left lamentable gaps in the text of Ramesses II's Karnak Treaty Stela.[7] This is especially unfortunate in places where the text named the

FIGURE 10.2. Ramesses II's Hittite Peace Treaty stela from Karnak Temple, the best preserved of two known examples of the hieroglyphic text that Ramesses II had published throughout Egypt; it contains a translation of the Akkadian silver tablet that Hattusili III sent to Egypt. The text also records the arrival of the Hittite and Egyptian ambassadors with the Silver Tablet and a provides a detailed description of the seals of Hattusili III and his queen Puduhepa. Courtesy of Mark Janzen.

Egyptian and Hittite ambassadors. For a long time, we did not know the names of any of Pharaoh's envoys.[8] Recently, French archaeologists discovered a tomb belonging to the first Egyptian envoy at Saqqara, the sprawling necropolis of ancient Memphis. We can now identify him as Necherwymes, a "royal messenger to every foreign land," the equivalent of an ambassador.[9] From his tomb inscriptions we know Netcherwymenes bore a second name, Parakhenawa. Under this alter ego, he appears frequently in the diplomatic letters that Ramesses II exchanged with Hattusili III. A plausible candidate for Pharaoh's second envoy is Mahu, a "royal messenger to the land of Hatti." The third Egyptian diplomat was perhaps a long-serving Egyptian functionary named Huy.[10] When Ramesses married the Hittite princess Maahorneferure, twelve years after he concluded the treaty, Huy escorted her to Egypt.[11] Later, Ramesses appointed Huy to be Viceroy of Kush.

Among their Hittite colleagues, we know of Tili-Teshub from other sources as an urbane diplomat.[12] Most intriguing of all is the second Hittite ambassador Ramose, who bears a good Egyptian name. An Egyptian expatriate, how he came to serve the Hittite king remains a mystery.[13]

The Silver Tablets

We can glean some idea of the appearance of the silver tablet Hattusili III sent to Egypt by analogy with a rare bronze treaty tablet his successor, Tudhaliya IV, concluded with a Hittite vassal king.[14] Close study of Ramesses II's Karnak stela also reveals something of its format. The silver tablet had two columns of cuneiform text arranged in horizontal lines on its front and back. When the Egyptian clerk transcribed Hattusili's silver tablet, he confused the proper order of the columns on its reverse. Due to this minor mix-up, the Egyptians placed some clauses recorded on the Karnak stela in the wrong order (fig. 10.3).[15]

Hittite kings did not "sign" state documents, rather they stamped them by impressing their official seal. Bureaucrats wrote these texts on moist clay tablets, marking the wedge-shaped cuneiform signs with a stylus. The king applied his official seal before the clay dried, sometimes into the tablet itself, but often into a separate clay lump called a bulla. As befitting a regal Hittite text, Hattusili's Silver Treaty tablet also bore his royal seal and that of his consort Queen Puduhepa. But how could the royal seals, designed to stamp soft clay, leave an impression on the silver plaque? Engraving them was an option. But the bronze treaty tablet from Hattusa reveals the actual method. It has two holes, through which short chains were attached to the slab. The chains secured the two clay seal impressions, encased in protective bronze capsules.[16]

FIGURE 10.3. Artist's reconstruction of the possible appearance of the Silver Treaty tablet Hattusili III sent to Ramesses II. Clay impressions of the seals of Hattusili III (right) and Puduhepa (left). Enclosed in metal capsules, the seals may have hung from chains. Artwork by Peter Brand.

Once it arrived in Egypt, Ramesses II's scribes did not just translate the silver tablet's wording for his Karnak Treaty Stela. They also described the Hittite royal seals in vivid detail, translating the texts on them. Clearly, these foreign insignia fascinated the Egyptians:[17]

> What is suspended from[18] the silver tablet on its front side: an image of the Storm God embracing the figure of the Great Chief of Hatti encircled by a border of words saying: "The seal of the Storm God, the ruler of the earth and heavens, the seal of the treaty that Hattusili III, the Great Chief of Hatti, the Hero, and son of Mursili II, the Great Chief of Hatti, the Hero, made." What is inside the circle (of words): an image of the seal of the Storm God, the ruler of earth and heaven.[19]

A border of text encircling the central image served as the treaty's formal title, listing Hattusili's royal name and titles, and those of his father Mursili II. Egyptian scribes also recorded Queen Puduhepa's seal in meticulous detail.[20]

We must applaud the Hittite scribes who made copies of the treaty they received, since Pharaoh's silver tablet vanished long ago.[21] Hittite copyists omitted any royal flourishes that Ramesses II's craftsmen applied to his silver tablet. But it was an immensely prestigious and important object, and the pharaohs delighted in recording their stately array of royal names and stylings on all official documents. We can be sure Ramesses II's cartouche names and titles in the hieroglyphic script appeared on its surface, or perhaps on seals attached to the tablet after the Hittite fashion.[22]

A Gentleman's Agreement?

To us, the Egyptian-Hittite peace treaty, with its orderly clauses and legalistic prose, resembles a modern legal document. Even the hieroglyphic transcription Ramesses II published on his Karnak stela lacks the hyperbole we find in most of his decrees.[23]

More striking than their actual stipulations is what the accords do *not* say. Although this treaty ended the long Egyptian-Hittite war over Syria, we find no language about international borders or territorial issues in either version. Diplomats negotiated these matters orally ahead of time. Or perhaps they ignored them altogether.[24]

By the time Ramesses II and Hattusili III exchanged silver tablets, they had resolved the sensitive question of their formal border in Syria. Ramesses conceded, at least tacitly, that the *de facto* border that Suppiluliuma I had established in Syria—when Kadesh and Amurru fell into Hittite hands—would stand permanently. Both kingdoms well knew the frontiers between their vassal provinces, so few technical issues hindered the settlement.

The pact was a "gentlemen's agreement," ignoring embarrassing issues deliberately, allowing Ramesses to save face. Their conspicuous silence on the matter extended to letters they exchanged just before they finalized the treaty. In none of these messages do they say anything about borders. Nor do they discuss any stipulations appearing in the final document. Instead, Ramesses and Hattusili restrict their formal "talking points" to the exchange of silver tablets and optimistic chatter about an imminent dawning of "good peace and good brotherhood" between them.

The Treaty and Its Stipulations

The impetus for these accords lay with Hatti, whose kings frequently imposed treaties of vassalage to regulate relations with their subject kingdoms.[25] Although Egypt concluded an earlier treaty with Hatti in the mid-Eighteenth Dynasty, this form of agreement was largely alien to the Egyptians.[26] Unlike the treaties Hittite rulers dictated to their vassals, Ramesses and Hattusili forged a parity agreement as two independent powers of equal status.[27] Therefore, every stipulation had to be amenable to both parties. They scrupulously evaded any issues to which either side might object, so almost every clause in the treaty was fully equal and reciprocal.

Both versions herald the "eternal treaty of perfect peace and perfect brotherhood," which now abolished all hostilities between them forever. Ramesses II's Karnak stela declares:

> Now long ago, from time immemorial, regarding the relationship between the Great Ruler of Egypt and the Great Chief of Hatti, the god prevented hostilities from occurring between them by means of a treaty. But in the time of Muwatalli II, the Great Chief of Hatti my brother, he fought wi[th Ramesses-Meramun] the Great Ruler of Egypt.
>
> But from now on, beginning today, see, Hattusili III, the Great Chief of Hatti [makes] a treaty to reestablish the relationship that Re made and the Storm God made for the land of Egypt and the land of Hatti to prevent hostilities from occurring between them forever.
>
> See, Hattusili III the Great Chief of Hatti binds himself by treaty with Usermaatre-Setepenre[28] the Great Ruler of Egypt starting today to bring about good peace and good brotherhood between us forever; he being brotherly with me and at peace with me, and I being brotherly with him and at peace with him forever.
>
> Now after Muwatalli II the Great Chief of Hatti, my brother, went to his fate, Hattusili III sat as the Great Chief of Hatti upon the throne of his father. See, I (Hattusili) am with Ramesses-Meramun, the Great Ruler of Egypt, and [the nature of our peace and our] brotherhood

> [is perfect]. It is more perfect than the peace and brotherhood which formerly existed in the [land].
>
> See, I, the Great Chief of Hatti, am with [Usermaatre-Setepenre] the Great Ruler of Egypt in perfect peace and perfect brotherhood. May the grandchildren of the Great Chief of Hatti make brotherhood and peace with the grandchildren of [Ramesses-Meramun] the Great Ruler of Egypt, for such is our plan for brotherhood and our plan [for peace: that the land of Egy]pt [might abide] with the land of Hatti in peace and brotherhood, just like us, forever, with no hostility occurring between them forever.[29]

The Akkadian document Ramesses sent to Hattusili opens with a preamble identifying both rulers and establishing their ancestry. Unlike the Egyptian translation at Karnak, where Hattusili is demoted to "Great Chief," here both have the title Great King. At last, Hattusili won the recognition he had craved for so long.[30]

> [The treaty which] Ramesses, [beloved] of Amun, Great King, King [of Egypt, Hero, concluded] on [a tablet of silver] with Hattusili, [Great King], King of Hatti, his brother, to establish [great] peace and great [brotherhood] between them forever.
>
> Thus says Ramesses, beloved of Amun, Great King, King of Egypt, Hero of all lands; the son of Minmuarea (Sety I), Great King, King of Egypt, Hero; and grandson of Minpahtarea (Ramesses I), Great King, King of Egypt, Hero, to Hattusili, Great King, King of Hatti, Hero; son of Mursili, Great King, King of Hatti, Hero; and grandson of Suppiluliuma, Great King, King of Hatti, Hero.[31]

The Akkadian version proclaims the goals to which the new allies aspired while briefly reflecting on past relations between their two kingdoms:

> I (Ramesses II) have now established good brotherhood and good peace between us forever, in order likewise to establish good peace and good brotherhood in [the relations] of Egypt with Hatti forever. As far as the relations of the Great King, King of Egypt, [and] the Great King, King of Hatti, are concerned, from the beginning of time and forever [by means of a treaty] the god has not allowed the making of war between them. Ramesses, beloved of Amun, Great King, King of Egypt, is doing this to bring about the relationship which [the Sun God] and the Storm God established for Egypt with Hatti in accordance with their relationship from the beginning of time, so that for eternity he might [not permit] the making of war between [them].[32]

Ramesses II and Hattusili III now inaugurated a permanent end to hostilities, obligating their successors to maintain this concord:

And Ramesses, beloved of Amun, Great King, King [of Egypt], has indeed created (this relationship) [on] this [day] by means of a treaty upon a tablet of silver with [Hattusili], Great King, King of Hatti, his brother, in order to establish good peace and good brotherhood [between them] forever. He is [my] brother, and I am his brother. <He is at peace with me>, and I am at peace with him [forever. And] we will create our brotherhood and our [peace], and they will be better than the former brotherhood and peace of [Egypt with] Hatti.... The sons of Ramesses, beloved of Amun, [Great King,] King of Egypt, will be at peace with [...] the sons of Hattusili, Great King, King of Hatti, forever. And they will remain (at peace) just like our our relationship of brotherhood [and of] peace, so that Egypt will be at peace with Hatti and they will be brothers like us forever.[33]

Both versions outline a series of reciprocal clauses incumbent on each party. In the first article, Egypt and Hatti vow never to make war on the other:

The Great Chief of Hatti will never invade the land of Egypt to take something from it. Usermaatre-Setepenre, the Great Ruler of Egypt, will never invade the land [of Hatti] to take anything from it.[34]

This clause ended Egypt's long struggle for control of Syria. With one stroke, the two kingdoms traded bitter enmity for a new alliance, and became responsible for their mutual defense against any foreign or domestic foes:

If another enemy should come against the lands of Usermaatre-Setepenre, the Great Ruler of Egypt, and he writes to the Great Chief of Hatti saying: "Come with me as an ally against him," then the Great Chief of Hatti should act by [coming to him as an ally], and the Great Chief of Hatti will kill his enemy. But if the Great Chief of Hatti does not wish to go, then he will send his army and his chariotry, and <they> will kill his enemy.

Or, if Ramesses-Meramun [the Great Ruler of Egypt] becomes enraged at his subjects, and they do some other evil act against him and he proceeds to kill them; then the Great Chief of Hatti must act with [him to destroy] all [those against whom he became enraged].[35]

Conforming to a standard provision of Hittite state treaties, the new pact included a clause requiring each side to extradite any fugitives who sought refuge from the other kingdom:

Or, if a great man should flee from the land of Hatti and [come to] Usermaatre-Setepenre, the [Great Ruler] of Egypt—or if a town, or a district, or [a city among] those belonging to the land of Hatti—if they come to Ramesses-Meramun the Great Ruler of Egypt, then Usermaatre-Setepenre, the Great Ruler of Egypt should not receive them. Ramesses-

Meramun, the Great Ruler of Egypt should have them returned to the
Great Chief [of Hatti]. They shall not be left there.

   Likewise, if one or two men, who are [un]known, flee and they come
to the land of Egypt to act as subjects of another (lord), then Usermaatre-
Setepenre, the Great Ruler of Egypt shall not leave them there. He should
have them returned to the Great Chief of Hatti.[36]

Did this mean Hattusili would get his rival, Urhi-Teshub, extradited?
If that was his hope, it would only happen under strict guarantees of
clemency:

But the Great Chief of Hatti shall not let [their crimes stand] against
them. Do not let his [house] be destroyed, or his wives, or his children.
Do not let him be killed, nor let his eyes, his ears, his mouth, or his legs
be harmed. Do not let any crime stand against him.[37]

An identical clause dealt with Egyptian fugitives. Notably, these extradition clauses apply both to vassal territories and individual subjects.
With this stipulation, ambitious liegemen like the kings of Amurru
could never again manipulate tensions between these empires by de-
fecting to the other side.

   Nearly all the terms in both versions are mutual, binding each side
with identical obligations. Just one clause deviates from this rigid pattern of reciprocity: Ramesses II pledged to recognize Hattusili III's dynastic successors as his legitimate heirs, and vowed to support them
militarily against any pretenders to Hatti's throne:

[See, the land] of Hatti and the [land of Egypt are at peace and in
brotherhood forever according to our] sworn oath. Another matter: I
(Hattusili) will go to my fate. But Ramesses-Meramun the Great Ruler
of Egypt shall live forever![38] *And someone will come [to the land of]*
Hatti [to ensure that they make my son their] lord and to prevent [them]
from making [someone else their lord]. Now if [they] should commit [a
crime against him] and oppose making him their lord, then Usermaatre-
Setepenre, the Great Ruler of Egypt should not remain silent about it
forever. He must come and destroy the land of Hatti and he should send
back an an[swer to] the Great Chief of Hatti and likewise [to] the [land
of Hatti].[39]

With different wording, this article also appears in the Akkadian version.[40] It indicates that Hattusili sought to shore up his legitimacy and
guarantee his heirs would succeed him.[41] But no such pledge obliged
Hattusili to support Ramesses II's dynastic line, for any notion that
Egypt's divine kingship might require foreign intervention was anath-
ema to the Egyptians.

A Sacred Oath

Treaties in the ancient Near East were religious oaths each party swore to their gods.[42] As befitting an accord of this magnitude, Ramesses II and Hattusili III bound themselves and their kingdoms with an oath sworn by "one thousand gods and goddesses of the land of Hatti and one thousand gods and goddesses of the land of Egypt (who) are here with me as witnesses who have heard these terms."[43] The Karnak stela lists over thirty Hittite deities, mostly local manifestations of their principal divinity, the Storm God of Hatti. The Egyptians identified the Hittite weather deity with their own god Seth who embodied violent storms and foreign lands. Several Egyptian divinities and elements of nature also witness the solemn oath:

> *Amun, Re, and Seth; the male gods and female goddesses; the Mountains and Rivers of the land of Egypt; Heaven and Earth, the Great Sea, Winds, and Clouds.*[44]

The treaty oath invokes a curse on any who violated these stipulations, for they would incur the wrath of two thousand avenging deities: "As for anyone who shall not keep these (terms), one thousand gods of the land of Hatti and one thousand gods of the land of Egypt will destroy his house, his land, and his subjects."[45]

In their conciliatory language, these accords contrast sharply with most Hittite treaties, which they imposed as loyalty oaths on vassal kings and defeated enemies, such as the rulers of Amurru and Hanigalbat.[46] A standard component of these treaties was the historical prologue, which reviews past conflicts between Hatti and its subject kings in frank terms.[47] Ultimate responsibility for the troubles always falls on the vassal. By contrast, a brief prologue that Hattusili III's scribes inserted in the document he sent to Egypt simply states his brother Muwatalli II and Ramesses II once fought, yet it provides no details about the causes and scope of these hostilities, and no blame adheres to either party.[48] Clearly, Hattusili wished to smooth over past differences and avoid embarrassing his new ally. The Egyptian version Ramesses sent to Hattusa omits any historical prologue.[49]

Once they exchanged silver tablets, Egypt and Hatti remained at peace until the Hittite Empire collapsed at the end of the Late Bronze Age. For Ramesses II, his alliance with Hattusili III proved his skill as a politician and his vision as a statesman. Yet, as the two former enemies embarked on this new era of peace, tensions remained and their contest of wills continued.

An Early Egyptian-Hittite Peace Treaty

When Ramesses II brokered his treaty with Hattusili III in the twenty-first year of his reign, the two sides restored a peace that was first broken in the Amarna period. Today, opinion differs on just how many treaties these rival empires concluded prior to Ramesses II's treaty. The earliest-known Egyptian-Hittite peace accord, the so-called Kurustama Treaty, dates to the middle of the Eighteenth Dynasty. It was still in effect when Suppiluliuma I came into conflict with the Amarna pharaohs over control of Amurru and Kadesh.[50] In the aftermath of these hostilities, some historians claim his grandson Muwatalli II concluded a second treaty with his Egyptian contemporary, either Horemheb or Sety I.[51] The basis for this questionable assessment is a passage in Ramesses II's Peace Treaty Stela from Karnak Temple:

> *As for the treaty that existed in the time of Suppiluliuma, the Great Chief of Hatti and likewise, the treaty which existed in the time of Muwatalli, the Great Chief of Hatti, my father, I take hold of it. See, Ramesses-Meramun, the Great Ruler of Egypt takes hold of the treaty which he made with us now, beginning from today. We both take hold of it and we shall behave according to the agreed upon stipulations.*[52]

In fact, there never were two previous treaties, only a single pact that "existed" under both Suppiluliuma I and Muwatalli II. Like Horemheb before him, Sety I waged aggressive war against the Hittites. Yet, despite his battlefield success, Sety could not hold on to Kadesh and Amurru, and they quickly reverted to Hittite control, either late in his reign or in the first years of Ramesses II's. Why should Horemheb or Sety humiliate themselves by revoking Egypt's claim on these lands through a peace treaty with Muwatalli II? Instead, the relentless belligerence of these pharaohs sparked a multi-generational war with Hatti that dragged on from Akhenaten's reign until Ramesses II forged the second Egyptian-Hittite peace treaty. Muwatalli's alleged treaty with Egypt is a phantom.[53]

Notes

1. The literature on the treaty is extensive. For the most recent and definitive critical edition of both the Akkadian and hieroglyphic versions, see Edel 1997. Recent translations of the Akkadian text include Beckman 2008, 96–100 (no. 15); Kitchen and Lawrence 2012, 1:573–82 (transliteration and translation) and 2:57–58 (commentary). Current translations of the hieroglyphic text translations include *RITA* II, 79–85 with commentary in *RITANC* II, 136–45; Allam 2018; Kitchen and Lawrence 2012, 1:583–94 (transliteration and translation) and 2:59–60 (commentary). Scholars have created a rich corpus of studies analyzing various historical, cultural, legal, and religious aspects of the treaty and its two versions: see Spalinger 1981; Sürenhagen 1985; Goelet and Levine 2000; Bryce 2006; Brand 2007a; Breyer 2010a, 230–47; Allam 2018; Mynářová 2014; Cordani 2017; V. Davies 2018; Jackson 2018; Jauß 2018.

2. For the bronze treaty tablet of Tudhaliya IV, see Otten 1988.

3. For detailed linguistic analyses, see Spalinger 1981; Edel 1997; Breyer 2010a, 242–44.

4. Written in Akkadian as LUGAL.GAL (*šarru rab*) in the cuneiform version Ramesses II sent to Hattusa. Here, the Akkadian document Pharaoh sent maintained a strict sense of parity and reciprocity toward his Hittite counterpart. It was not to last as his letters to the Hittite court reveal. See pp. 325–28 below. Interestingly, Ramesses identified himself only with his nomen in the document he sent to Hatti, not with his prenomen, nor with both names, as is often the case in his diplomatic letters. Mynářová (2011, 244) argues that this was from a need to maintain parity with Hattusili III. But why not include only his prenomen, like those of his father Mimmuaria (Sety I Menmaatre) and grandfather Minpahtaria (Ramesses I Menpehty)? Or, did the Hittite scribes who made this archival copy omit the pharaoh's—from their perspective—superfluous titles by reducing them to his nomen?

5. So, *ḥḳȝ-ʿȝ* and *wr-ʿȝ*. Discussed most recently by Jackson 2018, 52–54. On the other titles Ramesses II uses in the hieroglyphic version of the treaty, see Mynářová 2011, 242–45. Clearly this is a result of Egyptian ideological exceptionalism.

6. *KRI* II, 226:2–8; Edel 1997, 18*–20*.

7. Much of the damage arises from a kind of "pious vandalism" by generations of temple visitors who scraped away bits of the sandstone wall bearing Ramesses II's grand stela as they collected a few grains of pulverized stone for magical purposes. The rows of oval depressions, or "pilgrim's gouges," are a common sight at Karnak and other sandstone monuments in Luxor and across Upper Egypt. This practice began in pharaonic times, continuing after the end of paganism down into the modern era.

8. For a discussion of the envoys, see Breyer 2010a, 240–42.

9. Zivie 2006; Kitchen and Lawrence 2012, 2:58–59; Breyer 2010a, 279–80.

10. On Mahu and Huy as possible candidates for the second and third missing Egyptian diplomats from the treaty stela, see Kitchen and Lawrence 2012, 2:59. On Huy's career, see Davies, *RITANC* III, 70–71. If he took part in the peace accords, Huy had a relatively long career as a diplomat, lasting at least thirteen years.

11. See p. 369 below.

12. *ÄHK* I, nos. 43–44, 47, and 76(?); Cordani 2017, 22, 33, 34. A seal impression found at Ugarit gives his title as "messenger he (the Hittite king) sent to the land of Egypt." For Tili-Teshub's career as a Hittite royal envoy to Egypt, see Cordani 2017, 49–51; Breyer 2010a, 280.

13. Kitchen, *RITANC* II, 138; Cordani 2017, 49–50. Ramose also crops up in several of the diplomatic letters exchanged after the treaty. *ÄHK* I, nos. 30, 42–44, 46–48, 57; Cordani 2017, nos. 22–23, 29, 32–33.

14. This impressive bronze slab measures 13.75 × 9.25 inches (35 × 23.5 cm) and is 0.4 inches thick (1 cm). It weighs 2.2 lbs. (1 kg); see Otten 1988; Breyer 2010a, 237–38.

15. Spalinger 1981, 348–49. Breyer (2010a, 232–33) notes that the later discovery of the bronze treaty tablet confirmed Spalinger's brilliant deductions concerning the format of the silver tablet and how it confused the Egyptian scribes.

16. Breyer 2010a, 237–40. The clay seal impressions of the Hittite king and queen may have been encased in one capsule or a pair of them. See his figure 39. The seals were therefore not on both sides of the treaty tablet but were either on two sides of one capsule or in two side-by-side capsules.

17. The representation of the Hittite king on seal impressions influenced Egyptian artistic Egyptian representations of him; Devos 2004.

18. So not "what is in the center of the silver tablet." Breyer argues that the phrase *m-ḥri-ib*, "in the middle of" refers to the seal capsule or capsules attached by the chain, which in his reconstruction of the silver tablet would hang so that they lay against the middle of the plaque itself; Breyer 2010a, 238.

19. *KRI* II, 232:1–8; Edel 1997, *52–*53.

20. Kitchen, *RITANC* II, 144, §228.

21. Sliver was both highly valuable and recyclable. Both these silver plaques were smelted down once the texts they bore lost their political currency after the Hittite Empire fell in the twelfth century BCE.

22. Breyer (2010a, 238) makes the case that the Hittites could not have stamped impressions of the seals of Hattusili and Puduhepa on the silver tablet they sent Ramesses. But the Egyptians often engraved the pharaoh's names and titles on objects of copper, bronze, silver, and gold. Unless they slavishly conformed to the exact Hittite practice, it is conceivable the Egyptians could have engraved his cartouches and appropriate titles in the hieroglyphic script.

23. The introduction Egyptian scribes created to frame their translation of the Hittite document is certainly a product of Egyptian ideology and usage. The stela is couched in the manner of a royal decree. But it is not nearly as florid as contemporary royal stelae and lacks the panegyric verse typical of the genre. It contrasts sharply with other statements on Ramesses II's dealings with the Hittites in his Kadesh Narrative and the two Hittite Marriage Edicts and the Blessing of Ptah Decree; so Brand 2005, 30. Jackson (2018) makes several valid points about the ideological conceits that shine through the Treaty Stela, but he sometimes overstates his case. The introductory section is not as bombastic as he implies when compared to other monumental texts.

24. Brand 2007a, 31–32. See also Breyer (2010a, 246–47), who notes that the treaty language also ignored the issue of Urhi-Teshub. Nor does the mutual defense clause refer to Assyria. Breyer sees the avoidance of the issue of Kadesh as having arisen after the bitter exchange of letters over the Battle of Kadesh

(*ÄHK* I, no. 24; Cordani 2017, no. 13), assuming the surviving letter predates the treaty. But it likely dates to after the accords. See pp. 329–31 below.

25. Beckman 2006; 2008, 1–4; Altman 2004; Mynářová 2009. Scholars often take it for granted that the Hittites took the initiative in the exchange of treaties; Edel 1997, 85–88; Mynářová 2014, 5. But there are considerable differences between the two treaty texts, making it unlikely that the Akkadian document Ramesses sent to Hatti was modeled slavishly on the wording of the silver tablet he received from Hattusili; see Jauß 2018.

26. The so-called Kurustama Treaty, regarding which, see the sidebar on p. 313.

27. Sürenhagen 1985; *RITANC* II, 140–41.

28. For artistic effect, the Egyptian translation of the Hittite version of the treaty fluctuates between Ramesses II's prenomen Usermaatre-Setepenre and his nomen Ramesses-Meramun. In the original text the Hittites sent, only one name would have appeared, most likely his prenomen.

29. *KRI* II, 227; Edel 1997 22*–27*.

30. Some would view the pharaoh's use of the term "Great King" (LUGAL. GAL, Akk. *šarru rab*) for both Hattusili and himself as a concession. But we should distinguish the cuneiform treaty text and diplomatic letters from formal hieroglyphic texts in Egypt. The Akkadian documents were aimed at a foreign, external audience, while the monumental inscriptions were for internal Egyptian consumption. Much like the contradictory tone between a modern nation state's domestic propaganda and the niceties of its diplomatic communiques to other nations, Ramesses was talking out of both sides of his mouth.

31. Beckman 2008, 96–97. Egyptian scribes give Ramesses the superior epithet of "Hero of all lands."

32. Beckman 2008, 97.

33. Beckman 2008, 97.

34. *KRI* II, 227:15–228:1; Edel 1997, 27*.

35. *KRI* II, 228:3–8; Edel 1997 29*–30*.

36. *KRI* II, 229:6–11; Edel 1997, 37*–39*.

37. *KRI* II, 231:12–232:1; Edel 1997, 50*–51*.

38. This phrase is curious. Did an Egyptian scribe put words in the Hittite king's mouth, injecting this affirmation of Pharaoh's longevity in keeping with the Egyptian ideology?

39. *KRI* II, 228:12–229:2; Edel 1997, 33*–34*.

40. Beckman 2008, no. 15, 98.

41. Bryce 2006.

42. Goelet and Levine 2000; Beckman 2006.

43. *KRI* II, 229:12–13.

44. *KRI* II, 230:8–11; Edel 1997, 45*.

45. *KRI* II, 230:11–13.

46. Beckman 2006. For translations of many of these treaties, see Beckman 2008, nos. 1–18; Kitchen and Lawrence 2012, 1:nos. 50–70, 72–80, and, in Italian, Devecchi 2015.

47. Beckman 2006, 284–85; Altman 2004; Devecchi 2015, 35–39.

48. *KRI* II, 227:4; *RITA* II, 80. The pharaoh's name is missing in a gap in the text. Alternatively, it could have named Sety I, as Spalinger (1981, 309) and Murnane (1990, 37 n. 186) imply. This is doubtful. The rhetoric of this passage alludes to the whole period of hostilities between Ramesses and his Hittite contemporaries during the first two decades of his reign, as opposed to a single

event like the Battle of Kadesh, or even to the wars of his predecessors with Hatti. The reference to the royal ancestors of Ramesses and Hattusili is meant to establish their lineage, not to review prior relations. So, it comes as no surprise that Hattusili's document ignores the reign of his nephew Urhi-Teshub and even of his brother Muwatalli II; Spalinger 1981, 309.

49. We must keep in mind that the label "historical prologue" is modern terminology unrelated to the legalistic function of the Hittite vassal treaties. Taken at face value, the Akkadian text Ramesses sent to Hattusa implies that there never was an Egyptian-Hittite conflict, but the emphasis here is on how the gods have forbade warfare between the two kingdoms "from the beginning of time and forever [by means of a treaty]"; Beckman 2008, 97. The two treaty versions frame previous relations between the two kingdoms differently, with the Akkadian document Ramesses II's scribes composed denying prior hostilities; see Spalinger 1981, 203; Jackson 2018, 48–49.

50. See pp. 9–10 above.

51. According to one theory, Horemheb concluded a treaty with Muwatalli, which Sety I then violated by attacking Kadesh and Amurru; Murnane 1990, 34 and n. 169, 37–38; 1995b, 197–98; Brand 2007a, 18 with n. 19; Devecchi and Miller 2011, 142–46. Others claim Sety made peace after his Syrian campaigns, using his recent conquest of Kadesh as a "bargaining chip" to trade land for peace: Kitchen 1982, 25; Spalinger 1979a, 89 n. 99; Bryce 2005, 229–30.

52. *KRI* II, 228:1–3; Edel 1997, 28*. Regarding the earlier treaty that "existed" (*wnn*) under Suppiluliuma and Muwatalli, Ramesses and Hattusili agree to "take hold if *it*," (not "them"), meaning that they will abide by the terms of the previous treaty even as they conclude a new one. In his treaty with Ramesses II, Hattusili III seeks to contrast the hostile relations between the two kingdoms under his father Suppiluliuma and his brother Muwatalli with the renewed state of peace he has now established with Ramesses. Other scholars have also concluded there was only one treaty prior to Ramesses: Edel 1997, 29; Roth 2005, 186–87. While I have previously maintained (Brand 2007a, 18 with n. 19) that Horemheb, not Sety I, concluded a second treaty with Muwatalli, I am now convinced of Sürenhagen's (2006) view that only the Kurustama treaty existed prior to Ramesses II's alliance with Hattusili III.

Lacking a word for "treaty" in their language, Egyptian scribes employed two technical expressions, *nt-ꜥ* and *nt-ꜥ mty* in their transcription of the Akkadian document they received from the Hittites. Their precise meaning has occasioned much discussion; Spalinger 1981, 312 and 322; Murnane 1990, 73–74; Goelet and Levine 2000, 262–65. The term *nt-ꜥ* literally means "that which pertains to the document," and often references customary or habitual practice, while *mty* is a qualifier meaning "precisely." Hence, the Egyptians translated the Akkadian term for "treaty" in the silver tablet Hattusili sent as *nt-ꜥ* (*mty*), "the (precise) written document," here meaning "customary regulations" governing their peaceful relations.

Interestingly, the Egyptian terminology does not equate with the standard Akkadian term for "treaty" (*rikiltu*), which means "binding agreement," that is an oath. The Akkadian language version the Egyptians sent to Hattusili employs the term *rikiltu*. See Sürenhagen 1985, 80–82; Edel 1997, 5; Kitchen and Lawrence 2012, 1:573–82. On the Egyptian terminology used in Ramesses II Hittite Peace Treaty Stela see now: Mynářová 2014.

53. Sürenhagen (2006) offers further evidence that there was only a single treaty prior to Ramesses II.

CHAPTER ELEVEN

PEACE AND BROTHERHOOD: DIPLOMATIC RELATIONS BETWEEN THE EGYPTIAN AND HITTITE COURTS

After negotiating their Silver Treaty of "perfect peace and perfect brotherhood," Ramesses II and Hattusili III maintained intensive diplomatic contacts. Pharaoh and members of his court exchanged over one hundred letters with the Hittite king and queen in the years afterward.[1] Transferring his contest with the Hittites from Syrian battlefields to a game of great-power diplomacy, Ramesses II proved he was both a canny statesman and a master manipulator of his new ally Hattusili III. Both parties claimed to embrace the treaty as a sacred oath, regarding one another as beloved "brothers."[2] But unresolved issues and resentments lingered, and their chatter back and forth was rife with calculated snubs and endless recriminations.[3] There were several recurring irritants. The two monarchs bickered about the deposed Hittite ruler Urhi-Teshub—whose whereabouts they contested. They even squabbled over what happened at the Battle of Kadesh. These quarrels belied their professed fiction about brotherly affection.

Congratulatory Letters from the Royal Family

Judging from a barrage of epistles that Ramesses II's family and officials addressed to Hattusili III and Queen Puduhepa when peace came, we might imagine the Silver Treaty had transformed their relations for the better.[4] Amid much happy talk of peace and brotherhood, and even Ramesses II's fanciful claim that "our two countries have become one," each side showered the other with greetings and expensive gifts.[5] Reading between the lines, however, we discover the professed dawning of an era of good feelings was all too artificial (fig. 11.1).

The language the Egyptians use is formal and diplomatic, even stilted. Protocol and royal pride required both sides to maintain etiquette.[6] Only the lists of precious "greeting gifts" closing each message offers a jaded reader any genuine variety or interest.

But the political message is clear: Ramesses II now endorsed the Hittite regime. Crucially, these formal gestures would impress a wider audience: Hattusili's subjects, his vassal kings, and via their ambassadors, the other Great Kings in the ancient Near East.

These letters also revealed the power structure within both courts. Hattusili III and Puduhepa each received many letters from Pharaoh over the course of two decades. In fact, Ramesses often sent parallel epistles to Hattusili and his spouse. This reflects Puduhepa's well-deserved reputation as a formidable consort to her husband and a stateswoman on the international stage (fig. 11.2).[7] A definite pecking order emerges among Pharaoh's family and high officials. Only a handful of leading members of the Egyptian court were allowed to address letters to the Hittite king and queen, including the Vizier Paser, Ramesses II's mother Tuya, and the Great Royal Wife Nefertari, whose name is transcribed in Akkadian as Naptera.

Ramesses also permitted his designated heir Prince Amunhirkhopeshef to address a letter to Hattusili.[8] Another message salutes the Hittite king in the name of Pharaoh, his two eldest sons, and "the (other) sons of the Great King."[9] Nefertari dispatched two notes, both to her counterpart Queen Puduhepa.[10] The venerable Queen Mother Tuya wrote two missives to the Hittite king and queen.[11] Ramesses did not grant this honor to other royal women, neither his wives nor his daughters.[12] Indeed, after these celebratory messages from members of his court, Ramesses II never again authorized his family or his high officials to write to their Hittite counterparts.

Conforming to established protocol for exchanges between Great Kingdoms, members of the Egyptian court salute their Hittite counterparts in family terms. So, the Egyptian princes address Hattusili as their "father" and royal women on both sides are "sisters." Ramesses II himself also sent further congratulatory letters to his "sister" Puduhepa, and to Hittite princes named Kannuta, Teshub-Sharruma, and Tasmi-Sharruma, calling them his "sons."[13]

Each letter employs formulaic greetings full of platitudes and cliched small talk, but little real substance, as Queen Nefertari's first dispatch exemplifies:

> So (says) Naptera, the Great Queen of the Land of Egypt, to Puduhepa, the Great Queen of the land of Hatti, say (as follows): For me, your sister all is well and my country is well. For you, my sister, may all be well and may your land be well. I have now heard that you, my sister, have written to me to enquire about my well-being, and that you have written me about the relationship of good peace and good brotherhood in which the Great King, the King of the Land of Egypt, (now stands) with the Great King, the King of the Land of Hatti, his brother.
>
> May the Sun God and the Storm God exalt you and may the Sun God cause peace to flourish and bestow good brotherhood on the Great King, the King of the Land of Egypt, and the Great King, the King of the Land of Hatti, his brother forever. And I also am at peace and am sisterly with you, my sister, as well.
>
> Now, I have sent to you a present as a greetings-gift for you, my sister, that I have sent in the hands of Parikhnawa, the royal messenger:
>
> 1 (necklace) for the neck, multicolored, made of fine gold consisting of 12 strands, which weighs 88 shekels.
>
> 1 colorful cloak made from royal fabric.

FIGURE 11.2. Puduhepa (right) worshiping the Hittite Sun Goddess. Relief from Fraktin, Turkey. Courtesy Tayfun Bilgin, www.hittitemonuments.org.

1 colorful tunic made from royal fabric
5 colorful garments of excellent quality
5 colorful tunics of excellent quality
Total: 12 garments.[14]

Such effusive chatter rings trite in our ears today. In ancient hierarchical societies, however, where prestige and rank were paramount, these stereotyped communiques evoked the sender's renown and status and stroked the recipient's ego. In Egypt, Pharaoh's women surely envied Nefertari's privileged interaction with the Hittite Queen. Even commonplace bromides gratified the ear by affirming the royal recipient's eminence among members of the Great Powers Club dwelling in exotic, faraway kingdoms. But the rich assortment of "greeting gifts" were more highly valued than any written outporing of affection.[15] The gold necklace Nefertari sent Puduhepa weighed as much as 29 ounces (826 grams), and its bullion value alone would be at least $50,000—a queenly gift indeed.[16] More than stilted platitudes, precious gifts functioned as barometers of interstate relations, publicly declaring their mutual esteem.

Nor did recipients consider it gauche when donors spelled out in detail the form, quality, and value of the gifts they offered, including the weight in shekels of gold objects. Prince Amunhirkhopeshef gave his "father" Hattusili III a fine gold cup decorated with a bull's face, adorned with white stone inlays for its horns and obsidian for its eyes, all weighing a total of ninety-three shekels.[17] Unfortunately, most gift lists are fragmentary, so we cannot always appreciate the full generosity that Egyptian courtiers showed to their Hittite counterparts. While Puduhepa obtained an impressive golden neckless from Nefertari, Ramesses often gave Hattusili and his sons gold drinking cups, and in one case a team of horses. Remarkably, crumpled fragments of one of these golden cups has survived, inscribed in both cuneiform and hieroglyphic script. Part of this text reads "... [the Great] Ruler of Egypt ..." (fig. 11.3).[18]

More numerous and varied were the arrays of colorful dyed garments that Pharaoh bestowed on the Hittite royal pair, many being of "royal fabric" or of "excellent quality," along with others of "medium quality."[19] The highest quality textiles corresponded to Egyptian "royal linen," which women in Pharaoh's household produced. We should not

FIGURE 11.3. Two fragments of a gold cup Ramesses II sent to the Hittite king. The inscriptions are in hieroglyphs and cuneiform. The hieroglyphic texts reads "[the Great Ru]er of Egypt, Usermaatre-Setepenre." Photograph © Staatliches Museum Ägyptischer Kunst, München; ÄS 7208, 7209. Hieroglyphic script by Erika Feleg.

discount the costliness of these gifts.[20] All were examples of conspicuous generosity, enhancing the prestige and honor of donors and recipients alike.

An Ancient Superpower Summit?

Today heads of state from all but the most hostile nations will meet in
person. Among members of the Great Powers Club of the Late Bronze
Age, face-to-face visits rarely happened.[21] Great Kings preferred to hold
each other at arms' length, interacting through envoys and diplomatic
messages. In the Amarna Letters, the idea of a royal visit arises only
once—in a calculatedly fatuous vein—when Kadashman-Enlil I of Babylonia grumbled that Amenhotep III failed to invite him to his Jubilee
festival. He then offers Amenhotep a phony invite: "Your [en]voys have
seen [the new house and n]ow I am making the entry of the house. [So
you] come hither, [eat] with me and drink! [I am not doing wh]at you
did."[22] Even the irrepressible King Tushrata of Mitanni, despite endless
effusions of love for Amenhotep and Akhenaten, never once proposes
they should meet.

Often the hospitality a Great King provided, even to royal envoys,
proved to be objectionable. Messengers might endure unkind treatment
and petty slights that offended their master's honor.[23] Some were detained for extended periods—even years—before their host would let
them depart. A Great King would think twice about putting himself
in such a degrading position. If nothing more, in the role of guest he
would appear subordinate to that of host.

Nevertheless, after Ramesses II and Hattusili III concluded their Silver Treaty, the Hittite king responded positively, if only vaguely, when
Pharaoh pressed him to come to Egypt.[24] A dissembling game of offers ensued about logistics for the summit. Ramesses made gestures
of hospitality, which Hattusili countered with polite but noncommittal
noises intermixed with objections. Still, the idea must have intrigued
him. Even a consummate actor like Ramesses II occasionally let his
mask slip, revealing his human nature to viewers. Debriefing his envoys provided Hattusili with firsthand intelligence about his new peace
partner. But these anecdotes only whet his curiosity. When Ramesses
first suggested they meet, Hattusili nibbled at the bait.[25]

Hattusili wrote back: "[My] br[other] should write to me [sugges-
tions] regarding the pla[ces] where [we might me]et [each other]," po-
litely signaling he did *not* want to traverse the entire length of Egypt's
Asiatic empire before meeting him in Piramesses.[26] This tepid answer
failed to dampen Pharaoh's zeal for the visit. Ramesses now revised

the itinerary, suggesting they rendezvous in Canaan, from whence he would escort his guest into Egypt:

> *The Sun God and the Storm God, [and my gods and the gods of my brother will bring (?)] it to pass that my brother might see [his brother]; and [may] my brother [come to me and may] he [carry out] the good [proposal] to visit [me, and may] one [come] to the oth[er and may one look the other in] the face in the pla[ce where the (Egyptian) King] is to be found on [his throne (?)].*
>
> *[And I, the Great King, the King of the Land of Egypt, will] go to the land of Cana[an] to see [... the Great King, the King of Hatti(?) ...] and [look in]to the face of my brother [...].*[27]

However strongly Ramesses cajoled him, Hattusili finally balked. Perhaps he offered some medical pretext, such as the malady called "burning of the feet."[28] Or, he may have temporized that pressing business kept him at home. There was still a real risk, after all, of losing his throne to Urhi-Teshub's loyalists. Perhaps Hattusili feared that Ramesses might foist his deposed nephew on him, by arranging an awkward "family reunion" with Urhi-Teshub!

In the end Hattusili had nothing to gain from such a summit.[29] On the contrary, he knew well the diplomatic victory he would concede to Pharaoh by journeying to Egypt. Ramesses II would never present the visit, either to his own people or to the Great Kings, as a meeting of equals. Instead he would score a propaganda coup, depicting Hattusili's arrival as an act of abject homage by a Hittite chieftain "begging for the breath of life."[30]

Nor can we blame Ramesses, for this was the instinct of any Great King of the ancient Near East. Among these monarchs all diplomacy was a high-stakes, zero-sum game of enhancing their prestige at the expense of their royal peers. Diplomacy was "war by other means." Effusions of "brotherhood" did not obscure their inherent rivalry. Hattusili was too shrewd to make himself a witless tool of Egyptian triumphalism so the two "frenemies" never met.

Diplomatic Friction after the Treaty

Soon after Hattusili III and Ramesses II concluded their formal alliance and traded a slew of gushing missives extolling the new era of "good peace and good brotherhood," nettlesome issues quickly resurfaced. Neither king trusted his "brother." Animosities built up over half a century of hostilities did not evaporate overnight, and fulsome words and precious gifts could not dispel them. Their "good peace" soon gave way to rancor.[31] Both sides often resorted to waspish remarks, complaints, and snide comments. According to a modern diplomatic euphemism, Ramesses II and Hattusili III engaged in a "frank exchange of views."

There was no shortage of irritants to make the road forward a rocky one. The dossier of letters from Ramesses II discovered in the state archives at Hattusa offer vivid glimpses of a tense, acerbic discourse between uneasy allies. Two immovable poles governed the orbit of these exchanges. One was Hattusili III's aggrieved sense of political insecurity, and his acute sensitivity to any perceived slight. The second was Ramesses II's relentless, calculated arrogance, and his penchant for lobbing stinging comments at the Hittite king's expense (fig. 11.4).

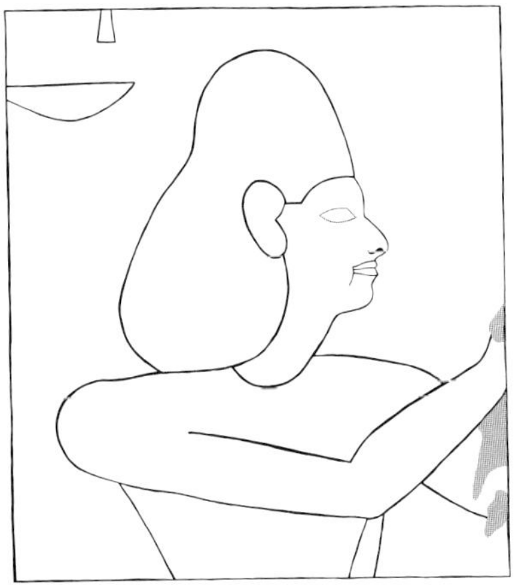

FIGURE 11.4. Drawing of a relief fragment with an Egyptian "portrait" of the Hittite king from the Ramesseum. The relief likely comes from the First Hittite Marriage Decree stela of Ramesses II's thirty-fourth regnal year. Drawing by Peter Brand after Leblanc 2019, pl. 15.

Pharaoh's Undiplomatic Tone

By exchanging letters with their "brothers," Great Kings of the ancient Near East's formally recognized each other as members of equal standing in their exclusive circle of powerful kingdoms. With every message, a Great King offered costly greeting gifts of luxury goods and of gold, showing his esteem for his fellow monarch. To preserve the impression of equality, they adhered strictly to the stately formulas of diplomatic protocol. This was not private mail. Amid the splendor of his court, the king received them from ambassadors before an audience of courtiers and envoys from other Great Kingdoms.[32] But Hattusili III often found Pharaoh's tone to be insufferably arrogant.

Diplomatic letters from the Amarna and Ramesside periods indicate that Great Kings suffered from a constant and acute sense of "status anxiety" in their dealings with one another. This manifested itself in repeated complaints by one correspondent that his fellow Great King had slighted him, compromising their equal standing through impolitic words and actions.[33] Egyptian monarchs were notorious for inflicting these indignities on their peers. Since the time of Amenhotep III, the kings of Assyria, Babylonia, Hatti, and Mitanni raised repeated objections to Pharaoh's affronts to their gravitas.

Hattusili III remained hypersensitive to his status as rightful king of Hatti. He carped peevishly about the tone and insinuations he read in Ramesses II's letters, because Pharaoh failed to accord him the equal standing he craved. The Hittite king's status anxiety, which Ramesses exploited masterfully, stands out as a constant sore point in their communications. Typical of this sniping is a message from Ramesses:

[I have] just [heard] these harsh [words] that you wrote to [me as follows]: "Why did you write to me these many words [as if I were a servant]?" [It is simply not true] that I [wrote to you like] a servant among [my] servants. Have [y]ou not attained the kingship? [Do] I [not know this?] Is it not firmly instilled in [my] heart? [Fulfill] your role as king! Moreover, I [have heard about] this [matter] of Urhi-Te[shub of which you have written]. You have written to me about him saying: "I have attained [the kingship in his place!]"[34]

Ramesses professed quite insincerely—that these complaints perplexed him. But there were real grounds for Hattusili's neurotic indignation. Ramesses projected a lofty, even arrogant tone when he addressed the Hittite king. Indeed, his manner of address must have offended other kings, for he flouted the protocols of interstate discourse with haughty disregard.[35]

In the diplomatic protocol current at the time of the Amarna Letters, it was mandatory for the addressee's name to come before the sender's when both were Great Kings. Only when addressing his vassals did he name himself first. Other monarchs objected strenuously when Egyptian pharaohs violated this etiquette. During the Amarna period, Suppiluliuma I resorted to threats, insults, and histrionics when Akhenaten named himself first in a letter.[36] Now, by regularly giving his own names and titles priority over those of Hatti's king, Ramesses implied that Hattusili was his subject, not his peer.[37] Even more galling, members of the Egyptian court, including the vizier and Ramesses's sons—all of them ranking well below the Hittite king—also addressed him in this demeaning fashion.

By Ramesses II's day, other Great Kings had resigned themselves, resentfully, to Pharaoh's supercilious tone. Refusing to let Ramesses defy long-standing customs without sanction, his contemporaries jettisoned the "Amarna rulebook" of diplomatic decorum and began placing their own names first when addressing their royal peers, as in Hattusili III's message to the king of Babylonia:

So says Hattusili, the Great King, the King of Hatti: Say [to] Kadashman-Enlil, the Great King, the King of Babylonia, my brother: I am well. My household, my wife, my sons, my infantry, my horses, [my chariots], and everything in my land is well. May you be well. May your household, your wives, your sons, your infantry, your horses, your chariots, and everything in your land be very well.[38]

Even so, the new greeting formula carefully balances each ruler's titles and the sender offers compliments about the mutual wellbeing of their two kingdoms. Although this long letter proceeds with a frank discussion of several points of contention in Babylonian-Hittite relations, Hattusili never complains that his Babylonian counterpart has "treated me like a servant." Yet, the Hittite remained acutely sensitive to slights from Ramesses II.[39]

In fact, Ramesses knew exactly how to get under Hattusili's skin. Pharaoh always multiplied his own titles and epithets at the expense of his correspondent when both should appear in equal ratios:[40]

> So (says) Wasmuaria-satepnaria, the Great King, the King of E[gypt], the Son of the Sun God, Riamasesa-maiamana, the Great King, the King of Egy[t]: [Say] to Hattusili, the Great King, the King of Hatti, my brother.[41]

Given the supreme importance ancient rulers attached to their official names and epithets as indicators of status and prestige, Ramesses was asserting that he outranked all other Great Kings when he claimed more titles for himself. This haughty attitude conformed to Egyptian ideology, and to Pharaoh's ingrained self-image, but it ruptured the polite fiction of reciprocity and "brotherhood" to which Great Kings normally adhered.[42] Ramesses got away with it too!

Hattusili grumbled repeatedly that Ramesses was treating him "like a servant," prompting Pharaoh to smooth his ruffled feathers with con-ciliatory—but insincere—reassurances:

> [I] see that you are great [...] in all lands [... you are the Great King (?)] of the countries of the land of Hatti ... [the Sun God] and the Storm God have granted you [to exercise kingship in the territories of] the land of Hatti in the place of your grandfather.
>
> [And why should I write to you like] a servant anyways? So you should not think [that I have written to you like a servant. You should write pleasing words to me] as follows: "May your heart be full of joy every day!" [You should not write to me] these empty worthless words![43]

Hattusili persisted in his complaints that Pharaoh was not holding to the spirit of the treaty of peace and brotherhood:

> Have you and I not achieved [brotherhood], and are we (not) as from one father, and are we (not) a[s from o]ne mother, and do we (not) live as in the same country? But see, you are abandoning the brotherhood of the land of Egypt (with Hatti) this (very) day![44]

Having none of it, Ramesses once again protested his good faith, re-sponding:

> Now look, this (bad) state of affairs, about which my brother wrote to me, does not exist! I have not committed any wrongdoing against

my brother. [I] am brotherly and [at pe]ace with my brother in my
relationship (with him) forever.[45]

While feigning puzzlement at Hattusili's ire, Ramesses never mended
his ways. At last, Hattusili stopped grumbling about breaches of protocol, while their war of words continued on other fronts.

Pharaoh's Sister-in-Law

It was not just Ramesses II's conceited tone and blatant defiance of diplomatic norms that irked Hattusili III. Pharaoh interlarded his messages
with gratuitous verbal barbs displaying an insufferable lack of tact. He
calculated these sneers for maximum impact on the recipient's self-es-
teem. A perfect example of his callous wordplay came when Hattusili'
requested help on behalf of his sister Matanazi, who had an embarrassing "family issue." Being a childless lady of advanced age, Matanazi
stood in desperate need of a fertility treatment.[46]

In keeping with the Hittite policy of betrothing royal women to vassal kings, Hattusili's married his sister Matanazi to King Masturi of the
Seha River Land, an important client kingdom in western Anatolia. Her
husband was aging but had not yet sired an heir to ensure the stability
of his realm. It was crucial for the infertile Matanazi to become pregnant—and soon—to bear her husband an heir linked to Hattusili III's
dynasty. Her regal brother was convinced Egyptian doctors and their
medicines could help. Unfortunately, she was well past her childbearing years, as Ramesses II's flippant and brutally undiplomatic response
makes clear:

> [About what my brother] wrote [to me concerning] his [sister] Matanazi:
> "Let my brother send me a man to prepare medicines for her, so that she
> might become pregnant." That is what my brother wrote to me. Say to
> my brother: Now I, the king, your brother, know about Matanazi, my
> brother's sister. She is said to be fifty or sixty years old! It is not possible
> to prepare medicines for a woman who has reached fifty or sixty years
> so that she might still become pregnant.
>
> May the Sun God and the Storm God command, so that the ritual
> which will be performed will be carried out fully for my brother's sister!
> And I, the King, your brother, shall send a competent incantation-priest
> and a competent [doctor] and they will prepare medicines for her in
> order that she might give birth.[47]

Egyptian medical arts were renowned and much sought after in the ancient world, but Pharaoh dismissed the unfortunate Matanazi as being
more in need of a magician than a doctor. Medicine and magic were, in
fact, intertwined for the ancient Egyptians, who relied on divine inter-

vention to effect healing. Yet, there were limits to what even the gods might do, and Egyptian doctors knew a hopeless case when they saw one. Ramesses II exploited the incident to score a point at his "brother's" expense.[48] Dripping with sarcasm, he coldly aimed his grossly impolitic rejoinder to Hattusili' earnest plea for its maximum psychological impact. This stung even more because Hattusili knew that Ramesses was correct in his assessment of Matanazi's age. And Pharaoh had most likely learned this from Hattusili's deposed nephew, Urhi-Teshub.

Refighting the Battle of Kadesh

As Ramesses II exchanged letters with Hattusili III, he reassured him he still held fast to the sacred Treaty Oath, which he had laid at the feet of Re-Horakhty in his temple at Heliopolis and that of the Storm God in Hattusa.[49] But a residue of bitter memories still provoked caustic disputes about the Battle of Kadesh. On that score, each king jealously guarded his preferred view of the encounter, and resented the other's official account. Ramesses II's grandiose celebration of the incident vexed and perplexed Hattusili III, leaving him incredulous and deeply offended.[50]

Hittite envoys and travelers returning from Egypt delivered lurid reports describing Pharaoh's extravagant rendition of the battle.[51] Ramesses II had emblazoned the walls of temples throughout Egypt and Nubia with his story of Kadesh, and circulated papyrus copies of the epic Poem among the Egyptian elite. Heralds read or sang it aloud, permitting even illiterate peasants to hear of their lord's self-proclaimed triumph over his foes. Foreign visitors could not evade the bombastic imagery of the Kadesh narrative, which confronted them on every temple façade and palace audience hall of Ramesses II's domains. This would have humiliated any Hittite, as they stood with envoys from rival Great Kingdoms before Pharaoh and his court.

Hattusili had fought at Kadesh under his brother Muwatalli II's command. But Pharaoh portrayed Muwatalli as "the despicable loser of Hatti," slandering him as an abject coward who, Ramesses claimed, hid among his reserve troops and refused to face him in battle.[52] All these insults mortified and outraged Hattusili. Livid over what he regarded as gross distortions of the events at Kadesh, and seething over Urhi-Teshub's unresolved status as Pharaoh's "guest," Hattusili fired off angry missives to Ramesses, picking quarrels about both issues.[53] He even raised the specter of past hostilities between them, implying they might return despite the recent treaty. Ramesses, in turn, took umbrage with these insinuations:

And you have written to m[e many] unpleasant [words] that [are] not
worth hearing as are my (own words) ... and after hearing of this matter,
could you not [write to me] as a man (worthy of the name) should? ...
but since you [heard] (these matters), you have written to your [brother]
these many words to pick a fight and you do not [think] about [our
brotherhood and our peace]. Further, you wrote to me ... as follows:
"Have you forgotten the days of enemies [from the land of Hatti?"] [54]

Ramesses now launched his own verbal onslaught, recounting in detail
his memories of Kadesh, which—unsurprisingly—conform to the official, monumental narrative:[55]

Look, that was the hostility of a god, and he [... But I] truly [penetrated (?)]
into the midst of the enemies from the land of Hatti, and [... the army
of (?)] of Muwatalli, King of the Land of Hatti, ca[me along with the
many countries that were with him], and while the armies of the Great
King, the King of the land of Egypt, were still i[n the land of Amurru, in
the land of ..., and in the land of Taminta].[56]

And since the vanguard of the Great King, the King of the land [of
Egypt ... there came two Bedouin from the army (?)] of the land of Hatti,
and they re[ached the King and said: "The King of Hatti is in the land
of Aleppo]."[57]

Three (Egyptian) armies marched on the road and had [not] yet
[reached the place where the King was (?)]. And the King sat on his
throne on the [western] side [of the Orontes River (?) ... the camp] they
were (still) setting up and occupying. And while the King knew th[at
Muwatalli, the King of the land of Hatti (?)] had departed [from Aleppo
(?)], the King (Ramesses) did not know [... And the King of the Land of
Hatti attacked him (?) ...] along with all the countries that were with
him. [But the King of the Land of Egypt defeated him/them (?) ...], all
alone, while my army was not with me, nor were [my] chari[ots with
me]. And I brought away enemy (prisoners) from these territories of the
Land of [Hatti ...] in the sight of the sons of the Land of Egypt and in
the sight of the sons of the Land of Hatti [...].

And since you would say about my army: "Was there no army there
[and were there really no chariots there?"... Look], one of my armies
was in the land of Amurru, another ar[my was in the land of ...], and
another army was in the land of Taminta—that's how it was![58]

In an earlier letter, Hattusili gloated that Muwatalli's forces pursued
the pharaoh's armies when they departed from Kadesh southward into
Egyptian territory, insisting that Muwatalli had forced Ramesses to retreat. This irked the pharaoh, who believed he had affected an orderly
withdrawal after achieving victory:

And since the King (of Egypt) [went] into the land of Canaan in th[at
same] year, [he established himself in the town of Sidon.[59] *This matter],*

of whi[ch the King of the land of Ha]tti then hea[rd], you have greatly exaggerated ... the land of Kad]esh, and the land of Khareta, and the la[nd of ... the]re.[60] And Muwatalli, King of the land of [Hatti ...]. But he (the Egyptian King) sat in the town of S[idon(?) ... the]re.[61] Why [did you write] this [to me? I do not understand these many matters] about which [you] have written to [me].[62]

Though fragmentary, Pharaoh's surviving letter was just one salvo in an ongoing epistolary duel between the two aging warlords, as they traded sneers and accusations disputing each other's account of events on that fateful day two decades earlier.[63] While their bickering looks petty to us, each fought to safeguard his personal honor. They soon let the matter drop, but with neither conceding the point, while their peevish discourse turned elsewhere.

The King of Mira's Letter

Even after the peace treaty, an air of political tension about Urhi-Teshub's fate lingered among Hatti's vassals.[64] Against this edgy backdrop, King Kupanta-Kurunta of the Hittite vassal kingdom of Mira sent an unexpected letter to Ramesses II. The whole affair was highly irregular and served as a test, intentional or not, of Pharaoh's commitment to his new ally. How Ramesses handled the situation deeply concerned Hattusili III. He still nursed deep bitterness toward his Egyptian counterpart, and genuine misgivings about his reliability as an ally. Meanwhile, Urhi-Teshub might still be in Ramesses's domains. Could Hattusili trust Pharaoh to uphold his crucial support for his regime?

Into this volatile atmosphere, the king of Mira blundered with a simple yet highly sensitive question: what was Ramesses II's stance on Urhi-Teshub now? Kupanta-Kurunta's original letter has vanished, but Pharaoh's rejoinder is among the best-preserved dispatches from the Hittite diplomatic archives. Ramesses rebuked the king of Mira's for his indiscreet query:[65]

Now, the Great King, the King of Egypt, has heard all the matters which [you wrote] to me about. No! Concerning the affair of Urhi-Teshub, I [have] not [done] that which [you wrote] to me about. Now, [... is] different. [...] The good relationship which (I), the Great King, the King of Egypt, have established with the Great King, [the King of Hatti], my brother, consists of good brotherhood and good peace. The Sun God and the [Storm God have granted it] forever. Furthermore, regarding the matter of Urhi-Teshub of which you [wrote to me], the Great King, the King of Hatti, dealt with (him/it) in accordance with [my wishes(?)].[66]

Pharaoh denied all knowledge of Urhi-Teshub's whereabouts:

[...] Indeed, the Great King, the King of Egypt, immediately [wrote] about these (matters) [to] the Great King, the King of Ha[tti] (as follows): "What about me? Should I know where/who he (Urhi-Teshub) is?"[67] [So] I [said]. But the Great King, the King of Hatti, did not write to me about this [matter]. Have my lips articulated plots?[68] [The words] that men speak to you are worthless. Do not trust them! I am happily in brotherhood and happily [at peace] forever with the Great King, the King of Hatti, my brother ...

I have sworn this Oath and I will not abandon it. In your heart [do] not [believe] the false words that you have heard. There is no sense in it. See the go[od] relationship [of brotherhood] and peace in which I [stand] together with the G[re]at King, [the King of Hatti, my brother.] I will keep it forever.[69]

Ramesses II walked a fine line by responding to the king of Mira, and he may have evaded a diplomatic snare. If so, who set the trap? By utterly rejecting any hint that he supported Urhi-Teshub's bid to regain his throne, Pharaoh proved to this overly inquisitive Hittite vassal that he remained committed to the treaty. Perhaps the king of Mira played a double game. Kupanta-Kurunta violated his oath of vassalage by writing to Ramesses in the first place. Great Kings forbade their subject kings from communicating directly with rival imperial powers. If Hattusili caught word of this illicit message, he could depose him from his throne for disloyalty.

Perhaps Kupanta-Kurunta was truly unsure where his loyalties should lie and uncertain about rumors of Urhi-Teshub's flight to Egypt. When Hattusili seized power he left his subjects, and many Hittite vassals, afraid that the sacred loyalty oaths they swore to Urhi-Teshub were still valid. The gods themselves might punish them for violating their vows. Had they not struck down even the mighty Suppululiuma I, and ravaged Hatti with plague for twenty years, for breaking a treaty oath with Egypt?

More worldly factors also entered the king of Mira's calculations. Urhi-Teshub had proved relentless in conniving to reinstate himself with the aid of foreign kings—first Babylonia, and now with Egypt. He also had an uncanny knack for eluding his uncle's clutches. What if he *did* regain his throne? How would a resurgent Urhi-Teshub hold vassals like Kupanta-Kurunta to account for their actions during the usurper's reign?

Ramesses II disdained Kupanta-Kurnunta's political quandary and remained blasé about any distress the affair inflicted on Hattusili III. Archaeologists unearthed Pharaoh's rejoinder to this unorthodox missive in the Hittite archives at Hattusa among the messages he sent to Hattusili. This is precisely where Ramesses sent it in the first place. By circumventing Mira's indiscrete king and forwarding his response directly to Hattusa, Ramesses openly proclaimed his fidelity to the Silver Treaty. Nor did Pharaoh resort to any of the gratuitous verbal barbs he usually deployed at Hattusili's expense. On the surface at least, there was nothing that Hattusili could object to.[70]

But Ramesses knew his response would embarrass his ally. Was this the first intelligence Hatti's king had of his vassal's duplicity? Had Kupanta-Kurunta blundered into deep geopolitical waters unwittingly? Had he informed Hattusil of the letter before sending it? Was he entreating Egyptian aide in restoring Urhi-Teshub, his former master, to power? Or did the king of Mira seek to lure Ramesses into going "on record" in support of either Hattusili or Urhi-Teshub?

Whatever the motive, reading Pharaoh's resounding endorsement of his regime was not an unalloyed pleasure for the Hittite king. Caught off guard, Hattusili's bile surely rose when he learned a key vassal had conversed—perhaps seditiously—with a rival Great King. This hint of treason only came to Hattusili when Ramesses *chose* to apprise him of the letter by forwarding his reply to Hattusha. Even as he presented himself as being faithful to the treaty and blameless in the Urhi-Teshub affair, Ramesses knew well the letter would mortify the Hittite king. Its unspoken implication was that the loyalty of a key Hittite vassal, and perhaps the stability of Hattusili's grip on power, might turn on Pharaoh's whim.

If we are ignorant of the full content of the king of Mira's dispatch, so too was Hattusili. In his carefully worded response, Ramesses never quotes Kupanta-Kurunta's letter; he only denies complicity in "all the matters which [you wrote] to me about ... concerning Urhi-Teshub."[71] This was enough to make Hattusili anxious. Had nasty gossip and talk of high treason flown back and forth across Hatti's vassal states, and as far as Piramesses?

Had Pharaoh so chosen, he could have discreetly ignored Kupanta-Kurunta's inquiry and pocketed a bit of juicy intelligence data on a potentially disloyal Hittite subject. He was firmly on record for upholding the treaty. But Ramesses could not resist the temptation to score a point against his ally's shaky sense of political security. Seen from this perspective, Ramesses played a subtle but effective game of psychological warfare.

But we could also interpret the king of Mira's letter as an ancient "false flag operation," one the Hittite king himself arranged. In this scenario, Hattusili III attempted to outmaneuver the cagey Pharaoh on the vexed question of Urhi-Teshub by sending a fake missive, purportedly from Kupanta-Kurunta. Its purpose: to probe Ramesses's true commitment to the peace accords by dangling the possibility of a local

Anatolian ally should Pharaoh choose to renounce the treaty and support Urhi-Teshub's comeback bid. Plots within plots? If Hattusili set such a cunning trap, Ramesses was too sharp witted to fall for it.

The most likely explanation is that the king of Mira's lost letter was just what it appeared to be; a delicate, if indiscrete, inquiry by a key Hittite vassal uncertain as to where his loyalties lay amid political dissention in the Hittite Empire. Wild rumors about Urhi-Teshub's location and intentions still circulated in Hatti. And despite Ramesses's ringing endorsement of Hattusili, the two allies sharply disagreed about Urhi-Teshub's current whereabouts and what should be done with him.

Urhi-Teshub at Large

Before Ramesses II concluded the Silver Treaty with Hattusili III, Urhi-Teshub had fled to Egypt. Hattusili demanded that Pharaoh hand over his nephew, but Ramesses refused. Urhi-Teshub was surely too shrewd to seek refuge in Egypt after Pharaoh concluded this treaty, which stated that exiles like him must be extradited. Yet, the clause was never invoked on his behalf.

None of the letters Ramesses sent after the treaty mentions Hattusili III's ultimatum for his nephew's extradition.[72] Nor does Ramesses refuse to hand him over. Just the opposite, for the gist of all their post-treaty dialogue is that Urhi-Teshub had absconded from the land of the Nile. Far from seeking his extradition, Hattusili now demanded Pharaoh exert himself to locate his errant nephew and bring him back to Egypt!

While Egypt and Hatti remained at war, and as they negotiated their peace accords, Ramesses II guarded Urhi-Teshub as a valuable bargaining chip. In turn, the exiled ruler hoped Pharaoh might aid him in regaining his throne. Their value to each other plummeted once Ramesses brokered the treaty and made it clear that he would abide by its terms. In several letters Pharaoh reaffirmed to Hattusili that he had laid the silver tablet at the feet of the sun god Re in Heliopolis. Typical in this vein is the conclusion of his message to Kupanta-Kurunta:

> The written text of the (Treaty) Oath that [I made] for the Great King, the King of Hatti, my brother, was set at the feet of [the Storm God] and before the Great Gods (of Hatti). They are the witnesses [to the words of the Oath ...]. And see, the written text of the (Treaty) Oath that the Great King, [the King of Hatti], has made for me [was set at] the feet of the Sun God of [Heliopolis], and before the Great Gods (of Egypt).
>
> I have sworn this Oath and I will not abandon it. In your heart [do] not [believe] the false words that you have heard. There is no sense in it. See the go[od] relationship [of brotherhood] and peace in which I

> *[stand] together with the G[re]at King, [the King of Hatti, my brother.]*
> *I will keep it forever.*[73]

Once Pharaoh's agents had debriefed Urhi-Teshub and squeezed every drop of intelligence out of him, his usefulness came to an end. The expatriate realized his Egyptian host would not renege on the peace deal on his behalf, and the threat of extradition loomed. It was time for Urhi-Teshub to seek his fortunes elsewhere. Perhaps through contacts with Hittite travelers visiting Egypt, he learned that his cause still inspired fierce loyalty among some of his former subjects and vassal states. They were willing to protect him and to fight for him. Ramesses reported as much to Hattusili, in his letter about the Battle of Kadesh:

> *[... they][74] came to me together with this man (Urhi-Teshub), and they*
> *[... said as follows]: "He is our [Lord (?)]. A king's daughter is his wife,"*
> *[...], and if evil should be done to [him ... we shall avenge (?)] it, and if*
> *(instead) good should be done [to/for ... him ... we shall ... repay it (?)*
> *...] so they all said."*[75]

But had Urhi-Teshub, in fact, sought refuge with Pharaoh in the first place, and if so, when and under what circumstances had he left Egypt? Certainly, given the political stakes, Hattusili might believe false rumors and Ramesses, likewise, would have every reason to deny them.[76] Rumors of Urhi-Teshub's continued residence in Egypt might be nothing more than a figment of Hattusili's paranoid imagination.[77] But how likely is this scenario?[78]

The chronology of the Urhi-Teshub affair is impossible to determine with precision; historians can only offer possible scenarios.[79] By the time Ramesses wrote his letter to Hattusili about the Battle of Kadesh and his missive to the king of Mira, he had received multiple letters from Hattusili harping on about the Urhi-Teshub affair. He was surely exasperated, but repeatedly insisted the man was not currently in Egypt.

Apparently Pharaoh did not guard his "guest" too closely. With aid from a cadre of Hittite loyalists, Urhi-Teshub likely slipped away and headed north. A very fragmentary message from Pharaoh makes an intriguing reference to someone "in a fisherman's boat."[80] Why would Ramesses mention such a humble craft in a diplomatic letter unless its passenger was someone of importance, perhaps the elusive Urhi-Teshub fleeing Egypt?

It is doubtful Ramesses would have confessed to letting Urhi-Teshub go, either through lax security or by intention. More likely Hittite merchants and diplomats told their king about his nephew's flight. Soon rumors began to circulate that Urhi-Teshub had resurfaced in Syria.[81] Hattusili, viewing this as an existential threat to his regime, wrote furiously to Pharaoh demanding to know where he was—and how Ramesses planned to apprehend him!

Doubtless reminding Ramesses of his treaty obligations to support him against this his greatest enemy, Hattusili enjoined his ally to spare no expense and make full use of his military forces to recapture the fugitive. Rather than invoking the treaty's extradition clause to repatriate Urhi-Teshub, his uncle at last decided he was simply uncontainable in Hittite custody. In his homeland, Urhi-Teshub might rally his former subjects in a counter coup. Ironically, it now seemed safer to keep him in Egypt. Still, someone had to catch him first. Hattusili's letters to Egypt have vanished, but Pharaoh rehashed this recurring ultimatum in his own messages. In his response to the king of Mira, Ramesses complained:

> He (Hattusili III) writes to me repeatedly about him (=Urhi-Teshub) as follows: "Let the Great King, the King of Egypt, have his infantry and [his chariotry] exert themselves, and let him expend his gold, his silver, his [ho]rses, his copper, [and his garmen]ts in order to bring Urhi-[Teshub back to Egypt...].[82] He should not allow him to become strong (?)] and to wage wa[r against Hatti..." That is what the Great King], the King [of Hatti, my brother wrote to me...].[83]

Impatient with these demands and baffled (perhaps) as to Urhi-Teshub's whereabouts, Ramesses lashed out in twin missives to Hattusili and Queen Puduhepa.[84] When Hattusili reminded him of his treaty obligations, Ramesses insisted he had done all he could, and denied any knowledge of Urhi-Teshub's location.[85] Taking a poke at his "beloved brother," Ramesses questioned, in sarcastic tones, whether Urhi-Teshub was running loose in Hittite-controlled territory, with support from vassal kings disloyal to Hattusili:

> See, this Ur[hi-Teshub] about whom [you have written me these m]any, many [words which are not] wor[th hearing, is it not the case that h]e went to the land of Kizzuwatna? [Would the king of Kizzuwatna have] re[ceived him] and [return]ed him to you? Is it not the case that he went to the land of Aleppo? [Would] the king [of Aleppo have received him and returned] him to you? Is it not the case that he went to the land of Shubari? [Would the king of Shubari have received him and return]ed him to you? Is it not the case that he went to the land of Kadesh? [Would the king of Kadesh received him and return]ed him to you?[86]

In another letter Ramesses repeats this list, and questions the loyalty of Hattusili's vassals: "Are they so [trust]worthy, as you have told me? [Trust not the words that you hear (from them). They are] worthless!"[87] Whether these charges rang true or not, it left Hattusili nonplussed and humiliated to have Ramesses II expose his political weakness.

A Cold Peace

Urhi-Teshub's trail now grows too faint for us to follow. Did he once again prove too wily and exceedingly lucky, thereby eluding his pursuers?[88] Was he apprehended and returned to Egypt, to live out his days in exile? Whatever his ultimate fate, he ceased to be a constant irritant between the Egyptian and Hittite courts. His name crops up later only once, in an acerbic remark by Puduhepa as she negotiated Ramesses's marriage to a Hittite princess.[89]

Despite a turbulent start to the era of eternal "good peace and good brotherhood" inaugurated with the Silver Treaty, the two kingdoms remained at peace. Having ceded all claims to Kadesh and Amurru, Ramesses's days of bravery in combat were at an end. Now he only waged epistolary battles.

In his irritable dialogue with his Hittite ally, Pharaoh excelled as a canny negotiator and skilled manipulator, adroitly exploiting Hattusili III's political insecurities through psychological warfare. Yet, diplomacy was not just a bloodless form of combat.

Ramesses also knew how to sweeten the pot, supplying Hattusili and Puduhepa with a slew of lavish greeting gifts: gold cups and ingots, jewelry, ebony logs and furniture, caskets and beds overlaid with gold, statuettes of lapis lazuli and other costly gemstones, expensive dyed fabrics, gold and silver vessels and tableware, ornate horse tack, and Nubian slaves.[90] He even honored special requests for Egyptian doctors and medicines to treat Hattusili' ailments.[91] We are less well-informed about the gifts the Hittites sent to Egypt, but these included horses, for which the Hittites were renowned, and perhaps weapons of iron, still an exotic rarity at the end of the Late Bronze Age.[92]

At home, Ramesses celebrated the Silver Treaty as a diplomatic triumph, the capstone to his long record of valor on the battlefield. To a domestic audience, he claimed his Hittite enemy came to him in submission, "begging for the breath of life." Yet, his letters to the Hittite court offer us a tantalizing glimpse of a different Ramesses. Here, in these clay fragments, the mask of royalty peels away, and we see him as a real man after all. Vain and boastful, to be sure; a clever and canny politician; but also, as the years went by, an experienced elder statesman.

Nearing the thirtieth anniversary of his accession to the throne, Ramesses began preparing for the first of his Jubilee festivals. Always more than a mere mortal to his people, he had made himself Egypt's all-conquering hero. Now, before their very eyes, Ramesses II would transform himself into a living god.

Notes

1. This remarkable dossier of letters is second only to the Amarna Letters and exceeds them in the number of messages sent by a single individual, Ramesses II himself. Edel's masterful set of translations with commentary (*ÄHK* I–II) is the culmination of a lifetime of work on this corpus. Most of these tablets are fragmentary and Edel is often daring in his restorations of broken passages, even when they are based on his meticulous scholarship, unrivaled knowledge of the corpus, and parallels from other texts. Many of these restorations are possible because Ramesses II seems to have dispatched duplicate copies of some of his letters addressed separately to Hattusili III and Queen Puduhepa. Likewise, the formulaic nature of portions of the texts, especially the greetings at the beginning of the letters; the use of certain stock phrases; and the tendency of the letters to quote from previous messages and to repeat the same "talking points" from letter to letter, all aid in reconstructing some portions of the fragmentary letters with a degree of confidence. Nevertheless, Edel's restorations are often conjectural, especially passages that are not strictly formulaic. These are, of course, also the most historically significant, leaving Edel open to the charge of having invented crucial elements of the texts he translates—and therefore the "historical events" they allegedly reference—for which several reviewers took him to task: Beckman 1997b; Isre'el 1997; Zaccagnini 2000a. Most trenchant in this regard is Singer's (2006) discussion of the tenuousness of Edel's reconstructions of passages related to Urhi-Teshub. Cordani offers a new set of translations of the more intact passages from the better-preserved documents while eschewing Edel's restorations: Cordani, 2017, 27–31. With these caveats in mind, I have accepted some of Edel's more plausible restorations while rejecting those that seem too audacious. Still, much of this is reconstructed history, and readers should understand that passages enclosed in brackets [ ], especially those marked with (?), are hypothetical.

2. On the ideology of brotherhood among the Great Kings, see Zaccagnini 2000b; Bryce 2003, 76–85; Jakob 2006; Podany 2012.

3. For Egyptian-Hittite diplomacy under Ramesses II, see Gundlach, Raedler, and Roth 2005; Roth 2006; Jakob 2006; Brand 2007a; Breyer 2010a, 247–94; Cordani 2017, 24–60.

4. Edel identifies thirteen letters as belonging to this group (*ÄHK* I, nos. 7–19), but some are badly preserved and Cordani includes only seven of them (2017, nos. 3–9). This is in addition to the earliest letters Ramesses II exchanged with Hattusili (*ÄHK* I, nos. 2–6; Cordani 2017, nos. 1–2, 10).

5. Jakob (2006, 13) wrongly sees the phrase "our two countries have become one" as a concession on the pharaoh's part, which he takes as a sign of Egypt's supposed strategic weakness. Rather, it is a timeworn cliché in Egyptian-Hittite diplomatic exchanges going back to the Kurustama Treaty in the Eighteenth Dynasty; Groddek 2008. It is also typical of the sort of glib pleasantries with which Great Kings stocked their messages to their fellow "brothers." The expression is traditional, appearing in the Amarna Letters, in a letter from the widow of Nipkhururiya (*ÄHK* I, no. 1 recto 6′), as well as in the so-called Kurustama Treaty. The sentiment crops up again in later marriage negotiations between Ramesses and the Hittite royal pair; Roth 2003, 2006. See p. 362 below.

6. On the rituals and protocol of "greetings," Akkadian *šulmu*, see Moran 1992, xxii–xxiv; Zaccagnini 2000b, 142–45; Bryce 2003, 63–64.

7. On Puduhepa's life and role in international diplomacy, see de Roos 2006.

8. *ÄHK* I, no. 9; Cordani 2017, no. 5. The letters use his northern Egyptian alias Sethirkhopeshef rendered in Akkadian as Shutahapashap.

9. *ÄHK* I, no. 7. Sethhirkhopeshef's name is not preserved in the fragmentary letter, but is likely to have come between that of the king and Prince Ramesses Junior.

10. *ÄHK* I, nos. 12–13; Cordani 2017, no. 3.

11. *ÄHK* I, nos. 10–11; Cordani 2017, no. 4.

12. Xekalaki (2007) takes an optimistic view of the diplomatic role of Egyptian royal women. Roth (2002) offers a more nuanced analysis, contrasting the idealized (*fiktiven*) presentation of Egyptian queens in the contexts of foreign relations and the pharaonic worldview with the documented historical (*realen*) diplomacy. See also Breyer 2010a, 286–93. The frequency and scope of Egyptian royal women's role in diplomatic activity was limited and was subordinated to that of the pharaoh. On the Hittite side, Puduhepa's diplomatic portfolio was exceptional; see de Roos 2006; Breyer 2010a, 288–93, where he contrasts her role with Nefertari's.

13. *ÄHK* I, nos. 14, 16–17; Cordani 2017, nos. 6–8.

14. *ÄHK* I, no. 12; Cordani 2017, no. 3. Translation adapted from Beckman 2008, no. 22B.

15. Zaccagnini 2000a; Bryce 2003, 95–106. On the "international style" of exotic luxury goods that circulated as gifts between royal courts of the Late Bronze Age Near East, see Cochavi-Rainey and Lilyquist 1999.

16. Most scholars accept Edel's reading of the necklace's weight as 88 shekels. So, Cordani (2017, 68 with n. 2), who points out that this is not unusual for Egyptian jewelry. Zaccagnini (2000b, 441–42) reads the text as only "8 shekels," or about 75.2 grams. The weight of a shekel in the Late Bronze Age varied between 9.4 and 13.64 grams; Zaccagnini 2018. If the Egyptians were using the heavier standard, Puduhepa may have received a necklace weighing as much as 1200 grams or 42 ounces worth almost $76,000. Even in the worst-case scenario, where the necklace weighed only eight "light" shekels, its bullion value would still be more than $4,370 in August 2021 prices.

17. *ÄHK* I, no. 9 verso 10–14.

18. See Petersen and Kehrer 2016, 380–81. Interestingly, the hieroglyphic text uses the Egyptian term "Great Ruler," *ḥḳꜣ ꜥꜣ*, as the equivalent of the Akkadian term for "Great King of Egypt" that also occurs in the Karnak Peace Treaty Stela.

19. Edel (1994) interprets the costliest type of fabric as being "Byssus cloth." Byssus cloth, also called sea silk, was a rare and exceedingly precious material. The ancients created it from ultra-fine filaments secreted by a large species of Mediterranean marine clam called *Pinna Nobilis*, the Noble Pen Shell. Fabric woven from this rare substance was even finer than traditional silk. But the highest category of cloth mentioned in the gift lists more likely refers to "royal fabric," corresponding to the Egyptian term "royal linen," *sšr nsw*, or even "garment of a king"; see Zaccagnini 2000b, 441; Cordani 2017, 38–39.

20. Vogelsang-Eastwood, Hense, and Wilson 1999.

21. We should view intimations of face-to-face meetings between the Great Kings with skepticism: Bryce 2003, 85–89. Some are unduly optimistic that such meetings took place; e.g., Abo-Elaz 2019. Certainly, a Great King met with

his vassals, either in the overlord's capital or while he was touring his imperial possessions.

22. EA 3: Rainey 2015, 61–71.

23. The Amarna Letters are full of complaints from the Great Kings about Pharaoh's mistreatment of the envoys of his "brother" kings; Avruch 2000; Liverani 2013, 240. Hattusili III also complained when Ramesses II detained a Hittite messenger named Zuwa; *ÄHK* I, no. 39 recto 2′–7′.

24. One damaged letter (KBo 28.1) seems to mention the proposed visit to Egypt: *ÄHK* I, no. 4; Edel 1960; Cordani 2017, no. 1. A second document (KBo 8.14) is poorly preserved and Edel's restorations of it (*ÄHK* I, no. 5) are highly speculative and unfounded. Zaccagnini (2000b, 441) dismisses them as "far-fetched." Scholars have debated whether KBo 8.14 even belongs to the Egyptian-Hittite dossier. See most recently Cordani 2017, 157–58 (no. 46). Even if it does, there is no convincing evidence that it refers to the proposed visit.

25. *ÄHK* I, no. 4 recto 1–3. How definite was Hattusili's response? At the mercy of a crumbled clay tablet, we can only guess. Hypothetically, Hattusili offered a polite but equivocal "yes." Whatever qualifications or excuses he then offered precluding a summit have disappeared, because we only have a single letter from Ramesses with large gaps in the texts, who quotes only Hattusili's most favorable murmurings about the issue. The passage Edel reconstructs is badly broken and may not deal with the visit. Still, there may have been an earlier exchange of missives on the subject.

26. *ÄHK* I, no. 4 recto 16′–17′.

27. *ÄHK* I, no. 4 recto 19′–24′. Cordani (2017, no. 1) takes a minimalist approach to the surviving traces and considers the notion of Hattusili's visit to Egypt to be possible, but not certain.

28. In KUB 15.3, Queen Puduhepa vows to make a donation of ten gold objects inlaid with lapis lazuli to the Hittite Sun Goddess when her husband recovers from "inflammation of the feet"; Edel 1960, 20; de Roos 2007, 108. Interestingly, she also promises to send "true tidings" to Egypt as well. Texts of Hattusili III and Puduhepa reference his bouts of ill health starting in childhood; Singer 2002, 101.

29. Kitchen (1982, 90–91) concludes that the summit did take place, but his reconstruction of these events is questionable.

30. Bryce 2003, 89; Liverani 1990, 215–16; 2013, 242. Liverani describes it as a trap the Hittite king avoided, but he also notes (2013, 240) that the Great Kings never met in person except indirectly on the battlefield. In his 1990 article about Hattusili III "grappling with" Ramesside propaganda, he examines how Egyptian triumphalist ideology vis-à-vis foreign kingdoms and the often grandiose propagandistic literary and artistic expressions of Pharaoh as world ruler were created for an internal Egyptian audience, but this was received skeptically by other kingdoms.

31. On the family/household model of interstate relations among the Great Kings and the ideology of brotherhood, see the varied remarks of David, Zaccagnini, Avruch, Jönsson, Cohen, and Westbrook in Cohen and Westbrook 2000. See also Bryce 2003, 76–78; Podany 2012.

32. For the Amarna period, see Cohen and Westbrook 2000, passim; Bryce 2003, 59–85. For the Egyptian and Hittite envoys who shuttled between Egypt and Hatti under Ramesses II, see Gundlach, Raedler, and Roth 2005; Roth 2005; Zivie 2006; Cordani 2017, 48–54.

33. Avruch 2000. A good illustration of this dates from the Amarna period (EA 1:88–98) when the Babylonian king complains to Amenhotep III that the chariots of his diplomats were placed among those of Egypt's vassals in a grand parade held at the Egyptian capital, thus implying he too was Pharaoh's subject. For the resulting culture clash, see Liverani 1990, 2013.

34. *ÄHK* I, no. 20 recto 5–9; Cordani 2017, 78–79 (no. 11).

35. Brand 2007a, 22–23.

36. EA 42; Rainey 2015, 362–63. Slighting the pharaoh in the same manner, Suppiluliuma even reduced Akhenaten's royal name to a demeaning diminutive "Huria"; see Murnane 1990, 35–37.

37. Mynářová (2009) discusses the change in epistolary forms between the Amarna and Hattusa archives. Clearly, protocol seems to have changed. Most of the Hattusa archive consists of letters from Ramesses II and his court to Hattusili III and Puduhepa. Yet, Hattusili also names himself first in a message to Kadashman-Enlil II; Beckman 2008, no. 23. Nor do we read of similar complaints about greeting protocols in this letter, or in others between Hittite and Assyrian kings in this period; Beckman 2008, nos. 24A and 24B. Could it be that Ramesses II's supercilious manner had prompted other Great Kings to abandon traditional etiquette?

38. Beckman 2008, 139.

39. *ÄHK* I, nos. 20 and 22; Cordani 2017, nos. 11–12.

40. For an inventory of the best-preserved permutations of the names and titles identifying Ramesses II and Hattusili III in the correspondence, see Mynářová 2011, 238–42. She excludes examples where Edel has wholly restored any of these.

41. *ÄHK* I, no. 76 recto 1–2; Cordani 2017, no. 38.

42. I see this differently from Mynářová (2011, 240–42), who argues that the use of Ramesses's names and titles are "purely functional," reflecting social and political parity between the pharaoh and his Hittite counterpart. But clearly something irked Hattusili in the pharaoh's tone. We should not assume that Egyptian kings always followed protocol in their diplomatic correspondence or maintained a diplomatic sense of parity and reciprocity in their international relations while expressing their innate sense of superiority only in their formal inscriptions targeting a domestic audience. The clash of these two conflicting viewpoints surfaces in the hieroglyphic text of the Hittite treaty stela at Karnak: Jackson 2018. See pp. 302–3 above. Egyptian exceptionalism often spilled over into the letters Ramesses II sent to Hattusa as he willfully ignored the rules of parity and reciprocity. Magnifying his status by including both his nomen and prenomen was one way to assert his superiority. Ramesses was not entirely consistent in his letters, and there are cases where he only used one of his two names: *ÄHK* nos. 14, 16, 19. Yet, the frequency with which he used both is telling. In the so-called *insibiya* letters dating to the forties or fifties of his reign, the pharaoh added unique Egyptian titles before his nomen and prenomen. See p. 424–25 below.

43. *ÄHK* I, no. 22 recto 13′–19′; Cordani 2017, no. 12.

44. *ÄHK* I, no. 32 recto: 20′–24′; Cordani 2017, no 14.

45. *ÄHK* I, no. 32 recto: 24′–27′; Cordani 2017, no 14.

46. *ÄHK* I, no. 75; Cordani 2017, no. 37. For translations and commentary, see also Bryce 1998; 2003, 121–23; Beckman 2008, 137–38.

47. *ÄHK* I, no. 75. Translation adapted from Beckman 2008, 138. See also Cordani 2017, no 37.

48. In a different vein, Cordani (2017, 145–46) views the letter as the product of Ramesses's acute embarrassment over the strange request, which he then tried to smooth over by proffering the requested medical aid even though he knew it was futile. Given the intermixing of insincere chatter about brotherhood and good will with gratuitous invective from both sides, I doubt Ramesses was trying to be conciliatory. Otherwise, why mention Matanazi's age in the first place?

49. KBo 1.15+1.19: *ÄHK* I, no. 24 recto 42´–verso 3; Cordani 2017, 86–87 (no. 13).

50. Liverani 1990.

51. Liverani 2013, 241.

52. Mynářová 2009; Prakash 2011. See pp. 155–56 and fig. 5.30 above.

53. Edel 1950; Liverani 1990, 211–13; *RITANC* II, 13–14; Bryce 2003, 89–90. Edel reconstructed the fragments (KBo 1.22 and KBo 1.15+1.19) as belonging to one letter, but they probably stem from two separate documents based on petrographic analysis. See Cordani 2017, 81–82.

54. KBo 1.15+1.19: *ÄHK* I, no. 24 recto 8´–16´; Cordani 2017, 85.

55. Edel restored broken passages in the letter(s) drawing on Ramesses II's formal commemoration of the battle in the Bulletin and the Poem. In eschewing most of these, Cordani (2017, 83) notes that the version of events the pharaoh outlines in his response to Hattusili III did not necessarily correspond to the monumental texts. But how likely is this considering that (a) preserved elements of the letters *do* in fact correspond to the official version, as when Ramesses states that his troops and chariots were not with him and Hattusili's ironic questioning of this statement, and (b) the likelihood that Pharaoh had long since come to believe his own version of events, and/or that (c) he would have maintained his preferred version of events in correspondence with his rival-cum-ally to save face, especially after the Hittite monarch had challenged it. See also Liverani 1990, 212.

56. Edel's restoration seems warranted by comparison with a similar passage: *ÄHK* I, no. 24 recto 32´–33´.

57. One might quibble with the precise wording of the broken passages Edel restores (followed by Kitchen, *RITANC* II, 13–14), but they likely referred to the same incidents recorded in Kadesh narrative. Still, I have included only some of them, marking the least-certain ones with (?).

58. *ÄHK* I, no. 24 recto 17´–33´; Cordani 2017, 85–86.

59. The name is not fully preserved. For Sidon as the town in question, see Kitchen, *RITANC* II, 20–21. Edel's reconstruction of the broken passage following this (*ÄHK* I, no. 24 recto 38´–39´) is speculative. See Cordani 2017, 86.

60. Edel restores and interprets this passage as a quote from Hattusili III's previous letter in which the Hittite king boasts of having conquered three kingdoms after the Egyptian armies retreated, the third, according to him, being Upe. So, *ÄHK* I, no. 24 recto 35´–37´. Followed by Kitchen, *RITANC* II, 14.

61. See n. 59. Obsomer's itinerary (2016, 128, fig. 26) required Ramesses II to move north once he reached the coast after coming inland from the southern end of the Beqaa Valley.

62. *ÄHK* I, no. 24 recto 34´–40´.

63. Another document (*ÄHK* I, no. 25) consisting of pair of fragments (KUB 30+31), also seems to refer to the Battle of Kadesh, but is not part of KBo 1.15+1.19 or of KBo 1.22 (*ÄHK* I, no. 24). Nor is it one of the "parallel letters" sent to Puduhepa, but likely a copy the Hittite chancery made of an Egyptian original; see *ÄHK* II, 97–98; Cordani 2017, 82. The fragments of KUB 30+31 are so poorly preserved that Edel's restorations must be viewed with considerable skepticism.

64. Bryce 2003, 2005.

65. *ÄHK* I, no. 28; Cordani 2017, no. 17.

66. *ÄHK* I, no. 28: 7–13.

67. Edel took this phrase as Ramesses II's denial of having recognized Urhi-Teshub as king, but the pharaoh is disclaiming knowledge either of *where* Urhi-Teshub is or—quite disingenuously—even *who* he is; see Singer 2006, 31, n. 19; Cordani 2017, 95 and n. 7.

68. Following Beckman 2008, 131. The phrase literally means: "Should I have mentioned it with my mouth?"; Cordani 2017, 96 and n. 1.

69. *ÄHK* I, no. 28 verso 4′–11′ and 20′–24′. Translation adapted from Beckman 2008, 130–31 (no. 22D) and Cordani 2017, 94–96 (no. 17).

70. Cordani (2017, 93–94) sees the letter as the means by which Ramesses could defend himself against charges of collusion with Urhi-Teshub while also signaling his irritation with Hattusili's repeated accusations regarding the fugitive.

71. The standard epistolary practice among the Great Kings was to repeat the wording of earlier messages verbatim in their responses to their correspondents. The absence of any such quotes from Kupanta-Kurunta's lost letter is noteworthy and was all the more troubling to his overlord Hattusili, who might never know what the king of Mira had said.

72. We only know of Hattusili's demand for extradition from his letter to the Babylonian king Kadashman-Enlil II. But this was before the Silver Treaty would have obliged Ramesses to do so. See pp. 291–92 above. See also Brand 2007a.

73. *ÄHK* I, no. 28 verso 13′–16′.

74. So a group of people, but not necessarily "sons of Hatti," as Edel restores; see Singer 2006, 32 n. 26.

75. KBo 1.22. Reconstructed by Edel *ÄHK* I, no. 24 verso 35–41. For a more judicious translation, see Cordani 2017, 84–85. Edel's restorations are perhaps too extensive, but the gist of the passage seems to be that the men who came before Pharaoh would take revenge for any evil done to Urhi-Teshub and reward those who aided him. A similar statement is made in *ÄHK* I, no. 25 (KUB 3.31 verso 7′ and 9′): "a king's son-[in-law], and we will not hand him over … [we will not] take him [away] and we will not hand him over." Although Ramesses only refers to him as "this man," it is hard to imagine who else the subject of this exchange could be other than the deposed Hittite ruler himself, especially since he names Urhi-Teshub directly elsewhere in the letter and the deposed ruler was an ongoing irritant in Egyptian-Hittite diplomacy. Why should this person be Hattusili III's son Nerikkaili, as Singer suggests (2006, 32–33)? Nerikkaili is not mentioned in this letter, and Singer is overly skeptical that the passage refers to Urhi-Teshub (followed by Cordani 2017, 85 n. 1). He is on firmer ground rejecting Edel's suggestion (*ÄHK* II, 120) that Urhi-Teshub had married the daughter of the Babylonian king Kadashman-Turgu.

76. Cordani (2017, 76–77) notes that the issue of Urhi-Teshub's flight to Egypt and the diplomatic fracas that resulted from it—starting with Hattusili III's complaint to the Babylonian King Kadashman-Enlil—cannot be verified today. This, she argues, would be true whether the controversy erupted before or after the Egyptian-Hittite peace accords. But she also asserts that Hattusili pursued the peace treaty to "stem the fracture in relations" with Egypt and to minimize Urhi-Teshub's threat to the stability of his regime.

77. And if so, did Hattusili misrepresent the pharaoh's denial that Urhi-Teshub was in Egypt as a refusal to extradite him in the Hittite king's famous letter to Kadashman-Enlil? This is unconvincing.

78. Singer (2006, 31–32) argues that Ramesses denied knowing about Urhi-Teshub, not because it was true, but as a pretext for refusing to extradite him.

79. Houink ten Cate 2006; Bryce 2003, 213–22; Singer 2006; Cordani 2017, 75–78; Bányai 2010.

80. KUB 3.27: *ÄHK* I, no. 26 verso 6´; *ÄHK* II, 122. The reading of this term as "fisherman's boat" is disputed by Singer (2006, 35 n. 37) but accepted by Cordani (2017, no. 15, 91). Given the striking similarities in phraseology between this letter and the missive Ramesses sent to the king of Mira, Singer's proposal that KUB 3.27 refers to payment for an Egyptian grain shipment to Hatti strains credulity. He is trading one "audacious scenario" for another.

81. Hattusili also directed his vassal, King Benteshina of Amurru, to apprehend "the enemy of His Majesty," presumably Urhi-Teshub, and to "capture him (and) bring him to me." In his reply to this directive (KUB 3.56), Benteshina denies that Urhi-Teshub was in Amurru, writing, "I do not know if he is in the land of Egypt or whether he is in some other land"; see Singer 2006, 33–33. It is not clear when Benteshina wrote this letter, but Urhi-Teshub was, in Singer's words, a "hot potato" and neither Ramesses II nor the king of Amurru cared to admit his presence in their lands.

82. Compare KUB 3.27 (*ÄHK* I, no. 26 verso 13´–14´): "and give silver and give [bronze and give garments and give horses, so that] this man can be [brought] to Egyp[t]."

83. *ÄHK* I, no. 28 recto 14–20. Compare Cordani 2017, 95. Translation adapted from Beckman 2008, 130.

84. *ÄHK* I, nos. 26–27; Cordani 2017, nos. 15–16. Despite their poor condition, the surviving traces from both documents bear striking resemblances to the letter Ramesses addressed to the king of Mira.

85. This appears to be the essence of damaged statements in two of the letters. *ÄHK* I, no. 24 verso 25 and no. 27 recto 13´. Edel's colorful restoration that has Ramesses describing Urhi-Teshub as having "flown" and been "set free" "like a bird" is unfounded. In these passages, and another (no. 20 verso 18´), the word "bird" is not preserved.

86. KBo 1.22: *ÄHK* I, no. 24 verso 29–34.

87. *ÄHK* I, no. 29 recto 20–21.

88. Our confusion about Urhi-Teshub's ultimate fate is chronological and geographical. Where did he end up and when? On this, the views are wide ranging. Bányai (2010) sees him as the king of Zulabi in Syria. Bryce (2003, 219–23) argues that he established an independent kingdom for himself and his descendants in southern Anatolia.

89. *ÄHK* I, no. 105 recto 11′–12′: "[Since Urhi-Tesh]ub is there, ask him if this is true or not!" See p. 361 below.

90. On the gifts, see Cochavi-Rainey and Lilyquist 1999, 195–210; Cordani 2017, 37–39.

91. Edel 1976; Bryce, 2003, 124–25.

92. In one letter (*ÄHK* I, no. 23; Cordani 2017, no. 31) Ramesses expresses his enthusiasm for a promised shipment of Hittite horses. Hattusili himself asked for stallions, in particular tall foals, from the Babylonian king Kadashman-Enlil II, expressing his concerns about older and shorter horses that Kadashman-Turgu had sent him, which did not survive the harsh winters in Hatti (Beckman 2008, 143). In a letter to Adad-nirari I, Hattusili demurs about a shipment of iron ingots and weapons the Assyrian king had requested, explaining that it was "a bad time for making iron" (Beckman 2008, 148). An iron dagger with a gold hilt and crystal pommel found on the mummy of Tutankhamun may have been a diplomatic gift from Hatti; Cochavi and Lilyquist 1999.

CHAPTER TWELVE

A TIME OF WONDERS: THE EARLIEST ROYAL JUBILEES OF RAMESSES II AND THE FIRST HITTITE MARRIAGE ALLIANCE

The Royal *Heb-Sed* Festival in Ancient Egypt

The origins of Egypt's royal *Heb-Sed*, meaning "Festival of the Tail," reach back into prehistoric times during the fourth millennium BCE.[1] Among the oldest written documents in human history is a miniature inventory control tag, made from ebony wood and inscribed with the name and image of King Den of Egypt's First Dynasty, about 3000 BCE (fig. 12.1). Den's ebony tablet bears a tiny pictorial scene of two important episodes from his *Sed*-festival. Here we see Den running a ritual race around a course marked at each end with three boundary stones. Wearing the Double Crown of dominion over Upper and Lower Egypt, he grasps ritual objects in his hands as he lopes along. Next, Den sits enthroned on a podium beneath the shelter of a pavilion. Both the ritual race and the enthronement ceremony became key episodes in the liturgy of the *Sed*-festival over the succeeding three millennia of pharaonic civilization.

Often called the Egyptian pharaonic "Jubilee," the *Sed*-festival differed from modern royal anniversary galas like those Queen Elizabeth II celebrated on the twenty-fifth, fiftieth, sixtieth, and seventieth anniversaries of her reign. The *Heb-Sed* originated in prehistoric rites the Egyptians devised to test their monarch's fitness to govern after he had ruled for three decades with rituals that recharged his depleted physical and spiritual energies.[2]

Traditionally Egyptian monarchs observed their first *Sed*-festival once they reached their thirtieth year on the throne. Thereafter, they might hold *Heb-Sed*s every three years. Exceptions to this rule sometimes occurred. While Thutmose III celebrated his *Sed* during his thirtieth regnal year, his co-ruler, the female Pharaoh Hatshepsut, observed at least one Jubilee before this milestone. When Amenhotep III planned his first *Sed*-festival, the tradition had stood in abeyance for more than a century. Beginning in his thirtieth year, he staged a series of three

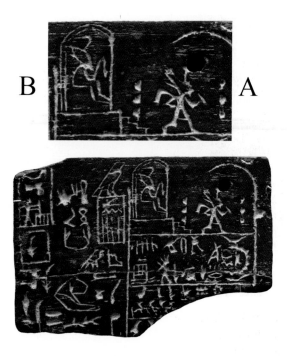

Figure 12.1. Ebony label of the First Dynasty king Den commemorating his *Sed*-festival. Above, detail of the upper-right corner showing the *Sed*-festival rites: (A) Den running a ritual race and (B) sitting enthroned in a pavilion. London, British Museum EA 32650. Wikimedia Commons.

Jubilees during the last decade of his reign.[3] His successor Akhenaten, a revolutionary in every way, celebrated a *Sed* in his early years as king.[4] Without breaking the thirty-year rule, few Egyptian rulers survived long enough to mark a *Sed*. Decades might elapse without a Jubilee.

Due to their rarity and antiquity, the rituals and procedures for staging a *Sed* evolved as historical memory of the original forms faded over the centuries. Amenhotep III reports how he delved into the archives and investigated the proper way to observe the feast. Amenhotep's three grand *Sed*-festivals blended innovation with time-honored ritual. Every ruler who held a *Sed*-festival adapted its observances to suit his needs, inventing new "traditions" and reinterpreting older ones.[5]

Evidence for this most ancient rite of pharaonic kingship lies strewn in isolated pockets across three millennia of Egyptian history. Our meager sources include Den's tiny ebony label; reliefs from the solar temple of the Fifth Dynasty king Niuserre; New Kingdom inscriptions of Amenhotep III, Akhenaten, and Ramesses II; and reliefs on the gateway of Osorkon II, which date to the Twenty-Second Dynasty.[6] All these sources are fragmentary, but enough remains to give us a broad overview.

A main event of the *Sed*-festival was a ritual race the king ran, without a competitor, around a field set with three stone boundary markers at each end. This course symbolized all Egyptian territory, and even the circuit of the entire world. By running around this track, a pharaoh proved his right to rule Egypt. In the earliest times, running this course

FIGURE 12.2. Ramesses II running a ritual race with a bull loping alongside him in the presence of Amun-Re. This idealized scene from the Great Hypostyle Hall at Karnak was carved in his first regnal year, three decades before his first *Sed*-fesival. Photograph by Peter Brand.

tested an aging king's physical fitness. After thirty years of rule, even a monarch who ascended his throne as a child had reached middle age when he marked his first *Sed*-festival (fig. 12.2).

As a king sprinted around the track, he carried various symbolic items. One was the *mekes*, a tubular case containing a papyrus scroll called a "household inventory document." This was the title deed to Egypt, declaring the pharaoh's ownership of every person, animal, and thing within his realm. Such inventories served as legal testaments, like a modern will, confirming the holder's ownership of his estate. In this case, Egypt was one grand household and the pharaoh was its master.

In a key observance of the *Sed*, the king paid homage to all Egypt's gods after gathering their cult statues in a great conclave. Resting within their booth-shrines lining the festival grounds, each deity received his adoration. In another ceremony, the king reconfirmed his rulership over the Two Lands by mounting twin thrones of Upper and Lower Egypt, placed side by side in a gilded royal pavilion atop a high dais.

Who was the audience for the *Sed*? Certainly Egypt's elite—courtiers, high priests, officials, and military officers—bore witnesses to its essential rituals. Some average folk from the lower ranks also enjoyed the spectacle. During the New Kingdom, vassal kings and envoys from other great kingdoms would attend as well.[7] The temple precinct of Ptah, in the historic capital of Memphis, often served as the traditional venue for the festival. Some kings held *Sed* rites in other cities. In Western Thebes, Amenhotep III built a huge, rambling complex of palaces and temples at Malkata.[8] There archaeologists found prodigious quantities of broken wine jars that once slaked the thirst of the revelers. The jars are dated to Amenhotep's three successive Jubilees, in his thirtieth, thirty-fourth, and thirty-seventh regnal years.[9]

An official of Amenhotep named Kheruef regarded these *Heb-Seds* as the highwater mark of his own career. He commissioned exquisite bas reliefs for his tomb informing us of their pomp and spectacle.[10] During his Jubilee decade Amenhotep built grand additions to temples in Thebes, including a vast solar court and his grand Colonnade Hall in Luxor Temple.[11] Even at Soleb, a remote site in distant Nubia, Amenhotep adorned a royal temple with carvings depicting scenes from his Jubilees.[12]

A few years later, his successor Akhenaten held an unorthodox *Sed*-festival after reigning for only three or four years.[13] Gone were the shrines of Egypt's traditional pantheon. Instead, this event marked a coming-out party for Akhenaten's new religion, focused exclusively on the sun god Aten. On a virgin site lying just east of Amun-Re's temple complex at Karnak, Akhenaten erected several new temples dedicated to the Aten. Chief among these was a building he dubbed the *Gem-pa-Aten*, or "the Sun Disk is Discovered." It consisted of a huge peristyle courtyard lined with columns on all four sides.[14] In the large open area at its center a privileged crowd witnessed Akhenaten and his young family arrive in their palanquins to stage his unique version of the *Sed*.

The climax of traditional *Heb-Seds* came when Egypt's gods in unison acclaimed the celebrant's right to rule.[15] Preparing for this momentous occasion, Pharaoh dispatched trusty officials to towns and cities all over Egypt to collect their sacred cult idols. Many were crafted from precious substances like gold and silver, and inlaid with gemstones of carnelian, lapis lazuli, and turquoise. Cult statues of prominent deities like Amun-Re of Karnak, Hathor of Dendera, Min of Coptos, and Re-Horakhty of Heliopolis were transported to Memphis, along with those of local gods and goddesses. This conclave of deities witnessed the pharaoh performing his *Sed* rituals. In exchange for his homage, they blessed his continued rule over Egypt and its Empire.

Mustering divine icons from every corner of the realm presented a daunting logistical challenge. They came from major centers like Thebes and Heliopolis and small towns up and down the Nile throughout Egypt and Nubia. In the Twentieth Dynasty, an inscription records how Ramesses III granted the vizier of Upper Egypt himself, a man named Tao, the honor of collecting the cultic effigies and escorting them to Memphis for his Jubilee in the thirtieth year of his reign.[16]

An even greater challenge—as often happens after a celebration filled with revelry and free-flowing wine—was ensuring all the gods and goddesses arrived home safely after the party. During the last four decades of Ramesses II's reign, these idols had shuttled back and forth between their hometowns and the Jubilee venue more than a dozen times. When Merenptah succeeded his aged father as king, he commissioned a scholar-priest named Ioti to hunt down every last one of the holy statues and ensure they had all returned to their proper shrines. Ioti left this short inscription commemorating his grand tour of inspection:

> Regnal year two, third month of the Inundation Season (Akhet), day twenty-seven, under the incarnation of the Dual King Baenre-Meramun, Son of Re Merenptah-Hetephermaat. His Person commanded to task the Royal Scribe, Chief Lector-Priest, and Great Chancellor Ioti, true of voice, with making a grand inventory of all the gods and goddesses of Upper and Lower Egypt.[17]

Ramesses II's First *Sed*-festival

As tradition dictated, Ramesses II celebrated his first *Sed*-festival in his thirtieth year.[18] As the first pharaoh to hold a Jubilee in decades, Ramesses eagerly awaited this milestone and laid ambitious plans to celebrate it in style. His bureaucrats accomplished countless logistical tasks before the festivities began. During their religious festivals the Egyptians consumed enormous quantities of food and drink, so a well-stocked larder was essential. Grand religious ceremonies involved processions of high dignitaries, sacred icons, sacrificial animals, musicians, dancers, soldiers, and charioteers. Someone had to marshal the requisite personnel, livestock, and equipment, and stock enough food, drink, and other consumables for the ravenous hordes of people who would soon descend on the festival grounds.

The guest list was extensive, a "who's who" of Egypt's elite: officials, courtiers, priests, military officers, and many more. Foreign guests were also prominent. From wall carvings depicting Akhenaten's *Sed*-festival we know he commanded Canaanite, Libyan, Nubian, and Syrian rulers from his vassal kingdoms, along with their personal retinues, to witnesses their overlord's Jubilee in person. Ambassadors from Great Kingdoms like Assyria, Babylonia, and Hatti also presented themselves.

When Ramesses II marked his inaugural *Sed*-festival, his first-born son Amunhirkhopeshef was dead and his second-born, Ramesses Junior, served as Crown Prince.[19] Sadly for the king, his favored wives Nefertari and Isetnofret were now years in their tombs. Although two of Nefertari's daughters succeeded her as great royal wives, it was Isetnofret's children who took center stage among Pharaoh's vast progeny. By year thirty Ramesses II had appointed the new Crown Prince's

FIGURE 12.3. A rock inscription from Aswan of Prince Khaemwaset commemorating his father's first three *Sed*-festivals. Lighter glyphs in the three rightmost columns are restored. Enhanced photograph by Peter Brand.

younger brother Khaemwaset as *Sem*-Priest of Ptah, the High Priest of Memphis. Given Ptah's special ties with the *Sed*-festival—Memphis being its traditional venue—Ramesses II appointed Khaemwaset as master of ceremonies.[20] In the final months before his inaugural Jubilee, Pharaoh directed Khaemwaset to announce it across the realm (fig. 12.3). As he traveled through Upper Egypt heralding the feast at every major town and city, Khaemwaset stopped at the sandstone quarries of Gebel es-Silsilah, where he left an inscription marking his pilgrimage in the shrine of King Horemheb:

> *Regnal year thirty, first occasion of the* Sed-*festival of the Lord of the Two Lands, Usermaatre-Setepenre, [given life eternally. His Person decreed] that the* Heb-Sed *be proclaimed in the entire land by the Sem-Priest Khaemwaset, true of voice.*[21]

Following Khaemwaset's pronouncement, throngs of officials, priests, courtiers, and the cult images of the gods themselves soon began migrating northward. Some fortunate servants and commoners hitched rides with social betters in need of their services. In droves they descended on Memphis for the great jamboree of Pharaoh and the gods.

At the receiving end of this jubilant mob of gods, men, and women stood various officials tasked with sorting out the affair's gargantuan logistics. A model letter a scribe named Mehy sent to Pawehem, a fellow penman, conveys the nervous excitement now gripping all these bureaucrats. Mehy admonishes his colleague to prepare chariots and stock provisions for ceremonies in Piramesses during Pharaoh's second Jubilee:

> *The Scribe Mehy of the Armory of Pharaoh, L.P.H., speaks to the scribe Pawehem as follows saying: Pay attention so as to accomplish all the*

orders given to your attention in a most proper and excellent way, and firmly like copper. Make sure to perform (all) the orders for the second Sed-festival in a most proper and excellent way and firmly like copper to ensure the chariots for the second Sed-festival are prepared.

Once they are ready, you should let me (know) to arrive at Piramesses-Meramun the Great Ka of Re-Horakhty. And you should inspect all that your associates have done, and you should do it (yourself). Do not sit around idly. The Sed-festival is coming to you! And you should give your attention to provisions for the festival offerings of Re-Horakhty in a most proper and excellent way and firmly like copper. And you should perform all these orders of yours. Do not let someone come to fight with you. You are a leader of men. As for all that they will do, you should do it too. Please know it! —end.[22]

This letter, and another like it, come from a collection of model writings used for training scribes. Mehy and Pawehem may not have been real men, but in advance of the Jubilee such missives flew about the kingdom from many an official to his underlings, all with a common battle cry: "The *Sed*-festival is coming to you!"

Despite its profound religious and ideological importance, Ramesses II's First Jubilee has left few traces in the historical record, forcing us to reconstruct it by comparing it to the better-attested *Sed*-festivals of Pharaohs like Amenhotep III.[23] Although no surviving temple reliefs depict Ramesses's *Sed*-festivals, he undertook an extensive campaign of monumental construction and decoration to herald them. In prodigious quantities, he directed his builders and sculptors to create new royal statues, obelisks, temple reliefs, and monumental inscriptions during his subsequent Jubilees, as he built new temples or enlarged existing ones at Memphis, Piramesses, and throughout Nubia.[24]

The main events of Ramesses II's Jubilees took place in Memphis and in Piramesses. At the west end of the temple precinct of Ptah in Memphis, he erected a large columned hall much like the Great Hypostyle Hall of Karnak.[25] A towering pylon gateway fronted this hall. Today the building is a shadow of its former glory: of its soaring columns, stout walls, and grand pylon gateways, only the granite bases are still intact, now standing in a fetid pool of groundwater. The main bulk of the structure consisted of limestone, which locals stripped away and recycled in later ages, leaving hardly a trace.

Relief decoration once covered this splendid building, but this too has mostly vanished. Eroded inscriptions indicate Ramesses built this hall during his Jubilee period. He raised another structure at Piramesses called "the Mansions of the *Sed*-festival." Only the name of this edifice has come down to us, recorded on a bronze ritual table that King Pseusennes I placed in his tomb at Tanis. The table is inscribed with texts referring to Ramesses II as beloved of Re-Hora-khty and Ptah-Tatchenen "in the Mansions of the *Sed*-festival."[26]

The Second Jubilee of Years 33/34

Ramesses II's first Jubilee, first in living memory, was only a warm-up act for his second *Heb-Sed*, which overshadows it in the historical record. From now on, these festivities extended for two weeks and they straddle the anniversary of the king's accession to the throne, on the twenty-seventh day of the third month of the Harvest Season (*Shomu*).[27] Thus, we date the second Jubilee to regnal years 33/34, the third to years 36/37, and so on. By a twist of fate, Ramesses's second *Sed* came at the exact midpoint of his reign. Later in his father's reign, Khaemwaset

Figure 12.4. Vizier Khay's announcement of Ramesses II's sixth *Sed*-festival in Regnal Year 45. Champollion's drawing of a stela from the shrine of Horemheb at Gebel es-Silsila. NYPL digital collections. Public domain.

retired from his triennial journeys across the realm, leaving it to other senior officials beginning with the Vizier Kay for the sixth jubilee in year 45 (fig. 12.4).

Years 33/34 also marked the pharaoh's zenith in terms of his achievements.[28] By ancient standards he had already ruled a lifetime. Most of his subjects were born after Ramesses became king, and few still remembered the days of Sety I. Ramesses had transformed Egypt's monumental landscape and the strategic face of the ancient Near East as the most senior and powerful king of his age.

After two decades of warfare, his peace treaty with Hattusili III had brought him a dozen years of stable relations with Egypt's former enemy. On the historic occasion of his second *Sed*-festival, Ramesses cemented his bonds with the Hittite Empire by taking Hattusili's daughter as his bride.

Diplomatic Marriage in New Kingdom Egypt

In the ancient Near East, Great Kings often gave their daughters or sisters in marriage to their fellow monarchs and acquired their colleagues' daughters in return.[29] To celebrate these marriage alliances Great Kings exchanged scintillating arrays of opulent gifts.[30] The bride's father bestowed a rich dowry, while the groom sent an equally spectacular bride price in exchange. On each side, this largess comprised prodigious quantities of luxury goods crafted from precious metals and rare commodities. Likewise, most Great Kings forged political ties with their vassal kings by marrying female relatives to them, as Hattusili III had done when he gave his sister Matanazi to King Masturi of the Seha River Land.[31]

New Kingdom rulers held themselves aloof from these two-way exchanges of princesses, insisting on a policy of Egyptian exceptionalism. They happily wed as many foreign brides as they could, both from their vassals and other Great Kings.[32] But they were loath to give their own royal women in marriage to any foreign ruler. When the Babylonian King Kadashman-Enlil I solicited Amenhotep III for an Egyptian princess, Pharaoh famously rebuffed him with the imperious rejoinder: "Never from the beginning of time has the daughter of the King of Egypt been given to anyone!"[33] Kadashman-Enlil retorted that Amenhotep could substitute another Egyptian maiden:

> *You are a king; you can [do] whatever you want. If you were to give (a daughter) who c[ould say] anything? ... There are grown daughters [of someone], beautiful women. Send one as if she were [yo]ur [daughter]. Who will say, "she is not the King's daughter?"*[34]

Although he scored a point with this sly innuendo, the Babylonian had to look elsewhere for a princess-bride. But he willingly offered his own daughter to Amenhotep.[35]

The Egyptians reversed this ban just once during the New Kingdom—with disastrous results—when the pharaoh Niphururiya's widow attempted a diplomatic marriage with the Hittite prince Zannanza. But when Zannanza died under mysterious circumstances while journeying to Egypt, his father Suppiluliuma accused the Egyptians of assassinating his son.[36] But as the Bible records, several hundred years later, in the tenth century BCE, when Egypt had lost its empire, an unnamed pharaoh offered his daughter to King Solomon, cementing an alliance with Israel:[37]

> *And Solomon became allied to Pharaoh, king of Egypt, by marriage, and took Pharaoh's daughter, and brought her into the city of David, until he had made an end of building his own house, and the house of the Lord, and the wall of Jerusalem around it.*[38]

In the New Kingdom, Egypt was a superpower and monarchs like Amenhotep III could dictate to other rulers that any movement of royal brides would flow in one direction—toward Egypt. His fellow Great Kings tolerated Pharaoh's conceit, knowing they might acquire staggering sums of gold and many prestigious gifts if they indulged his hubris. Indeed, Kadashman-Enlil I relented when Amenhotep requested a second Babylonian princess, but he haggled with the Egyptian monarch for a lavish bride price rich in gold. The pharaoh haughtily scorned his colleague's mercenary greed with the retort: "Is it fitting that you give your daughters in order to acquire a gift from your neighbors?"[39] Women exchanged between royal courts were indeed a valuable commodity, bringing treasure, enhancing prestige, and promoting good relations between the kingdoms of the ancient Near East. The daughter of Hattusili III would serve all these ends, surpassing any foreign bride in the queenly status Ramesses conferred upon her.

Ramesses II's First Hittite Marriage

Ramesses II welcomed multiple foreign princesses into his royal household but we only have hints of these alliances, which crop up in his diplomatic correspondence with the Hittites.[40] He wed at least one Babylonian princess, and may have obtained others from Assyria, Hanigalbat, and the Syrian kingdom of Zulabi.[41] Ramesses took advantage of any opportunity to enhance his prestige by acquiring foreign brides. And, although he begat over fifty daughters of his own, he surely spurned offers from other Great Kings to marry any of them.

Egypt's six decades of enmity with Hatti may have precluded any Hittite princess marrying a pharaoh. Even after the Silver Treaty, more than a decade elapsed before the two sides considered a marriage alliance.[42] Once Ramesses announced the union, his poet-scribes heralded his Hittite bride's arrival as a god-given wonder. Unlike his other diplomatic unions, Ramesses immortalized these nuptials in his First Hittite Marriage Stela. The edict's text is florid and bombastic, presenting the wedding as if Hatti's king came kowtowing before Pharaoh. The true story unfolded differently. We can observe behind the scenes as Ramesses II haggled with his future in-laws, thanks to remarkable letters he exchanged with Hattusili III and Queen Puduhepa.

Bartering for the Bride

We are not sure when Hattusili III broached the notion of a marriage deal, but it must have been at least a couple of years before the princess arrived in Egypt. The dickering over terms rambled on for months, with envoys shuttling back and forth between Piramesses and Hattusa, an overland trip of more than a thousand miles each way. By chariot, the journey took a month or so, longer for emissaries loaded with gifts and a retinue, but perhaps less for the speediest couriers traveling light.[43] If we add to this the weeks, or even months, when diplomats cooled their heels in either capital before the king released them, we can imagine the process took many months, if not years.

As with their exchanges on other matters, the "marriage dossier" blends fulsome expressions of harmony with hard bargaining and occasional invective. Although the prospective royal in-laws exchanged several sets of letters on the marriage question, they never named the Hittite princess, alluding to her simply as "the daughter." Today we know her only by her Egyptian name, Maahorneferure, which Ramesses II gave her when she arrived at his court. Nor do we know her rank among Hattusili III's many offspring. To boost his prestige, Ramesses II's First Hittite Marriage Decree claims she was the Hittite king's eldest daughter.[44]

Hattusili III took part in the discussion, but in the face of a wily customer like Ramesses II, the Hittite king played his trump card: a strong-willed mother who demanded the best for her daughter. Queen Puduhepa assumed primary responsibility for brokering the match. She proved to be a canny and feisty advocate for her daughter's interests. Puduhepa was one of the few persons on earth who ever dared to rebuke Ramesses, or confounded him in a contest of wills. An adept matchmaker, Puduhepa's chief priority was ensuring Ramesses II conferred the title of great royal wife on her daughter, surpassing all his foreign wives in status, including those from the kingdoms of Babylonia, Assyria, and Zulabi.[45]

Puduhepa also fretted about her daughter's fate once she reached Egypt, and with good reason. Egyptian pharaohs were notorious for collecting princesses from distant kingdoms and "warehousing" them in the palaces of Memphis or Mi-Wer, where many of Pharaoh's wives and children dwelt.[46] Once a foreign bride entered these quarters, her royal kinfolk had trouble staying in touch with her. A notorious case was the sister of the Babylonian king Kadashman-Enlil I, who married Amenhotep III. When Amenhotep later requested the hand of Kadashman-Enlil's daughter, the Babylonian objected that Pharaoh would not let his envoys meet with his sister, or even confirm she was still alive. Babylonian diplomats did not recognize the woman Amenhotep's palace officials produced for them. Kadashman-Enlil feared the worst, but Pharaoh batted away these complaints as rubbish:

> *The men you sent were nonentities. One of them was [...], the other was an ass herder...There was not one among them who [knows her] who was close to your father and who [can identify her].*[47]

Amenhotep advised his counterpart to dispatch more knowledgeable diplomats who could visit the princess and see her relationship with Pharaoh. Only then could they clear up the matter. Besides, Amenhotep insisted, "if yo[ur sister is] dead then why would they conceal [her] de[ath and why] would we present anoth[er (woman)]?"[48]

Alas, for such Babylonian princesses, history tended to repeat itself. A century later, a distressing bit of news the Babylonian ambassador had passed on to Puduhepa now perturbed her equanimity. She point-edly raised the issue with Ramesses in one of her letters:

> When messengers traveled to visit the daughter of (the king of) Babylonia who had been given to Egypt, they were left standing outside. Ellil-bel-nishe, the messenger of the king of Babylonia told [me] this information. Because [I] heard this, why would I not write to my brother about it?[49]

This must *not* happen to her daughter, Puduhepa insisted:

> I will send my [me]ssengers regularly and my messengers [should be able to see] the daughter [and] should be able [to speak with her]. And the daughter [should be able to speak (?)] in the presence of my messengers. .. [The daughter] from the land of Babylonia who re[sides] in Egypt [...] and (she) cannot see anyone. And in [her] presence, [no messenger has ever] spoken![50]

"Not so!" cried Ramesses. Babylonian envoys met with her regularly and even took meals in her presence. That anyone should say other-wise was pure slander, and Puduhepa must not take such wild rumors seriously.[51]

Meanwhile, Ramesses II continued negotiating with Hattusili and Puduhepa. He informed them about offers arriving from other king-doms, calculating this news to worry the Hittite royal couple as much as it might reassure them:

> [... the Kin]g of Babylonia and the King of Haniga[lbat have written to me saying (?) ... "the daughter of the King of Hatti (?)] is to be sent to the King of Egypt and [the King of Egypt will make her Queen of Egypt (?)]. But [y]ou should put my daughter in her place!"[52]

Ramesses II's "assurances" rankled Hattusili III as being too disingenu-ous for comfort. Was Ramesses now seeking a better offer? Did he wish to start a bidding war among the Great Kings to see who might place his daughter in Pharaoh's bed—and her rich dowry in his coffers?[53]

To pin their slippery future son-in-law down, the Hittite king and queen insisted on some kind of marriage contract.[54] To alay their mis-givings, Pharaoh graciously promised—as the gods themselves would guarantee—that he would bestow the highest queenly status in Egypt on Puduhepa's daughter.[55] Ramesses poured on the charm:

> The Sun God and the Storm God will see to the completion of all the arrangements that my sister desires to be made for her daughter. They will install her in the household of the King, your brother, since she is intended for rule [in] Egypt. They will satisfy (both) my sister and the

King (Ramesses), your brother, with the arrangements they will make
for her.[56]

Letters from the marriage dossier preserve lists of gifts consisting of
gold and silver objects, expensive fabrics, and various luxuries in magnificent quantities. Ramesses enticed his future in-laws with ostentatious displays of generosity. One gift registry itemized dozens of gold
ingots, cups, jewelry, and other items, whose weight added up to the
princely sum of at least 1,779 shekels,[57] more than a million dollars at
current prices.[58] This staggering sum is *only* the value of gold bullion in
just *one* consignment of gifts. There was even more, because the list is
fragmentary, but the consignment still included:

> *17 shekels of silver objects*
> *two falcon-statues of costly stone and two more in gold inlaid with*
> *   assorted gemstones*
> *10 rings of precious stone*
> *207 pieces of clothing, including 69 "royal garments"*
> *40 beams of ebony wood*
> *6 vases and 20 baskets of eye medicine*
> *Gold drinking cups weighing 96 shekels*
> *1 bronze helmet and 1 piece of leather body armor covered in bronze*
> *   scales.*

Of course, this was merely the appetizer to a much grander spend-
ing-fest, once the marriage pact came to fruition.[59] Unfortunately, we are
ignorant of the full extent of the bride price Pharaoh gave to the Hittites,
but we do know a sumptous dowry came with the princess to Egypt.

This dowry became a chief bone of contention between Ramesses II
and his plucky future mother-in-law, Queen Puduhepa. Undermining
her bargaining efforts, her husband Hattusili III, like many a big-spend-
ing father of the bride, promised his future son-in-law a stupendous
dowry and a quick marriage deal:

> *Truly, the woma[n will be given to you (?)...] in a hurry! [And I will]*
> *provide her [with a dowry], and [her dowry will be bigger (?)] than*
> *[that of the d]aughter of the King of Ba[bylonia or of the d]aughter of*
> *the King of Z[ulabi, and I have count]ed up all that the wo[man will*
> *bring].*[60]

Pharaoh was, of course, delighted. Ramesses even vowed to build a new
palace for his bride. Moreover, her father would recoup his expenses
thanks to his equally lavish wedding gift to the Hittite royal pair: "[...
and my bride price will be greater than those of all] the other Great
Kings, so [we will be e]ven!"[61]

Much of the proposed Hittite dowry consisted of living chattels, both human and the four-legged variety, as Hattusili outlined to Pharaoh:

> Se[e, truly, I] will give my daughter [a dowry consisting of peasants], horses, cat[tle, and sheep, and I will send my daughter w]ho will be brought [into the land of my brother. I]n whi[ch] territory [(and) to which man should she be handed over?][62]

Ramesses told Hattusili to send the bride, the people, and the herds of livestock to Egypt's Syrian province of Upe.[63] From there an Egyptian military force would escort them overland to Canaan and thence to Egypt. Pharaoh would care for and feed all this living property as soon as they entered Egypt's domains.[64]

The human component of the dowry consisted of a large group of the Kaska people, an unruly population on the fringes of the Hittite Empire. Hattusili had doubtless captured them as prisoners of war. Eager to be rid of them, he proposed resettling them in Egypt. Egypt craved such bonded manpower, and Pharaoh would set them to work in some remote corner of his realm, perhaps one of his new settlements in Nubia. Once there, any hope of escape was nil. But Queen Puduhepa worried they might make a run for it and flee to their homeland on Hatti's northern border. Ramesses, familiar with these desert wastes, knew better: "[Whoever w]ishes to go [should go there (the desert). L]et them perish there!"[65]

The Empress Writes Back

As negotiations dragged on, both sides became testy. Ramesses II grumbled about the endless delays. He also wanted the dowry to include gold, silver, and bronze, in addition to perishable livestock and slaves the Hittite couple had pledged. Complaining to Puduhepa, he wrote:

> My sister wrote to me: "[I will give] a daughter to you." [But you have withheld her and] now you are angry [with me]. Why have you not now given her to me?"[66]

By this point, the Hittite Queen had exhausted her store of patience with Ramesses's quibbling and demands. Her scribes took down a long letter that she dictated in Hittite.[67] Remarkably, this draft has survived largely intact (fig. 12.5). If it is anything like the letter Pharaoh received, it must have made his ears burn. Puduhepa let fly every arrow in her rhetorical quiver as she scolded, nitpicked, cajoled, and apologized to him. In a sarcastic aside, Puduhepa also taunted Ramesses for harboring her husband's old nemesis:

*[I have indeed withheld my daughter]. You will not disapprove of it;
(on the contrary) you will approve of it! At the moment [I am unable
to give] her to you. As you, my brother, know, the treasury of Hatti, do
I not [know that it is] a burned-out structure? And Urhi-Teshub gave
what remained to the Great God. [Since Urhi-Tesh]ub is there, ask him
if this is true or not!*[68]

Her verbal barb about Urhi-Teshub is puzzling. Did the deposed Hittite
king still reside in Egypt a dozen years after the Peace Treaty? Or did
Puduhepa tear the scab off this old wound merely to score a point?
Next, the queen extolled her daughter's virtues, before upbraiding Ramesses for "gold digging" about her dowry:

*With whom should I compare the daughter of heaven and earth whom
I will give to [my] brother? Should I compare her to the daughter of
Babylonia, of Zulabi, or of Assyria? If I am not to make her inferior to
them or make her (merely) their equal (?)[...]*[69]

    *Does my brother not possess anything at all? Only if the Son of the
Sun God, the Son of the Storm God and the Sea have nothing, do you
have nothing! But, my brother, you would enrich yourself at my expense.
That is worthy neither of prestige nor lordliness!*[70]

FIGURE 12.5. Queen Puduhepa's letter to Ramesses II responding to his complaints about delays in negotiations for his marriage to her daughter. KUB 21.38 (CTH 176). Alamy.

As for the tie-ups in sending the princess—and the Kaska folk and livestock of her dowry—Puduhepa offered a host of excuses. Messengers
from both sides had been delayed, since win-
ter had come and prevented the diplomats and
dowry from departing. If Ramesses did not believe her, he should ask his own envoys. Irked
herself with these hurdles, Puduhepa complained about the burden of feeding the living
dowry: "Regarding the prisoners, cattle, and
sheep that I will give for my daughter, in my
lands there is not even grain!"[71]

    Puduhepa now schooled Ramesses in the
twin issues of motherhood and diplomatic
protocol. "But my brother has [not accepted]
in his own mind my status as a sister and my
dignity," she complained.

*If [I had sent(?)] the daughter to my brother
[hastily(?)], or if I had [not] given [what was
due (the dowry) to] my brother or for his sister
(the Egyptian Queen), what would my brother
even then [have said]? Perhaps (he would say):
"May the woman whom they gave to me have*

some support, and [may] it [be generous] for her." That [would] be lordly behavior![72]

After tongue-lashing Ramesses with the unvarnished truth as she saw it, Puduhepa paints a portrait of herself as an emblem of Hittite motherhood and the soul of diplomatic courtesy, recalling her treatment of two foreign princesses her husband had married:

The daughter of Babylonia and [the daughter] of Amurru, whom I, the Queen, took for myself (as daughters-in-law)—were they not indeed a source of praise for me before the people of Hatti? It was I who did it. I took each daughter of a Great King, though a foreigner, as daughter-in-law. And if at some time his (the royal father's) messengers came in splendor to the daughter-in-law, or one of her brothers or sisters comes to her, is this not also a source of praise for me? Was there no woman available to me in Hatti? Did I not do this out of consideration for renown?[73]

Moreover, she insists, the marriage pact between Hatti and Babylonia redounded to the honor and glory of both kingdoms.[74]

Did my brother (the Babylonian king) have no wife at all? Did not my brother make these (marriage negotiations) because we are brother and sister and for our (mutual) honor? Did he not also marry the daughter of the Great King, the King of Hatti, the mighty King? If you (Ramesses) should say: "The King of Babylonia is not a Great King," then my brother does not know the rank of Babylonia![75]

After dispensing verbal jabs and candid advice to Ramesses, Puduhepa closes her letter on a more conciliatory note. Pharaoh asked the Queen to "write to me about any matters that might be on your mind and which you might wish to write to me about" when she turned her daughter over to his ambassadors.[76] To this open-ended invitation, ironically, to speak her mind, she responded in a friendlier tone:

This message is just what one would expect from my brother! Since the Queen is coming to Amurru, I will be near you, and from there I will write to my brother whatever matters are on the Queen's mind. You, my brother, will not disapprove of them; (rather) you will approve of them. When the daughter arrives at my brother's bed, these matters of the Queen will be settled.[77]

Near the end of her extended missive, Puduhepa expresses a highly idealized view of the impact of the marriage alliance on relations between their kingdoms, proclaiming: "Egypt and Hatti will become a single country."[78]

With, or perhaps despite, these heated negotiations, the two sides at last felt confident they had attained the desired outcome. Ramesses fired off parallel letters to Hattusili and Puduhepa expressing his delight at the forthcoming match, and assuring them their daughter would sit as queen by his side, just as Puduhepa had insisted:

> In respect to what my sister wrote [to] me regarding her daughter: "The Sun God has carried out my [wish], which I expressed to him, and he has made my heart rejoice." So, you, my sister, wrote to me. I am very [pl]eased about this relationship, which the Sun God created when he made [my] sister's heart rejoice regarding the wish she expressed to him.
> The Sun God and the Storm God will see to the completion of all the arrangements which my sister's heart desires for her daughter. They will install her in the household of the King, your brother, since she is intended for rulership [in] Egypt. They will satisfy my sister and the King (of Egypt), your brother, with the arrangements which they will make for her."[79]

At last, the parties reached a key milestone on the road to the marriage. Custom in the ancient Near East dictated that royalty should be anointed with oil. Now Hattusili III wrote to Pharaoh asking him to "seal the deal":

> [Let] people come and [pour oil of the finest quality on the head of my daughter, and may she be brought into the palace] of the Great King, [the King of Egypt, my brother].[80]

Ramesses complied happily and vowed to dispatch a messenger with aromatic oil to anoint the Hittite princess. Furthermore, he would send out troops to escort her to Egypt, so even the gods of the earth and the netherworld might witnesses their progress.

In the autumn of 1247 BCE, the bittersweet day came when Hattusili and Puduhepa saw their daughter off one last time. They chaperoned her as far as the Egyptian-Hittite border in Syria before saying their final goodbyes. As befitted her rank, and that of her parents, the Hittite princess traveled with a grand escort of ambassadors from both countries, Hittite troops and chariotry, and the myriad array of dowry gifts: Kaskean prisoners, herds of horses, droves of cattle, and flocks of sheep and goats. At the "Town of Ramesses," they joined up with a large contingent of Egyptian infantrymen and chariotry.[81] Now this grand cavalcade wended its way southward through Lebanon and Canaan and on to Egypt. From here, we must turn to Ramesses II's bombastic memorial of the wedding, his First Hittite Marriage Decree.

A Wondrous Event

With his second *Sed*-festival and his marriage to the Hittite princess, Ramesses II's thirty-fourth year marked the true noontide of his long reign, coming precisely halfway between his accession and his demise.[82] His poet-scribes reached unparalleled heights in the lofty rhetoric they composed for a matching pair of royal decrees the king now promulgated: The First Hittite Marriage Decree of year thirty-four[83] and the Blessing of Ptah Decree of year thirty-five (fig. 12.6).[84] Today their flamboyant verbiage seems "over the top," but to ancient ears it resounded as high poetry.

Insisting that the scale of the inscriptions must equal their epic grandiloquence, Ramesses ordered his sculptors to carve grand stelae on the walls of several temples throughout his realm. A few of these survive today in Upper Egypt and Nubia. The most imposing editions occupy the façade of the twin towers of the Ninth Pylon at Karnak. Here clever artist-scribes nimbly arranged Ramesses II's cartouches to alternate between the beginning and end of every line. This zig-zag pattern carries the eye from one cartouche to the next in a rhythmic flow as the viewer scans the text.[85]

The best-preserved version of the Marriage Decree comes from Abu Simbel. A scene at the top sets the tone, lauding Ramesses II as a warrior and a god and portrays the Hittite king as a supplicant. Pharaoh sits enthroned in a shrine between Seth and Ptah-Tatchenen, his fellow dieties. Approaching the shrine with their hands raised in adoration come the Hittite princess-bride and her father. The Egyptian scribe never dignifies the Hittite monarch with his own name, calling him "the Great Chief of Hatti" (fig. 12.7).

Although Ramesses II and Hattusili III never met, in the Egyptian worldview the Hittite monarch comes to Egypt to grovel before Pharaoh and offer all his property—even his own eldest daughter—as tribute. The caption invents a fawning speech as he bows and scrapes:

> Words spoken by the great chief of Hatti: "I have come before you, I adore your perfection as the one who subdues foreign lands. You are truly the son of Seth, for he has decreed for you the land of Hatti. I have plundered myself of all (my) possessions, my eldest daughter foremost among them, to bring them before you. Good is all you have decreed for us, I am under your feet forever and ever, along with the entire land of Hatti. You have appeared upon the throne of Re, and every land is under your feet forever."[86]

Having never seen a Hittite monarch in person, the Egyptian artists took inspiration from Hittite royal seal impressions like those affixed

FIGURE 12.6. Ramesses II's First Hitite Marriage Stela, Abu Simbel. Photograph by Peter Brand.

to the Silver Treaty tablet.[87] On the stela, the Hittite monarch wears a long cloak and a conical cap. His daughter has been transformed into an Egyptian consort, the Great Royal Wife Maahorneferure, bearing two sistra in her hands in adoration of her husband.[88]

The stela text consists of two main sections. First comes a laudatory hymn praising the king in epic verse. This paean has ten stanzas, dwelling on different aspects of his kingship and godhood.[89] The second half narrates events leading up to the wedding itself. Seth, dynastic god of the Ramesside kings, is the catalyst of a series of miraculous occurrences. Seth embodied foreign lands and powerful natural forces

FIGURE 12.7. Lepsius's drawing of the scene from the First Hittite Marriage Stela at Abu Simbel. At right, the Hittite ruler and Maahorneferure gesture in adoration before Ramesses II enthroned in a shrine between Ptah-Tatchenen to his right and Seth to his left. NYPL digital collections. Public domain.

like storms and extreme weather. The Egyptians equated him with the Hittite storm god.

The story begins with a chauvinistic reimagining of Ramesses II's military prowess and the dread he instilled in other kingdoms—with one exception:

> Then the great chiefs of every foreign land heard about this mysterious nature of His Person. They recoiled in fear; terror of His Person filled their minds and they extolled his power while giving praise to his perfect face. [... they a]ll presented their children to him from among the great lords of Syria and the mysterious foreign countries unknown (to Egypt), to placate the heart of the Mighty Bull and to beg peace from him.
>
> They plundered themselves of their property and were taxed according to their yearly production; their children were in front of their tribute-offerings in adoration and servility to his name. Then every foreign land was bowed down beneath the feet of this Perfect God who makes his border wherever he wishes. None opposed him except for that One of this land of Hatti. For he was not like these (other) chiefs.[90]

As the alleged solitary hold-out against Ramesses II's claim to universal rule, the Hittite king incurred his wrath on the battlefield. Without naming specific places or incidents, even Kadesh, the text conforms to time-worn doctrines of Pharaoh's invincibility as a solitary warrior:[91]

> Then His Person said: "As my father Atum praises me forever as Ruler of the Two Lands, and as I glitter like the sun disk when it shines like Re in heaven upon its four pillars, I will bring the attack to the land of Hatti; they will be cast prostrate beneath my feet forever! I will make them retreat from fighting on the battlefield. They will cease boasting in their land, for I know my father Seth has ordained victories for me against every land—for he has fortified my strong arm as high as heaven and my might as broad as the earth."

> *Then he readied his army and his chariotry and they departed to the land of Hatti. He plundered it by himself in front of his entire army, making an everlasting name for himself among them so that they remembered the triumphs of his strong arm. Against those who escaped his hand he laid a curse. His power is among them like a blazing torch, no chiefs can rest secure on their thrones nor can they revive the hearts of their minions.[92]*

Next the decree conjures up another familiar trope: foreign lands plunging into chaos and the Hittite ruler's fictive plea of surrender:

> *Now after they passed many years with their land being destroyed and savaged in turmoil, year after year, through the power of the great living god, the Lord of the Two Lands and ruler of the Nine Bows, the Dual King, Usermaatre-Setepenre, the Son of Re, Ramesses-Meramun.*
>
> *Then the Great Chief of Hatti sent messages to appease His Person, extolling his power and exalting his triumphs saying: "Relent in your refusal (to make peace), abate your malice, permit us to breathe the breath of life. You are truly the child of Seth, he has ordained the land of Hatti for you; we are taxed as much as you desire, and we will carry these (taxes) to your august palace. See, we are beneath your feet, O mighty king! Do to us all that you have decreed."[93]*

In this idealized version of events there are, perhaps, some nuggets of truth, like Pharaoh's former resistence to peace accords and drought in Anatolia:

> *Then the Great Chief of Hatti spoke to his army and his officials saying: "How screwed up is this![94] Our land is destroyed, our lord Seth is angry with us, the heavens do not give (rain)water properly for us.[95] Every foreign land is an enemy, fighting us all together. Let us plunder all our property with my eldest daughter at the vanguard, to carry tribute-offerings to the Perfect God so that he might give us peace and we might live."*
>
> *Then he had his eldest daughter brought, with august tribute-offerings before her, consisting of gold, silver, great quantities of copper, slaves, teams of horses without limit, herds of cattle, goats, and sheep by the tens of thousands. There was no end to the property they brought.[96]*

As is typical for such Egyptian "historical" texts, the First Hittite Marriage Decree grossly simplifies and distorts actual events to frame its ideological themes. It never mentions the Silver Treaty thirteen years earlier, implying peace came only in Ramesses II's thirty-fourth regnal year, when the Hittite king at last "surrendered" to him. Hatti's "tribute offerings" were in fact the princess's dowry and the categories of gifts broadly correspond to the types discussed in the diplomatic messages.[97] But Egyptian scribes ignore the fact that Pharaoh gave Hatti a rich bride price of his own.

The Marriage Decree then recounts the Hittite princess's arduous winter journey with her prodigious dowry. Ramesses sends an honor guard of troops to meet them and beseeches his divine patron Seth to intercede and ensure the wedding party might arrive safely in Egypt:

> *Then someone came to inform His Person saying: "See, the Great Chief of Hatti has caused his eldest daughter to be brought bearing multitudinous tribute-offerings, and they cover the road with their coming! The great chiefs of Hatti together with the great officials of the land of Hatti are carrying them. They have crossed many hidden mountains and difficult passes and have reached the borders of His Person. Let the army and the officials set out to receive them."*
>
> *Then His Person was overjoyed, [entering] the palace happily after he heard of this miraculous event that was completely unknown to Egypt (before this). He sent the army and the officials to receive them promptly. His Person deliberated (these) matters in his mind, saying: "How will they do it, those whom I have sent, who go on a mission to Djahy in these days of rain and snow that happen in winter?" Then he presented a great oblation to his father Seth, after he had petitioned him saying: "The heavens are in your hands, the earth is beneath your feet. Whatever you command is all that happens. Make no rain, cold wind, or snow until the wonders you have decreed for me reach me."*
>
> *Then his father Seth heard all he had said. So the skies calmed, and the days of summer happened in winter—and his army and the officials departed, their limbs being cheerful, and their hearts swelled in joy.*[98]

Once Seth effected this marvelous change of weather, he sparked a new miracle by transforming the diplomatic climate between the two sides when they joined up and escorted the princess from Syria to Egypt. Now that peace had come, the official narrative salutes the camaraderie among soldiers on both sides and reports the chagrin of other foreign rulers at this wondrous turn of events:

> *The daughter of the great chief of Hatti marched to Egypt, while the army, chariotry, and officials of His Person followed her. They mingled with the army, chariotry, and officials of Hatti—the* Teher-*warriors like the (Egyptian) infantrymen and like his chariotry. All the people from the land of Hatti mingled with those from Egypt. They ate and drank together. They were of one mind, like brothers, without one distrusting his fellow; they were at peace and brotherly toward each other according to the design of the god himself.*
>
> *As for all the great chiefs of every land through which they passed—their faces shrank back and turned away in weakness after they saw the men from the land of Hatti as they joined up with the army of the king:*

> *(namely) the Dual King, the Lord of the Two Lands, the sovereign of the
> victorious strong arm, who protects Egypt. Then one would say to his
> fellow among these chiefs: "It is true what His Person said ... How great
> are these [wonders] we have seen with our own faces! Every foreign land
> is in his hand as servants. What was once the Land of Hatti, see, it is
> now in his grasp like Egypt! Even the heavens are under his authority,
> acting according to his every command.*[99]

More down to earth is the brief statement of one of the Egyptian envoys
named Huy who describes himself as "the royal messenger to every
foreign country who came back from Hatti bringing its great lady (the
princess)."[100] For this deed of errantry Pharaoh later promoted Huy to
be Viceroy of Kush.[101] Hidden from our view today were the impressive
logistics of this operation, which involved large numbers of personnel,
livestock, and captives who had to be fed, watered, and supplied. No
wonder Ramesses sent the army. But this regal spectacle reflected the
combined prestige and authority of the Egyptian and Hittite thrones,
enhancing them further.[102]

Amid lavish festivities the Hittite princess, her magnificent dowry,
and her combined Egyptian and Hittite retinue reached Piramesses in
Ramesses II's thirty-fourth year, during the third month of the Season
of Emergence (*Proyet*; ca. January 1246 BCE). At court, attendants bedecked her in the finery and regalia of an Egyptian Great Royal Wife.
Heralds announced her by her new Egyptian name Maahorneferure,
meaning "She Who Sees Horus—the Perfection of Re." Once they ushered her in to meet her royal husband, the result, we are told, was love
at first sight:

> *Then the daughter of the Great Chief of Hatti who had come marching to
> Egypt was brought into His Person's presence—a great many gifts came
> with her, without limit and of every kind. Then His Person saw she was
> fair of countenance, the foremost among women, and that the officials
> adored her as a goddess. Now it was, indeed, a great and mysterious
> and splendid marvel, which was unknown; it had not been heard of by
> word of mouth, nor could it be recalled in the writings of the ancestors:
> (namely) how the daughter of the Great Chief of Hatti came marching
> to ... Egypt. She was perfect in the opinion of His Person. He loved her
> more than anything, as a fortunate occurrence and as a triumph his
> father Ptah-Tatchenen decreed for him.*
>
> *Her [name was proclaimed] (as): The Royal Wife Maahorneferure—
> may she live—the daughter of the Great Chief of Hatti, and daughter
> of the Great Mistress of Hatti. One made her happy in the palace of the
> royal household, following the sovereign every day, and they announced
> her name throughout the [entire] land.*[103]

Fittingly, due credit is given to "the Great Mistress of Hatti," Queen Puduhepa, as well as the Great Chief Hattusili. Perhaps Ramesses had come to admire her after all. The text closes on a triumphant note: "Thereafter, if a man or woman went out on a mission to Djahy, they could even reach the Land of Hatti without fear filling their minds because of the victories of His Person."[104] Ramesses II took evident pride in his First Hittite Marriage Decree, which is among the longest compositions of his reign. He even commissioned a shorter version and had it inscribed on a large calcite stela erected in the temple precinct of the goddess Mut at Karnak.[105]

Ten months after the Hittite princess arrived in Egypt, Ramesses II issued a text known as the Blessing of Ptah. It dates to his thirty-fifth year, first month of the Season of Emergence (*Proyet*), day thirteen (late October 1245 BCE), and serves as a literary mate to the Hittite Marriage Decree. Couched as a dialogue between the Memphite fertility god Ptah-Tatchenen and Ramesses himself (fig. 12.8), the Blessing is even more rhetorical, if possible, than its mate. It echoes themes like Pharaoh's divine nature, his military accomplishments, his building projects, and the marvels his divine father Ptah-Tatchenen ordained for him. Among these prodigies, Ptah inspired the ruler of Hatti to submit to Ramesses and bring his daughter as living tribute to Egypt as a "great and mysterious wonder,"[106] declaring:

> I shook (the earth) so I might foretell great and excellent wonders for you.[107] Heaven has trembled, and the Two Lands are in joy as those who are in them rejoice at what has happened for you. The mountains, the waters, and the walls upon earth tremble at your good name when they see the decree I have made for you: the land of Hatti to be serfs of your palace. I inspired them to present themselves humbly to your Ka, bearing their taxes, the plunder of their chiefs, and all their property as tribute-offerings to the power of His Person, L.P.H., (with) his (the Hittite ruler's) eldest daughter being at their head, to satisfy the heart of the Lord of the Two Lands, the Dual King Usermaatre-Setepenre, the Son of Re Ramesses-Meramun, given life.[108]

Happily Ever After?

After the festivities in Piramesses were over, Ramesses II's new Hittite bride confronted a less than storybook ending to her new life. She was indeed a great royal wife, a stipulation her mother Puduhepa had extracted from Pharaoh, surpassing all his foreign brides. But she may have been puzzled, if not shocked, that she shared this exalted rank with five more women—all of them Pharaoh's *daughters*.

After a year or so, Ramesses announced to Hattusili III that Maahorneferure had given birth to
a baby girl. Her father rejoiced at this news, as he
told Pharaoh in a congratulatory letter:

> [The gods have (?)] made [my wish] come true and
> [have blessed my brother and my daughter (?)] with
> a princess, [and] (I) the [G]reat [King see] in the
> daughter the (workings) of divine providence [... The
> other kings to whom I have (?) written [mes]sages
> [have not replied to me], nor will they answer my
> brother! I have rejoiced [over your daughter (?)] and
> the lands of Hatti [have rejoiced (?). The heavens],
> the earth, the mountains, and the rivers [were] in
> joy [because the gods have given [you] happiness.]
> ... But you, my brother, should not negl[ect] your
> daughter![109]

Ramesses endeavored to present his daughter's
birth as another case of divine intervention, sending a cuneiform tablet to Hattusa recording a decree of Seth in the guise of the Hittite Storm God.
The original missive is lost, but the first paragraph
of a Hittite copy of this divine oracle survives:

> Copy of the document that the Storm God decreed
> between the land of Egypt and the land of Hatti:
> Regarding the document that you (Ramesses) sent
> (saying): "A daughter was born to the king of the land of Egypt." so says
> the document, "And the great gods of the land of Egypt announced it"—
> and their words are true ...—"and they (the gods) said to him (Ramesses)
> as follows: '(As for) this daughter who was born to you, bring her to
> us and we will assign her [queen]ship over ano[the]r country. And the
> country to which we will give her to ex[ercise queenship] will be bound
> to the land of Egypt, and [shall be] a[s one land ...]'"[110]

FIGURE 12.8. Colossal
granite statue of
Ramesses and Ptah-
Tatchenen. A fertility
aspect of the Memphite
creator god, Ptah-
Tatchenen was the
patron of Ramesses II's
Sed-festivals. The statue
is typical of others
from the Jubilee period
depicting the king
with various deities.
Ny Carlsberg Museum
Copenhagen ÆIN 1483.
Alamy.

The document might confirm that the two sides hammered out a pre-
nuptial contract specifying any daughter Maahorneferure gave Ramesses II would later be married to a foreign king, just as her mother
had.[111] If so, it would seem to go against the ban on Egyptian princesses
marrying other kings, but the little princess could be an exception.[112]
This oracle also mirrored the Egyptian ideological conception of the
Hittite marriage itself as a wonder the gods performed for Ramesses.[113]

And what would have transpired had Maahorneferure produced a
son? In fact, once the initial excitement of this happy news began to
wear off, Hattusili III could not help noticing Pharaoh had *not* given

FIGURE 12.9. (Right) Siliceous sandstone colossus of Ramesses II originally from Piramesses but now in Tanis. (Center) damaged subsidiary figure of Maahorneferure on the colossus. Inscribed beside her, the text reads (center and right): "The Great Royal Wife and Mistress of the Two Lands, Maahorneferure, daughter of the Great Chief of Hatti." Photograph by Peter Brand.

him a grandson. He knew his royal brother and son-in-law Ramesses II had sired at least fifty sons by his many wives, but why had his own daughter not produced one? Perhaps Pharaoh was no longer up to the task. He was, after all, in his mid- to late fifties—old by ancient standards. Disappointed and resentful, the Hittite king fired off a letter hitting Ramesses "below the belt":

> [I would have given the l]and of Hatti to her son [if she had given birth to a son. But you] have not begat a son by my daughter [...] Is it not [possible], as has been said, for my brother [to sire a son]?[114]

Hattusili was rubbing salt in the wounds to no good end. He had already designated his own successor, Prince Tasmi-Sharuma, who ascended the throne after his death as King Tudhaliya IV.[115] Surviving letters never report any further children born to Ramesses II's first Hittite wife.

Just as he had with the Hittite peace treaty, Ramesses presented his Hittite nuptials both as an unprecedented wonder and a case of a foreign ruler kowtowing before him. The prominence he gave to the event surpassed all previous diplomatic alliances of an Egyptian pharaoh to foreign brides, including his earlier marriages to princesses from Assyria, Babylon, and Zulabi. But the triumphal ideology of his nuptial celebrations belied his diplomatic bartering with Puduhepa. Some view those exchanges as the genuine Ramesses, a mortal king who had to interact

FIGURE 12.10. A glazed plaque inscribed on one side with names and titles of Maahorneferure (left) and Ramesses II's cartouches on the other (right). London, Petrie Museum, University College London 61296. Courtesy Petrie Museum.

with other rulers as his equals since Egypt was in no position to dictate terms to other kingdoms.[116] Like most ancient kings and modern leaders, Ramesses presented one face to his people and another to the outside world. Still, in the triumphal bombast of his proclamations, Pharaoh saw the self he wished to see.

And what became of Maahorneferure? After the First Hittite Marriage Decree, we possess a few scraps of evidence testifying to her life in Egypt. As one of Ramesses II's great royal wives, she appears on a colossal statue from Piramesses (fig. 12.9).[117] Five small decorative plaques made of faience and steatite bear inscriptions with the names of Pharaoh and his Hittite queen.[118] Ramesses ordered craftsmen to produce these trinkets in large quantities and circulated them among the elite as keepsakes (fig. 12.10).

FIGURE 12.11. A papyrus fragment from the residential palace at Medinet Ghurob naming Maahorneferure. Wikimedia Commons.

At times Maahorneferure attended her husband during his sojourns in Piramesses and other cities of his realm, but the new queen soon found herself residing mainly in the royal family's palace at Mi-Wer. There, archaeologists found a papyrus naming her in an inventory of linen garments (fig. 12.11). After that, her trail grows cold. She probably died long before her husband Ramesses II and her mother Queen Puduhepa, both of whom survived to an advanced old age.

About a decade after Ramesses married Maahorneferure he wed a second Hittite princess.[119] Meanwhile he continued celebrating the *Sed*-festival every three years. As the pharaoh built new temples and monuments in his Jubilee years, his scribes and image makers increasingly emphasized his status as a living god.

Notes

1. Krol 2005.

2. Costa 2004.

3. Habachi 1971; Kozloff, Bryan, and Berman 1992, 38–42; O'Connor and Cline 1998, 15–17; Murnane 2000; Hornung 2013.

4. Hoffmeier 2015, 117–25.

5. The resulting order of service was a hybrid mix of new rituals and archaic customs, now imperfectly understood. A classic work on the phenomenon of invented traditions are essays in Hobsbawm and Ranger 1983. In the case of Amenhotep III's *Sed*-festivals, the (re)invention of traditions went hand in hand with antiquarian research into the customs of ancestral kings, a common ideological theme; see Redford 1986, 179–80; Kozloff, Bryan, and Berman 1992, 40; O'Connor and Cline 1998, 17; Hornung 2013.

6. Lange 2009.

7. From Eighteenth Dynasty temple and tomb scenes and from the Amarna Letters we know that Pharaoh's vassals and envoys from the Great Kings of the ancient Near East were practically dragooned to serve as witnesses to Egypt's imperial splendor during elaborate court ceremonies and festivals. This led to a culture clash, with the Egyptians and foreign diplomats viewing such ceremonies differently. For the Egyptians, these spectacles celebrated Pharaoh's universal dominion: Morris 2018, 253–66. Reports from their ambassadors prompted the kings of Assyria and Babylonia to complain to Amenhotep III and Akhenaten that their diplomats were being ill-used: Liverani 2013; Bryce 2003, 70–72.

8. Amenhotep III did not shun Memphis during his *Sed*-festivals, but archaeological relics of this once great city are so poorly preserved that we have limited archaeological evidence for what happened there during the Eighteenth Dynasty.

9. O'Connor and Cline 1998, *passim*.

10. Epigraphic Survey 1980.

11. On Amenhotep III's building program during his Jubilee decade, see Kozloff, Bryan, and Berman 1992, 93–115; Johnson 1998.

12. Schiff Giorgini et al. 1998; Murnane 2000.

13. Gohary 1992.

14. Hoffmeier 2015, 91–135.

15. Schiff Giorgini et al. 1998.

16. Gardiner 1948, 59, lines 15–16.

17. *KRI* IV, 26.

18. *RITANC* II, 233–38; Habachi 1971.

19. For discussion of the date of Prince Amunhirkhopeshef's death, see Fisher 2001, 67–70. See also pp.. 264 and 272 above.

20. For Khaemwaset's priestly titles and career, see Fisher 2001, 99–101 and 103–5. See pp. 265–69 above.

21. *KRI* II, 377.

22. P. Bologna 1094:7. Gardiner 1937, 4–5.

23. Habachi 1971; *RITANC* II, 233–38; Hornung 2013.

24. See pp. 410–28 below.

25. *RITANC* II, 342–48.

26. *KRI* II, 428; *RITANC* II, 288–89.

27. *RITANC* II, 238–41.

28. This was the anniversary of the king's accession. See pp. 381–82 and 411–13 below.

29. The scholarship on this issue is extensive. See Schulman 1979; Zaccagnini 1985; Meier 2000; Liverani 2001, 189–95; Roth 2002, 85–130; Bryce 2003, 107–20; Breyer 2010a, 294–97.

30. See Kitchen 1998, 250–61.

31. See pp. 328–29 above. On the mutual exchange of women between Great Kings and their vassals, see Meier 2000.

32. Amenhotep III collected several wives from the Great Kingdoms of Babylonia, Mitanni, and Arzawa. He also demanded multiple women from his vassal kings in the Levant and Nubia. However frequently these foreign unions took place, they have left few traces in the official Egyptian sources. When Amenhotep married Princess Giluhepa, daughter of King Shuttarna II of Mitanni, he acquired her retinue of 317 handmaidens. The pharaoh celebrated these nuptials by issuing a series of scarabs with inscriptions recording the event. But we know about most of Amenhotep III's foreign brides from the Amarna Letters. See Avruch 2000; Meier 2000; Bryce 2003, 109–13.

33. The issue is often raised and widely debated among scholars; e.g., Schulman 1979; Jansen-Winkeln 2000; Schipper 2002. Ultimately the ban on Pharaoh's daughters marrying abroad was a conceit of the Egyptian worldview and royal ideology that New Kingdom rulers could enforce due to their privileged status among the great kingdoms. Other Great Kings tolerated it, out of greed for the gold that was "like dust" in Egypt and through a different political calculus deriving from an alien cultural viewpoint. For contrasting views, see Avruch 2000; Meier 2000. Roth (2003, 177–78) views this embargo on Egyptian princesses marrying abroad as a practical one, involving a loss of prestige for the pharaoh, but she believes ideological concerns that such marriages might undermine the notion of his divine kingship was only secondary because these were not relevant in the international sphere. Such *Realpolitik* is not characteristic of Ramesses II in his diplomatic interactions. Rather, issues of prestige and the universal dominion of Egypt's ruler were central. His refusal—or inability—to conform fully with notions of parity and reciprocity in relations with other Great Kings reflects the primacy of ideology in his thinking and actions.

34. This infamous exchange is recorded in EA 4: 4–20; see Rainey 2015, 73.

35. EA 4: 21–22.

36. See pp. 9–10 above.

37. For contrasting views of this marriage, see Jansen-Winkeln 2000; Schipper 2002.

38. 1 Kgs 3:1.

39. EA 1 rev. 61: Rainey 2015, 63 and 1324. For a different translation, see Moran 1992, 2 with n. 21.

40. Unlike the remarkable Amarna Letters, which include messages from several other Great Kingdoms in the reigns of Amenhotep III and Akhenaten, no trace of Ramesses II's correspondence with any court other than that of the Hittites has come down to us.

41. *ÄHK* I, nos. 105 recto 13´; translation in Beckman 2008, 132–33.

42. Roth (2003, 180) believes the pharaoh took the initiative in requesting the marriage as was often the case in the Amarna period. See also Roth 2002, 108–10.

43. For these estimates and the itinerary of the diplomats, see Gundlach, Raedler, and Roth 2005, 41–43. Since there were multiple exchanges in the marriage negotiations, the process must have continued for well over a year, and likely longer. Breyer (2010a, 294) estimates they took at least three years.

44. The cuneiform letters never say this. It is hypothetically possible she was Hattusili's eldest daughter, or perhaps his eldest *unmarried* daughter. Given the fact that he concluded marriage alliances with other Great Kingdoms, including one with a Babylonian princess and with several of his vassal kings, it is unlikely his eldest daughter would have still been available to marry Ramesses some fourteen years after the treaty and perhaps two decades after Hattusili came to the throne. See also Bryce 2003, 115.

45. This seems to be the gist of KUB 26.53. Edel heavily restores the text (*ÄHK* I, no. 106: 5′–9′), while Cordani (2017 no. 20) is more cautious. On Puduhepa's diplomatic skills, see de Roos 2006.

46. The notion of Egyptian kings banishing their foreign brides to remote "harems" is as much a cliché among modern scholars as in the complaints of other ancient kings: Kitchen 1982, 88–89; Bryce 2003, 111.

47. EA 1: 18–21: Rainey 2015, 59.

48. EA 1: 44–46: Rainey 2015, 61.

49. *ÄHK* I, no. 105: verso 7–10; Cordani 2017, no. 19. Translation adapted from Beckman 2008, 135. Breyer (2010a, 294) views the Babylonian ambassador's report to Puduhepa as an attempt to sabotage the Egyptian-Hittite alliance. While intriguing, this is speculative, and one doubts whether such gossip could have dissuaded Puduhepa from entrusting Pharaoh with her daughter. Rather, she exploited the tidbit as a negotiating tactic.

50. KUB 26.89: *ÄHK* I, no. 104: 5′–11′. Translation adapted from Cordani 2017, no. 18. Written in Hittite, this badly damaged tablet is either a Hittite copy of an Akkadian original Ramesses II sent Puduhepa or a preliminary draft of a message she sent to the pharaoh: Cordani (2017, 102) notes the complex intermingling of quotations as both parties culled from the other's previous messages and even from their own earlier missives.

51. *ÄHK* I, no. 104: 11′–14′. In the draft of her long letter to Ramesses, Puduhepa quotes him as reassuring her that "[your messengers] shall speak freely to the daughter"; *ÄHK* I, no. 105: verso 41′. Roth (2003, 182) believes Puduhepa was anxious to exert influence over her daughter at the Egyptian court and that the princesses's brothers should also be able to visit her. Pharaoh's foreign brides were part of a system of permanent diplomatic relations that also included the continuous exchange of envoys. See Roth's comments in Gundlach, Raedler, and Roth 2005.

52. *ÄHK* I, no. 37: 11′–13′.

53. A large dowry, and a corresponding "bride price" that Ramesses would send to his Hittite in-laws, were sources of pride and prestige.

54. *ÄHK* I, no. 104: 7′. The term used can mean "binding agreement." Roth (2003, 183) takes this as a reference to a "treaty/contract." If so, it governed only the question of the eventual children born to Pharaoh and his Hittite wife. See Cordani 2017, 102.

55. Ramesses elevated the princess to the status of Great Royal Wife, *ḥmt nsw wrt*, in compliance with Hittite demands. Roth (2003, 180–82) sees this as a concession on Ramesses II's part because he wanted the marriage and had no basis for a counteroffer. Arguably, both sides wanted the match since it

mutually enhanced their prestige and bolstered the Egyptian-Hittite alliance. Certainly, it was unprecedented for a foreign princess to be elevated to the status of great royal wife. But as he had with the peace treaty, Ramesses touted the marriage alliance for maximal value in his innovative ideological program.

56. *ÄHK* I, no. 43: recto 37–43. Translation adapted from Beckman 2008, 136. See also Cordani 2017, no. 22.

57. According to Edel's reconstruction, two parallel letters Ramesses sent to Hattusili and Puduhepa record a total of 1,779 shekels of gold objects. *ÄHK* I, nos. 45: verso 13´–14´ and 46: verso 7´. The sums are damaged in both letters. 1,779 shekels of gold was a princely sum. Mursili II imposed an annual tribute of 300 shekels of gold in a vassal treaty with Tuppi-Teshub of Amurru (Beckman 2008, 61). Cordani's translation of the damaged total for gold and silver is more conservative (2017, 121 with n. 1), yielding a total of +96 shekels, but she notes that the presence of the *ME* (100) logogram suggests the sum is in the hundreds of shekels.

58. The value of a shekel in the ancient world varied between 0.335 and 0.481 oz (9.4 and 13.64 grams); see Zaccagnini 2018, 3–18. The range of values for 1779 shekels would add up to between 589 oz/16.7 kg and 853.6 oz/24.2 kg. In August 2021, gold reached a value of $1,808 per oz./$58,230 per kg.

59. So, in the Amarna period, we have two huge gift lists connected with Akhenaten's marriage to a princess from Mitanni: EA 22 and 25; see Rainey 2015, 160–83 and 242–75; O'Connor and Cline 1998, 258–60; Bryce 2003, 94–97.

60. *ÄHK* I, no. 54: recto 7´–12´. Cordani 2017, no. 28.

61. *ÄHK* I, no. 54: recto 16´–17´.

62. *ÄHK* I, no. 54: recto 19´–23´.

63. *ÄHK* I, no. 54: recto 25–verso 1´. On Upe and the Town-of-Ramesses-meramun, the name Ramesses gave to the administrative center of Kumidi (Kamid el-Loz) in the Beqaa Valley, see *RITANC* II, 15–16.

64. *ÄHK* I, no. 54: verso 1´–19´.

65. *ÄHK* I, no. 57: verso 7–8. Bryce's translation (2003, 117) is much freer. But see Cordani 2017, 130.

66. *ÄHK* I, no. 105: recto 7´–8´. Translation adapted from Beckman 2008, 132.

67. KUB 21.38: *ÄHK* I, no. 105; Cordani 2017, no. 19; Beckman 2008, 131–34.

68. *ÄHK* I, no. 105: recto 8´–12´. Translation adapted from Beckman 2008, 132.

69. The passage is obscure; see Cordani 2017, 107.

70. *ÄHK* I, no. 105: recto 12´–16´. Translation adapted from Beckman 2008, 132–33.

71. *ÄHK* I, no. 105: recto 17´. This statement is often taken as evidence for bad harvests and food shortages in thirteenth-century Hatti. On this issue, see Divon 2008. See p. 448 below. But the comment might be a rhetorical flourish. Cordani 2017, 108, n. 1.

72. *ÄHK* I, no. 105: recto 38´, 44´–46´. Translation adapted from Beckman 2008, 134.

73. *ÄHK* I, no. 105: recto 47´–52´. Translation adapted from Beckman 2008, 134.

74. In the Egyptian-Hittite marriage dossier, Babylonia was a convenient foil each side cited to score rhetorical points.

75. *ÄHK* I, no. 105: recto 55′–56′. Translation adapted from Beckman 2008, 134 and Cordani 2017, 109–10.

76. *ÄHK* I, no. 105: verso 1–2. Translation adapted from Beckman 2008, 134–35.

77. *ÄHK* I, no. 105: verso 2–6. Translation adapted from Beckman 2008, 135.

78. *ÄHK* I, no. 105: verso 13–14. The phrase "our two lands have become one" turns up elsewhere in the Egyptian-Hittite correspondence: *ÄHK* I, no. 51: recto 19–12; no. 53: recto 3′–4′ and 6′–7′; see Roth 2003, 176 and n. 1. See pp. 319 and 338 n. 5 above.

79. *ÄHK* I, no. 43: recto 30–43. Translation adapted from Beckman 2008, 136 and Cordani 2017, no. 22, 116–17.

80. *ÄHK* I, no. 49: recto 14–16; Cordani 2017, no. 24.

81. *ÄHK* I, no. 54: verso 11′–12′.

82. On the official Egyptian view of these events and its impact on Egyptian historical memory, see Kitchen 1982, 92–95; *RITANC* II, 150–55; Roth 2003; 2005, 205–7.

83. *KRI* II, 233–56; *RITA* II, 86–96; *RITANC* II, 146–59; Roth 2005. Five copies of the decree remain in various states of preservation from Karnak and Aswan in Upper Egypt and Abu Simbel, Aksha, and Amara West in Nubia. In addition, a block showing the image of the Hittite king found on the west bank of Thebes probably comes from an otherwise lost edition of the decree from the Ramesseum: Leblanc 2019, 35–36 and fig. 15. Further exemplars must have existed in the great urban centers of the north, including Heliopolis, Memphis, and Piramesses. A granite relief from Medinet el-Fayum depicts Hattusili III and his daughter in a scene like that on the Abu Simbel stela: Fisher 2013, 92–94 with figs. 9–10; Leblanc 2019, fig. 13.

84. *KRI* II, 258–81; *RITA* II, 99–110; *RITANC* II, 159–63.

85. *RITANC* II 151–52. This phenomenon, which Kitchen calls "visual poetry," is found on some of Ramesses II's rhetorical stelae during the second half of his reign; see Rashwan 2014; Dew 2017. Similarly, several parallel columns of royal titulary often appear on the large, flat rear surfaces of group statues of Ramesses and the gods.

86. *KRI* II, 234–35.

87. Bittel 1986; Devos 2004. In either case, the Egyptian artist-scribe represented Hattusili III as a figure wearing a tall conical headdress, perhaps confusing him with the image of the Hittite Storm God from the king's seal attached to the Silver Treaty tablet. In some hieroglyphic texts, including the filiation of Maahorneferure on a colossal statue from Tanis and on a fragment of the First Hittite Marriage Decree from Karnak, the hieroglyphic ideogram for "chief" in the title "great chief of Hatti," *wr ꜥꜣ n Ḫtꜣ*, depicts a figure wearing a similar headdress, either with his arms raised in adoration or stooped with his arms hanging beside him in submission.

88. This iconography reflects her cultic role as an Egyptian great royal wife, for which see Fisher 2013.

89. *RITANC* II, 151–53.

90. *KRI* II, 241–42.

91. Many conclude that this is a reference to the Battle of Kadesh. But this is likely a general allusion to Ramesses II's entire military career.

92. *KRI* II, 242–44.

93. *KRI* II, 244–45.

94. The verb *phr* means "to be twisted."

95. This conforms to a common theme about poor harvests and food short-ages in the late Hittite Empire; see Divon 2008. Anatolian crops were highly reliant on rainwater. For the Egyptians, the fact that many foreign lands could not depend on the Nile as a source of irrigation was yet another sign of their barbaric and alien character.

96. *KRI* II, 246–47.

97. Formal Egyptian texts had long presented diplomatic gifts from other Great Kings as being *inw*, or "tribute offering," while igoring any Egypitan reci-procity, as with Thutmose III's reference to gifts from Babylonia and Hatti after his Euphrates campaign against Mitanni. On the question of so-called tribute as an ideological disconnect between Egyptian internal versus external view-points, see Liverani 2001; Morris 2018, epilogue.

98. *KRI* II, 247–50.

99. *KRI* II, 250–53.

100. *KRI* III, 79:16–80:1. Compare an inscription of Huy on a statue in the Louvre (E 11770 bis) calling him: "[The one who brought] his royal daughter, (namely) the (royal) messenger to Hatti"; see Roth 2002, 118 and n. 365.

101. Davies, *RITANC* III, 70–71. On Huy's diplomatic career, see Breyer 2010a, 300.

102. See Breyer 2010a, 299. In one of his letters to Hattusili, Ramesses re-ports that he has commanded local governors to arrange for the escort of the princess and her dowry train when they entered Egyptian territory: *ÄHK* I, no. 54: recto 25′–verso 1′; Cordani 2017, 128.

103. *KRI* II, 253–55.

104. *KRI* II, 257.

105. *KRI* II, 256–57; *RITA* II, 96–99; *RITANC* II, 158–59.

106. So *biȝt ʿȝt štȝ*. For discussion, see Goelet 1991, 35–37; *RITANC* II, 162.

107. Some would take this as evidence for an earthquake around this time which may have shattered one of the four seated colossi on the façade of Abu Simbel. Inside the temple, the Blessing of Ptah appears on a later wall built be-tween the last two pillars on the south side of the outer hall, perhaps to shore them up after a seismic event: first theorized by Christophe (1965, 206–7) and endorsed by Kitchen 1982, 135–36.

108. *KRI* II, 273–75.

109. KBo 18.23: *ÄHK* I, no. 109: recto 1′–10′.

110. KBo 1.23: *ÄHK* I, no. 68; Cordani 2017, no. 30.

111. Roth (2003, 189–92) suggests the original document was engraved on a metal plaque in the same fashion as the Silver Treaty tablet and that the pharaoh's Hittite daughter was eventually married to a foreign ruler. But she deems it unlikely the daughter would have been sent back to Hatti since the text only says the princess would receive "queenship over another country."

112. So Jansen-Winkeln 2000. But such an exception does not necessarily mean the "rule" that Egyptian princesses could not marry foreign kings was already defunct in the thirteenth century BCE. Schipper (2002, 93–94), ques-tions the veracity of KBo 1.23 as an Egyptian document, but his objections are dubious. Why would the Hittites have "faked" such an oracular pronouncement and tucked it away in their archives? On the document itself, see Cordani 2017, 131–33. Indeed, she points out that the very fact the Hittite chancery copied and translated the Egyptian missive is proof of its exceptional importance.

113. For Roth (2003, 192), this is further evidence of the way Ramesses II's presentation of his Hittite marriage reconciled royal ideology with the realities of foreign relations.

114. KUB 23.105: *ÄHK* I, no. 110: recto 4´–6´. The statement is not proof that a son born to Pharaoh and his Hittite wife would be in line for the Hittite throne; see Roth 2003, 191.

115. Bryce 2005, 295–326. Prince Tasmi-Sharruma was one of Hattusili III's sons who received a letter from Ramesses II. *ÄHK* I, no. 17; Cordani 2017, 70–71 (no. 6). Cordani notes that his letter from the pharaoh was more elaborate than those his brother received, suggesting he outranked them.

116. Roth (2003, 193) emphasizes the discrepancy between pharaonic ideology on one side and diplomatic practice and *Realpolitik* on the other.

117. *KRI* II, 440; *RITANC* II, 296; Fisher 2013, 100–103; Sourouzian 2019, no. 46.

118. *RITANC* II, 570; Fisher 2013, 95–100.

119. See pp. 424–27 below.

Chapter Thirteen

Ramesses, the Great God

The Sun King at His Zenith

Ramesses II's second *Sed*-festival marked the apogee of his reign. During the second half of his reign, he continued building temples and monuments at a steady pace across Egypt and Nubia. After his second Jubilee, however, writing a continuous biography of the king becomes difficult.[1] Historians rely on the pharaoh's grand edicts to reconstruct his life, but he issued few of them in the second half of his reign, while diplomatic sources from Hattusa also dwindle. Historically, time seems to come to a virtual standstill after year thirty-four, giving way to a "living eternity" of Ramesses, the Great God.

Ideologically, his second *Sed*-festival marks a milestone in how Ramesses II envisaged his kingship. While temple art and inscriptions often affirm his divinity in the first three decades, image makers balanced this theme with an emphasis on his warlike deeds. By the second *Sed*-festival, his fighting days lay well behind him.[2] Ramesses the warrior now recedes, and Ramesses the god-king emerges (fig. 13.1).

Changes to Ramesses II's Titulary in Year 34

Ramesses II marked his second Jubilee by expanding his five ceremonial names and titles. His new epithets, introduced in his First Hittite Marriage Edict and the Blessing of Ptah decree, emphasized his divine qualities.[3] To his Horus name "Mighty Bull Beloved of Maat," scribes now added "Lord of *Sed*-festivals like his Father Ptah-Tatchenen."[4] This new name equated him with Ptah's fertility aspect, which brought about the annual Nile inundation, bestowing agricultural prosperity on Egypt.[5] Over forty more special Horus name variants occur on the monuments, expressing his warlike powers, kingship, and *Sed*-festivals.[6]

To his *Nebty* name, Ramesses II now added "a Re Whom the Gods Fashioned; Who Establishes the Two Lands."[7] The first one is intriguing, since we can also translate it: "A Re Who Fashions the Gods." Ramesses assumes Re's identity on earth, as the offspring of Egyptian deities. Simultaneously, he embodies Re's creative power, fashioning the gods as statuary. The key Egyptian term is *mesi*, meaning "to give birth," which also which also means "to create" or "to craft" something, as when a sculptor carves a statue. Perhaps Ramesses intended both meanings.[8]

FIGURE 13.1. Ramesses II before Re-Horakhty, the lion-headed goddess Iwasas, and his divine alter ego. The godly Ramesses is distinguished with a solar disk atop his head, a curved divine beard, and ram's horns. Like other gods, he grasps the *ankh*-sign of life. Inscribed horizontally above his head, his name is not enclosed in a cartouche. A. Ricci's watercolor of a relief from the great temple of Abu Simbel. Courtesy UK National Trust.

Living up to this sentiment, his artists sculpted immense quantities of statuary during his Jubilee period, including dyads and triads depicting him alongside various deities.[9] In Egypt, divine kingship was an ancient institution that ebbed and flowed for more than three millennia. But how did Ramesses II stand out in this lineage of god-kings?

Divine Kingship in the New Kingdom

Traditions of pharaonic godhood stretched back two millennia before the time of Ramesses II. Even before written records first surface, around 3300 BCE, Egyptians believed their monarchs possessed supernatural qualities. Among sacred kingship's oldest relics were mudbrick tombs the early kings built at Abydos and Saqqara during the First and Second Dynasties. Early in the Old Kingdom, King Djoser built his Step Pyramid Complex at Saqqara—history's first large stone building. Pyramid building reached its zenith in the Fourth Dynasty when Khufu and Khafre constructed the Great Pyramids at Giza. Giant pyramids were the ultimate expression of royal power and divinity. Yet, from late prehistory onward, Egyptians also wrestled with the contradictions in this doctrine.[10]

By the New Kingdom, a thousand years had elapsed since Khufu's time. During this interval Egyptian civilization experienced many crises and downturns, dispelling the aura of supreme authority and unrivaled power Khufu once exuded. As empire-building pharaohs like Thutmose III arose in the early Eighteenth Dynasty, they restored the potency and prestige of pharaonic kingship.[11]

While Egyptians believed their pharaoh was like a god, they never forgot he was also a mortal man. His human frailties were all too visible: he might be weak in mind or body, and someday he would age, sicken, and die. How did Egyptians resolve this contradiction between the king's transcendent and human natures? Over the centuries, sages contrived a sophisticated theology of his godly spirit, allowing them to reconcile it with his mortality.

Egyptian dogma overcame this disparity by seeing the pharaoh as a mortal vessel containing the sublime. Ancient texts refer to his human form as *khem-ef.* Literally meaning "His Incarnation," we can also translate it as "His Person" or, as Egyptologists traditionally have, as "His Majesty."[12] In Egyptian thought, a *khem*, written with the hieroglyph 〗, denotes a god's physical body as it exists on earth.[13] A *khem* could take the form of a sacred animal like the Apis Bull, the living incarnation of Ptah; a cult statue crafted from gold and precious stones; or the pharaoh's own body.[14] As the divine made flesh, Egyptians believed each sovereign was a living avatar of Horus.[15] His spiritual and mortal natures coexisted while he lived. He only became an absolute god in death, when his identity merged with Osiris.

While he lived, Egyptians constrained their ruler's supernatural qualities within strict boundaries.[16] He expressed his divinity by personifying certain gods on specific occasions—court ceremonies, festival pageants, and temple rituals—when his sublime heritage came to the fore. Sitting enthroned upon the dais, beneath his golden canopy of state, his courtiers hailed him declaring: "You are Re!" The Opet Festival in Thebes culminated each year in a mystical union of the king's *Ka* with that of Amun-Re, rejuvenating both of them.[17] In highly charged moments of action, too, he was said to embody one of the gods, as when he became the war god Monthu and raged in his battle frenzy.

Across centuries of sacred kingship, an ineffable barrier separated any pharaoh's mortal form from his divine aspect. This nuanced dogma prevented most New Kingdom rulers from claiming absolute godhood. Before Ramesses II, only Amenhotep III dared rule as a divinity on earth.[18] By the force of his will, his vast wealth, and legions of scribes and artisans, Ramesses II would also assert his apotheosis as a living god.

The God-King Arises

Sety I sought to revive Amenhotep III's style of divine kingship by building temples in Egypt and Nubia housing special avatars of his godhead.[19] To serve his cult, Sety also began to quarry colossal statues of himself shortly before his untimely death.[20] Taking power in his early twenties, Ramesses II continued his father's policy. From the outset of his reign, myriads of royal colossi poured forth from quarries and workshops. Ramesses set them up in temples at Coptos, Memphis, Pi-ramesses, and Thebes. He built royal cult temples called "Mansions of Millions of Years" for the adoration of his divine aspect, among them the Ramesseum in Thebes and his magnificent temple at Abu Simbel. During his Jubilee years, Ramesses merged his personal identity with those of Egypt's great gods, becoming a living incarnation of Amun-Re, Ptah, and especially Re-Horakhty.[21]

Precisely defining Ramesses II's concept of divine kingship remains a complex problem.[22] While emulating Amenhotep III and building on

FIGURE 13.2. Ramesses II offers incense to the falcon-headed moon god "Usermaatre-Setepenre-who Resides in the Domain of Ramesses-Meramun." From the main hall of the great temple of Abu Simbel. Drawing by Peter Brand.

Sety I's legacy, Ramesses surpassed them both in the scale of his royal cult and monumental construction.[23] During his seven decades as Lord of the Two Lands, he raised more temples and statues to his divinity than any other pharaoh. But how did Ramesses II's cult evolve across his long reign? Scholars long believed Ramesses assumed full godhood only during its second half.[24] We now know this distinction is false. By raising temples and statues to his personal cult, the king assumed the mantle of divinity long before his first *Sed*-festival in regnal year thirty.[25] This is clear from reliefs in the temples of Amara West and Abu Simbel (fig. 13.2).[26]

Still, Ramesses dedicated new monuments to his personal cult at an accelerated pace in his latter decades. This trend reached its zenith around his second Jubilee, when court scribes acclaimed his divinity in the poetic stanzas of The First Hittite Marriage Stela and the Blessing of Ptah decree. In his Jubilee era, icons depicting Ramesses as a god proliferated in wall reliefs embellishing his Nubian temples at Abu Simbel, Gerf Hussein, and Wadi es-Sebua. This shift in emphasis coincided with the king's political priorities as he aged.

In his first two decades as king, while he was still young, Ramesses II's ideological program evolved from that of Sety I and followed the traditional double path of a New Kingdom monarch.[27] Ramesses fought as a mighty warrior on the battlefields of Syria and Nubia, celebrating his valor in triumphal inscriptions and iconic war scenes. At the same time, he piously erected temples to Egypt's pantheon, endowing them with rich provisions even as he claimed to be their equal through state sanctioned worship of his colossal statues.

Military campaigning was a young man's pursuit. After the Hittite treaty in year twenty-one, Egypt's empire was at peace. Now, Ramesses the warrior pharaoh retired, as did his urge to project a bellicose image on his later monuments.[28] We hear his last hurrah in the belligerent hyperbole of his First Hittite Marriage Stela and the Blessing of Ptah decree. After year thirty-five, we usually see only the builder-king and divine ruler. Ramesses underscored this ideological shift when he changed his capital's name from "Piramesses-Great of Victories" to "Piramesses the Great *Ka* of Re-Horakhty."[29]

Ramesses the Great God

Today Ramesses II is famous for wall art portraying him worshiping his own deified persona. To modern viewers such auto-adoration smacks of crude egoism, even megalomania. But in New Kingdom Egypt's sophisticated dogma of divine kingship, Ramesses II's sacred avatars each guarded separate identities related to, but separate from, his human self.

We should not dismiss Pharaoh's ritual service to these entities merely as proof of supreme arrogance. Certainly, he lacked modesty. Yet, self-deification also served political ends by enhancing his earthly power and prestige. To express Ramesses II's wide-ranging conception of his own divinity, his scribes and artisans took delight in conceiving novel ways to represent their god-king (fig. 13.3).[30] His icons confront the viewer with a startling array of exotic forms, laden with divine symbolism. Yet, all share pictorial attributes and textual markers distinguishing Ramesses II's godhead from his mortal self.

Every reigning pharaoh was quasi-divine, and bore the title "perfect god" (*netcher nefer*). How did scribes set Ramesses II's divine form apart from his earthly persona? Building on precedents Amenhotep III and Sety I introduced, they classified the names of his avatars with distinctive epithets and graphic devices signaling their godhood. Texts

FIGURE 13.3. A. Ricci's watercolor of the Divine Ramesses II inserted between Amun and Isis. Relief from the inner hall of the great temple of Abu Simbel. Courtesy UK National Trust.

identify Ramesses the human king by enclosing his name with a cartouche. As a diety, his name sometimes lacks a cartouche—like those of Egypt's gods, who did not require such name rings (figs. 13.1 and 13.2).[31]

Scribes underscored the deified status of his avatars by affixing special epithets after his name. Most explicit were titles like "the god" or "the great god," as with "Ramesses-Meramun the Great God" who resided at Abu Simbel.[32] Major deities like Amun-Re and Re-Horakhty also bear the epithet "great god" in captions to ritual scenes.

All Egyptian deities possessed multiple forms emanating from diverse geographical regions and specific cult locations such as "Atum of Heliopolis," "Hathor Mistress of Dendara," and "Amun Preeminent in Karnak." Gods could also "reside in" specific temples like Amun's female counterpart "Amunet who Resides in Karnak." Several manifestations of the divine Ramesses II shared this distinction in his Nubian shrines including "Ramesses-Meramun who Resides in the Domain of Amun" at Wadi es-Sebua (fig. 13.4). Similar forms dwell in his temples at Abu Simbel and Gerf Hussein.[33]

Ramesses also signaled his divinity and union with Egypt's gods through the names he gave to his Nubian temples. Today, these shrines are known by their modern Arabic names: Abu Simbel, Derr, Gerf Hussein, and Wadi es-Sebua, among others. In antiquity, they were named for the unique form of the divine king residing there alongside Egypt's

major gods like Amun, Horus, Re-Horakhty, and Ptah. Wadi es-Sebua was called "The Temple of Ramesses-Meramun in the Domain of Amun" (fig. 13.4), while Gerf Hussein was "The Temple of Ramesses-Meramun in the Domain of Ptah." We find an identical pattern at Derr, equating him with Re. Although Ramesses consecrated his larger temple at Abu Simbel to both Amun-Re and Re-Horakhty, its official name was "The Domain of Ramesses-Meramun." Avatars of the divine Ramesses in these temples are both manifestations of major Egyptian gods and unique royal deities in their own right.[34]

FIGURE 13.4. A. Ricci's watercolor of the bark of the divine Ramesses II in the temple of Wadi es-Sebua, entitled "the sacred bark of Ramesses-Meramun in the Domain of Amun." Courtesy UK National Trust.

Artists used evocative pictorial symbolism to highlight Ramesses II's supernatural qualities, identifying him as a god who also fused with other deities. They expressed this mystical union by giving him iconographic attributes typical of solar gods, as we see at Abu Simbel (fig. 13.5) and Wadi es-Sebua. "Ramesses-Meramun the Great God" resembles a king but holds divine emblems: an *ankh*-sign of life and a *was*-scepter. A curved ram's horn emerges just above his ear, marking him as the son of Amun, to whom the ram was sacred.[35] A sun disk perched on his head expresses his solar attributes. At Abu Simbel and Aksha, the divine Ramesses mimics Re-Horakhty, portrayed as a falcon-headed man crowned with a large sun disk with an encircling uraeus serpent.[36] Increasingly during his Jubilee years, Ramesses II *was* Re. Another regal apotheosis shares Amun's characteristic headband with its long trailing ribbon.

FIGURE 13.5. Three manifestations of the deified Ramesses II, in the treasury chambers of the great temple of Abu Simbel. Image by Peter Brand.

At Soleb Temple in Nubia, Amenhotep III established his personal cult as a moon god named "Nebmaatre Lord of the Bow Land," referring to an Egyptian term for Nubia. Following this precedent, Ramesses II introduced his own lunar aspect at Wadi es-Sebua. He wears pharaonic costume and regalia, but the lunar crescent and disk sit atop his head-dress.[37] As a celestial companion to the sun, he accompanies Re-Hora-khty as the mortal Ramesses worships the pair. In other scenes, he is grouped with Amun-Re and Mut as a stand-in for their son, the lunar god Khonsu. At Abu Simbel another royal moon god, "Usermaatre-Sete-penre who Resides in the Domain of Ramesses-Meramun," blends attri-butes of Khonsu with those of a pharaoh (fig. 13.2). Wearing a divine kilt and grasping an *ankh*-sign, he is a falcon-headed man crowned with a lunar disk and crescent. But he has human ears and his corselet, *nemes*-headcloth, and staff are royal garb.

In other Nubian temple scenes the deified Ramesses II more closely resembles an earthly king. In the antechamber to Wadi es-Sebua's main sanctuary he wears kingly attire, sitting with various deities while his earthly persona adores them (fig. 13.6). In the temple of Derr, "Ramess-es-Meramun who is in the Divine Bark in the Domain of Re" sports kingly attire but grasps a god's *ankh*-sign and *was*-scepter. Once he embodies his own prenomen Usermaatre as a divine king with a solar disk atop his royal diadem, grasping the *user*-staff and *maat*-feather in his hands (fig. 13.7).[38]

Gods "of Ramesses"

All Egyptian gods possessed complex and fluid identities. They merge effortlessly with each other to form composite deities like Amun-Re and Ptah-Sokar-Osiris.[39] Ramesses II established a new class of gods

FIGURE 13.6. Ramesses II offers to his divine aspect named "Ramesses-Meramun in the Domain of Amun" who sits enthroned between Shu (right), Tefnut (center), and Nekhbet (left). From the temple of Wadi es-Sebua. Alamy.

FIGURE 13.7. The divine Ramesses II as an image of his own prenomen Usermaatre. Drawing by Peter Brand.

"of Ramesses-Meramun."[40] The Egyptian preposition *en* can mean "of," but also "belonging to" or "pertaining to," since the language lacked the verb "to have." Leading members of Egypt's pantheon now had special avatars like "Amun of Ramesses," "Ptah of Ramesses," "Re of Ramesses," and "Seth of Ramesses," whose identities were bound inextricably to the king's (fig. 13.8). This included goddesses like Anath, Hathor, Nepthys, and Wadjet. We encounter these deities in temple reliefs and on statuary, especially dyads and triads portraying Ramesses II alongside one or two gods.[41] An inscription on one dyad calls Anath "Mistress of the Gods of Ramesses-Meramun."[42]

What are we to make of these gods "of (or belonging to) Ramesses"? While Pharaoh's *Ka*-spirit could merge with Horus, Osiris, Re, and other deities—both on earth and in the netherworld—he did not relinquish his own autonomous identity. Neither did it fuse permanently with any god. Otherwise, we might expect merged entities like "Amun-Ramesses" or "Ramesses-Ptah," which never occur.[43]

Egyptian theologians drew a fine distinction here, blurring—but not erasing—the boundary separating Ramesses II's identity from those of other gods. We also see his special relationship with the pantheon in names he assigned to a group of his colossal statues at Gerf Hussein, dating to his later Jubilee period (see fig. 14.20 below). Each effigy is titled "Ramesses-Meramun Who Appears as the Gods."[44] The Gerf Hussein colossi express the dogma that Pharaoh has become an avatar of every god. As a new category of supernatural being, the gods "of Ramesses" transposed this doctrine, asserting the gods themselves were now components of his own complex identity.

Exalting the God-King in Poetry

Ramesses II marked his second *Sed*-festival and his marriage to his Hittite bride Maahorneferure by proclaiming his First Hittite Marriage Decree in regnal year thirty-four. In this grand edict, court poets acclaimed Pharaoh's symbiosis with Egypt's gods in a cycle of panegyric hymns prefacing the main record of the nuptials.[45] Dwelling at length on his mysterious and godly nature, they recounted the prodigious marvels his celestial fathers and mothers heaped upon him:

> *Living image of Re,*
>> *Offspring of Him who is in Heliopolis (Atum),*
> *His flesh is gold,*
>> *his bones are silver,*
>>> *and all his limbs are iron*
> *Son of Seth, warrior of Anath,*
>> *A Victorious Bull like Seth, He of Ombos*
> *Divine falcon whom people love*
> *A Great God among the gods*
>> *Who safeguards Egypt*
> *Who protects the Two Lands ...*
>> *Light*[46] *of the Two Riverbanks*
> *Everyone says in unison to Re when he rises:*
> *"Grant him eternity in the kingship*
> *May he shine for us daily as your equal*
> *May he be rejuvenated for us like the Moon God*
> *May he sparkle like the stars of heaven!*
> *Grant him eternal renown—*
>> *Just like your son Seth,*
>> *Who is in the Bark of Millions—*
> *(Namely), The Dual King Usermaatre-Setepenre,*
>> *The Son of Re Ramesses-Meramun—given life—*
>> *The living and perfect Re of gold,*
>> *The (very) electrum of the gods..."*[47]

This heady verse offers a taste of the florid rhetoric of these hymns. As Re personified, Ramesses II radiates a dazzling brilliance, and his lustrous flesh and gleaming limbs consist of precious metals: gold, electrum, silver, and iron.[48]

In regnal year thirty-five, Ramesses issued an edict called the Blessing of Ptah, which shares similar themes with the First Hittite Marriage Stela. It records an opulent dialogue between Ptah-Tatchenen, fertility aspect of the Memphite creator god, and Ramesses II. As divine patron of craftsmen, Ptah recounts how he inspires Pharaoh's own creative efforts:

> *I cause the mountains to give birth for you*
> *To very great and towering monuments*
> *I cause foreign lands to create for you every noble precious stone*
>   *To carve (them) as monuments in your name*
> *I cause every construction project to be productive for you*
>   *With every workshop laboring for you ...*
> *You have fashioned (my) children (the gods)*
> *You have built their shrines*
>   *Like I did at the moment of creation*
> *I have given to you (many) years of Sed-festivals,*
>   *My rulership, my position, and my throne*
> *I endow your flesh with life and dominion,*
>   *And protection envelops you with life, prosperity, and health*
> *I protect Egypt under your authority,*
>   *The Two Lands being imbued with life and dominion,*
> *O Dual King Usermaatre-Setepenre,*
> *O Son of Re Ramesses-Meramun—given life!*[49]

This is just one excerpt of Ptah's verbose address to Ramesses II, touching on his kingship, divinity, *Sed*-festivals, building projects, and the god's benediction on him and on Egypt. Pharaoh responds with an oration to his celestial father:

> *Speech by the divine king—*
>   *The Lord of the Two Lands,*
> *Who came into being as Khepri,*[50] *from his flesh*
>   *Who went forth from Re,*
> *Whom Ptah-Tatchenen begot: (namely)*
>   *The Dual King Usermaatre-Setepenre,*
>   *The Son of Re, Ramesses-Meramun, given life—*
>   *Before his Father, from whom he went forth,*
>   *Tatchenen, Father of the Gods:*
> *"I am your son whom you placed upon your throne*
>   *You decreed the kingship for me*
>   *You fashioned me in your image and your form*
>   *You endowed me with (all) your creation*
>   *I act continuously, achieving every good (thing) you desire*
>   *I am one who always does everything well,*
>   *according to your wish*
>   *I am the unique lord, as you were,*

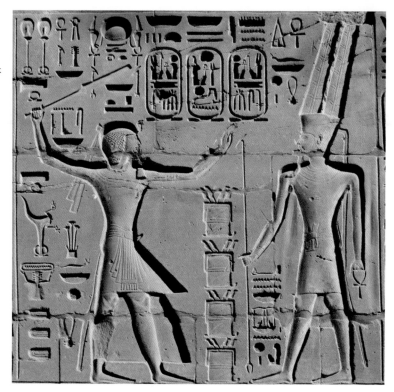

FIGURE 13.8. Ramesses II offers four *meret*-chests to Amun-of-Ramesses II in a relief from the enclosure wall of Karnak Temple. Photograph by Peter Brand.

doing what the country needs
creating Egypt anew for you,
I make it like it was in ancient times
I have cast (metal cult statues of) the gods—
Who came into being from your flesh—
(Crafted) from (precious) materials for their bodily forms[51]
I have established Egypt according to their desire
building it with temples
I have enlarged your temple in Hut-ka-Ptah (Memphis),
Constructed in the work of eternity,
Of excellent workmanship in stone,
Embellished with gold and genuine precious stones.[52]

Lofty rhetoric indeed, but based on genuine deeds. During Ramesses II's Jubilee years, quarries and construction sites across Egypt and colonial Nubia churned with activity, resounding at every strike of the masons' hammerstones and the sculptors' chisels. As he boasts in The Blessing of Ptah, Ramesses endeavored to remake his kingdom as a perfect replica of *zep tepy*, "The First Event," when Ptah created the universe at the dawn of time.

As time went on, Ramesses II blurred the distinction between his divine and human aspects until they converged in the Jubilee decades when he ruled as the sun god incarnate. How could this be so? Surely, we protest, astute priests and urbane courtiers knew their aging king was not a living god. Perhaps our rational skepticism of this ancient "cult of personality" misleads us. Such theological niceties were lost on Ramesses II's subjects, who were awed by the grandeur of his majestic colossi and monuments. The golden regalia of pharaonic power, its spectacular court ceremony, and the heady rhetoric of royal panegyrics sung aloud—all deeply impacted the emotions of those who beheld them. If we can still be moved at seeing his colossal statues, how much more did they overawe the god-king's contemporaries?

FIGURE 13.9. Lepsius's reconstruction of one of the standing colossi in the main hall of the great temple at Abu Simbel with its original colors, which were still visible in the nineteenth century. NYPL digital collections. Public domain.

The Cult of Royal Colossi

The most extravagant symbols of divine kingship were the mammoth statues pharaohs dedicated to their cult and glory.[53] Ramesses II created more royal statues, at every scale, than almost any monarch in Egyptian history (fig. 13.9).[54] These sculptures were not decorative, but sacred cult objects. They functioned as physical bodies in which the ethereal spirits of the gods or the dead could inhabit to receive ritual offerings of food, drink, incense, and other gifts.

Ramesses II's enormous colossi bore distinctive names marking them as idols housing his mystical identity. Inscribed on both shoulders, they consisted of a cartouche, often his nomen, plus one of several possible epithets.[55] These compound names expressed diverse aspects of the god-king's nature. Some epithets describe him as beloved of gods like Amun, Atum, Ptah, and Re-Horakhty. Others denote his suzerainty as "Ruler of the Two Lands" or "Ruler of Rulers."[56] A third variety acclaims him as "the God," "the Great God," and "Monthu in the Two Lands."[57]

The ancient Near Eastern honorific "King of kings" inspired an Egyptian equivalent "Ruler of rulers." Amenhotep III and Ramesses II eclipsed this sentiment by naming several colossi "Re of Rulers"—the Sun-god of kings! (fig. 13.10).[58] Each name belonged to a separate avatar of Pharaoh's sacred persona, but several colossal statues across his realm could bear the same identity. Ramesses erected colossi named "Re of Rulers" at Luxor, the Ramesseum, Abu Simbel, and Piramesses.[59]

Theologically, Ramesses II's many named colossi expressed his multifaceted divinity. On a more visceral level, they flaunted the raw power and immense prestige of Egypt's divine kingship. These behemoths overawed all who beheld them. Craftsmen artfully conveyed Pharaoh's serene aloofness. Standing in a striding pose with arms hanging at his sides, or enthroned with his hands laid neatly on his lap, his head is level and a slight smile plays across his lips. At first glance, the mammoth effigy does not seem to notice us. This sense of benign detachment vanishes when the viewer meets his gaze, for he seems to be staring back. The sculptor has tilted the statue's eyes downward, giving us the uncanny feeling the god-king is peering at us from on high. In antiquity its eyes were painted in lifelike colors, intensifying this surreal effect.[60]

FIGURE 13.10. Rebus inscription of the name of the colossus "Ramesses-Meramun the Re of Rulers" from the Ramesside forecourt in Luxor Temple. Photograph by Peter Brand.

Popular Worship of Ramesses II's Colossi

Unlike idols of the gods, which priests hid from view deep within temple sanctuaries, Ramesses II erected his colossal statues in the esplanades and outer courts of temple complexes. All levels of Egyptian society enjoyed access to these zones, and Pharaoh's colossi attracted many worshipers who left votive stelae attesting to their veneration (figs. 13.11–13.15).[61]

Colossi belonged to a special class of deities and images called "hearers of prayer." Acting as intercessors, they heard petitions from the Egyptian populace and conveyed them to the gods. In Ramesses II's fifth or sixth decade of rule, the High Priest of Amun-Re, Bakenkhonsu, built a shrine at Karnak dedicated to "Amun-Re who hears prayer." Positioned behind the main temple's inner sanctuary (where only the priests could go) people could visit this public shrine and ask one of Ramesses II's colossal effigies to intercede with Amun-Re on their behalf.

Through popular devotion to his colossi, Ramesses inserted himself into the spiritual lives of many Egyptians. The royal cult strengthened ties between Egypt's gods, its people, and the pharaoh, ties that Akhenaten's religious revolution had compromised. Shrines sprang up at the feet of Ramesses II's colossi as people offered their prayers and gifts.[62] Those who could afford it paid artists to craft votive stelae, which they set in these shrines as testaments to their piety and devotion.

From ancient Piramesses we are fortunate to possess the Horbeit stelae, a collection of fifty-four devotional tablets Egyptians from all walks of life presented to Ramesses II's grand statues.[63] These vary widely in their size and artistic quality. Well-to-do officials like the

FIGURE 13.11. Votive stela from Piramesses with images of two royal colossi: "Usermaatre-Setepenre-Beloved of Atum" (left) and "Ramesses-Meramun the God" (right). Hildesheim, Roemer- und Pelizaeus Museum, Inv. Nr. 410. Courtesy Roemer- und Pelizaeus Museum, Hildesheim.

FIGURE 13.12. Stela of the chantress Isis offering to the colossus "Usermaatre-Setepenre-is Monthu in the Two Lands." Hildesheim, Roemer- und Pelizaeus Museum, Inv. Nr. PM 380. © akg-images / De Agostini Picture Lib. / W. Buss.

FIGURE 13.13. Votive
stela of the soldier Anya.
In the upper register,
Ramesses II offers to his
colossal statue called
"Usermaatre-Setepenre
is Monthu in the Two
Lands." Below, Anya gives
praise to the colossus.
He holds a regimental
standard indicating that
he belongs to a military
unit named in honor of
another colossus called
"The Re of Rulers." Paris,
Louvre Museum E 27222.
Photograph by Peter
Brand.

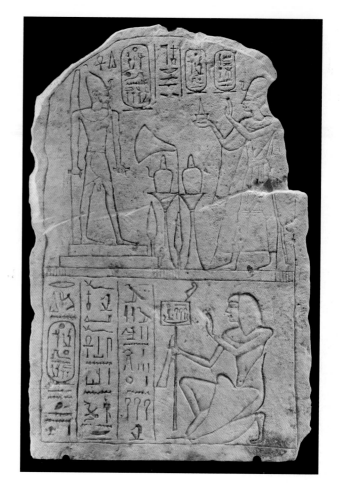

vizier offered larger votives with fine carvings depicting them adoring Pharaoh's colossi. Average folk—priests, soldiers, petty officials,
and women—presented smaller tablets, often bearing crude reliefs
and rudimentary texts (fig. 13.11).[64]

The Horbeit stelae typically depict specific colossi by name. Sculptors followed artistic conventions for portraying statuary in two-di-
mensional images, including the back pillar typical of Egyptian sculpture. In standing colossi, the king's arms hang at his sides, and he holds
a pair of dowel-like objects in his clenched fists. Where space allowed,
one or more donors appear, either standing or kneeling, raising their
hands to adore the statue. Some petitioners present food offerings. A
man named Setyerneheh kneels with women and children of his household before images of Amun-Re, Ptah, and a standing colossus called
"Usermaatre-Setepenre is Monthu in the Two Lands."[65] To ensure that
Pharaoh's massive likeness heard any supplicant's prayers, the sculptor
might carve multiple ears on its back support pillar as a magical device.

FIGURE 13.14. Stela of the soldier Mose from Piramesses. In the upper register, Ramesses II offers to Ptah (left) and rewards Mose with gifts from the royal Window of Appearances (right). Below, Ramesses stands on the lap of the "Re of Rulers" colossus as he rewards Mose and other soldiers with gold collars and various gifts. Hildesheim, Roemer- und Pelizaeus Museum, Inv. Nr. 374. Courtesy Roemer- und Pelizaeus Museum, Hildesheim.

But these surplus ears were artistic license, and never occur on Ramesses's actual colossi.

Some of the colossi from Piramesses that the Horbeit stelae depict have not survived, leaving these votives as the only evidence for their appearance. The colossus named "Ruler of Rulers" can be shown enthroned or standing. It wore a *nemes*-headcloth and a Double Crown of Upper and Lower Egypt, as did another called "Ramesses-Meramun Beloved of Atum." "Monthu in the Two Lands" always stands, wearing either the White Crown or the Double Crown.[66] "Ramesses-Meramun the God" was also a standing image.[67]

The names and images of donors inscribed on the Horbeit stelae reveal how each colossus attracted its own crowd of worshipers. Soldiers favored "Monthu in the Two Lands" because Monthu was a war god (fig. 13.13). This statue enjoyed its own cult establishment, including civilian worshipers who regularly paid their respects. Among its female devotees was a woman named Isis who served as a "chantress

FIGURE 13.15. Stela of
the Vizier Rahotep
from Pramesses. Above,
Ramesses II adores the
colossal statue named
"Ruler of Rulers." Ears
carved on its back pillar
enable it to hear the
prayers of the faithful.
Below, Rahotep intones
a hymn of praise to
"Ramesses II, the
Great God." Munich,
Staatliches Museum
Ägyptischer Kunst; ÄS
Gl 287. Drawing by
Peter Brand.

of Monthu in the Two Lands" (fig. 13.12).[68] Another woman called Kaemwia played the sistrum.[69] Both women provided musical liturgy to the statue's observances. A certain Shai's epithet, "mistress of the house," tells us she was a free woman.[70]

All three women were likely married to men who played some part in devotions to "Monthu in the Two Lands." So were Tentopet, a "royal sistrum player," and her husband Khaemwaset, who served as "fanbearer of the Lord of the Two Lands."[71] Devotees came from assorted social echelons, ranging from members of the court elite like Prince Meryatum and the Viceroy of Kush Setau to folks from everyday Egyptian society.[72] Some lacked sufficient means for personalized monuments. Instead they purchased readymade tablets without identifying inscriptions. Several stelae depict only the colossi; in others, Ramesses pays homage to his own statue.

The largest and most exceptional tablet from the Horbeit collection belongs to a soldier named Mose (fig. 13.14).[73] Mose once performed some act of bravery on the battlefield, or otherwise pleased his lord, for the stela commemorates his reward ceremony. On its upper register, Ramesses II worships Ptah at left. At right, he stands in a palace balcony, casting down precious objects to Mose. A caption proclaims: "The king himself gives silver and all (kinds of) good things from the King's House." A common soldier of modest means, Mose may have traded some of these gifts to pay the sculptor who fashioned this elaborate monument.

On the stela's lower register, we witness an extraordinary display of Pharaoh's bravado and generosity. Ramesses stands aloft on the lap of his own immense statue, "Re of Rulers," as he showers Mose and a crowd of his fellow soldiers with costly gifts: gold and silver cups, necklaces, and other precious items. Mose and his comrades eagerly reach with upstretched arms to receive their prizes. From his perch atop the colossus, Pharaoh addresses Mose and his comrades, and receives their collective adulation in return:

> *"May you see our action on behalf of the soldier who is beloved of His Person, Mose, in the presence of Pharaoh. How good is it (the reward) for him (Mose) who acted for him (the king) so very greatly!" Said by the whole army exalting their Lord: "You are Re—you are just like him when you shine, and we live by seeing you!"* [74]

Mose's stela exposes the theatrical side of the royal cult and its ties to politics. Did Ramesses II really scramble atop the lap of his own colossus as a ready-made balcony of appearances? This scene is idealized, so we cannot know for certain. Yet, this theatrical stunt is in keeping with the larger-than-life persona of Ramesses. This was as much a cult of personality—like those around modern authoritarian rulers—as a religious institution.

Senior courtiers also paid homage to their lord's gargantuan effigies. On the Vizier Rahotep's stela, Ramesses II offers incense and libation to a standing colossus called "Ramesses-Meramun the Ruler of Rulers" (fig. 13.15). Below the king, Rahotep kneels and intones a paean to the mammoth statue:

> *Giving praise to your Ka O Lord of Appearances Ramesses-Meramun– [the Ruler of Rulers]–the Great God who Hears the Prayers of Everyone. May he give life, prosperity, health, praise, alertness, and love, to [the Ka] of the hereditary nobleman and courtier, fanbearer on the King's right hand, city mayor, and Vizier, Rahotep, true of voice, of Piramesses.* [75]

The artist carved four human ears on the statue's back pillar, magically ensuring it could hear petitions. Rahotep's votive tablet emphasizes both the intercessory function of these colossi and the explicitly loyalist tone of Ramesses II's cult among his subjects.

Mansions of Millions of Years and the Royal Cult

Long before Ramesses II, Egyptian kings established cults for their sacred aspects, not just after their deaths, but during their lifetimes. They set up royal statues in temples for cultic worship, and endowed foundations with clergy and supplies of ritual offerings to sustain them. New Kingdom pharaohs solemnized their celestial alter egos in special royal cult temples called "Mansions of Millions of Years." [76] These "Mansions" include temple complexes that most Eighteenth, Nineteenth, and Twentieth Dynasty kings erected on the desert edge in Western Thebes. [77] In the past, because of their proximity to royal tombs in the nearby King's Valley, scholars often gave them misleading designations like "mortuary temples," "funerary temples," or "memorial temples," wrongly implying such devotions only began after a king had died.

Ramesses II finished building the Ramesseum during his first two decades of rule. There his cult functioned for half a century *before* he died. After a pharaoh "passed into the West," as Egyptians called the afterlife, these temples continued to nourish his spirit, in theory forever. In practice, administrative and economic entropy, and decay of the structure itself, caused most of these pious foundations to cease operating after a century or two.[78]

Like other temple complexes, massive mud-brick enclosure walls enclosed the Ramesseum. Its precinct walls enveloped dense blocks of administrative and economic buildings constructed largely of mud brick crowded around the stone-built temple itself. There was a small palace for occasional royal visits along with large blocks of workshops, storage magazines, granaries, and scribal offices. The compound functioned as a small city within the larger urban landscape of Western Thebes.[79] Beyond their precincts, Mansions of Millions of Years possessed economic assets including landed estates, fleets of ships, and other sources of wealth, all staffed by bureaucrats, priests, and personnel who might number in their thousands.

Each Mansion of Millions of Years in Western Thebes hallowed its royal builder as a unique aspect of Amun-Re who resided in this temple.[80] Here the identities of Amun and the pharaoh coalesced. Ramesside kings called each local form of Amun by the temple's official name. The temple we call the Ramesseum bore a more grandiloquent name in antiquity: "The Mansion of Millions of Years of Usermaatre-Setepenre who Unites with Thebes in the Domain of Amun." Here dwelled "Amun of United with Thebes," who was none other than Ramesses II as an avatar of Amun-Re.

New Kingdom pharaohs constructed Mansions of Millions of Years at many Egyptian religious centers. Eighteenth Dynasty kings like Thutmose III, Amenhotep III, and Tutankhamun also built Mansion temples in colonial settlements across Nubia.[81] The pace of Mansion construction picked up in the Nineteenth and Twentieth Dynasties. But Ramesses II built more of these shrines than any other pharaoh. Regardless of their patron or location, all these royal cult temples expressed the theology of divine kingship, and the pharaoh's mystical communion with one or more of Egypt's deities.

During the Jubilee decades, Ramesses II undertook waves of monumental construction and decoration celebrating his personal divinity and his assimilation with Egypt's gods. In cult centers across Egypt and Nubia, artisans embellished temples with hundreds of new inscriptions, wall reliefs, statues, and obelisks, especially in his showcase capital of Piramesses.

Notes

1. This is evident in previous studies of the reign; see Stadelmann 1981; Kitchen 1982; Obsomer 2012b.

2. Aside from conventional triumph scenes, battle art largely disappears from the decorative programs of the king's later temples at Gerf Hussein and Wadi es-Sebua, both of which date after the second *Sed*-festival. The last war scenes of Ramesses II are modest and depict him fighting nondescript Nubian and Syrian foes in his temple at Derr in Nubia, which date to this period between the Hittite peace and his first Jubilee (*PM* VII, 58 and 85; Wreszinski 1925, pl. 168a; *KRI* II, 200–204; *RITA* II, 64–65; *RITANC* II, 115–16; Heinz 2001, 262–64. On the date of the Derr temple, see Kitchen, *RITANC* II, 474). A Nubian war scene in his temple at Amara West may date to shortly after the Hittite peace; Spencer 2016, pls. 186–97. After his twenty-first year, the king also commissioned triumphal scenes in which he slays prisoners before the gods at Karnak, and in temples like Derr and Wadi es-Sebua, but these are entirely traditional and stereotyped and constitute a standard element of temple decoration. Also dating to after regnal year 21 are triumphal scenes on the vestibule of the Second Pylon at Karnak (*PM* II², 38; *KRI* II, 168–69; *RITA* II, 42–43; *RITANC* II, 78–79). Likewise, formal texts recording military actions also cease and monumental inscriptions from the latter half of the reign touch on past glories or repeat conventional verbiage about the king's prowess as a warrior, all of them being highly poetic and rhetorical. A partial exception are stelae from Wadi es-Sebua belonging to Setau, the Viceroy of Kush. One of these, dated to regnal year 44 (Cairo JdE 41395), records military actions in Nubia against Irem and Akuyata. In another (Cairo JdE 41403), Setau reports that the king commanded him to launch a raid in the western desert to capture Tjemehu Libyan prisoners who were put to work building the temple of Wadi es-Sebua: *KRI* II, 93–95; *RITA* II, 64–66; *RITANC* II, 81–82. The "historical" narrative about Ramesses II's conquests from the First Hittite Marriage Decree belongs to the rhetorical category. In a similar vein, inscriptions on an obelisk and a rhetorical stela refer to a battle against the Sherden in Ramesses II's earliest years as king, for which see pp. 102–3 above.

3. Kitchen 1987, 133–34; Brand 2005, 31–32.

4. Kitchen 1987, 183.

5. On Ramesses II's association with the god, see Manouvrier 1996, 645–52.

6. For a tally of many of these variant Horus names with translations, see Manouvrier 1996, 412–17; Leprohon 2013, 115–18. Many of these date to the Jubilee period. They are often found on architectural elements of the temples, especially architraves and soffits.

7. Kitchen 1987, 183–84. Ramesses also used over a dozen unique variations of his Nebty name on his monuments; see Leprohon 2013, 118.

8. Brand 2005, 31.

9. Eaton-Krauss 1991. This sentiment could also apply to statues of earlier kings Ramesses II reinscribed. See pp. 414–15 below. For an exhaustive catalog of Ramesses II's statuary and analysis of the corpus, see Sourouzian 2019 and 2020b.

10. Goedicke 1960; Posener 1960; Morris 2010. See the essays collected in O'Connor and Silverman 1995; Frandsen 2008. On divine kingship across the ancient world, see most recently Maret 2011.

11. Redford 1995, 157–84; Winnerman 2018.

12. In recent years, several Egyptologists have rejected the traditional translation of *ḥm=f* as "his majesty" in favor of "his person" or "his incarnation"; see Parkinson 1991; Murnane 1995b; Brand, Feleg, and Murnane 2018.

13. See Spiegel 1939; Shaw 2010, 175–79, esp. 179.

14. Like a cult statue fashioned from precious metals and gemstones, the king resplendent in his colorful crowns and regalia became a manifestation (*ḫprw*) of the gods themselves, imbued with their divine luminescence.

15. Examples of the term *ḥm* in reference to cult images are too numerous to mention here, but a few salient examples are in order. In the fragmentary oracular inscription from Hatshepsut's famous Red Chapel bark shrine from Karnak, Amen-Re addresses the queen in the form of his processional bark. The god is referred to as *ḥm=f*, "his incarnation" and *ḥm n nṯr pn*, "the incarnation of this god." From the context of Amun's oracular pronouncement, it is clear that the god's *ḥm*-incarnation is his sacred bark. Along with the cult statue housed in the cabin-shrine, the bark itself, and especially its figurehead, could function as the god's cult image housing his *Ka*; see Bell 1985; Karlshausen 2009, 159–69, 277–79. A dedicatory text from Karnak describes Amenhotep III as "One who endows [the temple of every god], who fashions their incarnate forms (*ḥmw*) from gold, and who perpetuates their offerings": *Urk.* IV, 1667:13–14. Another dedicatory inscription at Gebel Barkal gives a variant Golden Horus name of Amenhotep III as "Protector of the gods, who fashions their incarnate forms" (*nḏ nṯrw ms ḥmw=sn*): *Urk.* IV, 1751:13. In the divine birth legends of Hatshepsut from Deir el-Bahari and of Amenhotep III from Luxor Temple, Amun-Re's physical presence when he seduces the queen is consistently referred to as the "incarnate form of this august god" (*ḥm n nṯr pn šps*): *Urk.* IV, 1713–1715.

16. On ancient Egyptian and Near Eastern parallels to the medieval concept of "the king's two bodies," see Nuzzolo 2017.

17. Bell 1985, 1997.

18. Amenhotep also became a living deity and manifestation of all the gods as a result of his *Sed*-festival celebrations during the last decade of his reign; Johnson 1998; Bickel 2002. Amenhotep established a cult for a lunar form of his divine alter ego called Nebmaatre-Lord-of-Nubia; see Schiff Giorgini et al. 1998; Murnane 2000.

19. A unique divine avatar of Sety I entitled Menmaatre-the Great God appears in a relief in his Abydos temple; Calverley and Broome 1958, pl. 42. On the royal cult under Sety I, see Brand 2000, 384–93.

20. Brand 1997; 2000, 271–75 and 390–91.

21. Manouvrier 1996, 564–80.

22. The literature on this topic is vast. Classic studies include Goedicke 1960 and Posener 1960. Among the recent works, see Morris 2010; Winnerman 2018.

23. Amenhotep III served as a model for Ramesses II's kingship, who also reused many of his predecessor's statues: Sourouzian 2020a.

24. Habachi 1969a, 8–11; *RITANC* II, 481.

25. In her analysis of the decorative program of Abu Simbel, Ullmann (2011) persuasively challenged the notion that the deification of Ramesses II only came to fruition during the second half of his reign, refuting the interpretation of Habachi (1969a, 8) that Ramesses had not yet become divine when the four seated colossi on the façade were carved and inscribed.

26. There are palimpsest scenes on the columns of the temple's hypostyle hall depicting Ramesses II offering to deified images of himself and Queen Nefertari alongside other gods. The original scenes were smaller and feature the nomen form *Rʿ-ms-s*, indicating they date before regnal year twenty-one. The final scenes are larger and always have the nomen *Rʿ-ms-sw*, likely dating to after year twenty-one. Artsist often modified the king's regalia as well; see Spencer 2016, pls. 78–103.

27. On Egyptian kingship ideology, theology, and iconography in the early Nineteenth Dynasty, see Brand 2000, 38–44, 384–93; 2005; Spalinger 2009; Lurson 2016.

28. Plenty of monuments and texts dating from his earlier decades still proclaimed his warlike deeds in his later decades, and the glorious image of Ramesses "great of victories" was not in eclipse.

29. See p. 407 below. The epithets refer not to the city, but to the king himself, hence: "The House of Ramesses-Meramun who is great of victories" and "who is the great *Ka* of Re-Horakhty."

30. Habachi 1969a, 1–16 and pls. 1–7; Donadoni et al. 1975, pls. 5–6; Lurson 2001; Peters-Desteract 2003, 230–36, figs. 80, 85, 88; 245, fig. 104; and 253, fig. 118.; Ullmann 2011.

31. Bell 1985, 208 n. 142; Brand 2000, 42.

32. So "great god" (*nṯr-ʿȝ*) or "the great god" (*pȝ nṯr-ʿȝ*).

33. At Abu Simbel we find both "Ramesses-Meramun" and "Usermaatre-Setepenre," both of whom bear the epithet "Residing in the Domain of Ramesses-Meramun."

34. In their royal cult temples on the west bank of Thebes, special forms of the kings who built them merged with Amun-Re; Haeny 1997; Ullmann 2002, 2016. In Ramesses II's Nubian cult temples, his divine alter egos comingled with gods like Amun-Re, Ptah, and Re-Horakhty: Habachi 1969a, 27–39; Ullmann 2013a, 2013b, 2017.

35. Bell 1985.

36. Enany 2012. On other falcon-headed avatars of Ramesses II equating him with Horus or the moon good, see Bianchi 1989.

37. PM VII, 53–64; Ullmann 2013a, 31–33.

38. Habachi 1969a, 14–15.

39. Egyptian theologians expressed this communion of two or more deities by linking their names and epithets in hieroglyphic texts, and their iconographic attributes in temple iconography. An extreme example was the multivalent avatar uniting three distinct solar gods of Heliopolis with Amun of Thebes as the peerless "Amun-Re-Horakhty-Atum-Khepri the Great God"; see Brand, Feleg, and Murnane 2018, pl. 32.

40. Uphill 1984, 235–36; Manouvrier 1996, 674–77; Gulyás 2003; Römer 2004; Ullmann 2017, 665.

41. An unfinished granite dyad found at Giza depicts two figures with solar disks, one or both of which might be Ramesses II as a solar deity. Or, it could represent Ramesses II alongside Atum; see Willeitner 1996; Hawass 1997. A fragmentary granite triad, also from Giza, shows a king with a solar disk and *nemes*-headdress flanked by a male solar god, likely Atum, and a goddess, both of whom also have large solar disks on their heads. The facial features are eroded, and no inscriptions are preserved. The king's solar disk has an image of a

winged scarab beetle in low relief. It likely depicts Ramesses II's assimilation to both Atum and Khepri, the evening and morning aspects of Re.

42. *KRI* II, 446.

43. See Gulyás 2003, 59–61. After death, the king's "soul" (*bꜣ*) merged with those of Osiris and Re. In the New Kingdom underworld books inscribed in royal tombs from the Valley of the Kings, the souls of Osiris and Re also merge at the sixth hour of the night before going their separate ways. Neither loses his identity to the other god.

44. *KRI* II, 719:10; see Gulyás 2003, 58. See pp. 424 and 426, fig. 14.20.

45. For Kitchen's analysis, see *RITANC* II, 151–53.

46. Literally "Shu of the Two Banks." Shu, son of the creator Atum, was a god of the atmosphere and ambient light emanating from his father the solar god.

47. *KRI* II, 237–39.

48. In the late Bronze Age, iron remained an exotic rarity. Prior to the widespread adoption of iron-ore smelting at the beginning of the Iron Age in the first millennium BCE, the Egyptians only worked meteoric iron. They were aware of its celestial origins, calling it "wonder-metal from heaven," *biꜣwt n(t) pt*.

49. *KRI* II, 268–70.

50. The phrase "who came into being as Khepri" (*ḫpr m Ḫpri*) is a pun. Such word play was not humorous but expressed deeper theological meanings and connections between ideas. Khepri was the morning form of Re, who rose from the underworld at the eastern horizon. His name means "He Who Comes into Being."

51. Ramesses refers to casting cult statues of the gods from gold and other precious metals. These statues served as earthly "bodies" (*ḥmw*) of the gods.

52. *KRI* II, 276–78.

53. Habachi 1969a; Manouvrier 1996, 466–96; Leblanc 2011. On the typology and iconography of Ramesses II's colossi and smaller sculptures see now Sourouzian's (2020b) definitive synthesis of Nineteenth Dynasty royal statuary.

54. The one possible exception being Amenhotep III, whose artists sculpted vast numbers of royal and divine statues in granite, siliceous sandstone, and other stones ranging in size from statuettes to the two colossi of Memnon from his royal cult temple in Western Thebes.

55. Habachi 1969a; Price 2011. For an inventory of these monikers, see Manouvrier 1996, 466–92.

56. So "ruler of the Two Lands" (*ḥkꜣ-tꜣwy*) and "ruler of rulers" (*ḥkꜣ n ḥkꜣw*); see Manouvrier 1996, 480–18.

57. For references, see Manouvrier 1996, 472–76 (*Mnṯw m tꜣwy*); 478–79 (*pꜣ nṯr*); 479–80 (*pꜣ nṯr ꜥꜣ*).

58. So *Rꜥ n ḥkꜣw*: Manouvrier 1996, 480–81.

59. Habachi 1969a; Leblanc 2011.

60. A striking example of this is the life-sized enthroned statue of Thutmose III from Deir el-Bahari now housed in the Luxor Museum. Despite centuries of exposure to the elements, one occasionally sees traces of color on some of Ramesses II's granite colossi, especially on the stripes of his *nemes*-headdress, which were left rough so that the paint could adhere.

61. For a database of seventy-four known votive stelae from Piramesses, see Exell 2009, 179–85. Ninety-one percent are dedicated to the cult of Ramess-

es II's colossi. Exell also discusses the broader social phenomenon of Ramesside votive stelae.

62. Leblanc identified traces of a shrine in front of the massive pedestal of the Ozymandias colossus at the Ramesseum. It served both for the official cult of the colossus by the temple's priesthood and as a focal point for popular devotions, as the fragment of a small stela bearing images of Ptah and the colossus, titled Usermaatre-Setepenre-the-Re-of-Rulers attests; Leblanc 2011, 297–98 and figs. 6–7; 2019, pl. 68 opposite p. 142.

63. To date, no systematic publication of these stelae has appeared; see Roeder 1926. See also Exell 2009, 179–85 (table 5) for a comprehensive list of Piramesses votive stelae. For images of some of these, see Habachi 2001; Petersen and Kehrer 2016, cat. nos. 51–56. For discussion of this corpus, see *RITANC* II, 305–10; Habachi 1954, 527–59; 1969a, 27–39; Exell 2009, 102–3; Sourouzian 2020b, 47–49 and figs. 3–4, 17.

64. Habachi 1969a, 31, figs. 18, 19; Petersen and Kehrer 2016, cat nos. 52–55.

65. Hildesheim 375: *KRI* II, 452; *RITA* II, 279; *RITANC* II, 307–8; Habachi 1954, 536 and pl. 34B.

66. See examples in Petersen and Kehrer 2016, cat. nos. 52–56.

67. Hildesheim 410: *KRI* II, 453; *RITA* II, 280; *RITANC* II, 308–9; Habachi 1969a, 31, fig. 19. Hildesheim 1079, stela of Ramessu-menu: *KRI* III, 205; *RITA* III, 143; *RITANC* II, 173; Habachi 1954, 539–40; 1969a, 31, fig. 18.

68. Hildesheim 380: *KRI* II, 451; *RITA* II, 279; *RITANC* II, 306–7; Habachi 1954, 529; Exell 2009, pl. 15a; Petersen and Keher 2016, 108–9 (cat. no. 56).

69. Hildesheim 1080: *KRI* II, 451; *RITA* II, 279; *RITANC* II, 306–7; Habachi 1954, 529.

70. Hildesheim 376: *KRI* II, 452; *RITA* II, 279; *RITANC* II, 307–8; Habachi 1954, 529.

71. *KRI* II, 451; *RITA* II, 279; *RITANC* II, 306–7.

72. Prince Meryatum appears with a man named Akhpet who holds the cultic title "pure of hands in the Domain of Re" on Hildesheim 1102: *KRI* II, 906; *RITA* II, 591; *RITANC* II, 610–11; Habachi 1954, 541 and pl. 37; Leblanc 1999, 87, fig. 27.

73. Hildesheim 374: *KRI* III, 263–64; *RITA* III, 187–88; *RITANC* III, 216; Habachi 1969a, 30 and fig. 17; Exell 2009, pl. 14.

74. *KRI* III, 263–64.

75. Munich Egyptian Museum 287: *KRI* III, 52–53; *RITA* III, 35; *RITANC* III, 41–42; Habachi 1969a, 33–34 and fig. 21, pl. 13b.

76. In Egyptian *ḥwt nt nḥḥ n rnpwt*. A *ḥwt*, "mansion," literally means "enclosure." It refers to a style of architecture dating back to late prehistory and early dynastic times when the earliest pharaohs built walled enclosures containing temples and palaces. These culminated in the mud-brick enclosure of King Khasekhemwy at Abydos in the late Second Dynasty and his son Djoser's Step Pyramid Complex at Saqqara built of limestone. In the Middle and New Kingdoms, *ḥwt-nṯr*, "mansion of the god," referred to a temple with its enclosing complex of precinct walls, administrative structures, storage magazines, royal palaces or rest houses, and subsidiary shrines, not just the temple building itself.

77. On the religious function of these temples, see Haeny 1997; Ullmann 2002, 2016. See also the essays collected in Leblanc and Zaki 2010.

78. On the Ramesseum's decline, see Leblanc 2019, 289–310.

79. Haring (1997) elucidates the administration and economy of royal cult temples in western Thebes during the New Kingdom. Leblanc (2019, 171–280) synthesizes the archaeological data on the service buildings of the Ramesseum and its personnel.

80. Haeny 1997; Ullmann 2002.

81. For an overview, see Ullmann 2002.

CHAPTER FOURTEEN

RICH IN YEARS: MONUMENTAL CONSTRUCTION AND HITTITE RELATIONS IN THE JUBILEE PERIOD

The City of Piramesses

Nestled among a cluster of turtleback islands, called *gezira* in Arabic, Sety I founded a new royal residence in the eastern Nile Delta. Ramesses II expanded his father's palace into his showcase capital of Piramesses, the "Domain of Ramesses Great of Victories." In his Jubilee period, he rebranded it as "Piramesses the Great *Ka* of Re-Horakhty." It remains famous today as the biblical "City of Ramses" in Exodus. But where did Ramesses build his new metropolis?

Egyptologists long identified Tanis (modern San el-Hagar), an ancient city in the northeastern Delta, as the location of Piramesses.[1] Today the ruins at Tanis are an alien moonscape of sandy dunes, littered with ancient stone relics covered with hieroglyphic inscriptions (fig. 14.1). Beginning in the late nineteenth century archaeologists unearthed hundreds of granite and siliceous sandstone monoliths at the site: huge colossi and scores of smaller statues, dozens of obelisks, and numerous stelae and architectural components, all bearing Ramesses II's names, titles, and image.[2] More relics were scattered across the Delta.[3]

At Tanis early British and French excavators were certain they had uncovered lost Piramesses. Yet, doubts soon arose. Aside from these Ramesside monuments, the earliest pottery attesting to the occupation of Tanis dated no earlier than the first millennium BCE, when the Twenty-First Dynasty pharaohs made it their capital. Did they also change the city's name?

In the 1920s, glazed tiles with elegant decoration, which once graced the floors and walls of the palaces of Sety I and Ramesses II, turned up near the present-day village of Qantir in the eastern Delta. Qantir lies 37 miles (60 kilometers) northeast of Cairo and 19 miles (30 kilometers) south of Tanis. Close by lay ancient Avaris (modern Tel el-Dab'a), the former stronghold of the Hyksos rulers and ancestral seat of the Ramesside kings. In the 1940s, an Egyptian archaeologist uncovered proof

FIGURE 14.1. Ruins of Tanis strewn with blocks from Ramesses II's monuments that the Bubastite pharaohs transferred from the abandoned city of Piramesses. Photograph by Peter Brand.

that Ramesses II's capital once stood at Qantir.[4] But why were so many of his monuments found at Tanis?

More than a century after Ramesses died, the Nile channel on which he had built his once thriving capital silted up.[5] Abandoning the dying city, Twenty-First Dynasty pharaohs transported hundreds of monoliths to embellish their new capital at Tanis, on a nearby branch of the Nile. Ripped from their original context, it is hard to envision how all these monuments scattered across the ruins at Tanis once fit into Piramesses's urban landscape.

Ramesses II's grand capital remains an enigma. After three thousand years it has vanished from sight. At Qantir we see little trace of Piramesses amid the village houses and surrounding cropland: only a large pair of limestone feet, lying forlorn in a farmer's field. They once belonged to a colossus of Ramesses. Yet, just below the surface lie the foundations of this once thriving city. In recent decades a team of Austrian and German archaeologists have excavated parts of ancient Piramesses, revealing vital details of its urban design and economy.[6]

Its urban core occupied the largest of several islands in the ancient Nile's two westernmost branches, where the Waters of Avaris and the Waters of Re, diverge.[7] Given its strategic location on Egypt's northeastern frontier, Piramesses was also a garrison town, the gateway to Pharaoh's possessions in Sinai and the Levant. Here a large part of Egypt's chariot force was quartered in Ramesses II's extensive stables. Archaeologists estimate he once kept five hundred steeds here, along with their chariots and equipment.[8] In a military-industrial complex nearby, weaponsmiths manufactured armaments to equip his armies. An exceptional find was the stone template for an hourglass-shaped shield that Hittite soldiers used—an ancient example of technology transfer.

FIGURE 14.2. Arial view of a digital reconstruction of Piramesses based on magnetometer scans of the ruins of the city lying beneath the modern village of Qantir. Digital image courtesy Artefacts-Berlin: www.artefacts-berlin.de.

Archaeologists cannot excavate most of Piramesses without displacing the Qantir villagers. Instead, they rely on magnetometry, a type of remote sensing technology, to peer beneath local fields and map large portions of Ramesses II's lost capital. These magnetometer surveys revealed at least one major palace complex, housing estates belonging to court elites, and temples dedicated to national and local deities.[9] Ghostly outlines of one building complex resemble the Ramesseum in Thebes. Enclosed within its hulking mud-brick enclosure walls we see storage magazines and administrative structures. These granaries and warehouses inspired biblical accounts of the "store cities" of Pithom and Ramses.[10]

Only the foundations of the stone temple remain; later generations stripped away most of its masonry. We see the outlines of a pylon gateway, outer courts lined with columned porticos, hypostyle halls, and an inner sanctuary or audience chamber. Although smaller than the Ramesseum, these structures belonged either to a temple complex dedicated to pharaoh's cult or a ceremonial palace whose design resembles a temple. Digital technology now enables a virtual reconstruction of the city (fig. 14.2).[11]

We can better appreciate the city's vanished splendor from ancient poetic accounts preserved in a collection of model literary works.[12] One piece extolls Piramesses's beauties and describes its idealized layout, including colossal statues of Ramesses II. Referring to these grand statues by their descriptive epithets, the poet refers to them metaphorically as grand state officials:

Beginning the victory ode about the Lord of Egypt: His Person, L.P.H., has built a residence for himself called "Great of Victories." It lies between Djahy and Egypt and is filled with food and provisions. Its design is like Upper Egyptian Heliopolis (Thebes) and it endures like Memphis.

Shu shines in its horizon and he sets in its interior. Everyone leaves their towns. They settle in its district. Its western part is the Temple of Amun. Its southern part is the Temple of Seth. Astarte appears in its east. Wadjet is in its north. The palace-fortress which is in its center is like the horizon of heaven.

"Ramesses-Meramun" is in it like a god; "Monthu in the Two Lands" is herald; "Re of Rulers" is vizier; and "Pleasing the heart of Egypt–Beloved of Atum" is mayor.[13]

FIGURE 14.3. Pyramidion of an obelisk of Ramesses II, originally from Piramesses and now in the garden of the Egyptian Museum, Cairo. In the lower scene, Ramesses worships Ptah. Above, a rebus inscription of his nomen in a divine bark depicts the king's assimilation with the sun god Re. Photograph by Peter Brand.

Ramesses II's Jubilee years witnessed a burst of new construction activity at Piramesses, as he embellished it with scores of new monuments. Pharaoh's builders erected a dozen pairs of obelisks in the city, but all were later moved to Tanis. Some attained heights of forty-two to fifty-three feet (thirteen to seventeen meters), others were shorter, ranging from twenty to thirty feet (six to nine meters).[14] Although Ramesses II's twin Luxor obelisks dwarfed them all, the Piramesses obelisks impress us by their sheer numbers. Texts on some of these granite spires herald the king's *Sed*-festivals.[15] In scenes decorating their bases, upper shafts, and pyramidions, Ramesses adores gods like Atum, Ptah, and Shu, highlighting his role as Egypt's chief priest (fig. 14.3). On the pyramidions artists sometimes carved his name in rebus form—without a cartouche but resting in a solar bark. These word-pictures evoke his status as the Sun God incarnate, who sailed across the heavens each day in his celestial ship.

Numerous monoliths from Piramesses also found their way to Tanis, including at least thirteen granite stelae bearing rhetorical hymns praising Pharaoh's valor in combat.[16] Sadly, most are not well preserved, and their content runs more to high poetry than sober historical record. Ramesses also commissioned at least nine colossi of red and gray granite, black granodiorite, and red siliceous sandstone. Some date to his Jubilee period, like one red sandstone colossus with a small figure of Ramesses II's first Hittite wife, Maahorneferure, standing beside his massive leg (see fig. 12.9 above).[17]

From sites in Lower Egypt, Ramesses's men also removed several colossi and eight royal sphinxes belonging to Middle Kingdom rulers, transporting them to Piramesses and reinscribing them in his name.[18] He also dedicated much new statuary, smaller than his grand colossi but life-size or larger. More than a dozen statues depict Pharaoh seated or standing. In others he appears with assorted gods and goddesses, both pair-statues, called dyads, and triads depicting him with two deities. In these group statues he often stands or sits next to goddesses like Sekhmet, Wadjet, and Anath, a Canaanite warrior goddess. In one triad he accompanies Re-Horakhty and Ptah-Tatchenen, in another, Khepri and Hathor.[19] Ideologically, this statue program emphasizes Ramesses II's ties to Egypt's gods, not merely as their devoted servant and offspring, but as one of their number.

Monumental Inscriptions in the Jubilee Period

As he celebrated an unprecedented spate of thirteen *Sed*-festivals in the latter half of his reign, Ramesses II transformed Egypt's sacred landscape. He directed his sculptors to reengrave countless existing statues, obelisks, columns, gateways, and temple walls with new reliefs and hieroglyphic texts bearing his image, names, and titles.[20] His men carved these decorations on monuments with high visibility, both his own and those of his predecessors. Today scarcely any New Kingdom temple complex lacks at least one inscription attesting to his ceaseless activity. Nor did his artisans labor in a random or piecemeal fashion. This was a programmatic effort to renovate Egypt's entire sacred infrastructure as he prepared for his early *Sed*-festivals.[21]

Most of these inscriptions are undated, yet scribes left clues in the way they wrote Pharaoh's cartouches. By midway through his reign, Ramesses II had largely frozen the hieroglyphic spelling and arrangement of his nomen and prenomen. Gone were numerous eclectic variant cartouches we see in his early years. Beginning with the Hittite Peace Treaty stela in year twenty-one, the form and hieroglyphic spelling of his nomen changes from *Ramesses* to *Ramesssu*, especially in Upper Egypt and Nubia (fig. 14.4).[22] This lets us determine whether inscriptions date before or after year twenty-one. But examples with *Ramessu* often belong to his Jubilee period, a decade or more after the Hittite peace (fig. 14.5).[23]

Many of Ramesses II's epigraphs from his Jubilee era appear decorative, consisting of little more than strings of royal names and titles. Scholars call such marginal decorations "bandeau texts."[24] The

FIGURE 14.4. Relief from the enclosure wall of Karnak Temple showing Ramesses II wearing the *shebyu*-necklace. His elaborate crown and regalia consciously echo the baroque iconography of Amenhotep III's reliefs dating to the last decade of his reign. Photograph by Peter Brand.

FIGURE 14.5. Siliceous sandstone lintel from Piramesses, now in Tanis, depicting Ramesses II running in the presence of Re-Horakhty. Photograph by Peter Brand.

hieroglyphic script was versatile, allowing scribes to format texts horizontally or vertically, with signs facing either left or right. Although earlier pharaohs left bandeau texts on temple walls and gateways, Ramesses II set a new trend by inscribing them in huge quantities on monuments. Sculptors arranged them in horizontal bands along the bases and tops of walls and doorways and on pylon towers. They formatted others vertically on obelisk shafts, on the back pillars of dyad and triad statues, and as dividers between wall scenes.[25]

Despite their profusion, these inscriptions are stereotyped and ceremonial. Typically lacking a date, few indicate any specific historical event. Still, we should not dismiss them as meaningless "space fillers." Although they may be tedious to us, these royal names and titles guarded the king's sacred identity.[26] The hieroglyphic script itself, which Egyptians called the "divine words," was also sacred. Writing had magical potency because Thoth, patron god of scribes, first devised it. Displaying a pharaoh's name on monuments evoked his mystical presence, demonstrated his piety to the gods, and amplified his earthly prestige. Simply by carving such inscriptions, even on structures his ancestors built, the king was creating a new "monument" (Egyptian *menoo*), literally "something that endures."

Ramesses II authorized these new decorations in ambitious campaigns to refurbish temples before his *Sed*-festivals. We see this program unfolding at Sety I's cult temple at Gurnah in Western Thebes, where Ramesses commissioned new reliefs during the second half of his reign.[27] His father left most of Gurnah Temple undecorated when he died. Ramesses embellished its main chambers with reliefs in the earliest years of his reign before abandoning the project.[28]

Large portions of Gurnah Temple languished unadorned until Ramesses II's Jubilee period. Now, three decades after Sety's death, Ramesses revisited the project. Sculptors labored over blank wall surfaces
in Gurnah's solar court, side chambers, and exterior walls, carving new
ritual scenes naming Ramesses alone. In Gurnah's solar court they produced competent but uninspired reliefs.[29] At their worst, in the temple's
inner storage chambers, these efforts were perfunctory, even crude. Today many wrongly assume such maladroit carvings are representative
of all the king's later artistic output. Yet, there are also elegant and
sophisticated wall reliefs from all periods of his reign.

We should not interpret the slipshod carvings at Gurnah as signs
of a wider decline in Ramesside art. Racing to meet the deadline of a
Sed-festival the craftsmen sometimes fashioned inferior reliefs, especially in places likely to be seen by only a few priests. But ritual art
was magically potent, not merely decorative. Reliefs depicting pharaoh
conducting rites before the gods ensured that these ceremonies would
be repeated forever. They need not be elegant to be effective.[30]

Belying modern claims of declining standards are elaborate ritual scenes Ramesses added to Thutmose III's enclosure walls at Karnak
Temple.[31] Surrounding the main sanctuary, Thutmose left these long
walls blank, except for a dedicatory inscription along the top. Ramesses
now erased this text and added two registers of scenes, with a dedicatory bandeau along the base of the wall.[32] These reliefs date to the forties
or fifties of his reign and are of the finest workmanship. Craftsmen
engraved intricate details of costumes and regalia, which give hints of
Ramesses' divinity. They emulate reliefs from Amenhotep III's Jubilee
decade, when he too ruled as a living god. One key sign of Amenhotep's divinity was the *shebyu*-necklace he wore, along with assorted
exotic regalia.[33] These insignia now resurface in Ramesses II's reliefs at
Karnak and on some of his statuary from the jubilee years (fig. 14.6). Although none of the surviving scenes depicts Ramesses worshiping his
deified self, he makes offerings to certain gods "of Ramesses," including
Amun, Ptah, and Re (see fig. 13.8 above).

Ramesses II's preference for sunk relief, instead of the raised relief
Sety I employed, further prejudices modern assessments of his monumental art. Today many prefer raised relief, considering the sunken
medium aesthetically inferior.[34] Critics often assume Ramesses adopted sunken carvings so his sculptors could finish them quickly at their
impatient master's behest. This claim is overstated. Sunk relief offered
superior visibility in the dark interiors of Egyptian temples. On exteri-
or walls, harsh sunlight leaves bas reliefs looking washed out. But the
play of light and shadows on sunk reliefs makes them stand out in any
lighting conditions. To heighten their visibility, Ramesses ordered his

FIGURE 14.6. ⬆ Statue of Ramesses II bearing divine standards. Dating to the second half of his reign, the king wears the *shebyu*-necklace as a mark of his divine status during his jubilee period. Cairo, Egyptian Museum JdE 44668. Photograph by Peter Brand.

men to carve reliefs deeper and increase the size of hieroglyphic texts, especially his cartouches.

Over three millennia after Ramesses II created them, his temple reliefs now look drab and timeworn. In their heyday they rivaled the gaily painted (and better protected) walls of contemporary royal tombs. Artists finished these temple reliefs with a smooth coat of plaster and painted them in vivid colors. In exceptional cases—like the temples of Sety I and Ramesses II at Abydos—they still retain much of their color, hinting at the lost splendor of other Ramesside shrines.[35]

Reinscribing the Monuments

Ramesses II is infamous today for his habit of reinscribing monuments that his royal ancestors had raised with his own names and titles. Historians often condemn this practice as "usurpation," and single Ramesses out for robbing his forebears of credit for their works.[36] Indeed, his workmen often erased the original pharaoh's name before adding his. But earlier pharaohs also reinscribed old buildings and statues.[37] As with his other endeavors, the second Ramesses far outpaced his forebears.

Some pharaohs reinscribed monuments to suppress the official memory of kings they now considered illegitimate. In a notorious case, Thutmose III proscribed the memory of his onetime coregent Hatshepsut.[38] In Thutmose's view, she had violated Maat by assuming this inherently masculine office. Two decades after her death he methodically expunged Hatshepsut's names and images from temple reliefs and smashed her statues. At Karnak he often replaced her cartouches with those of his grandfather Thutmose I and his father Thutmose II. Later, as the Eighteenth Dynasty drew to a close, Horemheb targeted the Amarna pharaohs, demolishing Akhenaten's temples and reinscribing Tutankhamun's works with his own cartouches.[39]

Such replacement was not always hostile. Ramesses I erased the cartouches of his patron Horemheb on Karnak's Second Pylon, inserting his own instead.[40] During his Jubilee years, Ramesses II annexed numerous colossi and lesser statuary of past monarchs, either by carving his name in blank spaces alongside theirs, or erasing their names and inserting his own. Unlike Thutmose III's repudiation of Hatshepsut, Ramesses chose the statuary of pharaohs he admired and emulated, not those whose memory he sought to abolish.[41]

On the roster of illustrious bygone monarchs whose statues Ramesses II recarved are Middle Kingdom rulers like Senwosret I (fig. 14.7) and Amenemhet III, and the Eighteenth Dynasty paragon Amenhotep III. They often belong to a select group of rulers who celebrated at least one *Sed*-festival, suggesting Ramesses appropriated their statuary deliberately during one of his own Jubilees. Craftsmen often modified these effigies, especially their facial features.[42]

Ramesses II also reinscribed reliefs of earlier kings at Karnak Temple, especially on its main processional axis. He recarved cartouches of Horemheb, and even his grandfather Ramesses I and father Sety I on the Second Pylon and in the nave of the Great Hypostyle Hall. From the spelling of his nomen, we know this occurred sometime after his twenty-first year. Workmen erased the existing names by plastering over sunk reliefs or chiseling out raised reliefs, and then engraving his names in sunk relief (fig. 14.8).[43]

Unlike many today, who censure Ramesses II for pilfering works rightfully belonging to his ancestors, his descendants did not remember him as a thief. To understand why Ramesses reinscribed so many old monuments, we must first appreciate an Egyptian mindset and sense of history that strikes us as alien. Today, if an American president claimed

Figure 14.7. ← A colossal granite statue of the Twelfth Dynasty king Senwosret I, from ancient Memphis. Ramesses II reinscribed the statue with his own names and altered the facial features at some time during his Jubilee years. Photograph by Peter Brand.

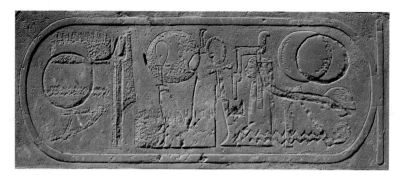

FIGURE 14.8. A palimpsest inscription from the Great Hypostyle Hall at Karnak Temple showing the prenomen cartouche of Ramesses II superimposed over that of Sety I. The sculptor partly erased the raised relief hieroglyphs of Sety's name before rapidly engraving Ramesses II's prenomen in sunk relief. J. Karkowski/Karnak Hypostyle Hall Project.

the Lincoln Memorial in Washington, D.C. for himself—engraving his name on it and replacing Abraham Lincoln's statue with his own— millions would denounce him for committing political sacrilege and historical desecration. Yet, for Egyptian pharaohs, reinscribing works their ancestors created was permissible, even legitimating.[44] It was the sincerest form of flattery, by kings who wished to emulate, not discredit, their forebears. After he died, some of Ramesses II's own statues and colossi fell victim to this strange breed of admiration, when later rulers—including his son Merenptah and his ardent emulator Ramesses IV—chiseled their names on them.[45]

Some now view Ramesses II's effort to insert countless inscriptions on monuments new and old as proof of his megalomania and the alleged decline in artistic standards during his reign. It is more productive to examine his actions in the historical and ideological context of his early Jubilees. When Ramesses observed his first *Sed*-festival in regnal year thirty, ca. 1249 BCE, most of his subjects were too young to recall Sety I's time. Memories of a Jubilee were even fainter, for more than half a century had elapsed since Akhenaten celebrated the last *Sed*-festival. Now, as Ramesses II prepared for this momentous occasion, who would object if he annexed the works of ancestral kings— even his father Sety's?

Whatever Ramesses II's appropriations, they pale in comparison with his creations. His Jubilee years witnessed new waves of building projects. A string of cult temples he built in Nubia are of special interest. In these shrines his program of self-deification reached its apogee.

Nubian Temples for a God-King

Following precedent earlier New Kingdom pharaohs established, but on an ambitious scale, Ramesses II founded several new urban settlements in Nubia, centered around temples dedicated to major gods of Egypt and to his own deification.[46] He launched two waves of temple building, one during his first two decades of rule, and a second in his

Jubilee years. By far the most spectacular and innovative of these sanctuaries were his twin temples at Abu Simbel. Ramesses constructed the larger temple in honor Amun-Re, Re-Horakhty, and his personal apotheosis.[47] He consecrated the smaller shrine to Hathor and his favored consort Nefertari as her living avatar. Abu Simbel, which the ancients called Meha, lies 140 miles (230 kilometers) southwest of Aswan on the Nile's west bank.[48] Both temples are grotto shrines, cut deep into the high cliffs skirting the river's western edge in Lower Nubia. Archaeologists call this type of rock hewn temple a *speos*.

The Great Temple of Abu Simbel

No monument encapsulates the awesome majesty and innovative spirit of Ramesses II's royal ideology more than his temple at Abu Simbel (fig. 14.9). Pharaoh's architects calculated every feature of this breathtaking edifice to overawe visitors. Its design, artwork, and inscriptions all promote the central themes of his regal ideology: Ramesses as builder, warlord, diplomat, family man, pious servant of the gods, and god-king.

To carry out their master's audacious vision, Pharaoh's engineers cut the grand temple's façade from the living sandstone of the moun-

FIGURE 14.9. The façade of the great temple of Abu Simbel with its four seated colossi. Alamy.

tainside, shaping it like a trapezoidal pylon tower. Masons and sculptors labored for years, hacking away uncounted tons of rocky overburden, to create the four gigantic statues of Ramesses II emerging from Abu Simbel's cliffs. These majestic colossi measured sixty-five feet (twenty meters) tall, dwarfing all who came within their purview.[49] The crowned head and torso of one lies shattered in ruins owing to an earthquake that struck the temple in antiquity.

All four colossi rest on large pedestals, embellished on their sides with carvings: rows of captive foreign rulers bound in fetters, kneeling prostrate beneath Pharaoh's massive feet. A staple of Egypt's iconography, these images of humiliated enemies serve as Ramesses's footstool.[50]

Standing beside and between the legs of Ramesses II's four giant statues are twelve smaller ones. They represent ten of the most prominent members of his huge family, including two effigies of his mother Tuya and two of Nefertari. Eight more statues depict favored offspring born to his consorts Nefertari and Isetnofret (see fig. 7.17 above).[51]

Just above the gateway leading to the rock-cut inner chambers, an architecturally unique niche depicts a large statue of Re-Horakhty (fig. 14.10). Beside his legs, two smaller statues represent hieroglyphs: a jackal's head staff ⁙ having the value *user*; and a squatting figure of Maat ⁙. Combined with Re's image, they form a type of cryptogram, also called a rebus, spelling out Ramesses II's prenomen Usermaatre. While it honors Re-Horakhty, this majestic iconic device is also a giant royal monogram, visually epitomizing the doctrine that Ramesses has assimilated with Egypt's preeminent solar deity. On the gateway below, an elaborate cryptogram spells out Ramesses II's cartouche names with figures of the gods (fig. 14.11).[52]

Inside the main hall, eight standing colossi line the main axis.[53] Behind them, wall scenes depict religious scenes and battle episodes including Kadesh. On the west wall, Ramesses leads foreign captives before divine triads that include his divine alter-ego.[54] The mortal Ramesses encounters his divine self in more scenes from the second pillared hall.[55] We also see images of two sacred barks carried by priests in procession. Amun's bark with its ram's head effigies appears on the south wall (fig. 14.12).[56] On the north wall, we might expect the bark of Re-Horakhty. But the falcon-headed deity in this bark is none other than Ramesses himself.[57] Once again, he assumes Re's identity.

This emphasis on the king's divinity culminates in the innermost sanctuary. Enthroned on its rear wall are four statues depicting Ptah, Amun-Re, Ramesses II, and Re-Horakhty. Twice a year at dawn, in late February and October, the sun's first rays pierce the temple's gloom, bathing the effigies of Amun, Ramesses, and Re-Horakhty in a golden glow, while barely touching Ptah's statue.[58]

FIGURE 14.10. ⬅ ⬅
Niche on the façade of the great temple of Abu Simbel. The large statue of Re-Horakhty has two smaller images of the jackal staff (left) and seated Maat goddess (right) below his fists. This forms a rebus spelling out of Ramesses II's prenomen Usermaatre. Images of Ramesses II in relief on either side of the niche offer Maat to the sun god, and effectively to his own divine aspect. Wikipedia Commons.

FIGURE 14.11. ⬅
A cryptographic inscription on the left side of the main gateway of the great temple of Abu Simbel. The figures of the gods represent the Egyptian pantheon but also spell out Ramesses II's nomen and prenomen. Photograph by Peter Brand.

Sometime after year twenty-one, masons excavated suites of treasuries and storage galleries off the outer hall (fig. 14.13).[59] Their proportions are irregular, and the quality of their relief carving is crude because workmen did a rush job. Yet, the gods in these scenes are rich in theological importance and iconic variety. Along with leading members of Egypt's pantheon, the king adores exotic forms of his divine avatars (see fig. 13.5 above).[60] The Abu Simbel treasuries are uniquely valuable for understanding Ramesses II's cult.

One suspects Ramesses II was especially proud of his magnificent shrine at Abu Simbel, revisiting it whenever his travels brought him to Nubia. We can imagine temple administrators getting word of their master's impending visit, with new orders to enlarge its interior chambers. In turn, they pressed the local workforce of masons and sculptors to hollow out and decorate these new rooms in a hurry. Abu Simbel lies in a remote and desolate stretch of the Nile Valley in Nubia with little arable land and a sparse population. After expending prodigious efforts to build this temple during Pharaoh's first two decades, the local workforce at Abu Simbel had dwindled when he ordered them to create these treasury chambers.

Figure 14.12. A. Ricci's watercolor sketch depicting Ramesses II and Nefertari offering to the sacred bark of Amun-Re carried by priests. South wall of the pillared hall of the the great temple at Abu Simbel. Courtesy UK National Trust.

When Europeans rediscovered Abu Simbel in the early nineteenth century, vast drifts of sand choked its mighty façade. These dunes sealed its inner chambers, preserving their delicate painted plaster. An Italian explorer named Giovanni Belzoni cleared much of this sand in 1817, revealing Abu Simbel's spectacular interior to human eyes for the first time since antiquity.[61]

Inside the grotto, Victorian travelers and early Egyptologists were astonished to discover exquisite colored plaster clinging to its interior walls and statues (fig. 14.14 and fig. 13.9). Pharaoh's artisans tinted every figure and hieroglyph in lavish detail. Early copyists documented some of these paintings in colored engravings that they published in massive folio volumes (fig. 14.15).[62] These precious illustrations are works of art in their own right, revealing the former splendor of

Figure 14.13. One of the treasury chambers added to the great temple of Abu Simbel in the later years of Ramesses II's reign. Alamy.

FIGURE 14.14. A. Ricci's watercolor sketch of two scenes from the main hall of the great temple of Abu Simbel. Left: the king kneels beneath the *Ished*-tree before Re-Horakhty while Thoth inscribes his name on the leaves. Right: Ramesses II offers to a special form of Amun-Re who dwells within the mountain of Gebel Barkal in Nubia, which also takes the form of an enormous cobra. Courtesy UK National Trust.

Ramesses II's glorious temple. Sadly, its beautiful murals soon began to decay from exposure to air and humidity. Two hundred years after Belzoni, Abu Simbel's vivid hues are all but lost to us.[63]

Abu Simbel itself was nearly lost when Egypt began building its Aswan High Dam, which would have flooded it completely. As we shall see in the last chapter, an international rescue effort unparalleled in human history saved this priceless heritage.

Nefertari's Abu Simbel Temple

Beside his own temple at Abu Simbel Ramesses II built another, dedicated to his Great Royal Wife Nefertari and Hathor of Ibchek, the goddess she embodied (fig. 14.16).[64] This was a rare honor for any Egyptian queen.[65] The architectural design and iconographic richness of Nefertari's temple make it extraordinary, a fitting tribute to Pharaoh's favored consort. Within wide niches on its sloping façade, two colossal images of the deified queen and four of Ramesses seem to stride out of the mountainside in lockstep. Inside each niche, smaller statues of Nefertari's children stand to either side of their parent's colossi. On the north side a dedication text proclaims:

> *The Dual King Usermaatre-Setepenre: He has made a temple by excavating in the mountain, of everlasting work in the Bow-Land (Nubia), which the Dual King Usermaatre-Setepenre has made [for] the Great Royal Wife Nefertari-Beloved of Mut in Nubia—like Re eternally and everlastingly. His Person decreed the making of a temple in Nubia by excavating in the mountain. Never had the like been achieved except by the "Beloved One of Amun" (the king).[66]*

On the south side, a shorter text describes this shrine as "a temple of great and grand monuments for the Great Royal Wife Nefertari-Beloved of Mut, she for whom the Sun does shine!"[67]

FIGURE 14.15. Rosellini's color facsimile of Ramesses II charging in his chariot from the main hall of the great temple of Abu Simbel. NYPL digital collections. Public domain.

Inside is a hall with six pillars supporting the ceiling. Their distinctive capitals are shaped like Hathor's heads: a woman's face with a long curled wig and bovine ears. Wall scenes highlight Nefertari's privileged role in Hathor's cult and those of other goddesses. She performs some rituals alongside her husband. But she also enjoys the rare honor of being the sole adoratrice before goddesses like Hathor and Anuket.[68] In one scene Nefertari grasps a queenly scepter and an *ankh*-sign, indicating her divinity, while Isis and Hathor set a lofty diadem upon her head (fig. 14.17). In the main sanctuary, wall scenes portray Ramesses II offering to deified images of himself and Nefertari.[69] Sadly, she could not savor the distinction her husband bestowed on her. Shortly after Pharaoh completed the temple, early in the twenties of his reign, Nefertari died.

Wadi es-Sebua

In the forty-fourth year of his reign, Ramesses II charged the Viceroy of Kush, Setau, with overseeing construction of a new temple at Wadi es-Sebua, a remote site in Lower Nubia.[70] While not as grand or elegant as Abu Simbel, Wadi es-Sebua is architecturally innovative. It is a hemi-speos, part inside and part outside a low escarpment. Pharaoh's architects excavated its hypostyle hall and inner chambers deep within

FIGURE 14.16. The façade of the temple of Nefertari at Abu Simbel. Four colossal images of Ramesses II flank two of Nefertari. To either side of their legs stand smaller statues of their most favored offspring. Alamy.

the shallow cliff. In front of this grotto they constructed a series of free-standing pylons, gateways, and courtyards.

Wadi es-Scbua is dedicated to both Amun-Re and the deified Ramesses.[71] In large scenes on its pylon façades and courtyard walls he worships his deified aspect, who sits with his fellow gods and goddesses, including Amun, Hathor, and Horus. In front of the pylons, large sandstone statues and an avenue of sphinxes (fig. 14.18) denote his supernatural presence. The sphinxes give Wadi es-Sebua its modern Arabic name, which means "Valley of the Lions." Most of them are conventional human-headed lions, but some have a falcon's head attached to their leonine bodies, depicting Ramesses as an avatar of Horus (fig. 14.19).[72]

On the courtyard walls we see a late example of the monumental lists of his sons and daughters.[73] Several of his offspring, including his firstborn son Prince Amunhirkhopeshef, died years before their father constructed Wadi es-Sebua. Yet, living or deceased, Ramesses chose to immortalize them here. Nefertari and Isetnofret had also passed away. Now Pharaoh's eldest daughter, the daughter-wife Bintanath, stands beside her father on one of his colossal statues.[74]

Wadi es-Sebua appears to confirm what Ramesses II's modern critics charge were low artistic standards during his reign. The Viceroy Setau and his men rapidly constructed the temple. Masons took short cuts in this sun-scorched, desolate stretch of far-flung Nubia. They never finished smoothing walls and other surfaces, leaving dense clouds of chisel marks on every block. Workmen applied heavy coatings of

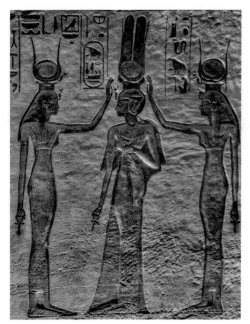

FIGURE 14.17. Nefertari crowned by Isis and Hathor, relief from her temple at Abu Simbel. The scene represents the queen's assimilation with these goddesses. Alamy.

plaster to hide these defects, but much has fallen away. But in a few places it is well preserved, offering a glimpse of Wadi es-Sebua in its heyday when its walls were smooth with colored reliefs in a rich palette of blues, greens, reds, and golds picked out against a brilliant white background. After thirty-two centuries, wind-blown sand has scoured away most of this fragile painted stucco. Here, as on many Ramesside temples, beauty was only skin deep.

Gerf Hussein

At Gerf Hussein in Lower Nubia, 56 miles (90 kilometers) south of Aswan, Ramesses II constructed the last of his Nubian speos temples, dedicating the shrine to Ptah-Tatchenen and his own divinity (fig. 14.20).[75] Sadly, most of its inner rooms were drowned beneath Lake Nasser after the Aswan High Dam was constructed in the 1960s. But portions of the temple were removed, including the best-preserved of the four colossi in the main hall, which still has much of its painted decoration. It is now the centerpiece of the Nubian Museum in Aswan.

The temple's most distinctive feature is a sequence of eight statue niches, each enclosing a triad of gods sculpted in high relief. The deified Ramesses II is the central figure, enthroned between various male and female deities.[76] Some of these are gods "of Ramesses," stressing his integration into the Egyptian pantheon, a theme that continues with the colossal statues named "Ramesses-Meramun-Appearing as the Gods."[77]

The Second Hittite Marriage

Some years after Ramesses II married his first Hittite wife Maahorneferure, he negotiated with the Hittite court to wed a second princess. Queen Puduhepa again led the negotiations.[78] By this time Maahorneferure may have died.[79] We can narrow the time frame from a letter Ramesses sent to Puduhepa, which belongs to a set of messages containing an expanded list of Pharaoh's names and titles. Before his prenomen, scribes now wrote his Egyptian titles in Akkadian: "Dual King," (Egyptian *nesu-bity*), and "Lord of the Two Lands," (Egyptian *neb tawy*), transcribing them in Akkadian as *insibiya* and *nib-tawa*. These

so-called *insibiya* letters also record his expanded nomen cartouche *Ramesses-Meramun-the God and Ruler of Heliopolis*, current from regnal years forty-two to fifty-six (fig. 14.21).[80] Although the Hittites had long since grown inured to their Egyptian in-law's pompous vanity, they could still only wince at his escalating egoism.[81]

FIGURE 14.18. View of the Wadi es-Sebua temple of Ramesses II with its avenue of lion- and falcon-headed sphinxes. Photograph by Peter Brand.

As before, Queen Puduhepa insisted Pharaoh confer the title of great royal wife on this princess. Ramesses agreed to these terms, replying with gifts for mother and daughter:

> [... I have sent you a fine gift as] a greeting gift for you ... and I have sent a gift as a greet]ing gift for the daughter of [my sister. And my sister has written to me as follows: "You should appoint] her as [Great King's] Wife [in the land of Egypt." So has my sister written to me.] Theref[ore, the daughter should be brought to me, and I shall appoint the daughter of] the Great [King], the King of the land of H[atti as Great King's Wife in my land ...].[82]

Did their haggling go more smoothly the second time around? Or did Puduhepa and Ramesses engage in the same contest of wills leading up to the first marriage pact? Regrettably, the rest of their correspondence is lost. One sticking point might have been visitation rights. If Pudehepa was willing to send a second daughter, we might assume that her envoys had visited Maahorneferure and found her situation satisfactory.

Our main source for Ramesses II's second Hittite marriage is a proclamation engraved on a stela from Coptos.[83] As with his first marriage edict, its tone is triumphant and presents the event as an act of homage by the Hittite king. But there is a notable difference in its ideological tone. In the First Marriage Decree, Pharaoh's military might vanquishes the Hittite king, who sues for peace and sends his daughter to Egypt

FIGURE 14.19. ⬆ A falcon-headed sphinx from Wadi es-Sebua repre-senting Ramesses II as the incarnation of Re-Horakhty. Photograph by Peter Brand.

FIGURE 14.20. ⬈ Nineteenth-century painting of the interior of Gerf Hussein by David Roberts. NYPL digital collections. Public domain.

as tribute. In the second, the gods alone bring her younger sister and the tribute of every foreign land to Ramesses:

> *The Great Chief of Hatti sent exceedingly abundant plunder from Hatti, exceedingly abundant plunder from Gasga, exceedingly abundant plunder from Arzawa, and exceedingly abundant plunder from Qode— which could not even be listed in writing—to the Dual King Usermaatre-Setepenre, the Son of Re, Ramesses-Meramun. And likewise, many droves of horses, many herds of cattle, many herds of goats, and many flocks of sheep, (all) in front of his other daughter, whom he sent to the Dual King Usermaatre-Setepenre, the Son of Re Ramesses-Meramun— given life—in Egypt, on the second occasion.*
>
> *It was not the troops who brought them. It was not the [chariotry] who brought them. It was the might of the gods of the land of Egypt, and (of) the gods of every foreign country! [They caused the great chiefs] to carry their gold, to carry their silver, and to carry their vessels of green [stone] to the Dual King Usermaatre-Setepenre, the Son of Re Ramesses-Meramun—given life—to bring their droves of horses, to bring their herds [of cattle, to bring] their flocks of goats, and to bring their flocks of sheep.... It was Ptah-Tatchenen, Father of the Gods, who places all flat lands and all hill countries under the feet of this perfect god—forever and ever![84]*

Aside from this idealized account, we know nothing about this second Hittite princess. Even her name escapes us. Nor does she appear beside

Ramesses II on his statues or monuments. After her nuptials, every trace of her vanishes from the records.

Egyptian Doctors at the Hittite Court

Meanwhile, Ramesses II continued his dialogue with the Hittite court. Hattusili III had suffered from poor health since childhood. Pharaoh offered precious gifts of medical aid to ilnesses that still tormented him. Egyptian doctors and their medicines earned renown in the Late Bronze Age. When Hattusili mentioned an eye disease afflicting him, Ramesses sent eye medicines to soothe him, along with an Egyptian doctor named Pariamahu to administer them.[85]

As the unfortunate case of Hattusili III's sister Matanazi shows, the price for airing medical needs to Pharaoh was a patronizing response. But when an important Hittite vassal named Kurunta—the son of Urhi-Teshub himself—fell gravely ill, Ramesses was all business. The first two Egyptian doctors he sent failed to cure Kurunta. Once again, it was Dr. Pariamahu to the rescue:

> I have now sent the Scribe and Doctor Pariamahu. He has been sent to prepare medicines for Kurunta, the king of the land of Tarhuntassa, and he will administer all types of medicines as you have written. As soon as he comes to you, place Kurunta ... in his care so he may prepare medicines for him. And dispatch these two doctors, who are there with Kurunta and let them come back to Egypt. As soon as the Scribe and Doctor Pariamahu reach him, on that day these other two doctors must terminate their activity.[86]

A Hittite Prince Visits Egypt

Some time after the Silver Treaty, a Hittite prince named Hismi-Sharruma journeyed to Egypt. Not just a goodwill mission, it was also a "business trip." In recent years Hatti had suffered recurrent droughts and crop failures leading to famine. When Puduhepa negotiated the marriage of her first daughter to Ramesses, she was eager for him to accept vast herds of livestock as the dowry, pleading: "I have no grain in my country."[87] As food shortages grew more dire, the Hittites began importing large amounts of grain from Egypt.[88] Contemporary documents mention bulk consignments ranging from fifteen to five hundred tons of wheat.[89] The Hittites marshalled their vassal kingdom of Ugarit's large merchant fleet to handle these cargos.

Egypt was the breadbasket of the ancient world. Annual Nile inundations and Egypt's fertile soil yielded bumper harvest year after year. Naturally, Hattusili turned to his new ally to relieve the hunger in his

FIGURE 14.21. Two nomen cartouches of Ramesses II from a dedicatory text on the enclosure wall of the main temple of Karnak showing the epithet "God and Ruler of Heliopolis" current in the 40s and 50s of his reign. Photograph by Peter Brand.

kingdom. The task was so urgent that the Hittite monarch sent his son to Egypt. Anxious for news of his mission, Hattusili wrote:

> [I have sent the Prince Hismi-Sharruma t]o the place [where] the (Egyptian) King is, [and I have sent] two messengers wi[th him (named) Kulazita and] Zitwalla. Has [my brother] not watched for a royal messenger from me? And see, truly, I have now sent these messengers as friends to the place where the King is. May the King allow him to be sent back to me![90]

Ramesses reassured Hattusili that the prince arrived safely during the winter. By spring, he announced that the prince was returning to his homeland with the life-giving freight:

> Let the Prince of the land of Hatti, Hismi-Sharruma, go with all the ships quickly, and quickly receive them. They have been replenished with barley and supplied with wheat. And he should return all the ships again and let them go to the land of Egypt to carry out deliveries ...[91]

In later decades the Hittites were still reliant on shiploads of food aid from the Nile, as Ramesses's successor Merenptah reports in a Karnak inscription: "To sustain this land of Hatti I caused grain to be taken in ships."[92]

In Ramesses II's later years, his correspondence with the Hittites tapers off. Whether this is due to accidents of preservation or diminished interest is unclear. Some years after Pharaoh married his second Hittite bride, her aged and sickly father Hattusili III died. His son Tudhaliya IV now succeeded him, even as Puduhepa lived on into ripe old age.[93] Tudhaliya's name never appears in the letters Ramesses sent to Hattusa. In the ruins of Piramesses, archaeologists unearthed a tiny scrap of a cuneiform tablet that may be a message from Hattusili III or Tudhaliya IV to Pharaoh, part of a lost archive of Hittite letters to Ramesses.[94]

Hattusili III's demise ended a long contest of arms and wills with Ramesses II that started at the Battle of Kadesh. Even after the Silver Treaty, their friendship was often as adversarial as it was amicable. Ramesses also outlived Puduhepa. Sadly, too, Pharaoh interred many of his wives and children in their tombs, even as his own life wore on, decade after decade. He had celebrated more *Sed*-festivals than anyone in history, and reigned as a living sun god. But, by the sixties and seventies of his reign, Pharaoh had grown exceedingly old and frail. Now, in the gathering gloom of his twilight years, Ramesses II faced his last opponent: death itself.

Notes

1. For a detailed critique of the debate on Piramesses's location, see Uphill 1968, 1969.

2. For an inventory of Ramesses II's monuments found at Tanis, see Uphill 1984, 8–94. For the inscriptions on various stele, obelisks, statuary, and other inscribed monuments of Ramesses II found at Tanis, see *KRI* II, 289–300, 407–61; *RITA* II, 118–34, 233–316; *RITANC* II, 173–80, 272–321.

3. Uphill 1984.

4. Habachi 1954, 2001.

5. Hodgkinson 2007.

6. Pusch 1991; Pusch, Becker, and Fassbinder 1999; Bietak and Forstner-Müller 2011; Pusch and Becker 2017. For a general overview with bibliography, see Pusch and Franzmeier 2016, online at: https://www.bibelwissenschaft.de/wibilex/das-bibellexikon/lexikon/sachwort/anzeigen/details/pi-ramesse/ch/971bd711359cfa47d5eb438c8a73f959/.

7. Bietak and Forstner-Müller 2011.

8. Herold 1999; Hageneuer 2016, 269, fig. 1; http://www.artefacts-berlin.de/portfolio-item/the-reconstruction-of-pi-ramesse/.

9. Pusch and Becker 2017.

10. Exodus 1:11.

11. Hageneuer 2016; http://www.artefacts-berlin.de/portfolio-item/the-reconstruction-of-pi-ramesse/.

12. Gardiner 1937; Caminos 1954.

13. P. Anastasi II.1: Gardiner 1937, 12; Caminos 1954, 37–40. Compare P. Anastasi III.2 and IV.10.

14. *RITANC* II, 273–88.

15. *RITANC* II, 286–87.

16. *KRI* II, 289–300, 407; *RITA* II, 118–34, 233; *RITANC* II, 173–80, 272–73.

17. For older references, see *RITANC* II, 293–304. For an exhaustive catalog of Ramesses II's statuary and iconographic analysis, see Sourouzian 2019 and 2020b.

18. Magen 2011; Sourouzian 2019, cat. nos. R-1 to R-8, R-28, R-44 to R-51, R-53 to R-54.

19. For Ramesses II's group statues, see Sourouzian 2019, cat nos. 263–334; 2020b, 231–70.

20. Brand 2005 and 2007b.

21. Brand 2007b.

22. As Kitchen (1979) first observed. This has widely been accepted by scholars ever since, e.g., Spalinger 1980, 2008, 2010; Brand, Feleg, and Murnane 2018; Obsomer 2012b. Goelet and Iskander (2012) have challenged this chronological interpretation but their findings are based solely on the Abydos Temple of Ramesses II. Built and decorated in the earliest months of his reign, this temple is not representative of the broader geographical and chronological patterns in the distribution of the variant forms and orthographies of the king's cartouche names on his early monuments. See following note.

23. But not exclusively so, as there are clear examples of R^c-*ms-s* and R^c-*ms-sw* coexisting on monuments inscribed after year one, when the long prenomen was adopted, and before the Hittite Peace Treaty stela was made in regnal year 21, as in some reliefs from the Ramesside forecourt of Luxor Temple:

Feleg 2020. Here, R^c-ms-sw can appear in some horizontal texts alongside the R^c-ms-s form that otherwise predominates in both vertical and horizontal texts. Moreover, Kitchen is wrong in asserting that the form R^c-ms-s did not occur in the north, for it occasionally turns up on monuments from Lower Egypt and in the Levant during this interval; contra Kitchen 1979, 2001. The forms and orthographies of Ramesses II's cartouches will be the subject of a future study by Erika Feleg and myself.

24. Kitchen 1984; Brand 2007b, 54–56; Wong 2018.

25. Brand 2007b, 2010b; Wong 2018. The use of columns of text to separate scenes is most obvious in Ramesses II's decoration on Thutmose III's curtain wall at Karnak and his later reliefs at Sety I's Gurnah Temple: Helck 1968; Osing 1977.

26. Leprohon 2013.

27. Osing 1977; Brand 2000, 245 and fig. 130; 2007b, 58 and figs. 5.10–5.11.

28. Brand 2000, 246–49.

29. Osing 1977.

30. The rear chambers and storerooms sculptors now decorated so hurriedly belonged to Gurnah Temple's most inaccessible zones.

31. Helck 1968; Brand 2007b, 57–58 and figs. 5.12–5.15.

32. For the dedicatory texts, see Helck 1968, 124–31; *KRI* II, 581–84; *RITA* II, 379–83; *RITANC* II, 397–98.

33. Johnson 1998.

34. Vandersleyen (1979) eloquently refutes this modern bias.

35. Sety I Abydos: Calverley and Broome 1933–1958. Ramesses II Abydos: Iskander and Goelet 2015; Karnak, Great Hypostyle Hall: Brand, Feleg, and Murnane 2018, frontispiece and figs. 363, 365–73; Medinet Habu: Epigraphic Survey, *Medinet Habu IV*, pls. 193, 198, 202, 208, 219–220, 222.

36. On the usurpation of monuments, see Brand 2010b. Although well established in Egyptology, the term usurpation carries a pejorative connotation that was alien to the Egyptians.

37. For the reused statuary, see now Magen 2011; Connor 2019; Sourouzian 2019, 2020b.

38. Dorman 2005.

39. So, in the wall scenes in the Colonnade Hall of Luxor Temple: Epigraphic Survey 1994, 1998. For the wider phenomenon of Horemheb's usurpations of Tutankhamun's monuments, see Brand 2010b, 2020a; Eaton-Krauss 2016, 42–44, 65–66.

40. Seele 1940, 7–22.

41. As with his reuse of Amenhotep III's statuary; Sourouzian 2020a, 2020b.

42. Kozloff and Bryan 1992, 172–75.

43. So, at Karnak on the Second Pylon and the main processional axis of the Great Hypostyle Hall; Seele 1940, 7–22; Brand, Feleg, and Murnane 2018, 23–24. On the decorative programs of the Second Pylon's eastern façade, see Audouit and Panaite 2019.

44. Brand 2010a.

45. Magen 2011, 17–19, 288–388; Sourouzian 2020b, 30–35.

46. On these temples and the royal cult, see Ullmann 2013a, 2013b, 2016, 2017; Epigraphic Survey, 1994, 1998.

47. Habachi 1969a, 1–16; Ullmann 2011.

48. *RITANC* II, 478–93; Christophe 1965; Peters-Destéract 2003; Willeitner 2010.

49. Habachi 1969a, 1–16; Sourouzian 2019, cat. nos. 175–178.

50. Sourouzian 2020b, 391–97.

51. Christophe 1956. See pp. 226–27 and fig. 7.17 above.

52. Peters-Destéract 2003, 168–71; Obsomer 2012b, 416–18. For an important reappraisal of New Kingdom cryptographic lexicography, see now Roberson 2020. In particular, Roberson corrects many of Drioton's misconceptions.

53. On both sides of the hall, the statues' names combine Ramesses II's cartouches with the epithets: "Beloved-of-Amun," "Beloved-of-Re-Horakhty," "Beloved-of-Atum," "Ruler-of-the-Two Lands," and "Beloved-of-the-Re-of-Rulers."

54. Rosellini 1832, I:pl. 87; Champollion, *Monuments*, 1:pls. 34–35; Wreszinski 1925, pl. 180; Habachi 1969a, pl. 3; Peters-Destéract 2003, 184–87; Salvoldi 2018, 344, pl. 18.1. Remarkably, sculptors revised both reliefs, separating the male and female gods and squeezing a deified Ramesses in between them. His nomen here is the new form, *Ramessu*, written without a cartouche to signify that he, too, is a god. These modifications must date after his twenty-first regnal year, when he largely stopped writing his name as R^c-*ms-s*.

55. PM VII, 109; *LD* III, pl. 189; *RITANC* II, 484–85; Habachi 1969a, pl. 4a–b; Peters-Destéract 2003, 214 and 219 and color plates 44 and 46; Salvoldi 2018, 346, pl. 20. For views of these pillars, see James 2002, 190–91. For Alessandro Ricci's watercolor facsimile of Ramesses II with his divine alter ego, see Salvoldi 2018, 343, pl. 17.3. Tellingly, his nomen here is the older form, *Ramesses*, but still written without cartouches, like a god. This shows that Ramesses II had already deified himself in the first two decades of his reign; Ullmann 2011.

56. PM VII, 109; *LD* III, pl. 189 (Amun bark); Habachi 1969a, 4–5, fig. 3; James 2002, 192–93.

57. Habachi 1969a, 5, fig. 4; *KRI* II, 758–59; *RITA* II, 500–501; *RITANC* II, 484–85.

58. PM VII, 110; *LD* III, pl. 180; *RITANC* II, 486–87; James 2002, 195.

59. PM VII, 106–8; *LD* III, 191; *RITANC* II, 487–89; Donadoni et al. 1975; Lurson 2001; Peters-Destéract 2003, 230–62. The king's nomen is consistently written in the *Ramessu* form, suggesting a date after regnal year twenty.

60. Donadoni et al. 1975; Lurson 2001; Peters-Destéract 2003, 232, 235, 245.

61. Christophe 1965; Peters-Destéract 2003, 31–110; Willeitner 2010, 11–28.

62. These facsimile paintings are themselves idealized, showing the ancient murals in perfect condition. They had likely lost some of their brilliance when Belzoni discovered them. Yet, the intricate details and fabulous polychrome in the color facsimiles of Champollion, Ricci, and Rosellini hint that most of it remained intact, much like wall paintings in many Egyptian tombs: Rosellini, 1832, I:pls. 79–86, 100–103; Champollion 1835–1845, I:pls. 3, 11–18, 26–29, 34–36. For Ricci's facsimiles, see Salvoldi 2018, 341–46, pls. 16–20. Lepsius recorded the colors on one of the standing colossi inside the main hall: *LD* III, pl. 190.

63. This sad decay is evident in recent photos of the interior; James 2002, 182–94.

64. Desroches-Noblecourt and Kuentz 1968; Peters-Destéract 2003, 153–280.

65. Among the other queens of the New Kingdom, only Amenhotep III's principal wife Tiy could boast of such a temple, at Sedinga in Nubia near her husband's royal cult temple at Soleb.

66. *KRI* II, 765:14–16; Desroches-Noblecourt and Kuentz 1968, pl. 11.

67. *KRI* II, 765:11–12; Desroches-Noblecourt and Kuentz 1968, pl. 11.

68. Desroches-Noblecourt and Kuentz 1968, pls. 26–27, 43–44, 47–48, 53–54, 57–58, 66–68, 73–76, 102–3, 107–9, 112, 114–16, 119–20.

69. Desroches-Noblecourt and Kuentz 1968, pls. 98–101 and 121–22.

70. PM VII, 53–63; *RITANC* II, 468–73. One of Setau's stelae at Wadi es-Sebua, dated to regnal year 44, relates how he employed Libyan captives to construct the temple on the king's orders: *KRI* III, 95; *RITA* II, 66; *RITANC* III, 82–83.

71. Ramesses II's grand Nubian temples are dedicated to the principal gods Amun-Re and Re-Horakhty (Abu Simbel), Amun (Wadi es-Sebua), Re-Horakhty (Derr), and Ptah (Gerf Hussein), with all four also serving the royal cult; see Ullmann 2011, 2013a, 2016, 2017.

72. Sourouzian 2019, cat. nos. 249–260; 2020b, 211–30.

73. Fisher 2001, 1:33–34 and pls. 5C-28A.

74. Sourouzian 2019, cat. nos. 89–90; 2020b, 366–68 and fig. 192b.

75. PM VII, 33–37; *RITANC* II, 464–68; Ullmann 2017.

76. Ullmann 2017.

77. *RITANC* II, 465. See p. 390 above.

78. Ramesses II's Second Hittite Marriage Decree refers to the princess as "his other daughter," *ßy=f kt šrit*, but her father is called only "the great chief of Hatti." The Hittite king's name is not preserved in the letter Ramesses II sent to Puduhepa about the match. The occasion may have been the accession of Hattusili III's successor, Tudhaliya IV. If so, perhaps the bride was his daughter instead of Hattusili's. From the Egyptian ideological perspective, it mattered not who the current Hittite ruler was, since neither the princess nor her father was called by name in the decree. If Tudhaliya IV had succeeded his father, the two kingdoms decided to reinforce their ties through a new marriage alliance.

79. So *RITANC* II, 164; Roth 2003, 185 and n. 63; Cordani 2017, 10, 27.

80. During these fourteen years, the king celebrated his fifth through ninth *Sed*-festivals while his cult as the living god-king and incarnation of Re-Horakhty approached its zenith. On the later jubilees, see *RITANC* II, 241–58. For the *insibiya* letters in the Egyptian-Hittite correspondence, see Edel 1976, 29–30. Other letters Edel includes in the *insibiya* group preserving elements of Ramesses II's expanded titles are *ÄHK* I, nos. 60–70, 72, 73, and 76. Sometimes *insibiya* and *nib-tawa* are missing and only the title "Son of the Sun God" occurs. Less certain are cases where Edel restores these titles: *ÄHK* I, nos. 74–75, 77, 81–82.

81. Conceivably, some of the letters Edel assigns to the negotiations for the first Hittite marriage may instead belong to the second; Cordani 2017, 100.

82. *ÄHK* I, no. 73: recto 10–19. Edel heavily restored this broken letter, but its content seems to be a promise by Ramesses to make his second Hittite bride a senior royal wife (Akkadian SAL-tu_4 [GAL]-ti); see Bloch 2010, 75–76. Presumably, this would have corresponded to Maahorneferure's title great royal wife, *ḥmt-nsw wrt*, but the Coptos stela does not record the second princesses's name or queenly title.

83. Only the last three lines of second copy survive in the temple of Sety I at Abydos. *KRI* II, 283: 14–16; Kitchen and Gaballa 1969, 17–18 and pls. 2–3. As with the First Hittite Marriage Decree and the Blessing of Ptah, Ramesses

II surely issued parallel copies in other centers across his realm, but none have yet come to light.

84. *KRI* II, 283.

85. *ÄHK* I, no. 30: recto 13´–14´.

86. *ÄHK* I, no. 71: recto 12´–verso 12; Cordani 2017, no. 35. Translation adapted from Bryce 2003, 125.

87. *ÄHK* I, no. 105: recto 17´.

88. Divon 2008.

89. Singer 1983.

90. *ÄHK* I, no. 78: recto 1´–7´; Cordani 2017, no. 39.

91. *ÄHK* I, no. 78: verso 15–20.

92. *KRI* IV, 5:3.

93. On Tudkhaliya IV's reign, see Bryce 2005, 296–326. Puduhepa lived into her seventies or eighties; see de Roos 2006.

94. Pusch and Jakob 2003; Breyer 2010b.

CHAPTER FIFTEEN

TWILIGHT OF THE GREAT GOD: RAMESSES II'S LAST YEARS AND HIS DESCENDANTS

Ramesses II in Old Age

Increasingly during the long, languid afternoon of his seven decades as Lord of the Two Lands, Ramesses II suffered from the ill effects of advanced old age. At the apogee of his rule, in regnal year 33/34, he was already in his fifties. Once he reached his sixties, to say nothing of his seventies or eighties, he was exceedingly old by ancient standards.[1] Possessing a tenacious will to live, excellent genes, and good fortune, Ramesses survived into his mid-eighties or early nineties.[2]

Unlike most of Egypt's ancient rulers, or indeed most significant figures in world history, we possess Ramesses II's mummified body as an artifact of his legendary reign (fig. 15.1). A century after his death, tomb robbers despoiled his burial and stripped him of his golden treasures. Fortunately they spared his mortal remains from destruction. The High Priests of Amun rewrapped and reburied it, in an extraordinary secret cache of royal mummies on the west bank of ancient Thebes.[3] Here many of Egypt's New Kingdom pharaohs escaped the worst catastro-

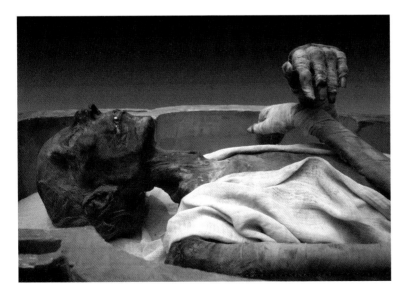

FIGURE 15.1. The mummy of Ramesses II. © akg-images / De Agostini Picture Lib. / W. Buss.

phe any ancient Egyptian could suffer: the destruction of their corpse. After slumbering undisturbed for more than three millennia, the mortal remains of Ramesses II and over twenty more pharaohs finally came to light in the 1880s, among them his grandfather Ramesses I, his father Sety I, and his son Merenptah. Gazing on his ancient corpse, we draw nearer than we otherwise could to Ramesses II the mortal man, who lurked behind the spectacular façade of Ramesses the Great God.[4] We see the gaunt face of an elderly man who had lived the ancient equivalent of three lifespans.

Scientists who examined his mummy discovered a host of medical ailments afflicting the pharaoh in old age, which made day-to-day living a formidable challenge, even without the extra duties of kingship. Ramesses endured a degenerative form of bone disease called diffuse idiopathic skeletal hyperostosis (DISH).[5] During the later years of his life, his spine became so curved, and his neck so bent forward, that he was always stooped over, leaving him with a prominent hunchback, while his neck was permanently angled up, which may have caused difficulty in swallowing.[6] After his death, embalmers were compelled to break his neck so they could lay his body flat. Hip dysplasia forced him to tread with a shuffle.[7] He needed a staff to walk. More often, he would have been carried around on a palanquin while he was still able to travel. He also suffered from severe atherosclerosis, a hardening of his arteries that was fairly common in ancient Egyptians.[8]

His teeth were in horrible shape. From middle age if not earlier, Ramesses suffered from periodontal disease, a severe inflammation of his gums.[9] A lifetime of access to honey and sweets, poor dental hygiene, the presence of grit from grinding stones used to make flour for bread (the staple of even a pharaoh's diet)—all contributed to dental decay and wearing down the enamel of his teeth. Loss of enamel often exposed the tooth's dentine, or even the pulp of its hypersensitive root. The second molar on his left jaw was also abscessed.

His dental conditions alone would have caused acute pain and extended agony. He may have resorted to cloves or a form of opium to relieve this misery. His diet and dental afflictions produced a vicious cycle, with the king increasingly relying on a soft and liquid diet including sweetened beer and wine and other high calorie carbohydrates.

However fragile he became, Ramesses was not always as emaciated as his desiccated mummy now appears. Long folds of excess skin on his lower abdomen and thighs reveal that he was overweight at some point in his life, likely in middle age. He may have lost weight in his old age.[10]

What of Ramesses II's other faculties? Delicate eye tissue does not survive mummification, and the process also removed his brain. We have no idea whether Ramesses could still see, or if cataracts and other eye ailments robbed him of his vision. Did he remain mentally lucid in his twilight years or had senility overcome the king? We also cannot know whether he became hard of hearing, perhaps even deaf.[11]

As he aged, servants kept Ramesses II safely harbored within the secluded recesses of his palaces, where they attempted to shield his all-too-human frailties from wider view. The last two Crown Princes, Khaemwaset and Merenptah, supervised a trusted staff of palace attendants who saw to their aged king's intimate physical needs. They alone were permitted to see his infirmities up close. For much of Egypt's population—even for members of the court elite—Ramesses became ever more remote. When courtiers saw him at all, it was on strictly controlled ceremonial occasions. The aged pharaoh became a human cult image, unlike the vigorous man he once had been.

Through it all, the Egyptians maintained the pretense of his divinity. Perhaps not coincidentally, a contemporary mythological text recounts how Re himself aged into a doddering old man, bent over, and drooling with senility.[12] Even in his dotage Ramesses II mimicked the sun god (fig. 15.2).

Ramesses II's Last Decades

A curious problem historians encounter is the rarity of monumental edicts following the Blessing of Ptah Decree of his thirty-fifth regnal year. Thereafter, dated royal inscriptions largely cease, except for terse triennial bulletins announcing his thirteen successive Jubilees. Historians have long viewed Ramesses's last three decades as a barren era of stagnation. Some compare it to the social and political lethargy late in the reigns of long-lived monarchs like Louis XIV of France.[13]

Despite these claims, we have no reason to suspect Egypt's government or economy suffered during these years. Even as Ramesses himself receded from view, the crown prince managed day-to-day affairs in his elderly father's name. To be sure, even an energetic pharaoh was a far-off, intangible figure for most of his subjects. Egyptian peasants

FIGURE 15.2. The sun god bent over in old age and leaning on his staff. Rosellini's drawing of a scene from the tomb of Sety I. NYPL digital collections. Public domain.

toiling in their fields rarely if ever saw their king, except perhaps for a glimpse of his royal barge. Still, Ramesses had regularly displayed himself to court elites, to soldiers in the army, and to the public at religious festivals in major cities. Now a cocoon of ritual enshrouded Pharaoh, shielding his human frailties from wider view.

In his fifth decade on the throne, Ramesses II reached sixty-five, an age when modern people often retire. Even for elite males in ancient Egypt, the average life expectancy was only thirty-five. Ramesses must have seemed—and felt—very old indeed.[14] He continued to observe *Sed*-festivals every three years, hoping to rejuvenate himself and restore his powers, but there can be no doubt he gained scant comfort from these now wearisome rites.

Despite his exceptional longevity, retirement was not an option for an Egyptian monarch. He was required to reign, at least in name, until he died. Nor would Ramesses, or any other Egyptian monarch, abdicate willingly. How did his people reconcile their wizened king's physical infirmities with his institutional duties? The solution lay in the doctrine of pharaonic divinity.

No later than his second Jubilee when he reached his mid-fifties, Ramesses II became the living incarnation of the sun god himself, "the Great *Ka*-Spirt of Re-Horakhty." He remained a fully visible and engaged god-king, actively governing Egypt for at least two more decades. By the fifties and sixties of his reign, however, Pharaoh's transformation into a living god served both a practical and a theological purpose. He limited his public duties to ceremonial functions, playing the role of an idol carried around on a palanquin, presiding in audience halls, and conducting temple rituals only as his strength allowed. He spent most of his time in the sanctuary of his palace, like a cult image in its temple. The mystique of being a living god now served as the perfect cover for a decrepit old man.

We may also attribute the silence of his later reign to the very success of his earlier policies and endeavors. By the end of his second decade of rule he had stopped campaigning abroad and concluded peace with Hatti. Projecting the image of a warrior king was less important after the Silver Treaty, and he dedicated few war monuments after his second decade.[15] Eventually even Ramesses ran out of things to build.

He had accomplished everything a pharaoh was supposed to do: monumental construction, warfare, and the formal inscriptions and artwork celebrating these activities. The business of government, recorded on fragile papyrus, hummed or lumbered along as it always had, but only a small fraction of these records have come down to us. Historical events, the kind "written in stone" on monuments, largely ceased in his last three decades, severing our tenuous connection to this ancient monarch.

Merenptah the Last Crown Prince

We know Ramesses II continued governing his kingdom through most of the forties and early fifties of his reign, as his correspondence with the Hittite court attests.[16] But as the king's winter years approached, he looked to his eldest surviving sons to assist him. Prince Ramesses Junior had served as crown prince for over two decades, at least from the earliest *Sed*-Festival in regnal year thirty until he died around year fifty-two.[17] His younger brother, the Scholar Prince and High Priest of Ptah Khaemwaset, then acted as designated heir until about year fifty-five.[18] It was Ramesses II's fate to survive many of his children and grandchildren. Finally Queen Isetnofret's youngest son Merenptah, his father's thirteenth eldest, became Ramesses's ultimate heir, assuming the daily burden of ruling on his behalf.

Merenptah was well advanced in age himself when the duty of acting as Ramesses II's "staff of old age" fell to him.[19] Crown Prince Merenptah left several monuments highlighting his exceptional role as pharaoh-in-waiting. Yet, this was not a coregency. Merenptah never appeared as a crowned ruler wearing the regalia of kingship while Ramesses lived. Nor did he enjoy the privilege of enclosing his name in cartouches until Ramesses died.[20] Still, Merenptah now ruled in his father's name (fig. 15.3).

Once Merenptah became heir, Ramesses II bestowed a series of exceptional titles signaling his status as Egypt's virtual ruler, like "chief of the Two Lands," "foremost of Two Lands," and "leader in the Two

FIGURE 15.3. A stela depicting Merenptah as Crown Prince adoring the Apis bull dating to the last decade of his father's reign. The prince holds the titles of "heir apparent" and "king's eldest son." The uraeus cobra on Merenptah's forehead was likely added later once he ascended the throne. He bears no other emblems of kingship. Paris, Louvre N 412. Photograph by Peter Brand.

Lands."[21] These distinctions expressed his authority over his father's government. Additional honors reflect Merenptah's portfolio of sacred and administrative duties. In accord with his sacerdotal role, he was "controller of the gods." We even see Merenptah officiating in sacred rites without Ramesses II, suggesting the crown prince now fulfilled the king's ritual duties. To manage Egypt's imperial possessions and foreign relations, Ramesses dubbed him "controller of the chiefs of every foreign land."[22] Another set of honorific titles hint at his quasi-regal prominence, even if it fell short of kingship:

> The Hereditary Prince, the successor of Geb, his heir, the divine seed that came forth from the Mighty Bull. (All) the lands and foreign countries are gathered in his grasp; who is skilled in doing Maat for his fathers, all the gods; the unique one without his equal, who controls the chiefs of every foreign country, preeminent in the Two Lands; Chief of [the Elite] and Common People; Leader of the Two Lands, the Royal Scribe, Great General of the Army, and King's Son, Merenptah, living forever.[23]

Merenptah fulfilled his role as king-in-waiting for a dozen years, until Ramesses II died early in his sixty-seventh regnal year.

The Sun-King's Twilight

By the seventh decade of his reign, Ramesses II had celebrated an unsurpassed record of thirteen jubilees. Inscriptions from a temple in Armant announced the last three Jubilees. The first reads:

> [Regnal year six]ty, first month of the Season of Emergence (Proyet), day seventeen under the incarnation of the Dual King Usermaatre-Setepenre, the Son of Re, Ramesses-Meramun, given life. His Person decreed that the City Mayor and Vizier Neferronpet be charged to proclaim the eleventh Sed-festival of the Dual King Usermaatre-Setepenre, the Son of Re, Ramesses-Meramun, in this [entire] land.[24]

Six years later, amid the fanfare of his final Sed-festival, an ailing Ramesses II neared the end of his days. It is doubtful he took much joy from the occasion, assuming he was even aware it was happening. By his sixty-sixth year, ca. 1214 BCE, he was at least eighty-five, and may have reached his ninety-second year on earth. Too frail to travel, he likely spent his last days within the confines of his palaces at Piramesses. The pitiable sight of this doddering Pharaoh in his dotage would have deeply unsettled his subjects. Yet, such a forceful personality did not yield power easily or willingly while he remained mentally lucid. He was also well prepared for his journey to the beyond.

Ramesses II's House of Eternity

From the earliest days of his long reign, Ramesses II began constructing his large tomb in the Valley of the Kings in Western Thebes (KV 7).[25] Sadly, despite being one of the largest and most complex tombs in the royal valley, the pharaoh's house of eternity has not fared well over the centuries. Ramesses and his tomb builders chose ill in situating his final resting place—along with the rambling catacombs he created for his children (KV 5)—in a flood-prone spot (fig. 15.4). Geologically, the entire Valley of the Kings suffers from the friable quality of its chalky limestone, which easily splits, cracks, and shatters. Beneath this thick layer of limestone bedrock lies a deeper stratum of porous shale.[26] This shale absorbs water like a sponge and swells up, further destabilizing the brittle limestone lying above it, the bedrock into which the Egyptians tunneled their royal tombs.

The local climate further endangers the burial vaults in the Valley of the Kings. Although located in the vast and arid Sahara Desert, the Valley suffers from periodic cloudbursts. These roll in off the desert and send torrents of debris-laden rainwater cascading through the Valley. KV 7 and KV 5 both sit in one of its lowest points, leaving them vulnerable to flooding. Since the thirteenth century BCE, both tombs suffered

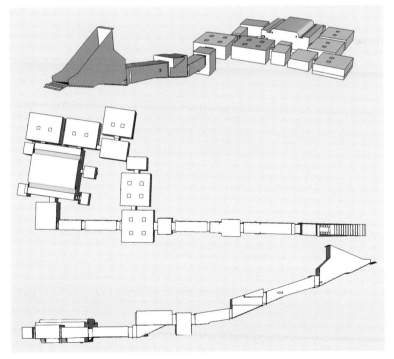

FIGURE 15.4. Tomb of Ramesses II. Once as beautiful as those of Sety I and Merenptah, catastrophic flooding has largely destroyed its painted relief decoration over the centuries. Wikimedia Commons.

repeated and disastrous inundations when violent storms washed tons of rocky debris and limestone sediment into them.[27]

Over the centuries, these torrents scoured away the finely sculpted and painted wall decoration in Ramesses II's cavernous sepulture. Flooding also undermined its structural integrity, wrecking pillars supporting its burial chamber, bringing parts of its ceiling crashing down, and rendering most of the tomb dangerously unstable. These devastating floods also choked it with limestone sediment, which often sets hard as concrete. All these catastrophes left Pharaoh's once spectacular tomb in a pitiable state, and deterred archaeologists from excavating it systematically until the 1990s.

Little of KV 7's once elaborate wall decoration still survives, although enough remains to show that its painted reliefs were of the highest quality. Craftsmen from the village of royal tomb makers at Deir el-Medina, whom Egyptians called the "servants in the Place of Truth," hewed out these catacombs and labored for decades sculpting their walls with delicate bas reliefs, painted in a dazzling palette of colors. In its original condition Ramesses II's tomb rivaled the splendid burial vault of his father Sety I and the exquisite tomb of his Great Royal Wife Nefertari in the nearby Valley of the Queens. Like most Ramesside royal tombs, including those of Sety I (KV 17) and Merenptah (KV 8), KV 7's decorative program included editions of several books charting the mysterious pathways of Underworld: The Book of Gates, The Book of Caverns, and The Litany of Re.[28]

Populated by the divine and demonic denizens of the underworld, these exotic compositions—which bewilder and puzzle us with their bizarre complexity—depict the sun god's nocturnal journey through vast subterranean caverns. The Egyptians believed Re grew old each afternoon and died at twilight as he entered the netherworld at the western horizon. Then, in his night bark, the *Ba*-soul of the dead solar deity plied a subterranean version of the Nile during the hours of darkness.[29] The *Ba*, often called the "soul," was a separate element of a human or god's identity, one different than its *Ka*-spirit. Both were etherial beings and their continued existence after death required them to receive food and drink offerings, allowing the deceased to be reborn in the netherworld. The exact natures of the *Ba* and *Ka* are difficult for us to grasp, but they were equally vital to the individual's well-being and were distinct from each other.

In his deceased form, Re appears as a man with the head of a ram, because the word for "ram" and "soul," *Ba*, sounded alike in the Egyptian language. A host of deities and spirits crewed Re's divine vessel as he voyaged through the night's twelve hours. The god Seth acted as Re's champion, defending the sun god against the malevolent forces of the demon serpent Apep who struggled to oppose Re's progress.[30] The fate of the universe itself stood in jeopardy each night. Had these agents of chaos succeeded, even once, in arresting Re's sacred journey, the sun would never dawn again, and all creation would cease to exist.

At the midnight hour, halfway through his nocturnal journey, Re's soul merged with Osiris, ruler of the netherworld. This mystical union united their identities and revitalized both of them, permitting Osiris to continue his eternal rule of the underworld and allowing Re to complete his arduous trek. As the twelfth hour of the night ended, Re was reborn at dawn each day, arising into the upper world at the eastern horizon. His new daily life cycle now began, and all living things on earth awoke from their deathlike sleep. Hieroglyphic legends in these scenes listed magical incantations the deceased pharaoh's spirit needed to merge his identity with Re and Osiris, assuring Pharaoh's own eternal life in this perpetual cycle of daily rebirth.

Ramesses II's Death and Burial

Of the king's last illness and precise cause his death we know nothing.[31] In records from the Twentieth Dynasty, we learn the royal-tomb builders in Thebes commemorated the sixth day of the second month of the Inundation Season (*Akhet*) as the "day of sailing" of Ramesses II.[32] So in mid-July, ca. 1213 BCE, Ramesses II breathed his last. He appears to have died in the north of Egypt, most likely at Piramesses.[33]

As news of Ramesses II's demise spread, it caused keening wails of deep mourning to ascend in every city, town, and village across Egypt. A fragmentary inscription discovered in the Valley of the Kings informs us that ten days later news had reached Thebes that something had happened to "the Falcon our [lord]."[34] By tradition, court officials announced Pharaoh's death by declaring "The Falcon has flown to heaven."[35]

Ramesses II's death, however long feared and expected, came as a profound shock to his subjects. Because of his extreme longevity, the passing of a pharaoh lay beyond living memory, for few still lived who recalled the days of Sety I. In western Thebes, the royal tomb builders' labors halted abruptly for several days, as they absorbed the enormity of what had happened. Reports of the king's death radiated like a shockwave throughout the Nile Valley and across Egypt's wide empire—from colonial Nubia to the vassal states of Canaan and Lebanon. Before Ramesses came to rest in his tomb two and a half months later, diplomats brought the news to Assyria, Babylon, and Hatti: The Great King of Egypt was dead!

The death of a pharaoh was always a calamity, endangering Maat, the stability of the universe, with the threat of engulfing chaos.

Politically, though, the succession was secure. Merenptah immediately arose as king, a task for which he was well prepared. Officials, priests, and attendants charged with preparing Ramesses II for his final journey now undertook the grim task of preserving his mortal remains by mummification. Others began to organize his elaborate burial equipment and costly personal goods for his grand tomb in the Valley of the Kings.[36]

Mummification traditionally required seventy days to complete. In Egypt's hot climate, where decay of a corpse immediately sets in, the embalmers lost no time in beginning their grisly work. In the embalming tent, they washed Pharaoh's corpse and purified it with natron, a naturally occurring carbonate salt. The Egyptians collected large quantities of this substance from rich deposits in the desert, and exploited its properties as a drying agent and antibacterial compound to mummify their dead. To avoid putrefaction, embalmers removed Pharaoh's internal soft tissues. Through a narrow incision on the left side of his abdomen, they extracted Ramesses's major organs—his intestines, liver, lungs, and stomach—preserving them separately in natron for placement in four canopic jars. One of the four sons of Horus guarded each jar containing these desiccated organs.

Embalmers removed Pharaoh's heart for mummification, after which they replaced it in the thorax. Egyptians viewed the heart as the seat of the mind. The deceased needed his wits about him when he journeyed through perilous realms of underworld, encountering divine and demonic forces. Ramesses II's heart was reinserted, bound in linen sewn with golden thread, in the left side of his chest.[37] As with most elite Egyptian mummies, the embalmers also removed the pharaoh's brain, breaking the tissue up and extracting the fragments with a long hook-like instrument they inserted via his nose. Not knowing what its function was, they simply discarded it. Next they carefully rinsed the cranial cavity with water and poured resin into his skull.

FIGURE 15.5. A gold bracelet inlaid with lapis lazuli inscribed for Ramesses II and discovered in Bubastis. It hints at similar riches once deposited in his tomb. Egyptian Museum, Cairo, Egyptian Museum CG 52576. Alamy.

After removing Pharaoh's internal tissues and flushing out all bodily fluids, embalmers packed his corpse in natron to desiccate it. This process freed his body of most residual moisture. But it still remained limber, allowing embalmers to arrange Pharaoh's arms crossed over his chest, a pose connoting his regal status. Sparing no expense, they anointed his corpse with costly perfumed oils and resins. They stuffed linen packing, soaked in resins and scented oils, inside his body cavity to give it a lifelike shape. Embalmers even put peppercorns with resin in the king's nose, magically restoring his sense of smell, with a small animal bone to secure it in place and restore its shape. Since the eyes could not be mummified, they filled the

FIGURE 15.6. The coffin of Ramesses II from the royal cache tomb. It was likely made for Ramesses I and was never gilded, thereby sparing it from destruction by tomb robbers. After their tombs were robbed at the end of the New Kingdom, Ramesses I's coffin was repurposed for his grandson. Egyptian Museum, Cairo, Egyptian Museum CG 61020. Photo © National Geographic, by permission.

sockets with linen packets and neatly drew his eyelids closed. They carefully wrapped Ramesses's body in long swathes of linen bandages, starting with his fingers and toes, until they had fully enveloped his corpse in many layers of cloth strips.[38]

From Tutankhamun's intact burial, we know embalmers inserted dozens of amulets, splendid pieces of jewelry (fig. 15.5), and kingly regalia between the layers of Ramesses's mummy wrappings. These precious objects were often fashioned of gold and inlaid with gemstones.[39] Although these treasures were worth a fortune, and later became a tar-

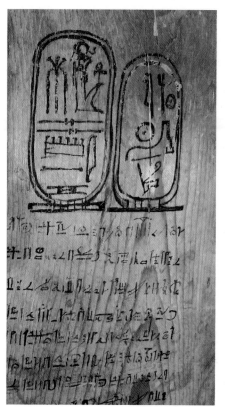

FIGURE 15.7. An ink docket on the coffin of Ramesses II. It records how the priests of Thebes rewrapped his mummy and deposited it in the royal cache tomb after thieves had despoiled the king's own tomb at the end of the New Kingdom. Wikimedia Commons.

get for tomb robbers, their original function was religious. Amulets served as magical talismans, preserving the body from harm and ensuring the king's *Ba*-soul and *Ka*-spirit would be reborn in the afterlife.

Once the embalmers and funerary priests completed all these elaborate preparations, they encased the pharaoh's mummified body in a nesting set of gilded, anthropoid, or "human-shaped," wood coffins (figs. 15.6 and 15.7). If Tutankhamun's burial equipment is any guide, Ramesses II's innermost coffin was likely fashioned of solid gold, as was the gold death mask placed over his head. An exquisite sarcophagus of translucent white calcite, so-called Egyptian alabaster, enclosed these gilded inner coffins. Like Sety I's magnificent example, this was inscribed with texts from the underworld books. French excavators discovered tiny fragments of this calcite sarcophagus, for ancient tomb robbers smashed it when they robbed Ramesses II's tomb. It must have been as remarkable as Sety I's, now the greatest treasure in London's Sloane Museum.[40]

By October of 1213 BCE, about two and a half months after he died, Ramesses II was ready to depart on his final earthly journey. His royal barge sailed southward from Piramesses, accompanied by his heir King Merenptah, his surviving children and grandchildren, and a crowd of courtiers and palace attendants. As the somber fleet passed every town and village along the Nile, the late king's subjects witnessed his final passing. After sailing for two weeks, the fleet, with its sacred cargo, arrived in Thebes, where the High Priest of Amun was waiting.

No records of Ramesses II's funeral have survived. Almost seven decades had elapsed since he laid his father Sety I to rest in the Valley of the Kings, and none still lived who recalled those solemnities. Priests and necropolis officials must have consulted records of earlier pharaonic burials. Workmen from the village of tomb makers were well acquainted by now with the burial rites of royalty, having already laid to rest many of Ramesses II's own wives and children, including three crown princes.[41]

In October the Valley was cooler than it had been that August, seven decades earlier, when Ramesses II presided over Sety I's burial. Merenptah led his father's mummy, in its nested set of gilded coffins set on a great ceremonial bier, through the arid canyon leading to his sepulture. Behind marched a funerary cortege of royal family, priests, and high officials. After them came a long file of necropolis personnel and palace attendants, carrying the king's burial equipment and personal belongings for his use in the afterlife. Performing the duty of any Egyptian son, Merenptah conducted final sacraments over his father's mummy, including the "opening of the mouth" ritual to reanimate Ramesses's spirit and restore his senses.

Once the bearers had placed his burial goods within the tomb, necropolis officials shut its outer doors and sealed them for eternity. The pharaoh's *Ba*-soul now entered the netherworld, where it would meld eternally with those of Re and Osiris, in an endless cycle of rebirth down through the ages.

The Reign of Merenptah

Merenptah was already old when he ascended his father's throne, probably in his later sixties (fig. 15.8).[42] The new pharaoh faced the daunting challenge of ruling in his father's lengthy shadow. Merenptah must have felt some urgency to distinguish himself in whatever time he had. His program of new artwork and construction was modest—relative to Ramesses II, anyway. Still, Merenptah's tomb in the Valley of the Kings (KV 8) is large and impressive, with a grand entrance, vaulted burial chamber, and high-quality wall decoration (fig. 15.9).[43] It has also fared better than his father's tomb, and remains an impressive sight for modern visitors who come to admire its fine painted carvings. In pre-

FIGURE 15.8. Statue of Merenptah as king. Cairo, Egyptian Museum CG 607. Alamy.

paring his final resting place, Merenptah followed his father and grandfather by having a calcite inner sarcophagus. He also started a new tradition by enclosing it in a nested set of three massive red granite sarcophagi.[44]

Merenptah's royal cult temple in Western Thebes is less than half the size of the Ramesseum, and his architects built it hastily, with stone blocks recycled from the temple of Amenhotep III, which had fallen into ruin.[45] In repurposing this older masonry, Merenptah's craftsmen often chiseled over Amenhotep's delicate bas reliefs, replacing them with crudely incised sunk relief. Among Merenptah's other significant building projects is a fine ceremonial palace he raised near the temple of Ptah in Memphis. Here his craftsmen produced relief decoration of the highest quality.[46]

Merenptah continued the practice of carving new inscriptions on older monuments and rein-scribing the statuary of his royal forebears, including some of Ramesses II's own sculptures. The king added minor epigraphs, including bandeau inscriptions, in temples throughout Egypt.[47] On a grander scale, he created cultic scenes and texts inside the court of the Seventh Pylon at Karnak (fig. 15.10).[48] Here we find his Libyan Triumphal Inscription, recording a major battle on the western fringes of the Nile Delta, although it is unlikely the aged king took an active role in the fighting (fig. 15.11).[49] Like his father's Kadesh narrative, Merenptah's Libyan Triumph Inscription is highly detailed and innovative. Sadly, it is not as well preserved.

On the international front, Merenptah's decade as ruler was not a quiet one. Egypt confronted new foreign threats in Libya and Canaan, but that was

FIGURE 15.9. Rosellini's color facsimile of a scene from the tomb of Merenptah in the Valley of the Kings. NYPL digital collections. Public domain.

far from the worst of it. In the last century of the Late Bronze Age (ca. 1200–1100 BCE), the ancient Near East underwent cataclysmic change. A cascade of natural and human-made disasters devastated Great Kingdoms and lesser states from the Aegean to the Nile.[50] The mighty Hittite Empire now sank into terminal decline, fallen prey to rebellious vassals and climatic disruptions that brought repeated crop failures and famine.[51] An inscription of Merenptah informs us he sent shiploads of grain to assuage his ally's needs.[52]

Closer to home, Merenptah's armies marched forth to war repeatedly on his western and northeastern frontiers. Prior to his fifth regnal year, the king mounted a military campaign in Canaan where his soldiers laid siege to the cities of Gezer, Yenoam, and Ashkelon.[53] Merenptah celebrated these battles in war scenes at Karnak and The-bes.[54] There, like his father and grandfather, idealized images show

FIGURE 15.10. Relief from the Court of the Seventh Pylon at Karnak showing Merenptah protected by Amun-Re in the form of a ram-headed sphinx. Amenmesse ordered Merenptah's cartouches erased (right), but the job was never finished and Merenptah's names can still be read amid the chisel gouges. Photograph by Peter Brand.

Merenptah attacking his enemies from his chariot or storming their towns on foot.

Merenptah's triumphal stela from Western Thebes is perfectly intact. It is famous today for preserving our earliest reference, outside the Bible, to the ancient Israelites (fig. 15.12).[55] Coming at the end of the hymn are these words "Israel is destroyed, its seed is nonexistent" (fig. 15.13).[56] This fleeting reference on what is now called the "Israel Stela" has fascinated Egyptologists and biblical scholars alike. By comparing it with the names of the Canaanite city-states, we know that in the thirteenth century BCE, the Egyptians understood the name "Israel" as referring to a group of people, not to a country.[57]

Merenptah's artists may have created the earliest-known images of the Israelites, in a battered relief from his Karnak war monument. In one scene

FIGURE 15.11. Merenptah slaying Libyan captives. Triumphal scene from Karnak beside his Great Libyan Inscription in the court of the Seventh Pylon. Photograph by Peter Brand.

Merenptah attacks a group of Canaanites in the open countryside, with no town in sight. The hieroglyphic captions to this scene have vanished, leaving no hint of who these people were.[58] Comparing the Karnak war scenes to Merenptah's Israel Stela suggests his opponents during this Canaanite expedition included the city of Ashkelon and a rural Canaanite ethnic group who called themselves "Israel."

Scholars still debate these issues fiercely, including the question of how this meagre record relates to the biblical exodus tradition. We can only be certain a group of people calling themselves Israelites existed in Canaan around 1210 BCE, when Merenptah claims to have defeated them in battle. For the pharaoh himself, the Israelites were a minor concern. He might have sent his troops to suppress a rebellion among his Canaanite vassals. Or, like his grandfather Sety I's inaugural campaign, it was perhaps little more than a show of force. In his fifth regnal year, however, a greater military threat emerged along Egypt's western border.

Libyan tribes, inhabiting the desert margins west of the Nile Delta, had seldom troubled Egypt since Sety I's day. Along Egypt's northwestern frontier, Ramesses II had built a string of forts to guard against Libyan tribes inhabiting the Western Desert.[59] Now, fortress commanders reported hostile Libyan tribes encroaching on Egyptian territory. Adding to this unrest was an influx of migrants from the Aegean. Among various ethnic groups were contingents of Sherden warriors, kin to those Ramesses II once defeated early in his reign. Now they joined forces with native Libyan tribes and other Sea Peoples including the

FIGURE 15.12. The Libyan Triumph Stela of Merenptah, also known as the "Israel Stela." The name of Israel is highlighted near the bottom of the stela. Cairo, Egyptian Museum CG 34025. Alamy.

Shekelesh, Teresh, Ekwesh, and Lukka. Having occupied the western desert oases, they threatened to invade the Delta.

In the summer of his fifth year, ca. 1208 BCE, Merenptah mobilized his armies, which descended on the Libyans and Sea Peoples. According to the king's Libyan Triumph Inscription at Karnak, the Egyptians fought the enemy in a six-hour battle and soundly defeated them.[60] Over six thousand enemies lay dead, while Pharaoh's troops rounded up thousands more and took them as prisoner back to Egypt.[61]

Meanwhile, the Libyans had stirred up rebellion in Lower Nubia, which the king's forces swiftly crushed.[62] For decades after Merenptah's campaigns, Egypt faced no major threats to her borders or her vassals. The reprieve he had won for Egypt, though, proved all too brief. After his death the most serious threat came not from without, but from within.

Name of Israel in hieroglyphs written right to left in original inscription.

Y - S - Y - R - I - A - L
1   2   3   4   5   6   7

1-7 Phonetic spelling of the name "Israel". The sign ⬭ indicates the sounds "R" & "L".

8 The bent stick sign indicates a foreign, non-Egyptian place or people.

9 The man & woman glyphs & 3 strokes signifies Israel was a group of people, not a territory.

FIGURE 15.13. The name of "Israel" on the Stela of Merenptah. The name is spelled out phonetically with additional determinative hieroglyphs indicating that the Egyptian's understood "Israel" to be a group of foreign peoples, not a country or city. Diagram by Peter Brand.

The End of the Nineteenth Dynasty

Merenptah's heir Sety II was in middle age when he succeeded his father (fig. 15.14).[63] Like his great-grandfather Sety I, his full nomen was Sety-Merenptah. Sety II reigned for about six years, during which he faced civil war and dynastic strife. Shortly after his reign began, a usurper named Amenmesse seized power in Upper Egypt and Nubia, styling himself as a rival pharaoh.[64]

Amenmesse's origins remain obscure, and Egyptologists still debate his heritage. Some identify him as a Viceroy of Kush named Messuy, who governed Nubia during Merenptah's reign.[65] On a statue depicting Amenmesse as pharaoh, a "king's mother" named Takhat appears.[66] Was she his mother? Who was his father?[67] We have no clear answers. Given the number of men who could trace their lineage to Ramesses II, the usurper may have had royal blood in his veins.

Soon after Sety II assumed power, Amenmesse challenged his claim. Initially, Sety retained control of Thebes and began work on his tomb in the Valley of the Kings.[68] This came to a sudden halt when Amenmesse took Thebes and the rest of southern Egypt along with Nubia. The usurper vandalized Sety's tomb, chiseling out his cartouches. Amenmesse also targeted Merenptah's monumental inscriptions, systematically erasing his cartouches in temple reliefs at Karnak and Luxor (fig. 15.10).[69]

FIGURE 15.14. Colossal siliceous sandstone statue of Amenmesse reinscribed for Sety II. Turin 1383. Courtesy Egyptian Museum, Turin.

Amenmesse's brief tenure as contra king lasted no more than three years, ending under circumstances lost to history. Sety II now methodically effaced the monuments Amenmesse left behind, destroying every inscription in the usurper's tomb.[70] He replaced Amenmesse's names with his own on a group of royal statues at Karnak.[71] Having regained control of Thebes, Sety repaired and completed his damaged tomb in the Valley of the Kings. He also restored his father's monuments, inscribing them with his own names now.[72] Sety took his revenge by usurping or defacing his rival's monuments.[73]

After facing down this challenge to his reign, Sety had to securely establish his designated heir. The prince was a young man also named Sety-Merenptah, who appears beside his father in reliefs from Karnak Temple.[74] Had he outlived his sire, the prince would have become "Sety III," but it was not to be. He died early, leaving his sickly younger brother, scarcely more than a child, to inherit his father's throne.[75]

As so often happens in history, political instability gave rise to an ambitious opportunist who exploited the weakness of his royal master. Such a man was Chancellor Bay, a high official of Syrian extraction.[76] Sety never made him one of Egypt's two viziers, yet it was Chancellor Bay who stood behind the pharaoh, in real life and on royal monuments like Sety II's bark chapel at Karnak.[77] Although the king later ordered sculptors to alter Bay's image on this chapel and replace his names and titles with those of the ill-fated Crown Prince Sety-Merenptah, this was only a temporary political setback for the influential courtier.

Sety II and his chosen heir both died less than two years after Amenmesse's downfall. The lineage of Ramesses II—as it descended through Merenptah—now fell into terminal decline. A disease-ravaged and physically disabled young prince with the nomen Ramesses-Siptah now assumed the throne. His mummy reveals that the scourge of disease had crippled him. Smallpox scarred his face, and may have killed him. He was also clubfooted. In his second regnal year, the young king changed his nomen to Merenptah-Siptah and he is better known today as Pharaoh Siptah.[78] His parentage remains uncertain. Some Egyptologists regard Siptah as a younger son of Sety II, while others claim Amenmesse was his father.[79]

Whatever his parentage, the ailing child king's accession was an irregular affair. Siptah reigned, but did not rule, as the protégé of Queen

Regent Twoseret, one of Sety II's wives, under the sway of the influential Chancellor Bay. Serving a weak young ruler, Bay now stood at the acme of his power and influence. In one inscription Bay boasts how he "placed the king on the throne of his father." Intoxicated with his own grandeur, he even dared to construct his tomb in the Valley of the Kings—one worthy of a pharaoh.[80]

Bay dominated court circles during the first four years of Siptah's reign, but in year five rivals engineered the chancellor's downfall. Recently, an extraordinary document from Deir el-Medina came to light, announcing his execution as an enemy of the state:

> *Regnal year five, third month of the Harvest Season (Shomu), day twenty-seven. On this day, the Scribe of the Tomb Paser arrived to say that Pharaoh, L.P.H; has killed the great enemy Bay.*[81]

A year later Siptah died. His mummy belongs to a youth in his teens.[82] Now, just two decades after Ramesses's death, Egypt's Nineteenth Dynasty was nearing its demise. With no rightful male heirs of Merenptah left, Sety II's dowager consort Twoseret assumed the throne, one of the rare female Pharaohs to rule the Nile Kingdom in over three thousand years.[83] She counted her regnal years as a continuation of Siptah's, but her rule did not last more than two years after his death. She oversaw Siptah's burial in his well-crafted tomb in the Valley of the Kings. Nearby she started her own royal tomb, but never occupied it.[84] Instead the next monach, Sethnakhte, founded a new line of Ramesside kings unrelated to Merenptah's lineage.

The Twentieth Dynasty

Around 1155 BCE, three decades after his grandfather Sethnakhte became king, Ramesses IV commissioned an anonymous master scribe to pen a vivid historical retrospective evoking the political chaos and social strife wracking Egypt at the end of the Nineteenth Dynasty:

> *The land of Egypt was abandoned, and every man was a law unto himself. They had no leader (for) many years previously, until other times, when the land of Egypt had (only) officials and city rulers, when one (man) slew his fellow, great and humble. Then another time came after it, consisting of empty years when Irsu, a Syrian, was with them as chief. He made the entire land tributary under him. One would gather his companions and steal their property. They treated gods just like men. No one proffered offerings within the temples. But when the gods inclined toward peace, to set the land to rights according to its natural state, (then) they established their son who came forth from their bodies to be Ruler, L.P.H., of every land, upon their great seat, (namely) ... Sethnakhte.*[85]

This statement is typical of a genre of royal decrees describing a time of troubles when chaos, the antithesis of Maat, wreaks havoc in the land. Although they often refer to genuine historical periods, these texts are intentionally vague about the duration and nature of the adversity. Their authors fill them with stock themes and hackneyed phrases like "one (man) slew his fellow," conjuring up an atmosphere of political and social pandemonium.[86] Such tribulations always cease when a new pharaoh—the king who authorized the text—ascends to power by divine will and sets Egypt aright by restoring Maat. Despite its well-worn ideological tropes and chronological ambiguity, this historical vignette from the Great Harris Papyrus does refer to at least one specific incident from the late Nineteenth Dynasty, the career of the upstart Chancellor Bay. Noting his Syrian heritage, it calls him Irsu, a pseudonym meaning "He who made himself."[87]

As for Sethnahkte himself, his origins remain obscure. Although some regard him as unrelated to Ramesses II, he was more likely descended from a cadet branch of the pharaoh's vast progeny—one not descending from Merenptah.[88] The Great Harris Papyrus relates how Sethnakhte's rise to power brought a generation of political strife, even civil war, to a close after the Nineteenth Dynasty's eclipse. Sethnakhte's stela from Elephantine tells us his claim to the throne did not go unchallenged:

> Regnal year two, second month of the Season of Harvest (Shomu), day ten … there were no more opponents against His Person, L.P.H., in any land.[89]

Sethnakhte spent his first year or so fighting unnamed enemies. Perhaps these included the Pharaoh-Queen Twoseret. Alternatively, what the Great Harris Papyrus calls "empty years" could refer to an interval when no pharaoh reigned, as Sethnakhte battled his rivals for the throne.[90] We can only speculate as to how long the conflict lasted or how widespread it was. The latest date we have for Sethnakhte is an inscription from regnal year four.[91] Soon thereafter he passed the throne on to an able successor, Ramesses III.

Ramesses III

Historians often consider Ramesses III the New Kingdom's last truly powerful king.[92] His thirty-one-year rule was beset with military crises as he warred against foreign invaders on his northern frontiers. Given the kingdom's internal turbulence, it was fortunate Egypt had faced no serious threats during the change of dynasties.[93] This peaceful interlude now ended abruptly. Beset on his northern and western borders with foreign enemies, Ramesses III fought, not to expand his empire, but to

FIGURE 15.15. Ramesses III fighting the Sea Peoples. Scene from the north exterior wall of his temple at Medinet Habu. The king stands on the prostrate bodies of his enemies. Photograph by Peter Brand.

defend Egypt's homeland against massive incursions of Libyan tribes and coalitions of Sea Peoples (fig. 15.15).[94]

Under his leadership, Egyptian armies repelled two Libyan assaults on the western Nile Delta during Ramesses III's fifth and eleventh regnal years. Between these conflicts, the pharaoh marshalled his forces on land and sea during his eighth year to repel an invasion by a coalition of the Sea Peoples. These consisting of several distinct ethnic groups, including the Danuna, Peleset, Tjekker, Sheklesh, Sherden, and Weshesh.[95] Ramesses immortalized these wars with elaborate battle scenes and grand historical inscriptions on the walls of his royal cult temple at Medinet Habu, and on two smaller temples he erected at Karnak.[96]

In keeping with pharaonic ideology, Egyptian scribes and artists presented Ramesses III's wars as famous victories, framing his own involvement as crucial to these triumphs. Despite their bombastic tone, his war narratives are innovative, introducing new textual and artistic themes.[97] In reliefs depicting the conflict against the Sea Peoples in year eight, Ramesses III's artists created the most dramatic depiction of a naval battle in pharaonic art.[98] While the Egyptian fleet engages a mass of enemy vessels at the mouth of the Nile, on shore Ramesses III and a large corps of Egyptian archers fire volley after volley into the ranks of the waterborne enemy (fig. 15.16).

Despite his victories in these three conflicts, the upshot of Ramesses III's wars was a decline in Egypt's imperial fortunes. Egypt was not alone: the entire Late Bronze Age system of empires collapsed between the thirteenth and twelfth centuries BCE.[99] Under Ramesses III's successors, Egypt would soon withdraw from its hegemony over the

FIGURE 15.16. Naval battle against the Sea Peoples from Ramesses III's temple at Medinet Habu. Egyptian soldiers fight with Sea Peoples, who wear their distinctive feathered headdresses. Many enemy warriors have fallen into the sea. Photograph by Peter Brand.

Levant. Meanwhile, Ramesses resettled large populations of Libyan prisoners of war in the Nile Delta.

Ramesses III sought to emulate his illustrious forebear Ramesses II by modeling every aspect of his kingship on his great namesake. His prenomen Usermaatre-Meramun was a variant of Ramesses II's Usermaatre-Setepenre. Ramesses III virtually replicated the Ramesseum when he built his own royal cult temple at Medinet Habu.[100] Within this temple the pharaoh dedicated a chapel to honor his illustrious namesake, claiming him as his "father."[101] Like his forebearer, Ramesses III portrayed his sons and daughters in processional lists on the walls of Medinet Habu, but only a handful of children appear in these sequences.[102]

Despite the vigorous military campaigns and building projects Ramesses III undertook, New Kingdom Egypt was now in decline. Economic setbacks, brought on by climatic stresses leading to poor harvests, caused severe dislocations in Egypt's government and agricultural economy.

From his twenty-ninth year, a remarkable document records how workmen from the village of royal tomb builders at Deir el-Medina abandoned their work in the Valley of the Kings and staged a series of strikes.[103] In history's first recorded labor dispute, the men walked off the job and staged sit-ins at temples in Western Thebes protesting their unpaid wages. Since they were paid in foodstuffs, especially grain, the whole village was going hungry.

We see further signs of hardship in contemporary economic texts, which document severe inflation in the price of grain and other staples during the Twentieth Dynasty.[104] These crises fueled a dramatic rise in tomb robbery. By the end of the Twentieth Dynasty, thieves had systematically plundered even the royal burials in the Valley of the Kings and Valley of the Queens.[105] Some of the hard-pressed tomb builders were among them.

Despite these political, military, and economic challenges, Ramesses III's reign appears to have been generally successful, and he projected an image of pharaonic kingship worthy of his model Ramesses II. Remarkably, he even celebrated a *Sed*-festival in his thirtieth regnal year, the first in six decades.

But Ramesses III's story has a tragic ending. After ruling for thirty-one years, he fell victim to assassins within his royal apartments. The conspirators murdered the pharaoh at the behest of a certain Tiye, one of his lesser wives, who plotted to set her son Pentaweret on his father's throne in place of the rightful heir. Often called the "harem conspiracy" by historians, the scheme involved over a dozen palace attendants and officials, and a group of women within the *kheneret*-household who abetted Tiye and her son.

Remarkably, a copy of the official court record of the investigation into Ramesses III's assassination has survived.[106] The conspirators were brought to trial and convicted of high treason. Many were executed, while authorities permitted the hapless Prince Pentaweret and a few others to commit suicide. Recently, a CT scan of Ramesses III's mummy led some to conclude the assassins had slit his throat.[107]

After his father's assassination, the rightful heir took the throne as Ramesses IV.[108] Although blameless of treason, the fourth Ramesses struggled to erase the taint of this sacrilegious murder.[109] He did this by striving to emulate, and even surpass, the achievements of Ramesses II. This ambitious monarch embarked on several grand projects, including a royal cult temple twice as large as the Ramesseum. But his architects had scarcely laid its foundations before he died.[110]

At Karnak, Ramesses IV's sculptors carved hundreds of new reliefs and inscriptions on the Great Hypostyle Hall of Sety I and Ramesses II, as he sought to legitimate himself by linking his name to theirs.[111] He decorated parts of the Temple of Khonsu at Karnak that Ramesses III had built with intricately carved reliefs of the highest quality (fig. 15.17).[112] As an act of filial piety, Ramesses IV commissioned the Great Harris Papyrus, a lengthy catalog of his father's donations of treasure and offerings to the cults of Egypt's gods.[113] He also bestowed endowments of his own. By his fourth regnal year, proud of his many gifts to the gods, he boldly implored Osiris to grant him a reign even longer than Ramesses II's:

> *And you shall be pleased with the land of Egypt, [your] land, in my time; and you shall double for me the long lifespan and the prolonged reign of King Usermaatre-Setepenre, the great god. Indeed, (more) numerous are*

FIGURE 15.17. Ramesses IV offers his prenomen to Khonsu with Isis in attendance. The king's name is substituted for the image of Maat. Along with his nomen epithet Maaty, "the just one," this stresses the Ramesses IV's desire to legitimate himself after his father Ramesses III was assassinated. From the Khonsu Temple at Karnak. Photograph by Peter Brand.

the deeds and benefactions which I have done for your temple to supply your sacred offerings, to search out every effective and beneficent deed, and to perform them [daily] in your precinct [in these] four years, than those (things) which King Usermaatre-Setepenre, the great god, did for you in his sixty-seven years. And (so) you shall give me the long lifetime and the prolonged [re]ign which you gave [him] as [king]...[114]

Despite his pious works and vast ambitions, the gods begrudged Ramesses IV two more years. He died after six years as king. But the name of his glorious forebear Ramesses II echoed throughout the Twentieth Dynasty, in a sequence of seven more pharaohs bearing the nomen Ramesses. Memories of Ramesses II would linger in Egypt's culture and history, and resound through other civilizations down into modern times.

Notes

1. Janssen and Janssen 1990.

2. Estimates for Ramesses II's age at death range between 85 and 92 years old; Wente 1980, 259–60; Balout and Roubet 1985; Hawass and Saleem 2016, 161. On the problems with determining the age at death of the royal mummies, where estimates based on observation of their remains contradicts historical data, see Krogman and Baer 1980; Wente 1980; Robins 1981. The same is true of human remains in modern times. Forensic examination of a thousand individuals buried in the Spitalfields cemetery in London during the eighteenth and nineteenth centuries yielded a consistent error in determining their ages at death when compared with records such as their coffin plates. Remains of individuals who were recorded as dying under the age of 40 were often estimated to be older, while older subjects were often determined to be younger; Reeve et al. 1993; Dodson 2016, 80–81.

3. For a recent overview of the royal cache tombs at Thebes, see Taylor 2019b. Dodson (2019, 115–18) recounts the history of the ancient robbery and reburial of the mummies of Sety I and Ramesses II.

4. Balout and Roubet 1985; Hawass and Saleem 2016, 160–66.

5. The bones did not fuse in the manner of ankylosing spondylitis as Balout and Roubet (1985) concluded; see Chhem, Schmit, and Fauré 2004; Hawass and Saleem 2016, 162. Ankylosing spondylitis typically strikes men in their 20s and fuses vertebrae so that strenuous physical activity and even bending becomes impossible. It is hard to imagine Rameses fighting at Kadesh and in his later Syrian wars in such a condition or living to the age he did. Still, calcification of his tendons and ligaments show that the king suffered severe degeneration of his joints including chronic osteoarthritis. Diffuse idiopathic skeletal hyperostosis is more common in men than women by a factor of 7:1 and strikes after the age of fifty. Comorbidities with DISH include obesity and cardiovascular disease, both of which affected Ramesses II. As DISH progresses, symptoms include the distortion of the spine. Some patients experience dysphagia, a difficulty swallowing; see Kuperus et al. 2020. I am grateful to Dr. Bradford Pendley of the University of Memphis for reviewing the scientific literature on Ramesses II's mummy and for advising me on the king's medical conditions and their implications for his health.

6. One result of pronounced spinal flexion (kyphosis) can be weight loss in advanced stages of the disease. See n. 10.

7. Hawass and Saleem 2016, 165–66.

8. Allam et al. 2009.

9. Balout and Roubet 1985; Hawass and Saleem 2016, 162. Severe erosion of tooth enamel and dentine of ancient Egyptians due to grit in their bread, a staple of the Egyptian diet, frequently exposed the pulp and caused dental abscesses even in individuals as young as thirty. Moreover, these dental problems afflicted all levels of Egyptian society. Having access to richer foods in large quantities exacerbated tooth decay in elites like Ramesses II.

10. If Ramesses lost weight late in life, it may have been sudden, preventing his body from reabsorbing excess skin. Drastic weigh loss often strikes the elderly who are terminally ill. Spinal distortion (kyphosis) and extreme dental decay could have resulted in weight loss toward the end of his life. Alternatively, he may have retained this weight or even gained it as he became more

sedentary and dental disease caused him to eat softer, high-calorie food and drinks. Suffering from DISH, Ramesses II would be predisposed to obesity and even diabetes mellitus (type 2 diabetes), as aging and a sedentary lifestyle set in. It is not, however, possible to diagnose diabetes from his mummified remains. Given his long life, it is perhaps less likely he became diabetic in middle age because he could not have survived so long without modern medical treatments like insulin. Two other historical figures who may have had type 2 diabetes were Henry VIII of England and Louis XIV of France. Henry, who became morbidly obese, died at the age of 55. Louis XIV—who died four days short of his 77th birthday—was infamous for his huge appetite and for a spate of maladies including, perhaps, diabetes. In his last days, he is known to have consumed large amounts of soft, sugary foods.

11. A common cause of geriatric hearing loss is calcification of the delicate bones in the inner ear.

12. Isis deceived the decrepit sun god by fashioning a serpent from mud mixed with spittle Re drooled on the ground, which bit and poisoned him. In his agony, he permitted Isis to know his secret name. The account is preserved in a magical spell for curing poison; see Borghouts 1978, 51–55. The aged sun god appears bent over his walking staff in scenes from the New Kingdom underworld books in royal tombs from the King's Valley.

13. Stadelmann 1981.

14. Horrific rates of infant and child mortality have dramatically skewed figures for ancient Egyptians' life expectancy at birth. Most Egyptians did not live beyond their twenties or thirties. Those that did could reasonably expect a relatively long life. However, Ramesses II's longevity was exceptional. Statistical data on ancient populations is sparse except for Roman Egypt, for which, see Scheidel 2012, 305–6. Other New Kingdom pharaohs with long reigns include Thutmose III (fifty-three years) and Amenhotep III (thirty-eight years), but both came to the throne in early childhood. Thutmose III would not have reached his early sixties, while Amenhotep III was probably in his mid-forties when he died.

15. See pp. 381 and 401 n. 2 above.

16. See pp. 427–28 above.

17. On Merenptah's monuments and career as a prince and his father's ultimate heir, see Sourouzian 1989, 1–30; *RITANC* II, 606–12; Fisher 2001; Servajean 2014, 14–19.

18. Fisher 2001, 1:116–17.

19. Merenptah's age at death is unclear, but Hawass and Saleem's estimate (2016, 167) of between fifty and sixty years old seems too young considering the historical record. As the thirteenth son, he must have been born early in Ramesses II's reign, if not late in Sety I's. Merenptah ruled for ten years after his father's death, suggesting at minimum that he was in his later 70s or 80s when he died.

20. Monumental reliefs of Merenptah as crown prince often show a uraeus cobra affixed to his forehead. These were inserted after his father's death when he became king in his own right, a practice well attested for Horemheb in his preroyal tomb at Saqqara.

21. So *ḥry-tp t3wy*, *ḥnty t3wy*, and *sšm m t3wy*. For Merenptah's epithets as prince, see Fisher 2001, 1:113–16.

22. So *ḥrp nṯrw* and *ḥrp wrw ḥ3swt nb*.

23. *KRI* II, 902–3.

24. *KRI* II, 397. For the last jubilees, see *KRI* II, 397–98; *RITA* II, 225–26; *RITANC* II, 254–58.

25. See Leblanc 2009a, 2010; Wilkinson and Weeks 2019, 204–6.

26. On the geology of the valley, see Wilkinson and Weeks 2019, 15–22.

27. For the hydrology of the King's Valley, see Wilkinson and Weeks 2019, 30–40.

28. On the books of the underworld, see Hornung 1990 and 1999; Roberson 2019.

29. Hornung 1990, 1999.

30. Hornung 1999.

31. This despite the presence of debilitating effects of old age including his poor dental hygiene and atherosclerosis of the arteries; Hawass and Saleem 2016, 166. One might speculate that the dental abscess on his left mandible went septic causing death by infection, but any number of diseases might have led to his demise without leaving a trace we can detect from his mummified remains.

32. The day of a New Kingdom Pharaoh's "sailing," (*ḥnw*), is a euphemism for his death. The term *ḥni* also designates processions of divine cult images during religious festivals.

33. The presence of marine sand in the mummy led French investigators to conclude the king died and was mummified in northern Egypt, presumably at Piramesses; Balout and Roubet 1985, 391.

34. Demarée 2016.

35. On euphemisms for the king's death, see Hsu 2014b; Lekov 2017.

36. See Wilkinson and Weeks 2019, 274–89.

37. Balout and Roubet 1985, 88–91.

38. The linen bandages enshrouding the mummy upon its discovery in the nineteenth century were placed by the priests of the Twenty-First Dynasty who restored the king's mummy after tomb robbers had despoiled it.

39. X-ray and CT scans of Ramesses II's mummy revealed the presence of an amulet the thieves overlooked; see Wilkinson and Weeks 2019, pl. 73.

40. A few fragments of Ramesses II's calcite sarcophagus attest that it compared faborably to Sety I's magnificent calcite sarcophagus, but indicate it was thoroughly smashed by tomb robbers.

41. On royal funerals in the New Kingdom and the role of the workmen of Deir el-Medina, see B. Davies 2018, 285–91.

42. On Merenptah's reign, see Servajean 2014, 14–52; Dodson 2016, 13–30.

43. Servajean 2014, 246–55.

44. Wilkinson and Weeks 2019, 253–54.

45. Servajean 2014, 241–45.

46. Sourouzian 1989, 33–45; Servajean 2014, 260–66.

47. Kitchen 1984, 549–50.

48. Sourouzian 1989, 142–52; Brand 2009. For an overview of Merenptah's Karnak monuments, see also Blyth 2006, 163–65.

49. Manassa 2003.

50. For overviews on the end of the Late Bronze Age, see Cline 2014; Knapp and Manning 2016.

51. Bryce 2005, 327–56.

52. *KRI* IV, 5:3.

53. Spalinger 2005, 235–48.

54. *RITANC* II, 72–78; Heinz 2001, 294–97; Brand 2011; Spalinger 2011, 141–47. The reliefs were wrongly attributed to Ramesses II because a prince named Khaemwaset appears in the scene and due to the obvious reworking of the cartouche names. This Khaemwaset was long assumed to be Merentpah's older brother. Yurco (1986, 1990, 1997a) first demonstrated that these war scenes were the work of Merenptah, a view endorsed by others including Kitchen, Spalinger, and myself. Yurco's findings raised the possibility that one of the reliefs depicted the early Israelites, leading to a polemical debate. Some prefer to credit Ramesses II. For an overview of the debate and arguments in favor of Yurco's dating, see *RITANC* II, 72–74. Brand (2009, 2011) further rebuts a dating under Ramesses II.

55. *KRI* IV, 12–19; *RITA* IV, 10–15; *RITANC* IV, 8–11; Hoffmeier 1996, 27–31. For an authoritative translation see Hoffmeier 2000, 40–41. For a textual and historiographical analysis of the Israel Stela, see now Spalinger 2021, 192–235.

56. *KRI* IV, 19:7. This snippet of rhetoric has caused Egyptologists and biblical scholars to spill oceans of ink. Among the more recent and original studies are Hasel 1994, 2008; Dever 2009.

57. Hasel 2008.

58. Heinz 2001, 296; Yurco 1986, 1990; Spalinger 2011, XXII, pl. 11.

59. For Ramesses II's fortress at Zawiyet Umm el-Rakham, one of several he constructed on the desert fringe of the western Nile Delta, see Snape 1997.

60. *KRI* IV, 2–12; *RITA* IV, 2–10; *RITANC* IV, 4–8; Manassa 2003; Spalinger 2005, 235–48; Servajean 2014, 36–47.

61. Manassa 2003, 55–61.

62. Servajean 2014, 47–51.

63. Dodson (2016, 79–81) concludes that the mummy attributed to Sety II is unlikely to have been his.

64. Hopper 2010; Schneider 2011; Servajean 2014, 62–81; Dodson 2016, 31–46.

65. This identification is controversial; see Hopper 2010, 585–632; Schneider 2011; Dodson 2016, 37–46; Yurco 1997b.

66. Dodson 2016, 40–42.

67. For overviews of the problem, see Hopper 2010, 630–32; Servajean 2014, 62–66; Dodson 2016, 40–45. On Takhat, see also Hopper 2010, 118–29.

68. Dodson (2016, 31–37) lays out compelling evidence that Amenmesse did not take power immediately upon Merenptah's death as evidenced by the decorative phases of Sety II's tomb, KV 15. On KV 15, see also Hopper 2010, 529–42.

69. Brand 2009, 2011. Amenmesse also effaced the name and titles of Sety II in a relief depicting him as Crown Prince Sety-Merenptah in one of Merenptah's war scenes at Karnak.

70. For a meticulous discussion of KV 10 and its defaced relief decoration, see Hopper 2010, 272–95.

71. Dodson (2016, 51–55) concludes that the statues were commissioned by Merenptah or Sety II upon his accession, but that Amenmesse completed them. Hopper (2010, 440–66) provides the most thorough epigraphic analysis of the erasures and palimpsest inscriptions on this corpus.

72. Brand 2009.

73. Hopper 2010, 343–584; Dodson 2016, 69–82.

74. Hopper 2010, 151–57; Johnson and Brand 2013; Dodson 2016, 70–71.

75. For Siptah's reign and monuments, see Johnson 2012; Servajean 2014, 94–123 and 300–303; Dodson 2011, 86–91; 2016, 83–110

76. Johnson 2012, 138–51; Safronov 2013; Dodson 2016, 86–91.

77. Johnson and Brand 2013.

78. Beckerath 1999, 160–61; Johnson 2012, 60–62; Dodson 2016, 85.

79. On Siptah's parentage, see Johnson 2012, 7–46.

80. On Bay's tomb (KV 13), see Altenmüller 1989; Dodson 2016, 89.

81. Grandet 2000; Roberson, *KRI* IX, 59.

82. Dodson 2016, 103.

83. Callender 2004; Johnson 2012; Wilkinson 2011, 2012; Servajean 2014, 124–46; Dodson 2016, 111–18.

84. Weeks 2006, 222–31; McCarthy 2008; Servajean 2014, 306–13; Dodson 2016, 113–14.

85. Grandet 1994. Translation adapted from Peden 1994a, 213.

86. Redford 1986, 267–69.

87. Other candidates for the individual behind the circumlocution Irsu are unconvincing. For Chancellor Bay as Irsu see most recently Johnson 2012, 98–99; Grandet 2014; Dodson 2016, 90–92, 120–22.

88. The evidence is inconclusive; see Johnson 2012, 48–51; Grandet 2014; Dodson 2016, 119–20; van Gils 2017.

89. *KRI* V, 672:10–11. On the Elephantine stela, see Johnson 2012, 96–97, 126–29, 159–60; Grandet 2014; Dodson 2016, 119–21.

90. On the meaning of the *rnpwt šwtyw*, "empty years," see Johnson 2012, 97–98.

91. Boraik 2007; Johnson 2012, 100–105.

92. The most thorough and authoritative treatment of the king's reign is: Cline and O'Connor 2012. See also Grandet 1993.

93. So between Merenptah's reign and the wars of Ramesses III. Still, Libyans and Sea Peoples were present in the oases and on the western margins of the Delta and the western desert; see Manassa 2003, 82–90; Kitchen 2012, 10–11; Servajean 2014, 36–47.

94. Kitchen 2012, 7–18; Cline and O'Connor 2012, 151–208. Redford's recent study (2018) of the military texts of Ramesses III is thorough, but his references are not fully up-to-date.

95. For perspectives on the so-called Sea Peoples, see Oren 2000; Cline and O'Connor, 2012, 180–208; Fischer and Bürge, 2017.

96. *Medinet Habu I–II*; Epigraphic Survey 1936; Heinz 2001, 298–322. For iconographic analysis, see Spalinger 2011, 190–201.

97. Simon 2016; Redford 2018; Spalinger 2021, 236–349.

98. The classic study is Nelson 1943. See now also Emanuel 2020.

99. The literature on the end of the Late Bronze Age and the end of Egyptian hegemony in the Levant during the twelfth century BCE is vast and their causes (human activity, climate change, systems collapse) are fiercely debated. See most recently Cline 2014; Knapp and Manning 2016; Cole 2017.

100. Nims 1976. For an in-depth analysis placing the temple in the context of New Kingdom royal cult temples in Western Thebes see Cline and O'Connor 2012, 209–70.

101. Epigraphic Survey, *Medinet Habu V*, pls. 335–37.

102. Epigraphic Survey, *Medinet Habu V*, pls. 250 (Prehirwenemef), 300 (royal daughters), 301–2 (royal sons). Two other scenes depict eight sons and

eight daughters bringing offerings before their father and the queen: Epigraphic Survey, *Medinet Habu V*, pls. 339–40. On these scenes see Cline and O'Connor 2012, 104–5, 284–85, and 407–14.

103. Gardiner 1948, 45–58a; Edgerton 1951; Vernus 2003, 50–69; Müller 2004; Cline and O'Connor 2012, 120–22; B. Davies 2018, 318–26.

104. See Cline and O'Connor 2012, 66–100.

105. Peet 1930; Cline and O'Connor 2012, 133–38; Goelet 2016; B. Davies 2018, 336–42.

106. For the Turin Juridical Papyrus, Papyrus Rollin-Lee, and Papyrus Rifaud, see *KRI* V, 350–66. Translations are in *RITA* V, 297–305; Peden 1994a, 195–210; Ritner 2002. Studies include Redford 2002; Vernus 2003, 108–20; Cline and O'Connor 2012, 411–13; Grandet 2014. Scholars do not agree on whether the assassins succeeded in murdering Ramesses III, but they failed to achieve their political objective to place Pentawreret on the throne. While some argue Ramesses III survived the plot, the introductory passage of the Turin Juridical Papyrus is couched as a statement from the dead king who declares: "I am among the righteous kings who are in the presence of Amun-Re, King of the Gods, and in the presence of Osiris, Ruler of Eternity."

107. Hawass et al. 2012; Hawass 2014. Grandet (2014) rejected this claim, arguing that the wound could easily have been inflicted *post mortem* during mummification or when the mummy was ransacked by tomb robbers.

108. Peden 1994b; Cline and O'Connor 2012, 410–15.

109. Grandet 2014.

110. Budka 2009.

111. Revez and Brand 2015; Brand 2018; Brand and Revez 2021.

112. *PM* II², 235–36.

113. Grandet 1994. Grandet (2014) places the composition of the document near the end of Ramesses III's reign, noting that it is dated III *šmw* 6, nine days before the king's death and the accession of Ramesses IV on III *šmw* 15. He argues that Ramesses IV ordered its composition in the aftermath of the harem conspiracy shortly before his father's death.

114. *KRI* VI, 19: 11–16; *RITA* VI, 20–21; Peden 1994a, 156–57.

Chapter Sixteen

Afterlife: The Legacy of Ramesses II, a Paragon of Pharaonic Kingship

Ramesses II was an inspiration for later Egyptian rulers, but he also lumbered them with an impossibly high standard of achievement. None could match Egypt's ultimate pharaoh, let alone surpass him. Yet, many strived to emulate their glorious ancestor. Ramesses IV was not the last Twentieth Dynasty pharaoh to adopt a royal titulary modeled on his namesake.[1] Seven more kings, Ramesses VI through XI, chose names mirroring those of Ramesses II. Beginning with Ramesses V, whose full nomen was Ramesses-Amunhirkhopeshef-Meramun, these rulers employed the name "Ramesses" as a prefixed title in the same way Roman emperors used "Caesar." Like Ramesses III, later Ramesside kings often chose Usermaatre for their prenomens with varying terminal epithets.[2]

After Ramesses XI died, the kings of the succeeding Twenty-First Dynasty (ca. 1069–945 BCE) retained elements of the Ramesside style of kingship. Ruling from Tanis in the eastern Delta, the new dynasty sought to recreate the glories of Ramesses's old capital of Piramesses by recycling many of his monuments. Removing dozens of statues, obelisks, stelae, and architectural elements, Tanite pharaohs installed these artifacts in their new capital after Piramesses lost its connection to the Nile and became uninhabitable. Abandoning the Valley of the Kings, they founded a royal necropolis within Amun's temple precinct in Tanis. Incredibly, these rich tombs remained intact when French archaeologists rediscovered them in the mid-twentieth century. In these splendid burials, excavators discovered Ramesside funerary monuments and treasures, including a sarcophagus lid belonging to Merenptah.

The Libyan monarchs of the Twenty-Second Dynasty (ca. 945–720 BCE) hailed from Bubastis, a city in the central Nile Delta. Modeling themselves on Ramesses II, kings like Osorkon II, Shoshenq III, and Osorkon IV adopted the prenomen Usermaatre, alone or with epithets. At Bubastis, alongside relics of Ramesses II's own day, these pharaohs fashioned new monuments emulating his style. When the Kushite kings of the Twenty-Fifth Dynasty (ca. 744–656 BCE) rose to power, however, they began to shift away from Ramesside models of authority. While the Kushite Pharaoh Piye conquered Egypt under the prenomen

Usermaatre, his successors broke with Ramesses II's legacy, preferring archetypes of kingship from Old Kingdom times.[3]

Egypt would later fall under the dominion of empires like Assyria and Persia, Macedonia, and Rome. (Egypt's most famed female pharaoh, Cleopatra, was of Macedonian heritage.) Native pharaohs recovered their country during the Twenty-Sixth and Thirtieth Dynasties. But Nectanebo II (ca. 360–342 BCE) was Egypt's last indigenous ruler for over two thousand years, until the Egyptian revolution in the 1950s of our modern era. But Ramesses II was no longer a paragon these pharaohs cared to emulate.

The Bentresh Stela—A Pious Forgery

Despite the passage of centuries, the grandeur of Ramesses II's monuments and legacy still inspired reverence. During the sixth and fifth centuries BCE, when Persian kings ruled the Nile Valley, priests of Khonsu in Thebes sought to enhance their god's status by appealing to the great pharaoh's memory.[4] They created an apocryphal decree in Ramesses II's name, modeling it on his First Hittite Marriage Stela (fig. 16.1).[5]

The Bentresh Stela's authors imitated the style of Ramesses II's Marriage Decree, complete with his pharaonic titles and a poetic eulogy, while the main text consists of a literary tale.[6] The story opens as Pharaoh embarks on his annual tour abroad, to receive homage and tribute from his Syrian vassals:

> Now His Person was in Naharin (i.e., Syria), according to his yearly practice. The chiefs of every foreign land came stooped down in peace due to the power of His Person, (from) as far as the most distant ends of the earth; their tribute-offerings of gold, silver, lapis lazuli, turquoise, and every pungent wood from the God's Land being (laden) on their backs as each one spurred on his companion.
>
> Then the Ruler of Bakhtan sent his tribute-offerings, having placed his eldest daughter before them while praising His Person and begging for life from him.[7] She was extremely beautiful to His Person's mind—more than anything. Then her titulary was recorded as: The Great Royal Wife Neferure. His Person arrived (back) in Egypt, (where) she performed all the acts of a king's wife.[8]

Although the Bentresh Stela parallels Ramesses II's First Hittite Marriage Decree, the Late-period scribes garbled the name of Hatti, transforming it into the fictional land of Bakhtan.[9] They also reduced the name of Ramesses's Hittite bride Maahorneferure to Neferure. By drawing on these period details, the authors endeavored to lend the Bentresh Stela an air of authenticity. But the account soon gives way to an ancient example of historical fiction.

FIGURE 16.1. Scene at the top of the Bentresh Stela. Paris, Louvre C 284. Photograph by Peter Brand.

After the marriage, an envoy from Bakhtan arrives and informs Pharaoh his new bride's younger sister Bentresh has fallen ill in the clutches of a demon. Ramesses sends an Egyptian doctor, who fails to cure her. Pharaoh dispatches a cult image imbued with the healing spirit of the moon god himself, bearing the impressive name "Khonsu the Counsellor–the Great God who expels demons of disease." Khonsu's entourage journeys for almost a year and a half to reach the ailing Bentresh.

As soon as Khonsu the Counsellor arrives in far off Bakhtan he expels the demon. Bentresh's grateful father holds a feast to honor this powerful Egyptian god, but detains the precious cult image in Bakhtan for four years. One night, this king dreams that Khonsu has transformed himself into a golden falcon and flown home to Egypt. Troubled by his vision, he now permits Khonsu and his retinue to depart without delay, laden with rich gifts.

In this colorful blend of storytelling and history, the priestly authors of the Bentresh Stela used Ramesses II's historical prestige to enhance the status of their Khonsu cult.[10] Ramesses II was still firmly lodged in Egypt's collective memory.[11]

The Tales of Prince Setne-Khaemwas

In the Greco-Roman period, a scribe recorded two stories from a cycle of traditional folk tales concerning the misadventures—amorous and magical—of Prince Khaemwaset, Ramesses II's fourth son.[12] He is now called the High Priest of Ptah Setne-Khaemwas, the son of Pharaoh Usermaatre. In his first adventure, Setne-Khaemwas and Naneferkaptah, the prince searches for the legendary *Scroll of Thoth*, a tome of potent magical power the god of wisdom himself had penned.[13] Setne-Khaem-was locates the scroll in the tomb of a long-dead prince named Naneferkaptah. When he enters the tomb, the spirits of Naneferkaptah and his wife admonish him to leave Thoth's book where he found it—for it had cost them their lives and that of their son. Setne-Khaemwas spurns their admonitions. Seizing the scroll, he escapes from the tomb, but not before Naneferkaptah lays a curse on the prince.

Pharaoh Usermaatre advises his son to return the book of his own volition before the tomb owner's vengeful spirit compels him. Prince Setne-Khaemwas ignores his father's advice and soon falls under the romantic spell of an alluring and mysterious woman named Tabubu. She beguiles the lustful prince into killing his own children, whom he murders to gain her favor. But Tabubu is merely an illusion Naneferkaptah has conjured to deceive Setne-Khaemwas. When the prince comes out of his reverie, he finds himself lying stark naked in a field. To his acute embarrassment, he sees an approaching retinue bearing his royal father on a palanquin. Pharaoh Usermaatre supplies his son with clothing and informs him his children are alive and well in Memphis.[14] After reuniting with his family, Setne-Khaemwas returns the *Scroll of Thoth* to its proper resting place in Naneferkaptah's tomb. Wishing to make amends to the aggrieved spirit, he requests a ship from Pharaoh and travels to Coptos in Upper Egypt. There he recovers the lost bodies of Naneferkaptah's wife and son and lays them to rest in his tomb in Memphis. Although Ramesses II plays a minor role in the story, the author presents him as a font of wisdom in contrast to the reckless actions of his son. These tales show that even a thousand years after his time, cultural memories of the king had not yet disappeared.[15]

Classical Greek and Roman Accounts of Ramesses II

Among ancient Greeks and Roman historians of the Classical Age, memories of Ramesses II had mingled with legends of other pharaohs, including Senwosret I, Amenhotep III, Sety I, and Ramesses III.[16] Classical authors knew Ramesses II by various names. He entered their historical memory through the writings of Manetho, an Egyptian priest who served one of the early Ptolemies, a line of Macedonian pharaohs who ruled Egypt after Alexander the Great.[17]

Manetho drew on archival sources to produce his account of Egypt's past, called the *Aegyptiaca*, or "History of Egypt." Its centerpiece was a king list beginning with the legendary founder of the First Dynasty, Menes. Manetho organized his tally of pharaohs into thirty dynasties, which remain the foundation of our chronology of ancient Egypt. Yet, Manetho often misconstrued the hoary annals he consulted, muddling his list of kings with redundant names and repeating colorful but bogus stories about various monarchs. Today, mere fragments of Manetho's *Aegyptiaca* survive, in jumbled excerpts and summaries from works by other ancient authors. They often contradict one another, offering baffling variations of Ramesses II's name and disparate figures for the length of his reign.[18]

The famous Greek historian Herodotus knew the pharaoh as Rhampsinitus, whom he credits with erecting a grand gateway and colossal statues in the Temple of Ptah in Memphis. Herodotus also relates fantastical stories about King Rhampsinitus's impregnable treasure room, which a clever thief nevertheless penetrates. As a reward, the king marries his daughter to the successful thief. In another colorful anecdote, Rhampsinitus embarks on a perilous journey to Hades, where he plays at dice with the goddess Demeter.[19] When he wins the game, Demeter permits him to return from the underworld alive.

In contrast to the garbled accounts of Manetho and Herodotus's fabulous tales, the Greek historian Diodorus Siculus offers a detailed description of the Ramesseum, which he credits to a certain King Ozymandias.[20] This name approximates Ramesses II's prenomen Usermaatre in Greek. Of the pharaoh's gigantic colossus, and another representing his mother Queen Tuya, Diodorus reports:

> *Beside the entrance are three statues, each of a single block of black stone from Syene (=Elephantine), of which one, that is seated, is the largest of any in Egypt, the foot measuring over seven cubits, while the other two at the knees of this, the one on the right and the other on the left, daughter, and mother respectively, are smaller than the one first mentioned. And it is not merely for its size that this work merits approbation, but it is also marvelous by reason of its artistic quality and excellent because of the nature of the stone, since in a block of so great a size there is not a single crack or blemish to be seen. The inscription upon it runs: "King of Kings am I, Ozymandias. If anyone would know how great I am and where I lie, let him surpass one of my works."[21]*

Diodorus also describes reliefs portraying the Battle of Kadesh, but he places the conflict in Bactria, where Ozymandias assaults a walled city surrounded by a river.[22] Diodorus credits the pharaoh with leading an impossibly huge army of four hundred thousand foot soldiers and twenty thousand horsemen arrayed in four divisions, each led by one of his sons. Diodorus also comments on the presence of his pet lion, stating:

> *He is accompanied by a lion, which aids him with terrifying effect. Of those who have explained the scene, some have said that in very truth a tame lion which the king kept accompanied him in the perils*

of battle and put the enemy to rout by his fierce onset; but others have maintained that the king, who was exceedingly brave and desirous of praising himself in a vulgar way, was trying to portray his own bold spirit in the figure of a lion.[23]

In book fourteen of his *Natural History*, the Roman scholar Pliny the Elder presents a fanciful tale of Pharaoh Rhamsesis, who erected two massive obelisks, one 140 cubits, the other 120 cubits in height. Pliny alleges Rhamsesis bound his own son to the larger monolith's summit, ensuring the workmen raising it would take care not to damage it or harm the prince.[24]

Diodorus Siculus and Pliny acquired their knowledge of Egypt's remote past at second or third hand. Only Herodotus visited Egypt personally.[25] All these classical authors drew on Egyptian folklore overflowing with distorted and erroneous stories about the kings of old. Once a millennium had passed since Ramesses's time, tall tales about his monuments colored fading memories.

The Modern Rediscovery of Ramesses II

As paganism declined across the Roman Empire in the fourth and fifth centuries CE, Christian emperors closed the temples of Egypt's gods, and knowledge of the hieroglyphic script died out. Now mystifying to all, pharaonic monuments fell mute for another fourteen centuries. Natural decay, reuse of old stones, superstitious iconoclasm, and careless vandalism destroyed or defaced what the ancients had called "the good work of eternity." Ramesses II and his fellow pharaohs languished in obscurity until scholars unlocked the hieroglyph script early in the nineteenth century.

The turning point came when Napoleon Bonaparte invaded Ottoman Egypt in 1798. Napoleon brought with him a contingent of 167 scholars and scientists who fanned out across the Nile Valley to record its cultural and scientific wonders, still largely unknown to Europeans. These savants created the earliest systematic copies of pharaonic monuments and their inscriptions. The French government published their results as the *Description de l'Égypte*, am impressive set of twenty-three large folio volumes illustrated with fine engravings representing ancient temples, tombs, and artifacts the expedition encountered during Napoleon's campaign.

In 1799 soldiers repairing a fortress at the site of Rosetta in the eastern Nile Delta uncovered a large fragment of a stela bearing a decree of Ptolemy V. Known as the Rosetta Stone, this remarkable discovery proved invaluable to science because Ptolemy had issued its text in in both Greek and Egyptian, transcribing the pharaonic

FIGURE 16.2. Abu Simbel from a nineteenth century painting by Hubert Sattler. Public domain. Wikimedia Commons.

language in the hieroglyphic and demotic scripts. Following pioneering work by scholars such as the English polymath Thomas Young, a French linguist named Jean François Champollion achieved a breakthrough in 1822.

He decoded the cartouches of Ptolemy V and Queen Cleopatra by comparing the Greek and hieroglyphic versions of the text. Soon Champollion became the first person in fifteen hundred years to read Ramesses II's name on his newly discovered temple at Abu Simbel (fig. 16.2).[26] His stunning revelations inspired further European explorers. Silenced for two millennia, Ramesses II now spoke with his own voice again, as pharaonic Egypt captured Europe's imagination.[27]

In 1828 Champollion and the Italian scholar Ippolito Rossellini mounted the joint Franco-Tuscan expedition to document monumental art and hieroglyphic texts from tombs and temples across Egypt and Nubia.[28] Published in two series of massive folio volumes, their facsimile engravings enabled scholars to translate these ancient texts with precision (fig. 16.3). Both series featured hundreds of plates, many of them intricately colored by hand. In 1842 Prussian linguist Karl Richard Lepsius led a fourth grand expedition to Egypt and Sudan. The Prussians copied hundreds of monumental inscriptions, publishing them with detailed notations on the hieroglyphic texts. Ramesses II's monuments are prominent in the folios of Champollion, Rosellini, and Lepsius. Each recognized the importance of his Kadesh narratives from Luxor, the Ramesseum, and Abu Simbel, reproducing them in meticulous detail.

Figure 16.3. Rosellini's color facsimile of Ramesses II parading in his chariot with a lion and bodyguard in a scene from the main hall of the great temple of Abu Simbel. New York Public Library digital collections. Public domain.

Shelley's *Ozymandias*

In 1821, the British Museum in London acquired a spectacular artifact, a colossal granodiorite bust from a broken colossus of Ramesses II at the Ramesseum (fig. 16.4).[29] Early in the nineteenth century, Europeans called his temple the Memnonium, following an ancient Greco-Roman legend linking it with Memnon, the legendary king of Ethiopia who fought in the Trojan War. Dubbed the "Younger Memnon," this colossal bust caused a sensation when the Italian adventurer and impresario Giovanni Belzoni removed it from the Ramesseum's ruins and delivered it to England for Henry Salt, Britain's Consul General in Egypt (fig. 16.5).[30]

Reports of the Younger Memnon's imminent arrival in England inspired the poet Percy Bysshe Shelley to pen his famous sonnet *Ozymandias*.[31] In an amiable contest with fellow poet Horace Smith—who wrote a less famous treatment of the subject—Shelly published his sonnet in *The Examiner*, a weekly intellectual newspaper, in January 1818. Having never seen the Younger Memnon statue itself, Shelly drew on his classical education, taking inspiration from Diodorus Siculus's evocative description of the much grander colossus, the Re of Rulers, which lay shattered in gargantuan fragments in the nineteenth century:[32]

I met a traveler from an antique land
Who said: Two vast and trunkless legs of stone
Stand in the desert ... near them, on the sand,
Half sunk, a shattered visage lies, whose frown,
And wrinkled lip, and sneer of cold command,
Tell that its sculptor well those passions read
Which yet survive, stamped on these lifeless things,
The hand that mocked them and the heart that fed;
And on the pedestal these words appear:
'My name is Ozymandias, king of kings;
Look on my works, ye Mighty, and despair!'
Nothing beside remains. Round the decay
Of that colossal wreck, boundless and bare
The lone and level sands stretch far away.[33]

In the second half of the nineteenth century the infant field of Egyptology rapidly matured. Pharaohs like Ramesses II materialized out of the mists of remote antiquity as archaeologists made spectacular discoveries, in endless quantities and at a dizzying pace we can only envy today. The British Museum and the Louvre, among other museums, formed large collections of Egyptian artifacts, attracting flocks of visitors. Like Rome and Constantinople in antiquity, western nations now decorated their leading cities with pharaonic obelisks, which the late Ottoman rulers of Egypt used as bargaining chips to curry favor in Britain and France. One of Ramesses II's Luxor obelisks was sent to Paris, where it stands in the Place de la Concorde.

Egypt's distant past enthralled all ranks of western society, leading to an aesthetic movement called Egyptomania. In response to the public's fascination with all things pharaonic, artists created Egyptianizing

Figure 16.4. The Young Memnon bust from an 1834 publication of Egyptian antiquities in the British Museum. Public domain.

Figure 16.5. Belzoni's painting depicting his removal of the Younger Memnon colossal bust from the Ramesseum. NYPL digital collections. Public domain.

architecture, artworks, furniture, and assorted luxury goods, while factories churned out bric-a-brac for middle-class consumers.[34] Books, magazines, and newspapers reported each sensational discovery of new monuments and artifacts to a mass audience. For Victorian scholars and the general public, pharaonic Egypt's connection to biblical tradition fired intense interest in the pharaohs. And none more so than the one they called Ramesses the Great.

An Oriental Despot

Soon after Ramesses II escaped from one and a half millennia of obscurity, scholars singled him out as the infamous pharaoh of the exodus and a paragon of oriental despotism (fig. 16.6). In his influential book *Egypt's Place in Universal History*, the nineteenth-century religious historian Christian Charles Bunsen expressed this jaundiced view of Ramesses:[35]

> *Not the slightest doubt, however, can be entertained as to his harsh and cruel disposition, by any one who feels bound to come to the conclusion that Ramses II, the son of Sethos, and no other, is the Pharaoh who drove the Israelites to desperation by his inhuman oppression ...*
>
> *All the facts tend, therefore, to give us the same picture of an unbridled despot, who took advantage of a reign of almost unparalleled length, and of the acquisitions of his father and ancestors, in order to torment his own subjects and strangers to the utmost of his power, and to employ them as instruments of his passion for war and building.*[36]

The Victorian novelist and traveler Amelia B. Edwards offered a more charitable assessment of the pharaoh in her famous travelogue *A Thousand Miles up the Nile*:[37]

> *The interest that one takes in Rameses II begins at Memphis and goes on increasing all the way up the river. It is a purely living, a purely personal interest; such as one feels in Athens for Pericles, or in Florence for Lorenzo the Magnificent. Other Pharaohs but languidly affect the imagination. Thothmes (Thutmose III) and Amenhotep (III) are to us as Darius or Artaxerxes—shadows that come and go in the distance. But with the second Rameses we are on terms of respectful intimacy. We seem to know the man—to feel his presence—to hear his name in the air. His features are as familiar to us as those of Henry VIII or Louis XIV. His cartouches meet us at every turn. Even to those who do not read the hieroglyphic character, those well-known signs convey by sheer force of association the name and style of Rameses, beloved of Amen.*[38]

Edwards admired Ramesses II for his exploits and grand monuments, but regarded his temperament as akin to other pharaohs:

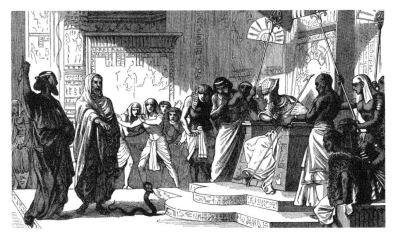

FIGURE 16.6. Moses and Aaron before the pharaoh of the exodus. Nineteenth-century illustration. Public domain.

For the rest, it is safe to conclude that he was neither better nor worse than the general run of oriental despots—that he was ruthless in war, prodigal in peace, rapacious of booty and unsparing in the exercise of almost boundless power. Such pride and such despotism were, however, in strict accordance with immemorial precedent and with the temper of the age in which he lived. The Egyptians would seem beyond all doubt to have believed that their king was always in some sense divine. They wrote hymns and offered up prayers to him, and regarded him as the living representative of deity. His princes and ministers habitually addressed him in the language of worship. Even his wives, who ought to have known better, are represented in the performance of acts of religious adoration before him. What wonder, then, if the man so deified believed himself a god?[39]

Victorian notions of pharaonic Egypt as the acme of oriental despotism ignited the visual arts. Indulging in fantasies of an exotic but decadent Orient, and intrigued by the mysteries of antiquity, artists captivated the public through engravings of their works in popular books and

FIGURE 16.7. The British artist Edward Poynter's 1867 masterpiece "Israel in Egypt." Poynter took inspiration from a colossal granite lion in the British Museum and early scientific publications of Egyptian monuments, including scenes of the Battle of Kadesh, which he reproduced on the pylon gateway. Alamy.

magazines. Even as they strove for historical accuracy, artists like the English painter Sir Edward John Poynter indulged in lurid Orientalist fancies about the ancient Nile kingdom and its place in biblical history.[40]

Poynter's masterpiece *Israel in Egypt* (1867) epitomizes this trend (fig. 16.7). Hebrew slaves, naked and miserable, struggle to move a colossal red granite lion statue toward a temple's pylon gateway. Pharaoh rides alongside in his chariot, aloof to their suffering, as other Egyptian grandees follow behind. Jubilant priests, musicians, and soldiers escort Amun-Re's sacred bark alongside the enslaved Hebrews.

Egyptian artifacts kept in the British Museum—like the two massive granite lions from Soleb in Nubia—and illustrations in the folios of Champollion, Rosellini, and Lepsius, inspired Poynter to intermix monuments from different eras and places into a composite fantasy setting.[41] This impressive painting evokes the splendor of pharaonic civilization, but juxtaposes its grandeur with the wretchedness of the enslaved Hebrews whom Pharaoh compels to build the biblical "City of Ramses."

The alleged degeneracy of Pharaoh's luxurious lifestyle also excited the imagination of the French artist Jean Jules Antoine Du Noüy.[42] In his 1886 painting *Ramses in His Harem*, Du Noüy depicts Pharaoh's life of voluptuous luxury (see fig. 7.2 above).[43] Ramesses lounges on cushions playing a board game with a naked concubine, while more women dance, play musical instruments, or recline in languid boredom in various states of dress and nudity around him. Du Noüy revisited this theme in his 1901 work *The Sadness of Pharaoh* (fig. 16.8). A listless Ramesses droops on his throne, absorbed in melancholy introspection. In his bemusement, he disregards a group of his harem women who bathe enticingly naked before him, while others arrive bearing musical instruments hoping to cheer him up. The works of Poynter, Du Noüy, and their colleagues fed into well-developed western stereotypes of the "decadent" Orient.[44]

Nineteenth century historians did not shy away from reading the moral and intellectual character of ancient kings, which they imagined were stamped on the features of their mummified corpses. Following the discovery of a cache of royal mummies on the west bank of Luxor in 1881, the French Egyptologist Gaston Maspero unwrapped Ramesses II's mummy in 1886, writing of his mortal remains:[45]

> *The mask of the mummy, in fact, gives a fair idea of that of the living king; the somewhat unintelligent expression, slightly brutish perhaps, but haughty and firm of purpose, displays itself with an air of royal majesty beneath the somber materials used by the embalmer.*[46]

By the early twentieth century, a hundred years after modern Egyptology emerged, Ramesses II was a familiar figure to scholars and the

public, a potent symbol of pharaonic excess. The pioneering American Egyptologist James Henry Breasted popularized Egyptian history with his books, reaching a wide English-speaking audience on both sides of the Atlantic. In his influential *History of Ancient Egypt*, Breasted offers a subjective and unflattering portrait of the king:

FIGURE 16.8. Engraving of *The Sadness of Pharaoh* (1901) by Jean Jules Antoine Lecompte Du Noüy. Public domain.

> *He was inordinately vain and made far more ostentatious display of his wars on his monuments than was ever done by Thutmose III. He loved ease and pleasure and gave himself up without restraint to voluptuous enjoyments ...*
>
> *... We are able to look into the withered face of the hoary nonagenarian, evidently little changed from what he was in those last days of splendor in the city of Ramses, and the resemblance to the face of the youth in the noble Turin statue is still very marked.*
>
> *Probably no Pharaoh ever left a more profound impression upon his age. A quarter of a century later began a line of ten kings bearing his name. One of them prayed that he might be granted a reign of sixty-seven years like that of his great ancestor, and all of them with varying success imitated his glory. He had set his stamp upon them all for a hundred and fifty years, and it was impossible to be a Pharaoh without being a Ramses.[47]*

During the first half of the twentieth century, Akhenaten, his wife Nefertiti, and his son Tutankhamun displaced Ramesses II in the public eye. New discoveries at Akhenaten's capital, El-Amarna, fed the public's insatiable appetite for all things pharaonic.[48] Egyptomania reached fever pitch when Howard Carter unearthed Tutankhamun's spectacular tomb treasures in 1922, sparking a worldwide sensation that has not abated since. In the meantime Ramesses II celebrity diminished—until he starred in a Hollywood movie of his own.

Ramesses the Movie Star

In Cecil B. DeMille's epic 1956 film, *The Ten Commandments*, actor Yul Brynner gives an incomparable performance as Ramesses II. Cast in the role of the story's main villain, Brynner exudes a stylish hauteur overflowing with elegant bravado and brooding malevolence. He meets his match in his half-brother Moses, played by Charleston Heston, and the regal but catty Princess Nefertari, played to the hilt by Anne Baxter (fig. 16.9).

DeMille strove for what he considered historical accuracy in recreating biblical history, but he allotted the majority of screen time to an extended pharaonic soap opera.[49] Egyptologists at the University of Chicago's Oriental Institute vetted the film's extravagant sets, costumes, and props.[50] Unlike most Hollywood movies about Egypt, we find real hieroglyphic inscriptions in *The Ten Commandments*, where we can read Ramesses II's cartouche names on Brynner's pharaonic garb (fig. 16.10). Still, this was Hollywood. The film's stylish sets and costumes owe as much to Art Deco and mid-century modern aesthetics as they do to New Kingdom Egypt.[51]

However spectacular its acting and stagecraft, *The Ten Commandments* has nothing whatsoever to do with the historical Ramesses II. DeMille looked beyond the Bible for source material, including the ancient Jewish authors Josephus and Philo of Alexandria, and from Islamic tradition in the Quran.[52] Still, in its portrayal of Ramesses II, *The Ten Commandments* conforms to traditional views of the pharaoh of the exodus as a cruel tyrant.[53] DeMille also conceived his "monument" as expressing American cultural and ideological values, anti-Communism in particular.[54] In his personal introduction to the film, DeMille even denounces Ramesses as a dictator, implying he is no different from Hitler or Stalin.[55]

Recent Hollywood takes on the exodus story are more familiar to younger audiences, but Stephen Spielberg's 1998 animated feature *The Prince of Egypt* and Ridley Scott's overwrought 2014 blockbuster *Exodus: Gods and Kings* lack the panache of DeMille's 1956 classic. Certainly no one of Yul Brynner's theatrical stature—or his elegant swagger—has ever brought a superior Ramesses to the silver screen. A close runner up is a 2010 French comic fantasy film, *The Extraordinary Adventures of Adèl Blanc-Sec*, where the mummies of Pharaoh and his court are revived by magic from an exhibition in the Louvre. Aristocratic and urbane despite his gaunt, ghoulish appearance, the reanimated Ramesses II takes an evening stroll through Paris. But he has a heart too and, with the help of his royal physician, revives Adèl's comatose sister with a kiss.[56]

Modern Egyptian Views of Ramesses II

As an icon of their pharaonic heritage, Ramesses II became a powerful nationalist symbol for modern Egyptians.[57] During the twenties and thirties, an ideological movement called Pharaonism emerged among Egypt's intellectual class. Advocating a native Egyptian cultural identity, Pharaonists looked to the country's pre-Islamic heritage. There they found inspiration for a modern national movement in the decades before Egypt won its independence from Great Britain.[58] The Pharaonists sparked controversy among Egypt's culturally conservative and deeply pious Muslim majority because they rejected both Islamic identity and pan-Arabic political solidarity.[59]

Along with the Great Pyramids and Tutankhamun's treasures, Pharaonists revered Ramesses II as a symbol of ancient Egypt's legacy. In 1923, a year after Howard Carter discovered the tomb of Tutankhamun and set off an explosion of patriotic fervor, the Egyptian playwright Mahmoud Murad staged his musical play *The Glory of Ramses*.[60] Other voices in Egypt looked to the pharaonic past, including the leading Egyptian politician Mohamed Husein Haykal, who wrote that "Ramesses was urging the Egyptians of today to regain the glory and grandeur which were Egypt's in the days of his power."[61]

The Pharaoh and Gamal Abdul Nasser

In 1952 the Egyptian Revolution toppled Egypt's last foreign ruler, King Farouk. By 1956, the same year *The Ten Commandments* premiered, Gamal Abdul Nasser became president of the Arab Republic of Egypt, only its second native ruler since Pharaoh Nectanebo II in the fourth century BCE.[62] Nasser's

FIGURE 16.9. Yul Brynner and Anne Baxter as Ramesses II and Nefertari from Cecil B. DeMille's 1956 epic film *The Ten Commandments*. Alamy.

FIGURE 16.10. Yul Brynner as Ramesses II in *The Ten Commandments*. Alamy.

regime strived to forge a modern, more secular Egyptian nation. As Prime Minister in 1955, Nasser ordered a granite colossus of Ramesses II moved to the square in front of Cairo's central railway station (fig. 16.11). Nasser renamed it Ramses Square. There Pharaoh's mammoth effigy presided for half a century over the bustle and traffic of central Cairo, a symbol of Egypt's ancient heritage and modern pride.[63]

Abu Simbel and the Nubian Rescue Campaign

During the 1960s, Nasser's government prioritized construction of the Aswan High Dam at the first cataract of the Nile. With financial and technical backing from the Soviet Union, the High Dam served as both a symbol and a vehicle for modernizing Egypt. This mega project would tame the Nile's annual flood, prevent droughts, and provide electricity to the nation. The project did not come without negative effects. It would drown much of Lower Nubia under a huge reservoir, Lake Nasser, displacing a hundred thousand people and drowning hundreds of archaeological sites.

Egypt appealed to the world community to rescue Nubia's imperiled heritage. The United Nations Cultural Organization, UNESCO, spearheaded a multinational rescue effort.[64] Archaeologists launched emergency excavations at sites throughout the flood zone, representing thousands of years of Nubian history.[65] The marquee component of this rescue campaign presented the most difficult challenge of all: saving Ramesses II's magnificent temples at Abu Simbel.

By the early 1960s, as construction of the Aswan High Dam progressed, the imposing and photogenic temples of Abu Simbel riveted world attention (fig. 16.12).[66] Fearing that these spectacular monuments would vanish beneath Lake Nasser, several nations offered plans for saving them. All these schemes were ambitious, but most appear harebrained today.[67]

The Egyptian government and UNESCO reluctantly accepted a Swedish proposal when other methods proved impractical. To save the temples of Abu Simbel, engineers would cut them into hundreds of pieces (fig. 16.13 and 9.4 above).[68] The scheme reduced the shrines to a giant three-dimensional jigsaw puzzle consisting of over a thousand blocks, some weighing thirty-three tons. Next, they would reassemble the temples on a pair of artificial mountainsides, two hundred feet (sixty meters) above their original site. Once Egypt and UNESCO authorized this audacious plan and secured international funding, a team of Egyptian and foreign engineers and stonemasons mounted an urgent, around-the-clock effort to move the temples ahead of the rising floodwaters.[69]

After removing thirty-three thousand tons of rocky overburden, they cut the outer and interior portions of both shrines from the mountainside. Above Lake Nasser's highest level, they reassembled the temples, enclosing them with artificial cliffs as in their original setting.

Ramesses II's builders had excavated the inner halls, treasuries, and sanctums deep within the mountainside. To protect these rebuilt grottos from collapsing under the crushing weight of the artificial mountains above them, engineers constructed massive reinforced concrete domes to support the overburden. (From within, the domed chamber above Ramesses II's larger temple resembles the secret lair of a supervillain in a James Bond movie.)

The international team extracted both temples just before Lake Nasser drowned their original site. Incredibly, once they had reassembled Ramesses II's temples, the masons camouflaged their work so carefully that not a seam is visible to the eye.

Alongside the Aswan High Dam itself, the Nubian salvage campaign was a triumphant symbol of mid-twentieth century notions of progress, engineering prowess, and international cooperation under the United Nations's banner. The world had rescued Abu Simbel and over a dozen more pharaonic temples, including Ramesses II's Nubian shrines at Beit el-Wali, Derr, and parts of Wadi es-Sebua.[70] In Nasser's fiercely nationalistic and assertive vision of modern Egypt, these ancient relics of a mighty past became potent symbols of a glorious present.[71] Millions of tourists have flocked to Ramesses II's temples at Abu Simbel, modern pilgrims paying homage to the grandeur of Egypt's ancient history and to Ramesses as its greatest icon.

Figure 16.11. Colossus of Ramesses II from ancient Memphis, formerly in Ramses Square in Cairo and now installed in the Grand Egyptian Museum in Giza, Cairo. Alamy.

Figure 16.12. Nigerian stamps commemorating the 1960s UNESCO campaign to salvage Abu Simbel.

Naguib Mahfouz—Judging the Pharaohs

In the early decades of the twentieth century, the Pharaonist movement exerted a profound influence on a young Egyptian novelist named Naguib Mahfouz, an avid nationalist and self-trained amateur Egyptologist. Mahfouz set most of his works in contemporary Egypt, especially in his beloved Cairo. These earned him Egypt's first Nobel Prize for literature in 1988. He also penned several works on Egypt's ancient past.[72] In 1983 Mahfouz pub-

lished *Before the Throne*, a novel of historical fantasy bearing a modern nationalist subtext.[73]

Sitting in judgment with a jury of ancient deities, Osiris, lord of the underworld, summons a series of Egyptian rulers, from the first Pharaoh Menes down to President Anwar Sadat, assassinated just two years earlier. Each leader gives a statement justifying his stewardship of the Egyptian nation. Osiris judges him either as worthy of joining the immortals in paradise or condemns him to hell. As each pharaoh, pasha, or president comes forward, his predecessors comment on his worthiness as leader of the Egyptian nation.

When Ramesses II's turn arrives, Horus heralds him as he enters the judgment hall still wrapped in his burial shroud. Thoth, god of wisdom and writing, proclaims his deeds on earth:

FIGURE 16.13. The UNESCO salvage of the great temple of Abu Simbel during the 1960s. Getty Images.

> *He buttressed Egypt's rule over Nubia and Asia. He waged war against the Hittites, then concluded with them a treaty of peace. Thenceforth he devoted the rest of his long life to a campaign of construction of a kind never before seen in the history of his country. It was an age of building and a blossoming of the arts, and of luxury. His life stretched to nearly a century, and he enjoyed it to the full, siring nearly three hundred children.*[74]

Granted the opportunity to plead his own case, Ramesses frankly admits usurping the throne from his elder brother after his father Sety I died: "I was certain that the hour demanded a man of power, while my brother's weakness, despite his legitimate claim to rule, would bring disaster to Egypt." Sety scolds his son for his treachery. Here, Mahfouz relies on outdated theories about Ramesses II's phantom elder brother.[75] Next Ramesses launches into a detailed account of his military accomplishments, justifying his actions at the Battle of Kadesh. He explains the Hittite ambush by pleading that he fell victim to bad luck. Yet, Ramesses insists, he repulsed the assault, so the battle still redounded upon him as a personal victory, due to his courage and excellence as a warrior.

Ramesses also justifies his treaty with Hatti and his subsequent marriage to a Hittite princess as necessary for bringing peace and security to Egypt. This defense fails to impress the great warrior Pharaoh Thutmose III, who demands to know why Ramesses made peace with Egypt's greatest foe and how he fell into a Hittite trap at Kadesh. Ramesses responds that enemy spies had deceived him. A debate ensues:

> *"You set off in haste when you should have waited for your army to reach you from the south," said Thutmose III. "You are courageous—there is no doubt about that—but you are not a prudent commander."*
>
> *"Yet I broke through the siege, then turned the attack back on the enemy with the rest of my army," Ramesses II protested. "They fell into the trap which they themselves had set for me—I tore them to pieces and scored a decisive victory."*
>
> *"Your objective was not merely to win a battle," Thutmose III said, moving to the point of his discourse. "Rather, you clearly wanted to conquer Qadesh, as I had done, because it controls the roads in every direction. Therefore, you have no right to claim a victory when you did not achieve the purpose of your expedition."*
>
> *"What do you say about my routing the enemy's army?" Ramesses II asked.*
>
> *"I say that you won a battle, but you lost the war," Thutmose III riposted, "while your enemy lost a battle but won the war."*[76]

This back-and-forth between the two dead pharaohs continues, until Ramesses forces Thutmose to admit that he, Ramesses, restored Egypt's empire to its former greatness. Thutmose concedes this point: "You restored to Egypt the greatest part of her empire, and were marked by your overwhelming personal valor, which put fear into the hearts of your enemies."[77]

Various ancestral kings object to Ramesses II's accounts of his peaceful exploits. Khufu disputes his claim to be Egypt's greatest builder, asking sarcastically if he had erected a pyramid: "'No, but one does not build pyramids alone,' said Ramesses II, 'there is not one province in Egypt without a temple or an obelisk or a statue of mine.'" Akhenaten denounces Ramesses's penchant for appropriating monuments his royal forebears created by inscribing his own name in place of theirs. When Ramesses dismisses Akhenaten as a heretic, Osiris compels him to apologize.

The probing inquisition turns to Ramesses II's family life and his legendary sexual prowess:

> "Did you use magic to preserve your marvelous manly vigor?" Amenhotep III inquired.
>
> "I performed my own magic myself," Ramesses II explained. "At the age of ninety, I would stand in the Great Hall while rows of chariots entered. In each rode one of my wives, naked, accompanied by a naked slave girl. They would keep rolling past me until there flowed in my aged veins the fresh blood of youth!"[78]

After concluding this bruising inquiry into all his deeds and shortcomings, the divine tribunal commends Ramesses II's spirit to eternal glory:

> Isis summarized, "This son returned Egypt to her former glory, while material comfort during his time spread from palace to house to reed hut alike. If we counted all his faults through all of his life, they would seem insignificant."
>
> And so Osiris turned to Ramesses II, "Go take your seat among the Immortals."[79]

Finally, when Egypt's modern presidents, Gamal Abdul Nasser and Anwar Sadat, stand before the divine tribunal, Mahfouz's Ramesses once more finds his voice. Ramesses judges Nasser as a great leader, like himself, who was tested by defeat in war. Unsatisfied with their own deeds, each took credit for those of their predecessors. Ramesses II's Egypt was the most powerful kingdom on earth. Nasser had a harder job, struggling against much greater powers.

At last, Anwar Sadat appears before the tribunal. Hanging in the air is Sadat's controversial peace treaty with Israel. Many Egyptians, and most Arab nations, condemned Sadat as a traitor. The treaty cost him his life when Islamic militants assassinated him in 1981. Even for secular Egyptians this remained a sensitive issue. With evident disdain, Thutmose III compares Sadat's efforts to Ramesses II's Hittite accords, to which Ramesses replies self-righteously: "A ruler is responsible first and foremost for the life of his people ... from this starting point, he resorts to war or turns to peace."[80] Thus, Mahfouz leverages Ramesses II's eternal prestige in defense of Anwar Sadat.

In Naguib Mahfouz's vision, Ramesses II embodies the contradictory impulses and complex judgments of modern Egyptian nationalism better than one-dimensional pharaohs like Khufu the pyramid builder, Thutmose III the empire builder, or Akhenaten the monotheist. Like Ramesses, Mahfouz presents Nasser as a colossal figure who dominated his age yet ran roughshod over the legacies of his predecessors. At war, Ramesses and Nasser both tasted glorious victory and humiliating defeat.[81]

Ramesses II's story also mirrors Sadat's, whose military achievement against Israel in the October War of 1973 was complex. Egyptians regarded it as a victory, but Sadat soon outraged many of his people by negotiating a treaty with their greatest foe.[82] For Mahfouz, Sadat bravely made peace for the nation's benefit, like his great pharaonic ancestor. In his telling, Osiris judges both Nasser and Sadat, like Ramesses II himself, as worthy to stand among Egypt's immortal sons.

Pharaoh's State Visit to France

During the 1970s, Anwar Sadat sought to reconcile Egypt with western nations like the United States, withdrawing from the Soviet orbit after 1973. Pharaonic heritage again became a cultural bargaining chip in Egypt's relations with the West. Throughout the seventies Sadat allowed spectacular artifacts from Tutankhamun's tomb, including the boy king's priceless gold death mask, to tour the United States, Canada, France, and the United Kingdom. "Tut fever" gripped America.[83]

But in France, Ramesses II reigned supreme. In 1976, another blockbuster exhibition traveled from Egypt to Paris: dozens of artifacts from the time of Ramesses II. It was not just his statues and artifacts that came to France that year—Pharaoh himself made an appearance. Officials at the Egyptian Museum in Cairo discovered that Ramesses II's mummy was decaying, a victim of bacteria and fungi. France offered an advanced radiation treatment to eradicate these infestations.[84] The Egyptian government decided to send the mummy to Paris for study and treatment (fig. 16.14). Sadat himself authorized the trip, but only after securing a promise from France: they would accord Ramesses the honors due to a visiting head of state. Pharaoh should get nothing less than a twenty-one-gun salute!

FIGURE 16.14. Egyptian President Anwar Sadat gazes at Ramesses II's mummy during its visit to Paris in 1976. Getty Images.

Equipping him for his journey, the Egyptian foreign ministry issued Ramesses with a passport, listing his occupation as "King (deceased)."[85] The royal mummy reached Charles de Gaulle Airport in Paris on the morning of September 26, 1976, where a French minister of state and a military honor guard turned out to receive him. Given the king's status, the arrival ceremony blended diplomatic protocol with the pomp of a state funeral.

Sadat found that appeals to Egypt's past could be a double-edged sword. Bowing to religious sensibilities, in 1980 he ordered the royal mummy room in Cairo's Egyptian Museum closed to visitors shortly after Ramesses II's mummy returned from Paris. "Egyptian kings are not to be made spectacles of," he insisted. When Islamic militants assassinated President Sadat in 1981, one of them shouted: "I have killed Pharaoh!" The title of "Pharaoh" remains a pejorative epithet in Egyptian politics, which critics have often hurled at Sadat's successors.[86]

The attitude of many Egyptians toward their distant past remains ambivalent. They take pride in the glories of their ancient forebearers and Egypt's legacy as a birthplace of civilization. As in the Bible, however, the Quran depicts the unnamed pharaoh of the exodus as a wicked tyrant, ignorant of God, who persecuted Moses and the Hebrews. So far as Ramesses II stands out among a crowded field of Egypt's ancient rulers, modern Egyptians may view him with contempt rather than national pride.[87] Unlike a handful of Pharaonist intellectuals in the early twentieth century, most Egyptians today look to pan-Arabism and Islam as the basis for their religious, personal, cultural, and national identities.

A Symbol of Pharaonic Egypt

Ramesses II remains today what he always wished to be: a larger-than-life icon of pharaonic power and splendor. For some he epitomizes the glory of Egypt's ancient past; his name and colossal image evoke antiquity like no others. Perhaps only Cleopatra, Tutankhamun, and Queen Nefertiti enjoy greater fame.

Ramesses occurs as a character in modern fiction, including Norman Mailer's *Ancient Evenings*—as a hypersexual king—and as the protagonist in a series of bad novels by Christian Jacq, a French Egyptologist who ought to know better.[88] Ann Rice even portrayed the pharaoh as a vampire and immortal villain in her novel *The Mummy, or Ramses the Damned*. Now a pop culture icon, Ramesses turns up in comics—ranging from *Tintin* to the *Watchmen*—and in video games. TV viewers often see him in programs, ranging from reruns of DeMille's *The Ten Commandments* and *The Prince of Egypt* to a slew of TV documentaries and the occasional cartoon.[89] As an emblem of sexual potency, his name appeared on a popular brand of condoms for several decades (fig. 16.15).[90] Ramesses II's name and image also peddled assorted tobacco products, perfumes and cosmetics, soft drinks, travel ads, tarot cards, children's toys, and countless souvenirs scooped up by foreign tourists visiting his homeland (figs. 16.16 and 16.17). Yet, he has also become a powerful symbol in modern discussions of race, identity, religion, and historical memory.

For many people of African descent, especially in North America and the United Kingdom, Ramesses was a black African king who remains

FIGURE 16.15. Package of Ramses brand condoms from the 1920s.

FIGURE 16.16. Coke and Pepsi bottles from the Ramesses II exhibit in Charlotte, North Carolina and Memphis, Tennessee in the 1980s.

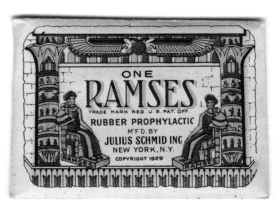

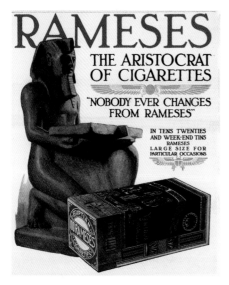

RAMESES

THE ARISTOCRAT
OF CIGARETTES

"NOBODY EVER CHANGES
FROM RAMESES"

IN TENS TWENTIES
AND WEEK-END TINS
RAMESES
LARGE SIZE FOR
PARTICULAR OCCASIONS

Figure 16.17. A 1920s era advertisement for Rameses brand cigarettes.

a source of pride for the global African diaspora. Like other famous Egyptian rulers, Ramesses is often caught up in questions about the African character of pharaonic civilization, debates that have raged since the nineteenth century.[91] Early Egyptologists held racist views about origins of pharaonic civilization. Popular books by Egyptologists like James Henry Breasted and William Mathew Flinders Petrie, penned a century ago, make for racially offensive and cringeworthy reading today. Beginning in the 1950s, however, a new generation of Egyptologists systematically discredited these racist Eurocentric theories, and none hold them today.[92]

Among late-nineteenth and early-twentieth century African-American intellectuals, a new school of thought emphasizing the importance of black people and African civilizations in world history challenged old Eurocentric views. Egypt was central to this world view.[93] Afrocentrism emerged to oppose all forms of white racism, from the enslavement of Africans throughout the Western Hemisphere and Jim Crow laws in the American South after the Civil War, to European colonialism in Africa, which finally collapsed after World War II. From its roots in the United States, what we now call Afrocentrism grew into a broad, world-wide scholarly and cultural movement, blossoming during the Civil Rights movement of the 1960s among the African diaspora in the Americas, Europe, and Africa.

This pan-Africanist ideology challenged outdated and racist notions of "white" Egyptians. Afrocentrism gained a strong advocate in the work of the Senegalese scholar Cheik Anta Diop, as former European colonies in Africa and around the globe rapidly became independent nations during the 1950s.[94] Many proponents view ancient Egypt as the true source of all civilization, including European ones starting with the ancient Greeks, whom Afrocentrists view as mere imitators of pharaonic culture. They object to the word "Egypt" itself, insisting it should be called "Kemet."[95]

Modern debates about race would have puzzled the ancient Egyptians.[96] But among the public, and in academia, many people still quarrel about whether figures like Akhenaten, Cleopatra, Nefertiti, and Ramesses II were "black" or "white." Today, amid heated debates about identity, divergent conspiracy theories, and internet shouting matches, louder voices drown out the dispassionate and meticulous work of scholars and more nuanced research by anthropologists or reject them outright. Afrocentrist critics object that mainstream American and European scholarship denies the common African heritage and blackness of ancient Egyptians, while accusing mainstream popular culture of "white-washing" the pharaohs.[97]

Some whites react to these charges defensively, with naïve responses that cherry pick certain ancient art objects, like the famous Bust of Nefertiti, as "proof" the Egyptians were "white."[98] Throughout the Nineteenth and Twentieth centuries, artwork depicting Egyptians in books, magazines, and popular media reinforced this racial fable. Today Hollywood still casts white actors to play the pharaohs in movies, television, and even videogames, just as it did in 1956 in *The Ten Commandments*.

Recent scientific research indicates the genetic makeup of the Egyptians was more diverse and complex than extreme views on either side care to admit. But the need to define the "true" heritage of these ancient people is caught up in modern identity politics and the common human tendency to seek validation by looking to the past, especially a great past like pharaonic Egypt.[99]

Not everyone looks back in admiration at pharaonic civilization. For some, Ramesses II is a villain. To his detractors Ramesses embodies the decadence and cruelty of oriental despots, the arrogance of kings, and the benighted ignorance of pagan antiquity. In the Judeo-Christian and Islamic traditions he has become *The Pharaoh* who oppressed the ancient Hebrews, the one God punished with the ten plagues, culminating in the death of his first-born son.[100] Others denounce him as a tyrant, a slave-master, an imperialist, and an oppressor of women. And, they insist, Ramesses was one of history's most notorious megalomaniacs.

To his admirers, Ramesses epitomizes the glory and sophistication of pharaonic Egypt at its height. From his royal descendants in the Ramesside age down to modern times, many hold him up as the ultimate paragon of Egyptian kingship: a bold warrior, colossal builder, and visionary statesman who signed one of history's first international peace treaties.

Even for most Egyptologists, Ramesses II typically inspires deep admiration or visceral distaste. Yet, his negative and positive qualities are not mutually exclusive. He was a complex figure concealing himself behind a carefully constructed, magnificent façade of the ideal pharaoh. For good or ill, Ramesses II is a mirror we hold up to our memories and fantasies of ancient Egypt. In assessing the pharaoh's reign and his achievements, we must confront our own ideologies as well as his.

Notes

1. Schlögl 2016.
2. Kitchen 1987; Leprohon 2010.
3. For archaism in the art and culture of the Third Intermediate period, see Tiradritti 2008.
4. Spalinger 1977; Morschauser 1988.
5. See now the comprehensive edition, commentary, and analysis of the stela in Witthuhn et al. 2015.
6. *KRI* II, 284–87; *RITA* II, 113–16; *RITANC* II, 165–68; Witthuhn et al. 2015, 49–61.
7. The traditional formula is "begging for the breath of life," *dbḥ ṯꜣw n ꜥnḫ*.
8. *KRI* II, 285.
9. Spalinger 1977.
10. Morschauser 1988; Bianchi 1991.
11. Lloyd 2019, 9–10.
12. Charron and Bartbotin 2016; Vinson 2018.
13. Translation: Simpson 2003, 453–69. For analysis, see Vinson 2018.
14. Translation: Simpson 2003, 470–89.
15. Lloyd 2019, 10–11. Bianchi (1991) examines Greco-Roman memories of and borrowings from the whole Ramesside era.
16. James 1991; Lloyd 2019. On ancient Greek and Roman fascination with pharaonic history and culture, see Fritze 2016, 71–107.
17. Waddell 1940.
18. Several ancient Greek and Jewish historians and early Christian authors brandished quotations from Manetho's history as weapons in their polemical debates concerning which of these civilizations was the most ancient. The Roman-era Jewish historian Josephus speaks of a Ramessês who ruled one year and four months, and so must be Rameses I while "his son Harmessês Miamûn (ruled) for sixty-six years, two months" and must be Ramesses II. Another copyist tells of Ramesses, also called Aegyptus, who ruled for sixty-eight years. Elsewhere, we have Rampsês the son of Sethôs, ruling for sixty-six years: Waddell 1940, 103, 119, 121.
19. Serrano Delgado 2011.
20. Leblanc 1993b.
21. Diodorus Siculus, *Bibliotheca historica* 1.47.
22. Bactria was known to the ancient Greeks and Romans as a country in central Asia, including parts of modern Afghanistan and Pakistan. It was completely unknown to New Kingdom Egypt.
23. Diodorus Siculus, *Bibliotheca historica* 1.47.
24. Pliny the Elder, *Natural History* 36.14. On classical accounts of Egyptian obelisks, see Obsomer 2010.
25. Likewise, the Roman historian Tacitus describes the visit of Augustus's stepson Germanicus to Thebes; Kelly 2010.
26. In 1813, the Swiss scholar Jean-Louis Burckhardt located the great temple, half buried in drifts of sand but was unable to explore it further. Burckhardt notified the Italian explorer Giovanni Belzoni who also failed to uncover the temple that year. Belzoni returned in 1817, excavating much of the temple and entering its interior where he made the earliest copies of its inscriptions. Peters-Destéract 2003, 31–109; Willeitner 2010, ch. 1.

AU

27. Lending et al. 2018.

28. Their arduous task, and the massive effort toward publishing their results in two separate series of giant folio volumes, taxed the health of both men. Each died in his early forties, Champollion in 1832 and Rosellini in 1843. But the copies they labored to produce were invaluable to the new field of Egyptology. Also participating in the Franco-Tuscan expedition was the Italian artist Alessandro Ricci; see Salvoldi 2018.

29. Leblanc and Esmoignt 1999; Garnett 2015. On the history of the colossal bust's arrival and presence in the British Museum and the development of the Egyptian collection and its impact on Victorian culture, see Moser 2006.

30. Colla 2007, 24–66.

31. Colla 2007, 67–71.

32. Rodenbeck 2004.

33. It is likely that Shelly confused the "Younger Memnon" statue with the much larger colossus called "the Re of Rulers." While Diodorus witnessed the great colossus when it was still intact, Shelley's "traveler from an antique land" describes it vividly as a "colossal wreck," as it now is. Was the traveler a contemporary of Shelley, or was he referring to Diodorus? In any case, we have to allow for a certain amount of artistic license. Christian or Muslim iconoclasts thoroughly destroyed the face of the great colossus in the Middle Ages. Ramesses II's statues, including the better-preserved "Younger Memnon," feature his characteristic benign smile. There never was a "wrinkled lip, and sneer of cold command." On the poet's inspiration, see Leblanc 1993b; Rodenbeck 2004.

34. See Fritze 2016 and the essays collected in MacDonald and Rice 2003; also the essays in Versluys 2020.

35. Bunsen was the first leading German historian of pharaonic Egypt and Lepsius's mentor.

36. Bunsen 1848, 3:183–84.

37. Edwards 1888, 262–83. On Edwards's life and influence on British Egyptology, see Moon 2006.

38. Edwards 1888, 262–63.

39. Edwards 1888, 283.

40. Conner 1983, 1985; Berko, Berko, and De Meulenaere 1992; Moser 2019.

41. Grouped with an Old Kingdom pyramid and a Ptolemaic structure resembling the Temple of Hathor at Dendera, we see a series of pylon gateways like those at Karnak and Luxor. Poynter even decorated the first pylon with scenes of the Battle of Kadesh.

42. Dierderen 2004.

43. Diederen 2004, 104–8, figs. 102 and 102a.

44. Dierderen 2004, 108: "the artist implies that, despite the absolute power of the pharaoh and his control of countless women, true love and happiness have eluded him." On Orientalism in western thought in general and Egyptology in particular, see Said 1979; Lewis 2004; Hellum forthcoming.

45. Smith 1912, 59.

46. Maspero 1904, 5:250.

47. Breasted 1905, 460–63.

48. Montserrat 2000; Fritze 2016, 222–44. In 1851 the architect and empresario Owen Jones built a series of large panoramas of Egyptian monuments for the Crystal Palace, including a mockup of the façade of the great temple of Abu Simbel; see Moser 2012.

49. For recent reassessments, see Tooze 2003; Joffe 2016.

50. Noerdlinger 1956. Among the scholars consulted in making the film were Keith C. Seele and John A. Wilson of the Oriental Institute of the University of Chicago, and William C. Hayes of the Metropolitan Museum of Art in New York. Noerdlinger also drew on the works of the early-American Egyptologist James Henry Breasted.

51. Even more lavish were the sets and props for DeMille's 1923 version of *The Ten Commandments* in the California desert, which became the object of an archaeological excavation in the 1990s when winds uncovered many of the plaster props; see Stokke 2018.

52. Noerdlinger 1956; Calabria 2015.

53. The historicity of the exodus tradition and how it might have unfolded remains a hotly debated topic among biblical scholars. Many Egyptologists hold themselves aloof from these polemics, aside from those like Michael Hasel, James K. Hoffmeier, Kenneth A. Kitchen, and Donald B. Redford, who have expertise and interest in both fields. Among Egyptologists, favorable assessments of the exodus as a genuine historical event include Kitchen 2003; Hoffmeier 1996; and Hoffmeier et al. 2016, while Redford (1992) rejects it. Assmann (2015) is more concerned with Moses and the exodus as an aspect of cultural memory. The literature on exodus is vast. For varying perspectives, see essays collected in Levy, Schneider, and Propp 2015; Hoffmeier et al. 2016; Janzen 2021.

54. Coming a decade after the defeat of Nazi fascism, *The Ten Commandments* appeared at the height of the Cold War as America's Red Scare reached its fevered peak. For DeMille, a fierce anti-Communist, pharaonic Egypt offered a vivid parallel to modern totalitarian regimes like those of Hitler's Germany and Stalin's Soviet Union. The movie also came a decade after the modern state of Israel was founded in 1948 in the aftermath of the Holocaust. On the film as a reflection of American society's fears and aspirations during the 1950s Cold War, see Nadel 1993. During the 1950s, Hollywood produced a spate of blockbuster films with pharaonic and biblical themes. On the former, see Serafy 2003.

55. DeMille states: "The theme of this picture is whether man ought to be ruled by God's laws or whether they are to be ruled by the whims of a dictator like Ramesses. Are men the property of the state or are they free souls under God? This same battle continues throughout the world today." ("Cecil B. DeMille's Introduction to the theatrical release," *The Ten Commandments*, directed by Cecil B. DeMille [Hollywood, CA: Paramount Pictures 1956]). Nadel (1993, 417), offers a decidedly postmodern interpretation.

56. In the film, Ramesses is portrayed as a computer-generated image, which resembles the king's emaciated mummy with its sharp aquiline nose yet is also subtly expressive. He admires the Louvre's courtyard in 1912 but recommends that the French build a pyramid at its center, a nod to the glass entrance to the museum erected almost a century later.

57. See Reid 2002, 200–212, 288–97; Colla 2007, passim, esp. 234–72.

58. Gershoni and Jankowski 1986, 164–90; Wood 1998, 179–96; Colla 2007, 172–226.

59. Pharaonists lionized Egypt's ancient past arguing that the country possessed a unique cultural identity different from neighboring Arab peoples, which, they claimed, should come before any pan-Arabic solidarity. Proponents of this ideology were secular, which raised the hackles of Islamic authorities

and critics, leaving the Pharaonists out of step with average Egyptians in this deeply religious society.

60. Gershoni and Jankowski 1986, 183.

61. Gershoni and Jankowski 1986, 171 and n. 42. His daughter, Prof. Faisal Haykal, would go on to become a leading Egyptian Egyptologist at the American University of Cairo.

62. Although De Mille filmed his epic in Egypt with Nasser's permission and the cooperation and approval of the Egyptian ministry of culture, Egyptian authorities banned the film upon its release, condemning it as "Zionist propaganda"; see Orrison 1999. Among the experts consulted on the film was the Egyptian Egyptologist Labib Habachi. De Mille attempted to make the film appealing to Muslims as well as Jews and Christians. Noerdlinger's (1956) documentation for the film reports that it drew on the Quran to reconstruct Moses's life. In his introduction to the book, De Mille states: "Here, I hope, Jewish, Christian, and Muslim believers and the clergy of all faiths will find the light of archaeological and historical science illuminating the Word of God" (Calabria 2015). Because the film visually portrayed the Prophet Moses, it offended Muslim doctrine that views depicting the voice or image of any prophet as idolatrous.

63. Wood 1998, 185; Reid 2015, 361–62; Labuhn 2018. The statue remained in the square until 2006 when concerns about the effect of pollution and the constant vibrations produced by traffic prompted the regime of Hosni Mubarak to move the colossus to a storage site near the Grand Egyptian Museum under construction in Giza near the Great Pyramids. In January 2018, the colossus was moved again to its final home in the cavernous foyer of the new museum.

64. Säve-Söderbergh 1987.

65. For an overview, see *The UNESCO Courier* (February-March 1980).

66. *National Geographic Magazine* chronicled the rescue of Abu Simbel throughout the 1960s: Gerster 1963, 1969; Nicholson and Gerster 1966; Desroches Noblecourt and Gerster 1968. *The UNESCO Courier* devoted its February 1960 and November 1961 issues to the plight of the Nubian monuments and cultural sites before a means to save Abu Simbel had been finalized.

67. French engineers proposed building a coffer dam around the temple site to hold back the waters and allow the temples to remain undisturbed, albeit as a kind of Nile Netherlands resting permanently below the water level of the lake. The Italians wanted to cut away parts of the surrounding cliff and enclose the great temple in a gigantic box of steel reinforced concrete. Next, hundreds of synchronized jacks would hoist the entire temple, millimeter by millimeter, until it rested safely above the floodwaters. This stupendous plan was highly impractical, and UNESCO declined it. Another idea, mercifully rejected, would have let nature take its course. Once the waters of Lake Nasser engulfed the temples, tourists could visit them via special underwater viewing chambers or even by scuba diving.

68. Allais 2013; Zaki 2019.

69. Dramatically recounted in the 1967 UNESCO film *The World Saves Abu Simbel*: http://www.unesco.org/archives/multimedia/document-67.

70. Allais 2013 and 2018.

71. The Arab-Israeli wars of 1967 and 1973 soon overshadowed the project's completion.

72. Even when writing on remote antiquity, Mahfouz's nationalistic sympathies, as well as his passion for exploring the concept of Truth, however complex, shine through in his work. His 1944 novel *Thebes at War* recalls the days of Pharaoh Ahmose who expelled the foreign Hyksos rulers at the beginning of the Eighteenth Dynasty. The book amounts to a parable about Egyptian national liberation in the waning days of the British Protectorate. Mahfouz later developed his interest in Truth and the nature of God in his 1985 novel *Akhenaten: Dweller in Truth*. This short novel follows a young scribe who interviews Akhenaten's contemporaries seeking to understand his religious revolution and its impact on Egypt. For Akhenaten's impact on the modern imagination, see Montserrat 2000.

73. First published in Arabic. For Stock's English translation and analysis of the novel, see Mahfouz 2016; Stock 2008, 2011.

74. Mahfouz 2016, ch. 26. As is often the case in popularizing accounts of Ramesses II, Mahfouz grossly exaggerates the number of children the king sired. We can only account for roughly one hundred sons and daughters. See pp. 256–57 above.

75. Mahfouz 2016, ch. 26. It is obvious here that Mahfouz was relying, as he often did, on outdated theories in nineteenth and early-twentieth century accounts, in particular the work of Breasted (1905). This was based on a misinterpretation of Sety I's war scenes at Karnak (for which, see pp. 53–54 and fig. 3.4 above).

76. Mahfouz 2016, ch. 26.

77. Mahfouz 2016, ch. 26.

78. Mahfouz 2016, ch. 26.

79. Mahfouz 2016, ch. 26.

80. Mahfouz 2016, ch. 63.

81. In summing up Nasser's legacy, the goddess Isis opines that "his magnificent accomplishments would need all the walls of the temples in order to record them. As for his faults, I do not know how to defend them"; Mahfouz 2016, ch. 62.

82. For differing perspectives on the 1973 war and the Egyptian-Israeli peace process, see Aly, Feldman, and Shikaki 2013. On Egyptian and Israeli perceptions of the war, see Johnson and Tierney 2006, 164–204.

83. Sømod 2018.

84. Balout and Roubet 1985.

85. Several images claiming to be of his passport circulate on the internet, but all of them are fake. The Egyptian government never published an image of the actual passport.

86. Indeed, as a political slur, the epithet "pharaoh" dates back to at least the nineteenth century; see Colla 2007, 169–71.

87. This ambivalence is present even among officials of the Ministry of Antiquities. A senior antiquities official in Upper Egypt once confessed to me his personally conflicted view of Ramesses II as Egypt's greatest pharaoh and as the impious tyrant who oppressed Moses, a revered prophet in Islam.

88. Mailer 1983. In the first novel of Christian Jacq's Ramses series (1997) a fourteen-year-old Prince Ramesses grows up in Sety I's court with a fictional elder brother bearing the improbable name of "Shaanar," along with the young Hebrew Prophet Moses (of course). Ramesses even rubs elbows with the Greek

poet Homer and Helen of Troy. The series goes downhill from here, as much mayhem, magic, weak plots, and bad writing ensue through four dreary sequels.

89. I was largely inspired to become an Egyptologist by the 1982 National Geographic television documentary *Egypt: Quest for Eternity* in which Ramesses II formed a key theme in the narrative, including the rescue of Abu Simbel and the Hittite Peace Treaty. Likewise, the show's coverage of Sety I's beautiful temple at Abydos and the University of Chicago's Epigraphic Survey inspired me to write my doctoral dissertation on Sety I's monuments and to become an epigraphist. My mentor William J. Murnane has a cameo role in the show. I studied with him at the University of Memphis in the early 1990s then Memphis State University—and fulfilled my dreams by joining him to record inscriptions of Sety I and Ramesses II at Karnak with Great Hypostyle Hall Project (www.memphis.edu/hypostyle). I became project director after Murnane's untimely death in 2000. The influence of the National Geographic TV special on my career came full circle beginning in the mid-2000s when I appeared in several cable television documentaries on Ramesses II and Egyptian monuments.

90. Other trade names for condoms associated with historical symbols of male sexual potency since the early twentieth century included the Sheik and Trojan brands. The Ramses and Sheik brands were discontinued in the late nineties.

91. Trafton 2004.

92. Typical of the pseudoscience early scholars once advocated is the "dynastic race theory," championed by none other than Sir William Matthew Flinders Petrie, the father of modern archaeology. In the late nineteenth century, Petrie claimed that pharaonic civilization only began in late prehistory when a Caucasian population group from Mesopotamia supposedly invaded the Nile Valley and established themselves as the ruling class over the indigenous black African population, which, Petrie alleged, was culturally and intellectually inferior. Early Egyptologists like Petrie and Breasted propagated this bogus view in scientific publications and popular history books throughout the late ninetieth and early twentieth centuries, until anthropologists discredited such racist pseudoscience between the fifties and seventies.

93. Fritze 2016, 300–335.

94. Diop challenged and discredited the old racist theories of early European anthropologists and Egyptologists. More controversially, he argued that all African civilizations and peoples, beginning with pharaonic Egypt, shared a common cultural and genetic heritage across the millennia and throughout the African continent. He fiercely challenged Eurocentric bias and argued that the Egyptians, like all Africans, were Black people.

95. The ancient Egyptians called their country Kemet, "the Black Land," and referred to themselves as "the People of the Black Land," (*rmṯt n Kmt*) or simply as "the People," (*rmṯt*). The term "Egypt," in all its modern variations in European languages like English, French (Égypte), German (Ägypten), Spanish (Egipto), etc., derive from the ancient Greek term Aigyptos (Αἴγυπτος). This name for the ancient Nile kingdom itself derives from one of the monikers of the Egyptian city of Memphis, in particular, the name of the Temple of Ptah. This shrine was called "The Mansion of the Ka-spirit of Ptah," transliterated by Egyptologists as *Ḥwt-k3-Ptḥ*. Ancient Egyptians vocalized it as something like Hei-ku-ptah, which the Greeks rendered as *Aigyptos*.

The modern name for "Memphis" derives from the Greek version of another Egyptian byname for the city, taken from the official name of the Sixth Dynasty Pharaoh Pepy I's pyramid complex called "Pepy-Is-Established-and-Perfect," transliterated *Ppy-mn-nfr*. Abbreviated and pronounced something like *Minnofe* by Egyptians, it became *Memphis* (Μέμφις) to the ancient Greeks, and *Memfi* (ⲙⲉⲙϥⲓ) in Coptic.

96. To be sure, the Egyptians looked down on foreign peoples, not for their skin color or physical appearance, but rather their lack of Egyptian culture. Yet foreign peoples, regardless of their origins or appearance, could settle within Egypt's borders and become Egyptian by adopting its language, dress, and culture. There was no sense of superior or inferior "races" based on skin tone or physical appearance among the Egyptians, but rather ethnic chauvinism based on the notion that their culture was superior.

97. Debates and anxieties about race are a subtext in Hollywood's portrayals of pharaonic Egypt; see Schroeder 2003.

98. Egyptian art often depicts women with lighter skin tones that are often yellow as well as light beige. By contrast, Egyptian men are depicted with darker pigmentation, usually reddish-brown or brown skin. Egyptologist still debate this iconographic distinction between genders and its ideological significance. But many Egyptian paintings show women with reddish skin tones as well, including numerous painted reliefs depicting Queen Nefertiti herself. Egyptian art is highly symbolic and stereotyped for ideological reasons. Pharaonic art also stereotypes foreign peoples. North and west of the Nile Valley, groups like the Canaanites, Hittites, Libyans, and Syrians have yellow or light-beige skin, implying that they are effeminate. Nubian peoples have dark-brown or black skin tones. The Egyptians also distinguished foreigners by their alien clothing, hairstyles, and personal adornment.

We see a perfect example of how artistic conventions and ethnic identities could clash in the case of a late Eighteenth Dynasty Nubian official named Heqanefer who lived during the reign of Tutankhamun. Heqanefer appears with black skin and Nubian attire and hairstyle in the Theban tomb of his superior, the Viceroy of Nubia Huy. In his own tomb in colonial Nubia, however, Heqanefer presents himself with the clothing and reddish skin tone of an Egyptian. As it is today, ethnic identity was mutable and subject to contrasting views by the individual and by other people; see Smith 2003, 2018; Matić 2020.

99. For an excellent study of Egypt as a cultural phenomenon and touchstone for various modern identities as expressed in cultural memories of the Amarna period, see Montserrat 2000.

100. There was great excitement in some circles when the American Egyptologist Kent Weeks uncovered the skeleton of a male adult in KV 5, the tomb of Ramesses II. Some were convinced that this must be the mummy of Prince Amunhirkhopeshef, but see pp. 271–72 above.

Glossary

Abu Simbel: Situated in Lower Nubia and called Meha in antiquity, Ramesses II built two temples carved into the mountainside here. He dedicated the larger shrine to Amun, Re, and his own divinity, and the smaller one to his consort Nefertari and the goddess Hathor.

Abydos: A town in Middle Egypt sacred to Osiris where the earliest Egyptian kings built their tombs during the First and Second Dynasty. Sety I and Ramesses II constructed royal cult temples here.

Adad-Nirari I: An Assyrian king and contemporary of Ramesses II and the Hittite kings Urhi-Teshub and Hattusili III. He conquered Hanigalbat during Urhi-Teshub's reign.

Akhenaten: He came to the throne as Amenhotep IV, before changing his name to Akhenaten. Ruling for seventeen years, Akhenaten rejected Egypt's traditional pantheon in favor of a solar god called the Aten, and conducted a wide-scale program of iconoclasm, defacing the names and images of the old gods.

Akhet. See Inundation Season.

Akkadian: The language of ancient Babylonia used as a common diplomatic language in the ancient Near East. It was inscribed in the cuneiform script on clay tablets.

Amarna Letters: An archive of 382 diplomatic letters the pharaohs Amenhotep III, Akhenaten, and Tutankhamun exchanged with the other Great Kingdoms and with Egypt's vassal kings in the Levant. The letters were written in Akkadian on clay tablets that were discovered in the ruins of the city of Akhetaten (El-Amarna).

Amarna period: A modern term for the reigns of Akhenaten and his immediate successors, Smenkhkare and Neferneferuaten.

Amenemopet: A viceroy of Kush during the reign of Sety I.

Amenhotep III: Among the greatest pharaohs, he reigned for thirty-seven years in the later Eighteenth Dynasty at the height of New Kingdom Egypt's power, wealth, and prestige.

Amenhotep IV: See Akhenaten.

Amurru: A small kingdom in Syria, Amurru was an Egyptian vassal until the Amarna period when its king, Aziru, renounced his allegiance to Akhenaten and became a dependent of the Hittite king Suppiluliuma I.

Amun-(Re): Amun, "The Hidden One," was a primordial deity from ancient Thebes. During the Middle and New Kingdoms, Theban kings elevated this local god to the head of the Egyptian pantheon, merging his identity with the solar god Re of Heliopolis. As the composite god Amun-Re, he was entitled "king of the gods." Amun-Re's main cult centers were at Thebes (modern Luxor) in the temple complexes of Karnak and Luxor.

Amunhirkhopeshef: The first born of all Ramesses II's sons, and the eldest child of his senior consort Nefertari.

Anath: Worship of this Canaanite war goddess increased in Egypt during the New Kingdom. She was a divine guardian of Ramesses II, who built a temple to her in his capital of Piramesses.

ancient Near East: A general term for the early civilizations located in the Middle East, including Assyria, Babylonia, Egypt, Hatti, and the petty kingdoms and peoples of ancient Canaan, Lebanon, and Syria.

Ankhesenamun: Tutankhamun's principal wife, she negotiated with the Hittite King Suppiluliuma I after her husband's death, in a failed bid to marry a Hittite prince named Zannanza.

Assyria: An ancient civilization in the northern part of modern Iraq, Assyria became one of the Great Kingdoms of the ancient Near East at the end of the Eighteenth Dynasty.

Astarte: Along with other Canaanite deities like Baal and Anath, worship of the Semitic goddess Astarte spread in Egypt during the New Kingdom.

Aswan: Modern Arabic name for a city in southern Egypt at the First Cataract of the Nile. In antiquity, the region was sacred to the god Khnum. Quarries in Aswan were the source for granite used in pharaonic monuments. The ancient town of Elephantine was located on an island just north of the First Cataract at Aswan.

Aten: Originally a term for the sun disk, Akhenaten worshiped the Aten exclusively as the unique form of the sun god Re after he rejected Egypt's traditional gods.

Atum: The creator god of Heliopolis, Atum embodied the setting sun. His name means "The Perfect One." An alter ego of the solar gods Re-Horakhty and Khepri, his main sanctuary was at Heliopolis.

Avaris: A town in the northeastern Delta of the Nile where the Hyksos kings established their capital. Seth was the city's divine patron. Ramesses II's ancestors hailed from Avaris and he built his new capital of Piramesses nearby.

Ay: This influential courtier served as chamberlain under Akhenaten, before assuming the throne after Tutankhamun died without an heir. Ay reigned for four years, but also died without a natural successor. His throne passed to Horemheb.

ba-(soul): An element of human and divine beings, *Ba* is often translated as "soul." The *Ba* is best known from its role in the afterlife and it is different from the *Ka*-spirit or "life force." The *Ba* took the form of a human headed bird that could fly in and out of the tomb but had to return to the mummified body of the deceased.

Baal: A Canaanite deity whom the Egyptians associated with their god Seth.

Babylonia: Located in southern Mesopotamia (Iraq), Babylonia was one of the Great Kingdoms of the ancient Near East.

bas-relief: See relief.

Beth Shean: An ancient town located at the junction of the Jezreel Valley and the Jordan River, Beth Shean was an administrative center of the Egyptian Empire in Canaan during the New Kingdom.

Beit el-Wali: A site in northern Nubia. Ramesses II built a small temple there during the first year of his reign.

Bintanath: Ramesses II's most favored daughter, she became one of her father's Great Royal Wives after her mother Isetnofret died. Bintanath's name means "Daughter of Anath."

cartouche: In Egyptian art and hieroglyphic writing, the cartouche was a loop of rope enclosing the pharaoh's prenomen and nomen, the most important of his five official names.

Coptos: A town in Upper Egypt sacred to the fertility god Min.

coregency: A term Egyptologists use for the notion that certain pairs of kings ruled jointly.

cuneiform: A complex writing system used in the ancient Near East, cuneiform consists of hundreds of wedge-shaped signs scribes made by impressing a reed stylus into soft clay tablets.

Dapur: A fortified town in western Syria near Tunip and the Orontes River, it was a Hittite vassal state when Ramesses II captured it in his eighth regnal year.

Djahy: A broad geographical designation the Egyptians gave to parts of the Levant, particularly Lebanon and northern Canaan.

Dual King: This title, *nesu-bity* in Egyptian, introduced the pharaoh's first cartouche name, called his prenomen. Egyptologists have traditionally translated *nesu-bity* as "King of Upper and Lower Egypt," but it refers to two aspects of kingship.

electrum: A naturally occuring alloy of gold and silver, which the Egyptians called *Djamu* in contrast to yellow gold, or *Nebu.*

Elephantine: An island in the Nile River at the First Cataract in modern day Aswan. Elephantine was the principal sanctuary of the god Khnum.

ennead: A Greek term for the group of nine gods, *Pesdjet* in Egyptian, that represented the plurality of pluralities, the sum total of all the gods.

faience: A type of glazed Egyptian ceramic widely used in ancient Egypt that is most commonly in a range of blue and blue-green shades. Small decorative objects of every sort were made of faience, including jewelry, ritual and funerary amulets and objects, and luxury goods.

Geb: The Egyptian god of the earth and father of Osiris and Isis. Egyptian kings were said to rule on "the Throne of Geb."

Gebel es-Silsilah: Arabic name for a barren site in Upper Egypt south of Edfu. During the New Kingdom, vast quarries on both sides of the Nile produced most of the sandstone for building the temples of ancient Thebes. Sety I and Ramesses II both left stelae at Gebel es-Silsilah, including a pair of shrines they dedicated to the god Hapi who embodied the annual Nile inundation.

Gerf Hussein: Arabic name for a remote site in Lower Nubia where Ramesses II dedicated a small rock cut temple, or speos, to the god Ptah and his own divine aspect. Far less elegant than the king's shrine at Abu Simbel, only parts of Gerf Hussein were salvaged during the Nubian Rescue Campaign in the 1960. Most of the temple now lies below Lake Nasser.

granodiorite: An igneous rock similar to granite and found in Aswan, New Kingdom pharaohs like Sety I and Ramesses II often used this grayish-black stone to make statuary, including royal colossi like those from Luxor Temple and the giant Ozymandias and smaller Younger Memnon colossi from the Ramesseum.

Great King: In the diplomatic system of the ancient Near East during the Late Bronze Age (sixteenth to twelfth centuries BCE), a Great King was an overlord subjugating "Little Kings" as his imperial vassals.

Great Royal Wife: Egyptian *khemet-nesu weret*, this title was reserved for the most favored royal consorts, who ranked above women holding the title "royal wife," *khemet-nesut*. A pharaoh might have multiple Great Royal Wives at one time.

Gurnah: Arabic name for the site on the west bank of ancient Thebes (modern Luxor) where Sety I built his royal cult temple.

Hanigalbat: Situated in the northern Tigris-Euphrates River Valley, Hanigalbat was core kingdom of the former Mitanni Empire after the Hittite King Suppiluliuma I destroyed Mitanni Empire's power during the Amarna period.

harvest season (*Shomu*): A four-month period that fell before the inundation season (*Akhet*) began. At the beginning of Ramesses II's reign, *Shomu* began in late February and continued until the end of June.

Hathor: Daughter of the sun god, this powerful and multifaceted goddess embodied love, sex, and fertility. In her wrath, she slayed the sun god's enemies. She also nurtured and protected the king. Ramesses II dedicated the smaller temple at Abu Simbel to Queen Nefertari as the living incarnation of Hathor.

Hatshepsut: One of the few women to rule in ancient Egypt, she became a female pharaoh in the early Eighteenth Dynasty after her husband Thutmose II died, sharing the throne with his young successor Thutmose III in a coregency.

Hatti: A powerful kingdom during the Late Bronze Age located in central and eastern Turkey.

Hattusa: The traditional capital of the Hittite Empire, Hattusa is located in east central Turkey at the modern site of Boğazköy.

Hattusili III: This Hittite king was the brother of Muwatalli II. Hattusili came to power in a coup d'etat against Muwatalli's son and successor Urhi-Teshub.

Heb-Sed: See *Sed*-festival.

Heliopolis: Called Iunu in Egyptian and On in the Bible, Heliopolis, or "City of the Sun," is the name the Greeks gave to the main cult center of the Egyptian solar god Re-Horakhty.

His Person: The Egyptian term *khem-ef*, meaning "His Person," literally "His Incarnation," designates the king's physical body and his mortal self. Egyptologists have often translated it as "His Majesty," but this does not reflect its true meaning. Pharaohs referred to themselves as *khem-i*, "My Person."

Hittite empire: See under Hatti.

Horemheb: Supreme general of the army and vizier under Tutankhamun and Ay, Horemheb succeeded Ay as the last ruler of the Eighteenth Dynasty. He is best known for his legal reforms and for suppressing the memory of the Amarna kings.

Horus: The son of Osiris and Isis, Horus was the god of Egyptian kingship. Every ruler was an incarnation of Horus.

Horus Name: The first and the oldest of the five royal names of Egyptian kings, the Horus Name originated with the prehistoric kings of Hierakonopolis in Upper Egypt before 3300 BCE.

hypostyle hall: A Greek term for a building having a roof supported by columns. In New Kingdom Egyptian temples, the hypostyle hall stood between outer courtyards and inner sanctuaries.

inundation season (*akhet*): The Egyptian civil year began with the four months of the Inundation Season (*Akhet*), traditionally when the annual Nile flood began. At the beginning of Ramesses II's reign, *Akhet* began in early July and finished in early November.

Isetnofret: One of Ramesses II's first wives, Isetnofret gave birth to at least six children, including the pharaoh's second eldest son Ramesses "Junior" and his favored daughter Bintanath.

isfet: An Egyptian word with a range of meanings including chaos, injustice, falsehood, wrongdoing, and general pandemonium. *Isfet* was the antithesis of *Maat*, or universal order and right.

Isis: An Egyptian goddess with great magical power, she was the sister and wife of Osiris.

iter: An Egyptian unit of distance measuring approximately 6.5 mi. (10.5 km).

ka-(spirit): The animating life force contained in every person and living thing, including the king and the gods.

Kadesh: A strategic Bronze Age city state located in southern Syria in the vicinity of modern Homs. Kadesh sat on the Orontes River at the site of Tell Nebi Mend.

Karnak: The modern Arabic name for the vast temple complex of the god Amun-Re on the east bank of Thebes (modern Luxor). The ancient name for Karnak was *Ipet-Suut*, "The Most Select of Places."

Khaemwaset: The fourth eldest son of Ramesses II, his mother was Queen Isetnofret. As High Priest of Ptah in Memphis, Khaemwaset heralded the king's early *Sed*-Festivals beginning in regnal year thirty.

Kharu: A generalized Egyptian term for the Levant, from Canaan northward into southern Syria.

kheneret-Household: This social and religious institution (*per kheneret*) was part of the larger royal estate (*per nesu*) and is often identified as the "harem" of the Egyptian king.

Khepri: Taking the form of a giant scarab beetle or a man with a beetle's body for its head, Khepri was the morning form of the sun god Re. Khepri's name means "He Who Comes into Being." He was worshiped alongside Atum and Re-Horakhty in their principal sanctuary at Heliopolis.

Khnum: The ram-headed god of Elephantine (modern Aswan), Khnum brought about the annual Nile inundation and created human beings by modeling their bodies from clay.

Khonsu: A moon god, Khonsu was the son of Amun-Re and his consort Mut.

Kurustama Treaty: An early treaty of friendship between Egypt and Hatti dating to the mid-Eighteenth Dynasty. It broke down during the Egyptian-Hittite conflict in the Amarna period.

Kush: The ancient name for the southern part of Nubia between the second and fourth cataracts of the Nile in modern Sudan. During the New Kingdom, a Viceroy of Kush administered colonial Nubia.

KV 5: Ramesses II built this tomb in the King's Valley for his numerous children. It is largest tomb ever built in Egypt.

KV 7: Ramesses II's tomb in the King's Valley.

KV 17: The tomb of Sety I in the King's Valley.

Late Bronze Age: A modern term for the era between 1550 and 1100 BCE in Egypt, the ancient Near East, and eastern Mediterranean. Contemporary with the Egyptian New Kingdom (Eighteenth to Twentieth Dynasties), the Late Bronze Age was a time of empires and intensive diplomacy, trade, and warfare.

Levant: A designation for the eastern coast of the Mediterranean Sea encompassing the modern nations of Israel, Lebanon, and Syria. The Egyptians had several broad terms referring to this region, including Djahy, the Fenkhu-lands, Kharu, and Retchenu.

L.P.H.: An abbreviation for the phrase "living! prosperous! healthy!" Egyptian scribes inserted this expression when referring to the Egyptian king, especially after his titles of "Pharaoh" and "His Person." The epithet was so common in Egyptian texts that ancient scribes, like Egyptologists today, abbreviated it.

Luxor Temple: A large temple complex on the east bank of Thebes dedicated to Amun-Re. Called the Southern Sanctuary in antiquity, it housed the fertility aspect of Amun and was the main venue for the annual Opet Festival.

***Maat* and the Goddess Maat:** This fundamental Egyptian concept denotes the cosmic order the creator god established at the beginning of time. It encompasses notions of truth, order, justice, right action, and harmony. The goddess Maat personified this idea. She appears as a woman with a single ostrich feather on her head.

Maahorneferure: The Egyptian name of Ramesses II's first Hittite wife, whom he married in his thirty-fourth regnal year. She was the daughter of Hattusili III.

Manetho: An Egyptian priest of the third century BCE and author of the *Ägyptiaca*, a lost history of pharaonic Egypt. Manetho wrote the work in Greek for Ptolemy I.

Mansion of Millions of Years: A class of Egyptian temple dedicated to both the gods and to the cult of the divine king.

Medinet Habu: The Arabic name for the site of Ramesses III's royal cult temple on the west bank of ancient Thebes, modern Luxor. Within the complex stood a smaller temple of Amun-Re built in the early Eighteenth Dynasty.

Memphis: The traditional capital of ancient Egypt since the First Dynasty, Memphis was also the primary cult center for the god Ptah.

***menat*-necklace:** Sacred to the goddess Hathor, a *menat*-necklace consisted of multiple strands of small globular beads joined to a counterpoise, which could take the form of the bust of Hathor or other goddesses.

Menmaatre: The prenomen of Sety I, it means "Enduring is the Order (*Maat*) of Re."

Merenptah: The thirteenth son of Ramesses II, and the youngest of Isetnofret, Merenptah became the fourth and final Heir Apparent in his father's fifty-fifth year. His own reign lasted for a decade.

Mi-Wer: Located in the Fayum lake region of Middle Egypt at the modern site of Abu Ghurob, the settlement of Mi-Wer included a residence palace housing the women and children of New Kingdom pharaohs.

Min: An ithyphallic male fertility god worshiped at Coptos in Upper Egypt. Min was closely related to the fertility aspect of the Theban god Amun-Kamutef.

Monthu: The falcon-headed god of war, Monthu's principal cult center was in Thebes. In battle, the pharaoh was often compared to this god of immense physical strength.

Mursili III: See Urhi-Teshub.

Mut: The consort of Amun-Re and mother of the moon god Khonsu, her name means "The Mother."

Muwatalli II: This Hittite king was a contemporary of Sety I, and later fought against Ramesses II at the Battle of Kadesh.

na'arin: A unit of elite troops that Ramesses II detached from his main army during his campaign against Kadesh. Their timely arrival turned the tide of battle against the Hittites.

Nebty **name:** The fourth of an Egyptian king's five official names, the title *nebty* means "the Two Ladies," referring to the tutelary goddesses: Nekhbet of Upper Egypt and Wadjet of Lower Egypt.

Nefertari: She married Ramesses II before he became king and gave him his first-born son Amunhirkhopeshef. Ramesses favored her as his senior queen until her death in the twenties of his reign. Her tomb in the Valley of the Queens (QV 66) is often considered the most beautiful Egyptian tomb.

Nekhbet: She was the tutelary vulture goddess of Upper Egypt who protected the king.

New Kingdom: A modern designation for the period between ca. 1550 and 1100 BCE comprising the Eighteenth, Nineteenth, and Twentieth Dynasties and corresponding to the Late Bronze Age in the ancient Near East. This was Egypt's imperial age.

Nine Bows: An Egyptian expression for the sum total of all the peoples of the world, including foreigners and Egyptians. The number nine symbolized a plurality of pluralities.

Niphururiya: The name of an Egyptian king as recorded in Hittite texts, his widow attempted to marry a Hittite prince named Zannanza, the son of Suppiluliuma I. Scholars debate whether Niphururiya should be identified as Akhenaten, Tutankhamun, or Smenkhkare.

nomen: The Egyptian king's second cartouche name. Preceded by the title "Son of Re," it usually corresponded to the name he received at birth.

Opet Festival: An annual festival in Thebes honoring Amun-Re. During Opet, the god's cult image journey from Karnak to Luxor Temple, the "Southern Sanctuary." During his stay, Amun's *Ka*-spirit merged with the king's *Ka*, thereby rejuvenating both of them.

Orontes: A river flowing northward from the Beqaa Valley in Lebanon into western Syria.

Osiris: The divine ruler of the Egyptian Underworld, he was the husband and brother of Isis. Their son was Horus.

ostracon: Plural ostraca. A flake of limestone or sherd of broken pottery. The Egyptians used ostraca as convenient writing material for brief inscriptions.

Ozymandias: A Greek approximation of Ramesses II's prenomen Usermaatre. The ancient Greek author Diodorus Siculus described the huge statue of the pharaoh Ozymandias he saw in the Ramesseum.

palimpsest: Egyptian pharaohs often erased inscriptions on older monuments and replaced them with their own. Traces of suppressed relief carvings and inscriptions visible beneath later ones are called palimpsests.

Paser: The Upper Egyptian vizier under Sety I and during the first two decades of Ramesses II's reign.

peristyle: An architectural term for rows of columns surrounding the perimeter of a building or courtyard, forming a porch.

Pharaoh: Meaning the "great house," (*per-a'a*) or "palace," this term became synonymous with the king himself during the New Kingdom.

Piramesses: Sety I built a royal residence near his family seat at Avaris in the northeastern Nile Delta that Ramesses II expanded into his capital city of Piramesses, meaning "The Estate of Ramesses."

post-Amarna period: Modern designation for the last part of the Eighteenth Dynasty, during the reigns of Tutankhamun, Ay, and Horemheb. These kings restored the cults of the traditional gods, especially that of Amun-Re.

Pramessu: An army general who rose to the highest military and administrative offices during the reign of Horemheb. Lacking a natural heir, Horemheb appointed Pramessu as his successor, who reigned briefly as Ramesses I.

prenomen: The Egyptian king's first cartouche name. Preceded by the title "Dual King." Each king chose his prenomen upon his accession. It was the most important of the five sequences of royal names and titles. Pharaohs compounded the prenomen with the name of Re.

Proyet. See Season of Emergence.

Ptah: The creator god of ancient Memphis, Ptah was also a patron of craftsmen. Along with Amun-Re and Re-Horakhty, he stood at the apex of the pantheon.

pylon: A type of monumental gateway standing in front of the entrances and outer courts of Egyptian temples in the New Kingdom. A pylon consists of two wide trapezoidal towers with a gateway between them. They were embellished with flag masts flying colorful pennants.

Puduhepa: The influental consort of the Hittite king Hattusili III, Puduhepa exchanged diplomatic letters with Ramesses II and negotiated her daughter's marriage with the pharaoh.

Qantir: See Piramesses.

quartzite: See siliceous sandstone.

Quban: A remote location in Nubia where Ramesses II set up a stela in his third regnal year commemorating a gold mining venture.

raised relief: See relief.

Ramesses I: When the General and Vizier Pramessu succeeded Horemheb, he became Ramesses I, the founder of the Nineteenth Dynasty. He was the father of Sety I and grandfather of Ramesses II.

Ramesses III: Second king of the Twentieth Dynasty, Ramesses III fought incursions of Libyan and Sea Peoples on Egypt's northern frontiers. His monuments and titulary emulate his revered ancestor Ramesses II.

Ramesses IV: The third king of the Twentieth Dynasty and his father's rightful heir, Ramesses IV came to the throne after Ramesses III was assassinated.

Ramesses "Junior": The second born son of Ramesses II, his mother was Isetnofret. When his older brother Amunhirkhopeshef died, Prince Ramesses "Junior" became Crown Prince, but died around the fifty-second year of his father's reign. "Junior" is a modern nickname to distinguish him from his royal father and from Ramesses III.

Ramesseum: A modern name for Ramesses II's royal cult temple on the west bank of Thebes. On its walls, the king carved two versions of his Battle of Kadesh narrative and a representation of the Battle of Dapur.

Ramesside period: The name historians give to the era of the Nineteenth and Twentieth Dynasties (ca. 1292–1077 BCE), which saw eleven kings named Ramesses.

Re: The name of the chief sun god and the ancient Egyptian word for "sun" and "day." Re was the solar god of Heliopolis who took many forms and assimilated with other deities. His alter egos included the beetle-headed Khepri who embodied the rising sun and Atum who was the setting sun. He also merged with other gods like Amun and Horus to form composite deities.

Re-Horakhty: New Kingdom Egypt's supreme solar deity and a composite of Re and Horus, his name means "Re-Horus the Horizon Dweller." He appears as a falcon-headed man with a large solar disk on his head. During the second half of his reign, Ramesses II became "the great *Ka*-spirit of Re-Horakhty."

regnal year: The Egyptian dating system was based on counting the years each king reigned from his accession to the throne until his death. A new regnal year began on the anniversary of his accession. The day after his predecessor died, a new king began the first regnal year of his own reign.

relief: In the first type of relief carving, called raised relief or bas-relief, the artist cut the figures, so that they project against a lower background of negative space surrounding them. Traditionally, this was used for interior surfaces inside temples and tombs. A second style of carving was sunk relief, in which the sculptor cut around the edges of the figures without removing the negative space around them as with raised relief. This leaves a trough with a beveled edge.

sacred bark: A model of a river boat that priests carried on a palanquin, the sacred bark served as a portable shrine housing the cult statue of a god or a king when it was transported from one temple to another during religious processions. Imbued with the divine presence, sacred barks could serve as oracles.

Sakhmet: The lion-headed goddess of Memphis and consort of Ptah. Her name means "She Who Is Powerful." Sakhmet embodied the destructive heat of the sun.

Saqqara: Modern Arabic name for the principal burial ground of ancient Memphis. High officials of the Eighteenth and Nineteenth Dynasty built their tombs here, including Horemheb before he became king. Here, too, was the Serapeum burial vaults of the Apis bulls.

Season of Emergence (*Proyet*): Denoting the end of the annual Nile inundation, the four months of the Season of Emergence began in early November and ended in early March at the beginning of Ramesses II's reign.

***Sed*-festival:** Called the *Heb-Sed*, or "Festival of the Tail," this was the so-called royal Jubilee in pharaonic Egypt. Traditionally, a king only celebrated the *Sed* after ruling for thirty years.

***Sep Tepy*:** The Egyptian term for the beginning of time when the creator god willed the universe into existence, *sep tepy* means "the First Event."

Serapeum: Ramesses II and his son Prince Khaemwaset, the High Priest of Memphis, expanded these extensive catacombs that Amenhotep III had begun in the necropolis of Saqqara to serve as the burial vaults of the sacred Apis bulls, who were living incarnations of Ptah.

Seth: The powerful Egyptian god of storms, foreign lands, and chaotic forces. He was the dynastic god of the Nineteenth Dynasty, which hailed from Avaris, Seth's major cult center in the eastern Delta.

Setne-Khaemwas: Based on the life of Prince Khaemwaset, Ramesses II's fourth son, the tales of Prince Setne-Khaemwas are part of a cycle of folk tales current a thousand years after his death and tell of his supernatural adventures.

Sety (father of Pramessu): Sety was a middle-ranking military officer in the late Eighteenth Dynasty and the father of General Pramessu who came to the throne as Ramesses I after Horemheb died. Sety's grandson became Sety I and his great grandson was Ramesses II.

Shasu Bedouin: A common term or nomadic peoples indigenous to Sinai and the Levant during the Late Bronze Age.

Sherden: One of several groups making up roving populations of raiders and sea farers known as the Sea Peoples at the end of the Late Bronze Age.

Shomu. See Harvest Season.

sistrum: Plural sistra. A sacred rattle used in rituals to soothe the gods with soft tinkling sounds. Elite women, including royal wives and daughters, often played this musical instrument during temple ceremony.

siliceous sandstone: Wrongly called Egyptian "quartzite," siliceous sandstone is a sedimentary rock containing quartz crystals that give the stone a glittery quality. Often of a reddish or warm brown hue, the Egyptians associated it with the sun god, calling it "wonder stone" and using it extensively in constructions at Heliopolis and for royal statuary. The main quarries for siliceous sandstone were located near Heliopolis in the eastern part of modern-day Cairo.

Sokar: A falcon-headed god from Memphis connected with the netherworld and funerary cults.

Son of Re: One of the pharaoh's five official sets of titles, Son of Re signaled the king's relationship to the sun god. It precedes his second cartouche name, the nomen.

speos and hemi-speos: A type of grotto temple hewn from the bedrock of a mountainside or cliff face. The grandest of these were Ramesses II's twin temples at Abu Simbel. Temples like Wadi es-Sebua and Gerf Hussein were hemi-speos, having their pylon gateways and outer courts built of stone blocks and mud brick, while their inner halls and sanctuaries consist of rock-cut grottos inside a cliff.

stela: Plural stelae. Formal hieroglyphic inscriptions were often carved on a free-standing upright slab of stone, on the wall of a temple, or etched onto a mountainside or rocky outcropping.

Storm God: The chief deity of the Hittite pantheon, the Storm God was a patron of Hittite kingship and guarantor of Hittite treaties, including the accords Hattusili III concluded with Ramesses II. The Egyptians identified him with their own deity Seth, who was also a god of powerful forces and foreign lands.

sunk relief: See relief.

Suppiluliuma I: This great Hittite king was a contemporary of the Amarna and post-Amarna pharaohs. His conquest of Syria destroyed the power of Mitanni, and deprived Egypt of its border provinces of Amurru, Kadesh, and Ugarit, resulting in six decades of bitter intermittent warfare. Suppiluliuma was the grandfather of Muwatali II and Hattusili III.

Tatchenen: The fertility aspect of Ptah, Tatchenen personified the annual Nile inundation. During his Jubilee years, Ramesses II added the epithet "Lord of *Sed*-festivals like his Father Ptah-Tatchenen" to his Horus Name.

Tanis: A city in the northeast Nile Delta that the kings of the Twenty-First and Twenty-Second Dynasties established as their capital.

Tcharu: A massive border fortress on the northeastern fringes of the Nile Delta at the western end of the Sinai. Tcharu was the gateway to the Ways of Horus and the traditional departure point for Egyptian military campaigns marching to the Levant.

Theban Triad: The principal gods of Thebes were Amun-Re, his consort Mut, and their son the moon god Khonsu. Such family triads of local gods were common in Egyptian religious thought.

Thebes: Called Waset in Egyptian, Thebes is the name the Greeks gave to the city of Amun-Re in Upper Egypt. Its importance as the cults center of Amun-Re rose with the kings of the Twelfth, Seventeenth, and Eighteenth Dynasties, all of whom originated here. The city remained an important religious center for the Ramesside kings, who built royal cult temples and their royal cemeteries in the Valley of the Kings and Valley of the Queens.

titulary: The term Egyptologists used for the official set of five royal titles, names, and epithets every Egyptian king adopted upon taking the throne. Most important were the nomen and prenomen, both enclosed within cartouches. Others were the Horus name, *Nebty* name, and the Golden Horus name. Each name was preceded by distinct title. For the nomen this included Son of Re and Lord of Appearances. Dual King and Lord of the Two Lands introduced the prenomen.

Tuya: Sety I's Great Royal Wife and mother of Ramesses II. Rarely seen on her husband's monuments, Tuy was prominent on those of her son, a reflection of her unique honor of being "mother of the god."

uraeus: Plural uraei. The cobra goddess emblem perched on the forehead of the king to protect him and as a mark of his royal status.

Urhi-Teshub: Ruling under the throne name Mursili III, Urhi-Teshub was the son and successor of Muwatali II.

Usermaatre-Setepenre: The prenomen or coronation name Ramesses II chose upon his accession. Usermaatre means "Powerful is the Order/Truth (*Maat*) of Re." During his second regnal year, the pharaoh added the epithet Setepenre, meaning "He-Whom-Re-Chose."

usurpation: A pejorative modern term for the practice by some pharaohs of reinscribing the monuments of earlier kings with their own names.

Valley of the Kings: Called the "Great Place" in antiquity, the King's Valley (KV) in Western Thebes served as the burial ground for the pharaohs of the New Kingdom. Members of the royal family could also be interred here, usually in small undecorated tombs.

Valley of the Queens: Called *Ta Set Neferu,* "The Place of Beauty," Ramesside pharaohs built the tombs of their high-ranking wives and children in the Queen's Valley (QV) in Western Thebes.

Viceroy of Kush: The "King's Son of Kush" was a high official who oversaw the administration of colonial Nubia during the New Kingdom. His authority and duties were comparable to the two viziers.

vizier: The viziers were the highest civilian officials in the pharaoh's government. During the New Kingdom, there were always two viziers, who administered Upper and Lower Egypt.

Wadjet: the tutelary cobra goddess of Lower Egypt who protected the king.

Ways of Horus: The ancient name of a military highway along the northern coast of Sinai leading from the border fortress of Tcharu at the northeast corner of the Nile Delta to the town of Pa-Canaan in southwest Canaan (modern Gaza).

Wadi es-Sebua: Meaning "Valley of the Lions," it is the modern Arabic name for the site of a temple Ramesses II built in Nubia in the second half of his reign.

Weret-Hekau: The name of this ferocious goddess means "Great Enchantress." Also called the Eye of Re, she personified the scorching heat of the sun and the uraeus cobra that protected Re and the pharaoh. Weret-Hekau often appeared as a lion-headed woman and was related to other powerful goddesses like Sakhmet and Mut.

Zannanza: The name of a Hittite prince, son of King Suppiluliuma I. After his father negotiated a marriage alliance with Tutankhamun's widow Queen Ankhesenamun, the prince was assassinated on his journey to Egypt.

Bibliography

Abbas, Mohamed Raafat. 2013. "A Survey of the Diplomatic Role of the Charioteers in the Ramesside Period." Pages 17–27 in *Chasing Chariots: Proceedings of the First International Chariot Conference (Cairo 2012)*. Edited by Salima Ikram and André J. Veldmeijer. Sidestone: Leiden.

———. 2016. "The Bodyguard of Ramesses II and the Battle of Kadesh." *Égypte Nilotique et Méditerranéenne* 9:113–23.

Abd el-Maksoud, Mohamed. 1998a. *Tell Heboua (1981–1991): Enquête archéologique sur la deuxième période intermédiaire et le nouvel empire à l'extrémité orientale du delta*. Paris: Ministère des Affaires Etrangères, Editions Recherche sur les Civilisations.

———. 1998b. "Tjarou, porte de l'Orient." Pages 61–65 in *Le Sinaï durant l'antiquité et le Moyen-Age: 4000 ans d'histoire pour un desert; Actes du colloque "Sinaï" qui s'est tenu à l'UNESCO du 19 au 21 septembre 1997*. Edited by Dominique Valbelle and Charles Bonnet. Paris: Errance.

Abd el-Maksoud, Mohamed, and Dominique Valbelle. 2011. "Tell Héboua II: Rapport préliminaire sur le décor et l'épigraphie des éléments architectoniques découverts au cours des campagnes 2008–2009 dans la zone centrale du Khétem de Tjarou." *RdÉ* 62:1–39.

Abd el-Razik, Mahmud. 1974. "The Dedicatory and Building Texts of Ramesses II in Luxor Temple. I: The Texts." *JEA* 60:142–60.

———. 1975. "The Dedicatory and Building Texts of Ramesses II in Luxor Temple. II: Interpretation." *JEA* 61:125–36.

Abo-Eleaz, Mohy-Eldin E. 2019. "Face to Face: Meetings between the Kings of Egypt, Ḫatti and Their Vassals in the Levant during the Late Bronze Age." *SAK* 48:1–21.

Allais, Lucia. 2013. "Integrities: The Salvage of Abu Simbel." *Grey Room* 50:6–45.

———. 2018. "Operation Egypt." Pages 170–71 in *Images of Egypt*. Edited by Mari Lending, Eirik Arff Gulseth Bøhn, and Tim Antsey. Oslo: Pax.

Allam, Adel H., et al. 2009. "Computed Tomographic Assessment of Atherosclerosis in Ancient Egyptian Mummies." *Journal of the American Medical Association* 302.19 (November 18, 2009):2091–94.

Allam, Schafik. 2018. *The Treaty of Peace and Alliance between Ramses II and Khattushili III, King of the Hittites*. Translated by Ola el-Aguizy. Cairo: Dar el Hilal.

Allon, Niv. 2021. "War and Order in Eighteenth Dynasty Egypt (1550–1295 BCE)." *ZÄS* 148:18–30.

Altenmüller, Hartwig. 1989. "Untersuchungen zum Grab des Bai (KV 13) im Tal der Könige von Theben." *GM* 107:43–54.

Altman, Amnon. 2004. "The Role of the 'Historical Prologue' in the Hittite Vassal Treaties: An Early Experiment in Securing Treaty Compliance." *Journal of the History of International Law* 6:43–63.

Aly, Said, Abdel Monem, Shai Feldman, and Khalil Shikaki. 2013. *Arabs and Israelis: Conflict and Peacemaking in the Middle East*. Basingstoke: Palgrave Macmillan.

Arnold, Dieter. 1991. *Building in Egypt: Pharaonic Stone Masonry.* Oxford: Oxford University Press.

Assmann, Jan. 1984. "Krieg und Frieden im alten Ägypten: Ramses II und die Schlacht bei Kadesch." *Mannheimer Forum* 1983/1984:175–231.

———. 2002. *The Mind of Egypt.* New York: Holt; Maidenhead: Melia.

———. 2015. *Exodus: Die Revolution der Alten Welt.* Munich: Beck.

Aston, David A. 2016. "In Vino Veritas: A Docketed History of the New Kingdom between Year 1 of Thutmosis III and Year 1 of Ramesses II." Pages 1–41 in *Another Mouthful of Dust: Egyptological Studies in Honour of Geoffrey Thorndike Martin.* Edited by Jacobus van Dijk. OLA 246. Leuven: Peeters.

Audouit, Clémentine, and Elena Panaite. 2019. "'The One Who Illuminates Thebes': An Epigraphic Study." *Egyptian Archaeology* 54:14–17.

Aufrère, Sydney. 1991. *L'univers minéral dans la pensée Égyptienne.* 2 vols. BiÉtud 105. Cairo: Institut français d'archéologie orientale.

Avruch, Kevin. 2000. "Reciprocity, Equality, and Status-Anxiety in the Amarna Letters." Pages 154–64, 256–58 in *Amarna Diplomacy: The Beginnings of International Relations.* Edited by Raymond Westbrook and Raymond Cohen. Baltimore: Johns Hopkins University Press.

Ayad, Mariam F. 2009. *God's Wife, God's Servant: The God's Wife of Amun (ca. 740–525 BC).* London: Routledge.

Bács, Tamás A. 2019. "Early Ramesside Royalty at Rosetau." *Saqqara Newsletter* 17:32–45.

Balout, Lionel, and C. Roubet. 1985. *La momie de Ramsès: Contribution scientifique à l'egyptologie.* Paris: Editions Recherche sur les Civilisations.

Bányai, Michael. 2010. "Ist Urḫi-Tešup der König von Zulapa?" *Anatolica* 36:1–16.

Baqué, Lucas 2002. "'On That Day When the Long-Horned Bull Was Lassoed' (Pt [254] 286): A Scene in the 'Corridor of the Bull' of the Cenotaph of Sethos I in Abydos; An Iconologic Approach." *SAK* 30:43–51.

Bárta, Miroslav. 2013. "Kings, Viziers, and Courtiers: Executive Power in the Third Millennium BC." Pages 153–85 in *Ancient Egyptian Administration.* Edited by Juan Carlos Moreno García. HdO 104. Leiden: Brill.

Barta, Winfried. 1980. "Thronbesteigung und Krönungsfeier als unterschiedliche Zeugnisse königlicher Herrschaftsübernahme." *SAK* 8:33–53.

Beal, Richard H. 1992. *The Organization of the Hittite Military.* THeth 20. Heidelberg: Winter.

———. 1995. "Hittite Military Organization." Pages 545–54 in vol. 1 of *Civilizations of the Ancient Near East.* Edited by Jack M. Sasson. 4 vols. New York: Scribners.

von Beckerath, Jürgen. 1999. *Handbuch der ägyptischen Königsnamen.* MÄS 49. Mainz: von Zabern.

Beckman, Gary. 1997a. "Plague Prayers of Muršili II." *COS* 1:156–60.

———. 1997b. Review of *Die ägyptisch-hethitische Korrespondenz aus Boghazköi in babylonischer und hethitischer Sprache,* by Elmar Edel." *BO* 54:423–27.

———. 2000. "Hittite Chronology." *Akkadica* 119–120:19–32.

———. 2006. "Hittite Treaties and the Development of the Cuneiform Treaty Tradition." Pages 279–301 in *Die deuteronomistischen Geschichtswerke: Redaktions und religionsgeschichtliche Perspektiven zur "Deuteronomismus"-Diskussion in Tora und Vorderen Propheten.* Edited by Jan Christian Gertz, Doris Prechel, Konrad Schmid, and Markus Witte. BZAW 365. Berlin: de Gruyter.

———. 2008. *Hittite Diplomatic Texts*. 2nd ed. WAW 7. Atlanta: Society of Biblical Literature.

Bell, Lanny. 1985. "Luxor Temple and the Cult of the Royal Ka." *JNES* 44:251–94.

———. 1997. "The New Kingdom 'Divine' Temple: The Example of Luxor." Pages 127–84 in *Temples of Ancient Egypt*. Edited by Byron E. Shafer. Ithaca, NY: Cornell University Press; London: Tauris.

Berko, Patrick, Viviane Berko, and Herman De Meulenaere. 1992. *Ancient Egypt in Nineteenth Century Painting*. Knokke-Het Zoute: Berko.

Bianchi, Robert S. 1989. "Ramesside Art as Reflected by a Dated Faience Statuette Identifying Ramesses II with Horus." *BES* 10:17–24.

———. 1991. "Graeco-Roman Uses and Abuses of Ramesside Traditions." Pages 1–8 in *Fragments of a Shattered Visage: The Proceedings of the International Symposium of Ramesses the Great*. Edited by Edward Bleiberg, Rita Freed, and Anna Kay Walker. Memphis, TN: Memphis State University.

Bianchi, Robert S., and John K. McDonald. 1992. *In the Tomb of Nefertari: Conservation of the Wall Paintings*. Santa Monica, CA: Getty.

Bickel, Susanne. 2002. "Aspects et fonctions de la déification d'Amenhotep III." *BIFAO* 102:63–90.

———. 2016. "Other Tombs: Queens and Commoners in KV." Pages 230–42 in *The Oxford Handbook of the Valley of the Kings*. Edited by Kent R. Weeks and Richard H. Wilkinson. Oxford: Oxford University Press.

Bietak, Manfred, and Irene Forstner-Müller. 2011. "The Topography of New Kingdom Avaris and Per-Ramesses." Pages 23–50 in *Ramesside Studies in Honour of K. A. Kitchen*. Edited by Mark Collier and Steven Snape. Bolton: Rutherford.

Bittel, Kurt. 1986. "Bildliche Darstellungen Ḫattušili's III. in Ägypten." Pages 39–48 in *Kaniššuwar: A Tribute to Hans G. Güterbock on His Seventy-Fifth Birthday, May 27, 1983*. Edited by Gary M. Beckman and Harry A. Hoffner. AS 23. Chicago: Oriental Institute of the University of Chicago.

Bloch, Yigal. 2010. "Setting the Dates: Re-Evaluation of the Chronology of Babylonia in the 14th–11th Centuries B.C.E. and Its Implications for the Reign of Ramesses II and Ḫattušili III." *UF* 42:41–95.

Blyth, Elizabeth. 2006. *Karnak: Evolution of a Temple*. London: Routledge.

Bolshakov, Andrey O., and Andrey G. Soushchevski. 1998a. "Hero and Society in Ancient Egypt." *GM* 163:7–25.

———. 1998b. "Hero and Society in Ancient Egypt II." *GM* 164:21–31.

Boraik, Mansour. 2007. "Stela of Bakenkhonsu, High Priest of Amun-Re." *Memnonia* 18:119–26.

———. 2008. "Inside the Mosque of Abu El-Haggag: Rediscovering Long Lost Parts of Luxor Temple; A Preliminary Report." *Memnonia* 19:123–49.

Borghouts, J. F. 1978. *Ancient Egyptian Magical Texts*. Nisaba 9. Leiden: Brill.

Brand, Peter J. 1997. "The 'Lost' Obelisks and Colossi of Seti I." *JARCE* 34:101–14.

———. 1999a. "Methods Used in Restoring Reliefs Vandalized during the Amarna Period." *GM* 170:37–48.

———. 1999b. "Secondary Restorations in the Post-Amarna Period." *JARCE* 36:113–34.

——. 2000. *The Monuments of Seti I: Epigraphic, Historical and Art Historical Analysis.* PÄe 16. Leiden: Brill.

——. 2005. "Ideology and Politics of the Early Ramesside Kings (13th Century BC): A Historical Approach." Pages 23–38 in *Prozesse des Wandels in historischen Spannungsfeldern Nordostafrikas/Westasiens: Akten zum 2. Symposium des SFB 295, Mainz, 15.10.–17.10.2001.* Edited by Ursula Verhoeven et al. Würzburg: Ergon.

——. 2007a. "Ideological Imperatives: Irrational Factors in Egyptian-Hittite Relations under Ramesses II." Pages 15–33 in *Moving across Borders: Foreign Relations, Religion and Cultural Interactions in the Ancient Mediterranean.* Edited by Kousoulis Kousoulis Panagiotis and Konstantinos Magliveras. OLA 159. Leuven: Peeters.

——. 2007b. "Veils, Votives, and Marginalia: The Use of Sacred Space at Karnak and Luxor." Pages 51–83 in *Sacred Space and Sacred Function in Ancient Thebes.* Edited by Betsy M. Bryan and Peter F. Dorman. SAOC 61. Chicago: Oriental Institute of the University of Chicago.

——. 2008. "La Restauration: L'Égypte de Toutânkhamon à Ramsès II." Pages 109–19 in *Akhénaton et Néfertiti: Soleil et ombres des pharaons.* Edited by Jean-Luc Chappaz, Francesco Tiradritti, and Marie Vandenbeusch. Milan: Silvana.

——. 2009. "Usurped Cartouches of Merenptah at Karnak and Luxor." Pages 28–48 in *Causing His Name to Live: Studies in Egyptian Epigraphy and History in Memory of William J. Murnane.* Edited by Peter J. Brand and Louise Cooper. CHANE 37. Leiden: Brill.

——. 2010a. "Reuse and Restoration." In *UCLA Encyclopedia of Egyptology.* https://escholarship.org/uc/item/2vp6065d.

——. 2010b. "Usurpation of Monuments." In *UCLA Encyclopedia of Egyptology.* https://escholarship.org/uc/item/5gj996k5.

——. 2011. "The Date of the War Scenes on the South Wall of the Great Hypostyle Hall and the West Wall of the *Cour de la Cachette* at Karnak and the History of the Late Nineteenth Dynasty." Pages 51–84 in *Ramesside Studies in Honour of K. A. Kitchen.* Edited by Mark Collier and Steven Snape. Bolton: Rutherford.

——. 2016. "Reconstructing the Royal Family of Ramesses II and Its Hierarchical Structure." *Journal of Ancient Civilizations* 31:7–44.

——. 2018. "Patterns of Innovation in the Monumental Art of Ramesside Thebes: The Example of the Great Hypostyle Hall of Karnak." Pages 45–61 in *The Ramesside Period in Egypt: Studies into Cultural and Historical Processes of the 19th and 20th Dynasties.* Edited by Sabine Kubisch and Ute Rummel. Berlin: de Gruyter.

——. 2020a. "Rameses II Redux: Of Colossi, Cartouches and Chronology." *KMT* 31.2:60–68.

——. 2020b. "The Historical Record." Pages 59–70 in *The Oxford Handbook of Egyptian Epigraphy and Palaeography.* Edited by Dimitri Laboury and Vanessa Davies. New York: Oxford University Press.

——. Forthcoming. "The Ideological Aspects of Ramesside Military Texts and Reliefs." In *Perspectives on the Ramesside Military System.* Edited by Mohammed Raafat Abbas, Alexander Schütze, and Friedhelm Hoffmann. Munich: Ludwig-Maximilians-Universität.

Brand, Peter J., Rosa Erika Feleg, and William J. Murnane. 2018. *The Great Hypostyle Hall in the Temple of Amun at Karnak, Parts 2 and 3.* 2 vols. OIP 142. Chicago: Oriental Institute of the University of Chicago.

Brand, Peter J., and Jean Revez. 2021. "The Cartouche Names of Ramesses IV in the Great Hypostyle Hall of Karnak: A Case of Royal Identity, Legitimation, and Historical Memory." Pages 291–316 in *His Good Name: Essays on Identity and Self-Presentation in Ancient Egypt in Honor of Ronald J. Leprohon.* Edited by Christina Geisen, Jean Li, and Kai Yamamoto. MVCAE 5. Atlanta: Lockwood Press.

Brand, Peter J., Jean Revez, Janusz Karkowski, Emmanuel Laroze, and Cédric Gobcil. 2013. "Karnak Hypostyle Hall Project, Report on the 2011 Field Season for the University of Memphis and the Université du Québec à Montréal." *Cahiers de Karnak* 14:193–229.

Breasted, James H. 1899. "Ramses II and the Princes in the Karnak Reliefs of Seti I." *ZÄS* 37:130–39.

———. 1904. *The Battle of Kadesh: A Study in the Earliest Known Military Strategy.* Decennial Publications of the University of Chicago 5. Chicago: University of Chicago Press.

———. 1905. *A History of Egypt: From the Earliest Times to the Persian Conquest.* New York: Scribners.

Breyer, Francis. 2010a. *Ägypten und Anatolien: Politische, kulturelle und sprachliche Kontakte zwischen dem Niltal und Kleinasien im 2. Jahrtausend v. Chr.* Vienna: Österreichischen Akademie der Wissenschaften.

———. 2010b. "Hethitologische Bemerkungen zum Keilschrift 'Zipfel' aus Qantir/Pi-Ramesse." *A&L* 20:43–48.

———. 2010c. "Thutmosis III. und die Hethiter: Bemerkungen zum Kurustama-Vertrag sowie zu anatolischen Toponymen und einer hethitischen Lehnübersetzung in den Annalen Thutmosis' III." *SAK* 39:67–83.

Broadhurst, Clive. 1989. "An Artistic Interpretation of Sety I's War Reliefs." *JEA* 75:229–34.

Brunner, Hellmut. 1986. *Die Geburt des Gottkönigs: Studien zur Überlieferung Eines Altägyptischen Mythos.* 2nd ed. ÄA 10. Wiesbaden: Harrassowitz.

de Bruyn, M. 1989. "The Battle of Qadesh: Some Reconsiderations." Pages 135–64 in *To the Euphrates and Beyond: Archaeological Studies in Honour of Maurits N. van Loon.* Edited by O. M. C. Haex, Hans H. Curvers, and Peter M. M. G. Akkermans. Rotterdam: Balkema.

Bryan, Betsy M. 1982. "The Etymology of *ḫnr* 'Group of Musical Performers.'" *BES* 4:35–54.

Bryce, Trevor. 1998. "How Old Was Matanazi?" *JEA* 84:212–15.

———. 2003. *Letters of the Great Kings of the Ancient Near East: The Royal Correspondence of the Late Bronze Age.* London: Routledge.

———. 2005. *The Kingdom of the Hittites.* 2nd ed. Oxford: Oxford University Press.

———. 2006. "The 'Eternal Treaty' from the Hittite Perspective." *BMSAES* 6:1–11.

———. 2010. "The Hittites at War." Pages 67–86 in *Studies on War in the Ancient Near East: Collected Essays on Military History.* Edited by Jordi Vidal. AOAT 372. Münster: Ugarit-Verlag.

Bryson, Karen Margaret. 2015. "Some Year Dates of Horemheb in Context." *JARCE* 51:285–301.

Budin, Stephanie Lynn, and Jean MacIntosh Turfa, eds. 2016. *Women in Antiquity. Real Women across the Ancient World.* London: Routledge.

Budka, Julia. 2009. "The Ramesside Temple in the Asasif: Observations on Its Construction and Function, Based on the Results of the Austrian Excavations." Pages 17–45 in *7. Ägyptologische Tempeltagung: Structuring Religion; Leuven, 28. September–1. Oktober 2005*. Edited by René Preys. Wiesbaden: Harrassowitz.

von Bunsen, Christian C. J. 1848. *Egypt's Place in Universal History: An Historical Investigation in Five Books*. Translated by Charles H. Cottrell. 5 vols. London: Longman, Brown, Green, & Longmans.

Calabria, Michael D. 2015. "The Movie Mogul, Moses and Muslims: Islamic Elements in Cecil B. DeMille's The Ten Commandments (1956)." *Journal of Religion and Film* 19.1:44. http://digitalcommons.unomaha.edu/jrf/vol19/iss1/44.

Callender, Vivienne Gae. 1994. "The Nature of the Egyptian 'Harim': Dynasties 1–20." *BACE* 5:7–25.

———. 2004. "Queen Tausret and the End of Dynasty 19." *SAK* 32:81–104.

Calverley, Amice M., and Myrtle F. Broome. 1933. *The Temple of King Sethos I at Abydos*. Vol. 1, *The Chapels of Osiris, Isis and Horus*. Edited by Alan H. Gardiner. London: Egypt Exploration Society; Chicago: University of Chicago Press.

———. 1935. *The Temple of King Sethos I at Abydos*. Vol. 2, *The Chapels of Amen-Rēʾ, Rēʾ-Ḥarakhti, Ptaḥ, and King Sethos*. Edited by Alan H. Gardiner. London: Egypt Exploration Society; Chicago: University of Chicago Press.

———. 1938. *The Temple of King Sethos I at Abydos*. Vol. 3, *The Osiris Complex*. Edited by Alan H. Gardiner. London: Egypt Exploration Society; Chicago: University of Chicago Press.

———. 1958. *The Temple of King Sethos I at Abydos*. Vol. 4, *The Second Hypostyle Hall*. Edited by Alan H. Gardiner. London: Egypt Exploration Society; Chicago: University of Chicago Press.

Caminos, Ricardo A. 1954. *Late-Egyptian Miscellanies*. London: Oxford University Press.

Cavillier, Giacomo. 2015. "From the Mediterranean Sea to the Nile: New Perspectives and Researches on the Sherden in Egypt." Pages 631–38 in vol. 1 of *Proceedings of the Tenth International Congress of Egyptologists: University of the Aegean, Rhodes, 22–29 May 2008*. Edited by Panagiotis Kousoulis and Nikolaos Lazaridis. 2 vols. OLA 218. Leuven: Peeters.

Černý, Jaroslav. 1929. "Papyrus Salt 124 (Brit. Mus. 10055)." *JEA* 15.3/4:243–58.

Champollion, Jean-François. 1835–1845. *Monuments de l'Egypte et de la Nubie: D'après les dessins exécutés sur les lieux sous la dir. de Champollion le-Jeune, et les descriptions autographes qu'il en a rédigées*. 4 vols. Paris: Didot.

Charaf, Hanan. 2017. "Kamid el-Loz." Pages 18–20 in vol. 15 of *Encyclopedia of the Bible and Its Reception*. Edited by Constance M. Furey et al. Berlin: de Gruyter.

Charron, Alain. 2020. "Les premières 'momies' de taureaux Apis." Pages 197–214 in *Les taureaux de l'Égypte ancienne: Publication éditée à l'occasion de la 14e Rencontre d'égyptologie de Nîmes*. Edited by Sydney H. Aufrère. Nîmes: Association égyptologique du Gard.

Charron, Alain, and Christophe Barbotin. 2016. *Khâemouaset, le prince archéologue: Savoir et pouvoir à l'époque de Ramsès II*. Arles: Musée départemental Arles antique; Ghent: Snoeck.

Chevrier, Henri. 1954. "Note sur l'érection des obélisques." *ASAE* 52:309–13.

Chhem, Rethy K., Pierre Schmit, and Clément Fauré. 2004. "Did Ramesses II Really Have Ankylosing Spondylitis? A Reappraisal." *Journal of the Canadian Association of Radiologists* 55:211–17.

Christophe, Louis-A. 1956. "Les temples d'Abou Simbel et la famille de Ramsès II." *Bulletin de l'Institut d'Égypte* 38.2:107–30.

———. 1965. *Abou-Simbel et l'épopée de sa Découverte*. Brussels: Merckx.

Cline, Eric H. 2014. *1177 BC: The Year Civilization Collapsed*. Princeton: Princeton University Press.

Cline, Eric H., and David O'Connor. 2012. *Ramesses III: The Life and Times of Egypt's Last Hero*. Ann Arbor: University of Michigan Press.

Cochavi-Rainey, Zipora. 2011. *The Akkadian Dialect of Egyptian Scribes in the 14th and 13th Centuries BCE*. AOAT 374. Münster: Ugarit-Verlag

Cochavi-Rainey, Zipora, and Christine Lilyquist. 1999. *Royal Gifts in the Late Bronze Age, Fourteenth to Thirteenth Centuries B.C.E.: Selected Texts Recording Gifts to Royal Personages*. Beer Sheva: Ben-Gurion University of the Negev Press.

Cohen, Raymond 2000. "Intelligence in the Amarna Letters." Pages 85–98, 247 in *Amarna Diplomacy: The Beginnings of International Relations*. Edited by Raymond Cohen and Raymond Westbrook. Baltimore: Johns Hopkins University Press.

Cohen, Raymond, and Raymond Westbrook, eds. 2000. *Amarna Diplomacy: The Beginnings of International Relations*. Baltimore: Johns Hopkins University Press.

Cole, Edward Mushett. 2017. "'The Years of Hyenas When There Was a Famine': An Assessment of Environmental Causes for the Events of the Twentieth Dynasty." Pages 3–17 in *Global Egyptology: Negotiations in the Production of Knowledges on Ancient Egypt in Global Contexts*. Edited by Juan Carlos Moreno García et al. London: Golden House.

Colla, Elliott. 2007. *Conflicted Antiquities: Egyptology, Egyptomania, Egyptian Modernity*. Durham, NC: Duke University Press.

Conner, Patrick. 1983. *The Inspiration of Egypt: Its Influence on British Artists, Travellers, and Designers, 1700–1900; An Exhibition Held at Brighton Museum, 7 May–17 July 1983, and at Manchester City Art Gallery, 4th August–17 September 1983*. Brighton: Brighton Borough Council.

———. 1985. "'Wedding Archaeology to Art': Poynter's Israel in Egypt." Pages 112–20 in *Influences in Victorian Art and Architecture*. Edited by Sarah Macready and F. H. Thompson. London: Society of Antiquaries.

Connor, Simon. 2017. *La statua di Ramesse II*. Turin: Museo Egizio; Modena: Franco Cosimo Panini.

———. 2019. "'Ramessiser' des statues." *BSFÉ* 202:83–102.

Connor, Simon, and Dimitri Laboury. 2020. *Tutankhamun: Discovering the Forgotten Pharaoh*. Liège: Presses Universitairs de Liège.

Cordani, Violetta. 2017. *Lettere fra Egiziani e Ittiti*. Turin: Paideia.

Costa, Salvador. 2004. "Muerte ritual del rey durante la fiesta Sed." *Boletín de la Asociación Andaluza de Egiptología* 2:43–59.

———. 2017. "A Comparative Study of Two Ramesses II Scenes in the Sety I Temple of Millions of Years at Gurna (West Thebes)." *AuOr* 35:251–59.

Crouwel, Joost. 2013. "Studying the Six Chariots from the Tomb of Tutankhamun: An Update." Pages 73–93 in *Chasing Chariots: Proceedings of the First International Chariot Conference (Cairo 2012).* Edited by Salima Ikram and André J. Veldmeijer. Leiden: Sidestone.

Cumming, Barbara, and Benedict G. Davies. 1982–1995. *Egyptian Historical Records of the Later Eighteenth Dynasty.* 6 fascicles. Warminster: Aris & Phillips.

Dalino, Edwin. 2017. "Le prince Mérenptah fut-il grand prêtre de Ptah? État de la question et focus sur Hori, fils de Khâemouaset." *Égypte Nilotique et Méditerranéenne* 10:1–5.

Darnell, John Coleman. 2010. "Opet Festival." In *UCLA Encyclopedia of Egyptology.* https://escholarship.org/uc/item/4739r3fr.

———. 2011. "A Stela of Seti I from the Region of Kurkur Oasis." Pages 127–41 in *Ramesside Studies in Honour of K. A. Kitchen.* Edited by Mark Collier and Steven Snape. Bolton: Rutherford.

Darnell, John Coleman, and Richard Jasnow. 1993. "On the Moabite Inscriptions of Ramesses II at Luxor Temple." *JNES* 52:263–74.

Darnell, John Coleman, and Colleen Manassa. 2007. *Tutankhamun's Armies: Battle and Conquest during Ancient Egypt's Late Eighteenth Dynasty.* Hoboken: Wiley.

David, Rosalie. 2018. *Temple Ritual at Abydos.* London: Egypt Exploration Society.

David, Steven R. 2020. "Realism, Constructivism, and the Amarna Letters." Pages 54–67, 244 in *Amarna Diplomacy: The Beginnings of International Relations.* Edited by Raymond Cohen and Raymond Westbrook. Baltimore: Johns Hopkins University Press.

Der Manuelian, Peter. 2006. "The End of the Reign and the Accession of Amenhotep II." Pages 413–29 in *Thutmose III: A New Biography.* Edited by Eric H. Cline and David O'Connor. Ann Arbor: University of Michigan Press.

Davies, Benedict G. 1997. *Egyptian Historical Inscriptions of the Nineteenth Dynasty.* Göteborg: Åströms.

———. 2018. *Life within the Five Walls: A Handbook to Deir el-Medina.* Wallasey: Abercromby.

Davies, Vanessa. 2018. *Peace in Ancient Egypt.* HES 5. Leiden: Brill.

De Backer, Fabrice. 2009. "Evolution of War Chariot Tactics in the Ancient Near East." *UF* 41:29–46.

Devos, Julien. 2004. "Les représentations égyptiennes de Khattusili III: À propos de l'usage des empreintes de sceaux royaux par la chancellerie égyptienne." Pages 175–200 in *Antiquus oriens: Mélanges offerts au professeur René Lebrun.* Edited by Michel Mazoyer and Olivier Casabonne. 2 vols. Paris: L'Harmattan.

Degrève, Agnès. 2006. "La campagne asiatique de l'an 1 de Séthy Ier représentée sur le mur extérieur nord de la salle hypostyle du temple d'Amon à Karnak." *RdÉ* 57:47–64.

Demarée, R. J. 2016. "Announcement of the Passing of Ramesses II." *Jaarbericht van Het Voorziatisch-Egyptisch Genootschap Ex Oriente Lux* 46:121–25.

Demas, Martha, and Neville Agnew. 2012–2016. *Valley of the Queens Assessment Report.* 2 vols. Los Angeles: Getty Conservation Institute. http://www.getty.edu/conservation/publications_resources/pdf_publications/valley_queens.html.

Desroches Noblecourt, Christiane. 1982. "Touy, mère de Ramsès II, la reine Tanedjmy et les reliques de l'expérience amarnienne." Pages 227–43 in vol.

2 of *L'Égyptologie En 1979: Axes Prioritaires de Recherches*. 2 vols. Paris: Éditions du Centre national de la recherche scientifique.

———. 1990. "Le mammisi de Ramsès au Ramesseum." *Memnonia* 1:25–46.

———. 1997. *Ramsès II: La véritable histoire*. Paris: Pygmalion.

Desroches Noblecourt, et al. 1971. *Grand temple d'Abou Simbel II: La bataille de Qadech; Description et inscriptions, dessins et photographies*. Cairo: Centre de documentation et d'études sur l'ancienne Égypte.

Desroches Noblecourt, Christiane, and Georg Gerster. 1968. *The World Saves Abu Simbel*. Vienna: Koska.

Desroches Noblecourt, Christiane, and Charles Kuentz. 1968. *Abou-Simbel: Petit temple*. 2 vols. Cairo: Centre de documentation et d'études sur l'ancienne Égypte.

Devecchi, Elena. 2013. "(Re-)Defining the Corpus of the Hittite Treaties." *Zeitschrift für Altorientalische und Biblische Rechtsgeschichte* 19:89–98.

———. 2015. *Trattati internazionali ittiti*. Brescia: Paideia.

Devecchi, Elena, and Jared L. Miller. 2011. "Hittite-Egyptian Synchronisms and Their Consequences for Ancient Near Eastern Chronology." Pages 139–76 in *Egypt and the Near East: The Crossroads Proceedings of an International Conference on the Relations of Egypt and the Near East in the Bronze Age, Prague, September 1–3, 2010*. Edited by Jana Mynářová. Prague: Charles University in Prague Czech Institute of Egyptology, Faculty of Arts.

Dever, William G. 2009. "Merenptah's 'Israel,' the Bible's, and Ours." Pages 89–96 in *Exploring the Longue Durée: Essays in Honor of Lawrence E. Stager*. Edited by J. David Schloen. Winona Lake, IN: Eisenbrauns.

Dew, Brenan. 2017. "Cartouches as a Structural Element upon Ramesside Rhetorical Stelae." Pages 263–72 in *The Cultural Manifestation of Religious Experience: Studies in Honour of Boyo G. Ockinga*. Edited by Heike Behlmer, Camilla Di Biasee-Dyson, and Leonie Donovan. AOAT 85. Münster: Ugarit-Verlag.

Dierderen, Roger. 2004. *From Homer to the Harem: The Art of Jean Lecomte du Nouÿ*. New York: Dahesh Museum of Art.

van Dijk, Jacobus. 1997. "The Family and Career of Tia." Pages 49–62 in *The Tomb of Tia and Tia: A Royal Monument of the Ramesside Period in the Memphite Necropolis*. Edited by Geoffrey Thorndike Martin et al. London: Egypt Exploration Society.

———. 2008. "New Evidence on the Length of the Reign of Horemheb." *JARCE* 44:193–200.

———. 2011. "The Date of the Gebel Barkal Stela of Seti I." Pages 325–32 in *Under the Potter's Tree: Studies on Ancient Egypt Presented to Janine Bourriau on the Occasion of Her 70th Birthday*. Edited by David Aston. OLA 204. Leuven: Peeters.

Divon, Shai. 2008. "A Survey of the Textual Evidence for 'Food Shortage' from the Late Hittite Empire." Pages 101–9 in *The City of Emar among the Late Bronze Age Empires: History, Landscape, and Society*. Edited by Lorenzo d'Alfonso, Yoram Cohen, and Dietrich Sürenhagen. AOAT 349. Münster: Ugarit-Verlag.

Dodson, Aidan. 1990. "Crown Prince Djhutmose and the Royal Sons of the Eighteenth Dynasty." *JEA* 76:87–96.

——. 2011. "Fade to Grey: The Chancellor Bay, *Éminence Grise* of the Late Nineteenth Dynasty." Pages 145-158 in *Ramesside Studies in Honour of K. A. Kitchen.* Edited by Mark Collier and Steven Snape. Bolton: Rutherford.

——. 2014a. *Amarna Sunrise: Egypt from Golden Age to Age of Heresy.* Cairo: American University in Cairo Press.

——. 2014b. "The Coregency Conundrum." *KMT* 25.2:28–35.

——. 2016. *Poisoned Legacy: The Decline and Fall of the Nineteenth Egyptian Dynasty.* Rev. ed. Cairo: American University in Cairo Press.

——. 2018. *Amarna Sunset: Nefertiti, Tutankhamun, Ay, Horemheb, and the Egyptian Counter-Reformation.* 2nd ed. Cairo: American University in Cairo Press.

——. 2019. *Sethy I, King of Egypt: His Life and Afterlife.* Cairo: American University in Cairo Press.

Dodson, Aidan, and Dyan Hilton. 2004. *The Complete Royal Families of Ancient Egypt.* London: Thames & Hudson.

Donadoni, Sergio H., et al. 1975. *Grand temple d'Abou Simbel III: Les salles du trésor sud.* 2 vols. Cairo: Centre d'études et de documentation sur l'ancienne Égypte.

Dorman, Peter F. 2005. "The Proscription of Hatshepsut." Pages 267–69 in *Hatshepsut: From Queen to Pharaoh.* Edited by Cathleen A. Keller, Catharine H. Roehrig, and Renée Dreyfus. New York: Metropolitan Museum of Art; New Haven: Yale University Press.

——. 2009. "The Long Coregency Revisited: Architectural and Iconographic Conundra in the Tomb of Kheruef." Pages 65–82 in *Causing His Name to Live: Studies in Egyptian Epigraphy and History in Memory of William J. Murnane.* Edited by Peter J. Brand and Louise Cooper. CHANE 37. Leiden: Brill.

Dorn, Andreas, and Stéphane Polis. 2016. "A Re-Examination of O. Cairo JdE 72460 (= O. Cairo SR 1475): Ending the Quest for a 19th Dynasty Queen's Tomb in the Valley of the Kings." Pages 129–61 in *Aere perennius: Mélanges égyptologiques en l'honneur de Pascal Vernus.* Edited by Philippe Collombert et al. OLA 252. Leuven: Peeters.

Drews, Robert. 1996. *The End of the Bronze Age: Changes in Warfare and the Catastrophe ca. 1200 BC.* Princeton: Princeton University Press.

Eaton, Katherine. 2007. "Types of Cult-Image Carried in Divine Barques and the Logistics of Performing Temple Ritual in the New Kingdom." *ZÄS* 134:15–25.

——. 2013. *Ancient Egyptian Temple Ritual: Performance, Pattern, and Practice.* New York: Routledge.

Eaton-Krauss, Marianne. 1991. "Ramesses: Re Who Creates the Gods." Pages 15–23 in *Fragments of a Shattered Visage: The Proceedings of the International Symposium of Ramesses the Great.* Edited by Edward Bleiberg, Rita Freed, and Anna Kay Walker. Memphis, TN: Memphis State University.

——. 2016. *The Unknown Tutankhamun.* London: Bloomsbury.

Edel, Elmar. 1950. "KBo I 15+19, ein Brief Ramses' II. mit einer Schilderung der Ḳadešschlacht." *ZA* 49:195–212.

——. 1960. "Der geplante Besuch Hattušilis III. in Ägypten." *Mitteilungen der Deutschen Orient-Gesellschaft Zu Berlin* 92:15–20.

——. 1976. *Ägyptische Ärzte und ägyptische Medizin am hethitischen Königshof: Neue Funde von Keilschriftbriefen Ramses' II. aus Boğazköy.* Göttingen: Westendeutscher.

——. 1994. *Die ägyptisch-hethitische Korrespondenz aus Boghazköi in babylonischer und hethitischer Sprache.* 2 vols. Opladen: Westdeutscher.

——. 1997. *Der Vertrag zwischen Ramses II. von Ägypten und Ḫattušili III. von Ḫatti.* Berlin: Mann.

Edgerton, William F. 1951. "The Strikes in Ramses III's Twenty-Ninth Year." *JNES* 10:137–45.

Edwards, Amelia B. 1888. *A Thousand Miles up the Nile.* 2nd ed. London: Routledge; New York: Dutton.

Elie, Serge D. 2004. "The Harem Syndrome: Moving beyond Anthropology's Discursive Colonization of Gender in the Middle East." *Alternatives* 29:139–68.

Elleithy, Hisham, and Christian Leblanc. 2016. *Nécropoles Royales.* Volume 1: *Vallée des Reines.* Cairo: American University in Cairo Press.

El-Sharkawy, Ali. 1997. *Der Amun-Tempel von Karnak: Die Funktion der Grossen Säulenhalle.* Wissenschaftliche Schriftenreihe Ägyptologie 1. Berlin: Köster.

Emanuel, Jeffrey P. 2013. "'Šrdn from the Sea': The Arrival, Integration, and Acculturation of a 'Sea People.'" *JAEI* 5:14–27.

——. 2020. *Naval Warfare and Maritime Conflict in the Late Bronze and Early Iron Age Mediterranean.* CHANE 117. Leiden: Brill.

Enany, Khaled El-. 2012. "Le pharaon hiéracocéphale Ramsès II." Pages 253–66 in vol. 2 of *Et in Ægypto et ad Ægyptum: Recueil d'études dédiées à Jean-Claude Grenier.* Edited by Annie Gasse, Frédéric Servajean, and Christophe Thiers. CENIM 5. Montpellier: Université Paul Valéry.

Epigraphic Survey. 1930–2009. *Medinet Habu.* 9 vols. OIP. Chicago: Oriental Institute of the University of Chicago.

——. 1936. *Reliefs and Inscriptions at Karnak: Ramses III's Temple within the Great Inclosure of Amon.* 2 vols. OIP 25, 35. Chicago: Oriental Institute of the University of Chicago.

——. 1980. *The Tomb of Kheruef: Theban Tomb 192.* OIP 102. Chicago: Oriental Institute of the University of Chicago.

——. 1986. *Reliefs and Inscriptions at Karnak.* Volume 4: *The Battle Reliefs of King Sety I.* OIP 107. Chicago: Oriental Institute of the University of Chicago.

——. 1994. *Reliefs and Inscriptions at Luxor Temple.* Volume 1: *The Festival Procession of Opet in the Colonnade Hall; With Translations of Texts, Commentary, and Glossary.* OIP 112. Chicago: Oriental Institute of the University of Chicago.

——. 1998. *Reliefs and Inscriptions at Luxor Temple.* Volume 2: *The Facade, Portals, Upper Register Scenes, Columns, Marginalia, and Statuary in the Colonnade Hall; With Translations of Texts, Commentary, and Glossary.* OIP 116. Chicago: Oriental Institute of the University of Chicago.

Eßbach, Nadine. 2020. *Ägypten und Ugarit: Kulturkontakte und die Folgen.* AOAT 499. Münster: Ugarit-Verlag.

Exell, Karen. 2009. *Soldiers, Sailors and Sandalmakers: A Social Reading of Ramesside Period Votive Stelae.* London: Golden House.

Fantechi, Silvana E., and Andrea P. Zingarelli. 2002. "Singers and Musicians in New Kingdom Egypt." *GM* 186:27–35.

Fecht, Gerhard. 1984. "Das 'Poème' über die Qadeš-Schlacht." *SAK* 11:281–333.

Feldman, Marian H., and Caroline Sauvage 2010. "Objects of Prestige? Chariots in the Late Bronze Age Eastern Mediterranean and Near East." *A&L* 20:67–181.

Feleg, Rosa Erika. 2020. "The Forecourt of Ramesses II at Luxor Temple: Cultic Features of the Interior Wall Reliefs." PhD diss., University of Memphis.

Feucht, Erika. 1985. "The *ḥrdw n Kȝp* Reconsidered." Pages 38–47 in *Pharaonic Egypt, the Bible and Christianity*. Edited by Sarah Israelit-Groll. Jerusalem: Magnes.

Fischer, Peter M., and Teresa Bürge, eds. 2017. *"Sea Peoples" Up-to-Date: New Research on Transformations in the Eastern Mediterranean in the 13th–11th Centuries BCE; Proceedings of the ESF-Workshop Held at the Austrian Academy of Sciences, Vienna, 3–4 November 2014*. Vienna: Österreichischen Akademie der Wissenschaften.

Fischer-Elfert, Hans-Werner. 1992. *Die satirische Streitschrift des Papyrus Anastasi I*. 2nd ed. Wiesbaden: Harrassowitz.

Fisher, Marjorie M. 2001. *The Sons of Ramesses II*. 2 vols. ÄAT 53. Wiesbaden: Harrassowitz.

———. 2013. "A Diplomatic Marriage in the Ramesside Period: Maathorneferure, Daughter of the Great Ruler of Hatti." Pages 75–119 in *Beyond Hatti: A Tribute to Gary Beckman*. Edited by Billie Jean Collins and Piotr Michalowski. Atlanta: Lockwood Press.

Foucart, George. 1921. "Un temple flottant: Le vaisseau d'or d'Amon-Râ." *Monuments et Mémoires de la Fondation Eugène Piot* 25:143–69.

Frandsen, Paul J. 2008. "Aspects of Kingship in Ancient Egypt." Pages 47–73 in *Religion and Power: Divine Kingship in the Ancient World and Beyond*. Edited by Nicole Brisch. Oriental Institute Seminars 4. Chicago: Oriental Institute of the University of Chicago.

Fraser, Antonia. 2007. *Love and Louis XIV: The Women in the Life of the Sun King*. New York: Anchor.

Freed, Rita E. 1987. *Ramesses the Great*. Memphis, TN: City of Memphis.

Fritze, Ronald H. 2016. *Egyptomania: A History of Fascination, Obsession and Fantasy*. London: Reaktion.

Frood, Elizabeth. 2007. *Biographical Texts from Ramessid Egypt*. WAW 26. Atlanta: Society of Biblical Literature.

Fukaya, Masashi. 2019. *The Festivals of Opet, the Valley, and the New Year: Their Socio-Religious Functions*. Archaeopress Egyptology 28. Oxford: Archaeopress.

Gaballa, Gaballa A. 1976. *Narrative in Egyptian Art*. Mainz: von Zabern.

Gaballa, Gaballa A., and Kenneth A. Kitchen. 1968. "Ramesside Varia I." *CdÉ* 43.86:259–70.

Gabolde, Luc. 2018. *Karnak, Amon-Rê: La Genèse d'un Temple, la Naissance d'un Dieu*. BiÉtud 167. Cairo: Institut français d'archéologie orientale.

Gabolde, Marc. 2015. *Toutankhamon*. Paris: Pygmalion.

Galán, José Manuel. 1993. *Victory and Border: Terminology Related to Egyptian Imperialism in the XVIIIth Dynasty*. HÄB 40. Hildesheim: Gerstenberg.

Gardiner, Alan H. 1911. *Egyptian Hieratic Texts Transcribed, Translated and Annotated, Series I: Literary Texts of the New Kingdom Part 1 The Papyrus*

Anastasi I and the Papyrus Koller, Together with the Parallel Texts. Leipzig: Hinrich.

———. 1935. *Hieratic Papyri in the British Museum, Series 3: Chester Beatty Gift.* London: British Museum Press.

———. 1937. *Late-Egyptian Miscellanies.* Brussels: Fondation égyptologique Reine Élisabeth.

———. 1948. *Ramesside Administrative Documents.* Oxford: Oxford University Press.

———. 1953. "The Coronation of King Ḥaremḥab." *JEA* 39:13–31.

———. 1960. *The Kadesh Inscriptions of Ramesses II.* Oxford: Griffith Institute.

———. 1961. *Egypt of the Pharaohs: An Introduction.* Oxford: Clarendon.

Garnett, A. 2015. *The Colossal Statue of Ramesses II.* London: British Museum Press.

Gasperini, Valentina. 2018. *Tomb Robberies at the End of the New Kingdom: The Gurob Burnt Groups Reinterpreted.* Oxford: Oxford University Press.

Genz, Hermann 2013. "The Introduction of the Light, Horse-Drawn Chariot and the Role of Archery in the Near East at the Transition from the Middle to the Late Bronze Ages: Is There a Connection?" Pages 95–105 in *Chasing Chariots: Proceedings of the First International Chariot Conference (Cairo 2012).* Edited by Salima Ikram and André J. Veldmeijer. Leiden: Sidestone.

Gershoni, Israel, and James P. Jankowski. 1986. *Egypt, Islam, and the Arabs: The Search for Egyptian Nationhood, 1900–1930.* New York: Oxford University Press.

Gerster, Georg. 1963. "Threatened Treasures of the Nile." *National Geographic* 124:586–621.

———. 1969. "Abu Simbel's Ancient Temples Reborn." *National Geographic* 135:724–44.

van Gils, Patrick. 2017. "Sethnakht, a Descendant of Ramses II?" Pages 10–30 in *Varia Aegyptiaca II.* Edited by Andreas Finger and Christain Huyeng. Kleine Berliner Schriften zum Alten Ägypten 4. Norderstedt: Books on Demand.

Goedicke, Hans. 1960. *Die Stellung des Königs Im Alten Reich.* ÄA 2. Wiesbaden: Harrassowitz.

———. 1985. "The 'Battle of Kadesh': A Reassessment." Pages 77–121 in *Perspectives on the Battle of Kadesh.* Edited by Hans Goedicke. Baltimore: Halgo.

Goelet, Ogden. 1991. "The Blessing of Ptah." Pages 28–37 in *Fragments of a Shattered Visage: The Proceedings of the International Symposium of Ramesses the Great.* Edited by Edward Bleiberg, Rita Freed, and Anna Kay Walker. Memphis, TN: Memphis State University.

———. 2016. "Tomb Robberies in the Valley of the Kings." Pages 448–66 in *The Oxford Handbook of the Valley of the Kings.* Edited by Kent R. Weeks and Richard H. Wilkinson. Oxford: Oxford University Press.

Goelet, Ogden, and Sameh Iskander. 2012. "The Epigraphic Record in the Temple of Ramesses II at Abydos: Preliminary Report." *JARCE* 48:143–83.

Goelet, Ogden, and Baruch A. Levine. 2000. "Making Peace in Heaven and on Earth: Religious and Legal Aspects of the Treaty between Ramesses II and Hattušili III." Pages 252–99 in *Boundaries of the Ancient Near Eastern World: A Tribute to Cyrus H. Gordon.* Edited by Claire Gottlieb, Sharon Keller, and Meir Lubetski. Sheffield: Sheffield Academic.

Gohary, Jocelyn. 1992. *Akhenaten's Sed-Festival at Karnak.* London: Kegan Paul.

Gohary, Said. 2009. *The Twin Tomb Chapel of Nebnefer and His Son Mahu at Sakkara*. Cairo: Supreme Council of Antiquities.

——. 2011. "A Chief Overseer of the Royal Harim at Memphis." Pages 199–205 in *Ramesside Studies in Honour of K. A. Kitchen*. Edited by Mark Collier and Steven Snape. Bolton: Rutherford.

Goldwasser, Orly, and Eliezer D. Oren 2015. "Marine Units on the 'Ways of Horus' in the Days of Seti I." *JAEI* 7.1:25–38

Golvin, Jean-Claude, and Jean-Claude Goyon. 1987. *Les Bâtisseurs de Karnak*. Paris: CNRS.

Gomaà, Farouk. 1973. *Chaemwese, Sohn Ramses' II. und Hoherpriester von Memphis*. ÄA 27. Wiesbaden: Harrassowitz.

Goyon, Jean-Claude, et al. 2004. *La construction pharaonique du Moyen Empire à l'époque Gréco-Romaine: Contexte et principes technologiques*. Paris: Picard.

Grandet, Pierre. 1993. *Ramsès III: Histoire d'un règne*. Paris: Pygmalion.

——. 1994. *Le Papyrus Harris I (BM 9999)*. 2 vols. BiÉtud 109. Cairo: Institut français d'archéologie orientale.

——. 2000. "L'exécution du chancelier Bay: O. IFAO 1864." *BIFAO* 100:339–45.

——. 2013. "The Ramesside State." Pages 831–99 in *Ancient Egyptian Administration*. Edited by Juan Carlos Moreno García. HdO 104. Leiden: Brill.

——. 2014. "Early–Mid 20th Dynasty." In *UCLA Encyclopedia of Egyptology*. https://escholarship.org/uc/item/0d84248t.

Greco, Christian. 2020. *Queen Nefertari's Egypt*. Fort Worth, TX: Kimbell Art Museum.

Grimal, Nicolas. 2018. "L'offrande d'un vétéran de l'an 16 d'Horemheb." *Comptes-rendus des inscriptions et belles-lettres* 2018:319–38.

Groddek, Detlev. 2008. "'Ägypten sei dem hethitischen Lande Bundesgenosse!': Zur textherstellung zweier Paragraphen des Kuruštama-Vertrages." *GM* 218:37–43.

Guégan, Izold 2020. "Le *ḫnr*: Recherches sur un group religieux de l'Ancien au Nouvel Empire." PhD diss., Sorbonne Université.

Guidotti, Maria Cristina, and Franca Pecchioli Daddi. 2002. *La battaglia di Qadesh: Ramesse II contro gli ittiti per la conquista della Siria*. Livorno: Sillabe.

Gulyás, András. 2003. "The Gods of the Type 'Amun of Ramesses' and Their Meaning in the Context of Religious Developments of the Ramesside Period." Pages 57–62 in *Proceedings of the Second Central European Conference of Young Egyptologists, Egypt 2001: Perspectives of Research, Warsaw 5–7 March 2001*. Edited by Joanna Popielska-Grzybowska. Warsaw: Institute of Archaeology, Warsaw University.

Gundlach, Rolf, Christine Raedler, and Silke Roth. 2005. "Der ägyptische Hof im Kontakt mit seinen vorderasiatischen Nachbarn: Gesandte und Gesandtschaftswesen in der Zeit Ramses' II." Pages 39–67 in *Prozesse des Wandels in historischen Spannungsfeldern Nordostafrikas/Westasiens: Akten zum 2. Symposium des SFB 295. Mainz, 15.10.–17.10.2001*. Edited by Ursula Verhoeven et al. Würzburg: Ergon.

Habachi, Labib. 1954. "Khatâ'na-Qantîr: Importance." *ASAE* 52:443–562.

——. 1969a. *Features of the Deification of Ramesses II*. Glückstadt: Augustin.

——. 1969b. "La reine Touy, femme de Séthi I, et ses proches parents inconnus." *RdÉ* 21:27–47.

——. 1971. "The Jubilees of Ramesses II and Amenophis III with Reference to Certain Aspects of Their Celebration." *ZÄS* 97:64–72.

——. 2001. *Tell El-Dab'a I: Tell El-Dab'a and Qantir; The Site and Its Connection with Avaris and Piramesse.* Edited by Eva-Maria Engel, Peter Jánosi, and Christa Mlinar. Vienna: Österreichischen Akademie der Wissenschaften.

Habicht, Michael E., et al. 2016. "Queen Nefertari, the Royal Spouse of Pharaoh Ramses II: A Multidisciplinary Investigation of the Mummified Remains Found in Her Tomb (QV66)." *PLoS One* 11.11:e0166571. DOI: 10.1371/journal.pone.0166571.

Haeny, Gerhard. 1997. "New Kingdom 'Mortuary Temples' and 'Mansions of Millions of Years.'" Pages 86–126 in *Temples of Ancient Egypt.* Edited by Byron E. Shafer. Ithaca NY: Cornell University Press; London: Tauris.

Hageneuer, Sebastian. 2016. "Die virtuelle Rekonstruktion von Pi-Ramesse." Pages 268–72 in *Ramses: Göttlicher Herrscher am Nil.* Edited by Nicole Kehrer and Lars Petersen. Petersberg: Imhof.

Hamada, A. 1938. "A Stela from Manshiyet Es-Sadr." *ASAE* 38:217–30.

Harari, Yuval Noah. 2007. "The Concept of 'Decisive Battles' in World History." *Journal of World History* 18:251–66.

Hari, Robert. 1979. "Mout-Nefertari, épouse de Ramses II: Une descendante de l'hérétique Aï?" *Aegyptus* 59.1–2:3–7.

Haring, B. J. J. 1997. *Divine Households: Administrative and Economic Aspects of the New Kingdom Royal Memorial Temples in Western Thebes.* Egyptologische Uitgaven 12. Leiden: Nederlands Instituut voor het Nabije Oosten.

Harrell, James A. 2013. "Ornamental Stones." In *UCLA Encyclopedia of Egyptology.* https://escholarship.org/uc/item/4xk4h68c.

——. 2016. "Varieties and Sources of Sandstone Used in Ancient Egyptian Temples." *Journal of Ancient Egyptian Architecture* 1:11–37.

Harrell, James A., and Per Storemyr. 2013. "Limestone and Sandstone Quarrying in Ancient Egypt: Tools, Methods, and Analogues." *Marmora* 9:19–43.

Harris, J. R. 1961. *Lexicographical Studies in Ancient Egyptian Minerals.* Berlin: Akademie.

Hasel, Michael G. 1994. "Israel in the Merneptah Stela." *BASOR* 295:45–61.

——. 1998. *Domination and Resistance: Egyptian Military Activity in the Southern Levant, ca. 1300–1185 B.C.* PÄe 11. Leiden: Brill.

——. 2008. "Merenptah's Reference to Israel: Critical Issues for the Origin of Israel." Pages 47–59 in *Critical Issues in Early Israelite History.* Edited by Richard S. Hess, Gerald A. Klingbeil, and Paul J. Ray Jr. BBRSup 3. Winona Lake, IN: Eisenbrauns.

Haslauer, Elfriede. 2001. "Harem." Pages 76–80 in vol. 2 of *Oxford Encyclopedia of Ancient Egypt.* Edited by Donald B. Redford. 3 vols. Oxford: Oxford University Press.

Hawass, Zahi. 1997. "The Discovery of a Pair-Statue near the Pyramid of Menkaure at Giza." *MDAIK* 53:289–93.

——. 2014. "The Assassination of Ramesses III: An Egyptological Approach." *ASAE* 87:259–67.

Hawass, Zahi, et al. 2012. "Revisiting the Harem Conspiracy and Death of Ramesses III: Anthropological, Forensic, Radiological, and Genetic Study." *British Medical Journal* 345:e8268. DOI: 10.1136/bmj.e8268.

Hawass, Zahi, and Sahar N. Saleem. 2016. *Scanning the Pharaohs: CT Imaging of the New Kingdom Royal Mummies*. Cairo: American University in Cairo Press.

Heagren, Brett H. 2007. "Logistics of the Egyptian Army in Asia." Pages 139–56 in *Moving across Borders: Foreign Relations, Religion and Cultural Interactions in the Ancient Mediterranean*. Edited by Kousoulis Kousoulis Panagiotis and Konstantinos Magliveras. OLA 159. Leuven: Peeters.

——. 2010. "The Art of War in Pharaonic Egypt: An Analysis of the Tactical, Logistic, and Operational Capabilities of the Egyptian Army (Dynasties XVII–XX)." PhD diss., University of Auckland.

Healy, Mark. 1993. *Qadesh 1300 BC: Clash of the Warrior Kings*. London: Osprey.

Heinz, Susanna Constanze. 2001. *Die Feldzugsdarstellungen des Neuen Reiches: Eine Bildanalyse*. Vienna: Österreichischen Akademie der Wissenschaften.

Helck, Wolfgang. 1955. *Urkunden der 18. Dynastie*. Urkunden des Ägyptischen Altertums 4.17–20. Berlin: Akademie.

——. 1959. "Bemerkungen zu den Thronbesteigungsdaten im Neuen Reich." Pages 113–29 in vol. 3 of *Studia biblica et orientalia*. Rome: Pontificio Istituto biblico.

——. 1968. *Die Ritualszenen auf der Umfassungsmauer Ramses' II. in Karnak*. ÄA 18. Wiesbaden: Harrassowitz.

——. 1973. "Die Lage der Stadt Tunip." *UF* 5:286–88.

Hellinckx, Bart R. 1999. "A New Daughter of Ramesses II?" *GM* 173:113–22.

Hellum, Jennifer. 2020. "The Questions of the Maidservant and the Concubine: Re-Examining Egyptian Female Lexography." Pages 269–78 in *Dust, Demons and Pots: Studies in Honour of Colin A. Hope*. Edited by Ashten R. Warfe et al. OLA 289. Leuven: Peeters.

——. Forthcoming. *The Legacy of Orientalism in Egyptology*. Leiden: Brill.

Herold, Anja, 1999. *Streitwagentechnologie in der Ramses-Stadt: Bronze an Pferd und Wagen*. Forschungen in der Ramses-Stadt. Grabungen des Pelizaeus-Museums Hildesheim in Qantir-Pi-Ramesse 2. Mainz: von Zabern.

——. 2006. *Streitwagentechnologie in der Ramses-Stadt: Knäufe, Knöpfe und Scheiben aus Stein*. Forschungen in der Ramses-Stadt. Grabungen des Pelizaeus-Museums Hildesheim in Qantir-Pi-Ramesse 3. Mainz: von Zabern.

Hobsbawm, E. J., and T. O. Ranger, eds. 1983. *The Invention of Tradition*. Cambridge: Cambridge University Press.

Hodgkinson, Anna Kathrin. 2007. "The Final Phase of Per-Ramesses: The History of the City in the Light of Its Natural Environment." Pages 99–115 in *Current Research in Egyptology 2006: Proceedings of the Seventh Annual Symposium*. Oxford: Oxbow.

Hoffmeier, James K. 1996. *Israel in Egypt: The Evidence for the Authenticity of the Exodus Tradition*. Oxford: Oxford University Press.

——. 2000. "The (Israel) Stela of Merenptah." *COS* 2:40–41.

——. 2015. *Akhenaten and the Origins of Monotheism*. Oxford: Oxford University Press.

Hoffmeier, James K., Alan R. Millard, and Gary A. Rendsburg, eds. 2016. *"Did I Not Bring Israel out of Egypt?" Biblical, Archaeological, and Egyptological Perspectives on the Exodus Narratives*. BBRSup 13. Winona Lake, IN: Eisenbrauns.

Hoffner, Harry A. 1997. "Deeds of Šuppiluliuma." *COS* 1:185–92.

Hopper, Roy W. 2010. "The Monuments of Amenmesse and Seti II: A Historical Inquiry." PhD diss., University of Memphis.

Hornung, Erik. 1990. *The Valley of the Kings: Horizon of Eternity*. Translated by David Warburton. New York: Timken.

———. 1991. *The Tomb of Pharaoh Seti I*. Zurich: Artemis.

———. 1999. *The Ancient Egyptian Books of the Afterlife*. Translated by David Lorton. Ithaca, NY: Cornell University Press.

———. 2013. "Amenhotep III as Renewer of the Sed-Festival." Pages 89–94 in *Soleb VI: Hommages à Michela Schiff Giorgini*. Edited by Nathalie Beaux and Nicolas Grimal. Cairo: Institut français d'archéologie orientale.

Hornung, Erik, Rolf Krauss, and David A. Warburton. 2006. *Ancient Egyptian Chronology*. HdO 83. Leiden: Brill.

van den Hout, Theo P. J. 1994. "Der Falke und das Kücken: Der neue Pharao und der hethitische Prinz?" *ZA* 84:60–88.

———. 1997a. "Apology of Hattusili III." *COS* 1:199–204.

———. 1997b. "The Proclamation of Telipinu." *COS* 1:194–98.

Houwink ten Cate, Philo H. J. 2006. "The Sudden Return of Urḫi-Teššub to His Former Place of Banishment in Syria." Pages 1–8 in *The Life and Times of Hattusili III and Tuthaliya IV: Proceedings of a Symposium Held in Honour of J. de Roos, 12–13 December 2003, Leiden*. Edited by Theo P. J. van den Hout and Carolien H. van Zoest. Leiden: Nederlands Instituut voor het Nabije Oosten.

Hsu, Shih-Wei. 2013. "Figurative Expressions Referring to Animals in Royal Inscriptions of the 18th Dynasty." *JEH* 6:1–18.

———. 2014a. "Pharaos Körper: Tiere als bildliche Ausdrücke in den Königsinschriften." *SAK* 43:143–57.

———. 2014b. "The Use of Figurative Language concerning the Death of the King." *Archív Orientální* 82.2:201–9.

———. 2015. "Der Stier als Symbol des Altägyptischen Königtums." *AuOr* 33:243–54.

Huyeng, Christian. 2014. "'Denn er erkannte wie sehr göttlich ihre Gestalt ist': Ein Krönungstext aus Deir El-Bahari?" Pages 7–24 in *Varia Aegyptiaca I*. Edited by Andreas Finger and Christian Huyeng. Kleine Berliner Schriften zum Alten Ägypten 2. Norderstedt: Books on Demand.

Irsay-Nagy, Balázs J. 2018. "Accession to the Throne in Ancient Egypt and Modern Japan: Parallels?" Pages 233–41 in vol. 1 of *Across the Mediterranean—Along the Nile: Studies in Egyptology, Nubiology and Late Antiquity Dedicated to Lásló Török on the Occasion of His 75th Birthday*. Edited by Tamás A. Bács, Ádám Bollók, and Tivadar Vida. 2 vols. Budapest: Institute of Archaeology; Research Centre for the Humanities; Hungarian Academy of Sciences; Museum of Fine Arts.

Iskander, Sameh, and Ogden Goelet. 2015. *The Temple of Ramesses II in Abydos*. Volume 1: *Wall Scenes*. 2 vols. Atlanta: Lockwood Press.

Isler, Martin. 1987. "The Curious Luxor Obelisks." *JEA* 73:137–47.

Izre'el, Shlomo. 1997. Review of *Die ägyptisch-hethitische Korrespondenz aus Boghazköi in babylonischer und hethitischer Sprache*, by Elmar Edel. *ZA* 87:141–47.

Izre'el, Shlomo, and Itmar Singer. 1990. *The General's Letter from Ugarit: A Linguistic and Historical Reevaluation of RS 20.33 (= Ugaritica V No. 20)*. Tel Aviv: Tel Aviv University.

Jackson, Samuel. 2018. "Contrasting Representations and the Egypto-Hittite Treaty." Pages 43–58 in *Registers and Modes of Communication in the Ancient Near East: Getting the Message Across*. Edited by Kyle H. Keimer and Gillan Davis. London: Routledge.

Jacq, Christian. 1997. *Ramses: The Son of the Light*. London: Simon & Schuster.

Jakob, Stefan. 2006. "Pharaoh and His Brothers." *BMSAES* 6:12–30.

James, T. G. H. 1991. "Ramesses II: Appearance and Reality." Pages 38–49 in *Fragments of a Shattered Visage: The Proceedings of the International Symposium of Ramesses the Great*. Edited by Edward Bleiberg, Rita Freed, and Anna Kay Walker. Memphis, TN: Memphis State University.

———. 2002. *Ramesses II*. Vercelli: White Star.

Jansen-Winkeln, Karl. 2000. "Anmerkungen Zu 'Pharaos Tochter.'" *BN* 103:23–29.

Janssen, Jac. J. 1963. "La Reine Nefertari et la succession de Ramsès II par Merenptah." *CdÉ* 38.75:30–36.

Janssen, Jac. J., and Rosalind M. Janssen. 1990. *Growing Up and Getting Old in Ancient Egypt*. London: Rubicon.

Janzen, Mark. 2013. "The Iconography of Humiliation: The Depiction and Treatment of Bound Foreigners in New Kingdom Art." PhD diss., University of Memphis.

———, ed. 2021. *Five Views on the Exodus: Historicity, Chronology, and Theological Implications*. Grand Rapids: Zondervan.

Jauß, Steffen M. 2018. "Zur Konzeption des Vertrages zwischen Pharao Ramses II. und Großkönig Ḫattušili III. (1259 v. Chr.)." *Zeitschrift der Savigny-Stiftung für Rechtsgeschichte, Romanistische Abteilung* 135:21–75. DOI: 10.26498/zrgra-2018-1350105.

Joffe, Alex. 2016. "'So It Is Written, So It Shall Be Done': The Ten Commandments at 60." *The Ancient Near East Today* 4.5. https://www.asor.org/anetoday/2016/05/so-it-is-written-so-it-shall-be-done-the-ten-commandments-at-60/.

Johnson, Dominic D. P., and Dominic Tierney, 2006. *Failing to Win: Perceptions of Victory and Defeat in International Politics*. Cambridge: Harvard University Press.

Johnson, Kevin L. 2012. "Transition and Legitimation in Egypt's Nineteenth and Twentieth Dynasties: A Study of the Reigns of Siptah, Tauseret, and Sethnakht." PhD diss., University of Memphis.

Johnson, Kevin L., and Peter J. Brand. 2013. "Prince Seti-Merenptah, Chancellor Bay, and the Bark Shrine of Seti II at Karnak." *JEH* 6:19–45.

Johnson, W. Raymond. 1992. "An Asiatic Battle Scene of Tutankhamun from Thebes: A Late Amarna Antecedent of the Ramesside Battle Narrative Tradition." PhD diss., University of Chicago.

———.1994. "Hidden Kings and Queens of the Luxor Temple Cachette." *Amarna Letters* 3:128–49.

———. 1998. "Monuments and Monumental Art under Amenhotep III: Evolution and Meaning." Pages 63–94 in *Amenhotep III: Perspectives on His Reign*. Edited by Eric H. Cline and David B. O'Connor. Ann Arbor: University of Michigan Press.

———. 2009. "Tutankhamen-Period Battle Narratives at Luxor." *KMT* 20.4:20–33.

Jönsson, Bryan. 2000. "Diplomatic Signaling in the Amarna Letters." Pages 191–204, 263–64 in *Amarna Diplomacy: The Beginnings of International Re-*

lations. Edited by Raymond Cohen and Raymond Westbrook. Baltimore: Johns Hopkins University Press.

Karlshausen, Christina. 2009. *L'iconographie de la barque processionnelle divine en Égypte au nouvel empire.* OLA 182. Leuven: Peeters.

Kawai, Nozomu. 2010. "Ay versus Horemheb: The Political Situation in the Late Eighteenth Dynasty Revisited." *JEH* 3:261–92.

———. 2014. "The New Kingdom Tomb Chapel of Isisnofret at Northwest Saqqara." Pages 69–90 in *Quest for the Dream of the Pharaohs: Studies in Honour of Sakuji Yoshimura.* Edited by Jiro Kondo. Cairo: Ministry of Antiquities.

Kelly, Benjamin. 2010. "Tacitus, Germanicus and the Kings of Egypt (Tac. *Ann.* 2.59 61)." *Classical Quarterly* 60:221–37.

Kemp, Barry J. 1976. Review of *Der königliche Harim im alten Ägypten und seine Verwaltung,* by Elfriede Reiser. *JEA* 62:191–92.

———. 1978. "The Harim-Palace at Medinet El-Ghurab." *ZÄS* 105:122–33.

Kitchen, Kenneth A. 1964. "Some New Light on the Asiatic Wars of Ramesses II." *JEA* 50:47–70.

———. 1979. "Aspects of Ramesside Egypt." Pages 383–89 in *Acts: First International Congress of Egyptology, Cairo October 2–10, 1976.* Edited by Walter F. Reineke. Berlin: Akademie.

———. 1980. Review of *Ancient Egyptian Coregencies,* by William J. Murnane. *JNES* 39:168–72.

———. 1982. *Pharaoh Triumphant: The Life and Times of Ramesses II.* Warminster: Aris & Phillips.

———. 1984. "A Note on Bandeau Texts in New Kingdom Temples." Pages 547–53 in vol. 1 of *Studien zu Sprache und Religion Ägyptens: Zu Ehren von Wolfhart Westendorf, überreicht von seinen Freunden und Schülern.* Edited by Friedrich Junge. 2 vols. Göttingen: Junge.

———. 1987. "The Titularies of the Ramesside Kings as Expression of Their Ideal Kingship." *ASAE* 71:131–41.

———. 1991. "Building the Ramesseum." *CRIPEL* 13:85–93.

———. 1998. "Amenhotep III and Mesopotamia." Pages 256–61 in *Amenhotep III: Perspectives on His Reign.* Edited by Eric H. Cline and David B. O'Connor. Ann Arbor: University of Michigan Press.

———. 1999. "Notes on a Stela of Ramesses II from near Damascus." *GM* 173:133–38.

———. 2001. Review of *The Monuments of Seti I: Epigraphic, Historical and Art Historical Analysis,* by Peter J. Brand. *Journal of the Royal Asiatic Society* 11:382–84.

———. 2003. *On the Reliability of the Old Testament.* Grand Rapids: Eerdmans.

———. 2007. "Moab in Egyptian and Other Sources: Fact and Fantasy." *GM* 212:119–28.

———. 2012. "Ramesses III and the Ramesside Period." Pages 1–26 in *Ramesses III: The Life and Times of Egypt's Last Hero.* Edited by Eric H. Cline and David O'Connor. Ann Arbor: University of Michigan Press.

Kitchen, Kenneth A., and Gaballa A. Gaballa. 1969. "Ramesside Varia II." *ZÄS* 96:14–28.

Kitchen, Kenneth A., and Paul J. N. Lawrence. 2012. *Treaty, Law and Covenant in the Ancient Near East.* 3 vols. Wiesbaden: Harrassowitz.

Klemm, Rosemarie, and Dietrich D. Klemm. 2008. *Stones and Quarries in Ancient Egypt.* London: British Museum Press.

Klengel, Horst. 1992. *Syria 3000 to 300 B.C.: A Handbook of Political History.* Berlin: Akademie.

Klotz, David. 2020. "The Enigmatic Frieze of Ramesses II at Luxor Temple." Pages 49–99 in *Enigmatic Writing in the Egyptian New Kingdom I: Revealing, Transforming, and Display in Egyptian Hieroglyphs.* Edited by David Klotz and Andréas Stauder. Berlin: de Gruyter.

Knapp, A. Bernard, and Sturt W. Manning. 2016. "Crisis in Context: The End of the Late Bronze Age in the Eastern Mediterranean." *American Journal of Archaeology* 120:99–149.

Knapp, Andrew. 2015. *Royal Apologetic in the Ancient Near East.* WAWSup 4. Atlanta: SBL Press.

Köhler, Ines. 2021. "Royal Rage and Private Anger in Ancient Egypt." Pages 88–102 in *The Expression of Emotions in Ancient Egypt and Mesopotamia.* Edited by Shih-Wei Hsu and Jaume Llop Raduà. CHANE 116. Leiden: Brill.

Köpp-Junk, Heidi. 2016. "Wagons and Carts and Their Significance in Ancient Egypt." *JAEI* 9:14–58.

Kozloff, Arielle P. 1996. "A Masterpiece with Three Lives: The Vatican's Statue of Tuya." Pages 477–85 in vol. 2 of *Studies in Honor of William Kelly Simpson.* Edited by Peter der Manuelian. 2 vols. Boston: Department of Ancient Egyptian, Nubian and Near Eastern Art, Museum of Fine Arts.

Kozloff, Arielle P., Betsy Morrell Bryan, and Lawrence Michael Berman. 1992. *Egypt's Dazzling Sun: Amenhotep III and His World.* Cleveland: Cleveland Museum of Art.

Krogman, Wilton Marion, and Melvyn J. Baer. 1980. "Age at Death of Pharaohs of the New Kingdom, Determined from X-Ray Films." Pages 188–233 in *An X-Ray Atlas of the Royal Mummies.* Edited by James E. Harris, Edward F. Wente, and Ibrahim el-Nawaway. Chicago: University of Chicago Press.

Krol, Alexej A. 2005. "Origins of the *Sd*-Festival: On the History of a Hypothesis." Pages 87–90 in *Modern Trends in European Egyptology: Papers from a Session Held at the European Association of Archaeologists Ninth Annual Meeting in St. Petersburg 2003.* Edited by Amanda-Alice Maravelia. BARIS 1448. Oxford: Archaeopress.

Kuentz, Charles. 1928. *La bataille de Qadech: Les textes ("Poème de Pentaour" et "Bulletin de Qadech") et les bas-reliefs.* MIFAO 55. Cairo: Imprimerie de l'Institut français d'archéologie orientale.

———. 1971. *La face sud du massif est du pylone de Ramses II à Louxor.* Cairo: Centre de documentation et d'études sur l'ancienne Égypte.

Kuperus, Jonneke S., et al. 2020. "Diffuse Ideopathic Skeletal Hyperostosis: Etiology and Clinical Relevence." *Best Practice and Research Clinical Rheumatology* 34:101527. DOI: 10.1016/j.berh.2020.101527.

Kuschke, Arnulf. 1979. "Das Terrain der Schlacht bei Qadeš und die Anmarschwege Ramses' II: Summarium einer ebenso kritischen wie selbstkritischen Bestandsaufnahme." *ZDPV* 95:7–35.

Laboury, Dimitri. 1998. *La statuaire de Thoutmosis III: Essai d'interprétation d'un portrait royal dans son contexte historique.* Aegyptiaca Leodiensia 5. Liège: C.I.P.L.

———. 2010. *Akhénaton.* Les grands pharaons. Paris: Pygmalion.

Labuhn, Beata. 2018. "Nasser Moving Ramesses." Pages 126–49 in *Images of Egypt.* Edited by Mari Lending, Eirik Arff Gulseth Bøhn, and Tim Antsey. Oslo: Pax.

Lacovara, Peter. 1997. "Gurob and the New Kingdom 'Harim' Palace." Pages 297–306 in vol. 2 of *Ancient Egypt, the Aegean, and the Near East: Studies in Honour of Martha Rhoads Bell*. Edited by Jacke Phillips. 2 vols. San Antonio, TX: Van Siclen.

Lal, Ruby. 2008. "Mughal Palace Women." Pages 96–114 in *Servants of the Dynasty: Palace Women in World History*. Edited by Anne Walthall. Berkeley: University of California Press.

Lange, Eva. 2009. "The Sed-Festival Reliefs of Osorkon II at Bubastis: New Investigations." Pages 203–18 in *The Libyan Period in Egypt: Historical and Cultural Studies into the 21st–24th Dynasties; Proceedings of a Conference at Leiden University, 25–27 October 2007*. Edited by Gerard P. F. Broekman, R. J. Demarée, and O. E. Kaper. Egyptologische uitgaven 23. Leiden: Nederlands Instituut voor het Nabije Oosten; Leuven: Peeters.

Leblanc, Christian. 1983. "Les tombes no 58 (anonyme) et no 60 (Nebet-Taouy) de la Vallée des Reines rapport préliminaire." *ASAE* 69:29–52.

———. 1984. "Les tombes no 58 (anonyme) et no 60 (Nebet-Taouy) de la Vallée des Reines: Achèvement des dégagements et conclusions." *ASAE* 70:51–68.

———. 1986. "Ḥenout-taouy et la tombe no 73 de la Vallée des Reines." *BIFAO* 86:203–26.

———. 1988. "L'identification de la tombe de Ḥenout-Mi-Rê': Fille de Ramsès II et grande épouse royale." *BIFAO* 88:131–46.

———. 1989. *Ta Set Neferou: Une nécropole de Thèbes-Ouest et son histoire*. Volume 1: *Géographie—toponymie historique de l'exploration scientifique du site*. Cairo: Nubar.

———. 1993a. "Isis-Nofret, grande épouse de Ramsès II: La reine, sa famille et Nofretari." *BIFAO* 93:313–33.

———. 1993b. "Les sources grecques et les colosses de Ramsès Rê-En-Hekaou et de Touy, au Ramesseum." *Memnonia* 4–5:71–101.

———. 1999. *Nefertari, "l'aimée-de-Mout": Épouses, filles et fils de Ramsès II*. Champollion. Monaco: Rocher.

———. 2009a. "La tombe de Ramsès II (KV.7): De la fouille archéologique à l'identification du programme iconographique." *Memnonia* 20:195–211.

———. 2009b. *Reines du Nil au Nouvel empire*. Paris: Introuvables.

———. 2010. "The Tomb of Ramesses II (KV 7): From Its Archaeological Excavation to the Identification of Its Iconographical Program." *MDAIK* 66:161–74.

———. 2011. "Ousermaâtrê Setepenrê 'Soleil-des-Princes': À propos de l'étude d'un apprenti-sculpteur ramesside." Pages 293–300 in *Ramesside Studies in Honour of K. A. Kitchen*. Edited by Mark Collier and Steven Snape. Bolton: Rutherford.

———. 2019. *Ramsès II et le Ramesseum: De la splendeur au déclin d'un temple de millions d'années*. Paris: L'Harmattan.

Leblanc, Christian, and Daniel Esmoingt. 1999. "Le 'jeune Memnon': Un colosse de Ramsès II nommé 'Ousermaâtrê-Setepenrê-Aimé-d'Amon-Rê.'" *Memnonia* 10:79–100.

———. 2014. "Le colosse de Touy, mère de Ramsès II, retrouve sa place dans la première cour du Ramesseum." *Memnonia* 25:89–105.

Leblanc, Christian, and Gihane Zaki. 2010. *Les temples de millions d'années et le pouvoir royal à Thèbes au Nouvel Empire: Sciences et nouvelles technologies appliquées à l'archéologie*. Memnonia Cahier Supplémentaire 2. Cairo: Dar el-Kutub.

Leclant, Jean, Marie-Ange Bonhême, and Annie Forgeau. 1988. *Pharaon: Les Secrets du Pouvoir*. Paris: Armand Colin.

Lekov, Teodor. 2017. "The Death of the Egyptian King." *Journal of Egyptological Studies* 5:30–44.

Lending, Mari, Eirik Arff Gulseth Bøhn, and Tim Antsey. 2018. *Images of Egypt*. Oslo: Pax.

Leprohon, Ronald J. 2010. "Patterns of Royal Name-Giving." In *UCLA Encyclopedia of Egyptology*. https://escholarship.org/uc/item/51b2647c.

———. 2013. *The Great Name: Ancient Egyptian Royal Titulary*. WAW 33. Atlanta: Society of Biblical Literature.

———. 2015. "Ideology and Propaganda." Pages 309–27 in *A Companion to Ancient Egyptian Art*. Edited by Melinda K. Hartwig. Chichester: Wiley Blackwell.

Levy, Eythan. 2017. "A Note on the Geographical Distribution of New Kingdom Egyptian Inscriptions from the Levant." *JAEI* 14:14–21.

Levy, Thomas E., Thomas Schneider, and William H. C. Propp. 2015. *Israel's Exodus in Transdisciplinary Perspective: Text, Archaeology, Culture, and Geoscience*. Cham: Springer.

Lewis, Reina. 2004. *Rethinking Orientalism: Women, Travel, and the Ottoman Harem*. New Brunswick, NJ: Rutgers University Press.

Lichtheim, Miriam. 1973. *Ancient Egyptian Literature: A Book of Readings*. Volume 1: *The Old and Middle Kingdoms*. Los Angeles: University of California Press.

———. 1976. *Ancient Egyptian Literature: A Book of Readings*. Volume 2: *The New Kingdom*. Los Angeles: University of California Press.

Liesegang, Diana. 2014. "The Phenomenon of 'Personal Religion' in the Ramesside Period, from the 'Poem' of Ramses II through to the Prayers of Ramses III." Pages 97–101 in *Cult and Belief in Ancient Egypt: Proceedings of the Fourth International Congress for Young Egyptologists, 25–27 September 2012, Sofia*. Edited by Teodor Lekov and Emil Buzov. Sofia: East West.

Lilyquist, Christine. 2003. *The Tomb of Three Foreign Wives of Tuthmosis III*. New Haven: Yale University Press.

Littauer, M. A., and J. H. Crouwel 1985. *Chariots and Related Equipment from the Tomb of Tutʿankhamūn*. Tutʿankhamūn's Tomb Series 8. Oxford: Griffith Institute.

———. 1996. "Robert Drews and the Role of Chariotry in Bronze Age Greece." *OJA* 15:297–305.

Liverani, Mario. 1982. "Pharaoh's Letters to Rib-Adda." Pages 3–13 in *Three Amarna Essays*. Malibu, CA: Undena.

———. 1990. "Hattushili alle prese con la propaganda ramesside." *Or* 59:207–17.

———. 2000. "The Great Power's Club." Pages 15–27, 237–39 in *Amarna Diplomacy: The Beginnings of International Relations*. Edited by Raymond Cohen and Raymond Westbrook. Baltimore: Johns Hopkins University Press.

———. 2001. *International Relations in the Ancient Near East 1600–1100 BC*. New York: Palgrave Macmillan.

———. 2013. "Under Northern Eyes: Egyptian Art and Ceremony as Received by Babylonians, Hurrians, and Hittites." Pages 238–43 in *Decorum and Experience: Essays on Ancient Culture for John Baines*. Edited by Elizabeth Frood and Angela McDonald. Oxford: Griffith Institute.

Llagostera Cuenca, Esteban. 1998. "The Mummy of a Daughter of Ramesses II in Madrid." Pages 691–96 in *Proceedings of the Seventh International Congress of Egyptologists, Cambridge, 3–9 September 1995.* Edited by C. J. Eyre. OLA 82. Leuven: Peeters.

Lloyd, Allan B. 2019. "Ramesses II in Legend." Pages 1–12 in *Some Organic Readings in Narrative, Ancient and Modern: Gathered and Originally Presented as a Book for John.* Edited by Ian Repath and Fritz-Gregor Herrmann. Ancient Narrative Supplementum 27. Groningen: Barkuis & Groningen University Library.

Loffet, Henri-Charles. 1999. "La stèle de Ramsès II en provenance de Tyr." *National Museum News* 9:2–5.

———. 2000. "Derechef Ramsès II, Tyr et la Stèle 2030 du Musée des Antiquités Nationales Libanaises de Beyrouth." *National Museum News* 11:2–7.

———. 2009. "Les reliefs de Ramsès II." Pages 195–239 in *Le site de Nahr El-Kalb.* Edited by Anne-Marie Maïla-Afeiche. Beirut: Ministère de la Culture, Direction Générale des Antiquités.

Lurson, Benoît. 2001. *Lire l'image Égyptienne: Les "Salles du Trésor" du grand temple d'Abou Simbel.* Paris: Geuthner.

———. 2005. "La Conception du décor d'un temple au début du règne de Ramsès II: Analyse du deuxième register de la moitié sud du mur ouest de a grande salle hypostyle de Karnak." *JEA* 91:107–24.

———. 2015. "Les scenes de la naissance merveilleuse de Ramsès II du temple contigu au Ramesseum: Réflexions autour d'un cycle iconographique novateu." Pages 113–38 in *Les naissances merveilleuses en Orient: Jacques Vermeylen (1942–2014) in memoriam.* Edited by Christian Cannuyer and Catherine Vialle. Acta Orientalia Belgica 28. Brussels: Académie royale des Sciences, des Lettres et des Beaux-Arts de Belgique.

———. 2016. *A Perfect King: Aspects of Ancient Egyptian Royal Ideology of the New Kingdom.* Paris: Geuthner.

———, ed. 2017a. *De la mère du roi à l'épouse du dieu/Von der Königsmutter zur Gottesgemahlin: Première synthèse des résultats des fouilles du temple de Touy et de la tombe de Karomama/Erste Synthese des Ausgrabungsergebnisse des Tempels von Tuja und des Grabes von Karomama.* Connaissance de l'Égypte ancienne 18. Brussels: Safran.

———. 2017b. "Historique et problématiques des fouilles du temple de Touy." Pages 11–26 in *De la mère du roi à l'épouse du dieu/Von der Königsmutter zur Gottesgemahlin: Première synthèse des résultats des fouilles du temple de Touy et de la tombe de Karomama/Erste Synthese des Ausgrabungsergebnisse des Tempels von Tuja und des Grabes von Karomama.* Edited by Benoît Lurson. Connaissance de l'Égypte Ancienne 18. Brussels: Safran.

Lynn, John A. 2002. *The French Wars 1667–1714: The Sun King at War.* Oxford: Osprey.

MacDonald, Sally, and Michael Rice. 2003. *Consuming Ancient Egypt.* Encounters with Ancient Egypt. London: UCL Press.

Magen, Barbara. 2011. *Steinerne Palimpseste: Zur Wiederverwendung von Statuen durch Ramses II. und seine Nachfolger.* Wiesbaden: Harrassowitz.

Mahfouz, Naguib. 2016. *Before the Throne.* Translated by Raymond T. Stock. Cairo: American University in Cairo Press.

Maïla-Afeiche, Anne-Marie. 2009. *Le site de Nahr El-Kalb.* Bulletin d'archéologie et d'architecture Libanaises, Hors-Série 5. Beirut: Ministère de la Culture, Direction Générale des Antiquités.

Mailer, Norman. 1983. *Ancient Evenings.* Boston: Little, Brown & Company.

Manassa, Colleen. 2003. *The Great Karnak Inscription of Merneptah: Grand Strategy in the 13th Century BC.* YES 5. New Haven: Yale Egyptological Seminar; Oxford: Oxbow.

Manouvrier, Colette J. 1996. *Ramsès le dieu et les dieux ou la théologie politique de Ramsès II.* 2 vols. Villeneuve d'Ascq: Presses universitaire du Septentrion.

de Maret, Pierre. 2011. "Divine Kings." Pages 1059–67 in *The Oxford Handbook of the Archaeology of Ritual and Religion.* Edited by Timothy Insoll. Oxford: Oxford University Press.

Mariette, Auguste. 1869–1880. *Abydos: Description des fouilles exécutées sur l'emplacement de cette ville.* 2 vols. Paris: Franck.

Martin, Geoffrey T., Jacobus van Dijk, Christopher J. Eyre, and Kenneth J. Frazer. 2016. *Tutankhamun's Regent: Scenes and Texts from the Memphite Tomb of Horemheb for Students of Egyptian Art, Iconography, Architecture, and History.* EES Excavation Memoir 111. London: Egypt Exploration Society.

Martin, Geoffrey T., Jacobus van Dijk, and David A. Aston. 1997. *The Tomb of Tia and Tia: A Royal Monument of the Ramesside Period in the Memphite Necropolis.* EES Excavation Memoir 58. London: Egypt Exploration Society.

Martinez, Philippe. 2009. "Une commande royale pour le Ramesseum: Une stèle inédite de Ramsés II au Gebel Es-Silsileh." *Memnonia* 20:133–72.

Maspero, Gaston. 1904. *History of Egypt, Chaldea, Syria, Babylonia, and Assyria.* Edited by A. H. Sayce. Translated by M. L. McClure. 13 vols. London: Grolier Society.

Masquelier-Loorius, Julie. 2013. *Séthi Ier et le début de la XIXe dynastie.* Paris: Pygmalion.

Mathieu, Bernard. 2000. "L'énigme du recrutement des 'enfants du kap': Une solution?" *GM* 177:41–48.

Matić, Uroš. 2019. *Body and Frames of War in New Kingdom Egypt: Violent Treatment of Enemies and Prisoners.* Philippika 134. Wiesbaden: Harrassowitz.

———. 2020. *Ethnic Identities in the Land of the Pharaohs: Past and Present Approaches in Egyptology.* Cambridge: Cambridge University Press.

———. 2021. *Violence and Gender in Ancient Egypt.* New York: Routledge.

Mauer, G. 1985. "Die Schlacht von Kadesch nach den Quellen aus Boghazköi." *Dielheimer Baltter zum Alten Testament* 21:86–93.

McCarthy, Heather Lee. 2002. "The Osiris Nefertari: A Case Study of Decorum, Gender, and Regeneration." *JARCE* 39:173–95.

———. 2005. "Place of the Beautiful Ones: When Egyptian Queens Got Elaborate Tombs of Their Own." *Archaeology Odyssey* 8.2:14–25, 48.

———. 2007. "The Beit El-Wali Temple of Ramesses II: A Cosmological Interpretation." Pages 127–45 in vol. 2 of *The Archaeology and Art of Ancient Egypt: Essays in Honor of David B. O'Connor.* Edited by Zahi A. Hawass and Janet E. Richards. 2 vols. Cairo: Supreme Council of Antiquities.

———. 2008. "Rules of Decorum and Expressions of Gender Fluidity in Tawosret's Tomb." Pages 83–11 in *Sex and Gender in Ancient Egypt: "Don Your*

Wig for a Joyful Hour." Edited by Carolyn Graves-Brown. Swansea: Classical Press of Wales.

——. 2011. "Queenship, Cosmography, and Regeneration: The Decorative Programs and Architecture of Ramesside Royal Women's Tombs." PhD diss., New York University.

McClain, Joseph Brett. 2007. "Restoration Inscriptions and the Tradition of Monumental Restoration." PhD diss., University of Chicago.

McDonald, Angela. 2002. "Animal Metaphor in the Egyptian Determinative System." PhD diss., Oxford University.

McDonald, John K. 1996. *House of Eternity: The Tomb of Nefertari.* Los Angeles: Getty Conservation Institute; J. Paul Getty Museum.

Meier, Samuel A. 2000. "Diplomacy and International Marriages." Pages 165–73, 259–62 in *Amarna Diplomacy: The Beginnings of International Relations.* Edited by Raymond Cohen and Raymond Westbrook. Baltimore: Johns Hopkins University Press.

Meltzer, Edmund S. 2001. "Children of the Kap: Upwardly Mobile, Talented Youth in Ancient Egypt." *Seshat* 5:20–26.

Meyer, Christine. 1984. "Zum Titel 'Ḥmt Njswt' bei den Töchtern Amenophis' III. und IV. und Ramses' II." *SAK* 11:253–63.

Middleton, Russell. 1962. "Brother-Sister and Father-Daughter Marriage in Ancient Egypt." *American Sociological Review* 27:603–11.

Miller, Jared L. 2007. "Amarna Age Chronology and the Identity of Nibḫururiya in the Light of a Newly Reconstructed Hittite Text." *AoF* 34:252–93.

——. 2008. "The Rebellion of Hatti's Syrian Vassals and Egypt's Meddling in Amurru." *Studi micenei ed egeo-anatolici* 50:533–54.

Mitchell, Peter 2018. *The Donkey in Human History: An Archaeological Perspective.* Oxford: Oxford University Press.

Monnier, Franck. 2020. "L'obélisque géant décrit sur le papyrus Anastasi I: Révision du problème." *Cahiers Caribéens d'égyptologie* 24–25:179–202.

Montserrat, Dominic. 2000. *Akhenaten: History, Fantasy and Ancient Egypt.* London: Routledge.

Moon, Brenda E. 2006. *More Usefully Employed: Amelia B. Edwards, Writer, Traveller and Campaigner for Ancient Egypt.* EES Occasional Publications 15. London: Egypt Exploration Society.

Moran, William L. 1992. *The Amarna Letters.* Baltimore: Johns Hopkins University Press.

Morkot, Robert G. 2007. "War and Economy: The International 'Arms Trade' in the Late Bronze Age and After." Pages 169–95 in *Egyptian Stories: A British Egyptological Tribute to Alan B. Lloyd on the Occasion of His Retirement.* Edited by Thomas Schneider and Kasia Szpakowska. AOAT 347. Münster: Ugarit-Verlag.

Morris, Ellen F. 2005. *The Architecture of Imperialism: Military Bases and the Evolution of Foreign Policy in Egypt's New Kingdom.* PAe 22. Leiden: Brill.

——. 2010. "The Pharaoh and Pharaonic Office." Pages 201–17 in vol. 1 of *A Companion to Ancient Egypt.* Edited by Alan B. Lloyd. 2 vols. Chichester: Wiley-Blackwell.

——. 2018. *Ancient Egyptian Imperialism.* Chichester: Wiley Blackwell.

Morschauser, Scott N. 1988. "Using History: Reflections on the Bentresh Stela." *SAK* 15.202–23.

Moser, Stephanie. 2006. *Wondrous Curiosities: Ancient Egypt at the British Museum.* Chicago: University of Chicago Press.

———. 2012. *Designing Antiquity: Owen Jones, Ancient Egypt and the Crystal Palace.* New Haven: Yale University Press.

———. 2019. *Painting Antiquity: Ancient Egypt in the Art of Lawrence Alma-Tadema, Edward Poynter and Edwin Long.* Oxford: Oxford University Press.

Müller, Matthias. 2004. "Der Turiner Streikpapyrus (PTurin 1880)." Pages 165–84 in *Texte zum Rechts- und Wirtschaftsleben.* Edited by Gernot Wilhelm and Bernd Janowski. Gütersloh: Gütersloher Verlagshaus.

———. 2005. "Die Krönungsinschrift der Hatschepsut." Pages 197–211 in *Staatsverträge, Herrscherinschriften und andere Dokumente zur politischen Geschichte.* Edited by Bernd Janowski and Gernot Wilhelm. Gütersloh: Gütersloher Verlagshaus.

———. 2010. *Akkadisch in Keilschrifttexten aus Ägypten: Deskriptive Grammatik einer Interlanguage des späten zweiten vorchristlichen Jahrtausends anhand der Ramses-Briefe.* AOAT 373. Münster: Ugarit-Verlag.

Murnane, William J. 1975. "The Earlier Reign of Ramesses II and His Coregency with Seti I." *JNES* 34:153–90.

———. 1977. *Ancient Egyptian Coregencies.* SAOC 40. Chicago: Oriental Institute of the University of Chicago.

———. 1990. *The Road to Kadesh: A Historical Interpretation of the Battle Reliefs of King Sety I at Karnak.* 2nd ed. SAOC 42. Chicago: University of Chicago Press.

———. 1995a. *Texts from the Amarna Period in Egypt.* WAW 5. Atlanta: Scholars Press.

———. 1995b. "The Kingship of the Nineteenth Dynasty: A Study in the Resilience of an Institution." Pages 185–217 in *Ancient Egyptian Kingship.* Edited by David O'Connor and David P. Silverman. PAe 9. Leiden: Brill.

———. 2000. "Soleb Renaissance: Reconsidering the Temple of Nebmaatre in Nubia." *Amarna Letters* 4:6–19.

Mynářová, Jana. 2009. "From Amarna to Ḫattušaš: Epistolary Traditions in the Amarna and Ramesside Correspondence." Pages 111–17 in *My Things Changed Things: Social Development and Cultural Exchange in Prehistory, Antiquity, and the Middle Ages.* Edited by Petra Maříková Vlčková, Jana Mynářová, and Martin Tomášek. Prague: Charles University in Prague, Faculty of Arts.

———. 2011. "Wretched Fallen One of Ḫatti or Hero? An Image of the Hittite King in the Egyptian Sources." Pages 235–47 in *Egypt and the Near East: The Crossroads; Proceedings of an International Conference on the Relations of Egypt and the Near East in the Bronze Age, Prague, September 1–3, 2010.* Edited by Jana Mynářová. Prague: Czech Institute of Egyptology.

———. 2014. "Lost in Translation: An Egyptological Perspective on the Egyptian-Hittite Treaties." *Annals of the Náprstek Museum Praha* 35.2:3–8.

Na'aman, Nadav. 2006. "Did Ramesses II Wage Campaign against the Land of Moab?" *GM* 209:63–69.

Nadel, Alan. 1993. "God's Law and the Wide Screen: The Ten Commandments as Cold War 'Epic.'" *Proceedings of the Modern Language Association* 108:415–30.

Navrátilová, Hana. 2016. "Khaemwaset in Dahshur: The Prince and the Stones." Pages 259–66 in *Rich and Great: Studies in Honour of Anthony J. Spalinger on the Occasion of His 70th Feast of Thot*. Edited by Renata Landgráfová and Jana Mynářová. Prague: Charles University in Prague, Faculty of Arts.

——. 2019. "Self-Presentation in the Eighteenth Dynasty." Pages 139–57 in *Living Forever: Self-Presentation in Ancient Egypt*. Edited by Hussein Bassir. Cairo: American University in Cairo Press.

Nefedkin, Alexander. 2005. "On Typical Tactics of Oriental Chariot Battle." *Ancient History Bulletin* 19.1–2:1–14.

Nelson, Harold H. 1943. "The Naval Battle Pictured at Medinet Habu." *JNES* 2:40–55.

Nicholson, R. W., and Georg Gerster. 1966. "Saving the Ancient Temples at Abu Simbel." *National Geographic* 129:694–742.

Nielsen, Nicky 2018. "Sety in Nubia: The Irem Rebellion." *Ancient Egypt Magazine* 109(19.1), 14–19.

Nims, Charles F. 1976. "Ramesseum Sources of Medinet Habu Reliefs." Pages 169–75 in *Studies in Honor of George R. Hughes: January 12, 1977*. Edited by Janet H. Johnson and Edward F. Wente. SAOC 39. Chicago: Oriental Institute of the University of Chicago.

Nishimoto, Shinichi. 2014. "The Mathematics of the Ideal Obelisk." Pages 91–94 in *Quest for the Dream of the Pharaohs: Studies in Honour of Sakuji Yoshimura*. Edited by Mamdouh El-Damati and Jiro Kondo. Cairo: Ministry of Antiquities.

Noerdlinger, Henry S. 1956. *Moses and Egypt: The Documentation to the Motion Picture* The Ten Commandments. Los Angeles: University of Southern California Press.

Nord, Del. 1970. "*Hkrt-Nswt* = 'Kings's Concubine'?" *Serapis* 2:1–16.

——. 1975. Review of *Der königliche Harim im alten Ägypten und seine Verwaltung*, by Elfriede Reiser. *JNES* 34:142–45.

——. 1981. "The Term *Hnr*: 'Harem' or 'Musical Performers'?" Pages 137–45 in *Studies in Ancient Egypt, the Aegean, and the Sudan: Essays in Honor of Dows Dunham on the Occasion of His 90th Birthday, June 1, 1980*. Edited by Whitney M. Davis and William Kelly Simpson. Boston: Department of Egyptian and Ancient Near Eastern Art, Museum of Fine Arts.

Nuzzolo, Massimiliano. 2017. "Human and Divine: The King's Two Bodies and the Royal Paradigm in Fifth Dynasty Egypt." Pages 185–214 in *Constructing Authority: Prestige, Reputation and the Perception of Power in Egyptian Kingship, Budapest, May 12–14, 2016; 8. Symposion zur Ägyptischen Königsideologie/8th Symposium on Egyptian Royal Ideology*. Edited by Tamás A. Bács and Horst Beinlich. Wiesbaden: Harrassowitz.

Obsomer, Claude. 2010. "Classical Accounts of Heliopolitan Obelisks." Pages 48–53 in *Heliopolis*. Edited by Marie-Cécile Bruwier and Anne van Loo. Brussels: Fonds Mercator.

——. 2012a. "L'épisode du couronnement de Ramsès II dans l'inscription dédicatoire d'Abydos." Pages 283–94 in *Regards sur l'orientalisme belge: Suivis d'études égyptologiques et orientales; Mélanges offerts à Claude Vandersleyen*. Edited by Christian Cannuyer, René Lebrun, and Daniel De Smet. Brussels: Société Belge d'Etudes Orientales.

——. 2012b. *Ramsès II: Abou Simbel, Louxor, Néfertary, Qadech*. Paris: Pygmalion.

——. 2016. "La bataille de Qadech de Ramsès II: Les n'arin, sekou tepy et questions d'itinéraires." Pages 81–170 in *De la Nubie à Qadech: La guerre dans* l'Égypte ancienne. Edited by Christina Karlshausen and Claude Obsomer. Brussels: Safran.

———. 2017. "Un nouveau titre pour la mère de Ramsès II: L'inscription du bloc de calcaire découvert en 2015 dans le temple de Touy adjacent au Ramesseum." Pages 42–50 in *De la mère du roi à l'épouse du dieu/Von der Königsmutter zur Gottesgemahlin: Première synthèse des résultats des fouilles du temple de Touy et de la tombe de Karomama/Erste Synthese des Ausgrabungsergebnisse des Tempels von Tuja und des Grabes von Karomama*. Edited by Benoît Lurson. Brussels: Safran.

Ockinga, Boyo G. 1987. "On the Interpretation of the Kadesh Record." *CdÉ* 62.123–124:38–48.

O'Connor, David. 2009. *Abydos: Egypt's First Pharaohs and the Cult of Osiris*. London: Thames & Hudson.

———. 2010. "The King's Palace at Malkata and the Purpose of the Royal Harem." Pages 55–80 in vol. 2 of *Millions of Jubilees: Studies in Honor of David P. Silverman*. Edited by Zahi Hawass and Jennifer Houser Wegner. Cairo: Supreme Council of Antiquities.

O'Connor, David, and Eric H. Cline. 1998. *Amenhotep III: Perspectives on His Reign*. University of Michigan Press.

O'Connor, David, and David P. Silverman. 1995. *Ancient Egyptian Kingship*. PAe 9. Leiden: Brill.

Onstine, Suzanne L. 2005. *The Role of the Chantress (Šmꜥyt) in Ancient Egypt*. BARIS 1401. Oxford: Archaeopress.

———. 2016. "Women's Participation in the Religious Hierarchy of Ancient Egypt." Pages 218–28 in *Women in Antiquity: Real Women across the Ancient World*. Edited by Stephanie Lynn Budin and Jean MacIntosh Turfa. London: Routledge.

Oren, Eliezer D., ed. 2000. *The Sea Peoples and Their World: A Reassessment*. University Museum Monograph 108. Philadelphia: University Museum, University of Pennsylvania.

Orrison, Katherine. 1999. *Written in Stone: Making Cecil B. DeMille's Epic* The Ten Commandments. Vestal, NY: Vestal Press.

Osing, Jürgen. 1977. *Der Tempel Sethos' I. in Gurna*. Volume 1: *Die Reliefs und Inschriften*. Sonderschrift Deutsches Archäologisches Institut, Abteilung Kairo 20. Mainz: von Zabern.

Otten, Heinrich. 1988. *Die Bronzetafel aus Bogazköy: Ein Staatsvertrag Tuthalijas IV*. Studien zu den Bogazköy-Texten 1. Wiesbaden: Harrassowitz.

Parkinson, R. B. 1991. *Voices from Ancient Egypt: An Anthology of Middle Kingdom Writings*. London: British Museum Press.

Parr, Peter J. 1991. "ISIS Archaeology Bulletin: Number Three—The Tell Nebi Mend Project; A Progress Report on the Institute of Archaeology's Excavations at Ancient Kadesh-on-the-Orontes in Syria." *Journal of the Ancient Chronology Forum* 4:78–85.

Payraudeau, Frédéric. 2020. "Une nouvelle fille-épouse de Ramsès II." *BIFAO* 120:253–64.

Pecchioli Daddi, Franca, and Maria Cristina Guidotti. 2005. *Narrare gli eventi: Atti del convegno degli egittologi e degli orientalisti italiani in margine alla mostra "la battaglia di Qadesh."* Studia Asiana 3. Rome: Herder.

Peden, A. J. 1994a. *Egyptian Historical Inscriptions of the Twentieth Dynasty*. Documenta Mundi: Aegyptiaca 3. Jonsered: Åströms.

———. 1994b. *The Reign of Ramesses IV*. Warminster: Aris & Phillips.

Peet, Thomas Eric. 1930. *The Great Tomb-Robberies of the Twentieth Egyptian Dynasty*. 2 vols. Oxford: Clarendon.

Peirce, Leslie P. 1993. *The Imperial Harem: Women and Sovereignty in the Ottoman Empire*. Oxford: Oxford University Press.

———. 2008. "Beyond Harem Walls: Ottoman Royal Women and the Exercise of Power." Pages 81–95 in *Servants of the Dynasty: Palace Women in World History*. Edited by Anne Walthall. Berkley: University of California Press.

Pereyra De Fidanza, Violeta. 2000. "A Queen Rewarding a Noblewoman in TT49." Pages 173–84 in *Les civilisations du bassin Méditerranéen: Hommages à Joachim Śliwa*. Edited by Krzysztof M. Ciałowicz and Janusz A. Ostrowski. Kraków: Université Jagaellonne, Institut d'Archéologie.

Peters-Destéract, Madeleine. 2003. *Abou Simbel, à la gloire de Ramsès*. Monaco: Rocher.

Petersen, Lars, and Nicole Kehrer. 2016. *Ramses: Göttlicher Herrscher am Nil*. Petersberg: Imhof.

Pézard, Maurice. 1931. *Qadesh: Mission à Tell Nebi Mend 1921–1922*. Paris: Geuthner.

Picton, Jan. 2016. "Living and Working in a New Kingdom 'Harem Town.'" Pages 229–42 in *Women in Antiquity: Real Women across the Ancient World*. Edited by Stephanie Lynn Budin and Jean MacIntosh Turfa. London: Routledge.

Pinch, Geraldine. 2006. *Magic in Ancient Egypt*. 2nd ed. London: British Museum Press.

Podany, Amanda H. 2012. *Brotherhood of Kings: How International Relations Shaped the Ancient Near East*. Oxford: Oxford University Press.

Politi, Janet. 2001. "Gurob: The Papyri and the 'Burnt Groups.'" *GM* 182:107–11.

Polz, Daniel. 1986. "Die Särge des (Pa-)Ramessu." *MDAIK* 42:145–66.

Posener, Georges. 1960. *De la divinité du Pharaon*. Cahiers de la Société Asiatique 15. Paris: Imprimerie Nationale.

Pouwels, Clément. 2014. "Les métamorphoses littéraires de Sésostris." Pages 236–41 in *Sésostris III: Pharaon de légende*. Edited by Guillemette Andreu-Lanoë, Fleur Morfoisse, and Clément Pouwels. Gand: Snoeck.

Prakash, Tara C. 2011. "King and Coward? The Representation of the Foreign Ruler in the Battle of Kadesh Reliefs." *JSSEA* 38:141–71.

Price, Campbell. 2011. "Ramesses, 'King of Kings': On the Context and Interpretation of Royal Colossi." Pages 403–11 in *Ramesside Studies in Honour of K. A. Kitchen*. Edited by Mark Collier and Steven Snape. Bolton: Rutherford.

Pusch, Edgar B. 1991. "Recent Work at Northern Piramesse: Results of Excavations by the Pelizaeus-Museum, Hildesheim, at Qantir." Pages 199–220 in *Fragments of a Shattered Visage: The Proceedings of the International Symposium of Ramesses the Great*. Edited by Edward Bleiberg, Rita Freed, and Anna Kay Walker. Memphis, TN: Memphis State University.

Pusch, Edgar B., and Helmut Becker. 2017. *Fenster in Die Vergangenheit: Einblicke in die Struktur der Ramses-Stadt durch magnetische Prospektion und Grabung*. 2 vols. Forschungen in der Ramses-Stadt. Grabungen des Pelizaeus-Museums Hildesheim in Qantir-Pi-Ramesse 9. Hildesheim: Gerstenberg.

Pusch, Edgar B., Helmut Becker, and Jörg Fassbinder. 1999. "Palast – Tempel – auswärtiges Amt? Oder: Sind Nilschlammauern magnetisch zu erfassen?" *A&L* 9:135–53.

Pusch, Edgar B., and Henning Franzmeier. 2016. "Pi-Ramesse." https://www.bibelwissenschaft.de/stichwort/32607/.

Pusch, Edgar B., and Anja Herold. 1999. *Streitwagentechnologie in der Ramses-Stadt: Bronze an Pferd und Wagen*. Forschungen in der Ramses-Stadt. Grabungen des Pelizaeus-Museums Hildesheim in Qantir-Pi-Ramesse 2. Mainz: von Zabern.

Pusch, Edgar B., and Stefan Jakob. 2003. "Der Zipfel des diplomatischen Archivs Ramses' II." *A&L* 13:143–53.

de Putter, Thierry. 1997. "Ramsès II, géologue? Un commentaire de la stèle de Manshiyet es-Sadr, dite 'de l'an 8.'" *ZÄS* 124:131–41.

Raedler, Christine. 2017. "Creating Authority: The High Priest of Osiris Wenennefer and a Special Deification of Ramesses II." Pages 215–40 in *Constructing Authority: Prestige, Reputation and the Perception of Power in Egyptian Kingship, Budapest, May 12–14, 2016; 8. Symposion zur Ägyptischen Königsideologie/8th Symposium on Egyptian Royal Ideology*. Edited by Tamás A. Bács and Horst Beinlich. Wiesbaden: Harrassowitz.

Ragazzoli, Chloé. 2016. "'The Pen Promoted My Station': Scholarship and Distinction in New Kingdom Biographies." Pages 153–78 in *Problems of Canonicity and Identity Formation in Ancient Egypt and Mesopotamia*. Edited by Kim Ryholt and Gojko Barjamovic. Copenhagen: Museum Tusculanum Press; Department of Cross-Cultural and Regional Studies, University of Copenhagen.

Rainey, Anson F. 1973. "Reflections on the Battle of Qedesh." *UF* 5:280–82.

———. 2015. *The El-Amarna Correspondence: A New Edition of the Cuneiform Letters from the Site of El-Amarna Based on Collations of All Extant Tablets*. Edited by William M. Schniedewind and Zipora Cochavi-Rainey. 2 vols. HdO 110. Leiden: Brill.

Rashwan, Hany. 2014. "A New Rhetorical Reading of the Zigzag Stela of Ramses II (Tanis V, Face C)." *Newsletter of the Society for the Study of Egyptian Antiquities* 2014.2:1–6.

Redford, Donald B. 1971. "The Earliest Years of Ramesses II, and the Building of the Ramesside Court at Luxor." *JEA* 57:110–19.

———. 1973. "New Light on the Asiatic Campaigning of Horemheb." *BASOR* 211:36–49.

———. 1986. *Pharaonic King-Lists, Annals and Day-Books: A Contribution to the Study of the Egyptian Sense of History*. Mississauga: Benben.

———. 1992. *Egypt, Canaan, and Israel in Ancient Times*. Princeton: Princeton University Press.

———. 1995. "The Concept of Kingship during the Eighteenth Dynasty." Pages 157–84 in *Ancient Egyptian Kingship*. Edited by David O'Connor and David P. Silverman. PAe 9. Leiden: Brill.

———. 2003. *The Wars in Syria and Palestine of Thutmose III*. CHANE 16. Leiden: Brill.

———. 2018. *The Medinet Habu Records of the Foreign Wars of Ramesses III*. CHANE 91. Leiden: Brill.

Redford, Susan. 2002. *The Harem Conspiracy: The Murder of Ramesses III*. Dekalb: Northern Illinois University Press.

Reeve, Jez, Max Adams, T. I Molleson, and Margaret Cox. 1993. *The Spitalfields Project I: The Archaeology across the Styx*. York: Council for British Archaeology.

Reeves, Nicholas, and Richard H. Wilkinson. 1996. *The Complete Valley of the Kings: Tombs and Treasures of Egypt's Greatest Pharaohs*. London: Thames & Hudson.

Reid, Donald M. 2002. *Whose Pharaohs? Archaeology, Museums, and Egyptian National Identity from Napoleon to World War I*. Los Angeles: University of California Press.

——. 2015. *Contesting Antiquity in Egypt: Archaeologies, Museums and the Struggle for Identities from World War I to Nasser*. Cairo: American University in Cairo Press.

Reiser, Elfriede. 1972. *Der königliche Harim im alten Ägypten und seine Verwaltung*. Vienna: Notring.

Revez, Jean. 2003. "The Metaphorical Use of the Kinship Term *sn* 'Brother.'" *JARCE* 40:123–31.

Revez, Jean, and Peter J. Brand. 2012. "Le programme décoratif des colonnes de la grande salle hypostyle de Karnak: Bilan de la Mission Canado-Américaine de 2011." *BSFÉ* 184:10–38.

——. 2015. "The Notion of Prime Space in the Layout of the Column Decoration in the Great Hypostyle Hall at Karnak." *Cahiers de Karnak* 15:253–310.

Ricke, Herbert, George R. Hughes, and Edward F. Wente. 1967. *The Beit El-Wali Temple of Ramesses II*. 2 vols. Chicago: University of Chicago Press.

Ridley, Ronald T. 2019. *Akhenaten: A Historian's View*. Cairo: American University in Cairo Press.

Ritner, Robert K. 2002. "The Turin Juridical Papyrus (The Harem Conspiracy Against Ramses III) and Papyri Rollin and Lee (Magic in the Harem Conspiracy Against Ramses III)." *COS* 3:27–31.

Roberson, Joshua A. 2016. "Anatomy of a Palimpsest: The Not-so-Strange Case of the 'Abydos Helicopter.'" *KMT* 27:61–66.

——. 2019. "The Royal Funerary Books: The Subject Matter of the Scenes and Texts." Pages 316–34 in *The Oxford Handbook of the Valley of the Kings*. Edited by Richard H. Wilkinson and Kent R. Weeks. Oxford: Oxford University Press.

——. 2020. *Enigmatic Writing in the Egyptian New Kingdom II: A Lexicon of Ancient Egyptian Cryptography of the New Kingdom*. ZÄS Beihefte 12. Berlin: de Gruyter.

Robins, Gay. 1981. "The Value of the Estimated Ages of the Royal Mummies at Death as Historical Evidence." *GM* 45:63–68.

——. 1994. "Women and Children in Peril: Pregnancy, Birth and Infant Mortality in Ancient Egypt." *KMT* 5.4:24–35.

——. 2008. "Ideal Beauty and Divine Attributes." Pages 118–30 in *Queens of Egypt: From Hetepheres to Cleopatra*. Edited by Christiane Ziegler. Monaco: Grimaldi Forum; Paris: Somogy.

Robinson, Joanne-Marie. 2020. *"Blood Is Thicker than Water": Non-Royal Consanguineous Marriage in Ancient Egypt; An Exploration of Economic and Biological Outcomes*. Archaeopress Egyptology 29. Oxford: Archaeopress.

Rodenbeck, John. 2004. "Travelers from an Antique Land: Shelley's Inspiration for 'Ozymandias.'" *Alif: Journal of Comparative Poetics* 24:121–48.

Roeder, Günther. 1926. "Ramses II. als Gott: Nach den Hildesheimer Denksteinen aus Horbêt." *ZÄS* 61:57–67.

Romano, James F. 1979. *The Luxor Museum of Ancient Egyptian Art: Catalogue.* Cairo: American Research Center in Egypt.

Römer, Malte. 2004. "Königssöhne – Königsstatuen – Königsgötter." *ZÄS* 131:73–82.

de Roos, Johan. 2006. "Materials for a Biography: The Correspondence of Puduḫepa with Egypt and Ugarit." Pages 17–26 in *The Life and Times of Hattusili III and Tuthaliya IV: Proceedings of a Symposium Held in Honour of J. de Roos, 12–13 December 2003, Leiden.* Edited by Theo P. J. van den Hout and Carolien H. van Zoest. Leiden: Nederlands Instituut voor Het Nabije Oosten.

———. 2007. *Hittite Votive Texts.* PIHANS 109. Leiden: Nederlands Instituut voor Het Nabije Oosten.

Rosellini, Ippolito. 1832. *I monumenti dell'Egitto e della Nubia: Disegnati dalla spedizione scientifico-letteraria Toscana in egitto.* 12 vols. Pisa: Capurro.

Roth, Ann Macy. 1999. "The Absent Spouse: Patterns and Taboos in Egyptian Tomb Decoration." *JARCE* 36:37–53.

Roth, Silke. 2001. *Die Königsmutter des alten Ägypten von der Frühzeit bis zum Ende der 12. Dynastie.* ÄAT 46. Wiesbaden: Harrassowitz.

———. 2002. *Gebieterin aller Länder: Die Rolle der königlichen Frauen in der fiktiven und realen Außenpolitik des ägyptischen Neuen Reiches.* OBO 185. Fribourg: Academic Press; Göttingen: Vandenhoeck & Ruprecht.

———. 2003. "'Da wurden an diesem Tage die zwei großen Länder zu einem Lande': Zum Verhältnis von Königsideologie und internationaler Heiratspolitik in der Zeit Ramses' II." Pages 175–95 in *Das königtum der Ramessidenzeit: Voraussetzungen – Verwirklichung – Vermächtnis; Akten des 3. Symposions zur ägyptischen Königsideologie in Bonn 7.–9.6.2001.* Edited by Rolf Gundlach and Ursula Rößler-Köhler. ÄAT 36. Wiesbaden: Harrassowitz.

———. 2005. "'Im schönen Frieden befriedet und in schöner Bruderschaft verbrüdert': Zu Motivation und Mechanismen der ägyptisch-hethitischen diplomatischen Kontakte in der Zeit Ramses II." Pages 179–226 in *Motivation und Mechanismen des Kulturkontaktes in der späten Bronzezeit.* Edited by Doris Prechel. Eothen 13. Florence: LoGisma.

———. 2006. "Internationale Diplomatie am Hof Ramses' II." Pages 89–118 in *Der ägyptische Hof des Neuen Reiches: Seine Gesellschaft und Kultur im Spannungsfeld zwischen Innen- und Außenpolitik; Akten des internationalen Kolloquiums vom 27.–29. Mai 2002 an der Johannes Gutenberg-Universtitat Mainz.* Edited by Rolf Gundlach and Andrea Klug. Wiesbaden: Harrassowitz.

———. 2009. "Queen." In *UCLA Encyclopedia of Egyptology.* https://escholarship.org/uc/item/3416c82m.

———. 2012. "Harem." In *UCLA Encyclopedia of Egyptology.* https://escholarship.org/uc/item/1k3663r3.

Rowton, M. B. 1959. "The Background of the Treaty between Ramesses II and Hattušiliš III." *JCS* 13:1–11.

el-Saady, Hassan. 2011. "Egypt in Nubia during the Reign of Seti I." Pages 433–37 in *Ramesside Studies in Honour of K. A. Kitchen.* Edited by Mark Collier and Steven Snape. Bolton: Rutherford.

Sabbahy, Lisa 2018. "Moving Pictures: Context of Use and Iconography of Chariots in the New Kingdom." Pages 120–49 in *Chariots in Ancient Egypt: The Tano Chariot, a Case Study*. Edited by Salima Ikram, Lisa Sabbahy, André J. Veldmeijer, Ole Herslund, and Lucy Skinner. Leiden: Sidestone.

Safronov, Alexander. 2013. "New Titles of the Great Chancellor Bay." *JEA* 99:290–95.

Said, Edward W. 1979. *Orientalism*. New York: Random House.

Salvoldi, Daniele. 2018. *From Siena to Nubia: Alessandro Ricci in Egypt and Sudan, 1817–22*. Cairo: American University in Cairo Press.

Säve-Söderbergh, Torgny, ed. 1987. *Temples and Tombs of Ancient Nubia: The International Rescue Campaign at Abu Simbel, Philae and Other Sites*. London: Thames & Hudson.

Scalf, Foy. 2022. "Oriental Institute Museum Notes 17: The Setting for Osiris Sety I, Establishing the Abydos Provenience for OIM E10507." *JNES* 81:85–98.

Scheidel, Walter. 2012. "Age and Health." Pages 305–16 in *The Oxford Handbook of Roman Egypt*. Edited by Christina Riggs. Oxford: Oxford University Press.

Schiff Giorgini, Michela, Clément Robichon, Jean Leclant, Nathalie Beaux, and Liza Majerus. 1998. *Soleb V: Le temple; Bas-reliefs et inscriptions*. Bibliothèque Générale 19. Cairo: Institut français d'archéologie orientale.

Schipper, Bernd Ulrich. 2002. "Nocheinmal zur Pharaonentochter: Ein Gespräch mit Karl Jansen-Winkeln." *BN* 111:90–98.

Schlögl, Hermann A. 2016. "Ramses II. Leitbild und Bürde seiner Nachfolger." *Sokar* 33:68–75.

Schmidt, Heike C., and Joachim Willeitner. 1994. *Nefertari: Gemahlin Ramses' II*. Antike Welt Sondernummer. Mainz: von Zabern.

Schneider, Thomas. 2011. "Conjectures about Amenmesse: Historical, Biographical, Chronological." Pages 445–51 in *Ramesside Studies in Honour of K. A. Kitchen*. Edited by Mark Collier and Steven Snape. Bolton: Rutherford.

Schott, Siegfried. 1964. *Der Denkstein Sethos' I. für die Kapelle Ramses' I. in Abydos*. Göttingen: Vandenhoeck & Ruprecht.

Schroeder, Caroline. 2003. "Ancient Egyptian Religion on the Silver Screen: Modern Anxieties about Race, Ethnicity, and Religion." *Journal of Religion & Film* 7.2:1. https://digitalcommons.unomaha.edu/jrf/vol7/iss2/1.

Schulman, Alan Richard 1957. Egyptian Representations of Horsemen and Riding in the New Kingdom. *JNES* 16:263–71.

———.1963. The Egyptian Chariotry: A Reexamination. *JARCE* 2:75–98.

———.1976. "The Royal Butler Ramessesemperrē." *JARCE* 13:117–30.

———. 1979. "Diplomatic Marriage in the Egyptian New Kingdom." *JNES* 38:177–93.

———.1980. "Chariots, Chariotry, and the Hyksos." *JSSEA* 10:105–53.

Schulz, Regine. 2016. "Dapur: Ein Triumph über die Feinde von Hatti; Die Idealisierung einer Schlacht zur Glorifizierung des Königs und Ehrenrettung der Prinzen." Pages 269–91 in *Mit archäologischen Schichten Geschichte schreiben: Festschrift für Edgar B. Pusch zum 70. Geburtstag*. Edited by Thilo Rehren, Regine Schulz, and Henning Franzmeier. Hildesheim: Gerstenberg.

Schwela, Dietrich. 2012. "A New Solution for the Ramp Problem in Papyrus Anastasi I." *GM* 232:115–21.

Seele, Keith Cedric. 1940. *The Coregency of Ramses II with Seti I and the Date of the Great Hypostyle Hall at Karnak*. SAOC 19. Chicago: University of Chicago Press.

Seidlmayer, Stephan J. 1999. "New Rock Inscriptions at Elephantine." *Egyptian Archaeology* 14:41–43.

———. 2003. "New Rock Inscriptions on Elephantine Island." Pages 440–47 in vol. 1 of *Egyptology at the Dawn of the Twenty-First Century: Proceedings of the Eighth International Congress of Egyptologists, Cairo, 2000*. Edited by Zahi Hawass and Lyla Pinch Brock. Cairo: American University in Cairo Press.

Serafy, Sam. 2003. "Egypt in Hollywood: Pharaohs of the Fifties." Pages 77–86 in *Consuming Ancient Egypt*. Edited by Michael Rice and Sally MacDonald. London: UCL Press.

Serrano Delgado, Jose M. 2011. "Rhampsinitus, Setne Khamwas and the Descent to the Netherworld: Some Remarks on Herodotus II, 122.1." *Journal of Ancient Near Eastern Religions* 11:94–108.

Servajean, Frédéric. 2012. *Quatre études sur la bataille de Qadech*. Cahiers de l'ENIM 6. Montpellier: Université Paul Valéry.

———. 2014. *Mérenptah et la fin de la XIXe dynastie: Moïse, Exode, la reine Taousret*. Paris: Pygmalion.

Sethe, Kurt. 1927. "Die Jahresrechnung unter Ramses II. und der Namenswechsel dieses Königs." *ZÄS* 62:110–14.

Shaikh Al Arab, Walid. 2019. "A (Re)Investigation of the So-Called King List in the Abydos Temple." *ANKH: Revue d'Égyptologie et des Civilisations Africaines* 28/29:78–97.

Shaw, Garry J. 2010. "The Meaning of the Phrase *m ḥm n Stp-s3*." *JEA* 96:175–90.

Shaw, Ian. 2011. "Seeking the Ramesside Royal Harem: New Fieldwork at Medinet El-Gurob." Pages 453–63 in *Ramesside Studies in Honour of K. A. Kitchen*. Edited by Mark Collier and Steven Snape. Bolton: Rutherford.

Shirun-Grumach, Irene. 1998. "Kadesh Inscriptions and Königsnovelle." Pages 1067–73 in *Proceedings of the Seventh International Congress of Egyptologists, Cambridge, 3–9 September 1995*. Edited by C. J. Eyre. OLA 82. Leuven: Peeters.

Shorter, Alan W. 1934. "Reliefs Showing the Coronation of Ramesses II." *JEA* 20:18–19.

Simon, Camille. 2016. "Les campagnes militaires de Ramsès III à Médinet Habou: Entre vérité et propogande." Pages 179–94 in *De la Nubie à Qadech: La guerre dans l'Égypte ancienne*. Edited by Christina Karlshausen and Claude Obsomer. Brussels: Safran.

Simon, Zsolt. 2007. "Zur Datierung des Kuruštama-Vertrages." Pages 373–85 in *Proceedings of the Fourth Central European Conference of Young Egyptologists:31 August–2 September 2006, Budapest*. Edited by András Gulyás and Kata Endreffy. Budapest: NKTH.

———. 2009. "Kann Armā mit Haremhab gleichgesetzt werden?" *AoF* 36:340–48.

Simpson, William Kelly, ed. 2003. *The Literature of Ancient Egypt: An Anthology of Stories, Instructions, Stelae, Autobiographies, and Poetry*. 3rd ed. New Haven: Yale University Press.

Singer, Itamar. 1983. "Takuḫlinu and Ḫaya: Two Governors in the Ugarit Letter from Tel Aphek." *Tel Aviv* 10:3–25.

———. 2002. *Hittite Prayers*. WAW 11. Atlanta: Society of Biblical Literature.

——. 2004. "The Kurustama Treaty Revisited." Pages 591–607 in *Šarnikzel: Hethitologische Studien zum Gedenken an Emil Orgetorix Forrer*. Edited by Detlev Groddek and Sylvester Rößle. Dresden: Technischen Universität Dresden.

——. 2006. "The Urḫi-Teššub Affair in the Hittite-Egyptian Correspondence." Pages 27–38 in *The Life and Times of Hattusili III and Tuthaliya IV: Proceedings of a Symposium Held in Hhonour of J. de Roos, 12–13 December 2003, Leiden*. Edited by Theo P. J. van den Hout and Carolien H. van Zoest. Leiden: Nederlands Instituut voor Het Nabije Oosten.

Smith, G. Elliot. 1912. *The Royal Mummies: Nos. 61051–61100*. Catalogue Général des Antiquités Égyptiennes du Musée du Caire 59. Cairo: L'institut français d'archéologie orientale.

Smith, Stuart Tyson. 2003. *Wretched Kush: Ethnic Identities and Boundaries in Egypt's Nubian Empire*. London: Routledge.

——. 2018. "Ethnicity: Constructions of Self and Other in Ancient Egypt." *JEH* 11:113–46.

Snape, Steven. 1997. "Ramesses II's Forgotten Frontier." *Egyptian Archaeology* 11:23–24.

——. 2011. "Khaemwese and the Present Past: History and the Individual in Ramesside Egypt." Pages 465–73 in *Ramesside Studies in Honour of K. A. Kitchen*. Edited by Mark Collier and Steven Snape. Bolton: Rutherford.

——. 2017. "Some Ramesside Appropriations of Ancient Memphis." Pages 187–95 in *Egypt 2015: Perspectives of Research; Proceedings of the Seventh European Conference of Egyptologists, 2nd–7th June 2015, Zagreb, Croatia*. Edited by Joanna Popielska-Grzybowska and Mladen Tomorad. Archaeopresss Egyptology 18. Oxford: Archaeopress.

Solvang, Elna K. 2006. "Another Look 'Inside': Harems and the Interpretation of Women." Pages 374–98 in *Orientalism, Assyriology and the Bible*. Edited by Steven W. Holloway. Hebrew Bible Monographs 10. Sheffield: Sheffield Phoenix.

Sømod, Robert. 2018. "Tutmania: Geopolitics and the Museum Shop." Pages 260–71 in *Images of Egypt*. Edited by Mari Lending, Eirik Arff Gulseth Bøhn, and Tim Antsey. Oslo: Pax.

Sourouzian, Hourig. 1983. "Ḥenout-Mi-Rê, Fille de Ramsès II et Grande Épouse du Roi." *ASAE* 69:365–71.

——. 1989. *Les monuments du roi Merenptah*. Sonderschrift, Deutsches Archäologisches Institut, Abteilung Kairo 22. Mainz: von Zabern.

——. 2019. *Catalogue de la statuaire royale de la XIXe dynastie*. BiÉtud 177. Cairo: Institut français d'archéologie orientale. https://www.ifao.egnet.net/uploads/publications/enligne/BiEtud177.pdf.

——. 2020a. "La fascination de Ramsès II pour Amenhotep III." *Égypte, Afrique & Orient* 97:13–22.

——. 2020b. *Recherches sur la statuaire royale de la XIXe dynastie*. BiÉtud 173. Cairo: Institut français d'archéologie orientale.

Spalinger, Anthony J. 1977. "On the Bentresh Stela and Related Problems." *JSSEA* 8:11–18.

——. 1978. "Traces of the Early Career of Seti I." *JSSEA* 9:227–40.

——. 1979a. "Egyptian-Hittite Relations at the Close of the Amarna Period and Some Notes on Hittite Military Strategy in North Syria." *BES* 1:55–89.

———. 1979b. "The Northern Wars of Seti I: An Integrative Study." *JARCE* 16:29–47.

———. 1979c. "Traces of the Early Career of Ramesses II." *JNES* 38:271–86.

———. 1980. "Historical Observations on the Military Reliefs of Abu Simbel and Other Ramesside Temples in Nubia." *JEA* 66:83–99.

———. 1981. "Considerations on the Hittite Treaty between Egypt and Hatti." *SAK* 9:299–358.

———. 1982. *Aspects of the Military Documents of the Ancient Egyptians.* Yale Near Eastern Researches 9. New Haven: Yale University Press.

———. 1985a. "Notes on the Reliefs on the Battle of Kadesh." Pages 1–42 in *Perspectives on the Battle of Kadesh.* Edited by Hans Goedicke. Baltimore: HALGO.

———. 1985b. "Remarks on the Kadesh Inscriptions of Ramesses II: The 'Bulletin.'" Pages 43–75 in *Perspectives on the Battle of Kadesh.* Edited by Hans Goedicke. Baltimore: HALGO.

———. 2002. *The Transformation of an Ancient Egyptian Narrative: P. Salier III and the Battle of Kadesh.* Wiesbaden: Harrassowitz.

———. 2003a. "Epigraphs in the Battle of Kadesh Reliefs." *Eretz-Israel* 27:222–39.

———. 2003b. "The Battle of Kadesh: The Chariot Frieze at Abydos." *A&L* 13:163–99.

———. 2005. *War in Ancient Egypt: The New Kingdom.* Ancient World at War. Oxford: Blackwell.

———. 2006. *Five Views on Egypt.* Lingua Aegyptia Studia Monographica 6. Göttingen: Seminar für Ägyptologie und Koptologie.

———. 2007a. "Ramesses Ludens et Alii." Pages 71–86 in *Studies on the Ancient Egyptian Cultures and Foreign Relations.* Edited by Panagiotis Kousoulis. University of the Aegean Egyptological Series 1. Rhodes: Department of Mediteranean Studies University of the Aegean. http://aegeanegyptology.gr/wp-content/uploads/2014/09/Studies-in-the-anc-eg-cultures.pdf.

———. 2007b. "Some Notes on the Chariot Arm of Egypt in the Early Eighteenth Dynasty." Pages 119–37 in *Moving across Borders: Foreign Relations, Religion and Cultural Interactions in the Ancient Mediterranean.* Edited by Panagiotis Kousoulis and Konstantinos Magliveras. OLA 159. Leuven: Peeters.

———. 2008. "Early Writings of Ramesses II's Names." *CdÉ* 83:75–89.

———. 2009. *The Great Dedicatory Inscription of Ramesses II: A Solar-Osirian Tractate at Abydos.* CHANE 33. Leiden: Brill.

———. 2010. "Ramesses II at Luxor: Mental Gymnastics." *Or* 79:425–79.

———. 2011. *Icons of Power: A Strategy of Reinterpretation.* Prague: Charles University in Prague, Faculty of Arts.

———. 2012. "Divisions in Monumental Texts and Their Images: The Issue of Kadesh and Megiddo." Pages 373–93 in *All the Wisdom of the East: Studies in Near Eastern Archaeology and History in Honor of Eliezer D. Oren.* Edited by Shmuel Aḥituv et al. OBO 255. Fribourg: Academic Press; Göttingen: Vandenhoeck & Ruprecht.

———. 2013. "Egyptian Chariots: Departing for War." Pages 237–56 in *Chasing Chariots: Proceedings of the First International Chariot Conference (Cairo 2012).* Edited by Salima Ikram and André J. Veldmeijer. Leiden: Sidestone.

——. 2016. "Operational Bases: Gaza and Beth Shan." Pages 63–80 in *De la Nubie à Qadech: La guerre dans l'Égypte ancienne*. Edited by Christina Karlshausen and Claude Obsomer. Brussels: Safran.

——. 2018a. "Mathmatical Factors of the Battle of Kadesh." Pages 89–108 in *Feasts and Fights: Essays on Time in Ancient Egypt*. YES 10. New Haven: Yale Egyptological Institute.

——. 2018b. "The Sinai of Seti I." Pages 109–28 in *Feasts and Fights: Essays on Time in Ancient Egypt*. YES 10. New Haven: Yale Egyptological Institute.

——. 2020. *Leadership under Fire: The Pressures of Warfare in Ancient Egypt*. Études d'égyptologie 20. Paris: Soleb. https://www.soleb.com/pdf/leadership-under-fire/Anthony-Spalinger-Leadership-under-Fire.pdf.

——. 2021. *The Books behind the Masks: Sources of Warfare Leadership in Ancient Egypt*. CHANE 124. Leiden: Brill.

——. Forthcoming. "Horse Names and Chariots." In *Signs of Life: Egyptian Script, Language and Writing; Studies in honor of Orly Goldwasser*. Edited by Niv Allon. Turnhout: Brepols.

Spencer, Patricia. 2016. *Amara West III: The Scenes and Texts of the Ramesside Temple*. EES Excavation Memoir 114. London: Egypt Exploration Society.

Spiegel, Joachim. 1939. "Die Grundbedeutung des Stammes Ḥm." *ZÄS* 75:112–21.

Stadelmann, Rainer. 1981. "Die Lange Regierung Ramses' II." *MDAIK* 37:457–63.

——. 2010. "The Mystery of the Unification of King and Amun in the Mortuary Temple of Seti I at Qurna." Pages 99–103 in *Les temples de millions d'années et le pouvoir royal à Thèbes au Nouvel Empire: Sciences et nouvelles technologies appliquées à l'archéologie*. Edited by Christian Leblanc and Gihane Zaki. Cairo: Dar el-Kutub.

——. 2013. "The Mortuary Temple of Seti I as Symbol of Legitimacy and Power in the Nineteenth Dynasty." *Études et Travaux* 26:625–36.

——. 2015. "The Temple of Millions of Years of Seti I at Qurna/El Templo de millones de años de Seti I en Qurna." Pages 167–93 in *Los templos de millones de años en Tebas/The Temples of Millions of Years in Thebes*. Edited by Myriam Seco Álvarez and Asunción Jódar Miñarro. Granada: Universidad de Granada.

——. Forthcoming. *Der Temple Sethos I. in Gurna*.

Stavi, Boaz. 2015. *The Reign of Tudhaliya II and Šuppiluliuma I: The Contribution of the Hittite Documentation to a Reconstruction of the Armana Age*. THeth 31. Heidelberg: Winter.

Stefanović, Danijela. 2015. "The Ḫkrt-Nswt on the Monuments of the Ꜣṯw n Tt Ḥkꜣ." Pages 861–71 in vol. 1 of *Proceedings of the Tenth International Congress of Egyptologists: University of the Aegean, Rhodes. 22–29 May 2008*. Edited by Panagiotis Kousoulis and Nikolaos Lazaridis. 2 vols. OLA 218. Leuven: Peeters.

Steindorff, George, and Keith C. Steele. 1957. *When Egypt Ruled the East*. Chicago: University of Chicago Press.

Stock, Raymond T. 2008. "A Mummy Awakens: The Pharaonic Fiction of Naguib Mahfouz." PhD diss., University of Pennsylvania.

——. 2011. "Egypt's Revolution Foreseen in Fiction: *Before the Throne*, by Naguib Mahfouz." Foreign Policy Research Institute. https://www.fpri.org/article/2011/05/egypts-revolution-foreseen-in-fiction-before-the-throne-by-naguib-mahfouz/.

Stokke, Eirik. 2018. "Unearthing Cecil B. DeMille's Californian Egypt." Pages 272–85 in *Images of Egypt*. Edited by Mari Lending, Eirik Arff Gulseth Bøhn, and Tim Antsey. Oslo: Pax.

Strouhal, Eugen. 2008. *The Memphite Tomb of Horemheb, Commander-in-Chief of Tutankhamun, IV: Human Skeletal Remains*. EES Excavation Memoir 87. London: Egypt Exploration Society.

Strouhal, Eugen, and Ladislava Horáčková. 2011. "Human Skeletal Remains." Pages 304–64 in *The Memphite Tomb of Horemheb, Commander-in-Chief of Tutankhamun V: The Forecourt and the Area South of the Tomb with Some Notes on the Tomb of Tia*. Edited by Maarten J. Raven et al. Turnhout: Brepols.

Sürenhagen, Dietrich. 1985. *Paritätische Staatsverträge aus hethitischer Sicht: Zu historischen Aussagen und literarischer Stellung des Textes CTH 379*. Pavia: Iuculano.

———. 2006. "Forerunners of the Hattusili-Ramesses Treaty." *BMSAES* 6:59–67.

Taraqji, Ahmad Ferzat. 1999. "Nouvelles découvertes sur les relations avec l'Égypte à Tel Sakka et à Keswé, dans la région de Damas." *BSFÉ* 144:27–43.

Taylor, John H. 2017. *Sir John Soane's Greatest Treasure: The Sarcophagus of Seti I*. London: Pimpernel.

———. 2019a. "The Egyptian Concept of a Royal Necropolis." Pages 41–53 in *The Oxford Handbook of the Valley of the Kings*. Edited by Richard H. Wilkinson and Kent R. Weeks. Oxford: Oxford University Press.

———. 2019b. "Intrusive Burials and Caches." Pages 360–74 in *The Oxford Handbook of the Valley of the Kings*. Edited by Richard H. Wilkinson and Kent R. Weeks. Oxford: Oxford University Press.

Thausing, Gertrud, and Hans Goedicke. 1971. *Nofretari: Eine Dokumentation der Wandgemälde ihres grabes*. Graz: Akademische Druck- und Verlagsanstalt.

Thijs, Ad. 2018. "The Ramesside Section of the Serapeum." *SAK* 47:293–318.

Thum, Jen. 2016. "When Pharaoh Turned the Landscape into a Stela." *NEA* 79.2:68–77.

Tiradritti, Francesco. 2008. *Pharaonic Renaissance: Archaism and the Sense of History; Cankarjev Dom, Ljubljana 4th March–20th July 2008*. Ljubljana: Culture and Congress Center.

Tooze, G. Andrew. 2003. "Moses and the Reel Exodus." *Journal of Religion & Film* 7.1:3. https://digitalcommons.unomaha.edu/jrf/vol7/iss1/3.

Trafton, Scott. 2004. *Egypt Land: Race and Nineteenth-Century American Egyptomania*. Durham, NC: Duke University Press.

Trimm, Charlie. 2017. *Fighting for the King and the Gods: A Survey of Warfare in the Ancient Near East*. Resources for Biblical Study 88. Atlanta: SBL Press.

Trope, Betsy Teasley, and Peter Lacovara. 2003. "A Pharaoh in Atlanta? The Apparently Royal Mummy in the Michael C. Carlos Museum Collection Is Probably the Missing Rameses I." *KMT* 14:45–51.

Troy, Lana. 1986. *Patterns of Queenship in Ancient Egyptian Myth and History*. Acta Universitatis Upsaliensis, Boreas 14. Stockholm: Almqvist & Wiksell.

———. 2008. "The Queen as a Female Counterpart of the Pharaoh." Pages 154–70 in *Queens of Egypt: From Hetepheres to Cleopatra*. Edited by Christiane Ziegler. Monaco: Grimaldi Forum; Paris: Somogy.

Turner, Susan. 2021. *The Horse in New Kingdom Egypt: Its Introduction, Nature, Role and Impact*. Wallasey: Abercromby.

Ullmann, Martina. 2002. *Die Häuser der Millionen von Jahren: Eine Untersu-chung zu Königskult und Tempeltypologie in Ägypten.* ÄAT 51. Wiesbaden: Harrassowitz.

———. 2011. "Der Göttliche Ramses II. im Großen Tempel von Abu Simbel." Pages 301–15 in *From Illahun to Djeme: Papers Presented in Honour of Ulrich Luft.* Edited by András Gulyás, Eszter Bechtold, and Andrea Hasznos. BARIS 2311. Oxford: Archaeopress.

———. 2013a. "Von Beit El-Wali nach Abu Simbel: Zur Neugestaltung der sakra-len Landschaft Unternubiens in der Regierungszeit Ramses' II." *Der An-tike Sudan: Mitteilungen der Sudanarchäologischen Gesellschaft zu Berlin* 24:23–37.

———. 2013b. "Von Theben nach Nubien: Überlegungen zum Kultkomplex Ramses' II. in Abu Simbel." Pages 503–24 in *Kleine Götter – große Götter: Festschrift für Dieter Kessler zum 65. Geburtstag.* Edited by Friedhelm Hoff-mann et al. Vaterstetten: Brose.

———. 2016. "The Temples of Millions of Years at Western Thebes." Pages 417–32 in *The Oxford Handbook of the Valley of the Kings.* Edited by Kent R. Weeks and Richard H. Wilkinson. Oxford: Oxford University Press.

———. 2017. "Tradition and Innovation within the Decoration Program of the Temple of Ramesses II at Gerf Hussein." Pages 661–66 in *Proceedings of the XI International Congress of Egyptologists, Florence Egyptian Museum, Florence, 23–30 August 2015.* Edited by Maria Cristina Guidotti and Gloria Rosati. Archaeopress Egyptology 19. Oxford: Archeopress.

Uphill, Eric P. 1968. "Pithom and Raamses: Their Location and Significance Part I." *JNES* 27:291–315.

———. 1969. "Pithom and Raamses: Their Location and Significance Part II." *JNES* 28:15–39.

———. 1984. *The Temples of Per Ramesses.* Warminster: Aris & Phillips.

Van de Mieroop, Marc. 2007. *The Eastern Mediterranean in the Age of Ramesses II.* Oxford: Blackwell.

Vandersleyen, Claude. 1979. "De l'usage du Relief dans le creux à l'époque ra-messide." *BSFÉ* 86:16–38.

Vasiljević, Vera. 2016. "Orientalism Oblige: A Case Study." Pages 341–58 in *Egypt and Austria IX: Perception of the Orient in Central Europe (1800–1918); Proceedings of the Symposium Held at Betliar, Slovakia (October 21st to 24th, 2013).* Edited by Jozef Hudec and Ľubica Hudáková. Krakow: Aigyptos Foundation.

Veldmeijer, André J., and Salima Ikram. 2018. *Chariots in Ancient Egypt: The Tano Chariot, a Case Study.* Leiden: Sidestone.

Vernus, Pascal. 2003. *Affairs and Scandals in Ancient Egypt.* Translated by David Lorton. Ithaca, NY: Cornell University Press.

———. 2013. "The Royal Command (*Wḏ-Nsw*): A Basic Deed of Executive Power." Pages 259–340 in *Ancient Egyptian Administration.* Edited by Juan Carlos Moreno García. HdO 104. Leiden: Brill.

Versluys, Miguel John. 2020. *Beyond Egyptomania: Objects, Style and Agency.* Berlin: de Gruyter.

Vinson, Steve. 2018. *The Craft of a Good Scribe. History, Narrative and Meaning in the First Tale of Setne Khaemwas.* HES 3. Leiden: Brill.

Vogelsang-Eastwood, G. M., Martin Hense, and Kelvin Wilson. 1999. *Tutankhamun's Wardrobe: Garments from the Tomb of Tutankhamun.* Rotterdam: Barjesteh van Waalwijk van Doorn.

Waddell, W. G. 1940. *Manetho: With an English Translation.* Loeb Classical Library. Cambridge: Harvard University Press; London: Heinemann.

Walthall, Anne, ed. 2008. *Servants of the Dynasty: Palace Women in World History.* Berkeley: University of California Press.

Warburton, David. 1997. "Kadesh and the Egyptian Empire." *Journal of Ancient Civilizations* 12:125–47.

Ward, William A. 1983. "Reflections on Some Egyptian Terms Presumed to Mean 'Harem, Harem-Woman, Concubine.'" *Berytus* 31:67–74.

Watson Andaya, Barbara. 2008. "Women and the Performance of Power in Early Modern Southeast Asia." Pages 22–44 in *Servants of the Dynasty: Palace Women in World History.* Edited by Anne Walthall. Berkeley: University of California Press.

von der Way, Thomas. 1984. *Die Textüberlieferung Ramses' II. zur Qadeš-Schlacht: Analyse und Struktur.* HÄB 22. Hildesheim: Gerstenberg.

Weeks, Kent R. 1998. *The Lost Tomb: The Greatest Discovery at the Valley of the Kings since Tutankhamun.* London: Weidenfeld & Nicolson.

———. 2006. *KV 5: A Preliminary Report on the Excavation of the Tomb of the Sons of Rameses II in the Valley of the Kings.* Rev. ed. Publications of the Theban Mapping Project 2. Cairo: American University in Cairo Press.

Weeks, Kent R., and Araldo De Luca. 2002. *Valley of the Kings: The Tombs and the Funerary Temples of Thebes West.* Vercelli: White Star.

Wente, Edward F. 1980. "Age at Death of Pharaohs of the New Kingdom, Determined from Historical Sources." Pages 234–85 in *An X-Ray Atlas of the Royal Mummies.* Edited by James E. Harris, Edward F. Wente, and Ibrahim el-Nawaway. Chicago: University of Chicago Press.

———. 1990. *Letters from Ancient Egypt.* WAW 1. Atlanta: Scholars Press.

Wernick, Nicholas. 2013. "K(No)w More Spears from the Backs of Chariots: Problems with the Battle of Kadesh's Thrusting Spears." *JAEI* 5.2:48–51.

Westbrook, Raymond. 2020. "International Law in the Amarna Age." Pages 28–41, 239–42 in *Amarna Diplomacy: The Beginnings of International Relations.* Edited by Raymond Cohen and Raymond Westbrook. Baltimore: Johns Hopkins University Press.

Widmer, Ghislaine. 2014. "Sésostris, figure de légende dans la littérature greque et démotique." Pages 232–35 in *Sésostris III: Pharaon de légende.* Edited by Guillemette Andreu-Lanoë, Fleur Morfoisse, and Clément Pouwels. Gand: Snoeck.

Wiener, Malcolm H. 2015. "Oh, No—Not Another Chronology!" *BES* 19:649–63.

Wilhelm, Gernot. 2009. "Muršilis II. Konflikt mit Ägypten und Haremhabs Thronbesteigung." *Die Welt des Orients* 39:108–16.

———. 2012. "Šuppiluliuma I. und die Chronologie der Amarna-Zeit." Pages 225–57 in *Kāmid El-Lōz, 20: Die Keilschriftbriefe und der Horizont von El-Amarna.* Edited by Rolf Hachmann. Bonn: Habelt.

———. 2015. "Suppiluliuma and the Decline of the Mittanian Kingdom." Pages 69–79 in *Qaṭna and the Networks of Bronze Age Globalism: Proceedings of an International Conference in Stuttgart and Tübingen in October 2009.* Edited by Peter Pfälzner and Mīšāl al-Maqdisī. Qaṭna Studien Supplementa 2. Wiesbaden: Harrassowitz.

Wilkinson, Caroline M. 2008. "The Facial Reconstruction of Ancient Egyptians." Pages 162–78 in *Egyptian Mummies and Modern Science.* Edited by Rosalie David. Cambridge: Cambridge University Press.

Wilkinson, Richard H. 2011. *The Temple of Tausret: The University of Arizona Egyptian Expedition Tausret Temple Project, 2004–2011.* Arizona: University of Arizona Egyptian Expedition.

———. 2012. *Tausret: Forgotten Queen and Pharaoh of Egypt.* Oxford: Oxford University Press.

Wilkinson, Richard H., and Kent R. Weeks, eds. 2019. *The Oxford Handbook of the Valley of the Kings.* Oxford: Oxford University Press.

Willeitner, Joachim. 1996. "Rätselhafter Gottkönig: Ein Statuenfund in Giza wirft ein neues Licht auf die Vergöttlichung Ramses' II." *Antike Welt* 27:359–64.

———. 2010. *Abu Simbel: Die Felsentempel Ramses' II. von der Pharaonenzeit bis heute.* Zaberns Bildbände zur Archäologie. Mainz: von Zabern.

Wilson, John A. 1956. *The Culture of Ancient Egypt.* Chicago: University of Chicago Press.

Wimmer, Stefan Jakob. 2002. "A New Stela of Ramesses II in Jordan in the Context of Egyptian Royal Stelae in the Levant." Paper presented at the Third International Congress on the Archaeology of the Ancient Near East. Paris, 18 April 2002.

Winkler, Andreas. 2013. "A Royal Star: On the 'Miracle of the Star' in Thutmoses III's Gebel Barkal Stela and a Note on the King as a Star in Personal Names." *RdÉ* 64:231–47.

Winlock, Herbert E. 1921. *Bas-Reliefs from the Temple of Rameses I at Abydos.* The Metropolitan Museum of Art Papers 1. New York: Metropolitan Museum of Art.

———. 1937. *The Temple of Ramesses I at Abydos.* The Metropolitan Museum of Art Papers 5. New York: Metropolitan Museum of Art.

Winnerman, Jonathan. 2018. "Rethinking the Royal *Ka.*" PhD diss., University of Chicago.

Witthuhn, Orell, *et al.* 2015. *Die Bentresch-Stele: Ein Quellen- und Lesebuch; Forschungsgeschichte und Perspektiven eines ptolemäerzeitlichen Denkmals aus Theben (Ägypten).* Göttinger Miszellen, Occasional Studies 2. Göttingen: Seminar für Ägyptologie und Koptologie der Georg-August-Universität Göttingen.

Wong, Jun Yi. 2018. "Notes on the Marginal Inscriptions of Ramesses II." *Bulletin de le Société d'Éyptologie Genève* 31:129–37.

Wood, Michael. 1998. "The Use of the Pharaonic Past in Modern Egyptian Nationalism." *JARCE* 35:179–96.

Woods, Alexandra. 2015. "Relief." Pages 219–48 in *A Companion to Ancient Egyptian Art.* Edited by Melinda K. Hartwig. Chichester: Wiley Blackwell.

Wouters, Werner. 1989. "Urḫi-Tešub and the Ramses-Letters from Boghazköy." *JCS* 41:226–34.

Wreszinski, Walter. 1925. *Atlas zur altaegyptischen Kulturgeschichte,* Zweiter Teil. Leipzig: Hinrichs.

Xekalaki, Georgia. 2007. "Egyptian Royal Women and Diplomatic Activity during the New Kingdom." Pages 163–73 in *Current Research in Egyptology 2005: Proceedings of the Sixth Annual Symposium, University of Cambridge,*

6–8 January 2005. Edited by Rachel Mairs and Alice Stevenson. Oxford: Oxbow.

———. 2011. *Symbolism in the Representation of Royal Children during the New Kingdom.* BARIS 2314. Oxford: Archaeopress.

———. 2015. "The Royal Children as Signs: Reading New Kingdom Princely Iconography." Pages 1911–22 in vol. 2 of *Proceedings of the Tenth International Congress of Egyptologists: University of the Aegean, Rhodes, 22–29 May 2008.* Edited by Panagiotis Kousoulis and Nikolaos Lazaridis. 2 vols. OLA 241. Leuven: Peeters.

Xekalaki, Georgia, and Reem Khodary. 2011. "Aspects of the Cultic Role of Queen Nefertari and the Royal Children during the Reign of Ramesses II." Pages 561–71 in *Ramesside Studies in Honour of K. A. Kitchen.* Edited by Mark Collier and Steven Snape. Bolton: Rutherford.

Yoshimura, Sakuji, and Nozomu Kawai. 2010. "Report on the Waseda University Excavations at North Saqqara, 2009-I." *ASAE* 84:467–83.

Youssef, A. A.-H., Ch. Leblanc, and M. Maher. 1977. *Le Ramesseum IV: Les batailles de Tunip et de Dapour.* Cairo: Centre d'études et de documentation sur l'ancienne Égypte.

Yoyotte, Marine. 2008. "The Harem in Ancient Egypt." Pages 76–90 in *Queens of Egypt: From Hetepheres to Cleopatra.* Edited by Christiane Ziegler. Monaco: Grimaldi Forum; Paris: Somogy.

Yurco, Frank J. 1986. "Merenptah's Canaanite Campaign." *JARCE* 23:189–215.

———. 1990. "3,200-Year-Old Picture of Israelites Found in Egypt." *Biblical Archaeology Review* 16.5:20–38.

———. 1997a. "Merneptah's Canaanite Campaign and Israel's Origins." Pages 27–55 in *Exodus: The Egyptian Evidence.* Edited by Leonard H. Lesko and Ernest S. Frerichs. Winona Lake, IN: Eisenbrauns.

———. 1997b. "Was Amenmesse the Viceroy of Kush, Messuwy?" *JARCE* 34:49–56.

Zaccagnini, Carlo. 1985. "On Late Bronze Age Marriages." Pages 593–605 in *Studi in Onore Di Edda Bresciani.* Edited by Sandro Filippo Bondì et al. Pisa: Giardini.

———. 2000a. Review of *Die ägyptisch-hethitische Korrespondenz aus Boghazköi in babylonischer und hethitischer Sprache,* by Elmar Edel. *Or* 69:439–42.

———. 2000b. "The Interdependence of the Great Powers." Pages 141–53, 253–56 in *Amarna Diplomacy: The Beginnings of International Relations.* Edited by Raymond Cohen and Raymond Westbrook. Baltimore: Johns Hopkins University Press.

———. 2018. "'Heavy Shekels' in Late Bronze Age Syria." *Annali Sezione Orientale* 78:3–18.

Zaki, Gihane. 2019. "Abu Simbel: The Story of an Extraordinary Rescue." *World Heritage* 90:22–30.

Ziegler, Christiane. 2008. *Queens of Egypt: From Hetepheres to Cleopatra.* Monaco: Grimaldi Forum; Paris: Somogy.

Zivie, Alain-Pierre. 2006. "Le messager royal egyptien Pirikhnawa." *BMSAES* 6:68–78.

INDEX

Page numbers in italics reference the illustrations and/or their captions.

A

cattle, 58–*60*, 361, 363, 367, 426. *See also* Apis Bull

Champollion, Jean-François, 471, 476, 491n28

chantresses, 22, 207, 218, 228, 253, 275n41, *395*, 397

chaos (*isfet*), 13, 24–25, 30, 185, 195, 293, 443, 454

chapels, 24–25, 28–29, *35*, 37, 42n23, 79, 111n94, 245 46n168, 456; at Gurnah, 25, 82, 109n79; at Kar- nak, 402n15, 452; *Sed*-festival, 349–50; tombs, 240–41n94, 268, 270, 281nn124 and 128

chariots/chariotry, 21, 47, 120, 122–24, 132–33, 143–44, 157, 166n54, 291, 303, 326, 330, 336, 341n33, 342n55, 356, 363, 368, 408, 426; Egyptian, 124, 138–39, 141, 144, 148, 150, 177n163, 184, 367; Eighteenth Dynasty, 123–24, 166–67n55, 176n153; elite status of, 122, 124; at festivals, 351–53; fragility of, 130, 168n71; Hittite, 120, 121, 123–25, 141–46, 148–49, 150–52, 153–54, 156, 162n7, 168nn65–66, 174n131, 175n145, 177n163, 184, 310; iconography and ideology of, *123*, 126, 166n50, 167n60, 176n153, 200n43; logistics and performance, 122–25; maintenance and manufac- ture, 124–25, 129, 166–67nn53–55; modern portrayals of, *125*, 167nn61 and 64, 484, *479*; numbers of, 122, 141, 164nn35, 165n38, 184; Ramesses II's chariot and horses, *117*, *119*, 146, 151–52, 155, 157–*58*, *160*, 189–*90*, *422*, *472*; Ramesses II's sons and, 200n47, 258–*59*, 260, 262, 266; Ro- man, 166nn50 and 53; runners,*144*, 148, 176–77nn159–60; of Sety I, *33*, 167n60; speed and maneuverability of, 125–26, 148, 167n63, 168–69n75; tactics and weaponry, 126–27, 147–48, 165–66nn44–47, 166n60, 168nn66 and 69; 175n146, 176n158, 177nn160, 162, and 63; transported on supply carts, 122, 125, 127, 130, *138*–39, 141, 165n41, 168n75; weight of, 124–25, 167n63

charioteers/chariot officers, 20, 52, 102, 122, 126, 137, 141, 143, 154–55, 164n34, 165n45, 166n54, 175n146, 177n162, 184, 210, 262, 303, 351; Menna, 119, 125, 146–47, 155, 167n59, 176n153; Pharaoh as, 66–67n26, *117*, 147, 183, 449

City of Ramses (biblical), 407, 476

colossal statues, *5*, *92*–96, 112n117, 245n163, 394–99, 404nn53–54, 414–16, *452*; Abu Simbel, 96, 227, 231, 244n149, 246n174, 265, 275n47, 295, 379n107, 393, 395, 402n25, 408, 417–18, 421–23, 482; from Akhmim, 231, 245–46nn168–69; from Canopus (Abukir), 232, 246n178; Classical accounts of, 95, 213, 469; cult of, 385, 394–99; 404–5nn61 and 62, 472, 491n33; Gerf Hussein, 390, 424, 426; at Luxor Temple, 69n64, 90, 92–94, 216, 241n98, 263, 394; names of, *94*–95, 389–90, 394–98, 405n62, 410, 424, 431n53, 472, 491n33; Nasser transports to Cairo, 480–81, 493n63; of Nefertari, 231, 246n174; paint- ed decoration of, 393–94, 404n60, 431; at Piramesses and Tanis, 1–2, 112n127, 230, 245n166, *372–73*, 378n87, 384, 394, 407–10; quarrying of, 95–99, 384; Sety I commissions, 39–40, 50–51, 63, 70n67, 93, 384; subsidiary figures, 216, *220–21*, 226– *27*, 228–*29*, 230–*32*, 241n98, 244n149, 245n163, 246nn169 and 178, 263, *265*, 275n47, *372–73*, 378n87, *417–18*, 421, *423*; transporting of, 50–51, 94, 111n115; of Tuya, 212–13, 469. *See also* granite/grandiorite; sandstone: siliceous

conspiracy theories (modern), 82–*84*, 283n142, 488

coregencies, 26, 65nn5–6; Sety I and Ramesses II (alleged), 49, 61–63, 67n27, 69n56, 82, 276n59

coronation, *38*, 45n68, 60, 68n52, 69n55, 105n5; of Ramesses II, 47, 49, 71, *72*, 80, 82, *83*, 105nn2–6, 108n62

correspondence, international: Assyrian-Hittite, 288, 290, 297n12, 345n92; Babylonian-Hittite, 291–92, 341n37, 343n72, 344n77, 345n92;